Theory of Motivation

THEORY

OF

MOTIVATION

Robert C. Bolles

UNIVERSITY OF WASHINGTON

HARPER & ROW

PUBLISHERS

New York, Evanston, and London

Library of Congress Catalog Card Number: 67–10251

Contents

Preface

❖❖❖❖❖❖❖❖❖

The concept of motivation has taken many forms. It appears in our folklore, in our traditions and customs, in our great philosophical systems, and in our more recent science of behavior. Sometimes it is made explicit so that it may be scrutinized, but more often it is implicit, unanalyzed, and unquestioned. The concept of motivation has been variously identified as an unquestionable fact of human experience, as an indisputable fact of behavior, and as a mere explanatory fiction.

The common and unifying element in these diverse conceptions is that motivation is an agency or factor or force that helps to explain behavior. Motivation is a hypothetical cause of behavior. This book is concerned with this single idea. We will see where the idea comes from, how it has developed, some of the uses it has been put to, and how in recent years it has been challenged by other ideas about how behavior can best be explained. This narrative will involve us to some extent in the philosophy of science because we will have to consider carefully just what it means to "explain" behavior. We will also become involved to some extent in the history of psychology because the roots of the concept of motivation lie in its history rather than in any contemporary analysis of behavior. The concept of motivation makes sense only when viewed in historical perspective.

The science of behavior is too new to nurture historians, so while the historians of psychology have written many fine books about the history of man's attempts to study what and how he senses, perceives, and knows, they have told almost nothing about man's attempts to study how he behaves.[1] The present book is not intended to fill the gap

[1] The general histories have tended to neglect the motivation field. Boring (1950) devotes one chapter to "dynamic" psychology, or at least to some of the men who pioneered in it. Spearman (1937) presents several chapters; they deal mainly, however, with problems of classification and are limited almost exclusively to the preexperimental area. Troland (1928) has a four-chapter introduction to the preexperimental theories of motivation. Young (1936) is the definitive work on the early experimental period but it is now hopelessly dated. The several books (Bindra, 1959; Brown, 1961; Hall, 1961; Cofer & Appley, 1964) that are

and it is not a history in any technical sense. But perhaps it will indicate some of the problems a modern history of psychology must consider.

As our narrative moves into contemporary times it will be dominated by the experimental research, mostly animal research, on motivation. This too will be organized along historical lines. The reason for this is that motivation as a research area is in a state of rapid change. The science of behavior is too young and unstructured at this point to progress merely by the accumulation of facts or by the elaboration of great theoretical systems. We are at the stage where progress is made by the clarification of methodological issues and the reorganization of conceptual issues. An understanding of these issues and an appreciation of how they change are critically important because it is they rather than the great theoretical structures that guide our research efforts.

I view science not as a search for imperishable truth but more as a kind of game, a game we play partly for the fun of it, but partly also because we believe it will increase our understanding. This book is dedicated to those rare men, like Tolman and Hull, who taught us how to play the game and who made it seem worth playing. It is addressed to all those who would do research to improve our understanding of behavior.

I am indebted to a number of editors, colleagues, and students who read and commented on portions of the manuscript. I am greatly indebted to the National Science Foundation, which for several years has supported my own research, enabled me to do research and write during the summer, and borne some of the cost of preparing the manuscript. I am also grateful for permission to reproduce quotations and figures generously granted by a number of authors and by the *American Journal of Psychology;* American Physiological Society; American Psychological Association; Holt, Rinehart and Winston; the *Journal of the Experimental Analysis of Behavior;* The Journal Press; the New York Academy of Sciences; *Psychological Reports;* and Williams & Wilkins.

ROBERT C. BOLLES

strong on recent experimental work convey little sense of historical background and suggest little of where we are going. On the other hand, Smith (1960) and Madsen (1961) survey the philosophical basis of motivation theory and give some sense of its history but ignore the experimental literature.

Theory of Motivation

1

INTRODUCTION

The notion of cause is replaced by the notion of law. Instead of causal relation, we have the conception of a continuous succession of events logically connected with one another by an underlying principle . . .

SIR EDMUND WHITTAKER

Only rarely is motivation said to be a fact of human experience, that is, a mental event, which determines the course of action. The idea of motivation does not originate from what men say either about their own experience or about their own behavior. It is not one of the "indigenous problems" of psychology.

Nor is motivation a fact of behavior. There is not one feature or aspect or characteristic of behavior to which we invariably have reference when we say that some behavior is motivated. Although some writers have suggested behavioral criteria to define motivation, these attempts to specify what is meant by motivation are not very compelling. There is little agreement among the different proposals about what the defining criteria should be. We may say, for example, that an animal that has been deprived of food is hungry, or that it has a hunger drive, or that it "looks" motivated. But even though we may agree on this, it is not so clear that we can agree on what characteristic of its behavior makes the animal look motivated.

What one proposes as a definition of motivated behavior seems to depend more upon his theoretical commitments than upon anything in the

behavior itself. Any solution to the problem of what it is about a particular behavior that makes it appear motivated will therefore depend upon
how we regard behavior in general and how we explain it in general.
Thus, motivation seems to be neither a fact of experience nor a fact of
behavior, but rather an idea or concept we introduce when we undertake
to explain behavior.

THE EXPLANATION OF BEHAVIOR

Sometimes we are fortunate enough to observe behavior occurring as
a direct response to prevailing stimulus conditions in the environment.
In such cases no very elaborate explanation is necessary; we may simply
cite the eliciting conditions. In these cases of reflexive responses, the behavior of the organism becomes nearly as predictable as the behavior
of simple physical systems, and our explanation can be correspondingly
simple. More frequently, though, no identifiable external stimulus can be
specified for a certain act. In this case behavior might be explained indirectly as the result of stimuli that have been effective in the past or
it might be explained indirectly as a result of the physical structure of the
individual, or of its prior experience. But all such explanations would be
relatively indirect compared with the simple idea that there is a single
active internal agency which, if it could be located, would provide a
direct explanation. If such an internal agency or cause of behavior could
be found, our explanation of all behavior could then be as simple as it is
in the case of the reflex. Typically, the search for such an agency is fruit-
less, and it is then that we take the much easier course of hypothesizing
the existence of an appropriate agency.[1] Different theories of motivation
are distinguished primarily by the different sorts of motivating agencies
that they hypothesize.

In this sense the most enduring theory of motivation is that which attributes a man's behavior to the results of his own mental processes. We
can designate this traditional approach to the problem of explaining behavior by any name we wish, since it has no accepted name (prevailing
doctrines often don't). Let us call it rationalism or, more precisely,
traditional rationalism.

Traditional Rationalism. The naive and traditional explanation of
human behavior is that we act because we have reasons for acting. Because
we have free will, our reasons constitute a sufficient account of the whole

[1] Skinner makes the point this way: "A rat does not always respond to food
placed before it, and a factor called its 'hunger' is invoked by way of explanation.
The rat is said to eat only when it is hungry. It is because eating is not inevitable
that we are led to hypothesize an internal state to which we may assign the variability. Where there is a no variability, no state is needed. Since the rat usually
responds to a shock to its foot by flexing its leg, no 'flexing drive' comparable to
hunger is felt to be required" (Skinner, 1938, p. 341).

matter. Such was the common view of the Greek philosophers, and such is the common view of the layman today. Traditional rationalism, of course, receives considerable support from our continuing use of it in our day-to-day contact with people. We hold our fellow man personally responsible as the author of his actions, and society expects him to describe his own actions in terms of intention, awareness, and purpose. We teach our children to use these words by making our transactions with them contingent upon what we consider to be their proper usage. We all do this, even the most behavioristic of us, because that is, in turn, what we have learned to do.

We attribute a man's behavior to events going on in his mind. This is the common and familiar variety of explanation which provides the point of departure for all other theories of motivation. All alternative conceptions of motivation and all alternative motivation constructs arise as reactions to this traditional rationalistic doctrine.

There are two distinguishing characteristics of traditional rationalistic explanations of behavior. These explanations are almost invariably (1) teleological and (2) untestable.

Teleology. When we speak in everyday language about the reasons for some behavior or about its purpose, we usually have reference to the mind, and more specifically to the conscious intentions of the person behaving. And to the extent that the individual has some purpose or intention that is focused upon the future, such an explanation is said to be teleological. Today we tend to restrict teleological explanations to human behavior because of our conviction that only man can foresee the consequences of his actions. The idea that purpose always implies intention and that some reasoning intellect, either man's or God's, must be the author of the intention is a feature of Christian philosophy; it was formalized by Augustine and the other codifiers of Christian theology.[2] By contrast, Greek philosophers found it possible to consider purpose, and even reason, as characteristics of nature quite apart from any conscious intention on the part of man. Thus, Aristotle proclaims that in some cases an event is explained when we know what end it serves.

> Another sort of cause is that on account of which a thing is done. For example, bodily health is a cause of walking exercise. Why does a man take exercise? We say it is in order to have good health; in this way we mean to specify the cause of walking.[3]

---

[2] The idea that man is personally, morally responsible for his own acts is also due to the early Church Fathers. The blamable part of the human personality was called the soul. The Greeks, on the assumption that man always sought to do good, attributed evil to human error or ignorance.

[3] Aristotle's views on causation are given in *Physics,* Book 2, ch. 3, and *de Anima,* Book 2, ch. 4. He believed a phenomenon was not fully explained until its purpose, its final form, and its physical causes had all been accounted for.

This earlier teleological concept, the idea of final cause as something apart from intention, was most suited to processes of growth, development, and fulfillment. For example, a block of stone becomes a statue with the sculptor as a causal agent or a child grows up and becomes a man. The stone and the child represent the unfulfilled but potential matter to which the statue and the man give form and fulfillment. They in turn are the final causes of their respective developments.

Whether we speak of purpose in the sense of final cause or purpose in the sense of intentions, both usages have a common element; some events are explained for some people when a justification for them is found. Justification is one variety of explanation. Some, like Aristotle, insist that there are certain events in the world that can be given meaning only in terms of the reasons for which they occur. But the meaning that is found in these instances is invariably evaluative; it is justification. Consider as an example the ancient argument that the appearance of purpose throughout nature is proof of the existence of a Creator. Aside from the difficulty that the argument presupposes what it purports to prove (i.e., the existence of purpose), it has the additional difficulty that after invoking a Creator such an explanation, or justification, stops with its account of nature as though nothing more were of interest. Invoking a Creator perhaps justifies creation but tells us nothing about creation; it has only restated the problem.[4] So, too, when we demand of a person the reason for his actions, his statement that he behaved as he did for such and such a reason only restates the problem; at best, we still have to explain why he had the reason he had. In the meantime, however, we may attach blame or praise to his purposes, and, indeed, it is probably just the evaluative freedom we have with another person's motives that gives us such a sense that his purposes are important. If we were to give up the notion of purpose as the cause of action we would lose one of the principal objects of our own affections and aggressions.

Untestability.   The most serious limitation of traditional rationalism is not that its explanations are teleological, but that they are inherently untestable. The events that are presumed to explain behavior are supposed to occur in the mind and be available only to the individual himself. Others have no ready or certain access to the hypothesized events. Moreover, there are no explicit hypotheses about how the mind is supposed to work so as to produce behavior; the relationships between these inaccessible mental events and observable behavior are so ill-defined and

---

[4] The point was made by Hume (1779) when he said that the argument (for the existence of God) from design was invalid because it involves the assumption that the existence of a creator was a sufficient cause of creation, whereas at most the existence of a creator is only necessary. The argument itself is that the world presents endless indications of means adapting themselves to ends, which could only have occurred as the deliberate action of a powerful intellect.

elusive that we cannot lay down any rules to indicate how the mind itself works. How does an intention to act (granting that an intention to act can produce the action) itself arise from the individual's perceptions, knowledge, feelings, and so on? There are no rules to guide us.

We should note that it is not just the case that such rules have not been found; typically, the proponents of traditional rationalism insist that there are no such rules. They say that the mind of man cannot be bound by lawfulness; it operates creatively and dynamically rather than according to fixed, predictable principles. Plato said that the psyche is that which moves itself; it has laws of its own being and needs no others. Similar statements about the inherent unpredictability, the untrammeled freedom of the human mind have come rattling down the ages. These assertions are, in fact, a crucial part of the traditional rationalistic doctrine and it is for this reason, as we will see later in this chaper, that traditional rationalism does not constitute a "theory" of motivation; nor does it provide an explanation of behavior in any real sense. That is, it is not a coherent, consistent, testable set of propositions about behavior; indeed, it is in large measure a denial that such a set of propositions can be found.

MECHANISM

In his restless quest for understanding and certainty man has sought to find the causes of all natural events, including, sometimes, human behavior. One of the oldest and most time-honored alternatives to the traditional rationalistic approach to explanation is mechanism or physicalism. To summarize it briefly, this is the doctrine that all natural events have physical causes, and that if we knew enough about physical and mechanical systems we would then be able to explain, at least in principle, all natural phenomena. The mechanist has the faith that when all the mechanical factors have been accounted for there will be nothing else left to explain.

This faith is supported in part by the predictability of physical objects in everyday life. We throw rocks and we observe that they behave in a reasonably predictable manner. If we make our observations on a billiard table we find that the predictability of the balls appears to be limited only by our skill in applying energy to them. The mechanist starts on the basis of a number of such observations and proceeds by analogy to the hypothesis that all events in nature have a similar machine-like predictability.

The doctrine of mechanism is based upon several distinct precepts, and it is important not to confuse them. Mechanism views all the phenomena of nature in the same light; while the rationalist makes a special case of man's ability to reason, the mechanist is concerned with finding principles that will include the behavior of man among the other phenomena of nature. Man's ability to reason provides no grounds for introducing exceptions to the laws of nature. His intellectual activity must be derived somehow from other, simpler principles.

The mechanist is also a determinist. While the rationalist assumes free will, the mechanist assumes that there are systematic laws of behavior that can be discovered. He assumes that if these laws were known they would permit behavior to be predicted. He may or may not involve the mind of man in his explanatory schemes, but if the mind is included, then it too must follow determinate laws.

The third distinguishing characteristic of the mechanist is his assumption that the world of physical events not only provides the pattern of what is natural and what is lawfully determined in nature but also provides the substance for all phenomena. Thus, he is a materialist. Behavior is not only a natural phenomenon, and lawfully determined, but is determined by precisely the same physical laws and forces that apply throughout nature. The ultimate and only reality, it is assumed, is physical in character.

There were Greek mechanists, but they were a minority group, and their influence was small compared with that of either Plato or Aristotle. Any substantial gains for the mechanistic position had to await its development and success in the physical realm itself; this occurred only in the seventeenth century through the work of such giants as Galileo and Newton. Wider scientific acceptance of mechanism had to wait still longer until it had been applied to the phenomena of the biological sciences.

Faith in the mechanistic doctrine has usually extended far beyond its usefulness in explaining the phenomena to which it has been applied. For example, most and perhaps all of our motivational concepts, such as drive and incentive, were developed and popularized during the interval between the introduction of mechanistic assumptions into psychology and the time when these concepts were put to empirical test. As a consequence, our theorizing made considerable use of drives and incentives and their postulated properties long before the usefulness of these concepts had been demonstrated by their ability to explain behavior. Indeed, virtually the entire history of motivation theory is devoted to declarations by this or that theorist that we must find the forces underlying behavior and the physiological causes of behavior if we are ever to explain it. The urgency with which this program has been proclaimed has, unfortunately, not always been matched by the development of what we now consider to be the proper fruits of science, namely, adequate explanatory theories. We will consider shortly what is meant by an adequate explanatory theory, but first we must note some objections that have been raised to the mechanistic doctrine.

EMPIRICAL DETERMINISM

The traditional difference of opinion regarding what constitutes an adequate explanation of any natural phenomenon has centered about purpose and teleology. The scientist has always been reluctant to admit that there are purposes operating in nature, preferring to rely upon what he views as the "real" or physical causes of things. On the other hand, rationalists, humanists, the clergy, and most thoughtful laymen have felt most at ease with, or even insisted upon, teleological accounts of certain natural phenomena, such as human behavior. The question at issue has traditionally been whether physical causes provide a total explanation, or whether teleological principles had to be added for some phenomena. Before David Hume (1739) did so, no one seemed to question whether physical causes were necessary, but only whether they were sufficient. Hume asked, How can we know the nature of causation? How can we know if causes really produce their effects? Hume's skeptical epistemology led him to the realization that the best evidence we can ever obtain is that two events invariably occur together, one preceding the other, always in the same order, and neither occurring alone. The imputation of causation, the abstract conception that the prior event necessitates the subsequent event, is an inference which goes beyond the evidence. There may be such a thing as physical or material causation, of course, but we can never be sure whether nature operates mechanistically since all we can know is the successive experience of successive events. It is in the nature of the human mind, Hume asserted, to transcend the data and infer a causal relationship between the two events if we invariably experience them one before the other.

Although scientists have characteristically operated in an empirical and pragmatic manner, philosophers, even philosophers of science, have tended to lag conceptually behind. Hence, for many years Hume's point was regarded as undue skepticism or as mere sophistry. Most men felt bound to commit themselves metaphysically either to a rationalistic position, to a mechanistic position, or to some dualistic combination of the two.

As far as science is concerned, its object is not to discover the ultimate nature of reality, but rather to explore empirical relationships and derive useful generalizations from them. The question of what sort of causation is involved in explanation is an unnecessary impediment, a philosophical encumbrance, to the conduct of science. It is futile for the scientist to be concerned with whether an event occurred because some other event compelled it to occur; much more to the point is that an event occurs and its occurrence can be correlated with certain sets of conditions. Of course we wish to refine our observations and improve our ability to control conditions until a point is reached where perfect or near-perfect correlations are possible and where very powerful general descriptive laws can be found.[5] But science does not wait for the final solution of the causation problem. We must proceed to view empirical correlations as the subject matter of science without committing ourselves to either a teleological, purposive, or materialistic philosophy. Nor do we need to go as far as Hume and say that we can never transcend empirical correlations. We may believe that, or we may take the more optimistic position that the empirical correlations we observe will ultimately be undergirded by a more profound understanding of causation. By adhering to a descriptive or correlational approach we may at least leave the way open for such a possibility.

The empirical approach is noncommittal; it provides a convenient vantage point from which we may survey other, more highly committed approaches. Psychology, particularly the area of motivation, is confused enough by the practice of regarding motives, or drives, or instincts, or needs, as the causes of behavior. If we are to describe behavior from a point of view which does not restrict us to any particular theoretical or philosophical position, then it is necessary that we adopt a terminology which leaves these questions open. Thus the relationship which exists, for example, between a stimulus and a response will be described throughout this book, not in causal terms, but in neutral and descriptive terms. We will say that deprivation and stimulus conditions *determine* behavior, or that some behavior is under the *control* of some stimulus.

The crucial insight here is that the empirical attitude does not imply a rejection of the principle of determinism. Quite the contrary; it will be argued that behavior is determined, not because forces act on the organism to make it behave, nor because the behavior was willed by some reasoning intellect, but is determined simply in the sense that it is intrinsically predictable. Behavior is determined in that it is lawful.

The doctrine that I have called empirical determinism thus keeps the first two propositions of the mechanistic doctrine, namely, that behavior is a natural phenomenon and that it is determined, and rejects only its mechanistic or materialistic bias. It will be argued that a "causeless" account of a phenomenon can constitute an explanation of it even though it fails to provide any justification, or indicate its physical basis. It will also be argued that accordance with an empirical law constitutes just the kind of explanation we want, provided only that the empirical law is contained in a systematic theory. Before proceeding with this argument

---

[5] Recent scholars have sought to analyze more carefully the meaning of terms like "cause," "effect," and "necessitate" (Bunge, 1959; Smith, 1960). Usually, the conditions of temporal and spacial contiguity between cause and effect call for their most serious consideration. These considerations are serious, weighty, and highly involved logically—particularly when contrasted with the elegance of the empirical laws to which they are purported to be relevant.

let us digress briefly to consider some objections that might be raised to this position.

Hempel and Oppenheim (1948) have discussed a number of such objections. They consider, for example, the argument that a strictly empirical explanatory system is not applicable to behavior in humans because of the enormous complexity of the human subject and the unique character of his behavior. Hempel and Oppenheim contend that the only real question here is whether phenomena as complex as human behavior are susceptible to adequate explanation. This is an empirical question; can laws of sufficient breadth and generality be discovered and can sufficient precision be obtained in specifying the appropriate antecedent conditions? The uniqueness and the irrepeatability of observations do not distinguish behavior from other observable phenomena. Irrepeatability is no less a problem in physics, or even astronomy, than it is in psychology; all observations are unique. The only strategy by which science can proceed at all is to concern itself with common features of and abstractions from unique observations.

Is such a system of explanation applicable to psychological phenomena in view of the fact that so many of the theoretical entities in psychology are not directly observable? The answer, again, is that psychological phenomena and theoretical constructs do not differ appreciably from those in physics or from those in any other science in this respect. So long as there are methods for determining with reasonable clarity and precision the hypothesized variables there is no special problem here at all. The only real question is whether psychological theories are to be based entirely upon empirical observations or whether they are to be based partly upon other, "transempirical," sources of knowledge.

Another question is whether psychological explanations, which have historically involved reference to purposive behavior, call for a different mode of explanation. If "purposive" pertains to Divine purpose or to some inscrutable intention on the part of the individual, then, it is true, the approach fails to provide an adequate explanation. But if these kinds of purpose really have no empirical reference, then it is not clear that behavior which is purposive in this sense is susceptible to any sort of explanation. On the other hand, if we mean by "purposive behavior" only that form of behavior which is highly correlated with its consequences, i.e., if we use the phrase in a purely descriptive or empirical manner, then there is no difference in principle between purposive behavior and any other kind of phenomena.

Perhaps the most fundamental practical objection that might be raised to empirical determinism is that it fails to tell *why* an event occurs; it only describes how and when events occur. When all is said and done a phenomenon is explained when it is put into terms with which we are familiar and shown to be an instance of a principle with which we are familiar. As Bridgman (1932) has said, an explanation is that kind of account that puts the curiosity at rest.[6] We may ask what is the frame of mind of a man whose curiosity is only "put at rest" by an account of why things happen. What are such men really looking for? In the case of behavior, there seem to be two different kinds of accounts that men may be seeking when they ask "why?" One is justification, and the other is an application of the mechanistic doctrine. Thus, some of the time when someone is asked "why did you do that?", what is expected is a justification of the action. At other times it seems clear that what is demanded is an understanding of the physiological or neurological machinery that produced the effect.

In general, a satisfactory answer to a "why" question is a statement involving terms with which the inquirer is familiar. The difficulty of explanation in psychology is that those who ask the psychologist "why" come to him quite familiar with justifying action and quite familiar with the reality of the physical body and seek some explanation in these terms. On the other hand, the scientist, who is familiar with the empirical regularities in his science, does not seek the why of them. Insofar as the psychologist asks why, it is because he is curious about moral questions of justification or about the mysteries of neurology, either of which he may have legitimate reasons for wanting to relate to behavior. But the psychologist asks why only when he wants to transcend or extend the boundaries of his science and not when he is working within them.

THE EVALUATION OF THEORIES

It was noted above that if an empirical law is to provide an explanation of a phenomenon it must be part of a systematic theory. All this means in effect is that explanation in science requires that a phenomenon be systematically related to other phenomena. When we have a model for producing such a systemization, then we have a theory. Since there is ample opportunity in current usage for confusion about what does and what does not constitute a theory, let us consider in some detail just what is involved.

Formal Properties of Theories. From a logical point of view, a theory involves at least (1) a number of terms, and (2) a number of relational rules tying the terms together or interrelating them in some way. In purely formal systems, such as the different branches of mathematics, the terms are undefined. However, if a theory is to have empirical usefulness and testability it must have a third property: its terms have to be defined or

---

[6] ". . . an explanation consists in reducing a situation to elements with which we are so familiar that we accept them as a matter of course, so that our curiosity rests" (Bridgman, 1932, p. 37).

related in some way to empirical events. There are a few examples of theories in psychology in which the primary emphasis is placed upon formal structure and in which little interest is attached to the problem of relating to empirical events. One such example is Lewin's topological psychology (1936). Lewin went to considerable effort to develop a formal (or what might be called a preexperimental) structure which would be able to encompass the full richness and complexity of human behavior as the facts became known. The terms that constitute the formal language of the theory, i.e., terms like "valence," "force," and "tension," are explicitly related to each other, but are only poorly tied to observable events in the empirical world. Lewin's theory demonstrates a remarkable degree of sophistication, complexity, and internal coherence quite apart from the empirical question of whether people actually behave in the way the system prescribes. One could entertain oneself at length with the purely formal properties of the theory without applying it to the explanation of behavior.

As another example of a theory which provides a certain measure of formal adequacy we might cite Hull's hypothetico-deductive theory of rote learning (Hull et al., 1940). This theory was admittedly just a model to describe the "behavior" of an idealized "subject" learning a list of nonsense syllables, and again, it would be of considerable formal interest even if it should turn out that no actual subject ever demonstrated such behavior. What makes these semiformal systems of interest, apart from their empirical possibilities, is that they contain sets of relational rules which together give structure to the theory. Such a structure is called the *syntax* of a theory. The syntactical rules indicate how the terms of the theory fit together to provide an explanatory network; they describe how to operate with the theoretical terms in order to relate them to each other and to the data.

The syntax of a theory may be precise and formally rigid, as in Hull's hypothetico-deductive theory where mathematical relationships were formulated between all of the terms; or it may be left loose and qualitative; and terms may be left undefined, as in mathematical systems. All gradations occur. But since it is by relating the terms of the theory to each other (and to the data) that a theory is used, a theory without adequate syntactical rules is no theory at all. For example, the traditional view that man's behavior is explained by his rationality lacks any syntax because it assumes that man's behavior cannot be described by any set of rules. And this, the most serious limitation of traditional rationalism, is why this doctrine cannot properly be called a theory of behavior. One property we may require of a theory is that it should have an explicit syntax.

Empirical Base of a Theory. Philosophers of science and model builders may be chiefly interested in the structure of a theory considered just as a formal system. But to the scientist a much more interesting and important matter is the tying down of the logical or formal structure of the theory to empirical data so that the theory may be tested. This tying-down process is often called "anchoring." It is a different kind of process from the construction of the formal structure of the theory, and in many instances occurs quite independently of it. The branch of logic which deals with such definitions is called *semantics*. One difficulty in semantics is that a theory will ordinarily possess two kinds of terms: those that are theoretical, or not directly observable, and those that are empirical, or more-or-less directly observable. The theoretical terms of a theory (which I will call its *theoretical constructs*) are known by the fact that they are interrelated syntactically; they constitute the terms in the formal theory. But they must also be given empirical reference by being tied semantically to empirical terms (which, for reasons given below, I will call the *empirical constructs* of the theory).

From the point of view of the formal purist, some of the most popular theories have unfortunately been developed by theorists who have not paid enough attention to the empirical roots of theory making. For example, in psychoanalysis the semantic linkages of the theoretical constructs to empirical observations are so weak that it sometimes appears as though only the theorist himself could possibly know what he was theorizing about. Psychoanalysts seem at times to make a deliberate effort to create a mystique: the empirical anchoring of the terms of the theory is supposed to be left intuitive and loose. Freud believed that the rigid definition of theoretical terms should be the end rather than the means of theoretical advancement.

> The view is often defended that sciences should be built up on clear and sharply defined basal concepts. In actual fact no science, not even the most exact, begins with such definitions. The true beginning of scientific activity consists rather in describing phenomena and then in proceeding to group, classify and correlate them. Even at the stage of description it is not possible to avoid applying certain abstract ideas to the material in hand, ideas derived from various sources and certainly not the fruit of new experience only. Still more indispensable are such ideas—which will later become the basal concepts of the science—as the material is further elaborated. They must at first necessarily possess some measure of uncertainty; there can be no question of any clear delimitation of their content. So long as they remain in this condition, we come to an understanding about their meaning by repeated references to the material of observation, from which we seem to have deduced our abstract ideas, but which is in point of fact subject to them . . . It is only after more searching investigation of the field in question that we are able to formulate

with increased clarity the scientific concepts underlying it, and progressively so to modify these concepts that they become widely applicable and at the same time consistent logically. Then, indeed, it may be time to immure them in definitions. (Freud, 1915, pp. 60–61)

Although some might despair at such laxity, Freud always put difficult problems into historical perspective, and here he has indicated quite realistically how a scientific theory develops. We find that the logical analysis of the formal structure of a theory into its syntax and semantics does not tell us all about it, and in fact, such an analysis may have little historical or practical validity.

Still, the most useful theories of behavior are those in which theoretical constructs are coordinated at least tentatively with behavioral data. A theory must contain hypothetical relationships that tie together the empirical and theoretical terms. A second property we may require of a theory is that it have an explicit semantics.

Data Language. It should be noted that the specification of the empirical terms of a theory, the selection of facts which it is to explain, is not entirely arbitrary but is dependent also upon usage and habits of observation. "Response" is usually considered an empirical term, but it is not purely empirical. Its meaning is determined as much by the theory in which it is designated an "empirical observation" as by what happens in the real world. Thus, it is only relatively empirical. It is empirical by comparison with the theoretical constructs, but it is theoretical compared with the more basic terms of everyday language. To emphasize the quasi-empirical-quasi-theoretical nature of such terms we will call them *empirical constructs*. The empirical constructs, taken together, constitute what we will call the *data language*.

Data language serves as a foundation for a theory by tying it down empirically; it is also the language scientists use to talk among themselves. As Estes has put it,

> the data language . . . includes the terminology needed for the description of observations and operations. In psychology the chief function of the data language is the description of behaviors and of the situations in which they occur. The terms used in description must be limited to those for which agreement upon usage can be obtained from workers in the field regardless of theoretical biases and which are free of any reference to theory (that is, to the theory for which the set of terms in question functions as data language). (Estes, 1954, p. 321)[7]

[7] I have taken much of the language Estes uses in the logical analysis of theories for the present discussion. One point Estes makes I cannot agree to, however, and that is that a data language is theoretically neutral. It seems to me

Some writers define the data language of their theory explicitly (e.g., Skinner) but more often they leave it unanalyzed, implicit (e.g., Lewin, or the Gestalt psychologists).

One of the difficulties in assessing different theories of behavior is that the different theories have tended to isolate themselves by the use of data languages which are unintelligible to theorists of other persuasions. Thus, it is only with considerable effort that a S-R-learning theorist and a psychoanalyst can communicate with each other. The difficulty is that what one accepts as an empirical observation the other may not. Each has no difficulty in a linguistic community which accepts the same data language, but the mixture of data languages from two independent sets of workers can be disastrous. Some of the great conflicts in the history of theoretical psychology can be traced to the problem of mutually un-intelligible data languages. For example, the continuing lack of harmony between molar and molecular points of view may be attributed to the use of the word "response" for very different kinds of events for which very different kinds of psychological theories seem appropriate.

Consequently, we must consider that the semantic problems in a theory of behavior extend not only from the theoretical constructs down to the empirical constructs of the data language, but from there on down to facts of experience upon which anyone speaking the language can agree—what Carnap (1936) has called the physical-thing language. Ideally, the data language would be linked to the thing language, the language of common perceptual experience, through operational definitions. As an alternative to such rigid linkages, the theorist may use the technique commonly employed in the physical sciences, *sets* of reductions. That is, he might identify a term by means of several functional properties.

An important question is whether the ultimate language to which the data language is reduced *must* be the physical-thing language. This question lies at the very heart of the traditional difficulty of studying complex human behavior. In the rationalistic variety of explanation, the language of human experience is asserted to be the only one that is valid for the study of man. To be sure, there may be a perfectly good language of human experience which is more or less independent of the language of physical things, but this language has shown itself to be of relatively little use for the purpose of developing a theory of human behavior. There

---

that much of a data language is determined in the same way as the other contents of a theory, namely by the constraints of our own experience, and by our previously established habits of speculation and observation. In the storybooks, the scientist is able to study a perfectly arbitrary selection from among possible phenomena, but in fact, this selection is determined in large part by what he believes to underlie what he observes. Stevens put it: "There are *only* constructs . . . A datum *is* a construct" (1935, p. 523). Margenau (1950) has examined thoroughly the implications of this position for physical theory.

is so much trouble communicating with such languages that we cannot test assertions stated in them. And perhaps above all else we require that a theory of behavior be testable. Therefore we may require of a theory that it have a precise and explicit data language, precise enough and explicit enough that it is possible to test assertions derived from the theory.

Figure 1-1 depicts some of the formal properties of theories we have been considering.

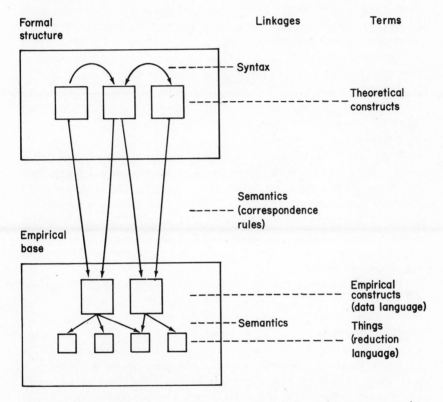

Fig. 1-1. An analysis of the kinds of terms and linkages between terms that occur in a theory.

THE CONSTRUCTS OF A THEORY

Viewed solely as part of a conceptual model, the set of theoretical constructs in a theory are all of the same sort, viz., symbols to be put down on paper. But imbued with the purposes and presuppositions (and biases) of the theorist, the theory takes on new dimensions, and all its constituent constructs acquire conceptual properties of their own. They differ in temporal duration; some are enduring, like "dispositions," others are temporary state variables, like "drive," while still others are fleeting determinants of behavior like "percepts." They differ also in temporal order; the consequences of stimulation precede the final determinants of the response. Constructs also differ with respect to their causal relationships; stimuli are generally assumed to *cause* the responses they control.

Empirical Reference of Constructs. Perhaps the most striking way in which constructs differ is with respect to their hypothetical or actual empirical reference. Spence (1944) has suggested a four-fold classification of the referents commonly used in psychological theories: animistic, neurophysiological, response-inferred, and intervening. With constructs of the animistic variety there is no anchoring to empirical observables. Presumably everyone is just supposed to *know* the signs of these intuitive psychological variables. The reason these sorts of constructs are called animistic is clear: they operate on the individual as though they had reason and will of their own, and these cognitive and volitional powers are not subject to further analysis.

Physiological Reference. The neurophysiological type of construct is another favorite; its empirical reference is most frequently to a hypothetical neurological mechanism which is not now directly observable, but which, at least in principle, could be observed. One example is the concept of decreased synaptic resistance as a basis of learning. As a mechanism it sounds plausible, but as an empirical fact it has the status of a "promissory note," that is, we invoke it hoping that some day the physiologist will confirm its existence for us.

It is not clear that either the physiologist or the psychologist has gained much by the one telling the other what he should look for. It is also not certain that the surplus meaning that the psychologist attaches to his constructs by means of these promissory notes makes them any more valuable. Certainly they become no more useful for describing the facts of behavior; their only possible utility would seem to be to establish a true bridge science of physiological psychology. But their major application is not ordinarily as constructs in new physiological theories, but as ancillary elements in behavioral theories. In this application they would seem to be something like status symbols.

The theorist may be simply indicating his faith in a mechanistic variety of explanation when he posits neurophysiological constructs; he may simply be showing that he believes that ultimately the facts and laws of psychology will be reducible to the facts and laws of physiology. But if the theorist would validate a theoretical construct in terms of, say, neural synapses, then neural synapses must be included in the data language of his theory, and he would then have a theory *about* neural synapses rather than one *invoking* them. He still would not have validated the original behavioral construct; that can only be done empirically. If the theorist attempts a reductionistic coup by translating all his data language into the language of physiology, then he is thrown back by the fact that physiology lies no closer to "reality" but is itself only an organization of empirical correlations. The reductionistic psychologist might just as well have stayed where he started. Translation of the stimulus into its neurological correlate and the response into its neurological correlate has brought him no nearer to demonstrating that the stimulus really causes the response. After the translation, the psychological theorist (who has now become a physiological theorist) may observe a correlation between this neural activity and that, but he is no closer to having shown that the one causes the other.

Mentalistic Reference. In an earlier day it was more frequent for the psychologist to seek validation of his constructs by shifting to quite another level, that of "human experience." Again, this sort of validation of a theoretical construct is inadmissible. If human experience can be included in the data language, then so much the better, but it cannot be invoked to lend ancillary validity to a construct that is otherwise anchored to behavioral phenomena. Because its reference is outside the theory, introducing it does nothing to bind together the structure of the theory. Its surplus meaning must always remain surplus.

Response-Inferred Constructs. The other two categories of theoretical constructs which Spence lists, response-inferred and intervening, are the bread and butter of psychological theorizing. Response-inferred constructs are those that are linked by coordinating definitions to just one kind of empirical construct—some single response phenomenon. Now, there is a hazard in relying upon a single semantic linkage. It means that, in one sense, the construct cannot be used to explain the phenomena with which it is linked because such an explanation would be circular. Theorists are rarely so naive, however, and certainly they rarely work with such uninteresting constructs, and perhaps he has in mind some more or less implicit secondary linkages which give further conceptual properties to his constructs. Or the theorist may simply not feel ready to incorporate them into the definition (the primary linkages) of the construct, preferring to leave them tentative. The onus of circularity that is often put on response-inferred constructs is really only justifiable in those cases where the theoretical construct is used to explain exactly the same features of behavior from which its existence is inferred. To the extent that a variable is used across different situations or different subjects or different behavioral events, it acquires some practical sort of validity.

Intervening Constructs. The intervening-variable type of constructs are those which are embedded in a network involving several empirical constructs, and in particular, they intervene between the stimulus and the response.[8] If they are given semantic and/or syntactical linkages to both the stimulus and the response, then they are said to be anchored on both the antecedent and the consequent side. Spence has tried to make a sharp distinction between the intervening-variable and the response-inferred type of construct, and he has made clear his preference for the intervening variety. However, I doubt that the distinction can be maintained as sharply as Spence would like. It frequently turns out that the stimulus is not empirically independent of the response; we sometimes don't know what the effective stimulus is until the responses of the subject are analyzed. Consequently, an intervening construct variable is often logically reducible to one of the response-inferred variety.

But the point of Spence's argument remains and it is a critically important one: our theoretical constructs have to be tied by two or more semantic relationships (possibly via some further syntactical linkages) to two or more empirical constructs. The whole set of theoretical and empirical constructs then may be visualized as a sort of network. Sometimes it is called a nomological net. A theory in which there is a simple one-to-one correspondence between empirical and theoretical constructs is hardly better than a theory with none. Such a theory would consist merely of a restatement of empirical relationships that had been obtained, and would contribute no economy, power, or possibility of further insight to a purely empirical description.

Radical Empiricism. One way to adhere to the formal criteria of science is to exclude all theoretical constructs from consideration, i.e., to use no terms that cannot be immediately reduced operationally to the physical-thing language. This means a dedication to finding lawfulness among empirical constructs. This approach may be called radical empiricism. The scientist who adheres to the program of radical empiricism gains some safety from it since he never has to revise his theoretical constructs or his syntactical structure—because he doesn't have any. But there is relatively little else to recommend this approach.

Of course, those who speak loudest against theories may only be voicing their distaste for the animistic and neurophysiological sorts of constructs that so frequently occur in them.[9] Or the advocates of atheorism

---

[8] The designation "intervening variable" was coined by Tolman (1936). Skinner has pointed out, however, that this designation is not a particularly good one unless what is meant is some sort of transempirical, i.e., mentalistic or physicalistic, intervention between stimulus and response (Skinner, 1959, p. 320). Tolman probably had no such intention.

[9] I am referring here particularly to Skinner's disavowal of theory (1950). He says that he would have theory excluded from a science of behavior if that word refers to "any explanation of an observed fact which appeals to events taking place somewhere else, at some other level of observation, described in different terms, and measured, if at all, in different dimensions" (p. 193). Skinner clarifies further the object of his dissatisfaction: theories incorporating real and conceptual mental and

may be against the sort of causation that tends to be implied in many psychological theories. But one does not have to abandon theory altogether to overcome the limitations of animistic and neurological constructs. In fact, the formal and empirical structure of most of our theories of behavior may be quite easily divorced from the surplus meaning that is characteristically associated with them. It is certainly possible to have a theory of behavior involving terms with no surplus meaning, terms which do not commit the theorist to a particular variety of explanation, or betray his personal belief in one.[10]

Radical empiricism is too big a price to pay. All that it buys can be purchased more cheaply by demanding that constructs be validated solely by being tied syntactically and semantically to the data language. This demand appears simple and straightforward, but it is contrary to the common practice of attempting to validate a construct or give it greater reality status by transcending the data or by going to another level of discourse. What makes one construct "better" than another is not that it is more real, but that it is tied in more different ways to empirical constructs, that it has what Koch (1941, p. 30) has called a "plurality of observable symptoms."[11] It is not the theorist's inclusion of a neurological or mentalistic construct which is wrong but his insistence that a construct can be given status within a theory by means outside the theory itself. He is subscribing to the belief in some transempirical validation. He believes that he has somehow really gotten hold of the causal agencies when he refers to a synapse, or a S-R connection, or a drive, or a cell assembly,

---

neural terms. "When we attribute behavior to a neural or mental event, real or conceptual, we are likely to forget that we still have the task of accounting for the neural or mental event. When we assert that an animal acts in a given way because it expects to receive food, then what began as the task of accounting for learned behavior becomes the task of accounting for expectancy. The problem is at least equally complex and probably more difficult. We are likely to close our eyes to it and to use the theory to give us answers in place of the answers we might find through further study" (p. 194).

[10] Undeniably there is a correlation between what variety of explanation a theorist favors and the sort of constructs he puts into his theory. But there is no necessary connection between the two. Thus, animistic constructs tend to be teleological, but they are not necessarily so. Neurophysiological constructs may indicate the theorist's faith in material and efficient causation, but they may have reference only to the empirical regularities in physiology. The response-inferred and intervening types of constructs tend more than the others to be of a purely empirical or mathematical nature, but they too may be based upon other varieties of explanation. Thus, Hull generally believed that the constructs in his theory had physiological reality, and Tolman believed that behavior was intrinsically teleological. A response-inferred or intervening type of construct may be proposed by a theorist with an acausal view of nature, or one who, for some other reason, prefers a purely empirical approach.

[11] The plurality of empirical symptoms is a measure of the *fruitfulness* of the construct, as opposed to the commonness of the symptoms which is a measure of its *generality*. Another way to state the importance of a plurality of empirical symptoms is to say that a construct should be "overdetermined" by its empirical coordinations.

or an expectancy. But at our present stage of understanding we can know no more than that our observations correlate. The fourth and final thing we should require of a theory, then, is that its theoretical terms be validated solely by their empirical usefulness. We will give no weight to any sort of claimed transempirical validation.

Compromise Character of a Theory. We have come to a point where logical analysis fails us. We want to require of a theory that its terms be anchored to empirical observations as definitively as possible, but at the same time we must recognize that these linkages are always tentative; theories are always in a process of formulation, or should be. The skill of a theorist is shown by his ability to alter the semantic structure of his theory as new evidence becomes available. And at the same time, the structure of the theory dictates to some extent what observations will get made and even how they will be made and recorded. So a theory must specify its constructs with some precision, but it must also allow for further conceptual reorganizations. We want to require of a theory that it provide some measure of economy over a raw description of certain phenomena, but it must not be too economical; it must provide for some syntactical complexity if it is to prove useful. We want to require that a theorist speak out as plainly and explicitly as possible, but we have to recognize that the formal statement of a theory must always remain somewhat behind the insight of the theorist.

So our portrait of the useful theory begins to take shape. A good theory is a tentative compromise between economy and complexity, explanatory power and mere descriptive tautology, precision and richness. We require that a theory meet certain standards of formal adequacy: its syntax, semantics, and data language must be set forth with some precision and explicitness. But we may wish to relax these formal standards if doing so can lead to further theoretical gains in the long run. We can expect an occasional departure from these standards, particularly with the more interesting and important theories.

2

HISTORICAL ORIGINS OF MOTIVATIONAL CONCEPTS

✦⟨⟨

. . . the hope of progress—moral and intellectual as well as material—in the future is bound up with the fortunes of science, and every obstacle placed in the way of scientific discovery is a wrong to humanity.

J. G. FRAZER

The experimental psychologist today assumes with little question that systematic laws of behavior can be discovered. This deterministic outlook would seem to be firmly enough established that we would not have to examine it further. We might just acknowledge that we have arrived at this position and pass on quickly to other problems. But the idea of universal determinism is new and exciting, even today. We who regard behavior as determined by natural law occupy a unique position. The present chapter is a document to celebrate our arrival at this position and a testimonial to some of the men who have led us to it.

The gradually growing confidence in the power of some form of determinism to explain human behavior must be considered against the perennial background of the rationalistic doctrine. Our brief history will show that rationalism has provided a continuing challenge, first to the mechanist and then to the more empirically oriented scientist. (In a later chapter we will see how modern incentive theory has attempted to meet this challenge.) We will see that naive forms of the mechanistic philosophy have been advanced with fond hopes and great faith and that mechanism has been extended to encompass an ever-widening range of topics, only to be replaced in turn by a more subtle variety of determinism. We should be able to discover in the course of this history not only the origins of the general concept of motivation, but also the beginnings of such specific concepts as instinct, drive, incentive, and reinforcement.

THE RATIONALISTIC ERA

For Plato, as for most of the Greek philosophers, what we would call the motivational determinants of behavior had little direct bearing on a man's behavior because they could always be overridden by his faculty of reason. As long as the intellect is free to decide upon a course of action, a man's ability to select goals makes his choice of goal the determinant of his subsequent course of action. The will is free because it is always directed toward the future; it is not constrained by the situation (except insofar as a man's reason is limited by his education). Plato did recognize "forced" movements, those produced by emotion or by the animal passions, but he considered them awkward, graceless, and lacking in purpose. He thought of them as essentially random or lawless in character and surely not like man's usual, natural activities.[1]

Plato's position is noted here, not just because of his enormous contribution to the history of ideas, but also because it provides an interesting example of a comprehensive philosophy of man that includes no motivational concepts. The reason for this omission is clear: no such concept was necessary because man was viewed as an active and rational agent; he was free to do what he wanted to do. Man's intellect and will were felt to provide a sufficient account of his actions. Such an attitude, of course, shuts the door to further possible investigation. Shut long ago, the door has been very difficult to open.

The evaluative elements of Greek rationalistic philosophy have also endured. They have dominated not only western philosophical thought

---

[1] Here I have followed Zeller (1883)—a particularly useful source because Zeller seemed to be remarkably aware of the problems inherent in explaining behavior and the Greek's failure to cope with them. Another useful classic, for similar reasons, is Lange (1873).

but, via Christian theology, have permeated our whole culture to a degree that is difficult to overestimate. Consider the following quotation:

> . . . man has sensuous desire, and rational desire or will. He is not absolutely determined in his desires and actions by sense impressions as is the brute, but possesses a faculty of self-determination, whereby he is able to act or not to act. . . . The will is determined by what intelligence conceives to be the good, by a rational purpose. This, however, is not compulsion; compulsion exists where a being is inevitably determined by an external cause. Man is free because he is rational, because he is not driven into action by an external cause without his consent, and because he can choose between the means of realizing the good or the purpose which his reason conceives.

This quotation sounds as though it could have been taken directly from Plato or perhaps Aristotle. It is, however, from a discussion of the philosophy of Thomas Aquinas, who wrote 1500 years later. Moreover, it is the position taken today by most Catholic writers on the question of psychological determinism.[2]

The First Mechanists. From the earliest times there was a small group of thinkers who dissented from this position. Democritus, a contemporary of Plato, based his elaborate philosophical system upon the mechanistic principle that all substances, animate as well as inanimate, were reducible to atoms of different sizes and shapes. Events in both the physical world and the mental world occur because of the constant motion of the respective atoms. The atoms of the psyche are smooth and round which enables them to interpenetrate other, coarser atoms; and it is because of this penetrating power of its atoms that the psyche can get in contact with and come to have knowledge about the physical world.

This philosophy was all the more remarkable for its time because it was supplemented by a principle that has become known as ethical hedonism. There had always been agreement that pleasure and pain were related in some way to man's conduct and that pleasure sprang from the exercise of the animal passions, e.g., eating, drinking, and sex. Rationalists, like Plato, had dealt with this persistent fact by asserting

[2] The quotation is from Thilly and Wood (1957, pp. 232–233). This is another useful history of philosophy for our purposes because the writers pay particular attention to the problem of determinism. For the Catholic, the question of free will is not just academic; it is an important theological matter. The Catholic's salvation depends upon his choosing good instead of evil. Confronted with this special problem, most Catholic psychologists hold the will to be free axiomatically (see, e.g., Harmon, 1951). For a further discussion of this problem and of the research done by Catholic psychologists to demonstrate the existence of the will and how to train it, see Misiak and Staudt (1954). The best discussions of theories of the will (like the theory that it is awareness of effort) is still James (1890). The clearest sympathetic treatment of Aquinas is Gilson (1956).

that pleasures so derived were ethically or morally inferior to those obtained through the exercise of the higher mental capacities. What Democritus argued was that all of the pleasures were equally good and that the rational and virtuous man is simply one who regulates his life so that in the end he would have obtained the greatest possible total of pleasure. The problem of the animal appetites in this view is not that they are intrinsically evil, or less desirable than the intellectual pursuits, but rather that they entail certain dangers. The wise man, therefore, will seek to satisfy his bodily needs and to attain physical pleasures only in moderation.[3]

Epicurus, following Democritus, proposed an improved atomistic system, but he held what appears to be an incongruous view of determinism. He argued that there was a chain of mechanical causation from the atoms of the soul to the atoms of the body. But he allowed for the atoms of the soul to "swerve" slightly through volition so that the subsequent chain of movements of the atoms would pursue the desired end. The causal chain of events could be altered by volition. This inconsistency was deliberately installed into the system in order to make moral responsibility more plausible.

Epicurus' solution to the problem of moral responsibility was symptomatic of the treatment the problem was to receive for the next 2,000 years. During this long interval there was no real opposition to the doctrine that man is a free agent, and therefore morally responsible for his acts.[4] For most of this period dissension was held in check by self-appointed keepers of revelation who crystallized what they called knowledge.

THE INTELLECTUAL REVOLUTION

The established orthodoxies were not shattered by any single blow. But gradually man began to enter a new age, an age of discovery. He discovered himself (the renaissance) and the outer world (the Copernican revolution). Some of the participants in this great awakening were concerned with overthrowing Aristotle's philosophy, others with reforming the Church. Still others were dedicated to the new scientific methodology; Bacon, for example, attributed the success of the new science to the collection of data, while Galileo was concerned primarily with determining

[3] Watson (1895) and Bailey (1928) give specialized accounts of this period.

[4] However, the glorious autonomy we appear to have gained through the rationalistic doctrine has been bought at considerable price. We may hold man to be free, but we also hold him to be responsible. And therefore, because he is free, and because he is responsible, he is liable to punishment. Someday we may be able to show that men consider themselves free *because* they are held responsible (Bolles, 1963a). Thus, it may not be that the burden of responsibility attaches to the glory of freedom, rather, it may be that a sense of freedom is all that can be salvaged from the bondage of being held responsible!

the empirical laws which would best provide a concise mathematical account of certain facts he hoped to explain.[5]

With the decline in prestige of Aristotelian philosophy, other philosophers were inspired to propose bold new world-views based upon the new physicalistic account of the heavens. Rather than despair because Copernicus had displaced man from the station he had assumed at the center of the universe, philosophers of that day, at least some of them, found a new optimism.

René Descartes. Descartes (1649) introduced a bold new dualism of mind and matter to replace the prevailing scholastic philosophy. He held that all physical phenomena could be adequately explained mechanically. The solar system, Descartes observed, could be likened to a great clockwork. Descartes contended that it was not necessary to suppose divine intervention in the solar machinery. Divine creation was assumed to be necessary to create and set the system in motion, but once in motion it could be assumed to proceed by its own purely physical laws.

According to this view, animals, lacking rational souls, were merely automata. Their behavior was held to be due to the physical forces acting upon them. Some forces were external but other forces were internal, caused by agitations within the physical organism. For example, if an animal was without food its physiology would be disturbed in such a way that it would eat; it was compelled to eat by its physical structure. Although Descartes' physiology has failed to survive, it was important for establishing a break with traditional scholastic doctrines and for its postulation of explanatory mechanisms where previous analysis had been in terms of Aristotelian capacities and functions. As Descartes saw it, organisms functioned largely through agitations entering the brain and being reflected (reflect = reflex) back out into the muscles (Fearing, 1930). In the case of animals, reflection was entirely automatic; what went in completely determined what came out. But in the case of man, reasoning intervened between input and output so that man was free to choose, to select, to determine his behavior according to his knowledge. Because man possessed a reasoning soul, his nature transcended the physical realm.

The popularity of Descartes' dualism derived from the fact that it retained rationality where it was important, i.e., in man, but espoused determinism in the physical realm where it was becoming increasingly hard to deny it. This dualism of mind and matter constitutes the starting point for any discussion of the mind-body problem; indeed, it may be said that Descartes created the problem.

[5] A great deal has been written on the scientific reawakening of the sixteenth and seventeenth centuries. Perhaps the best introduction is Crombie (1959). Crombie is especially interested in the divergent views about causation entertained at this time. Crombie, and most recent students of this period, have emphasized that the awakening was a gradual process which took many centuries, and was marked by many setbacks.

Descartes presented his own solution to the mind-body problem in *The Passions of the Soul* (1649). He held that man's conduct was mediated through complex interactions of mind and body in which the body as much as the mind could be said to initiate action. The mind is subject to certain passions (literally, agitations) which might come to it either from its own reflections or from the body. Agitations from the body might come from the receptors or might depend upon bodily conditions like hunger and sexual appetite, or might arise from other internal disturbances such as the emotions, e.g., joy and anger.

Descartes believed that the emotions were critically important because of the way they can change the flow of animal spirits which, in turn, determine action. He was concerned with showing how six primary emotions in combination could give rise to the large number and gradation of feelings that are known introspectively. The modus operandi of the emotions was complex. The passions "dispose the soul to desire those things which nature tells us are of use, and to persist in this desire, and also bring about that same agitation of spirits which customarily causes them to dispose the body to the movement which serves for the carrying into effect of these things" (1649, article 52).

The emotions appear from this to have four functions. They cause:

1. an appropriate flow of animal spirits in the body;
2. the body to be ready for certain goal objects;
3. the soul to desire the objects (which nature tells us are of use) ;
4. persistence of the desire for these objects.

Descartes' optimistic theorizing stands as the first real attempt to build a theory to correlate physiological, behavioral, and experiential events. He was quite explicit in stating that it was not sufficient to look merely to the mind itself in order to understand its activity; appropriate behavior must be accounted for as well as the underlying substrate of physiological events. Thus he broke with and went considerably beyond the old rationalism. His account was deterministic in spirit, although it still left considerable room for the free play of man's rationality. Although Descartes still retained teleological elements (e.g., he viewed the nature of man as organized in such a way as to serve his natural ends) he made some effort to rid his system of teleology, and he said (1677), "All the phenomena of nature may be explained by their means." On the other hand, Descartes assumed that it was God who had so built man and given him his rationality and his wondrously adapted biological nature.

Here Descartes had seized upon a new concept, one which was to have considerable impact, for in discussing man's God-given nature which guides him to satisfy his appetites and which is organized in such a way as to make behavior adaptable, Descartes was talking about the seventeenth-century concept of instinct. Instinct was, at first, the source of the forces that impel man to satisfy his appetites. It should be noted that in this early usage instincts were not the impelling forces themselves but the source of such forces. It should also be noted that in this early usage there was no implication of a mechanical principle; quite the contrary, instinct (the word was used in the singular) was evidence of the hand of God, of His divine plan. Instinct, being God given, was considered to be perfectly normal and natural. Instinct was thus the natural origin of the biologically important motives.

Although the word "instinct" was first used in this sense in English at the end of the sixteenth century (Shakespeare, *Henry IV, 2*), the concept had a much earlier origin. Thomas Aquinas had said,

> There are some things which act not from any choice, but, as they are moved and made to act by others; just as an arrow is directed to the target by the archer. Others act from some kind of choice, but not from free choice, such as irrational animals, for the sheep flies from the wolf by a kind of judgment whereby it considers it to be hurtful to itself; such a judgment is not a free one but implanted by nature.

Thus, nature has given animals (and man, according to Descartes) a remarkable constitution which produces the right kind of behavior and the right kind of mental attitude and a readiness to do just those things which will promote their welfare.

Thomas Hobbes and Materialism. The pinnacle of seventeenth-century scientistic optimism was reached by Hobbes (1651) who sought to build upon the materialism of Democritus a philosophy of great breadth and subtlety that accepted little of traditional doctrines.[6] Hobbes was a resolute materialist for whom the explanation of all things was to be found in their physical motions. Hobbes supposed that there were two sorts of motion in the body. One kind, vital motion, was concerned with the circulation of the blood, breathing, nutrition, and other biological processes. The other kind of motion, animal or voluntary motion, manifested itself in locomotion, in speaking, and so on. Animal or voluntary motion was asserted to be "first fancied in our minds." But these contents of the mind, together with thinking and the other intellectual activities, were held to follow the same physical laws of motion as corporal bodies. The unique nature of mental activity was due entirely to its location in the head. The appetitive life and the life of the emotions and feelings were held to be merely motions in the head which are produced by motions in the heart.

Pleasure, in Hobbes' system, was due to a speeding up of the flow of blood, while pain was attributed to an impediment of the blood. The

[6] A useful discussion of Hobbes, particularly since it is written by a motivation psychologist, is Peters (1956).

changing rate of these physiological processes was alleged to produce not only these emotional feelings but, more importantly, general bodily reactions that augmented or inhibited a tendency to action. An action was initiated, however, in Hobbes' psychology by an "endeavor." Endeavors were hypothesized to be small, incipient actions, or beginnings of actions. Whenever an endeavor was directed toward an object known by experience to be pleasant, an appetite was aroused; and with an appetite the vital motion of the body is enhanced, the endeavor gains energy, the blood is speeded up, and the action must necessarily follow. On the other hand, if an endeavor was directed toward an object known by experience to be painful, then an aversion was aroused, the vital motions were impeded, and the blood congealed to prevent action directed toward the object. This crude physiological scheme is interesting because it is the forerunner of a number of similar schemes, and, like them, it proposes a singularly important role for pleasure and pain: they, or their physiological correlates, are the essential agents for motivating the organism, or else for governing what it learns.

By endeavor, Hobbes did not mean just a readiness or desire to act—it was not a mental event—he meant a small incipient motion. This remarkable concept of endeavor is clearly in the same spirit, and is implemented with many of the same hypothetical properties, that we attribute today to the anticipatory goal response, r_G. Hobbes' startling innovation appears to have no precedent; it evidently arose out of what he considered to be the necessity to explain mechanistically what had always been one of the principal tenets of the rationalistic position, namely, that man can anticipate what he is about to do.

Hobbes was also the originator of a new kind of hedonism. He said that no matter how much we may deceive ourselves, all of our actions are motivated by the desire for pleasure or the desire to avoid pain. In contrast to ethical hedonism, which is based upon the premise that man's tendency to pursue pleasure and avoid pain is ethically good, psychological hedonism, which was what Hobbes was proposing, strips the pleasure-pain principle of all ethical implications and makes it a principle of motivation. According to psychological hedonism, the pursuit of pleasure and the avoidance of pain are the only agencies that can move an organism to action. Thus, for the psychological hedonist, whether the hedonistic nature of man is good or bad is inconsequential; the ethical question is transcended by a law of nature: men are hedonistic.

As a group, the proponents of psychological hedonism stand in opposition to the rationalistic tradition. Whereas the rationalist is willing to admit that men do indeed tend to pursue pleasure, he usually insists that man ought to exercise his higher mental capacities to overcome this tendency. A psychological hedonist, on the other hand, argues that the will cannot be free if man invariably chooses that course of action the consequences of which are believed to be most pleasant or the least painful.

Hobbes believed that the will was simply an idea that man has about himself. What are the facts about the will, Hobbes asked. We deliberate. We alternately think of fear and pride; we are alternatively given to aversion and appetite; we alternately experience anticipated pleasure and pain. The last of these conditions to be present prior to action is presumably the strongest, and we think of it in retrospect as our own volition. Hobbes admitted that during the deliberation prior to an act many ideas (all governed by the laws of association, to be sure) may come to mind. Many of these ideas will have associated with them separate endeavors and the associated ideas of pain and pleasure.

Hobbes made many contributions to the history being described here. Descartes had offered a mechanistic explanation of the behavior of animals. The next logical step—a step Descartes had perhaps been afraid to take—was that man too could be viewed as a machine. That step was taken by Hobbes, awkwardly perhaps but bravely. By taking that step he became the first thoroughgoing opponent of rationalism and he became the first determinist. Hobbes' psychology provided an impetus for the subsequent development of British associationism, and contributed appreciably to the secularization of the study of man. One issue Hobbes raised which subsequent thinkers could not ignore was whether it was advisable, or even possible, to conceive of man purely as a biological-mechanical entity. Correlated with Hobbes' determinism was the concept that man's motives must be prior to his actions (this was the principle which led him to postulate a device such as endeavor). Hobbes was perhaps the first to note that the explanation of behavior did not have to be teleological. The goal of an action influenced that act only through its anticipation, and only through previous experience. He contended that man's actions were determined by his knowledge of how his ends were to be achieved, and by his knowledge of the pleasure to be derived from his acts. Descartes had hinted that teleology could be rejected, but he could not do it himself. Hobbes could.

ASSOCIATIONISM

Descartes and Hobbes had presented the case for a mechanistic philosophy in which the behavior of animals, and some of the behavior of man could be understood in terms of mechanical principles alone. They thus shared in launching one of the critical movements against the traditional rationalistic view of man.

A second and perhaps even more devastating movement was associationism, which was based on the premise that there are psychological laws which, like Newton's law of gravity (see p. 45), need not commit one to materialism or to dualism or to any particular theological position, but which describe what a man would think, what he could know, and what he might do. It should be emphasized that the mechanistic doctrine and the associationistic idea are logically independent and although they do often occur together (for example in Hobbes, and later in Hartley and in Watson) it is possible to endorse one without endorsing the other.[7] One may, like Hume, be an associationist without being a mechanist; or one may be a mechanist without being an associationist, like La Mettrie, for example, who based his materialism entirely upon Descartes' prior speculations by simply omitting the theological dogma. Sometimes the separation is not clear. For example, with Freud we invariably find strong associationistic principles which are sometimes accompanied by a mechanical model but which at other times stand alone. The most important point is that the mechanist and the associationist share a common denial of free will, and a common espousal of determinism.

John Locke.   Although Hobbes might be said to be the father of British associationism, Locke (1690) is usually credited with being its founder. Like Hobbes, Locke was an opponent of the traditional rationalism, but he was not a materialist. On the assumption that the innate mind is a *tabula rasa* (cleared slate) and that all knowledge is attributable to experience, Locke sought to understand the contents of the adult mind in terms of the gradual building up of ideas from experience. He conceived the mind to be passive, capable only of receiving sensations and of remembering them as ideas. The mind, he contended, cannot create original ideas, nor are ideas given to it innately; it can only form simple ideas from sensations, and complex ideas from simple ones.

On the question of what moves man to action, Locke contended that the will is always determined by some pressing "uneasiness" that not only establishes the will but also initiates action. The will is strictly determined by that particular uneasiness which is most pressing. The uneasiness was said to be a desire, "an uneasiness of the mind for want of some absent good. . . . God has put into man the uneasiness of hunger and thirst, and other natural desires . . . to move and determine their wills for the preservation of themselves and the continuation of their species."[8] The emotions and the will, like pleasure and pain, were said to be merely ideas that arise from sensations in the body and present themselves to the mind. That a man knows his own will tells us only that he can have an

---

[7] Even though a commitment to determinism does not necessarily commit one to physicalism, or preclude a belief in mentalism, many writers mistakenly see free-willist mentalism and deterministic physicalism as the only possible alternatives. For example, Krutch (1956), by rejecting determinism, finds nature full of teleology; and Farrer (1959), by rejecting determinism, finds God.

[8] This passage from Locke (1690, Book 2, ch. 21, No. 31, 34) makes it rather clear that he espoused the instinct concept.

idea of his action or his preference for a particular action, and nothing more.

For Locke, the virtuous man was characterized by his ability to deliberate on the consequences of alternative actions so that he might choose that which offered the greatest pleasure in the long run. The man without virtue lacks this ability to deliberate. Not having the advantage of a suitable education and not having established suitable habits, the virtueless man chooses that course of action which leads to the greatest immediate pleasure. For example, when the virtuous man deliberates on the pleasure of intoxication and the pain of the subsequent hangover he abstains, whereas the man without virtue, imagining only the short-term pleasure, indulges. (Locke noted in this connection that if the hangover were to precede the intoxication few men would drink.) Both the man with virtue and the man without it, however, follow the same general hedonistic principle of acting so as to maximize their expected pleasure; they differ only in what they expect.

After Locke, others offered alternative solutions to the problem of how to account for moral or ethical behavior in view of man's natural hedonistic tendencies. Psychological hedonism had become by this time a well-accepted psychological precept. Hutcheson (1728), for example, proposed that men have two basic motives, one egotistical, which seeks pleasure for themselves, and a second, altruistic, which seeks pleasure for others.

Hutcheson was also concerned with the instinct concept. He noted that we often have a propensity to act "without any prior conception of good, which is neither a desire nor a sensation, and which determines our actions before we can think of the consequences, indeed before we could have learned about the consequences." Recall that just 30 years before, Locke had retained the original theological flavor of instinct; it was a source of motivation that "God had put into man to determine his will." Hutcheson was here changing the emphasis so that instinct became the force itself rather than the natural origin of the motivating force. Hutcheson was also adding to the concept of instinct the idea that instinct produces action prior to any thought of the consequences of action. This too was a clear break with earlier tradition. Thus, in Hutcheson we find the first really modern view of instinct as a force which impels to action without the idea of the object of the action. The other clause of Hutcheson's definition, which asserts that instincts occur prior to education about an action or the consequence of an action, was not new. In fact this is about the only common strand linking the diverse interpretations of instinct.

Hutcheson was not an intellectual descendant of Locke; quite the contrary. He invoked instinct at this point to attack British associationism which was then beginning to gain some favor, and according to which man does what he does because he knows and desires the consequences of his act. Hutcheson was primarily attacking Locke's *tabula rasa* doctrine. It was only the seriousness of Hutcheson's opposition to that doctrine that made plausible the introduction of a mechanistic instinct concept into a philosophy which otherwise was in the rationalistic tradition. The incongruous blind impulse type of instinct was evidently a sort of concession to some of the strength of Locke's position; it was small price to pay to avoid confronting the main force of Locke's argument.

David Hume. Hume (1739) gave the concept of will a new and different treatment, first by recognizing that much of what man calls his will may really be just an impression of effort, and second by his famous treatment of the problem of causation, which was outlined in the previous chapter. Hume's determinism, like that of Locke, was mentalistic. That is, the determining conditions for man's actions were his ideas, his sensations, and his desires. He made no reference to an underlying physiological or materialistic causal substrate. Perhaps Hume's greatest contribution was to question the validity of traditional ways of explaining man's thoughts, feelings, and behavior. It is a man's experience, i.e., his history of sensations, that governs his thoughts and his behavior, not some fixed unalterable "human nature." A man's experience not only limits his thoughts and behavior, but even imposes limits upon the knowledge he may have of himself and the world he lives in. This was Hume's great message.

The mentalistic determinism of Locke and Hume might have given rise to a viable psychology of the mind, or even a psychology of behavior, but it did not. It did, however, have considerable impact upon the philosophers of the Enlightenment. The importance of this early deterministic movement therefore lay not in the growth of a science of psychology, but rather in the development of sociological reform through the efforts of wise political leaders, and an aroused citizenry.[9]

THE REACTIONARY COUNTERREVOLUTION

There was a rationalistic reaction against these developments. The reaction was led in Scotland by Reid, and was derived mainly from a moral conception of man designed to combat the materialistic view of Hobbes and the French philosophers. Reid also sought to salvage certain aspects of the associationism of Hobbes, Locke, and Hume which appealed to common sense. Reid sought to establish a new realism by making the final authority on all empirical matters the intuition of the ordinary man. The result of such analysis was a multiplication of the faculties and powers of the mind, each of which was held to be more or less discrete

[9] See Bury's (1913) enthusiastic treatment of this subject. The best overall history of associationism is Warren (1921).

and incapable of analysis. Faculty psychology admitted faculties of the will, courage, nobility, etc.—in short, all of the "noble" motives. The variety of faculties that arose appeared to be limited only by the philosopher's verbal agility.

The concept of instinct as an impulse to action prior to thought or to knowledge about its consequences played an important part in this "common-sense" or "faculty" psychology. And again we may note the incongruity of the notion of a blind force to action in Reid's otherwise rationalistic philosophy. To understand this it is important to note that here, as with Hutcheson, motivational concepts had a compromise character. The admission of instinct is the concession that tender-minded writers have made.[10] In comparison with the tough-minded principle of hedonism, instinct represents a somewhat smaller concession, somewhat less of a compromise, on the part of the tender-minded since they usually admit that only some behavior is determined by instinct whereas the tough-minded mechanist usually holds hedonism to be a universal principle. The tender-minded, by invoking instincts and making some concessions in the direction of determinism, may still retain in his philosophy some spirituality, some purposes, and some rationality.

Within the framework of faculty psychology man did what he did because he wanted to, except on those occasions when he was moved by instinctive forces. The will was free again, and man's motives were considered to be of concern not so much to the psychologist as to the moralist. Men's motives were viewed as reflecting his choice of action and hence were not subject to such questions as how they arose.[11]

The counterrevolution spread to France. French thinkers, who had a generation or two before been leaders in the original intellectual revolt and had espoused a variety of naturalistic ideologies, suddenly reverted to earlier orthodoxies. Early in the nineteenth century there appeared what Robertson (1930) has called a "sentimental" return to religion and to the thinking of a much earlier era.[12] The effects on French psychology in particular were disastrous. The French spiritualism that evolved led to a sort of pervasive, uncritical dogmatism that did little to

---

[10] James (1914) suggested that psychologists tended to be either tender-minded, or tough-minded. The tender-minded were supposed to be rationalistic, idealistic, optimistic, religious, free-willist. In contrast, the tough-minded were supposed to be empiricalistic, empiricistic, sensationistic, materialistic, pessimistic, irreligious, and fatalistic. It is too much to expect that these traits would always go together so that men could be divided neatly into two groups, but they go together well enough to make this a useful distinction.

[11] The principal works of the Scottish school were Reid (1785, 1788), Stewart (1792–1827), Brown (1820), and Hamilton (1858). The whole movement has been discussed by one of the last of their number, McCosh (1874); Warren (1921) is more objective.

[12] That there is a historical connection between the rationalistic position and religiousness (or at least piety) seems inescapable (see Bury, 1913).

advance psychology, and French psychology has not yet, 150 years later, managed to escape from a sort of complacent unsystematic attitude toward man.[13]

Experimental Psychology.   It is not certain that the explanation of behavior was proceeding any better in Germany where the "new psychology" was being developed. At first sight, it might appear surprising that Boring's *History* (1950), which is so rich an account of the early experimental psychology, would contain almost no mention of how behavior was explained in this system. This is scarcely an oversight on Boring's part; it is an indication of the nature of that early science. Structuralism was a marriage of two deterministic traditions, one physiological, and the other the mentalistic associationism of Locke and Hume. The marriage appears to have been one of convenience, however, for the structuralist never allowed it to be consummated. Man's action was always viewed entirely as a physiological problem; it could not be illuminated by any knowledge of how the mind functions. At the same time, the activity of the mind was assumed to depend upon and to be determined by its underlying neural substrate. But the laws of its activity were never to be found by recourse to physiological observables, much less to behavioral data; they were always to be revealed by an introspective analysis of the mind's own contents. Utter dedication to this schematic program precluded such questions as what motivates man's actions. The traditional explanatory devices, hedonism, free will, emotions, were treated just as the ideational contents of the mind were treated, i.e., they were analyzed into more elemental sensations and their relationships to action were wholly ignored.

Abnormal Psychology.   In his *History of Medical Psychology,* Zilboorg (1941) has provided evidence of a parallel in abnormal psychology to this paradoxical attitude toward determinism in experimental psychology. In the medical world there was little doubt that behavior was physiologically determined, and that physiological research could discover the determinants of all behavioral phenomena. Curiously, though, medical men were reluctant to apply the same sort of positivistic attitude to the problems of mental illness. Up until the eighteenth century, insanity had been explained by means of demonic possession. But when that was gradually abandoned during the Enlightenment, no alternative account of mental illness was proposed. The problem of insanity became, to a surprising

[13] This indictment follows Baldwin (1913). The same situation also prevailed for a time in this country. Baldwin said "Early American psychology was written by theologians and educators or both in the same person" and thus laconically dismissed a large part of our history. He was right though; counting just some of the educators who were college presidents and also theological psychologists we have: Bascom at Wisconsin, Hill at Rochester, Hopkins at Williams, McCosh at Princeton, Porter at Yale, and Wilson at Cornell. This era, fortunately, ended about 1890 (see Fey, 1939).

degree, a purely legalistic matter. Medical men were, to be sure, in charge of mental institutions, and they promoted the use of various kinds of restraint and shock therapy, but they did little in an attempt to understand or explain the behavior of their patients. The law enters the picture because it is obliged to have some criterion for meting out the judgments it has to make; the law must cope with behavior—particularly abnormal behavior—and the working assumption that has stood unquestioned in the legal profession from the earliest times down to our own is that man is morally responsible for his actions.[14]

The New Rationalism. The Enlightenment was over. And as it ended a new rationalism emerged which was similar in some respects to the old Greek rationalism. Man's reason still had its sovereignty; it was still held to be unanalyzable. Man was still assumed to have an autonomous will. The faculty psychologists were, of course, in the forefront of the new rationalistic movement. One contribution of the later psychologists in this tradition was their popularization of the faculty of conation. By the turn of the century British writers such as Stout and Ward, and in this country, James, were emphasizing that man strives for his goals. James said, "Desire, wish, will, are states of mind which everyone knows, and which no definition can make plainer" (1890, II, p. 486).[15] Stout (1903) said behavior was to be explained in terms either of (1) "the motive for" our actions (i.e., the reasons we assign for choosing to do the things we do), or (2) "the motive of" our actions (i.e., the factors which influenced the deliberation or choice of action).

This revised rationalism has continued with some vitality to the present day. One spokesman, Peters (1958), has recently written "the most obvious and usual answer to the question 'Why' about human actions is to find the goal or end towards which an action is directed or the rule in accordance with which it is performed" (p. 149). In this view the goals and ends in question are to be found by asking a man why he performed the act. Whereas Peters recognizes that the man's stated reasons and the "real" reasons for his actions may not be the same, still, he insists, they do correspond most of the time. Men are assumed to be rational and to direct their behavior to their own ends. Peters

---

[14] Zilboorg went on to observe that the freedom of the will was so incontestable that, during the sixteenth-century witch hunts, it led "to its most terrifying, although most preposterous, conclusion. Man, whatever he does, even if he succumbs to an illness which perverts his perceptions, imagination, and intellectual functions, does it of his own free will; he voluntarily bows to the wishes of the Evil One. The devil does not lure and trap man; man chooses to succumb to the devil and he must be held responsible for this free choice. He must be punished; he must be eliminated from the community. More than that, his soul, held in such sinful captivity by the corrupted, criminal will within the body, must be set free again; it *must* be delivered. The body must be burned" (Zilboorg, 1941, p. 156).

[15] This is not really fair to James. I will try to straighten accounts in discussing his theory of instinct in Chapter 4.

insists that it is only when this purposive approach to the explanation of behavior fails that we seek to explain behavior deterministically (we will consider Peters' discussion of psychoanalysis on p. 63).

The new rationalists are eclectic. They are willing to accept the occurrence of an occasional unconscious act, they may recognize automisms of behavior, they acknowledge the existence or reflexes and habitual behavior governed by external or internal stimuli, but they are not willing to accept any sort of universal law of behavioral determination. Man's behavior may be determined some of the time, or even most of the time, but a place must be left for the operation of man's higher moral and creative activities.[16]

The Challenge of Rationalism. It must be admitted that while rationalism is not likely to take us very far in the explanation of behavior, it does provide stimulation in one respect. The rationalist's conception of man's free and fluid mind, and the loose ties between man's mental activity and his behavior, lead to a very pat and simple account of many sorts of complex behavior. The great challenge to the modern behaviorist is how can he design scientifically acceptable explanatory mechanisms which allow the human organism the same flexibility that the rationalist can allow him. How can the behaviorist build a model to explain the behavior of man which is congruent with the phenomena that the rationalist is talking about when he speaks of purpose, thinking, and creativity? This is the challenge of rationalism which has only recently been squarely faced.

THE ADVENT OF DETERMINISM

By the beginning of the nineteenth century, the appeal and the practical utility of the deterministic assumption were becoming apparent. It seems clear that educated men, at least, were ready to accept some forms of determinism, or some more sophisticated form of materialism. Witness the popularity of a number of naturalists and the remarkable acceptance of phrenology in France and England.[17] In classical mechanics, and in

[16] Evidently the rationalist feels able to explain behavior without having to tie the behavior mechanistically, empirically, or in any other way to its determinants. The explanation of behavior simply does not involve behavior. A nice illustration of this is found in Moslem theology. The Moslem philosophers liked to concern themselves with the attributes of God, and frequent lists were drawn up of properties and powers that a god would have to have in order to fulfill his godly functions as revealed in the Koran. One popular list included the following attributes: life, knowledge, hearing and sight, will, and speech. The point is that speech was the only motor possibility allowed Allah. Not that he was powerless to act except to speak to his prophets, but that in the tenth and eleventh centuries no one conceived it necessary to have any rules translating knowledge and will into action.

[17] It is quite evident that uneducated men have always been far more willing

physiology, in the newly successful chemical sciences, and in the newly formulated economic philosophies men could see their success in applying deterministic principles.

Charles Darwin. At mid-nineteenth century there were apparently limits to how far determinism was supposed to extend, however, and Darwin's biological determinism exceeded accepted bounds. He contended (1859) that the variety of living forms which we see before us could be explained entirely in terms of random variation and natural selection. There was no need for teleology or divine intervention in evolution, nor for revelation as a source of knowledge about evolution. For the rationalistic philosophers, and for the clergy, such a position was deplorable; but for the scientist, new realms of nature were now open for systematic investigation. This was Darwin's great contribution. The problem of creation was, at least in large measure, now solved and the naturalistic approach which had yielded the solution now strongly suggested itself as the way to solve other age-old problems.

To appreciate fully Darwin's contribution it is necessary to contrast his ideas with the prevailing background of thought. Prior speculation about evolution tended to interpret phylogenetic development as evidence of a divine plan. The existence of the higher animals and man was taken to be evidence for a teleological principle of evolution. This view was consonant with the older idea of instinct as the guiding hand of nature which directs impulses. Early in the nineteenth century as distinguished a scientist as Magendie could define instincts as "propensities or inclinations or wants by which animals are constantly excited and forced to fulfill the intentions of nature."[18]

It had become clear by this time that a sharp line could not be drawn between intelligence, such as found in man, and instinct, such as found in animals. Lamarck had emphasized that the mark of instinctive behavior in animals was not its stereotypy (this was a late nineteenth-century contention which arose when the mechanistic philosophy had become more highly developed and widely applied) but rather its adaptiveness, or apparent intelligence. Lamarck proposed that this appearance of intelligence represented the gradual accumulation over many generations of the slight learning that was possible with a low level of intelligence. Adaptiveness, when it becomes habitual and passed on to succeeding generations as part of the evolutionary heritage could, after

---

to attribute their behavior to bumps on their skulls, wrinkles in their hands, their body chemistry, or the location of the planets, than to their own psychological experience.

[18] Quoted from Drever, 1917 (p. 74). Magendie (1831) was by no means a conservative thinker; he was perhaps the first experimental biologist in the sense that he was the first to use live animal preparations—much to the horror of his peers. Biology before and biology after Darwin have been nicely contrasted by Eiseley (1958).

a sufficient number of generations, take on the appearance of intelligent behavior. This was an optimistic theory; it carried the implication that man or beast could help his descendants through his own efforts, slight though they might be. Thus the life and effort of an animal have purpose. The species learns so that the individual may react instinctively.

Darwin's idea of evolution was characterized by quite a different spirit. He contended that instinct which looked like blind impulse was indeed just that. It was present because the animal that had it, out of a random variation of possible blind impulses, had been lucky enough to survive and procreate.

> . . . if it can be shown that instincts do vary ever so little, then I can see no difficulty in natural selection preserving and continually accumulating variations of instincts to any extent that may be profitable. It is thus, as I believe, that all the most complex and wonderful instincts have originated. (Darwin, 1859, p. 209)

It is unnecessary, Darwin tells us, to suppose that nature has purpose— the only criterion is whether a particular aspect of behavior promotes survival. If it does it will persist in evolution, and if it does not it will disappear. As wondrous as the variety of instinctive adaptations appears to be, we must recall that there are multitudes of different animal forms, they are prolific, and they have been evolving for an immense period of time. It is therefore perhaps not surprising that a variety of remarkable adaptations have survived.

Darwin went on to argue that if random variation and natural selection suffice to account for the diversity of the lower animal forms, the same principles are logically extendable to account for the evolution of the entire animal kingdom, including man. It is only necessary to suppose, Darwin asserted, that intelligence in lower animal forms has survival value. It then follows that evolution is likely to proceed along this line, and that more and more intelligent members of the animal kingdom will evolve. Given the perpetual adaptive value of higher intelligence it is likely that animals as intelligent as man (or even more so) will eventually evolve.

Biological Determinism. Darwin's theory of evolution involved four precepts, each of which was to have widespread implications for research and theory. First, there is a constant struggle for survival. Nature is a battlefield on which the species compete for space, food, and the necessities of life. This competition leads to a *natural selection* of the best fit.[19] Those that survive the competition do so by possession of some specialized adaptation. This Malthusian idea bears the crucial burden in Darwin's

---

[19] The full title of Darwin's *Origin* pretty well tells the story: "On the Origin of Species by Means of Natural Selection or The Preservation of Favoured Races in the Struggle for Life."

theory of accounting for selection; if it were not for natural selection, all sorts of different animal forms, presumably, would survive. But as it is we find in nature's realm only those forms which are specialized in their own peculiar ways while their forebears, generally speaking, have all been superseded.

A second but closely related aspect of Darwin's theory is that whenever a characteristic of an animal or man is found to be strikingly unique to a species, or contrarily, strikingly general across species, we may suppose that it has played some crucial role in survival. If it had not been important in survival it would not have become general or, as the case may be, specific. For example, Darwin makes it clear that the relatively general characteristic of birds to build nests is biologically useful, but at the same time he points out that the idiosyncratic way birds of a given species build their particular type of nest is also useful for that species. Survival thus becomes a criterion against which we may judge any behavior. We may ask of any instinctive behavior, how does it aid the survival, maintenance, and adaptation of the organism.

The great animal psychologists of the last century and the learning theorists of the last two generations have nearly all invoked at one time or another the criterion of survival. And clearly, any adequate theory of motivation or of learning must at least be compatible with the survival criterion.

The third precept of Darwin's theory that demands our attention is his utter rejection of his predecessors' teleology. This aspect of his theory provided biology, and indeed, all the Western world, with a new outlook on nature. Darwin supposed that nature has neither purpose nor plan. The only mechanisms that are required to explain the diversification of animals is some random variation in original characteristics and then the continued operation of natural selection. From the assumptions of random variation and natural selection the entire realm of nature can be predicted to unfold, without cause or purpose, without insight or guidance, without foresight or hindsight. Whether this brand of biological determinism provides a sufficient account of the awe-inspiring spectacle of nature has been hotly debated, but we cannot pursue that subject here.[20]

The fourth aspect of Darwin's theory follows if the first three are granted: Phylogeny is continuous. The point is simply that the Darwinian theory of evolution implies the continuity of man and beast. Biologists and psychologists, regardless of how they may feel about the metaphysical

[20] The effect of modern discoveries in genetics has not been to change the force of the argument, but merely to speed up the process, to allow for more change in the same time, or the same change in less time. Because of genetics we have an explanation of variation without having to suppose, with Darwin, that it is "random." Darwin later made considerable concession to the Lamarckian proponents; this was particularly true of his treatment of instinctive and emotional behavior (Darwin, 1872), but even so there was no more purpose or teleology in evolution.

or moralistic problems involved, have found it most useful to accept the continuity assumption. Even though some psychologists (e.g., Allport, 1947) feel that their science would be better off if the gap were not bridged, the acceptance of continuity has proved to be one of the most crucial points in the history of human thought. It was a point which had to be passed in order for the explanation of behavior to pass from philosophy to science, from theology to naturalism, and from speculation to investigation.

Animal Psychology. One group of writers, working from the assumption of phylogenetic continuity, sought to develop an animal psychology by looking for the mental faculties of man in animals. The advocates of this approach, writers such as Carus (1866) and Romanes (1882), expected to find the same kind of mental faculties in animals as in man, although developed to a lesser extent.[21] The fate of this enterprise was doomed by the weakness of the methodology that was used. Carus relied primarily upon allegories to demonstrate the gradual growth of consciousness in the animal mind, and Romanes relied perhaps too heavily on anecdotal evidence, although he himself was evidently a very competent observer.

More conducive to a successful inquiry was the experimental method developed by the great German physiologists and the animal psychologists at the end of the last century whose approach was, in effect, to downgrade man to the level of animals by seeking to explain all behavior mechanistically. These workers gave great impetus to the development of conceptions of reflex and instinct that could be applied equally to man and to animals.

The continuity assumption also opened up a number of purely quantitative problems. For example, if we assume that intelligence does not emerge suddenly with man, but is present to some degree in lower animals, then it is natural to ask to what extent it is present in any given animal species. A great deal of experimental work has been addressed to just this problem, and for a while the issue of intelligence versus instinct became a favorite for both theorists and experimenters.[22]

Darwin initiated the modern era in instinct theory. It was he who

---

[21] Keller (1937) has observed that Darwin closed the Cartesian gap; he gave animals back their minds—with interest.

[22] The instinct vs. intelligence debate, which really began long before the Darwinian revolution and continued on into the present century, might appear from here as a great waste of words. However, it was symptomatic of profound changes occurring in man's view of himself and his fellow creatures. And directly out of it came much of the animal research of the period, research with a genuinely comparative outlook. Some of the best surveys of this research, and of the theoretical positions that marked the age, are Morgan (1894), Hobhouse (1901), Washburn (1908), Holmes (1911), and Warden et al. (1936). One outcome of this work, of course, has been the realization that the distinction between instinct and intelligence is not a useful one.

proposed the first objective definition of instincts in terms of animal behavior; his predecessors had derived their concept of instinct from the subjective emotional experience of man.[23] He was also one of the first to come to grips with the question of how instincts arise. Darwin treated instincts as though they were merely complex reflexes, hoping thereby to be able to analyze them into units that were compatible with the assumed mechanisms of random variation and natural selection. Evolution must proceed in small steps. Therefore the evolved instinct must be constituted of small parts. In his later writing (e.g., 1872), Darwin made bold attempts to analyze instinctive and emotional reactions into their basic elemental and inheritable units.

One important consequence of this molecular approach was that men began to think of behavior in man as well as in animals as dependent upon a number of specific stimulus-response reflexes. This interpretation of instinctive behavior as merely complex reflexes, and indeed the whole approach of analyzing behavior in terms of elemental units, provided a clear alternative to traditional modes of thought. Such an account of behavior, being free from intellectualistic bias, is inherently deterministic and antirationalistic. Darwin thus indirectly gave a tremendous boost to the mechanistic position.

By the turn of the century, animal psychology had developed a very powerful explanatory concept, a concept which would in time totally change the content and even the definition of psychology: the reflex arc. We need not dwell upon the central position that this concept held in the behavioristic revolution. The success of that revolution is evidence enough that psychologists had finally addressed themselves to the question of behavior and how to explain it mechanistically. Before turning to these developments and the beginning of the experimental psychology of motivation it is necessary to note briefly a final crucial contribution by a philosopher.

Herbert Spencer and the New Hedonism. Up to this point, hedonism had always referred to the seeking of pleasure and the avoidance of pain. Spencer proposed a new and conceptually powerful form of hedonism that shifted the attempt to explain behavior hedonistically out of philosophy and into biology and psychology. For Spencer, pain and pleasure were critically important determinants of behavior, not because they are what we seek, but because they control what we learn. Here was a materialistic and hedonistic determinism that would have delighted old Thomas Hobbes.

Spencer suggested that if Darwin's naturalistic conception of the survival of the fittest works so well for biological phenomena, it might

---

[23] This nice distinction between objective and subjective definitions of instinct is due to Drever (1917). He has written a valuable history of the subjective instinct concept. Wilm (1925) is a better history of the objective instinct concept.

be applicable to psychological and sociological phenomena as well. Hence Spencer argued that during the course of evolution, a correlation must develop between those behaviors that yield pleasure and those behaviors that promote survival.

> If we substitute for the word Pleasure the equivalent phrase—a feeling which we seek to bring into consciousness and retain there, and if we substitute for the word Pain the equivalent phrase—a feeling which we seek to get out of consciousness and to keep out; we see at once that, if the states of consciousness which a creature endeavours to maintain are correlatives of injurious actions, and if the states of consciousness which it endeavours to expel are the correlatives of beneficial actions, it must quickly disappear through persistence in the injurious and avoidance of the beneficial. In other words, those races of beings only can have survived in which, on the average, agreeable or desired feelings went along with activities conducive to the maintenance of life [and in which disagreeable feelings went along with detrimental activities]. (Spencer, 1880, I, p. 280)

With the survival of species accounted for by means of the hedonistic principle, Spencer went on to account for the survival of the individual organism. An animal in an uncomfortable situation, Spencer supposed, goes through a series of random movements. The pleasurable ones are beneficial, and the painful ones are injurious; after many repetitions, whenever by chance an organism happens to make a movement which leads to pleasure, there will be a concomitant increase in nervous activity involving those nerves which have just participated in the movement. Thus stimulated, the nerves are rendered "more permeable" than before. When these circumstances recur, those muscle movements that were followed by success are likely to be repeated so that what was initially an accidental motion will acquire considerable probability.

Physiological speculation, reminiscent of Hobbes', follows:

> For when on such subsequent occasion the visual impressions have produced nascent tendencies to the acts approximately fitted to [attain some end], and when through these there are nascently excited all the states, sensory and motor, which accompany [that end], it must happen that among the links in the connected excitation there will be excitations of those fibres and cells through which on the previous occasion, the diffused discharge brought about the actions that caused success. The tendency for the diffused discharge to follow these lines will obviously be greater than before; and the probability of a successfully modified action will therefore be greater than before. Every repetition of it will make still more permeable the new channels, and increase the probability of subsequent repetitions; until

at length the nervous connections become organized. (Spencer, 1880, I, p. 545)

There are a number of respects in which this remarkable theory of Spencer's has proved to be important. First of all, it is built upon a new type of psychological hedonism: man's actions are governed by pleasure and pain, not because they serve as goals, or as motives, but because they have served as reinforcement in the past. Pleasure and pain explain action by accounting for what has been learned. All teleology is rejected. The "purpose" of action was not egotistical for Spencer; it is not pleasure, qua pleasure, that rules the behavioral domain, but only survival. Only that behavior survives which has proven its survival value; the explanatory principle of "survival of the fittest" applies to responses as well as to species. The antecedent effects of pleasure and pain are real, and effective, but they are historical rather than immediate or teleological.[24]

Spencer's explanation of behavior was in the deterministic tradition of Hobbes, but added to the tradition some evolutionary considerations, the concept of habit, and some nineteenth-century physiology. Before we condemn Spencer's overzealous physiological speculation, we should ask what we have to replace it with today. If we substitute for Spencer's term "pleasure" the modern phrase "drive reduction," and if we substitute for his "lines of nervous communication" the modern term "S-R association," we arrive at the position: drive reduction strengthens S-R associations. This is not to say that Spencer's theory of learning was the same as Hull's; the point is that the assumed physiological mediation was not appreciably different.

Spencer's concept of nascent excitation is particularly interesting. It was clearly a revival of Hobbes' notion of endeavor, but it is also reminiscent of the modern concept of mediating response. Note, in this latter connection, that the nascently excited states were asserted to be both sensory and motor, just as mediating responses are supposed to have both sensory and motor properties. The flexible properties of these nascent excitations, or endeavors, or mediating responses, were particularly emphasized by Bain (1864). Bain, following the central lines of Spencer's theory, said that when pleasure occurs a number of things become associated. The association includes not only a situation and the successful act, but also the idea of the situation, the idea of the successful act, and the idea of the pleasurable consequences. Thus, when any one of these components occurs in the future, any of the others may be reinstated by virtue of the laws of association.

Bain's psychology retained a good deal of traditional rationalism: man's actions were still largely governed by events occurring in the mind.

---

[24] The hedonism of Epicurus, Locke, and Spencer have been characterized by Troland (1928) as hedonisms of the future, present, and past.

The crucial acquisition in learning was the idea of the successful act. Thus, Bain was in no real sense a behaviorist; that important step was taken by Thorndike and by others in the twentieth century.

Most of our motivational concepts have stemmed from the materialistic tradition, the tradition which includes Darwin and Spencer, and excludes Bain. Darwin had initiated the modern era of instinct theory which, as we will see in Chapter 4, was the direct and immediate ancestor of our modern drive concept. Spencer, too, made a crucial contribution. We have just seen that he supplied us with most of the ingredients for a law of reinforcement and a behavioristic account of learning. Spencer also had suggested in his concept of nascent excitation all of the important ingredients for an incentive theory of motivation. Thus, we find in the materialistic tradition the roots of the incentive theory and the reinforcement theory of our own era. The instinct concept had a more tender-minded origin. It seems that by as early as about 1880 we had fairly clear expositions of the motivational constructs which were eventually to dominate contemporary theories of motivation.

EMPIRICAL DETERMINISM

At the end of the century one essential element still had to be supplied before we could have theories of motivation. Theorists had to learn to view their constructs as constructs rather than as approximations to an underlying reality. The origins of this development may be traced to a small rebellion that took place toward the end of the nineteenth century within the scientific community. This rebellion was directed against mechanism, and more specifically against the physicalistic bias which had played such a prominent role in the development of mechanistic ideas. What was wanted was a determinism which was not mechanistic in character, i.e., an empirical determinism. This rebellion was not touched off by any one person, and it had no single leader. Rather, the idea has grown slowly and has gradually accumulated support and status until today, still growing, it is one of the leading contenders along with rationalism and materialism as an explanatory position.

Empirical determinism is primarily a protest against the assumption that there must be some mechanical or material (or mental) basis for causation. It is opposed to the ancient precept underlying materialism that was formulated by the Greek philosophers: "action at a distance is impossible." An event cannot occur, it was said, unless there is some medium or material through which energy that makes the event occur can be transferred. The mover must "touch" the moved. The "action at a distance is impossible" principle would seem to be so obvious that no one could question it.

Yet it turns out that it is just in physics, where the principle might seem, naively, to have the highest validity, that it has been most hotly debated and was most quickly abandoned. The battle raged over Newton's law of gravitation. Here was a case of action at a distance which had to be accepted because of its descriptive utility, even though the law of gravity required forces acting through empty space. Newton ended the *Principia* (1687) with the words, "I have not been able to discover the cause of these properties of gravity, and I make no hypotheses. . . . It is enough that gravity act according to the laws which we have found." Newton had constructed what we could call a mathematical model which accounted for a variety of observations and he would make no hypotheses regarding the physical reality that underlay the observations. This attitude was not new with Newton; it had also been characteristic of Galileo. It is interesting to note that at its outset classical mechanics could dispense with a materialistic or mechanistic interpretation of nature and use a purely mathematical or empirical explanation of its findings.

Materialistic varieties of explanation were not abandoned so easily, however. Many physicists, and particularly philosophers writing about physics, insisted upon maintaining a mechanistic outlook. The late, great historian of science, Charles Singer, observed that

> The course of the new science, as a progression from the observation of a few phenomena to a world-outlook, was transmuted into a world-outlook imposed on those phenomena . . . No sooner was the conception of inert bodies passively following the dictates of blind forces seen to be applicable to the motion of mass-points, than it was immediately generalized into a world-philosophy. Instead of being accepted as what it was [a model] it became a principle of universal . . . materialism . . .

Singer went on to note the irony in the misapplication of the empirical nature of science. The mathematical, empirical *method* of Galileo and Newton was what was revolutionary, not that they were studying physical systems. The mechanistic philosophy which was later superimposed on the method totally ignored the principal lesson to be learned from the scientific revolution.

> It is to this cause that we owe the great conflicts between science and religion, and science and humanistic feeling, that reached their culmination in the second half of the nineteenth century. Science was justified by its success, and it was incompatible with religion and with art; therefore religion and art were illusions or fancies. What was not realized was that the success of science was due to the faithfulness of its practice, while its destructiveness arose from the error of its philosophy. . . . (Singer, 1959, pp. 419–420)

For two hundred years after Newton the mechanistic view of nature gradually gained currency, as we have seen, leaving behind the real contribution of the seventeenth century to the methodology of science. A crisis for the concept of material causation and for the mechanistic doctrine finally came when it was deemed necessary to postulate a medium through which light waves could travel in space. The "ether" was accepted as a necessary compromise, and it really was a compromise because the hypothesized ether was required to have properties quite unlike anything that had ever been observed.

By the turn of the century Karl Pearson could observe: "Step by step men of science are coming to recognize that mechanism is not at the bottom of phenomena, but is only the conceptual shorthand by aid of which they can briefly describe and resume phenomena" (Pearson, 1911, viii).[25] Even before Planck and Einstein had destroyed the mechanical world-view we had begun to see that it was inadequate.

Reductionism.   In spite of the lesson to be learned from the history of physics, psychologists seem reluctant to abandon the concept of material causation. This reluctance may be attributable to the plausibility of reductionism in psychology. The physicist has had to cope with the problem of matter in one way or another; he could not relegate the responsibility to another discipline. But the psychologist has been able to postpone facing the problem by arguing that the material underlying his studies is the subject matter of biology, or physiology, or neurology. The behaviorist, especially, has grown up with the belief that eventually he would be superfluous because of the promised success of the biological sciences in explaining at the material level any phenomenon which he might explain at the empirical level.

However, it is purely an article of faith for the psychologist to believe that the biologist can do any better with his substrate of phenomena than the physicist has done with his. The biologist, of course, faces the same problem: whether to reduce his science to the terms of organic chemistry, or to accept it for what it is, i.e., sets of laws or principles for relating diverse biological phenomena. We may doubt if the biologist will prove to be in any position to provide the material substrate for the psychologist's requirements of material causation. However successful reductionism may eventually prove to be, it seems clear that the psychologist will continue to have a place in science as long as it proves to be more economical to explain psychological phenomena with psychological terms than to reduce them to biological ones.

Meteorology is in a similar situation: no meteorologist would deny that the subject matter of his science is directly reducible to classical,

---

[25] It seems likely that Pearson worked so hard to develop tools of correlational analysis just because he believed correlation rather than causation should be the guiding principle in science.

well-worked-out problems of hydrodynamics and thermodynamics. Yet scientists in the latter fields have little interest in the phenomena which the meteorologist has managed to explain in his more molar terms. With molarity goes economy. The specialized applications of science do not lead to reductionism but to the establishment of bridge sciences such as physical-chemistry, bio-chemistry, astro-physics, and physiological-psychology. What has happened throughout science is not the breaking down of interdisciplinary boundaries through the success of reductionism, but rather, the establishment of new sciences, bridge sciences, at the boundaries.

Despite the poor prospects for an effective reductionism, psychologists persist in the faith that whatever they can find at an experiential or behavioral level will have its correlate in the physiological and especially in the neurological substrate. No one seems to question that the nerves are the material cause of behavior. There is, of course, some justification for this belief in the high correlations obtainable between neural activity and behavior. But both the nerves and behavior have properties which have made it difficult to benefit very much so far from the observed correlations. Of course, such correlations provide the phenomena for another bridge science, physiological psychology, but they are not part of psychology qua psychology, i.e., as the science of behavior. While it might be possible to sharpen a psychological definition of "response" so that it corresponded precisely with what a neurologist means by "response," it cannot be guaranteed that such a definition would have any use in a psychological theory of behavior.

Distinguishing sharply between psychological and physiological varieties of behaviorism, Tolman observed:

> Science demands, of course, in the end, the final development of both sorts of behaviorism. And the facts and laws of physiological behaviorism, when obtained, will presumably provide the explanation for the facts and laws of psychological behaviorism. But the psychological facts and laws are also to be gathered and established in their own right. A psychology cannot be explained by a physiology until one has a psychology to explain. (Tolman, 1936, p. 118) [26]

But Tolman was too generous and perhaps too optimistic with respect to the future potentialities of reductionism. Charles Singer was perhaps more realistic:

> . . . science, true to its principle of limited attacks and limited objectives, has its own working rules of causality. It follows Galileo

[26] Compare Woodworth (1924), Skinner (1938, especially ch. 12) on the question of why psychology doesn't need reductionism. Perhaps the most urbane rejection of reductionism is Kantor (1947). What it all comes down to is not whether the terms and laws of psychology can be reduced to those of physiology but whether they would be deduced from them.

in agreeing to discuss only certain particular types of sequence and treating them as related, the relation being regarded as cause and effect. Thus the physicist will deal only with physical, the chemist only with chemical sequences, the biologist only with biological sequences. In the course of this process new relationships may be discerned or become more apparent, as for instance in the physical state of the heavenly bodies or the relative constitution of parents and offspring. Thus will arise new sciences—astro physics and genetics —which will limit their scope to the relations in their particular fields. (Singer, 1959, p. 258)

Psychological Forces. When physics gave up the materalistic doctrine, it still retained the concept of force. But modern physics has given the term "force" a meaning somewhat different from its historical connotation and quite different from the layman's use of the term. Force is given a very elegant mathematical definition as the second derivative with respect to time of the displacement of a mass. Technically, this is all "force" means, whether we are speaking of gravitation, magnetism, kinetics, or whatever. But the separation of this mathematical abstraction from the older historical connotation of a causal agency has taken a long time and has required a good deal of discussion (Jammer, 1957).

In psychology, the concept of force has sometimes been used as though it were nothing but an analogy from the modern physicist's use of the term, i.e., as a term which describes changes in behavior. More often, however, force is given surplus meaning, it is used to imply some sort of internal agency or mechanical causation. Perhaps it is the same promise of an effective reductionism in psychology that maintains our faith in physical causes which also leads us to perpetuate the idea that the motivating agents (motives, tensions, drives, etc.) goad or force or drive the organism into action.

A good example of such mechanistic thinking is provided by the etymology of the word "drive," which was introduced into American psychology by Woodworth in 1918.[27] Woodworth was primarily concerned with showing that a large part of behavior could be thought of as the product of the psychophysical machinery, machinery which revealed itself in innate and habitual dispositions to action. Like any other machine, Woodworth contended, it won't go without fuel, without some source of motive power or force. Woodworth sought a word to denote this psychological force, and disliking the mentalistic connotations of "impulse" and "desire," he suggested "drive" which conveyed, he felt, the proper mechanistic connotation. Subsequently, drives have always been

---

[27] Young (1936) has published an interesting letter from Woodworth discussing how he came to use the word, and how that usage caught on among animal psychologists.

assumed to have the ability to goad an organism into action. A drive makes itself known to the observer, it is asserted, through its power of raising the subject's activity level.

This conception of force was implicit in psychology, however, long before Woodworth helped popularize the word "drive" for it. The idea that behavior occurs when psychological forces exist stood pretty much unquestioned until 1949 when Hebb suggested that motivation might better be thought of as an organization of behavior, as a coordination of behavior in a particular direction, rather than in the mere production of behavior. Hebb pointed out that even at the neural level the "motivated" animal shows no more over-all activity than the "unmotivated" animal; the most one might hope to observe would be a difference in the *pattern* of neural activity of the two animals.[28]

We have now traced the history of motivational concepts, and the idea of motivation itself, up to about 1900. We have seen the concepts which gave rise to the modern explanatory constructs of drive, incentive, and reinforcement. There was still one impediment, however, to the application of deterministic principles to the explanation of human behavior; namely, that no one except a very small minority believed it could be done. The rationalist still reigned supreme; he could argue that the reflex-arc concept and the encroaching deterministic attitude, particularly the mechanistic variety, had no bearing upon what went on in the human mind. The reality of the soul and the freedom of the will could not be changed by what the mechanist said.

The case for the rationalist ultimately rests on the argument that man's will must be free in order that he can be held responsible for his behavior. It is probably not just a historical accident that the evidence which provided the breakthrough, the insights from which Freud deduced his theory of motivation, came from neurotics, i.e., people who are not held wholly responsible for their behavior. Freud's contribution is so great that we will consider it in some detail in the following chapter. But there is one aspect of Freud's contribution that needs to be brought

[28] The idea that motives supply the energy for behavior has recently been spoofed by Littman (1958) and Kelly (1958). Kelly says that in school counseling teachers often make the complaint that some pupils just aren't motivated. "Often the teacher would insist that the child would do nothing—absolutely nothing—just sit! Then we would suggest that she try a nonmotivational approach and let him 'just sit.' We would ask her to observe how he went about 'just sitting.' Invariably the teacher would be able to report some extremely interesting goings on. An analysis of what the 'lazy' child did while he was being lazy often furnished her with her first glimpse into the child's world and provided her with her first solid grounds for communication with him. Some teachers found that their laziest pupils were those who could produce the most novel ideas; others that the term 'laziness' had been applied to activities that they had simply been unable to understand or appreciate" (pp. 46–47). Kelly observed further: "There is no doubt that the construct of motives is widely used, but it usually turns out to be a part of the language of complaint about the behavior of other people" (p. 46).

out here in order to complete our historical outline: the shattering of man's faith in his own rationality. Freud contended that the rationality that is supposed to guide our actions is only a facade with which we keep ourselves from knowing what we are really doing and why we are doing it. He made it plausible to suppose that there are always real reasons for our actions, although they can sometimes only be known through psychoanalysis.

Parallel to the history of determinism is a history of man's loss of his own high regard for himself. Man's elevated self-regard has suffered three blows. The first was the cosmological blow administered by Copernicus. Man no longer occupied the center of the universe. But he still had an advantage over other animals; he surely had acquired a dominant position over them. "Not content with this supremacy, however, he began to place a gulf between his nature and theirs. He denied possession of reason to them, and to himself he attributed an immortal soul, and made claims to a divine descent."[29] Darwin, in doing away with this bit of arrogance, delivered the second, the biological blow, to man's elevated regard for himself. But man still retained his rationality and his high moral nature. Freud found, however, that the ego is not master in its own house, and thereby delivered the third and most wounding, the psychological, blow to man's self-esteem. Man had to start conceiving of himself as a natural phenomenon.

[29] Original authorship of the idea of three blows, or revolutions, has been attributed to several writers. I am paraphrasing here Freud's own version (1917).

3

DYNAMIC PSYCHOLOGY

. . . no therapist or, indeed, anyone who has to deal in a practical way with human beings, can get along without some notion of motivational force . . .

HENRY MURRAY

In the preceding chapter the growth of the deterministic attitude was described, and we saw how this attitude gradually became applied to the explanation of human behavior, replacing traditional rationalistic and mentalistic explanations. The following chapters will be concerned primarily with the study of animal behavior, where the deterministic attitude has become strongly established, where theories of behavior have been stated with considerable precision, and where, consequently, we may hope to find some promising models for theories of human motivation. But in the present chapter we must consider another sort of theory that has arisen primarily from the very practical need to assess human motives. We will be concerned here with theories written by men who had to build their theoretical structures because of pressing commitments to provide usable tools for everyday human problems without waiting for fundamental research findings.

The theories which resulted from this practical need to deal with human affairs show some strain from the lack of a firm empirical base, but they can be readily recognized nonetheless as transitional between the traditional rationalistic approach to human behavior and modern behavior theory. We will see first how Freud shattered the widespread complacent reliance upon traditional rationalism. The rationalist doctrine maintains that man acts in any particular instance because he has reasons for acting as he does, and although we may often be able to discover his reasons by asking him what they are or were, more often his reasons are forever lost in the privacy of his own mind—he alone may know why he acts as he does. This doctrine accepts that some behavior may be due to emotion (passion), or habit, or instinct, or reflex, but insists that all of the important reasons for action are intellectual in nature, which makes them something apart from all of the mechanical causes just noted. It sets them apart by exempting them from natural law.

Freud also maintained that men act because they have reasons for their action, but there is a difference. Freud would not accept what a man gives as the reasons for his actions, so the purely intellectual reasons, to which the rationalist is accustomed, are not allowed. In their place we find a new explanatory principle: the reasons for an action can be found by certain procedures of psychological analysis ("psychoanalysis," for short) which can disclose the pattern of forces and energies which led to the action. A man's private intellectual reasons are replaced by a theoretical array of forces and energies which constitute the real reasons for his actions. The potential advantage of this approach is that *all* behavior now becomes subject to psychological law. This was the sense in which Freud was a determinist. We will discover that psychoanalysis is inadequate as a formal theory of behavior because, while Freud elaborated a systematic account of the reasons for action, he paid little attention to how these reasons became transformed into behavior. The lawfulness in psychoanalysis pertains to the reasons for, or the motives of, behavior, and not to behavior itself.

We will consider next Lewin's theory of motivation. Lewin also postulated that behavior is a result of forces and tensions, but the nature and origin of these dynamic factors are much different from what they are in psychoanalysis; and the time perspective is quite different for the two theories. Although Lewin, in contrast to Freud, devoted considerable attention to the relationships between the hypothetical dynamic causes of behavior and their behavioral consequences, he unfortunately neglected the equally important explanatory task of accounting for the forces and tensions themselves, so that, again, we do not have a strictly deterministic system, nor one which is acceptable as a theory of behavior. Although we have to grant that Freud and Lewin both handed down to us a variety of conceptual tools to enrich our understanding of behavior, we also recognize that they each retained a little too much of the traditional rationalism.

Finally, we will consider briefly Murray's theory of motivation, partly just to present a third variation on the dynamic-psychology theme, and partly to illustrate the versatility of the motivation concept. Murray applied this concept, with considerable success, to the problem of analyzing personality, which is surely the most intractable problem in all of psychology.

These three theorists, Freud, Lewin, and Murray, represent contrasting points of view, they were interested in entirely different sorts of behavior, and, of course, their total systematic positions are quite different. Our concern in this chapter is by no means to assess or even to survey their complete theoretical systems. We will look only at the motivational aspects of the theories, paying particular attention to the evolution of the concept of drive in the context of human motivation. In succeeding chapters we will see that there has been a parallel evolution of a similar drive concept in the context of animal motivation. In both cases we will find that motivation theorists have tried to maintain a sharp distinction between energy and structure. Freud, Lewin, and Murray have all argued that the explanation of psychological phenomena requires more than an account of the conditions under which an event occurs, more than just a description of the observed relationships between events. Such structural accounts must be supplemented, it is argued, by the postulation of psychological forces which make the necessary conditions *produce* the observed event, and *bring about* the observed relationships between events. Each theorist can cite some psychological phenomena which, he insists, cannot be explained in terms of structure alone; it is necessary to adopt some form of energy conception for these phenomena, and the logical extension of postulating an energy or force for all behavior follows. This is what makes a theory motivational. Let us begin by seeing how this energy vs. structure distinction first came into psychology with Freud.

THE ORIGINS OF PSYCHOANALYSIS

It has become customary in tracing the history of psychoanalysis to start with the development of hypnosis in the eighteeenth and nineteenth centuries. This history usually runs up to Charcot and emphasizes Charcot's use of hypnosis in treating hysteria. The beginnings of psychoanalysis are then attributed to the impact of Charcot's work on Freud. Certainly some of the phenomena and concepts of psychoanalysis, namely, the concept of the unconscious mind, the idea of getting at unconscious material through hypnosis, and the underlying importance of sex, are evident in Charcot's work. It is also certain that some of the data of psychoanalysis and some of its hypotheses about underlying processes were derived from the phenomena of hypnotism and neurotic hysteria. There was nothing motivational about Charcot's treatment of these phenomena, however. If they contributed to the origin of psychoanalysis, it was by providing it with structural content. Nor is either hypnosis or hysteria generally given a motivational interpretation except in the context of psychoanalysis. Freud must have derived his dynamic concepts from another source.

Although neither hypnosis nor hysteria might seem therefore to have a place in a history of motivation, they do quite properly belong to our narrative simply because they both were phenomena which demonstrated the inadequacy of traditional explanation of behavior. As Cofer and Appley have described the situation:

> . . . when hypnotism and psychoneurosis came to be regarded as natural phenomena, involving neither magnetic, spiritual nor willful aspects, they yet remained phenomena requiring explanation. The great systems of philosophy, in general, and in their psychological principles, had almost always been constructed by and with a view to normal, rational men. Their principles, even the motivational ones . . . could not easily accommodate the phenomena of mental disorder and hypnotism. (Cofer & Appley, 1964, p. 51)

In short, toward the end of the last century it was no longer acceptable to deal with hypnosis or hysteria by means of any accustomed variety of explanation. The challenging problem for Freud was that these phenomena had to be explained naturalistically, and there were at that time no adequate conceptual tools for doing it. If he did not get a motivational model from Charcot, where did Freud's idea of motivation come from? The answer is to be found in his continuous commitment to determinism.

At first Freud adhered to the only kind of determinism then available, materialism, and only later did he become a psychological determinist, a variety of determinism he virtually had to construct himself. Freud trained as a medical student from 1876 to 1881 under Brucke, who was the arch-materialist of his day. Brucke was the man who had pledged with Du Bois-Reymond to fight vitalism by demonstrating that "no other forces than common physical chemical ones are active within the organism," and Brucke's students were trained in the same spirit.[1] This background was apparent as a strong physicalistic bias in Freud's early work. In 1895 Freud wrote a radically reductionistic psychology, his *Project for a Scientific Psychology,* in which physical and physiological bases for psychological phenomena were boldly hypothesized. Although he had no sooner committed these ideas to writing than he repudiated them (they were not published during his lifetime), it is interesting to note that many of his earliest explanatory principles survived his subsequent efforts to translate this early work into purely psychological terms. As this transition occurred his determinism changed from being physi-

[1] See Bernfeld (1944) and Jones (1953). Brucke's pledge is quoted from Boring (1950, p. 708).

calistic to psychological, and as his system became no longer mechanical, it became motivational. Freud's biographer, Jones (1953), has given very little indication of how Freud's earlier physicalistic, materialistic, and reductionistic psychology became transformed into a psychological system. Jones said only that he became emancipated. Freud himself commented only that the mechanistic view is intellectually crippling (1925, p. 166).

If we seem to be belaboring the point that Freud shifted from a physical to a psychological variety of determinism, it is because the point is so crucial in understanding the origin of the idea of motivation. It is characteristic of all of our motivational concepts, whether they be drive, incentive, or reinforcement, that they are initially visualized in physical or physiological terms, and only later conceptualized in behavioral terms. What makes Freud's case so interesting is that while usually this transition has occurred only as one theorist has superseded another, Freud made the transition for himself. In the following section we shall look at the evolution of some of the basic motivational concepts of psychoanalysis. We will see how the evolution of these concepts reflected Freud's growing conception of psychological determinism.

EXPLANATORY PRINCIPLES

The Concept of Equilibrium. Throughout the years that Freud developed his theory, certain concepts kept recurring. One such perennial concept is *equilibrium* (probably more literally translated as constancy). Equilibrium is the tendency of the nervous system to discharge any increase in excitation. In 1892 Freud and Breuer declared:

> The nervous system endeavours to keep constant something in its functional condition that may be described as the "sum of excitation." It seeks to establish this necessary precondition of health by dealing with every sensible increase of excitation along associative lines or by discharging it by an appropriate motor reaction. (Freud & Breuer, 1892, p. 30)

Freud elaborated the concept of equilibrium in the *Project for a Scientific Psychology,* where it was put into strict physicalistic and reductionistic form. The nerves were said to function to maintain a constant amount of energy; if they are stimulated, they will seek to discharge the input energy. At this point there was nothing very psychological in the equilibrium concept, but by 1900 the situation had changed. In *Interpretation of Dreams* Freud abandoned the earlier mechanistic orientation when he wrote that the work of the primitive psychic apparatus

. . . is regulated by the effort to avoid accumulation of excitation, and as far as possible to maintain itself free from excitation. For this reason it was constructed after the plan of a reflex apparatus; motility, in the first place as the path to changes within the body, was the channel of discharge at its disposal . . . the accumulation of excitation . . . is felt as pain, and sets the apparatus in operation in order to bring about again a state of gratification, in which the diminution of excitation is perceived as pleasure. Such a current in the apparatus, issuing from pain and striving for pleasure, we call a wish. (Freud, 1900, p. 533)

Then, in 1915, he referred to the great complexity introduced into a reflexive conception of the nervous system by the instincts, i.e., internal sources of stimulation. Although the task of the nervous system was still considered to be the mastery of stimulation, internal stimuli lend an aspect of purpose to how this is accomplished, since the individual must adapt its means to the end of abolishing stimulation.[2]

Thus, over a period of 20 years Freud stated in somewhat different ways his belief in the concept of equilibrium, and the different statements indicate profound changes in orientation. Later, the maintenance of equilibrium served as a prototype for what was called the "primary process." Before the child finds out how to cope with the problems of the real world, tension may be discharged through hallucinatory images in the absence of appropriate motor activity. A direct but unrealistic discharge of energy also occurs in adults in wish-fulfilling dreams.

We may note another aspect of Freud's theoretical treatment of the equilibrium concept. He always made the implicit assumption that stimuli were "bad," not just because the organism sought to maintain a condition of equilibrium, but also because stimuli by their very nature in some way posed a threat to the continued health of the organism. He observed that, historically,

. . . the concept of *stimuli* and the scheme of the reflex arc, according to which a stimulus applied *from the outside world* to living tissue (nervous substance) is discharged by action *towards the outer world*. The action answers the purpose of withdrawing the substance affected from the operation of the stimulus, removing it out of range of the stimulus. (Freud, 1915, p. 61)

The early animal physiologists had indeed arrived at the concepts of stimulus and reflex arc on the basis of their observations that animals would react to avoid externally applied irritations; these withdrawal reactions (e.g., the flexion reflex in mammals) formed the experimental

---

[2] These ideas were remarkably similar to those being developed quite independently by Tolman and other instinct theorists about 1920 (see Chapter 4).

basis of their early work. In all of Freud's examples stimuli are assumed to have the same aversive nature. For example, he speaks of a strong light striking the eye, and of certain stimuli that can be avoided, and even more explicitly he says, "external stimuli impose on the organism the single task of withdrawing itself from their action." It seems that Freud invoked the concept of instinctual drive as a stimulus to action in large measure because he had taken such a narrow definition of stimulus. Stimuli were ipso facto dangerous or threatening to the welfare of the organism. It is no wonder then that he discovered that the organism was dedicated to minimizing stimulation. This view of stimuli was not idiosyncratic of Freud. In fact, we must wait another whole generation to find writers proposing that some stimuli are "good" and to be sought.[3]

The Concept of Structure. Freud's *Project* emphasized another concept which was adopted from physics but given a characteristically Freudian twist. While it is possible to hold that neurons (or states of awareness) tend to discharge their excitation, it must also be recognized that discharge is only possible through specific preestablished channels. A neuron can only discharge its energy through other neurons with which it is connected, and this limitation on the possible consequences of excitation must be dealt with, Freud believed, if the theory is to have any validity. This tendency of excitation to be discharged according to some established pattern is recognizable as a prototype of what Freud later called the *secondary process,* i.e., tension can only be reduced by finding an outlet through the constraints and inhibitions that the structure of the ego places upon its discharge. To extend the analogy, it may be supposed that such outlet, once found to be useful in the discharge of excitation, would come to be used habitually. The individual might even develop a fixation on the particular means of relieving excitation.

Here we have come to the all-important distinction between energy and structure. In order to explain what the individual does the psychoanalyst must determine not only what energy or motive force lies behind the behavior, but also what structure of the ego enables the motivating forces to be expressed in ways that are characteristic of a particular individual. We have also come to another characteristic of Freudian theory, viz., Freud's tendency to view any consequence of a man's psychological makeup as the result of conflict. Excitation is never just discharged, it is always met with some opposition—from the external world, from the structure of the ego, from the superego, from some contrary primitive instinct, or from some other conceptual barrier, so that what is manifest in behavior is never a direct consequence of the motivating

---

[3] The realization that stimuli might be sought, that there could be a "stimulus hunger," first occurred to Fenichel (1934), Lashley (1938), and Lorenz (1937). This more or less independent formulation of the concept by at least three men provides an interesting example of simultaneous discovery.

energy, but is always a resultant, a compromise, or a disguised consequence of the underlying excitation.

To explain behavior, then, it is necessary to look first for the motivating force, and then for a counterforce, before the details of the explanation can be filled in. At first, Freud viewed the balance of the effects of the equilibrium principle and the limitations of the neuronal circuity as a type of conflict. Later, he emphasized the constant conflict between libidinal impulses and the structure of the ego. Neurotic symptoms, dreams, slips of the tongue, and other sorts of behavior which have no apparent motivation were regarded as the effects of conflict. In cases where there is no superficial motive, or where the motive is not known to the individual himself, some motive must be postulated, and its apparent absence explained by postulating countermotives that hide it from view.

Freud argued that the nature of these repressed motives was revealed clinically when the resistance of the patient was overcome. In neurotic patients these repressed motives invariably turned out to be sexual. Hence, according to Freud, a systematic picture of the neurotic may be formulated which involves (1) a powerful sexual wish as the basic motivation which strives to flood the patient with stimulation but which is inhibited by (2) powerful counterforces originating from the demands of the real world; the result is (3) a loss from awareness of the initial sexual wish, and (4) a disguised expression of the initial wish in the form of a neurotic symptom. We will see shortly how the counterforces were characterized, and how they were assumed to develop. But first let us look at the nature of the assumed initial motivating forces.

PSYCHOANALYTIC THEORY OF INSTINCTUAL DRIVES

Freud's most important paper on motivation was "Instincts and their vicissitudes," written in 1915. In it Freud distinguished between instincts and stimuli, and asserted that the former were the principal (or at least the most interesting) motivators of behavior. Simuli were regarded as necessarily (or by definition) external to the organism and necessarily to be avoided. Freud admitted to considerable difficulty in arriving at a choice of a word to describe the internal counterpart of stimulus before deciding on the German word *Trieb*. At the time the early translations of Freud's works were being made into English, *Trieb* was rendered as "instinct"; today "drive" would be more accurate. Literally, *Trieb* means a mechanical provocation to action. Probably the best semantic strategy is to speak of these psychoanalytic motivators as "instinctual drives."

By 1915 Freud had completely given up his early physiological model with its reductionistic philosophy, and adopted a very broad outlook on drive and instinct, transcending even the relatively broad mentalistic viewpoint he had assumed in the *Interpretation of Dreams* (1900). According to his 1915 essay, an instinct or instinctual drive could be characterized by its impetus, its aim, its object, and its source.[4]

By the *impetus* of an instinct we understand its motor element, the amount of force or the measure of the demand upon energy which it represents. The characteristic of impulsion is common to all instincts, is in fact the very essence of them . . .

The *aim* of an instinct is in every instance satisfaction, which can only be obtained by abolishing the condition of stimulation in the source of the instinct . . . . this remains invariably the final goal of every instinct . . .[5]

The *object* of an instinct is that in or through which it can achieve its aim. It is the most variable thing about an instinct and is not originally connected with it, but becomes attached to it only in consequence of being peculiarly fitted to provide satisfaction . . .

By the *source* of an instinct is meant that somatic process in an organ or part of the body from which there results a stimulus represented in mental life by an instinct. We do not know whether this process is regularly of a chemical nature or whether it may also correspond with the release of other, e.g., mechanical, forces. The study of the sources of instinct is outside the scope of psychology; although its source in the body is what gives the instinct its distinct and essential character, yet in mental life we know it merely by its aims. (Freud, 1915, pp. 65–66)

Instincts thus have some of the same properties as external sources of stimulation: they have the same aim (to be rid of stimulation) and a comparable impetus (motivational). The differences lie in the source and in the necessity of realizing a particular relationship with some par-

---

[4] It may be of some significance that some 40 years earlier Freud had been a student of Brentano. Barclay (1959) has suggested that Freud's theory of motivation owes a great deal to the influence of Brentano's teaching. Brentano's "act psychology" was built in large part upon the philosophy of Aquinas and Aristotle taught at that time by Catholic scholars. Evidence for Barclay's argument is suggested by the parallel between Freud's discussion of the impetus, aim, object, and source of an instinct, and Aristotle's distinctions among the efficient, final, formal, and material causes of an event. Indeed, a better modern exemplar of Aristotle's fourfold approach to explanation can hardly be found. The point was also made by Merlan (1945). Boring (1950) seems intrigued by the possibility of Brentano being one of Freud's intellectual fathers; however, Jones (1953), after noting that Freud took courses under Brentano, observes that so did everyone in Vienna! Jones does not entertain the possibility of any influence.

[5] But Freud sometimes (even in the 1915 paper) used "aim" to refer to the particular consummatory activity through which the stimulating condition is abolished, rather than the abolition itself.

ticular external goal object. Flight is of no avail against the internal stimulation of an instinct. Hence, the instinct provides a steady and continuing source of stimulation, whereas external stimuli are reduced to momentary disturbances by reflex action.

The Alteration of the Instincts.   Having stated that instinctual drives are the universal motivators in psychoanalytic theory, it is necessary to point out immediately that there are some qualifications that must be attached to the statement. The vicissitudes of the original instinct may carry it so far from its initial manifestation that it becomes practically unrecognizable. The object of an instinct and its means of expression may become so changed that only a historical tie with the original remains. Freud devoted the last part of his *instincts* paper to a discussion of how instincts may change in their object and in their aim, and how they may become reversed or inverted, repressed or sublimated.[6] The way that this sort of change is assumed to occur has been outlined by Rapaport:

> When an instinctual drive reaches threshold intensity and the drive object is absent, and therefore no consummatory action can take place, a change in threshold is assumed to occur. This change is conceptualized as a heightening of threshold by means of a superimposed cathetic barrier termed "anticathexis." When such anti-cathexes structuralize, we speak of them as defenses. . . . Anti-cathexis, like any other energy, manifests itself as a force. (Rapaport, 1960, p. 212)

For example, altruism may result from frustrated aggression. These defenses result in differentiation of the original motives into a variety of derivative motivations, that is, motivations with displaced objects and with diversified means of object attainment. The original instinctive force may become increasingly hampered as these defense structures continue to ramify and diversify. It may even be the case that the initial drive becomes devoid of its initial emotional potential; it may be said then to have become neutralized or sublimated. Sufficient energy may even get bound up in these anticathectic structures that they become semi-autonomous, running on their own borrowed energy. These ego structures, whether they be activated by diverted instinctual energy or by their own bound energy, may be said to be determinants of behavior every bit as much as were the primal sexual instincts. To this extent, the behavior of the adult can be virtually independent of its original motivational source, that is, independent in all senses except the historical.

_____

[6] In 1920 Freud reorganized his view of the instincts and their incessant struggle. Roughly, he grouped the ego and id instincts together, calling them life instincts, and opposed them by the newly conceived Death instinct. There has been a good deal of dissension among psychoanalysts about the value of this reorganization. The reorganization affected only the details, however, and not the general nature of what Freud considered to be an adequate explanation of human behavior.

Perhaps the Freudian view of instinctual drives can be restated as follows: Instinctual drives are characterized by their energy, or impulse to action. Men learn to attain certain objects, or goals, that make possible the discharge of this energy. This discharge makes the goals more valuable and reduces the original impulse to action. Psychoanalysis is a theory about the goals of behavior, what they are, and how they become goals.

PSYCHOANALYTIC EXPLANATIONS OF BEHAVIOR

Although the theory incorporates a vast explanatory network to deal with the establishment of motives and goals, psychoanalysis provides a dearth of explanatory hypotheses to account for how goals are attained. Freud's psychology deals with the wish and goal object and proclaims that we can understand the individual if we know these components of his mental life. But the motility component (the regulation of behavior) is only given in barest outline. Freud tells us *why*, but not *how* a man does what he does. The actual behavior of the individual is viewed by the psychoanalyst principally as a means of inferring the underlying structure of the personality. But a complete account of behavior requires something more than this. It requires a complimentary theory of the ego, some explanation of how the ego goes about its business.[7]

Passivity of the Ego. Allport, among others, has criticized psychoanalysis for the passive role it gives the ego. Allport has said that in psychoanalysis, egoism

. . . is not ascribed to the ego, but to the urges arising from the id. For Freud the ego proper is a passive percipient, devoid of dynamic power, "a coherent organization of mental processes" that is aware of the warring forces of id, superego, and external environment. The ego, having no dynamic power, tries as well as it can to conciliate and to steer the warring forces, but when it fails, as it often does, it breaks out in anxiety. (Allport, 1943, pp. 455–456)[8]

There is a major fallacy, however, in Allport's analysis: There is only one limited sense in which the ego has been dethroned, namely, that it has no autonomy for establishing its own goals. The goals it serves are

[7] A number of psychoanalytic writers in the last 20 years have tended to give much more attention to the ego than Freud did, even in his later years (e.g., Hartmann, 1958). To the end, Freud provoked ego psychologists with statements like: The ego develops "as an *intermediary* between the id and the external world" (italics mine) (Freud, 1940, p. 15).

[8] Allport takes offense at psychoanalysis, not only because of its denial of the ego's autonomy, but also because of its insistence upon historical explanations of men's motives (Allport, 1937a), and its failure to recognize the uniqueness of the individual (Allport, 1937).

established at best through principles of expediency and compromise. Nor can the ego produce its own energy; ultimately its dynamic power is derived. In these matters the ego is legislated to by the other components of the personality. Nonetheless, the ego is, for good reason, called the executive of the personality.

> The ego is said to be the executive of the personality because it controls the gateways to action, selects the features of the environment to which it will respond, and decides what instincts will be satisfied and in what manner. (Hall & Lindzey, 1957, p. 34)

How can Allport designate as passive any agency which controls, selects, and decides, and which is essentially autonomous in performing these functions? The behaviorist sees a limitation of psychoanalytic theory which is just the opposite of that which Allport sees: the ego is too active, too removed from explanatory mechanisms, and too free of lawful determination. The behaviorist suspects that a psychoanalytic explanation of behavior is considered complete when the psychoanalyst has discovered the motive and the goal of the behavior.

Defense Mechanisms. According to some writers on psychoanalytic theory (e.g., Anna Freud), the nature of the ego is best revealed by analyzing the way in which it learns to cope with anxiety. The first confrontation with reality is the birth trauma; since the ego is essentially passive at this point it has no means of coping with the flood of external stimulation with which it is suddenly faced. This initial overpowering excitation presents a model for all subsequent traumatic experience. To cope with the fear of too much stimulation, the ego may acquire further mechanisms of defense, further techniques for dealing with the threat of being overwhelmed.

In acquiring and using these defense mechanisms the ego is going beyond a passive role, and taking a hand in the regulation of the total personality. Some of the mechanisms which Freud stressed were repression, projection, fixation, and regression. Each of these is a technique for coping with anxiety. Each of these modes of adjustment may, if used exclusively, lead to personality abnormalities. On the other hand, it is just the characteristic limited use of these mechanisms that provides the structure of the individual personality. It is important to note that the defense mechanisms are not motivational concepts per se. In every case the motivational components of behavior lie beneath the ego and dictate to it what it has to do. Defense mechanisms are essentially structural conceptions—they are descriptive of how the ego handles its task of warding off anxiety.

Freud did not even regard anxiety itself as a motivational force, but emphasized its role as a signal or a cue (1926). Little Hans was anxious about horses; he was frightened of them. Freud's interpretation of Little

Hans' phobia was based on the assumption that the boy unconsciously feared his father for the threat of castration which the father represented. This fear of damage at the hands of his father was symbolized as a fear of being bitten by a horse. The function, therefore, served by the anxiety about horses was a cue, a signal to the ego to repair or strengthen the defense (in this case repression) against fear of the father. If Little Hans could keep away from horses he could keep away from the to-be-repressed fear of the father and the Oedipal reasons for the fear. Anxiety is thus a signal to the ego to get to work or to avoid a potentially more dangerous situation; it is not in itself, according to Freud, a motive or a source of energy.

Specifying when the ego must act and what it must do is about as far as Freud went in developing an ego psychology. Beyond this, psychoanalysis has very little to say about how the ego works, and how it serves its executive role. We may note again that the psychoanalytic theory of motivation is essentially a *theory of the structure and historical development of motives*. A complete theory of motivation would encompass not only these aspects of the determination of behavior, but would also include an explanatory account of behavior itself, i.e., how behavior is mediated. In this respect psychoanalysis represents very little gain over the traditional rationalistic explanation that men do what they want to do.

The Scope of Psychoanalysis. Another serious limitation to psychoanalytic theory is that it was never intended to apply to all behavior.[9] Although the unconscious libidinal strivings, particularly those associated with sex, are in one sense universal, it is a misinterpretation to suppose that Freud wanted to explain all behavior in the same way he explained neurotic symptoms. He formulated the concept of unconscious instinctual drives to make sense out of a relatively small class of clinical phenomena. The phenomena that were to be included were (1) certain pathological phenomena (like hysteria), (2) certain irrational ideas or behavior that are not necessarily pathological, (3) the origin of certain phenomena that are subjectively felt as being beyond voluntary control, and (4) "spontaneous" ideas and behavior which are not obvious responses to known stimuli.[10] These categories clearly do not encompass all behavior; they probably exclude the majority of the things people do.

Peters (1958, pp. 53–61) has made the same point quite insistently. Peters argues that outside his specialized field of interest, Freud accepted traditional varieties of explanation:

. . . there are a great number of cases . . . which have such an

---

[9] Psychoanalysis "has never dreamt of trying to explain 'everything,' and even the neuroses it has traced back not to sexuality alone but to the conflict between the sexual impulses and the ego" (Freud, 1922, p. 127).

[10] This analysis of the scope of psychoanalysis is taken from Rapaport (1960), which is one of the best analyses of the psychoanalytic theory of motivation.

obvious and acceptable explanation in terms of conscious reasons that it seems absurd to look around for unconscious motives. This, I think, Freud would have been perfectly prepared to accept; for, though he held that much of the ego was unconscious, he thought that the ego-instincts, concerned with self-preservation, were more influenced by the reality principle and less subject to repression than the sex instincts. In such cases the conscious reasons are obviously sufficient to explain what a man does. . . . (Peters, 1958, pp. 60–61)

Perhaps Peters is right that psychoanalysis is only suitable for explaining the bizarre, the pathological, and the inexplicable, and that it falls back upon other, mundane rationalistic principles, for explaining the bulk of things that men do.

This is a serious indictment of Freudian psychology, and I should hasten to add that there are some outstanding respects in which psychoanalysis is far from impotent in dealing with normal behavior. Much behavior which appears to be motivated by ordinary, reasonable, and time-honored interests and attitudes can be explained developmentally or historically in terms of more basic, primitive, and unifying motives. For example, the ordinary virtue of tidiness can frequently be traced back (by a psychoanalyst) to an individual's adjustment to the stresses of his anal period.

Moreover there seems to be no limit to the circumstances under which psychoanalytic principles can be invoked. Our appreciation of literature, our understanding of social structure, of family relationships, and of religion and art have all been enriched by the introduction of psychoanalytic concepts. It may be that in explaining the abnormal Freud had discovered new principles of explanation and that having become acquainted with these new principles we can no longer accept the old ones. One such feature of Freud's view of man is that it emphasizes underlying sources of motivation and it denies the importance of superficial motives, particularly those which the individual cites in explanation of his own behavior. It is difficult to accept any longer as an explanation of a man's behavior that he had "no reason" for it, or that he "just felt like it." Still another feature of psychoanalysis that cannot be dismissed in the explanation of everyday behavior is its emphasis upon the historical and developmental determinants of behavior. Characteristically, what is attributable to structural features of the individual's adult personality may often be understood in terms of the energetic features of his earlier personality. An adult motive, functionally autonomous though it may be, may often only be explained in terms of its motivational origins; and, in many cases, to ignore its origins may be to eliminate the only grounds on which a motive can be explained. We have to conclude that although

Peters' point is well taken, he is wrong in dismissing psychoanalysis as a serious challenge to the rationalistic position. After Freud, the student of behavior can no longer accept a rationalistic account for the explanation of any behavior.

Freud's Paradox. There is still another aspect of psychoanalytic theory which deserves comment in relation to the traditional rationalistic account of behavior. We have emphasized that one of the enduring contributions of psychoanalysis was Freud's demonstration that man's sense of rationality and will power are essentially illusory. Now we are confronted by a paradox: while a central tenet of psychoanalysis had been a denial of man's rationality and will, at the same time these same faculties have been retained and pressed into service as tools of the ego. Put another way, behavior is explained deterministically, but at the same time, the ego is free to get along in any way it can in meeting the demands placed upon it. Freud said repeatedly that the ego learns, perceives, remembers, imagines, thinks, etc. In short, the ego seems to have all of the powers that a nineteenth-century faculty psychologist might suppose it to have. And yet it would also be fair to conclude that people do the things they do because of powerful unconscious sexual motives; and even though these be disguised during the course of individual development, their motive power can be discerned by the use of appropriate analytic techniques.

A resolution of the paradox can be based upon the fact that Freud felt that his own contribution to human thought was primarily a humanitarian one.[11] The classical picture of man as a rational being had attributed all mental functioning to a conscious ego (or mind or soul) and had set the conscious ego apart from unconscious instinctive activities such as eating and sexual behavior. Freud complicated this dichotomous scheme by inserting a third level. There were instincts to be sure, and also a conscious part of the ego, but there was a third part of the mind which obeyed determinate laws of mental organization as though it was conscious, but which was, in fact, not conscious. This third element of the mind represented a limitation upon the sovereignty of rationality and the will, even though it functioned like the volitional and rational part of the mind. All of us to some extent, but especially the neurotic, suffer a grim tyranny of the mind which prevents us from being wholly rational or completely in command of our actions. Freud viewed psychoanalysis as a technique for minimizing the power of this third realm, for liberating

[11] See, e.g., Zweig (1932) and Zilboorg (1951). Zilboorg said "One always feels an undertone of pessimism, or a cold rejection of fate, circumstances, society, whenever one reads Freud very carefully. Freud set very little store in possible changes of mankind in general, in man's social structures, or in any other set of environmental forces . . . they always seemed to him to interfere with the inner freedom of man" (p. 25). According to Zilboorg, Freud conceived of mental health as a "new, special kind of strength and freedom."

man, for restoring him to the dichotomous condition depicted by the traditionalist.

FORMAL ADEQUACY AS A THEORY OF BEHAVIOR

Our final concern with psychoanalysis is not with its status as a new political, social, or humane philosophy but rather with its status as a formal theory of behavior. As an explanatory model it is much in need of a firmer empirical foundation and more explicit rules for the use of its theoretical constructs. That is, we need to know how to relate the theoretical terms both to each other (the syntactical problem) and to observable events (the semantic problem). Psychoanalysts have concerned themselves primarily with inferring central events or structures of a non-directly observable character from certain manifestations of overt behavior, but they have not told us the rules for such inferences. The trouble here, of course, is that the analyst is not very interested in explaining behavior itself, or in constructing a theory that would permit him to do so. The traditional belief seems to prevail that it is sufficient to explain an individual's motives or reasons for acting; this done, the behavior follows as a matter of course. Therefore, dream analysis, associative recall, catharsis, and all of the other behavior-eliciting techniques of the analyst are considered to be merely means for getting at the all-important motivational factors of the individual. As Janis (1958) and others have pointed out, it is possible for the psychoanalytic interview to be a useful research tool, and some steps in realizing this promise have already been taken, but there is a great deal of work yet to be done to establish an unambiguous set of principles and hypotheses.

Historically, the behavioral observations upon which psychoanalysis was built did not come from the laboratory, or even from systematic work in a clinical setting, but rather from case histories, from Freud's own self-analysis, and partly also from the fields of art and literature. Freud himself attached little importance to external verification of the events his patients described; it was much more important that his patient's reports held together in a pattern which was consistent with psychoanalytic principles than that they be empirically verifiable. When the analyst comes to the conclusion, for example, that a patient's symptoms, associations, and emotional characteristics can be best interpreted in terms of an unresolved Oedipus problem, he is quite concerned that all of the patient's current behavior is consistent with this interpretation, but he is relatively unconcerned with whether the individual has, in fact, always loved his mother and feared his father. In part, this bias reflects the demand, mentioned in the introduction to this chapter, put upon the analyst to adjust the patient's current behavior to his current situation.

On the other hand, it seems unlikely that psychoanalysis is wholly without empirical content. Freud and others have assured us that during a series of psychoanalytic interviews the structure of the patient's mental world becomes clear. And the analyst assures us that during this process he is discovering the determinants of the patient's behavior in an empirical manner. Freud insisted that his conclusions were in many cases "forced" upon him by his clinical findings, often in contradiction to his prior conceptions. Unfortunately, Freud has not told us how to arrive at an empirically compelling confirmation of the theory. It is commonly said that verification of the hypotheses of psychoanalysis requires considerable clinical sophistication and experience. If this is true, it indicates the seriousness of the inherent semantic difficulties of the theory.

The theory also presents certain problems of syntax. There is rarely an unequivocal way of fitting the theoretical terms of the theory together to constitute an explanation of behavior. More often, there is a diversity of possible interpretations of a given phenomenon; and the rules of syntax are not clear enough to permit us to say which of the alternative interpretations is preferable, much less to permit us to test between them. Discrepant and even contradictory interpretations are often possible. More often than not, psychoanalytic theory "underdetermines" the phenomena it is expressly designed to explain. Thus, although psychoanalysis provides a deterministic account of behavior, and lends itself to an ad hoc account of any behavioral happening, where in Freud's writing can we find a prediction of behavior?

The value of psychoanalysis lies in its challenge to the traditional rationalistic interpretations of behavior. For centuries we had come to accept the proposition that a man does what he wants to do because he wants to do it. Psychoanalysis impressed upon us that men frequently act for reasons which are quite different from those they articulate. But a psychoanalytic explanation of behavior still adheres to the principle that a man does what he is motivated to do, and it is addressed not so much to explaining behavior as to explaining the motives that are assumed to underlie behavior. The syntactical rules of psychoanalysis rarely, if ever, include overt behavior in their terms. They tell us what a man wants to do and why he wants to do it, but never how he does it. This limitation of psychoanalytic theory is, of course, not unique among the theoretical accounts of human behavior. Indeed, it seems to be symptomatic, and perhaps it is too easy to criticize Freud for attempting to explain no more than why a man has the motives that he has.

Pratt has aptly summarized for us the essence of Freud's contribution:

> Freud will be remembered long after the names of most scientific psychologists have been forgotten . . . [He was] a brilliant artist whose glamorous perceptions and piercing intuitions have held the

modern intellectual world enthralled. The tremendous sweep of his imagination has enabled him to see connections where narrower minds see nothing. Whether the connections are *really* there or not, no one knows, not even Freud himself; or if he does, he has committed an unpardonable scientific sin by not revealing to the rest of the world the secret of his knowledge. Many generations of psychologists will spend their lives trying to translate the poetry of Freud into the prose of science. (Pratt, 1939, p. 164)

ENERGY VERSUS STRUCTURE

In German psychology at the turn of the century, the dominant viewpoint was Wundt's structuralism, which was based on the premise that psychology could solve all its problems through an investigation of the mind. It was supposed that the functioning of the mind would be revealed by an analysis of its contents. Of course, the easiest associative elements to investigate were sensations, and accordingly the bulk of the structuralists' research involved sensations. But emotions, feelings, acts of will, and automatic impulses to action were all supposed to yield to the same introspective mode of analysis. The basic belief was that to understand the mind (which implied an understanding of the whole individual) it is necessary only to know what is associated with what in the mind.

The Discoveries at Würzburg. This purely structural approach was extended to the problem of the higher mental processes (thinking) by a dedicated group of psychologists at Würzburg under the leadership of Külpe. But although these investigations were initiated in complete faith in structuralism, they soon led to the demise of the structuralistic position.

In the first place, it was found that thinking could occur without any mental content at all, i.e., so-called imageless thoughts were discovered. Later, these contentless elements or processes were held to be the fundamental elements of thinking.[12] Secondly, and more important, the Würzburgers found that they had to introduce other, new, and nonassociative explanatory terms. For example, they began to concern themselves with the effects of instructions (Aufgabe) in producing a set (Einstellung). The Würzburg psychologists began to consider the selectiv-

---

[12] This was the view of Messer (1906). The best account of the Würzberg school in general is Humphrey (1951). Boring (1950) gives a shorter survey of Würzburg but relates it better to the stream of history. Thus, he cites not only the Würzburgers but also the men in the tradition of Leibnitz and Herbart as the creators of the dynamic principle. I mention the former and slight the latter. Earlier in the chapter I ignored (also in defiance of Boring's example) the psychopathologists prior to Freud on the grounds that they had little or no influence upon him, at least as far as his motivational concepts were concerned.

ity of attention and the importance of experimentally induced sets in the selection of associations. Of course, instructions might be viewed as stimuli, as particular stimuli that are presented prior to the stimulus which actually elicits the response.[13] The Würzburgers did not handle the problem this way however; instead they contended that an Einstellung was a new kind of mental process.

According to Ach (1905) and Watt (1905), a subject could have a "determining tendency" which could operate upon the associative structure of the mind by selecting from among available associations. Watt contended that, therefore, the selective principle, the determining tendency, must have a different nature from the processes which it governed. Because focusing of attention and maintaining a set were largely under voluntary control, a function of the will, this additional principle was held to be a "dynamic" factor in mental processes. This dynamic factor was viewed as something distinct from the purely structural features of the mind. Humphrey has observed that for Watt,

> . . . this is a dichotomy separating the mechanical from the non-mechanical factors in thinking . . . Watt assumes as a groundwork the conventional associational theory that if experience A has occurred together with experience B, then if either A or B occurs later, there is a tendency for the other to recur. This theory Watt has overlaid with the stipulation that before this tendency can be realized, there must be a task present, which will itself contribute energy that may reinforce or inhibit any particular association. (Humphrey, 1951, pp. 98–99)

Humphrey goes on to note that the assumption by the Würzburgers of a dynamic factor, an energizing force, which activates the associative content and causes an event in our mental experience to occur, is the root idea behind the modern theory of drive or motive. The implication is that the material of past experience, the associative structure of the mind, is simply the material to be *used by* the energizing task, and does not itself have any power to cause a mental event.

In spite of some differences of opinion regarding the interpretation of the Würzburg findings, psychologists of that time generally concluded that a purely structuralistic psychology would not suffice because (1) certain mental processes (e.g., thinking) could occur in the absence of any associative content, and (2) because such a system failed to provide the energy needed to make the mental processes operate.

---

[13] A stimulus interpretation of set and other attitudinal concepts is possible (Graham, 1950, 1952). The best overall review of the tortured concepts of set is Gibson (1941).

It should be emphasized that structuralism was not rejected on empirical grounds, or at least not on these empirical grounds. Actually, the dynamic principle upon which the psychologists at Würzburg (and later those at Berlin) insisted is necessary only to the extent that one insists upon having it. There are no compelling logical or empirical reasons for rejecting a psychological theory just because it lacks a dynamic principle. We will see in the present chapter and in succeeding ones that the theorist assumes the concept of energy as necessary to complement the concept of structure. It never emerges from a survey of the facts, and it never emerges from the theoretical structure; it is always lurking in the background as a basic presupposition.

LEWIN'S THEORY OF MOTIVATION

No one made more of the energy vs. structure distinction than did Kurt Lewin. He began by extending and giving a broader interpretation to the work of Ach and Watt. Whereas the Würzburg investigators had argued that determining tendencies (produced by appropriate instructions) could either facilitate or interfere with associative tendencies, Lewin (1917, 1922) contended that the conflict here was not between associative and determining tendencies, but rather between the determining tendencies. He maintained that all mental processes, even those which appeared to be entirely under associative control, are in fact caused by some tension or psychic energy. In the laboratory the subject is always following some task, either one set for him or else one he sets himself. And in the course of everyday life, again, the individual's behavior is always governed by some intention to do one thing or another. In other words, all behavior is motivated. Lewin always adhered to this basic postulate.

A second postulate to which Lewin held consistently was that if psychology hopes to find causal laws to explain its phenomena, these laws must be based upon psychological "realities," and not just fictions. He contrasted realities with what he called achievement concepts (1926a). Achievement concepts, when applied to behavior, are definitions of behavior in terms of its consequences. Lewin cited as an example the case of learning to type where, he says, the beginner and the expert are engaged in psychologically different activities. The beginning typist is really hunting for letters, whereas the expert typist is really punching out words. It is only when we have determined what the psychologically real processes are that we can hope to explain them adequately. Where we miss the real phenomena we are concerning ourselves with mere semblances of the underlying processes. In some cases such semblances might be valid indications of their underlying causes but we can never assume that they are, so we should not build our theories upon them.[14]

A third important postulate, or axiomatic assumption, in Lewin's work was that conventional associationism was inadequate to the task of explaining man's behavior. He distinguished between "controlled" and "intentional" actions. Controlled actions, being those controlled by direct associative connections, may depend upon simple linkages between the occasion for an action and the action itself; but intentional or voluntary or willed behavior follows "field" principles. In a willed action the organism brings his whole psychological being into the production of his behavior. It is not sufficient to look for simple associative links or direct forces; we must look for more global factors (i.e., field factors). This position, long a part of the rationalistic doctrine, did not mean to Lewin that voluntary behavior was not lawful. Quite the contrary, as we will see, he attempted to furnish a much-needed syntactical structure to fill the void the rationalists had left between man's mind and his behavior.

There is a fourth characteristic feature of Lewin's motivation theory that should be mentioned before we proceed to consider his theoretical constructs in any detail. He believed there was little doubt about the basic facts of motivation, and little question about how they should be explained. He never claimed to have a "theory"; an explanatory theory was really not necessary. Lewin was concerned with "representing" or clarifying the understanding of behavior that was already in the public domain. He said that "the main objective of [his 1938 book] is to bring into the open some of the basic concepts and assumptions which objectively are presupposed in practically all psychological research in this field" (1938, p. 18). Lewin's attempts to find a satisfactory representation consumed a large part of his theoretical efforts, and he was evidently never thoroughly satisfied with any of his representational schemes. The logical structure of the theory and particularly the conceptual properties of its constructs are what concern us here, however, and it is quite possible to deal with these features of the theory without becoming involved with the arrows, Easter eggs, and gerrymanders to which Lewin himself was so devoted.[15]

---

[14] See also Lewin (1927) for his further views on explanation. This point in Lewin illustrates one of those "polarized" issues about which it is difficult to be indifferent; one reacts either "what a good way to put it" or else "what a lot of nonsense." The issue basically is whether science should properly be concerned with realities or with conventionalisms, i.e., constructs. If we are to deal with realities, then *whose* should we accept?

[15] Some writers have said that the representations cannot be given up without losing the theory, but we will follow the example of others who have done so. Cartwright (1959) and Heider (1960) are recent sympathetic reviews; Leeper (1943) is more critical; Estes (1954) is very critical, especially of the failure of Lewin's theory to meet acceptable standards for explanatory models. Only Leeper of these four writers found it necessary to make extensive use of diagrams, and Heider used none at all.

LEWIN'S MOTIVATIONAL CONSTRUCTS

In brief, Lewin asserts that a man's actions are to be explained on the grounds that he perceives particular ways and means of discharging certain tensions. Those activities which an individual perceives as making possible the release of tension will attract him; they will have positive valence for him and he will experience a force moving him to engage in these activities. Certain other activities may have the opposite effect; they are seen as increasing tension; they are said to have a negative valence, and to generate repulsive forces. Heider says of Lewin's theory:

> Essentially, this is an explication in systematic terms of the simple fact that when I think that I can reach goal y by doing x, I will do x in order to get what I want. It is not an explanation; it is a representation in a language which is supposed to help in disentangling more complicated means-end situations, and which also is supposed to help in spotting relevant variables. (Heider, 1960, p. 158)

Later Heider sketches it ". . . tension induces valence and valence directs behavior . . ." (p. 164).

We can already see illustrated in this summary outline all of the characteristics of Lewin's theorizing noted above. All behavior, or at least all intentional behavior, is motivated; it is driven by tensions, moved by forces, directed by valences, and addressed to goals. Lewin does not question the reality status of these terms; they are not constructs but facts of behavior as far as he is concerned. For Lewin, behavior is not just an associative response to a stimulus—it is potentially subject to influence by anything the individual may perceive, feel, or think. Finally, we may note that there is little that is inconsistent between Lewin's account of behavior and the traditional rationalist's account. Certainly the kinds of determinants Lewin introduced were acceptable to the traditionalist. Where Lewin went beyond the rationalist was in attempting to supply syntactical rules for the determination of behavior. The important question as we proceed is whether the syntactical and semantic linkages of Lewin's theoretical constructs meet the criteria (given in Chapter 1) that would make the theory scientifically acceptable. Let us look at the four motivational constructs—tension, need, valence, and force.

Tension. Lewin's basic explanatory premise was that a voluntary intention to perform some act created in the organism a state of tension which would persist until the tension could become dissipated by the performance of the intended act.

For instance, someone intends to drop a letter in the mailbox. The first mailbox he passes serves as a signal and reminds him of the action. He drops the letter. The mailboxes he passes thereafter leave him altogether cold. . . . According to the laws of association, dropping the letter into the first mailbox should create an association between the mailbox and the dropping of the letter; the forces, whether associative or any other kind, which lead to dropping the letter, should also be reinforced by it. This is a stumbling block for association psychology; moreover it casts doubt upon whether the coupling between occasion and consummation . . . plays really the essential role here. If the effect of the act of intending is that a tendency toward consummation arises when the occasion implied by the act of intending occurs, then it is hard to see why on a second occasion this tendency should not appear to the same and even to a greater degree . . . Thus, the cause of the process does not seem to be simply that the coupling between the [mailbox and consummation] drives toward action when the occasion arises. (Lewin, 1926, pp. 97–98)

Some other sort of explanation besides associationism is required, Lewin believed; and he suggested that we view the causal factor in the mailbox example as a tension which is aroused by the intention to mail the letter.

There was a second class of phenomena which seemed to Lewin to require a tension concept, namely, that in the absence of a suitable goal object the tension to fulfill an intention may be discharged by a substitute action which attains the same end. For example, if a person has the intention to write to a friend, this establishes a certain tension which would ordinarily persist until the letter was written. But seeing a telephone might remind him to communicate with his friend; the substitute activity of phoning discharges the tension aroused by the intention to write.

Third, a task that has been interrupted is likely to be subsequently resumed. Were the coupling between the occasion and consummation decisive, nothing would happen without a repeated recurrence of the occasion. In point of fact though, as Ovsiankina had shown (reported in 1928), an interrupted task is more likely to be resumed than one which was allowed to go to completion.

Fourth and finally, Lewin noted that frequently we forget our intentions. This occurs generally either because the occasion for the consummatory activity is not perceived or because the tension to consummate the intention is swamped by some greater demand upon psychic energy. Lewin concluded that

The experiments on forgetting of intentions, and even more those on resumption of interrupted activities, prove that . . . intention is a force . . . *There exists rather an internal pressure of a definite direction, an internal tension-state which presses to carry out the intention* even if no predetermined [associatively established] occasion invites the action. (Lewin, 1926. pp. 113–114)

So here, as early as 1926, is a clear statement of the motivational idea, the dynamic principle.[16]

Need. In this same 1926 paper Lewin defined, more or less permanently, the concept of need. He distinguished between genuine needs and quasi-needs. The genuine needs arise from conditions such as hunger, relief from which serves the organism biologically. Tensions arising from intentions, acts of will, and other more or less arbitrary commitments of the individual person are quasi-needs; they are purely psychic needs. This distinction is approximately the same as that which was current in this country at about the same time between primary and secondary (or acquired) drives (e.g., Tolman, 1926). It might just be noted that now, 40 years later, we are not in any better position than Lewin was in making or defending such a distinction.

This distinction does not turn out to play a very important part in Lewin's theorizing, however, because of his insistence upon the principle of "contemporary action." It does not make much difference, except for purposes of historical analysis, where a need comes from, or how it arises, because the causes of action must be contemporary with the action. Wherever a number of needs may have come from, the principle of contemporary action makes them all functionally equivalent.

For Lewin, one of the important classes of motivating tension includes those which arise from needs which characterize a given individual. Every person has a characteristic need structure which may be more or less stable, but which may also vary somewhat from moment to moment. The needs of an individual may be real or quasi; they may arise as the result of any circumstance that gives the individual a reason for acting in a particular way.

Lewin's failure to delimit more precisely what and how tensions are induced provides at once both theoretical strength and weakness. On the one hand, by leaving open the question of how needs arise Lewin was free to consider the effects on the individual of any reason at all for acting. But on the other hand, by neglecting the antecedent conditions which produce tensions we are immediately deprived of the opportunity to investigate a large important class of determinants of behavior. Further-

---

[16] Lewin's intention here was evidently to be able to arrive at an inductive definition of tension. This strategy calls for focusing many loosely tied linkages between data and construct, no one of which can be held to be a strict definition. Compare this strategy with that of Murray, to be described shortly, and J. S. Brown, given in a later chapter, for defining what seems to be much the same concept. Quite another Brown is J. F. (1932), who reported that the rate of tension discharge depends upon the structure of the system. In 1938 Lewin had added this as well as Zeigarnik's finding (1927) that tension diffuses with time to the above "evidences" of tension.

more, by ignoring these antecedents tension becomes, in effect, a response-inferred type of construct, with all the problems noted in Chapter 1 that attend such constructs.

The hypothetical relationship between need and tension is described in terms of conceptual properties: ". . . whenever a psychological need exists, a system in a state of tension exists within the individual" (1938, p. 99). And another: A tension is a "state of a system which tries to change itself in such a way that it becomes equal to the state of surrounding systems . . ." (p. 98). It seems clear that tensions are supposed to be caused by needs (or quasi-needs), and that they persist until the needs are alleviated.

These conceptual distinctions would suggest that we could distinguish empirically between needs and tensions. Both constructs, however, are so poorly linked operationally to experimental variables that the hypothetical connections between them can hardly be confirmed. For example, it is not clear how one might demonstrate a need in the absence of a corresponding tension, or a tension without an underlying need. Moreover, in Lewin's writings, need and tension are frequently referred to almost interchangeably. For example, Lewin sometimes equated the psychic reality of tension with the experimentally manipulated variable hours of deprivation. But neither need nor tension was systematically anchored to a set of experimental conditions or to a specific behavioral phenomenon. Lewin always left the linkages between constructs and the data language loose and intuitive.

Force and Valence. In addition to generating tensions and thereby providing the "push" in behavior, needs also set the occasion for the two "pulling" constructs, force and valence, to take effect. As a general rule, perception of the possibility of engaging in some activity, the desirability of that activity (its valence), and the tendency to engage in it (the force it exerts) all go together. The conceptual differences emerge principally as a matter of emphasis. Valence helps to account for choice, but force may be more useful if we are concerned with the speed or persistence of behavior. (Note that it is not the object or the end that is the teleological terminus, but rather, the aim, the consummatory activity itself. On this point, Lewin's position is more like that of the ethologists, which we will consider in Chapter 4, than that of Freud.)

Lewin tells us that when a need exists there will arise a force, or a field of forces, signifying a valenced activity. If an individual has no need (e.g., if he is not hungry), then the environment registers no valences for him nor does it generate any forces for him (e.g., he will not be inclined to eat anything). The attainment of goals is, typically, perceived as possible only by engaging in certain intermediary activities. Each of these intermediaries may hold a valence itself, and all the valences may be viewed as generating forces directed either toward or away from the particular activities. The resulting behavior is assumed to be determined by some sort of psychological summation of these different forces.

It should be easy to separate force from valence conceptually, but it is not. Force is given three explicit attributes. It has magnitude (but so does valence), direction (a valence has location which is topologically equivalent to direction), and it has a point of application (and so does valence insofar as it is a valence for the individual). These conceptual properties of the construct justify the designation "force," by analogy with "force" in physics. There is a fourth, implicit, property of force which is also relevant, namely, that forces are what make things go. A force makes something happen, whereas a valence is passive; it is an abstract value which is merely implicated in action.

In conclusion, it seems that both in the case of need and tension, and also in the case of valence and force, there is an unnecessary redundancy of constructs. Moreover, there seems to be further redundancy between the pullers and the pushers of action. If all four constructs are merely different manifestations of the same underlying principle, then we would like to know what the underlying principle is. And if the four constructs are to be viewed as four more or less independent agencies, then we feel that a more parsimonious theory ought to be possible.

FORMAL ADEQUACY OF LEWIN'S THEORY

Although Lewin claimed he did not have a theory, he did formulate specific constructs, and indicate how they might be linked to empirical phenomena. There are also hypothethical syntactical linkages, i.e., hypotheses, to relate the different constructs. The system as a whole deals with the individual, his tensions, and his perceptions, indicating how they determine behavior. The "laws and definitions are a network of statements which only as a whole can be viewed as right or wrong" (1938, p. 16). And it is as a whole that we shall consider them.

Lewin's Variety of Explanation. What did Lewin consider to be an explanation of behavior? He made no reference to physical or physiological causation; quite the contrary, his network of terms and laws, like that of Freud, was expressly designed to apply to psychological phenomena. And the causes in Lewin's system, as in Freud's, are invariably analogous to mechanical causes—they are tensions and forces. Needs and tensions both are necessary for action, although they are not in themselves sufficient. An additional component is required, namely, a perception of certain behavioral possibilities, certain goals. The goals of behavior play an explanatory role, but their action in behavior is transferred to the construct of force. When Lewin speaks of goals, there is nothing teleological in the account. In this he broke sharply with the rationalist tradition.

A goal does not have a future reference; rather it has its effect by changing the individual's contemporary perception. He sees or feels or knows what he wants to do. Unfortunately, the simple elegance of the motivational model is purchased at a terrible cost; all of the vague, lawless, inherently untestable, and rationalistic characteristics that have been kept out of the motivational hypotheses, pop up immediately in the perceptual hypotheses, i.e., in the structural properties of the life space. Lewin can tell us precisely how a man's perceptions go over in a determinate manner to fix his behavior, but what can he tell us about the man's perception? The trouble is that all we can know of another's perception must be an inference based upon his behavior.

Lewin was a determinist. Whereas he frequently spoke of the organism choosing between one course of action and another, or choosing between one goal and another, choice was always a metaphor, since the behavior in question was always assumed to be strictly determined by the resolution of conflicting forces. Choice was recognized as a kind of activity which the organism may perceive himself engaged in, but that was as much reality status as it was given. Lewin was clearly a determinist of the psychological variety, inasmuch as the determining conditions for behavior are explicitly stated to be dynamic and structural psychological occurrences.

Semantic Problems. The major inadequacies of Lewin's theory are due to its uncertain semantics. There is little indication of how one could possibly validate the constructs of the theory. How do we know what the needs of an organism are? How can we tell whether these needs have created tension? How do we know that the tension is reciprocated in a force or in a valence perceived by the individual? How can we know how the individual perceives his behavioral possibilities? The constructs of the theory are not even provisionally tied to empirical observations; there are no semantic rules for translating between the construct language of the theory and the data language.

This problem is somewhat greater for the Lewinian than for most other theorists because he claims (1) to know reality, and (2) to have discovered laws that are universal and determinate. If a theorist leaves a certain margin of fuzziness either in the definition of his constructs (as Freud did) or in the linkages between constructs (as Tolman did), then the theory is open to improvement. But when the theory remains rigid from construct to construct, then fuzziness at the level of linking the theory to the data would seem to leave the theory itself untestable.[17] To the extent that Lewin was not building a theory but only attempting to represent what he regarded as the generally accepted facts of behavior, he might have been willing to go along with this charge of untestability.

Syntactical Problems. Lewin's theory presents some syntactical prob-

[17] Brunswik (1952) said of Lewin's theory that it was "encapsulated."

lems, too. It has an overabundance of what can be called accessory hypotheses, that is, hypotheses which are not deductions from the basic hypotheses of the theory but which seem to have been added to the theory as afterthoughts. For example, Lewin said that with an increase in tension (or need) there will be a force to quit an on-going activity. This is evidently a translation into the terms of the theory of the "generally accepted knowledge" that the motivated organism becomes restless. A more formally adequate theory than Lewin's would, of course, either deduce this hypothesis as a "theorem" from more fundamental hypotheses, or state it as a fundamental hypothesis. A more empirically adequate theory would indicate, in addition, how we might go about confirming or rejecting the hypothesis.

As another example, when Lewin (1938) discussed the possibility that motivation might influence the speed of learning, he observed that learning is speeded up if force (or valence) is increased. But then he went on to say, "If the force in the direction toward the goal is too great, a decrease in learning probably will result, because learning requires a *sufficient survey* of the total situation" (italics mine) (pp. 160–161). This assertion seems intuitively plausible, but how would one test it empirically; in particular, how would one know if a "sufficient survey" has been taken?

Data-Language Problems. The Lewinian psychologist typically refers to the structure of the organism's private world (his life space) as though he could observe it himself. The structuralists (e.g., Titchener) occasionally spoke this way also—and surely the psychophysical dualism of that era led psychologists to believe that their statements about the sensations of the subject were statements in the data language—but Titchener told us in more or less operational terms how we might train a subject and how we could establish a stimulus situation in precise physical terms so that at least sensations were empirically anchored antecedently.

Lewin refers to energy, tension, force, and the rest as "psychological facts." He says in defense,

> The reality of the psychological forces is the same as that of the "biological forces governing the brain" . . . It is often asked whether psychological force is something "real" or only an "'analogy." The problem of the reality of a dynamic construct is a peculiar one in any science . . . It will suffice here to emphasize that a psychological force is as real as any other kind of dynamical construct in psychology and certainly as real as a physical force. The situation is not merely one in which the person *appears* to locomote in the direction to a goal. A change in the position of the goal easily proves that the dynamical interrelation between person and goal expressed in the term force is a real one . . . (Lewin, 1938, p. 87)

So Lewin's theory can be seen as a system in which the linkages between constructs and experimentally manipulable physical conditions are either ignored or intuited.[18]

As promising as the syntactical features of Lewin's theory are, the semantic problems and the data-language problems are so serious that the theory can not really be put to empirical test. This is not to say that there is no relation between the theory and the empirical world, but only that most of those who have tried to work with Lewin's theory have been forced to intuit the coordination between the level of the formal model and the level of behavioral data as best they could. It seems likely that Lewin's own, highly imaginative, laboratory work flowed primarily from his abundant supply of "accessory" hypotheses rather than from the systematic or formal properties of the theory.

In spite of the limitation of untestability, the motivational model has enjoyed considerable popular acceptance. Perhaps one reason for this acceptance is that Lewin's account of behavior was so compatible with traditional rationalistic modes of thought. Indeed, the only serious departure from the rationalistic position was Lewin's "postulate" (see page 70) that all behavior was a result of forces acting upon the individual. Because force was said explicitly to be merely analogous to physical force, and because Lewin emphasized the necessity of "field factors" to explain human behavior, there was no danger that his theory would be mistaken for a mechanical explanation. What he gave us then was the promise of a deterministic calculus of forces with which we could describe the psychological causes of behavior—provided only that we could measure the forces.

Lewin's three other postulates have not fared so well. In fact, his insistence upon speaking about realities (implying that other people's constructs are illusory), his utter rejection of associationism (on the grounds that it was too mechanical, rather than because of any empirical shortcomings), and his extravagant dedication to representational problems (when theoretical problems might more profitably have occupied his time) may have kept Lewin's work from being as widely regarded as it

---

[18] At first glance, Lewin might seem to have been a phenomenologist. He was not. Indeed, one might complain that Lewin failed to take sufficient account of immediate experience, and didn't use it enough to check out his theoretical formulations. For example, does an individual really perceive a variety of possible activities and decide upon a course of action on the basis of their various attractivenesses? Or does the individual more nearly only perceive one possibility, that one which is a consequence of some unconscious decisional process? In any case, only one possibility at a time can be registered; any good introspectionist could have told Lewin that. Consequently, the life space, which Lewin assumed to be fixed at one time point, must be more nearly the summation of processes occurring over a short period of time. One wonders if the order in which these sequential processes occur is a factor itself in the determination of behavior. However that may be, the point should be emphasized that Lewin used intuition, but not introspection. Lewin was logical in orientation rather than empirical.

might otherwise have been. The first two of these postulates have given us Field Theory, and the third has been even less consequential.

MURRAY'S CONCEPT OF NEED

It is perhaps appropriate to conclude this brief sampling of human motivation theories with a sketch of Henry Murray's position. Because Murray is an extremely eclectic motivation theorist, his views encompass pretty well those of many modern workers, and he summarizes many of the implicit views of others regarding how behavior should be explained. Many of his concepts are derived from Freud, from Lewin, and particularly from Tolman (see Chapter 4).

According to Murray, the behavior of an individual person reveals rhythms of rest and activity. The cycles are interwoven in a dense network of total behavior, but the task of the psychologist is to discover the individual threads that go to make up the whole fabric. If we consider just one cycle of activity, we may observe that the organism will invariably react in such a way that its behavior shows a "unitary trend." The trend may not be noticed if the reactions are analyzed simply into muscle movements because muscle movements are not themselves organized so as to display purposiveness or adaptability.[19] But viewed in molar terms, particularly if the behavior is analyzed in terms of its effects upon the organism and upon the environment, its adaptive unity will be apparent. This molar analysis of the units of behavior has the principal practical advantage of permitting us to deal directly with the biological usefulness of behavior; it also has the convenience of providing units which are nearly universal across individuals and across time.

Behavior, defined in these molar terms, generally serves to take the organism from some prior state into some consequent state—that is what the unitary trend of behavior consists in. These trends are assumed to be due to a hypothetical force (a drive, need, or propensity), which operates homeostatically. That is, a motivating force carries the organism away from the prior or initiating condition into a state like satiation in which the force disappears. Because motivating forces are not directly observable, we have to infer them from observations of and communications with the individual. Sometimes the needs or drives of the individual can be related to specific physiological disturbances; this is true in the case of hunger, thirst, sex, and the avoidance of various kinds of harmful stimulation. Murray felt that the physiological conditions underlying

[19] Thus Murray summarily dismissed simple associationistic and mechanistic approaches to the explanation of behavior. I am following here Murray's *Explorations on Personality* (1938), which seems to have escaped critical reviewers except for Hall and Lindzey (1957).

these viscerogenic drives, and their subsequent effects upon behavior were fairly well understood. Much more interesting, and much more relevant for human psychology, Murray argues, are the psychogenic drives or needs, of which he has listed about thirty.[20] The psychogenic needs are also, of course, less crucial to the survival and the long-term adaptation of the organism, but they are, perhaps just for this reason, all the more important in understanding human behavior and experience. Both psychogenic and viscerogenic drives are viewed as central states of the organism ultimately localizable in the brain.

Homeostatic Nature of Needs. Needs, in Murray's system, may arise from physiological disturbances, but more typically they are aroused by particular events in the environment which offer certain threats or promises to the individual. These stimulus actions upon the organism Murray calls "presses."

The purposive motivational model includes the following sequence of events: (1) some stimulus feature in the environment promises to have some effect upon the organism, either desirable or undesirable; (2) a drive or need is aroused; (3) the organism is activated to engage in certain kinds of activity which may be motor, verbal, merely ideational, or even unconscious; (4) this activity has the effect of causing a trend in the overall behavior of the organism which tends to restore equilibrium; (5) the achievement of a demotivated state is only possible in many cases through the attainment of some particular goal object. Goal objects acquire, through learning, a value, or valence, or cathexis. Finally (6), this reestablishment of equilibrium, dispelling the drive, arouses a pleasurable affect. (Murray did not emphasize this affective element, nor indicate what it might mean for learning.) We can recognize in this simply stated homeostatic scheme the same conception of equilibrium that Freud had proposed and the same sequence of tension-force-release of tension that Lewin had proposed. In Chapter 4 we will discover that the concepts of instinct and drive were also largely based upon the same paradigm. Our interest in it here is that it arose from the consideration of such different behavioral events in Murray's case. What it was designed to accomplish was to account for the uniqueness of integration of human personalities. This purpose could not be achieved immediately, however; first it was necessary to embellish the homeostatic model with a number of syntactical properties.

Functional Properties of Needs. Murray admits that one could translate motivational constructs into purely behavioral terms; but he insists that there are good reasons, at least 10 of them, for not making

---

[20] The distinction between need and drive for Murray is not very clear-cut. Needs are somewhat more on the antecedent or perceptual side of the organism, whereas drives are more directly related to motor behavior (similar to Lewin's distinction between need and tension).

such a translation. (Again, we may observe the similarity of his arguments to those that had been advanced by McDougall, Lewin, Freud, Lorenz, and others). (1) There is the problem of the persistence of behavior, particularly in the face of barriers to its realization. Overall trends may be found in behavior even when the details of the muscle movements are without apparent significance. The unitary trend is not given in the behavorial data, but is assumed to be a property of an underlying agent, the need. (2) The organism will persist in a variety of attempts to get at its goals or to fulfill its purposes. Again, the motive lends a unity to what would otherwise be simply a variety of different behaviors. (3) Even in an experimental context it is found that what response a particular stimulus will evoke depends upon the needs of the individual. (4) Occasionally behavior will go off in the absence of an appropriate goal object (so-called vacuum activity). (5) Behavior frequently occurs not because it was elicited by a stimulus but because a stimulus is absent (i.e., there may be seeking for a stimulus).

Murray continued the list with evidence of a more subjective sort: (6) Fantasy is evidence of the direct action of some need. (7) Subjective experience of desire or feeling of an urge helps to corroborate and validate the construct. (8) Needs are more important in an explanation of behavior than S-R associations because they are more closely linked with the emotions of the organism. (9) Needs may interact either by summation or in conflict to yield effects which are not predictable on the basis simply of the available stimulation. (10) Most of the phenomena of abnormal psychology—compulsion, conflict, repression, conversion, displacement— would be wholly unintelligible without a concept of motivating force. This list of 10 arguments doesn't seem to be so much evidence of needs as an enumeration of the sort of phenomena which Murray intends to explain by invoking needs. Whether they can be explained without invoking needs is quite a separate question, which Murray begs. It might be a worthwhile exercise to see if it could be done, or in how many different ways it could be done.

A Lexicon of Human Needs. After demonstrating the need for the need concept (or the drive for the drive concept), Murray proceeds by classifying and cataloging the different needs and indicating some of the relationships between them. Murray's characterization of the different needs evolved from his clinical studies of the needs underlying the activities of his subjects. The needs discovered in these clinical cases range alphabetically from need-Abasement (the need to surrender, to self-deprecate), and the now-popular need-Achievement, down to need-Understanding (which is the need to analyze experience, to define relations, to synthesize ideas). These needs were discovered in a wide variety of behavior situations: casual interviews (and the subject's subsequent recollection of them); autobiographical writings; childhood memories;

questionnaires; highly structured interviews; casual conversations; interest and ability tests; aesthetic tests; a hypnotism test; a level-of-aspiration test; tests of memory for failure, ethical standards, and emotionality. The subjects were also observed at play and were given TAT and Rorschach tests.

The assumption underlying the assessment of motives is that if an individual is characterized by a few salient needs, then these needs should keep reappearing in a number of different contexts. The different contexts thus provide a means of cross-validating the motivational structure (and consequently the analysis of the personality) of the individual. At the same time, enough observations of the subject are made to ensure that some of his less salient needs would also be disclosed.

Murray's position does not really constitute a theory of behavior because it provides so few syntactical rules telling us how to operate with the theoretical terms. Consequently we do not know how to fit them together to form an explanatory network. We are not told how different individuals come to react differently to environmental presses. Why, for example, does failure characteristically induce need-Abasement in one man and need-Achievement in another? Even though Murray tells us that such differences constitute the basic source of difference between individual personalities, he provides no analytical tools for explaining them. Nor does he consider the question of how a given pattern of needs comes to characterize a given individual. Still more serious is that we are not told how these particular needs, once given as part of the individual, are expressed in ways characteristic of him; we do not know from Murray's scheme how to predict any particular behavior from the knowledge that an individual is subject to or has been previously subjected to a particular press.

The semantics of Murray's formulation, on the other hand, provides a considerably improved set of constructs over those proposed by his predecessors, Lewin, for example. He admits that the ties between the data language and construct language are rather loose. But this looseness obtains only within a single observational context, and certainly we cannot demand that the observation of a single bit of behavior within a single environmental context be itself of particular interest, scientific or otherwise; "it is an outcast fact begging to be understood and to be accepted with others of its kind" (1938, p. 127). If we would know what motivates a man, then we must make use of a diversity of indices. Even though the linkages between empirical data and the constructs are not defined operationally, nor tied down in any rigid way, the psychologist has an opportunity in Murray's system to use a variety of semantic tricks. He may use, in effect, any behavioral measure he wishes. Whatever variety of evidence is available, it is used to "converge" upon the organism's needs. Thus, a potent safeguard was provided against the too facile and too simple postulation of drives to account for particular instances of behavior. With Murray, human motivation theory began to lose its linear or simple "this causes that" character and began to assume the form of a network of functional relationships.

THE DRIVE CONCEPT IN HUMAN MOTIVATION THEORY

The motivational theories of Freud, Lewin, and Murray present many points of difference. The three men had different points of view and different philosophical commitments; their backgrounds and the times in which they lived were different. They concerned themselves with quite different sorts of problems, and they certainly had in mind quite different applications for their theories. Nonetheless, there are certain areas of basic correspondence. In each case the theorist was a determinist and attempted to explain behavior in determinate ways by means of certain psychological constructs. In each case behavior is partly "pushed" through the action of motivating drives, and partly "pulled" through the perception of valuable objects, valences, or goals in the environment. In each case an individual is to be described by his characteristic drives and by the characteristic goals he uses to discharge the tension his drives produce.

The drive construct, as it is formulated by Freud, Lewin, or Murray always operates homeostatically; the individual is constantly seeking to rid himself of tension which threatens his well-being. The greater the threat the greater the drive and the more likely the individual is to seek and find a suitable goal. For Freud, behavior ultimately depends upon one drive, sex; whereas for Murray there are a large number of social as well as biological drives; and for Lewin there is nearly an infinite number of possible tension systems that could stir an individual to action. However, Freud's unitary drive is found by viewing the subject historically; even a Freudian sees a large number of energy systems when he views the subject more contemporaneously. This is what Murray sees from his viewpoint. Lewin, by freezing his subject in time, and attributing energy to whatever he sees happening, sees it everywhere. Nothing just happens; for each of our three theorists there must always be some force of energy or drive which makes it happen. Where they find the drive depends mainly on where they look for it. It may be back in the repressed memories of the individual, or it may be lurking in the most inconsequential movement, but it must be there somewhere. These three theorists share a common belief: Behavior is to be explained by discovering the underlying forces that make it happen.

4

INSTINCTS

❖❧❧❧❧❧❧❧❧❧❧❧❧❧❧❧❧❧❧❧❧❧❧❧❧❧❧

There are reflexes—then vastly more important and complex are instincts—emotionally toned activities which are inborn reaction tendencies. They furnish a fundamental basis for likes and dislikes—they are the great primitive drives in our lives.

WILLIAM McDOUGALL

As a general rule the concept of instinct is introduced to account for the apparent intelligence of behavior when it does not seem reasonable to attribute intelligence to the organism. The problem arose originally because intelligence was considered to be a faculty of man alone. Therefore the adaptiveness and apparent intelligence of animals had to be explained by a special faculty, instinct. After the Darwinian revolution it became reasonable to attribute intelligence, at least in some measure, to animals; but careful naturalistic observation indicated that the adaptability of behavior, especially the behavior of the lower animals, far exceeded the amount of intelligence that could be afforded them, so the instinct concept was retained.

The next step is that the theorist, in defense of the instinct concept, studies behavior and discovers still more marvelous adaptation which cannot be accounted for except by assuming the operation of instinctive forces.

But the instinct concept does not have a cohesive and consistent form which fixes its conceptual properties; it changes shape to suit the circumstances, the problem, and the range of alternatives that are acceptable at a given time. For example, when James or McDougall wrote about instincts it was permissible to make subjective experience an important part of the definition of instincts, and they did. Later writers could not.

When the mentalist talks about instinct he is admitting that at least some behavior, that which is instinctive, is not due to mental causes but is governed instead by other, mechanical-like principles of some sort. When the tough-minded mechanist or empiricist talks about instinct he is admitting that at least some behavior is innately organized along functional lines, or that at least some behavior is not learned.[1]

In the present chapter we will discover that instincts have been invoked and defended mainly by tender-minded theorists in protest against mechanistic theories because they consider such theories to be lacking in the proper appreciation of either the adaptability of behavior, its goal-directedness, its energetic properties, or its emotional concomitants. Different instinct theorists differ largely in what they consider to be the strongest attack upon the mechanistic position.

It might be expected that because of the flexible conceptual properties of the instinct concept explanations of behavior couched in terms of instincts would come to acquire considerable popular acceptance, and that is just what happened. Indeed, after McDougall such explanations became so popular, so universal, and so all-encompassing that the instinct concept could no longer be used by the serious student of behavior. We will see how some theorists, most notably Tolman, began to transform the instinct concept into what we now know as the drive concept. Finally, we will note the contribution of a new discipline, ethology, which has recently revitalized the instinct concept, changing and sharpening it considerably, but not altogether altering its basic character. As the story proceeds, we will see that various conceptual properties have gradually been stripped away from instinct—first its opposition to intelligence, then the subjective experience component, then the emotional component, and most recently, the idea of instinct energy.

WILLIAM JAMES' INSTINCTS

The early development of the instinct concept was outlined in Chapter 2. We noted there that it had gained considerable acceptance by the proponents of the common-sense or faculty psychology of the nineteenth century. In that school of thought instinct was still sharply contrasted with intelligence, instinct supposedly being the source of adaptive behavior in animals (and occasionally in man) while intelligence was regarded as

---

[1] James' distinction between tough- and tender-mindedness was described on p. 33.

the principal source of adaptive human behavior. Toward the end of the century the ancient dichotomy between the animal mind and the human mind had begun to evaporate, mainly as a consequence of Darwin's influence; and some type of conceptual reorganization was desperately needed. This was the problem to which William James addressed himself.

James (1890) defied the popular view that since man has a superior intellect he possesses few instincts. Quite the contrary, James argued, man has many more different instincts than the other animals, they are merely more apt to be obscured by the operation of his superior mental apparatus. Man's great facility for learning can readily disguise or modify his native instinctive endowment. Moreover, he argued, the traditional interpretation of instinct as a blind impulse or force, as something opposed to intelligence, is valid only at a very shallow level of analysis; there are many tangled relationships between learning and instinctive impulses. For example, he noted that an instinct could only properly be said to be blind on its first occurrence; after that it must be accompanied by some amount of foresight of its end.[2]

James stressed that with an instinct appropriate objects capture the organism's attention at the appropriate time. This is the hypothesis of "instinct meaning" or "instinct interest," which suggests that when the organism is being acted upon by instinctive forces, these forces will make known what is the appropriate goal object, and will give the goal object a value appropriate for the instinct. Thus, James suggests that a hen sits on an egg because the egg looks to the hen as though it is just right for sitting on; we should not ask why it does, it just does. ". . . to the animal which obeys it, every impulse and every step of every instinct shines with its own sufficient light, and seems at the moment the only eternally right and proper thing to do" (1890, II, p. 387).

Instinct was defined as "the faculty of acting in such a way as to produce certain ends, without foresight of the ends, and without previous education in the performance" (1890, II, p. 383). Although this definition of instinct seems clear enough, James did not adhere to it in his examples; he included as instincts simple reflexes such as sneezing and coughing, some much more complex motor adjustments such as walking, and some emotional dispositions like fear and love. He also listed as instincts some very complicated patterns of behavior, such as hunting and kleptomania, where there was certainly little likelihood of meeting his

---

[2] James anticipated two phenomena that have attracted much attention recently in connection with imprinting. He proposed a "law of inhibition" of instincts: sometimes only the first object of an instinct can occupy the central role on its subsequent performance. After the first object of an instinct has become associated with it, other objects could not readily take its place. His "law of nonuniformity" was a clear anticipation of the modern critical-period hypothesis. James tells us that if an instinct has not found a suitable object by some certain time, it may never find one.

defining criteria of no previous education, and occurrence without foresight.

We can see in James, transitional figure that he was, the merging of a
number of apparently disparate viewpoints encompassing both the old
and the new: Darwin's conception of biological adaptation, the prevailing mentalism, a tough-minded dependence upon the underlying neural
basis of behavior and consciousness, and a tender-minded acceptance of
spiritual values and of the then popular faculty psychology. For example,
his famous treatment of emotions in terms of the feedback from bodily
reactions was frankly materialistic, but on the free-will vs. determinism
issue, he took the side of free will (this was clearer in some of his later
writings, e.g., 1914, than in *The Principles*).

Atkinson (1964) has observed that in the gradual transition between
traditional, mentalistic accounts of behavior and the more scientifically
adequate models we have today, James stands among the last of the traditionalists. To put his contribution into proper perspective, it is necessary
to note that the doctrine of instincts constituted only a minor part of
James' total view of behavior. James proposed three distinct devices to
explain behavior: (1) the ideomotor theory of voluntary action in which
the idea of the occurrence of a voluntary act is sufficient to make the act
occur; (2) habit, which was a sort of short-circuiting of consciousness
which occurs with repetition of a voluntary act; and (3) instinct.

If we think of instinct as Lamarck did (and as did most other theorists of the times), as a sort of short-circuiting of habit that occurs over
evolutionary time, then we have the following overall scheme for the explanation of behavior: All behavior is originally voluntary, but after sufficient exercise of the voluntary act it becomes habitual, and after sufficient
exercise of the habit it becomes hereditary or instinctive. Even Darwin
(1872) subscribed to this position. Thus, none of James' three explanatory
devices was, strictly speaking, original with him, but he spelled them out,
especially the ideomotor theory, so clearly that everyone knew what they
meant. James was a mentalistic psychologist, and to that extent among
the last of the traditionalists; his use of three mediating devices to explain
behavior prevents us from classifying him as a rationalist, and to that
extent he belonged to the new era rather than the old.

INSTINCTS AS UNIVERSAL MOTIVATORS

William McDougall. It would be possible to cite a number of theorists
after James who had a hand in the development of the instinct concept,
but none of their contributions compares with that of McDougall. Even
though James had broken with the traditional view that instinct applied
to animals and intelligence applied to man, he still gave instincts a role

secondary to that of ideation and habit in the determination of behavior. James sought to explain only certain bits and pieces of behavior in terms of instincts. McDougall went much farther; for him *all* human behavior had an instinctive origin. He contended that if it were not for instincts man would lie inert, like an intricate clockwork with a broken mainspring. His position was that it was not sufficient to explain a man's actions in terms of his having an idea to act in a certain way, it was much more important and basic to explain *why* he wanted to act as he did. For McDougall, that part of psychology which is of the greatest importance is

. . . that which deals with the springs of human action, the impulses and motives that sustain mental and bodily activity and regulate conduct; and this, of all the departments of psychology, is the one that has remained in the most backward state. . . . It is the mental forces, the sources of energy, which set the ends and sustain the course of all human activity—of which forces the intellectual processes are but the servants, instruments, or means—that must be clearly defined . . . before the social sciences can build on a firm psychological foundation. . . ." (McDougall, 1914, p. 3) [3]

We have seen earlier that Stout (1903) had recognized the importance of men's motives in the explanation of behavior, but it had not occurred to Stout to make motivation a universal principle, that was where McDougall parted with the long line of rationalists who had come before him. The importance which McDougall attached to active or dynamic principles in human behavior was all the more remarkable because he had little precedent for it. Few theorists (Freud was one exception) had proposed that men acted because they were made to do so by particular forces acting upon them.

For McDougall, these psychological forces were definitely not to be conceived as mechanical in operation. He stood in violent opposition to the application of the mechanistic philosophy to psychological problems, and he was, accordingly, opposed to the idea that instincts were merely complex reflexes. He was, in fact, the leading critic in his day of this idea. Reflexes are immutable and unchanging, he asserted, while instinctive behavior is modifiable and adaptable to changing circumstances. An instinct is to be defined and recognized not by the kind of movements in which it finds expression but rather by its goal, i.e., by the kind of change in the organism's environment which brings the sequence of behavior to a close. Behavior manifests a striving toward its natural goal, and if the behavior is frustrated by an obstacle, the striving merely intensifies until

[3] I have quoted the 8th edition of McDouglall's *Social Psychology*, but the other 28 editions, starting with the first in 1908, were all quite similar. So were many of his other books.

the appropriate end process of the instinct is finally achieved. This type of action, striving toward a goal, is characteristic of psychological phenomena and is to be contrasted with mechanical action; mechanical laws are not applicable here, McDougall tells us.

An instinct, in McDougall's view, not only regulated behavior, it also provided the basis of the subjective experience of striving and goal directedness; all of our wants and desires were supposed to stem from the instincts. In addition, each instinct had associated with it a characteristic emotion. Indeed, McDougall sometimes asserted that the emotional aspect of the instinct was its most important and constant feature. The emotion, together with the sense of striving and desire, constituted the subjective aspect of the instinct, while the resulting behavior which achieved the goal was the objective aspect of the instinct, the part which man shared with other animals.

Putting these different features of McDougall's concept together, we can say that an instinct is an innate predisposition

> . . . to perceive, and to pay attention to, objects of a certain class, to experience an emotional excitement of a particular quality upon perceiving such an object, and to act in regard to it in a particular manner. . . ." (McDougall, 1914, p. 29)

It would seem that McDougall made what may have been an indispensable contribution to the development of our thinking about motivation. It seems possible that motivation theory would bear little resemblance to its current form if McDougall had not held the theoretical position he did, nor written as insistently and persistently as he did about this position. To appreciate this it must be remembered that he wrote at a time when Watson's behaviorism was beginning to consume behavior theory. Conditioning, both the physiological concept and the method, was coming to occupy a central position in psychological theory. Psychologists were entering a self-confident materialistic era in which teleology had no place and in which man's mental life was to be excluded. What men thought were their motives for action could be dealt with in terms of physiological constructs and conditioning. In this setting it was McDougall who reminded us that man can be characterized by his purposiveness, and his emotional life. And it was he perhaps as much as Freud or any other man who popularized the idea that we act because of forces operating on us: all behavior is due to motivating forces, or energies, which push us toward some goal.

The Decline of Instinct.   The increasing popularity of explaining behavior in terms of instincts rapidly led to the crisis that may be called "The Great Instinct Controversy." During the second decade of the century, sociologists and economists as well as psychologists began to invoke instincts to explain any and all kinds of human activity. For any activity, it was possible to introduce an instinct of which the activity in question was the manifestation. No criteria were employed to determine if the alleged instinctive behavior was unlearned, or universal, or done without foresight, or if it was purposive. Instincts were invoked ad hoc and ad lib. If the connotation had been purely descriptive, little harm would have been done; however, the attitude common in these accounts was that nothing more needed to be said of any behavior to explain it once an instinct had been invoked.

It was clear that such a state of affairs could not endure, and a lively critical movement was soon underway. Ayres (1921) was provoked to write a paper subtitled "The instinct of belief-in-instincts," Dunlap (1919) wrote one titled "Are there ·any instincts?" and there were others in a similar vein. The best review of the controversy has been written by Tolman (1923). Tolman presented the issues fully and fairly, and made an attempt to reconstruct a serviceable conception of instinct.

Tolman began by noting some of the objections critics had raised to the instinct concept. First, they contended that the arbitrary and ad hoc designation of instincts deprived the concept of explanatory value. This criticism was valid insofar as all existing lists of the principal instincts had been drawn up on the basis of the most casual sort of observation. Nothing stood in the way of a systematic investigation of just what constituted the instinct repertoire of animals (including man), but unfortunately the lack of systematic observation was only part of the trouble. Equally serious was the lack of generally acceptable criteria for distinguishing between what was instinctive and what was not; the proponents of the instinct concept had failed to embellish it with adequate semantic and syntactical rules for its proper scientific use. As Tolman noted in defense of the concept, the critics could be disarmed on this point by the development of adequate theories and observational techniques. There was, he concluded, nothing necessarily erroneous in the basic conception of instinctive behavior.

Second, some critics thought the instinct concept had come to look like a modern version of the doctrine of preestablished harmony, or the doctrine of innate ideas. Tolman argued, as McDougall had before, that this charge was largely fallacious since ultimately it is an empirical question whether instinctive reactions are so adaptive that they make the animal appear to have intelligence or some special form of knowledge.

Third, according to some critics the instincts were no more than class names for certain kinds of behavior; they were just new names for the old and discredited mental "faculties." If there was any further implication, it was that the behavior in question was caused by some sort of drive or mystical force. The assumption of an instinct adds nothing to a descriptive account of the behavior. Tolman observed, and certainly we must agree, that the same charge could be leveled against any theoretical position; theories are necessarily tautological to some extent. But a theoretical statement offers a possibility of economy and order and added perspective beyond that given by a bare description of the data—which is just why we entertain theories.

Finally, it was frequently pointed out that the instincts were often confused with habits. McDougall had argued, for example, that the widespread occurrence of combat and war could be taken as evidence of an aggressive instinct in man, i.e., an innate disposition common to all men. This argument is far from compelling; we have only McDougall's assurance of the universality of combatitiveness. We cannot tell if the peaceful men we know have learned to overcome their original combatitive dispositions, or whether, perhaps, the aggressive men we know have learned to overcome an originally peaceful nature. Surely few of the arguments about man's original nature have been based upon substantial data. Tolman's reaction to this criticism was that it had merit but that the critics went too far with it, for in the absence of the appropriate data it took just as much faith to maintain that a particular behavior was learned as to hold that it was instinctive. His opinion was, as on all these issues, that more data were needed to settle the question.

All of these criticisms have some validity when directed against the interpretation of instincts which identifies them as direct sensory-motor mechanisms, i.e., complex reflexes. However, the mechanistic theorist who advances this interpretation gains very little by classifying some behavior as instinctive. His recognition of such a classification is no more than a concession that at least some behavior is innately organized. This is not to say that the mechanist should not make the concession and attempt to distinguish between native and acquired behavior, but only that once he has made the distinction he has extracted all the meanings from the broader conception of instinct that he can use in his system. None of the other features of the instinct concept, namely, those which we have just seen attacked, are compatible with his account of behavior. This is why, on the one hand, the mechanists attacked the concept, and on the other hand, why the concept was so ardently defended by McDougall and Tolman; they stood in opposition to the mechanists, men like Pavlov, Watson, and Thorndike. How else was one to defend the idea of motivation, emphasize the idea of psychological energy and force in human conduct, and explain the apparent purposive character of behavior except by promoting the instinct doctrine?

Tolman's Behavioral Teleology.   Tolman proposed that if the instinct concept was to be reconstructed usefully it had to be based upon teleological principles; a mechanistic orientation would not do. On this he followed McDougall. Tolman thought that a new, empirically well-founded, teleological interpretation could meet all of the objections that had been raised against the older instinct doctrines. There are different possible teleological frames of reference that could be employed, but our choice is pretty much determined by our dedication to the problem of behavior. First, Tolman argued, we may reject the possibility of a biological teleology, one which stresses the biological utility of instinctive behavior. Some of the most important instincts, e.g., those that promote racial preservation, lack behavioral meaning for the individual. Racial continuity may very well be served by sexual behavior, but in what sense is the individual animal served? Tolman's basic assumption was that *the ends of behavior must be found in the organism that behaves.*[4]

A mentalistic teleology, like that proposed by McDougall, meets the previous requirement, but is empirically inadequate. Consider, as an example, McDougall's position that we infer the "pugnacious instinct" when the emotion of anger occurs. Tolman asks, is this not just the reverse of what we actually do? Is it not more nearly correct to say that we infer the emotion of anger from the observation of pugnacious behavior? We observe the persistence of pugnacious behavior; the supposition of an underlying explanatory instinct and the associated emotion is an inference (Tolman, 1923a).[5]

Tolman concluded that the only acceptable possibility would be a purely behavioral teleology, according to which behavior is to be understood in its own terms, by its own ends. Behavior, in this view, is characteristically purposive, which means that it can be best defined in terms of its goals or consequences, rather than in terms of its mediating processes. As individual psychologists, we may elect to focus our attention either upon the goal and its effect upon the mediating processes, or upon these processes themselves; but the entire initiation-means-end relationship is to be taken as the inherent and defining function of an instinct. Once the instinct is initiated, either by internal or external stimulation or by some physiological condition of the organism, it determines what adjustments the organism must make to reinstate a neutral condition. The instinct does not determine, however, how the final adjustment or end is to be brought about, that is governed by environmental conditions, by previous training in particular means-ends relationships, by the influence of competing instincts, and so on. Thus, Tolman arrived at the proposition that behavioral ends are fixed but behavioral means are variable. This point, fundamental to his whole approach to motivation, marks a critical turning point in the history of the instinct concept at least as important as any we have noted so far.

Today we might wonder why this behavioral teleology was couched

---

[4] Modern ethologists have tended to reverse this emphasis by concentrating on ecological and evolutionary factors and minimizing the importance of learning in adaptive behavior.

[5] I have nothing more to say in this book about emotion except to recommend Beebe-Center's brilliant historical analysis of the problem (1951) and the exciting research of Schachter and Singer (1962).

in terms of instincts when it could have been stated in terms of motives, or drives, or tensions, or more simply just in terms of purposive behavior itself. The answer is that it was really only a matter of historical accident. The explanatory concept of the day was instinct; motivational ideas were either formulated in terms of instincts or not at all. Tolman was concerned with maintaining a theory of motivation, and his use of the instinct idea was simply a means toward that end. As it turned out, his theory of motivation came to occupy a prominent historical position, while his reconstructed instinct concept, as such, was neglected. In contrast with James and McDougall, whose conceptions of instinct were frankly mentalistic, since their times required that behavior be explained by events going on in the mind, Tolman cast the functional properties of instincts into behavioral language. Wants, desires, and subjective sense of striving became simply persistent behavior. Tolman was known as a "cognitive" theorist, but it is wrong to suppose he was not a behaviorist on that account. The mentalistic language he adapted (1932) was to be considered no more than a heuristic device to build a better theoretical model for the explanation of behavior. Even then, all his mentalesque terms were carefully defined operationally in behavioral terms.

Tolman, in his review of these events, modestly minimized his own contribution to them. The fundamental idea of behavioral teleology, the idea that behavior could be explained in terms of its behavioral consequences, Tolman attributed to his teacher Perry (1918, 1921).[6] Tolman also acknowledged that the essential features of his teleological account of behavior had been proposed by three other men, namely, Craig, Woodworth, and Dunlap, all more or less independently; and he pointed out that there had emerged a surprising degree of agreement among the different positions in spite of their differences in detail and nomenclature. The consensus was that instincts are aroused by certain physiological conditions of the organism which signify some biological distress, like a sexual or food need. Instincts also characteristically involve particular kinds of motivated behavior: a sequence of restless seeking behavior which may be highly variable but which is invariably terminated by a fixed innate reaction that has the effect of relieving the initiating condition. In 1923 this conception was called "instinct"; five years later, and ever since, it has been called "drive." Let us look at some of the variations of this new instinct concept.

Wallace Craig. One variation was formulated by the naturalist Wal-

---

[6] Tolman's new teleology was introduced in 1920. Students of E. A. Singer have told me that in his lectures Singer had anticipated both Tolman and Perry by about 10 years; I have not been able to find the anticipation in print, however. Tolman might have cited also Russell (1916), and particularly Holt (1915). But questions of historical priority should not obscure the fact that it was Tolman who developed the idea, made it popular, built it into a general theory of behavior, and above all, tried to put it to empirical test.

lace Craig (1918). He noted that the overt behavior of adult animals (Craig spoke principally about birds) occurs not so much in fixed stimulus-response elements, but rather in flexible cycles or chains of behavior, only some parts of which may be fixed. We should not let the fixed part of an instinct prevent us from seeing that for each instinct there is a characteristic appetitive or aversive sequence of behavior that is not fixed. Appetitive behavior (or appetence, as Craig preferred to call it) is a state of agitation which continues as long as a certain stimulus, the appeted stimulus, is absent. When the stimulus is present it stimulates a *consummatory reaction,* which terminates the behavior cycle. When the appeted stimulus is absent there will still be a "readiness" to make the innate consummatory reaction. The best evidence for its fixity and innateness is the occurrence (even on the first manifestation) of incipient consummatory action when the appeted stimulus has not yet been presented. (This is called "vacuum activity" by present-day ethologists, and is rather common in the sexual behavior of birds, but occurs elsewhere as well.)

Aversion was treated in an analogous way; whenever a stimulus evokes in an animal an agitation, a particular restlessness, which continues until the animal takes flight, we may say that the animal is showing aversion to that stimulus. In this case flight is the instinctive consummatory reaction. For either appetence or aversion, the agitation consists of (1) phasic and static contractions of skeletal and dermal muscles, giving rise to body postures and gestures which are readily recognizable "signs" of the appetite or aversion; (2) restlessness; (3) activity; (4) varied effort; and (5) the readiness to engage in the consummatory activity.

Craig admitted that there were probably a number of gradations between true reflexes and a mere readiness to act in a certain way. Instinctive readiness patterns, though, differ in principle from reflexes in that they may involve trial-and-error learning: a number of trials takes place until one response pays off. Those modes of behavior which were immediately followed by the appeted stimulus are later repeated while the other behaviors drop out. Sometimes, of course, such trial and error is not evident, but even in this case it is useless to seek the environmental stimuli that elicit the behavior because appetitive behavior is characterized by its variability in the absence of the appeted stimulus, rather than by fixed stimulus-response relationships. Thus, for Craig, instinctive behavior was defined by the kind of consummatory reaction it involves, and by the occurrence of variable, restless, agitated behavior that precedes the consummatory reaction.[7]

[7] Craig placed, perhaps, even greater reliance upon behavioral data than Tolman did. He also put less weight on the energy vs. structure distinction than any of the theorists we have considered here. He was thus much more in the spirit of modern behaviorism than were his contemporaries. Craig supposed, interestingly, that it was necessary to assume the existence of internal stimuli to help account for appetitive behavior since it is not regularly elicited by external stimulus conditions.

Robert Woodworth.   For many years Woodworth was concerned with
what he called dynamic psychology, which he defined at one point as
the study of cause and effect in psychology. The study of cause and effect
is the "attempt to gain a clear view of the action or process in the system
studied . . . noting whatever uniformities occur, and what laws enable
us to conceive the whole process in an orderly fashion" (Woodworth,
1918, p. 35).[8]

This approach introduces two problems, one the problem of mechanism, i.e., how a thing is done, and the other the problem of drive, i.e.,
what induces us to do it. It may be noted that "how" questions are relevant to mechanisms while "why" questions lead us to inquire about
drives. In the case of a machine, the mechanism is the machine itself,
which is inert until power is supplied to it to make it go. On the other
hand, the energy supplied to the machine—its drive—requires the machine to guide, channel, and direct it. Now, if all behavior were of a
simple reflex type, dynamic psychology would be relatively simple: the
mechanisms would be the whole organism, and the drive would be the
stimulus to which it responds. The situation is complicated, however, by
the fact that once a neural center is aroused by an external stimulus it
stays in a state of activity that outlasts its excitation. Moreover, a mechanism may be excited to a subthreshold level by one drive, and triggered
off by a second.

The principal justification of dynamic psychology, and the main reason for distinguishing between mechanisms and drives, is the phenomenon
of instinctive behavior, which, following Sherrington (1906), Woodworth
characterized in terms of preparatory and consummatory reactions.

A consummatory reaction is one of direct value to the animal—one
directly bringing satisfaction—such as eating or escaping from danger. The objective mark of a consummatory reaction is that it terminates a series of acts, and is followed by rest or perhaps by a shift to
some new series. Introspectively, we know such reactions by the satisfaction and sense of finality that they bring. The preparatory
reactions are only mediately of benefit to the organism, their value
lying in the fact that they lead to, and make possible, a consummatory
reaction. Objectively, the mark of a preparatory reaction is that it
occurs as a preliminary stage in a series of acts leading up to a con-

[8] Compare McDougall, 1932, p. 9. He tells us that so long as any science is
content merely to describe, it does not require the conception of energy. The
energy concept introduces order and system into an explanation of events when we
seek the causal laws of a science. It seems as though the notion of force, or energy,
arises in psychology when a theorist wants to disavow mechanistic explanations
but doesn't have a sound alternative. James did not do this because he had mentalism to rely upon, but most of the theorists we are considering here discovered the
"dynamic principle" when they gave up mechanism. So did Freud; and so did the
psychologists at Berlin, including Lewin, as we saw in the last chapter.

summatory reaction. Consciously, a preparatory reaction is marked
by a state of tension (Woodworth, 1918, p. 40)

Some preparatory reactions, like looking and listening, may occur
when the animal is in a passive state; but a more interesting set of preparatory reactions are those that arise only when the mechanism for a
consummatory reaction has been aroused, as when the animal is hungry.
Then we find that while each preparatory reaction is in part a response
to some external stimulus, it is also dependent upon the drive towards the
consummatory reaction.

Woodworth parted company with McDougall most emphatically on
the question of the universality of instincts as motivating agents. Mc-
Dougall had posited that all behavior was directly or indirectly motivated
by the instinct. Woodworth, denying this view, held that "any mechanism
—except perhaps some of the most rudimentary that give the simple reflexes—once it is aroused, is capable of furnishing its own drive and also
of lending drive to other connected mechanisms" (p. 67).

Thus, Woodworth denied the proposition that all the mechanisms of
the human adult, all the things he is capable of doing, are wholly passive,
requiring the drive of a few instincts, like sex, hunger, curiosity, etc., to
put them into action. Sometimes, especially upon their first occurrence,
instincts do drive these mechanisms into action; but after a time they
become more or less autonomous. Typically, we find that any mechanism
that is habitually exercised tends to behave as though it were itself a
drive, and comes to acquire the ability to drive other mechanisms so that
the latter are freed from their direct dependence upon the primitive instincts. "Mechanisms can become drives."

Dunlap and Others. The third theorist, whom Tolman felt had also
arrived at a similar position regarding the new teleology, was Dunlap
(1922, 1923). Historically his contribution has not been as important as
the contributions made by Craig, Woodworth, or Tolman. What Dunlap
did was to draw up a list of "fundamental desires." These desires had
reference to some of the physiological disturbances of the organism and
provided the springs of social conduct.

Dunlap was just one of a number of writers urging that the current
conception of instinct should be discarded or replaced. All of these men
shared certain broad theoretical commitments. Like all instinct theorists,
they sought to account for the seeming intelligence, adaptability, and
goal-directedness of behavior without invoking rationalism (James could
endorse rationalism, but later writers could not), or without invoking
mentalism (James and McDougall could do that but subsequent theorists could not). They all had the conviction that the task could not be
accomplished by the mechanists or the reflexologists, because behavior
was a different type of realm from the world of physical laws. Some, like

Tolman, retained mentalistic-sounding concepts to help do the job, while others, like Craig, were able to see enough lawfulness in behavior itself that they could accept this lawfulness as providing a sufficient account. However, most instinct theorists have insisted upon adding "something else," such as energy, to explain purposive behavior.

THE OUTCOME OF THE CONTROVERSY

With the added perspective of 40 years we can see the Great Instinct Controversy somewhat more clearly than the participants could.[9] It appears that three distinct issues were involved, although they were not always sharply distinguished at the time. The issues in contention were (1) whether adaptive behavior is learned or innate, (2) whether adaptive behavior is best explained with purely structural concepts or with dynamic ones, and (3) whether the explanation of behavior should be mechanistic or mentalistic.

McDougall was the leading spokesman for the extreme tender-minded position on all these questions. He argued that both biological and social motivations were innate, that behavior had to be explained in terms of instinctive forces, and that mentalistic terms, particularly those referring to feelings and emotions, had to be kept within psychology. Watson (1919) and Kuo (1924) were the outstanding extremists for the tough-minded side of these issues. They argued that what were called instincts were either just reflexes or else involved learning, that the explanation of behavior should be exclusively in associationistic terms without reference to dynamic forces or energies, and that a mechanistic account of behavior was sufficient to encompass all the facts. The critics of the instinct concept also attacked it on the grounds that it lacked scientific rigor. For example, Kuo (1924) argued that the propositions of the instinct theorists were untestable; instinct psychology was a "finished psychology," discontinuing its study of behavior at just the point where behaviorism would wish to begin. It proposed answers where questions were more in order. Had he adhered to this position Kuo's attack upon the instinct theorists might have had a better reception. But as it was, he overstated his case and defended with great passion (and largely in the absence of experimental support) the position that there were no instincts, nor indeed any evidence of hereditary factors in psychology. He argued not only that there was no innate organization of behavior, but even that there was no predetermination of behavior in the structure of the nervous system. This

---

[9] Judging from contributions to *The Psychological Review*, 1923 was the year of crisis. See, for example, Perrin (1923), Tolman (1923a), Wells (1923), Zigler (1923), and the remarkable paper of Thurstone (1923). A slightly earlier anticipation of what was to come was English (1921).

latter position could not bear up under the first reports of the empirical work of Carmichael (1926), or even the work of Kuo himself (1929).

As might be expected, neither extreme position won a clear victory; the outcome was mixed. In 40 years we have not arbitrated the question of what is learned and what is innate. However, it has become apparent that the truth of the matter does not lie anywhere between Kuo's and McDougall's positions, but somewhat off to the side. We have discovered that there are species-specific constraints upon what animals can learn and, at the same time, much species-specific behavior involves unique kinds of learning (e.g., imprinting). Hence, one writer has been led to wonder "Since learned behavior is innate, and vice versa, what now?" (Verplanck, 1955). But this is a recent dilemma; for many years the initial deadlock was considered to have been resolved by means of a compromise: There are a few basic innate drives such as hunger and thirst, while the other varieties of motivation, for example, those in social situations, derive from (are learned on the basis of) the basic ones (see Chapter 11).

The tender-minded carried the day on the question of structure vs. energy.

> The psychology of instincts was a dynamics of imaginary forces and the anti-instinct movement was primarily a crusade against such a conceptual dynamism. Somehow the argument got twisted. Heredity was made the scapegoat and the hypostatization of psychic energies goes merrily on. (Lashley, 1938, p. 447)

What Lashley called the hypostatization of psychic energies has continued to the present day. In fact, it is one of the principal subjects of the present book.

Of the three theoretical issues of the 1920s, probably the most important was the third, which was whether man's behavior could be explained mechanistically (and if it could, whether it should) or, on the other hand, whether the traditional rationalistic variety of explanation had to be retained.

Indeed, the instinct controversy of the 1920s could only have occurred if men saw mentalism and mechanism as the only real alternative explanatory systems. This controversy has gradually become resolved as we have begun to see that behavior can be explained in its own terms without recourse to either mentalism or mechanism. This was, of course, the change which Tolman, Craig, and Woodworth sought to bring about. However, this solution was not generally seen as the proper course and this final resolution is still being brought about, its slowness perhaps resulting from the seeming appropriateness of mechanistic and mentalistic approaches to our problems. At the time, neither side won a clear victory on this question. Mentalism was dethroned; Watson had won that much. But Watson's stark physicalistic alternative to mentalism was not widely accepted. The definition of psychology changed from the study of the mind to the study of behavior, but this too was only accomplished gradually.

The only obvious immediate outcome of the Great Instinct Controversy was that the word "instinct" was banished; it virtually disappeared from the psychological literature for the next 15 or 20 years. When it began to reappear (e.g., Lashley, 1938) it was purely as a descriptive term designating unlearned behavior. It had been stripped of its prior connotations of emotion, biological adaptiveness, unconscious impulses, and teleology. These connotations did not perish when the word was banished, however, they merely became attached, with varying degrees of persistence, to the new word "drive."

Drive was an even better compromise concept than instinct had been. It gave the mechanist just the principle of mechanical causation he wanted; and the drives promised to have objective physiological or physical bases, which the instincts lacked. Drives also permitted the vitalist and the mentalist to keep at least a descriptive teleology of the kind Craig and Tolman had proposed. Drives were manifest in behavior, had physiological correlates, and gave rise to man's desires. Thus, they bridged all of the interdisciplinary gaps that instincts were supposed to bridge.

In England and in Germany the instinct idea became embodied in a new set of theoretical trimmings. It is undoubtedly not just a coincidence that the new revitalized instinct concept arose from a relatively new realm of behavioral data to which neither the mechanistic nor the mentalistic philosophy had previously been applied in a wholesale manner. This new area emphasized the behavior of submammalian forms, primarily birds and fishes. This new subject matter and the new approach of its students led to the rapid growth of a new discipline, ethology. In later chapters we will consider the development, the vogue, and the subsequent decline of the drive concept, all primarily as the result of research in animal laboratories in this country. It will not be digressing too far, however, to look at the rise and decline in popularity of some ethological concepts because that story provides some very nice parallels.

THE ETHOLOGIST'S INSTINCTS

Ethology may fairly be said to have begun with the publication in 1935 of Lorenz's paper "Companions in the life of birds." Lorenz begins this paper by calling our attention to the principle that different animals must have different perceptions of objects. Man, by virtue of his good sensory equipment and highly differentiated nervous system, can perceive or respond to many different aspects of a stimulus situation. By contrast, lower animals tend to respond only to a given aspect or to some fixed feature of the objects in its world. Lorenz proceeds then to note a further restriction on the behavior of lower animals, namely, that the response to the limited perception is again limited, restricted by the animal's simpler nervous organization. In the most characteristic cases the response which occurs is innately organized into adaptive patterns. When these responses occur, they are not so much elicited by the appropriate stimulus events as they are *released* by them. Lorenz observes that in order for behavior of the simple animal to be adaptive, it is sufficient that an appropriate fixed action pattern be released by the appropriate stimulus.

What gives individuality and specificity to each animal species is that both the particular releasing stimulus and the particular response which it releases are highly specific to a given species. We may credit evolution with producing both the diversity of particular instinctive behaviors observed in nature, and the development of structures and behaviors in other members of a species which serve as releasers for the appropriate behavior (appropriate in the sense of being biologically adaptive). Thus, for example, birds mate with members of their own species because both the male and female, under the proper hormonal conditions, engage in behavior which presents stimulation which releases just the appropriate behavior in the mate; and these mechanisms are specific enough that the corresponding behavior is not produced except by animals of the proper sex and the proper species. The specificity of these instinctive mechanisms gives them a certain general improbability in much the same way that a key fits only a particular lock and has a low probability of fitting locks in general.

Lorenz distinguishes sharply between the final act of instinctive behavior, which he assumes is innately organized and released by appropriate stimuli, and all of the prior, more or less motivated, behavior which precedes it. It is only the final fixed action pattern which is properly referred to as the instinct. Whatever other behavior precedes it, including whatever instrumental (i.e., learned) behavior there may be which makes it possible for the instinct to run off, this behavior is not to be confused with the instinct itself, but is to be referred to as appetitive behavior. It is only the final act, the behavioral end point which is necessarily fixed because it is innately given. Lorenz denies emphatically that the instinct itself is modifiable through experience.

Lorenz cites as an example of instinctive behavior the "following" response of geese and other birds. Ordinarily, the young goose follows its mother in a characteristic manner which provides some safety for the individual and some integrity for the family group. This behavior turns out however, not to be purely instinctive, nor to be learned, but to be a unique blend of the two processes. The following response itself is assumed to be fixed, but the particular releaser is not. Rather, it depends upon what objects happen to occupy the bird's world at a particular stage in its development. If the young animal is surrounded by members of its own species at a certain "critical period" in its development, then it will follow in a normal manner. But if it is isolated from members of its species, it will follow other objects, including people, that happen to be present during the critical period. Lorenz argued that this flexibility in the behavior is not an instance of learning since (1) it is irreversible; for example, having been imprinted on a human, the duck will always follow the human and may even direct sexual behavior toward the human rather than to members of its own species; and (2) plasticity in the behavior is limited to a very short period lasting only a few hours early in the animal's development.

Lorenz cited and gave ample credit to his forerunners. His idea of the lower animal's unique and limited perception of objects was based largely on von Uexküll's profound and often poetic appreciation of the perceptual worlds of animals (1909). The distinction between the modifiable appetitive component in a sequence of behavior and the fixed end point was attributed to Craig (1918). His description of imprinting followed that of Heinroth (1911).

The picture we get, then, of adaptive behavior is that such behavior, crucial for the survival and normal functioning of the animal, is innately organized into fixed action patterns which normally occur when released by certain specific stimuli. However, the integrated and coherent nature of the fixed action pattern, Lorenz argues, is most convincingly demonstrated by its tendency to go off "in a vacuum" in the absence of the characteristic releasing stimuli if it has not been released appropriately for a long period time. In fact, it is this separation of the innate releasing mechanism from the normal releaser which tells us what part of the behavior is fixed and innately organized as an instinctive pattern (Lorenz, 1937).

One of the great values of the ethological approach for the psychologist is the wealth of descriptive material about animal behavior it has produced. The ethologist insists, moreover, that behavior is seen at its best in its natural setting, i.e., in nature, so that its appearance will be governed by the characteristics of the animal rather than by the constraints of the laboratory situation. Ethology makes the constant discovery that the behavior of one species is often no more than analogous to the behavior of another. Each animal form has its own characteristic ways of solving its problems. It may share its manner of solution to some extent with other species, but the range of generalizability must always be determined empirically. We cannot expect the psychology of the rat to apply immediately to the stickleback, or to the jackdaw, or to man. The psychologist, with his great haste to generalize, can learn a valuable lesson from the ethologist's respect for the diversity of behavior.

ENERGY MODELS

Up to this point the account of behavior Lorenz had given us was purely structural; dynamic or motivational elements played little part in it. Moreover, much of subsequent ethological theory and research has developed along purely structural lines. For example, there has been considerable discussion of the conditions under which imprinting occurs, the variety of species in which it may be found, the variety of objects upon which birds may be imprinted, and the determination of the other behavioral effects that the imprinted object may have. All such questions can be put in structural form, without introducing motivational concepts; and perhaps that is the best way to put such questions if we wish to get answers to them.

However, Lorenz's theoretical model was soon motivationalized, both by Lorenz himself and by Tinbergen. For Lorenz (1937, 1950), each fixed action pattern, i.e., each instinct, was motivated by its own source of energy, its own action-specific energy. Lorenz likened the source of energy for each instinct to a reservoir in which the energy specific to a given instinct would gradually accumulate in the absence of the appropriate releaser, and then be discharged when the releasing stimulus was presented. This analogy illustrated several hypothetical properties of the fixed action pattern: the specificity of the fixed action pattern, its weakening with continued elicitation, its strengthening with the withdrawal of the appropriate releaser, and even the overflow of energy in vacuum activity when the organism is sufficiently aroused but the appropriate releasing conditions are absent.

Tinbergen (1951) elaborated this model by proposing first that the different sources of action-specific energy were arranged in a hierarchical system so that the energy pertinent to one basic class of functional activity, such as reproduction, would motivate a number of different but related behaviors, such as mating, aggression, nest building, and tending the young. Each of these specific patterns of behavior was assumed to be organized around and motivated by energy associated with a particular center, presumably localizable somewhere in the central nervous system. Tinbergen further elaborated this model by supposing that a surplus of energy in any one center, if blocked or prevented from being discharged, or in the absence of the appropriate releaser, could "spark over" to other centers, even centers controlling quite unrelated behaviors (Tinbergen, 1940, 1951). It had been noted by a number of ethologists that instinctive behavior patterns often occur out of context, and most typically in situations in which the behavior of another instinctive pattern is blocked or frustrated in some way. This out-of-context occurrence of behavior has been called *displacement activity* (Armstrong, 1947, 1950). Most characteristically, displacement activity takes the form of some sort of grooming behavior. For example, if an animal is thwarted in mating it may groom. Grooming, itself an innately organized behavior, is supposed to occur in this instance because it is motivated by the displaced energy normally residing in the center controlling mating.[10]

The view of behavior which we have just described has been criticized on several grounds, and it should be noted that partly as a result of this criticism ethology, which was at its inception characterized by an extremely naturalistic approach (i.e., an approach which maximizes the richness of descriptive observation while minimizing experimental intervention in the natural order of events to be observed), has proceeded to become less naturalistic in orientation. For example, recent work in this field has tended to become more analytical both with respect to the physiological determinants of behavior, and also with respect to the immediate psychological conditions that govern the behavior. Moreover, there has been increasing concern about the genetic basis of instinctive behavior, and considerable progress has been made in the direction of manipulating the genetic substrata (Fuller & Thompson, 1960). At the same time, there has been an increasing concentration upon the details of the behavior itself, and as a consequence of this analysis we have come to realize that a sharp distinction between learned behavior and innate behavior frequently cannot be maintained (Lehrman, 1953; Kennedy, 1954). Nor indeed is it possible to adhere empirically to the conceptual distinction which Lorenz has made between the fixed action pattern and the more labile appetitive behavior which precedes it; they merge one into the other.

The most immediate concern here is not with the criticisms that have been made of these structural aspects of the ethologist's instinct theory, but rather the criticisms that have been made of the ethologist's use of motivational concepts and, more specifically, of the energy concept of motivation. Some of this criticism has been directed at the motivation idea itself (Hebb, 1955; Hinde, 1959, 1960). Some critics have stressed that motivational models, especially the one proposed by Tinbergen, do not correspond with what is known about the workings of the central nervous system (Hinde, 1954, 1956). Hinde observes that we know of

[10] The theoretical importance of displacement is further emphasized by Tinbergen in terms of the concept of ritualization. This concept arises from the problem of attempting to account for the evolutionary development of fixed action patterns. Why is it that a bird of a particular species displays in a particular manner? Tinbergen's answer is that particular forms of behavior such as grooming that occur as displacement behavior early in the evolutionary history of the animal become, through the pressure of natural selection, a necessary part of the releaser in later evolutionary time. Hence the importance of plumage, spectacular colorations, and display patterns found in mating. Displacement behavior therefore can be viewed as a source of variation in the process of evolution.

nothing in the field of neurology that corresponds with Tinbergen's "sparking-over" phenomenon.[11]

The most telling argument against Tinbergen's motivational model is that which has arisen from the recent experimental analysis of displacement activity. Recall that displacement and vacuum activity are the two principal sources of support for the motivation idea in ethology. These are the phenomena which cannot be explained, it has been argued, without recourse to motivational or dynamic concepts; how else are we to account for the sudden occurrence of grooming or aggression when the animal has been frustrated in the midst of mating?

Quite recently, however, it has become apparent that a purely structural or associative account of displacement behavior can be formulated. The necessary assumption is that displacement activities, such as grooming, are very high in the animal's repertoire of available responses because the stimulus conditions which ordinarily elicit them are nearly always present (Andrew, 1956). It is certainly the case that grooming constitutes one of the most common behavior patterns under normal circumstances, and it is precisely this sort of behavior which is most frequently observed as a displacement activity. If the animal has nothing else to do, if it is not responding to some more insistent stimulus, it grooms. However, grooming is easily supplanted by other sorts of behavior. In conflict situations, when a response such as a part of the mating ritual is simultaneously evoked and inhibited, the response which would ordinarily take precedence over grooming is blocked and then grooming proceeds as the next most probable response. So-called displacement activities therefore can be viewed simply as the occurrence of the next strongest response in the animal's repertoire on those occasions when the strongest response or responses are prevented from occurring.

Rowell (1961) has recently given experimental support to this competing response interpretation of displacement grooming. Rowell varied the presence of conflict and the presence of the external stimuli which ordinarily produce grooming (water was sprayed on the feathers of a chaffinch, or sticky material was placed on the bird's bill). By varying the kind and intensity of stimuli to elicit characteristic forms of grooming (preening or bill-wiping) Rowell demonstrated that both the amount of grooming and the form which it took were appropriate to the stimulus conditions and the experimentally produced conflict conditions. Thus, displacement behavior, which was supposedly inexplicable simply in terms of stimulation, appears to be readily explained in structural terms.

---

[11] Hinde recognizes that a model need not necessarily represent everything about the system being modeled. But he argues that since Tinbergen speaks about "neural centers," his model should at least not be inconsistent with what is known in neurology. The history and current status of the motivation concept in ethology have been ably surveyed by Kortlandt (1959) and Beer (1963–1964).

The way now seems clear to give vacuum activity a similiar systematic structural interpretation. Thus, for example, mounting of inappropriate objects when an animal is "sexually aroused" does not necessarily have to be understood in motivational terms as an "overflowing" of the reservoir. We might also regard it merely as an instance of stimulus generalization (Beach, 1942a), or we might conceive of it as indicating the breadth of stimulus and hormonal conditions which ordinarily produce it. It is only if we think of mounting as a response released by, or given exclusively to, the female of the species that its occurrence in the absence of the female appears incongruous. If we think of mounting as a response which occurs whenever there are enough stimuli from a pool of possible stimulation including the female, hormonal effects upon the nervous system, gonadal tension, and the animal's postural and kinesthetic feedback, then there is nothing at all incongruous about its occurrence in the absence of one of these potential sources of stimulation.

Some writers (Hinde, 1960; Zeigler, 1964) have seen an object lesson in the doubt suddenly cast upon the utility of energy models in ethology by the experimental work of Andrew and Rowell. Tinbergen's theoretical account of displacement had a great deal of appeal, it was simple and elegant, but it did not foster an empirical attack upon the problems presented by the displacement phenomenon. Hinde and Zeigler have both suggested that Tinbergen's energy model was too pat, too facile— it discouraged an experimental analysis of the behavior. Like McDougall's analysis of instinctive behavior a generation before, it proposed answers when questions might have been more valuable.

Hinde (1960) has pointed out that there is another lesson to be learned from the case history of the energy model of instinctive behavior. (We should note carefully the lesson to be learned here from ethology, because we will come to precisely the same conclusion in subsequent chapters when we consider the status of the drive concept in behavior theory.) Hinde's point is that it is a mistake to provide a purely motivational account of behavior, one which emphasizes the motivational determinants, if that means that it neglects the associative determinants. We know enough about behavior now to find no explanation satisfactory unless it describes the structural, i.e., associative, facts of the case. But when these facts are known in any specific instance, the further attribution of motivating agencies may add nothing more to our understanding of the case. For example, when and if we know precisely the stimulus conditions that control grooming, it will be foolish to explain displacement grooming as a "sparking over" of instinctive energy. At this point, we may begin to wonder whether instincts (or drives) are invoked only when not enough is known about some behavior to explain it structurally.

5

THE DRIVE CONCEPT

We believe, however, that spontaneous activity arises from certain underlying physiological origins. We shall attempt to show from studies chiefly on the white rat what some of these origins are. . . .

C. P. RICHTER

The concept of drive was recognized, even from the first, as being similar to the concept of instinct; but drives were supposed to have certain theoretical advantages over the discredited instincts. Drives were like instincts in that they were believed to motivate behavior. They were also like instincts in that they were supposed to provide a substantial and scientific basis for the subjective aspects of motivation; they were supposed to explain men's wants. Finally, drives were like instincts in that they were considered to be biologically important. The drive concept had one theoretical advantage in that it was based upon a new conceptual distinction between energy and structure which replaced the time-worn distinction between vitalism and mechanism that had supported the concept of instinct.

But the principal virtue of the early conception of drives was that they were assumed to have a discernible, tangible, easily accessible physiological basis. Instincts were assumed to have physiological bases too, of course, but these bases were not immediately accessible; they were bound up in the intricacies of the genetic mechanisms. The only tangible reference for the instincts was the relatively permanent nature of hereditary behavior traits. Certainly one reason for the widespread acceptance of the drive concept was the general belief that physiological research would soon disclose the "real roots" of motivation. The drive concept, which was already gaining considerable currency in the explanation of both human and animal behavior, needed only to be tied down empirically to physiological observables to be thoroughly acceptable to all parties. Some of the first experimental reports looked encouraging; they were eagerly seized upon as scientific proof of the motivational ideas which few psychologists doubted. We were so convinced of the legitimacy of the concept that supporting evidence was accepted quite uncritically.

In the present chapter we will consider some of these early attempts to get at the "real roots" of motivation. We will find that four sorts of evidence, originating from different laboratories, focused upon quite different aspects of motivation, and involving initially entirely different conceptions, began to converge upon a unified (and unifying) set of ideas which gave the drive concept its present form. The first of these sources of ideas was the failure, or what was taken to be the failure, of the "local" theory of hunger and thirst proposed by Cannon. Cannon attempted to defend the position that hunger and thirst were merely stimuli, certain special localized sensations to be sure, but nonetheless stimuli, to which motivated behavior became associated. As data began to accumulate which indicated that Cannon's particular local theory was incorrect, the most attractive alternative was the position that hunger and thirst were dynamic central states, definitely something other than stimuli.

At about the same time, Richter and his collaborators were discovering that animals became more active as biological needs were imposed upon them. This result suggested that an animal's drives not only were directed toward specific goals, such as food and water, but that drives had a diffuse and generalized effect as well. Drives not only led to specific adaptive behavior, they were also reflected in general activity level.

Third, the discovery of specific hungers helped to shape the drive concept. Animals appeared to be motivated for just those things they needed for their well-being. For example, an animal maintained on a salt-free diet seemed to develop a specific motivation for salt.

The fourth, and in some ways the most exciting, development was the belief that Warden and his coworkers at Columbia had actually measured the strengths of the animal drives.

Some of these early research findings were pressed into service as a means of establishing operational definitions of drive. But we will see that these proposed definitions failed to survive because they could not cope adequately with the broad range of facts that were becoming known about motivated behavior. An adequate theoretical anchoring of the drive concept had to await a more detailed and sophisticated analysis. But in the interim there was little question that this either had been or soon would be accomplished. Everyone (or nearly everyone) believed in the validity of the drive concept.

STIMULI AS DRIVES TO ACTION

In the early days of behavior theory "stimulus" nearly always referred to events external to the organism. But it soon occurred to some theorists that it might be useful to consider the possibility of internal stimuli. They began to conceive of certain events in the organism's internal environment that could register on the nervous system and to which the organism could react.[1]

We have already seen that Freud had developed a similar view in 1915, and had called attention to the fact that until that time stimuli had always been regarded as noxious as well as external. Freud's theory of motivation was built on the fact that an organism cannot escape noxious internal stimuli in the same way it can flee external ones. A noxious internal stimulus requires some special arrangement with the environment in order to bring about an adequate adjustment.

Local Theory of Motivation. At about the same time certain physiologists, most notably Walter B. Cannon, were beginning to develop similar ideas about the importance of internal stimulation. Cannon guessed from internal noises that hunger sensations, "pangs," were caused by stomach contractions.[2] He persuaded Washburn to swallow a balloon on the end of a tube which was connected to a pneumatic kymograph on which were also recorded marks made by pushing a button whenever Washburn felt a hunger pang. The correlation of contractions with hunger sensations indicated that Cannon's guess had been correct (Cannon & Washburn, 1912). Substantiation for this conclusion came from Carlson's laboratory and from x-ray observation (Carlson, 1912, 1913; Rogers & Martin, 1926). Carlson (1916) then came out strongly in support of a local theory of hunger.

Quite recently, some doubt has arisen regarding the legitimacy of Cannon's conclusion that hunger pangs can be identified with stomach contractions; but for nearly a half century it was generally accepted that Cannon had found the source of those stimuli we perceive as hunger pangs.[3] On the other hand, there has been a great deal of discussion about the wisdom of Cannon's next step, which was to label these sensa-

[1] Verworn (1889) was one of the first to suggest that internal stimuli should be considered in the explanation of behavior. Others, e.g., Morgan (1894) and Jennings (1906), also emphasized the importance of internal stimulation and physiological conditions for the behavior of lower animals.

[2] This was not an entirely novel conception, nor was Cannon by any means the originator of the "local" theory. The long history of these matters has been nicely surveyed by Rosenzweig (1962).

[3] Davis et al. (1959) measured gastric motility in terms of electric activity

tions "hunger." He defined hunger as a ". . . disagreeable ache or pang or sense of gnawing or pressure which is referred to the epigastrium, the region just below the tip of the breast bone" (1934, p. 248).[4] Cannon said that he had made the identification of hunger with the sensations from stomach contractions mainly to combat the notion that hunger was a "general" sensation, a sort of diffuse awareness, which was not based upon any particular localizable sensation.

Cannon was well aware that people eat without being goaded into eating by hunger pangs; he said: "In any discussion of hunger and thirst it is important at the outset . . . to distinguish carefully between these sensations [of hunger] and appetite" (Cannon, 1934, p. 247). Cannon paid very little attention to appetite, however; he indicated only that it depends upon previous experience with sensations which are so agreeable that we desire to repeat them. He acknowledged that appetite was an important determinant of how and when people eat, and particularly of what they eat; but he was almost exclusively concerned with showing that hunger was a local sensation.[5]

In 1918 Cannon developed a similar local theory of thirst. He adduced a variety of evidence to support the view that the sensation of thirst arose from a dry, parched mouth and throat. Some of the relevant observations are that a small mouthful of water, or anesthetic drugs, or saliva produced by acid in the mouth, all abolish the thirst sensation.[6] He observed at one point that "All accounts of well-marked thirst agree

---

measured by electrodes placed externally on the upper abdomen. They found no evidence of the classical gastric activity cycle demonstrated in balloon studies until *after* a balloon had been inflated in the stomach. Essentially the same results have been reported by Penick et al. (1963) using a miniature pressure-sensitive telemetering device taken into the stomach. It would appear that the contractions reported by Cannon, and others, are *produced* by filling the stomach with a balloon, and are not just a phenomenon measured by the balloon. This wonderful illustration of the principle that a measuring device can distort the phenomenon to be measured should not obscure the fact that many people do report having hunger pangs or cramps. Moreover, it is certain that many people eat in order to stop these sensations. See Hoelzel and Carlson (1952) and Hoelzel (1957) on the question of whether these sensations disappear with continued food deprivation—the sensations do but hunger does not.

[4] An expert introspective study of hunger and appetite was conducted by Boring and Luce (1917). The closest agreement with Cannon's perception came from the subject Dimmick: hunger is a "bright burny thing at the base of the stomach" (p. 445). Boring concluded that hunger differed from appetite in many ways: certain stomach sensation, certain oral factors (like salivation), presence of imagery, and the general attitude or disposition. Thus, for some subjects, the main component of appetite was the desire to grab the food and eat it.

[5] Cannon never made clear who he thought his opposition was. Wolf (1958) (who examines Cannon's position in merciless detail) believes he was opposing Bernard (1878), but points out that this was unjustified because Bernard believed thirst was a general *need*, not a general sensation. In other words, Cannon may have been attacking a straw man.

[6] Cannon (1918) gives only a short account; Cannon (1929, 1934) gives fuller accounts and attempts to deal with some of the criticisms that had come up.

that its main characteristic is the dry mouth" (1934, p. 254). We may wonder how Cannon could have failed to note that all accounts of thirst agree that its main characteristic is that the individual wants a drink.

There are really two distinct questions here: one is the semantic question of whether the subjective experiences of hunger and thirst are actually due to local sensations arising from the stomach and the oral cavity. The second question, a syntactical one, is perhaps more interesting. Granted for the moment that Cannon really found the psychophysical correlates of what we call hunger and thirst, what can we say then about the behavior of hungry or thirsty organisms? Cannon himself was so busy defending his answer to the first question that he neglected the second. On the other hand, it now seems clear that those who most bitterly attacked Cannon did so because they were primarily interested in developing concepts of hunger and thirst which would permit them to deal with the second question rather than with the first. Even if Cannon had provided an answer to the first question, the semantic rigidity with which hunger and thirst were tied down made them virtually useless for explaining what or how or when the organism will eat or drink (Grossman, 1955). Cannon's sensations from the stomach and from the mouth could tell him only that he was hungry or thirsty and never how much to consume or how to get consumable commodities.

The syntactical poverty of Cannon's local theory was not recognized at first. From the point of view of the early animal psychologists it was easy to suppose that an internal noxious stimulus such as a hunger pang or a parched throat would stir the organism to action, and lead it to do something to relieve the condition. Experimental psychologists had generally been so preoccupied with problems of sensation and perception and so imbued with the traditional structural account of behavior that for them too the problems of hunger and thirst were largely solved once stimulus correlates for each could be found. But psychologists eventually began to distrust Cannon's theory as they came to develop the notion that drives were something other than stimuli, and particularly as they gained more insight into the behavioral facts of motivation, i.e., as they began to see that motivation was a problem in the organization and explanation of behavior rather than a problem in perception. At the same time, physiologists became dissatisfied with Cannon's local theory, first, as they probed further into the brain and found more central mechanisms in motivated behavior, and second, as they began to accumulate evidence that was incompatible with the theory. Let us look at some of this evidence.

Evidence Against Local Theory. Hoelzel (1927) and Wangensteen and Carlson (1931) had patients who had the stomach removed and the esophagus tied directly to the intestine. These patients' eating habits and experience of hunger were said to be normal, even to the experience of hunger pangs. More systematic observations of a similar sort were made by Tsang (1938) who surgically removed the stomachs of rats. Again, except for the fact that the animals ate somewhat more frequently than usual (due no doubt to their limited storage capacity) they ate normally and showed the normal pattern of activity in an activity wheel. Wolf and Wolff (1943) found that a patient with a stomach fistula, which permitted gastric activity to be observed directly, showed no correlation between stomach activity and subjective hunger. Other experimenters (Bash, 1939; Morgan & Morgan, 1940a) found that cutting the neural pathway from the stomach had little effect either upon a rat's consummatory behavior or its instrumental food-getting behavior.

Cannon's local theory of thirst was not faring any better. According to Weir et al. (1922), in cases of diabetes insipidus drugs such as pilocarpine and atropine (which have the effects of facilitating and inhibiting salivation respectively) had little effect either upon the patients' reports of thirst or upon their drinking behavior. Moreover, extensive application of cocaine to the throat (which Cannon had found eliminated the sensation of dryness) failed to alleviate the craving for water characteristic of the disease. Similar studies with dogs (e.g., Montgomery, 1931) have failed to show that dryness or wetness of the mouth has a determining effect upon water consumption. Studies by Bruce (1937, 1938) and Morgan and Fields (1938) showed that animals were more motivated for food or water, in the sense that they ran faster for it, if they were prefed or prewatered a small part of their daily ration just before running. The optimum amounts for the fastest running turn out to be large enough that they would be expected to stop stomach contractions and to alleviate the parched throat.[7]

Perhaps the studies that were the most damaging for Cannon's local theory, and at the same time the most interesting in terms of methodology, were those reported by Adolph (1939) and Bellows (1939) with fistulated dogs. These dogs were allowed to drink but the water was prevented from getting to the stomach by a fistula connected to the esophagus which drained it all back out. Such dogs "sham drank" great quantities of water each day, keeping the mouth wet, but evidently not reducing the desire to drink. These studies also indicated that if water is poured into the dog's stomach directly through the fistula without letting it enter the mouth, subsequent drinking would be inhibited provided some time elapsed between the stomach loading and the subsequent drinking test. The interesting finding was that a lapse of 10 to 15 min. was sufficient to obtain a marked inhibition of drinking, and this is ordinarily considered

---

[7] Carlson (1916) had found that stomach contractions stopped with the first mouthful of food. This reaction is evidently conditionable since Lorber et al. (1950) found that the first mouthful of food stopped contractions even when the food was sham eaten.

to be too short a time for an appreciable amount of water to be absorbed from the stomach (but see below, p. 166).

It was inevitable that the local theory of motivation would be extended to sexual motivation. However, Bard (1935) and Root and Bard (1937) showed that cutting the afferent pathways from the genital region of female cats failed to disrupt their sexual behavior. So it seemed that this behavior was like eating and drinking in that it too could not be explained solely in terms of unique localizable eliciting stimuli.

The systematic importance of all these studies was soon overshadowed, however, by the excitement that followed application of the recently rediscovered Horsley-Clarke stereotaxic technique in making hypothalamic lesions. Bard (1940) found that there was a region of the hypothalamus which appeared to be critical for the appearance of sexual behavior. He showed that if this region was destroyed, or if appropriate hormones were not present, female cats could not be brought into heat; normal behavior required both. Other "centers" controlling other sorts of motivated behavior (sleep and eating) were located about the same time by Ranson (1939) and Hetherington and Ranson (1940).

This sort of evidence made it plain that Cannon's "spit and rumble" theory of motivation would not suffice. Finding a motivating stimulus simply would not account for the animal's consummatory or instrumental behavior. For such an explanation it seemed more profitable to seek mechanisms, or explanatory constructs, which would have more generalized, widespread, and organizing effects upon the organism.

Central Theory of Motivation. Beach (1942) surveyed the evidence then available on male sexual behavior and postulated that there is what he called a "central excitatory mechanism" which, aroused by stimulus and hormonal and even experiential factors, acts to initiate and sustain the variety of behavior patterns that constitute the male's sexual activity. Morgan (1943) proposed a similar concept; he suggested that there were a number of "Central Motive States," each of which governed one of the different kinds of motivation (Morgan allowed for the possibility of some overlap between states). The hypothetical properties of a Central Motive State (CMS) were:

1. Persistence—a CMS endures in a more continuous form than either the initiating conditions or the consequent behavior.
2. General activity—the motivated animal has a heightened level of bodily activity.
3. Specific activity—a CMS evokes specific forms of behavior which do not seem to depend upon any special environmental conditions.
4. Preparatory condition—the most important feature of a CMS is that it "primes" the organism for appropriate consummatory behavior when the right environmental onditions appear.

This view of the motivated organism, emphasizing the central state, has dominated subsequent physiological research. Typically, the neural and hormonal bases of the state are discovered, their effects upon behavior noted, and the controlling antecedent conditions are hunted down. Explanations of specific behavior result that may quite legitimately be considered to constitute a theory of motivation. The physiologist's concern here is ordinarily, however, not with explaining behavior but rather with elucidating the nature of the central state. The consequent linkages to behavior are often considered as more properly of concern to the psychologist. Thus, it has been fairly common to follow Adolph (1943) and speak of hunger and thirst as the "urges" to eat and drink.[8] Work in this area has progressed at a remarkable rate in the 20 to 25 years since these pioneering discoveries. We have now begun to get a rather good, albeit complex, picture of the various physiological factors that control specific behaviors such as eating, drinking, and mating. Although it is not the purpose of this book to describe our present understanding of the physiological mechanisms underlying motivated behavior, we will have occasion in subsequent chapters to look at some of this material.

DRIVES AS STIMULI TO ACTIVITY

If a rat is put in a revolving wheel (first used by Stewart, 1898), or a cage mounted on tambours (first used by Szymanski, 1914), then it will engage in different kinds of behavior that result in turning the drum, or tilting the tambour cage. Munn (1950) has observed that this behavior sometimes seems random because it is

> . . . without the kind of specific direction that we observe when an animal runs toward food, toward water, or toward a sexual partner. What the animal does is run around in its cage or run in a revolving drum. Two terms have been used to designate this apparently random activity. One of these is *spontaneous activity,* and the other, *general activity.* The first term involves the assumption that no external stimulation, or at least no experimentally varied external stimulation, is responsible for eliciting or regulating the behavior. It has also been used to mean that the stimulus for the activity is un-

---

[8] The urge is measured, ordinarily, only in terms of the animal's consummatory behavior. Hence, the construct is not particularly well anchored behaviorally, and the psychologist may become a bit uneasy to see such a basically mentalistic term bandied about by men who he may feel have a better claim than he does to be called scientists. We have become accustomed to thinking of psychology as issuing promissory notes to physiology, and we are a little shocked to find that physiologists may also at times use the same currency. When a physiologist speaks of an urge, he seems to be revealing a faith either that psychology knows all about urges, or that it soon will.

known. The second term makes no assumptions about stimulation and, being just as descriptive as the first, is to be preferred. (Munn, 1950, p. 52)

Further justification for calling it *general* activity is that it is usually not analyzed; we count wheel revolutions when we don't care to know or don't bother to find out what animals do under some particular condition, or what the controlling stimuli are. Recent work has confirmed Munn's suspicions that the stimuli which control general activity are more complex and more external than was thought at first.

The Effect of Drive on General Activity. The historical importance of the early studies of general activity was that they called attention to the internal and constitutional determinants of behavior. No one played a larger part in this movement than Curt Richter. Richter first discovered that general activity tended to occur periodically rather than continuously (1922, 1927). He then attempted to correlate the periodic activity of different animals, including humans, with periodic physiological disturbances, such as stomach contractions. Richter (1927) has described the technical difficulties and disappointing initial results of trying to get stomach balloons to stay down. Finally, when Wada (1922) managed to obtain records from medical students while they were sleeping, gross bodily movements were indeed found to occur more or less simultaneously with stomach contractions as registered by balloons swallowed just before retiring. Further supporting evidence of a somewhat more circumstantial nature was obtained from rats living in a tambour cage attached to an eating cage, also mounted on tambours. Kymograph records were obtained of bodily general activity which showed not only more or less periodic bursts of activity at approximately 4-hr. intervals, but also that these active periods correlated with the times at which food was taken.[9]

Richter reported further that activity records of very young rats showed their activity to be more or less continuous, and that only after the age of 2 weeks or so does the continuous activity pattern break up into discrete periods of activity. This change in pattern was attributed to learning. Richter supposed that through more or less continuous activity and by virtue of reflexive sucking in the young animal there will become gradually conditioned an association between the discomfort due to stomach contractions, and nursing, which leads to subsequent relief. In the infant rat activity always ends with feeding. In the adult rat, the

[9] It is clear even from Wada's and Cannon's published records that stomach contractions don't necessarily precede the overt activity. Powelson (1925) has made a special point of this, and has suggested that perhaps waking up and running around stimulates stomach contractions, rather than the other way around. This interpretation has been defended by Richards (1936). Bolles (1960) has also reported that when rats wake up in their home cages they typically don't start to eat until after they have groomed or engaged in some other activity.

same preliminary restlessness, due to contractions, becomes diverted into specific food-seeking activities, which again, lead to quiescence.

Wang (1923), also working in Richter's laboratory, showed that there was a similar correlation between activity in a rotating drum and phases of the female rat's estrus cycle. When the female rat is in heat (approximately every 4 days, as judged either by her receptivity to males or by histological examination of the vagina), she may run three to ten times as much as normally. Slonaker (1924), confirming this, was also able to show that this cyclicity persists from puberty to menopause. This vivid cyclicity is destroyed and the level of activity markedly reduced during pregnancy, lactation, or in pseudopregnancy.

In the male rat, too, there seems to be a hormonal contribution to general activity in rotating cages, inasmuch as castration markedly reduces activity level (Hoskins, 1925). The dependence of activity upon hormones is not as clear in the case of the male as it is for the female since injection of testosterone does not reestablish a high activity level. Transplantation of ovaries to male rats, however, has been reported (Wang et al., 1925) to lead to heightened activity with a 4-day rhythm. Also, whereas sexual consummatory activity immediately reduces general activity in the female, it has little effect in the male (Slonaker, 1924).

Other studies from Richter's laboratory indicated that there was also periodicity in drinking. elimination, and nest-building activity (Richter, 1927). It should be emphasized, however, that when Richter speaks of cyclic or periodic behavior he sometimes means behavior with a fixed period, as in the case of the estrus cycle, and sometimes he means merely behavior which does not occur continuously. In the case of eating, which he calls periodic, the data he gives for the time intervals between feedings reveal a very broad distribution of intervals. Bash (1939) and Baker (1953) have also demonstrated that there is no strict periodicity of the order of 2 to 4 hours in eating in rats (see p. 185). There is abundant evidence for a 24-hr. periodicity, however, as we will see later. But in any case, Richter's contention that the drives have a basically cyclic character was widely accepted for many years as valid.

Another important implication of Richter's work is that if the animal is deprived of anything necessary for its well-being, it responds by becoming more active. In support of this bold hypothesis Hitchcock (1928) reported that rats became more active on a low protein diet (although their activity level soon drops as they become progressively weakened). Wald and Jackson (1944) found that deprivation of water, or food and water, or thiamin increased running in activity wheels.[10] How could anyone doubt the power, much less the validity, of the drive concept?

Other, Specific, Effects of Drive. In 1916 Evvard reported that hogs

[10] Wald and Jackson contend that the unconditioned reaction to any deprivation is "activity, as such."

which were permitted to balance their own diet from a variety of foods showed far superior weight gains, to those ordinarily obtainable on regular fixed diets. These results were soon followed by others with chickens (Pearl & Fairchild, 1921), with human infants (Davis, 1928), and with rats (Richter et al., 1938), all testifying to the ability of organisms to select for themselves diets appropriate for their needs. Subsequent work with better controls has revealed a number of complicating factors in testing for the adequacy of self-selected diets (Young, 1949, 1959).

There can be little doubt that sometimes animals show specific hungers: i.e., selective preference for substances in which their diet is deficient. Some of the more vivid and better established phenomena are the preference of adrenalectomized animals for salt (Richter, 1936) and the preference of cattle deficient in phosphorus for bones (Green, 1925). Richter (1939, 1942) proposed that appetites always come from some physiological need, and that the preference for the needed object arises innately through an automatic adjustment of the sensory receptors.[11]

In 1925 Dashiell reported, in a paper titled "A quantitative demonstration of animal drive," that animals deprived of food would explore more in the complex maze he had designed than would animals that were satiated. Again, it looked as though the need for food, by arousing a hunger drive, had stimulated the subjects to "explore" for food.

For many years this diverse group of studies was uncritically accepted as evidence to support two broad conclusions. First, certain stimulus or hormonal conditions of an organism lead it to engage in that behavior which alleviates the motivating condition. If an animal needs food it will eat, if it needs water it will drink, if it needs salt it will eat salt, if it is cold it will build a nest, and so on presumably through the gamut of biological necessities. In short, the biological needs of animals (including man) lead to appropriate behavior which occurs with little or no training when the appropriate occasion for it arises.[12]

The second general conclusion that was drawn from these early

[11] It is important to stress that the phenomenon is one of preference since subsequent research has shown that it is not just due to a modification of the receptors. For example, Harriman and MacLeod (1953) found that normal rats could be trained to have thresholds for salt discrimination at least as low as adrenalectomized rats. Young began a long series of food preference studies quite in sympathy with Richter's position, but his findings led him to change his opinion (compare Young, 1941 and Young, 1948, 1949). Young found that rats would acquire strong habitual preferences for foods which might or might not serve their needs.

[12] It is not yet settled how much learning is involved in some of these effects. For example, Scott and Verney (1949) and Smith et al. (1958) have shown that the specific hungers, or preferences, for thiamin and salt in animals deprived of these specific necessities are learned. But Rozin (1965) and Bolles et al. (1964) have shown that these preferences are unlearned. It is not unthinkable that there are unlearned initial preferences for these substances when they are needed, but that the preference increases with experience.

studies was that in the absence of the appropriate goal object, the organism will engage in general or diffuse activity, even when in some particular circumstances this is evidently not beneficial. Thus, in the absence of food, the animal will run in an activity drum; so will the animal with normal sexual hormones, so will the thirsty animal, and so will the animal that is cold, or one that has specific dietary deficiencies. During the 1920s and the 1930s when this evidence was first becoming available, it was eagerly seized upon as supporting the notion that an animal's needs determine its drives and that its drives determine its behavior.

In recent years all of these different lines of evidence for this picture of need $\rightarrow$ drive $\rightarrow$ goal seeking have come under experimental and theoretical attack. The day now seems far removed when Rignano (1923) and Raup (1925) could enthusiastically propose that homeostatic principles could explain all psychological activity (however, see Stagner & Karwoski, 1952). We now know that this picture of automatic adjustment was much too simple. But it was important historically because it confirmed the psychologist's belief that direct and relatively simple physiological bases could be found for all of the organism's biological needs and that they would be directly and simply translated into motivational terms. Thus, it did not seem unreasonable in 1943 for Hull to *equate* needs and drives. This early physiological research gave the drive concept an aspect of empirical testability and tangibility which the instinct concept had never had. To help press the concept into active service, just one more thing needed to be done: the different drives had to be quantified. Psychologists like Warden optimistically set out to measure drive strength.

The Columbia Obstruction Box Studies. Warden objected to activity-wheel measures as indices of the strength of motivation on the grounds that, while they may have provided a valid index of the general tendency of animals to be active, they failed to differentiate among the different drives and they failed to indicate the directionality of motivated behavior.

> Certainly, the knowledge that a hungry rat is excited by food in the offing and is bending its energies to secure the food, to the exclusion of other types of activity, presents a more adequate biological and psychological picture of its behavior than the knowledge that, when equally hungry the same rat will turn a wheel round and round so many times per hour. (Warden et al., 1931, p. 5)

To meet this objection, the well-known Columbia obstruction box was developed (Jenkins et al., 1926). With this apparatus, Warden argued, it would be possible to define and measure the strength of the animal's drive in terms of its tendency to approach a particular goal.[13]

---

[13] The method had been developed a little earlier by Morgan (1916, 1923) and Moss (1924). Their studies were highly imaginative but rather casually con-

Warden and his co-workers ran a series of studies measuring the number of times an animal under a given deprivation condition would cross an electric grid in a 20-min. observation period in order to have momentary contact with the incentive. The results for a number of different drives—hunger, thirst, sex (both male and female), exploration (no incentive), and maternal (returning to the litter and nest)—are summarized in Fig. 5-1.

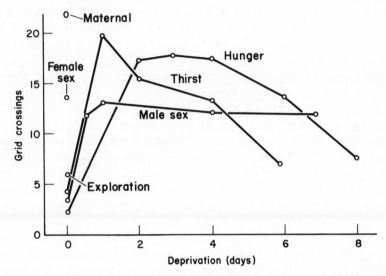

Fig. 5-1. Grid crossings in the Columbia obstruction box as a function of deprivation of food, water, or sexual behavior. The number of grid crossings is also indicated for female animals returning to their nest and young (maternal), crossing for a male animal (female sex), and for animals given no incentive (exploration). (From Warden et al., 1931)

These systematic investigations provided some information about the effects of different deprivation conditions upon the strength of a single drive (e.g., that the maximum strength of hunger occurred with a deprivation of about 3 days). The guiding idea behind the Columbia obstruction-box studies, however, was to make possible the comparison of different drives within a single experimental context; and it has certainly been this possibility of comparisons across drives (e.g., the strongest thirst is stronger than the strongest hunger) that has caught the imagination of

ducted for which Warden scorned them severely. Warden attributed the origin of the basic idea that the strength of a motive can be measured in terms of how hard the animal will work for an incentive to Lubbock (1882), but the connection seems dubious.

subsequent psychologists. (Witness the studies by Simmons, 1924; Tsai, 1925; Stone & Sturman-Huble, 1927; and Stone & Ferguson, 1938, all attempting to compare hunger and sex.) Unfortunately, it is just at the point of comparing different drives, where the Columbia obstruction-box studies offered the greatest promise, that the results are most subject to criticism.

The difficulty of interpreting the results of these studies comes from the unique definition that had been given drive. For most psychologists around 1930, the term "drive" referred to a physiological state of the organism which was aroused by a particular goal or by a particular deprivation condition. But for Warden et al., "drive" meant just the behavioral tendency which resulted from such an arousal. It was recognized, of course, that approach behavior depends not only upon the conditions of deprivation, but also on the fact that the organism's activity is always directed toward or away from some incentive, i.e., some object such as food or water or an animal of the opposite sex which is capable of arousing and then satisfying the animal's seeking tendency. In all of the Columbia studies, then, the strength of approach behavior, which was said to be drive strength, was really a measure both of drive and incentive factors, combined in some unknown proportion. After recognizing the important distinctions between deprivation and incentive conditions, Warden proceeded to study deprivation conditions almost to the exclusion of incentive factors.[14]

We cannot deny that Warden et al. did good and important work, but at such an early date it would have perhaps been more valuable had they mapped out a wider variety of experimental variables, even if this meant that the work had to be done with less precision. Let us see what some of the implications might have been. Their own data show that early in the test session the results are markedly different from what they are over the whole session; such changes are found both in the effect of deprivation upon the strength of a single drive and also in apparent relative strengths of different drives. Thus, with 5-min. test sessions quite a different picture of drive strength is obtained from that with the standard 20-min. tests.

Second, consider the effects of pretraining. In all of the obstruction-box studies, animals received 5 pretraining trials, 4 without shock, and 1 with the shock grid activated. We wonder whether different strengths of learning under the different motivation conditions were obtained with the use of a fixed number of pretraining trials and whether 5 trials provides a "normal drive," as Warden claimed. We wonder, too, whether the performance which was measured during the immediately following 20-min. test should be thought of as extinction of the approach tendency built up in the pretraining trials, or whether it is better to think of it as a

---

[14] Hamilton (1929) is a notable exception. She studied the effect of delay of reinforcement upon the rate of grid crossing.

learned aversion of the shock grid. It may be noted in this connection that the rate of grid crossing falls off during the 20-min. test, i.e., the subjects extinguish.

Thirdly, Warden et al. went to some trouble to maximize the stimulus properties of the incentive; the experimental apparatus was arranged so that the animal could see and smell the food, mate, litter, etc. But we must wonder how one can equate the stimulus values of these diverse sorts of incentives. Finally, we must wonder how one equates the effect of contact with the different incentive objects, that is, how does one insure that a comparable amount of consummatory activity has been guaranteed by permitting the animal a "nibble of food," or a "lick of water," or a "nosing of the female."

The concept of drive presents both semantic and syntactical problems. Warden's approach was to solve the semantic problems in one stroke with an operational definition: strength of drive equals the number of grid crossings. But the equally important syntactical properties of the drive construct remained in the dark, and no amount of definitional rigidity or experimental precision could shed any light on them. Clarification could only come from discovering how behavior is dependent upon the many variables that affect it. Thus, the standardization of conditions under which the Columbia studies were conducted, which made them so outstanding for their day, also led to their greatest limitation.[15]

The trouble with the Columbia obstruction-box studies was that the same word, "drive," was used on the one hand by Warden to designate grid crossing behavior, and on the other hand by most psychologists to designate hypothetical motivational or physiological states of the organism. It was popularly believed that Warden had measured the intensity of these motivational states, and not just a particular behavior tendency motivated by them. Had Warden et al. studied the effect of different incentives under the same deprivaton conditions, we now know that he would have found marked differences in what he called drive, and the confusion between what he called drive and what others called drive could not have occurred. Most psychologists were no more ready to accept Warden's explicit definition of drive than they were to accept Richter's implicit definition in terms of activity level, or Cannon's in terms of localized

---

[15] It might be objected that the use of operational definitions under "standardized conditions" has proved of great value in the physical sciences, so we ought to emulate the practice of standardization. The difference is that reference to a physical standard (such as a platinum meter in Paris) is only useful when we have a very good understanding of what the variables are that affect the construct (in this case length). The arbitrariness of the standard meter is only defensible to the extent that we can refer to it after making corrections for pressure and temperature without worrying about how it may change as a function of other physical manipulations. We know the variables of which length is a function, and we know how it depends upon them. In short, semantic rigidity of the length construct pays off because it also has a well-established syntax. Drive does not.

sensations; drive always meant something more than any one of these. Historically, we started in bravely to define drive in a way we thought was convenient; but we were caught up by the discovery that we had not come to grips with the many phenomena we wanted the concept to explain.

DEFINITIONS OF DRIVE

Sometimes in science we can define a term operationally in a way which arouses virtually no opposition. The principal reason for the success of the operational definitions in these cases is that they are applied to new phenomena. No one had concerned himself with these concepts or with anything like them until they had been discovered and named. Consider, for example, proactive and retroactive inhibition. No one except the verbal learning psychologist wants these terms to mean anything. Consequently, they can mean precisely what he wants them to.

But more often in science we must cope with concepts which have been thought about and talked about a great deal, concepts for which there is a rich background of prior associations. To the extent that such concepts enjoy common usage they have a sort of primitive inherent meaning, even though they are not really encompassed by any one explicit definition. Each person knows what he means even though he cannot explain it quite to anyone else's satisfaction. These terms ordinarily also lack syntactical rigor; their conceptual properties are not agreed upon. Drive has been such a concept. We have already met it in different forms and guises. Freud, Tolman, Woodworth, and many others proposed dynamic or motivating principles, and although their different principles and concepts had some common semantic and syntactical features, the essence of the thing eluded them—and so did an adequate definition.

The way we ordinarily proceed in the development of such concepts is from primitive meanings implicit in common usage to tentative definitions that are highly selective if not completely arbitrary, i.e., definitions which emphasize some one feature of the concept. Such a transition in the development of the drive concept occurred, as we have seen, in the 1920s. This era started with a variety of intuitive definitions and ended with a variety of rigid operational ones. Just as the earlier definitions of drive had been too loose, so the later ones, those of Cannon, Richter, and Warden, were too tight.[16]

[16] In the last analysis it is common usage rather than formal definition which dictates meaning. We may note that we always have the option of accepting or rejecting any definition, operational or otherwise. Acceptance depends upon the defining properties being those we wish to imply by the word. There are a number of phenomena which we want to be able to explain with the drive concept. The empirical question is to find out if all of the implications of the word follow when

There has always been an insistent feeling that motivation is not a feature or aspect of action but rather that which moves the organism to action. Both the loose intuitive approaches and the rigid operational ones were, I believe, attempts to get at some elusive central core of meaning. What was being sought was a general or universal cause of behavior. The various attempts to define drive perhaps should not be considered as attempts to get at what drive "really is," but rather as hopeful tentative attempts to link an important feature of behavior to an ineffable explanatory something else. Such operational definitions should be regarded as working hypotheses rather than formal definitions (see also Pribram, 1962).

More optimistically, we may note that the research that has been done in support of one or another view of the drive concept has borne considerable empirical fruit. A number of highly reliable, easily reproducible, and widely general phenomena have been found which can be attributed to, and hence, explained by, almost any version of a drive concept. Thus, Cannon's definition of drive in terms of stimulation has led to a recognition of the importance of internal stimuli in the determination of behavior, and to considerable research on the physiological conditions accompanying deprivation. Miller and Dollard's (1941) definition of drive as any strong stimulus has led to a wealth of work on acquired drives and aversive behavior. Definitions of drive as a central state of the organism (e.g., Morgan, 1943) have had very wide empirical and theoretical ramifications. Definitions in terms of particular kinds or aspects of behavior, such as Richter's or Warden's, opened up new techniques for the investigation of behavior. Drives have also been defined fruitfully in terms of antecedent conditions, and in terms of the total energy released in behavior (e.g., Young, 1936).

One vs. Many Drives. As soon as the drive concept was seen as useful in psychological theorizing, the question immediately arose as to whether there should be a multiplicity of drives—say, a drive for food, a drive for water, and a drive for sex objects—or whether, on the other hand, there should be only a single drive—drive itself—which may have different sources and different objects. The question is whether we should regard drives as the motivators of specific kinds of behavior, or whether we should use the concept more broadly, making it synonymous with motivation in general (always recognizing, of course, that it may affect different specific forms of behavior).

If we assume a multiplicity of drives, then each one is specific, so we

one of them has been established. If they do, then that one (or any of the others) may be used to provide a popular definition. In Warden's case, this meant that when he had defined drive as the tendency to approach a particular incentive, he should have seen if the other manifestations of drive, for example, activity level in a wheel, would also follow quantitatively.

end up referring to a drive *for* this or that object or a drive *from* this or that disturbance. This concept of specific drives is relatively close to the ancestral concept of instincts. Just as there was a plurality of instincts, so there could be a plurality of drives, and this was the most common assumption in the early days of drive theory. From the beginning, however, some writers referred in the singular to "animal drive" (e.g., Dashiell, 1925), while others (e.g., Fryer, 1931; Young, 1936) who spoke of drive as the energy of behavior also clung to the singular concept.

A closely related and much discussed question is whether drives contribute to the direction and regulation of behavior, or to the energy of behavior, or to both the directing and the energization of behavior. Again, if a theorist subscribes to the concept of multiple specific drives, he gets as a bonus drives directing behavior. But if he thinks mainly in terms of a single, generalized drive, then he finds that it serves primarily just to energize behavior. The ethologists are a good example of the first approach, while Hull is the outstanding spokesman for the latter position.

Drives in the plural are not very secure logically. Their very specificity deprives them of functional properties that give value to the singular construct. Consider, for example, hunger and sex. The primary evidence of the sexual drive is a single consequent relationship, viz., it motivates sexual behavior. The sex drive may also be related on the antecedent side to various hormonal and stimulus conditions which have been found to be related to sexual behavior. On both the antecedent and consequent sides, then, the sex drive is tied by functional properties different from those of food deprivation and the motivation of eating which constitute the primary evidence of the hunger drive. We are left in the very difficult position of having an explanatory concept which is empty in the sense that invoking it contributes nothing beyond specifying the original empirical relationships. Under these circumstances, we are free to invoke a drive to explain all conceivable kinds of behavior; a drive for activity, a drive to explore, a drive to perceive, a drive for competence (these are all recent examples of drives that have been hypothesized to explain the indicated kinds of behavior). In the case of some of these hypothetical drives there is additional evidence for further semantic linkages and hence they have further explanatory value. But the danger is clear; there is nothing to prevent us from invoking drives to explain twiddling the thumbs, or not twiddling the thumbs, or even believing in drives.

The solution to the problem of circularity is apparent. To give explanatory usefulness to the concept of specific drives, it is necessary to anchor them on the response side in more than one way, through two or more functional properties. It is not enough to say that a drive for food motivates eating, it must also be shown that additional features of behavior, such as heightened activity in a rotating wheel or the ability to learn the location of food, also follow.

As we will see next, the drive concept was saved from the danger of inadequate anchoring by the bold, brilliant theorizing of Clark L. Hull (1943) and his students. Hull's basic strategy was to embed the drive construct in a network of many semantic and syntactical relationships. After Hull, drive is no longer merely a concept, it is a well-defined theoretical construct.

ASSOCIATIVE ACCOUNT OF MOTIVATION

It would not be correct to conclude that there was no dissension from the widely accepted concept of motivation during the period we have been considering. There was a small but vocal group of theorists who had argued all along that there was no need to have special dynamic concepts to handle the facts of motivation.

To illustrate the thinking of this group, let us see how they might have dealt with the arguments advanced by Morgan (1943) in support of his Central Motive State construct. Recall that his CMS construct was based upon four sets of phenomena which, he said, could not be explained by a purely associative or structural account. These were: (1) persistence of motivation after the initiating conditions were removed, (2) increased activity level, (3) occurrence of specific consummatory responses, and (4) preparation of the organism to make appropriate consummatory responses. The question here is whether Morgan was really justified in his contention that stimuli alone cannot have these behavioral effects.

Let us conceive of a consummatory response as being innately connected to an internal stimulus which persists until the occurrence of certain supporting external stimuli make possible the particular consummatory response. And let us suppose further that the internal stimulus in question is abolished only as a consequence of this consummatory response. Such a stimulus would then be persistent. It might also well be that if it were of sufficient intensity it would increase general activity. It has specific responses innately connected to it by definition, so that the continual presence of such a stimulus would "set" the organism for making the consummatory response when the goal object was presented. Such a stimulus would then seem to have all of the properties that Morgan attributed to his Central Motive State. All that would distinguish such a stimulus from any other type of stimulus would be its innate association with a particular consummatory response and its persistence.

Even if we grant that because of these special properties it would be desirable to call this state of affairs by some name other than "stimulus," still, logically, such a state would have its effect upon the nervous system by initiating particular patterns of nerve impulses; and at that point it would become the adequate stimulus for its neurological consequences.

Thus the only real criterion for distinguishing between such a "motivating" stimulus and any other stimulus is that we do not yet know if it has a unique psychophysical correlate (Cannon's proposals, as we have seen, will not do). But the inability to identify corresponding physical stimulus objects has not deterred psychologists from hypothesizing stimuli. So there seems to be nothing to prevent us from proposing that stimuli are the motivators of behavior as long as we admit that such stimuli would have to have properties which other stimuli lack, such as persistence and innate association with particular consummatory responses.

This purely associationistic point of view has been given its best known (and most enduring) formulation by Smith and Guthrie (1921). For many years Guthrie insisted that what we call hunger, for example, is just the effect of some stimulus (he never subscribed to any particular theory of its somatic sources) which he called a *maintaining stimulus* because, until terminated by eating, it persists and maintains whatever behavior makes the animal act hungry.

Guthrie argued that if a hungry animal makes energetic movements in running to food, it must be because it has learned to do so; these energetic movements are the ones that have become conditioned to the hunger stimulus; without it they would not occur. The same principle is held to account for the apparent purposefulness of the preparatory responses; they too have all become conditioned to the maintaining stimulus and will persist as long as it does. Guthrie has been charged with ignoring the obvious purposive character of behavior; the animal "wants" to get to the goal box, and "tries" to get there. The answer to the charge is that the "want" and the "try" are inferences the observer makes. Such inferences are evidently based upon some feature of the animal's behavior, sometimes just the occurrence of the learned response that gets the animal to the goal box. In more complicated situations, the animal may be said to "try" to get to the goal box when it makes responses which are similar to the responses that would get it there.

According to Guthrie, motivated behavior is identical in principle to any other behavior except that it is characterized by the presence of this persistent maintaining stimulus. This kind of argument deals with the phenomena of motivation in terms of stimulation but without making the additional assumption that the stimulus is good or bad, i.e., that it must be reacted to either appetitively or aversively.[17] This purely associative account of motivated behavior has been defended over the years by Guthrie (1935, 1952), by Copeland (1926), Kuo (1928), Hollingworth (1931),

---

[17] The "neutrality-of-stimuli" plank of Guthrie's theoretical platform is really a by-product of his particular view on association by contiguity. Miller and Dollard (1941) also adhere to the idea that stimuli maintain behavior and can be drives, but their commitment to a drive-reduction theory of reinforcement has the consequence that for them stimuli must be noxious.

Rexroad (1933), Wolpe (1950), and Estes (1958), among others.[18]

Such an amotivational approach to the phenomena of motivation offers the obvious advantages of parsimony and elegance. It explains the phenomena with a simple conditioning model. However, in higher animals, where the effect of stimulation cannot generally be traced through to response consequences, it is common practice to infer the eliciting stimulus from the occurrence of the response. The specification of the stimulus then raises all of the problems of circularity that invoking a drive or an instinct would. In the last analysis, if we are to have theories with constructs (and we should not call them theories otherwise), it would seem to be pretty much optional whether our constructs are maintaining stimuli or Central Motive States or drives.

The choice between motivational and nonmotivational explanatory schemes cannot be made simply on the basis of a few well-selected observations. The theorists (e.g., Morgan, Lewin, Murray) who have attempted to prove the logical or empirical necessity of dynamic concepts by citing features of behavior that associationists could not explain, have been taking on a straw man in the form of nineteenth century associationism. Modern sophisticated associationistic models (e.g., Estes, 1958) present a very serious challenge to dynamic theories. But this quite recent development required extensive data about the structure of behavior, and before we knew as much as we now know about behavior the drive concept flourished almost unchallenged.

[18] Hull too subscribed to this position at one time (1930, 1931), as we shall see shortly. Guthrie attributed the basic notion of a maintaining stimulus to Sherrington (1906), although, of course, Sherrington worked with "surface" stimuli rather than internal ones. The best systematic statement of the associationistic position has been made by Brown (1961). Brown's account is particularly valuable since, being a drive theorist, he is most concerned with drive theory and associationistic theory as competitive positions.

6

HULL'S THEORY OF
MOTIVATION

+((((

*One really does not have a scientific theory until constructs are
introduced in some such precise fashion as Hull employs, for it is
only under such conditions that the possibility of verification or
refutation exists.*

K. W. SPENCE

By 1940 almost everyone believed in some form of drive concept, although, as we have seen, there was considerable disagreement about just
what form it should take. Hull and his students entered the picture at this
point. They reformulated the prevailing consensus about drives, embedded
the motivational concepts of the time into a unified theory of behavior,
and crystallized the basic theoretical issues in the form of a number of
specific and testable empirical propositions. In Hull's theory, drive was
hypothesized to have a number of explicit functional relationships both
with antecedent conditions, such as the biological needs of the organism,
and with those aspects of the organism's behavior that make us say it is
motivated.

This chapter is concerned simply with presenting Hull's theoretical
treatment of motivation, while the following four chapters are devoted to
a presentation of the evidence that has been amassed to test the theory.
It may seem that this is giving an undue amount of attention to one
theoretical construct in one man's theory. But it must be noted that Hull

was speaking not only on his own behalf but for most psychologists concerned with the explanation of behavior; there was such wide acceptance of one or another variant of the drive construct that a test of Hull's drive theory of motivation provides at least an indirect test of the underlying logical and philosophical precepts of the prevailing idea of motivation. However, there was a great superiority of Hull's formulation over any that had preceded it; and this superiority was shown in the fact that it stimulated a vast amount of research. From this wealth of material it is possible to evaluate not only the large theoretical questions entailed in the theory, but also a great number of smaller but nonetheless important conceptual issues which it has generated. Finally, it must be said that much of the empirical work that has been stimulated by Hull's theory is important because it has produced the basic empirical building blocks in the area. Hull showed us not only how to construct a theory to explain motivated behavior, but also how to establish what the fundamental behavioral phenomena of motivation are.

Hull actually developed three quite different but partially overlapping theories of motivation. First, there was a strictly associative theory which he formulated during the early 1930s. Next, there was the drive theory which began to take shape in the late 1930s and reached a dominant position in *The Principles of Behavior* (1943). Then, at the time of his death in 1952, Hull had begun to develop an incentive theory of motivation.

In one sense, each of these theories replaced its predecessor by providing more powerful explanatory mechanisms. But the different explanatory devices also supplemented each other, and the older ones were never completely abandoned when the newer ones were introduced. The associative principles were not discarded when the drive construct was added, nor was drive dismissed later when incentive motivation concepts were introduced. In the following chapters, we will attempt to look at each of these theories in isolation, to the extent this is possible, even though this may mean doing some violence to the overall structure and integrity of Hull's behavior theory. The justification for this type of analysis is that we will wish to view the phases of Hull's evolving theory as representative of associative, drive, and incentive theories in general, rather than try to assess Hull's overall prowess as a theorist.

We will conclude this chapter with a short summary, a brief look back at the territory we have covered thus far.

HULL'S EARLY ASSOCIATIVE THEORY

Motivation per se played a relatively minor part in Hull's earliest theoretical statements. In 1930 he held a view that was very similar to that of Guthrie which we discussed in the last chapter. He assumed that a particular response occurring in a learning situation, e.g., a left turn in a maze, becomes attached exclusively through Pavlovian conditioning to whatever stimuli are present at that point. The question to which he addressed himself was: How is it possible for behavior which is based merely upon conditioning principles to make the organism look as though it is striving toward a goal? That is, how can conditioning, ordinarily conceived to be a process that automatically connects a specific response to specific stimulus, account for the appearance of flexible, adaptive, purposive behavior? Hull postulated that there is a residual core of stimuli which binds together and organizes the series of learned responses into a coordinated chain. It is also this persistent core of constant stimulation which makes the hungry animal look hungry, and makes possible the anticipation of food at the goal.[1] Anticipation occurs to the extent that the different instrumental responses constituting a behavior chain all become conditioned to these maintaining stimuli, S_D. To the extent that these responses are elicited by S_D they will tend to occur prior to the occurrence of the environmental stimuli which would ordinarily elicit them. When this occurs, the later members of a chain of responses move forward in the chain, and the animal will appear to anticipate what he is going to do next.

As Hull developed the implications of this position, it became apparent that it was no longer necessary for the S-R psychologist to conceive of behavior as being immediately dependent upon external stimulation. The animal could exhibit anticipation of a goal; it could behave as though it had knowledge (1930). It could also vary its behavior in the face of obstacles (1934); it could assemble segments of behavior into novel combinations (1935); and its behavior in general could have an aspect of adaptiveness (1937).

The Anticipatory Goal Reaction.   In any trial-and-error situation, the last response, the one which brings the sequence or chain of responses to a close, is some sort of consummatory response or goal response, which may be symbolized R_G. R_G is elicited by the joint action of deprivation-produced stimuli, S_D, and certain external stimuli such as the sight and smell of food. After a number of trials, we may expect that through Pavlovian conditioning the environmental stimuli that characterize the goal situation would also tend to elicit R_G so that, for example, the animal would show a greater readiness to eat in a familiar goal box where it had eaten before than it would in a novel box.

In the absence of an appropriate goal object, such as food, both

[1] Hull tentatively attributed this persistent core of stimulation to stomach contractions in the case of hunger. But whatever the somatic source of these stimuli, we may call them deprivation-produced stimuli, or drive stimuli, or S_D.

the situational stimuli and S_D will tend to elicit R_G, but this tendency cannot be fully realized, first, because the stimuli arising from food are necessary for eating, and second, because the animal may be engaged in some other kind of activity, such as running, which is more or less incompatible with R_G and which therefore inhibits it. Nonetheless, Hull suggested, certain fractional components of R_G, certain parts and pieces of the total consummatory response which are compatible with the ongoing behavior (such as, perhaps, salivation and small mouth movements), may be elicited, and he designated this the fractional goal response, r_G. We may suppose that whenever r_G occurs it will have certain stimulus consequences, e.g., proprioceptive feedback, which may be designated s_G. Now, s_G will persist throughout the learning situation once a particular r_G has been conditioned to S_D and to environmental stimuli there. This other source of persistent stimulation, s_G, will summate with S_D to augment its function as a maintaining stimulus, and help to integrate the sequence of responses that lead to the goal.

Why, Hull asked (1931), do we need two sorts of maintaining stimuli? He gave two reasons. First, he noted that an animal may learn to anticipate a particular goal by virtue of the specificity of a particular s_G which results from a particular r_G, which depends in turn upon what food is present or what sort of consummatory activity occurs at the goal. Second, Hull observed that the phenomena of extinction seem to point to the importance of s_G rather than S_D in maintaining a chain of behavior. During extinction the whole chain usually collapses at once, whereas from what we know of conditioning and extinction, the last response elements should extinguish first, just as they are the first to be strengthened in acquisition. If S_D was all-important in integrating the chain of responses, it should continue to elicit the early members of the chain in extinction. But the extinction of R_G at the end of the chain would be expected to generalize back to the earlier members of the chain so that r_G and the stimulus support provided by s_G would fail to occur there. The fact that the whole chain does collapse, therefore, is indicative of the importance of s_G in maintaining the integrity of the chain.

It should be emphasized that in this discussion of the consummatory response the r_G-s_G mechanism was given only associative attributes. There was nothing motivational here, nothing like drive or incentive. Nor did r_G-s_G imply anything about secondary reinforcement. Indeed, at this stage in his theorizing, Hull had proposed no mechanism for primary reinforcement. While it is certainly true that Hull later implicated the r_G-s_G conceptualization both in the explanation of secondary motivation (i.e., incentive motivation) and also in the concept of secondary reinforcement, he did so only at the terminal stage of his theorizing (1952). We will consider these developments, and Hull's third variety of motivation theory, in due course, but in the present chapter we are primarily concerned with the development of his second type of theory, the drive theory.

THE EMERGENCE OF HULL'S DRIVE THEORY

Before 1937, Hull had dealt with the two classical forms of learning, Pavlovian conditioning and Thorndike's trial-and-error learning, by explaining the latter in terms of the former. The conditioning model was primary; all that was necessary for learning was the occurrence of the stimulus and the response in close contiguity. The function of the goal response was only to terminate the behavior chain, and it occurred only because unconditioned stimuli elicited it. According to the associative theory of motivation which we have just reviewed, a Pavlovian conditioning model provided the primary set of principles which encompassed the phenomena of trial-and-error learning; explanation of the latter did not require a separate set of principles (Hull, 1930a).

In 1937 the situation was suddenly reversed; Thorndike's law of effect was made the primary principle of learning, and the phenomena of Pavlovian conditioning were derived from it.[2] In Hull's 1937 analysis, learning was supposed to occur *because* the stimuli which are encountered at the goal (S_G) elicit the goal reaction or the consummatory response (R_G). Hull contended that it was this encounter with the goal object and the consummatory reaction to it that produces learning, rather than the mere contiguous association of stimulus and response. Postulate 3 of the 1937 miniature system states:

> A characteristic stimulus-reaction combination $S_G \rightarrow R_G$ always marks reinforcing states of affairs . . . The particular stimulus-response combination marking the reinforcing state of affairs in the case of specific drives is determined empirically, i.e., by observation and experiment.

This statement is of central importance in the history of Hull's theorizing not only because it indicates a transition from a contiguity account to a reinforcement account of learning, but also because for the first time drive is credited with having more than just associative properties. Previously its sole behavior property was that the specific drives (note that Hull referred to plural "drives") gave rise to specific S_D's; here drives are implicated in determining what constitutes reinforcement. It is interesting

[2] Thorndike's position, which we will consider in its proper context in Chapter 15, was based on the "law of effect," which asserts that learning occurs when and only when a response is followed by certain "effects" or consequences which constitute reinforcement. This position grew from and seems most easily applied to trial-and-error learning, or to operant behavior.

that, in this first statement connecting drive with reinforcement, Hull emphasized that the relationship between the two was a problem that could only be solved empirically. By 1943, with little more data, he was speculating much more freely about the ultimate basis of reinforcement. He argued that during evolution there have arisen correlations between certain biological needs of organisms and appropriate patterns of behavior tending to alleviate these needs. In the lower animal forms, needs may be satisfied by relatively direct reflex action; but in the higher forms, in animals whose behavior patterns are mainly learned, a special mode of adaptation has evolved. Many of the animal's needs make themselves known by means of specialized receptors within the body which pour stimulation into the central nervous system. Whatever immediate associative effects these "need receptor discharges" may have, they also have the effect of increasing drive. Hull then suggested that if drive reduction were to have a reinforcing effect, we would have a mechanism whereby animals would learn adaptive behavior patterns, i.e., those that are likely in the future to be effective in alleviating their needs.

Hull, accordingly, hypothesized that reinforcing states of affairs are those involving "a diminution of the receptor discharge characteristic of a need" (Hull, 1943, p. 80). He states at another point, however, that reinforcement is a "diminution in a need (and the associated diminution in the drive, D, and in the drive receptor discharge, S_D)" (p. 71). Hull was quite aware of and evidently uncomfortable about the ambiguity here. He noted that usually the need, the receptor response to the need (S_D), and drive (D) all tend to go together—up during motivation and down during reinforcement—but he indicated that with experimentation it should be possible to separate the different factors and show which was basic. "Meanwhile, in the interest of definiteness, the alternative of reduction in drive receptor response [S_D] is chosen for use in the present work as the more probable" (p. 81). (See also Hull, 1952, p. 153.)

Prior to Hull's 1943 statement about reinforcement, those who were working with him at Yale were already suggesting, not only how drive and drive reduction could be incorporated into a unified theory of behavior, but also how far the resulting theory might go toward explaining human behavior. Thus, in 1938 Mowrer criticized what he considered to be the widespread acceptance of Pavlovian conditioning as a model for all learning. Mowrer pointed out that the results one obtained in classical conditioning were largely dependent upon the subject's *expectations* in the test situation. He suggested that anticipatory tension, or preparatory set might well be

. . . capable of functioning as a drive or motive . . . , not only is it possible to account for the formation of conditioned defence reactions on the basis of the law of effect and thus remove what would seem

. . . to be the final objection to the universality of the law of effect as a theory of learning process; it also thus becomes clear why in the case of human beings, learning can be produced without recourse to any of the common forms of motivation used with animals. (Mowrer, 1938, pp. 74–75)

Mowrer proposed that learning might occur whenever any sort of preparatory set or anticipatory tension becomes discharged: "It is conjectured that the occurrence of the response for which a preparatory set is specifically appropriate . . . normally reduces the tension of which this preparatory set is composed" (Mowrer, 1938, p. 77). The implication was spelled out more explicitly later: "The truth of the matter seems to be that all learning presupposes (i) an increase of motivation (striving) and (ii) a decrease of motivation (success) and that the essential features of the process are much the same, regardless of the specific source of motivation or of the particular circumstances of its elimination" (Mowrer, 1939, p. 562). On the basis of this formulation, Mowrer hoped to be able to explain all manner of social behaviors, including such abnormal behavior as neurotic symptoms.

The theory was put in still simpler terms by Miller and Dollard (1941). Miller and Dollard suggested that any strong stimulation might serve as a source of drive.

Drive impels the person to make responses to cues in the stimulus situation. Whether these responses will be repeated depends on whether or not they are rewarded. . . . As the dominant response is weakened by non-reward, the next response in the hierarchy becomes dominant. As successive responses are eliminated by nonreward, the individual exhibits variable or what has perhaps been misnamed *random behavior*. It is this variability that may lead to the production of a response that will be rewarded. If one of the so-called random responses is followed by an event producing a reduction in the drive, the tendency to make this response on subsequent exposure to the same cues is increased. (Miller & Dollard, 1941, p. 28)

In short, drives are the universal agencies that impel organisms to action, and drive reduction is the universal reinforcing state of affairs. Miller and Dollard also saw the far-reaching explanatory power of this conception; they proceeded to generalize it to acquired drives in order to explain all sorts of social learning.

The group at Yale was not restricting its activities to theory construction, however. Mowrer and Miller began to conduct pioneering studies of the acquired fear drive (which we will consider in Chapter 11).

Hull started his students on a systematic investigation of hunger. We will turn now to one of these hunger studies, one conducted by Perin (1942). Because it was from Perin's results that Hull derived many of the hypothetical properties he gave the drive construct, this study proved to be one of the most important experiments ever run with rats.

The Perin-Williams Experiment. It had been generally presumed for some time that the strength of a learned response increases with both practice and motivation. Although there was some experimental evidence to indicate the importance of both practice and motivational variables varied separately, there were no data to show how the two kinds of variable interacted, i.e., what happens to the strength of a response when practice and motivational variables are manipulated at the same time. Perin measured the resistance to extinction of a bar-press response as a function of the strength of the habit, i.e., the number of prior reinforcements. His data, taken together with those of Williams (1938), who had already done a similar experiment at Yale, provided a map of the strength of this response as a joint function of practice and motivation.

Perin (1942) trained four groups of 40 rats to press a bar for food. All subjects were trained under 23-hr. food deprivation but with different numbers of reinforced trials (5, 8, 30, or 70). All animals were then extinguished under 3-hr. deprivation. The results are given in the lower curve of Fig. 6-1, while the results from the Williams study are given in the upper curve. Williams had also trained four groups under 23-hr. food deprivation with varying numbers of reinforcement (5, 10, 30, and 90), but his animals were all extinguished under 22-hr. deprivation. For both sets of data the dependent variable is the number of bar presses animals made before meeting a criterion of 5 min. with no responding.

Two features of these curves should be noted. One is the regular growth of resistance to extinction as a continuous increasing function of the number of reinforcements the response received during training. Although the level of performance was a function of the motivation existing at the time behavior was tested, the relative *rate* of growth was not. This finding led Hull to conclude that behavior strength was a function of a construct habit, designated $_sH_R$, which presumably reflected a more or less permanent change in the organism's nervous system, and which was independent of the animal's transient state of deprivation. That is, the *relative* performance did not depend upon whether subjects were tested under high- or low-motivation conditions, but only upon the number of prior reinforcements. The second crucial feature of these curves is that they do differ as a function of test deprivation conditions, so that a second construct, drive, may also be assumed to contribute to the strength of behavior. Moreover, it is apparent from the independence of learning

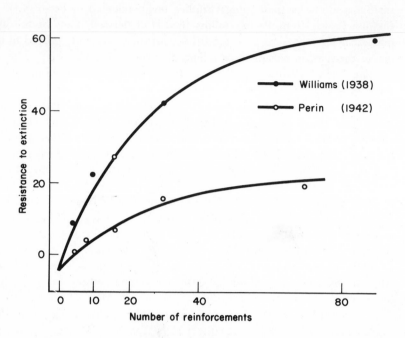

Fig. 6-1. The Perin-Williams data showing how resistance to extinction depends upon both deprivation conditions (D) and the number of reinforcements ($_sH_R$). (Adapted from Perin, 1942)

and motivational effects that $_sH_R$ and drive, D, combine multiplicatively to determine overt behavior.[3]

Perin ran four other groups. They were all trained with 16 reinforcements under 23-hr. deprivation, but they were extinguished under differing hours of deprivation. The results, measured in terms of resistance to extinction, are presented in Fig. 6-2.

In view of the multiplicative equation just established, this curve represents the general relationship describing behavior strength as a function of hours deprivation; it should be (or was hypothesized to be) independent of the number of reinforcements. Increasing or decreasing the number of reinforcements from 16 should simply generate a family of curves lying above or below the given one, but all of the same form.

These results reported by Perin and Williams provided virtually the whole of the empirical base for Hull's 1943 drive theory of motivation.

[3] Both curves are represented by equations of the form $H = A(1 - 10^{-BN})$ where A indicates the asymptote of performance reached for a given drive intensity, N is the number of reinforcements, and B is the "growth constant." The Perin and Williams data are fitted by curves whose growth constants are .0185 and .0180, i.e., very nearly the same.

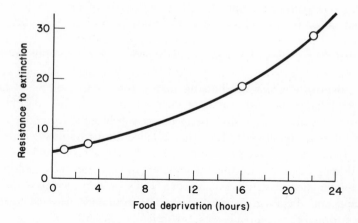

Fig. 6-2. Perin's data showing how resistance to extinction depends upon deprivation conditions (D). (From Perin, 1942)

Let us consider a little more rigorously the functional properties Hull gave the drive construct.

THE FINAL FORM OF HULL'S DRIVE CONSTRUCT

The drive construct in Hull's system was defined by a set of hypothesized relationships which may be briefly outlined here for purposes of exposition.

1. *Antecedent Conditions of D.* Drive is to be anchored by tying it on the antecedent side to the organism's physiological needs. The only specific case which Hull worked out in any detail was hunger, and by hunger he usually meant some number of hours of food deprivation. Needs were supposed to make themselves known to the organism by means of specialized need receptors which were sensitive to the physiological conditions that produce drive.

2. *Drive Stimuli.* Although the same physiological conditions that produce drive are also credited with producing characteristic stimulus effects, these drive-related stimuli affect behavior only by their ability to acquire habit strength; they have no effect at all upon the organism's motivation, per se. By this stratagem Hull retained in his explanatory model virtually all the features of the earlier stimulus theory of motivation, and added to it all the implications of the new drive construct. On the one hand, each of the drive-producing conditions is supposed to be accompanied by a characteristic drive stimulus, S_D, which can give direction to motivated behavior; but on the other hand, drive itself is something other than a stimulus and cannot direct behavior.

The distinction here between the eliciting power of those stimuli which accompany drive and the energizing effect of drive itself is conceptual rather than empirical. It is never possible to have more than circumstantial evidence for the distinction. Some circumstantial evidence is provided by the part of Perin's results shown in Fig. 6-2. Hull assumed here that approximately one-half of the behavior strength obtained under 22-hr. deprivation was attributable to the contribution of S_D to habit strength. Under the lower hours of deprivation the relative contribution would be considerably less since performance was being tested under somewhat different stimulus conditions than applied during training.

3. *Independence of Drive and Habit.* D and $_sH_R$ are independent, and although neither one alone is manifest in behavior, their multiplicative combination determines behavior. Hull's primary evidence for this principle was the Perin-Williams data. The distinction between learning and performance was already well established, however.[4]

4. *Energizing Effect of Drive.* Drive is to be tied on the consequent side by several effects upon behavior. The most fundamental of the hypothesized behavioral effects is the energizing of behavior. The difference in response strength found by Perin and Williams under 3-hr. and 22-hr. deprivation respectively represents a difference in the activation of presumably the same given habit. The activation or energizing role of drive can be manifest in any behavior—in the performance of learned instrumental acts such as running in a maze; in the readiness to engage in certain forms of consummatory activity, such as eating; and in an increase in the organism's general activity level, such as running in an activity wheel.

5. *Reinforcing Effect of Drive Reduction.* Drive is also to be tied on the consequent side to behavior by means of the hypothesis that drive reduction is the underlying event characterizing all reinforcing states of affairs.[5]

6. *Generalized Character of D.* Drive is nonspecific; there is only one drive, D, and though it may be produced by food deprivation, water deprivation, electric shock, or whatever, and even though these different drive-producing conditions may produce different stimuli, they all contribute alike (although perhaps in different degree) to D. Hence D cannot direct behavior; it can only energize. All of the steering of behavior is done associatively by stimuli. Hull cited Perin (1942) once again in

---

[4] See Chapter 9. All of these hypothetical properties of D will be spelled out in more detail and put in their proper theoretical contexts in the following chapters; they are just being listed and defined here.

[5] Hull evidenced some doubt about the sufficiency of drive reduction as the basis of reinforcement. In 1943 he noted that for classical conditioning and for escape learning, the *onset* of the reinforcing stimulus might be the critical element in reinforcement, even though this was accompanied by a momentary increase in drive.

support of the generalized drive effect. Note that extrapolating from Perin's data points (Fig. 6-2) back to 0-hr. deprivation we can expect there would still be some resistance to extinction. Hull attributed this residual behavior potentiality to the miscellaneous sexual, fear, and exploratory tendencies that would persist in the situation in the absence of hunger and maintain the hunger-learned behavior.

7. *Individual Differences in D.* We may expect that one individual might be characteristically more or less motivated than others in his group. For a given standardized set of drive-producing conditions there ought to be consistent individual differences which hold across the various response consequences of drive intensity. Such individual differences would be apparent across different test situations, and might even have some generality across different drive-producing conditions. Hull did not make explicit his thoughts on individual differences in 1943, but it seems clear from his other writings (Hull, 1939, 1945) and from the writings of his students (e.g., Spence, 1956) that there ought to be individual differences in D.

No one of these relationships taken by itself provides a definition of drive. Hull's different hypothetical relationships comprise a network which interrelates all the theoretical constructs of the theory, so that the whole ensemble must be defined at once. For example, the Perin-Williams results portray the functional properties of D and $_sH_R$ together; nothing can be asserted about either D or $_sH_R$ without making at least some tentative assumptions about the other. Recall too that in the preceding interpretation of the Perin-Williams data we had to make certain assumptions, such as that learning effects are more nearly permanent than motivational effects. Fortunately, we need not be concerned here with an analysis of Hull's constructs at this level.[6]

Another way to describe the situation is to point out that many of these properties of drives are syntactical. Only one property, viz., antecedent connection with need, has a clearly semantic character, since only it relates D directly to observable events. None of the hypothetical properties that point to the behavioral consequences of drive can be semantic in any simple sense because all of the effects of D and $_sH_R$ are mediated

---

[6] Although it might be interesting to determine just what assumptions Hull made at this presystematic level, we have more urgent things to do. Hull's presentation was not entirely consistent from a purely logical point of view; and it is not too difficult to document inconsistencies, some of them potentially quite serious (Koch, 1954). Hull's systematic presentations are also marred by his frequent casual references to events going on in the nervous system. The theory itself in no way depends upon such references, however, and it would perhaps be better just to omit mention of any possible surplus meaning that his constructs might convey in the physiological area. (The one exception is the antecedent anchoring of D to need; this is an essential linkage.) Accordingly, we will give Hull the benefit of any doubt regarding the logic of his presentation and regarding his personal faith in the reality status of his constructs; we will confine the discussion to the structure of the theory itself.

through a chain of further hypothetical linkages involving two kinds of inhibition, behavioral oscillation, and the various response measure transformations. We will simplify these relationships as much as possible, as Hull and his students did, when looking at the particular relationships involving drive. The Perin-Williams experiment, for example, was run with distributed trials to minimize inhibition effects and made use of large numbers of animals to provide stable means of the oscillation function. This experiment thereby affords a relatively straightforward picture of the $D \times {}_sH_R$ relationship, and it is reasonably safe to interpret it accordingly. In the case of some other motivation studies, however, we shall see that inferences about the motivational variables involved are quite unjustified. But usually we will not have to be caught in the full complexity of the theoretical model, which is considerably greater than is suggested by just those relationships that involve D. We will be concerned in the next few chapters primarily with the seven hypothetical properties of drive considering them more or less in isolation from the rest of the system. Certainly it is not our purpose to evaluate or even to examine Hull's whole theoretical structure; we are addressing our present discussion only to his construct D.

It may be noted that some of these functional properties of D are more fundamental than others in the sense that they reflect broader consensus about what conceptual properties a drive construct should have. No doubt the most fundamental hypothetical property in this sense is the energizing function. It represented the rather commonly held view that drive should be like a force which makes behavior happen. Hull's principle that D energizes habit structures rather than energizing behavior directly was a real innovation, however—one which accumulated evidence has continued to justify. There was also relatively little general disagreement, at first, with Hull's formulation of the relationship between need and drive, or of the connection between drive and drive stimuli. On the other hand, a great deal of comment and research was generated by the proposition that drive reduction constituted primary reinforcement. Considerable concern was also evident about the strategy of making drive general, i.e., not specific to the particular source of drive, and independent of habit. For many theorists, the basic motivational agency should give direction as well as energy to behavior. Therefore there was some feeling that drive should be plural, and that the various specific drives should be considered as learned. One of the things the hungry animal learns, it could be argued, for example, is to be hungry, and this hunger necessarily is specific to, and directs the animal to, food. Because of the unsettled status of this argument, and the absence of experimental data bearing on it, Hull's postulation of a generalized drive construct may be regarded as the boldest step in his theorizing about motivation.

Hull's long-range plan was to build a theory, a mathematical model for the explanation of behavior. Where empirical regularities were well-established, for instance in the area of classical conditioning, this material was incorporated; and where adequate data were lacking, as was the case in the area of motivation, tentative extrapolations were made from what was available. The important consideration for Hull was the integrity of the complete system. So, whereas it would have been a simple matter to define drive by means of a rigid semantic linkage (as Warden et al., 1931, attempted to do), e.g., so much D for so many hours of food deprivation, he chose instead to leave this particular relationship open for future determination and indicated merely that D would increase according to some as yet unknown function of hours of food deprivation. This strategy permits the theorist to develop the syntactical properties of the model without having to wait for solutions to all the semantic problems. Drive is that which has the hypothesized properties, it is therefore theoretically something other than just an attribute of behavior, or an antecedent condition of behavior, it is in fact a theoretical construct in the technical sense discussed in Chapter 1.

There are, of course, hazards in this type of theorizing. First of all, the propositions, the hypothetical functional relations between terms, have to be empirically testable if the theory is to have any value. This does not mean that any given proposition must be directly and immediately confirmable empirically—this is not possible with propositions of the type we are discussing—but only that the theory be tied semantically at various points to observable events so that it can be established whether observation corresponds with what is derived from the whole structure of the theory.[7] Lewin too had a theory, a syntactical structure, for the explanation of behavior; but, as we saw in Chapter 3, he failed to provide sufficient contact between theoretical constructs and empirical constructs. Hull's model was much better anchored. Stimulation can be followed from the external object, through the receptors, into the nervous system, and precisely correlated with the S in $_sH_R$. Similarly, the responses that the theory predicts are generally defined so that they can be observed.[8] In the case of drive we have another contact with the manipulable and ob-

---

[7] This kind of approach leads to what Deutsch (1960) has called a structural explanation. Deutsch contrasts such explanations with those which simply cite a phenomenon as a member of a class of similar phenomena which regularly behave in the same way. (This is probably the point Lewin was trying to make in distinguishing between Aristotelian and Galilean explanations.) "Structural explanation" is a good name for it. Unfortunately Deutsch derives the name from the notion that theoretical constructs are guesses at the underlying causal *structures* (again following Lewin). I would use the same phrase to indicate that the explanation flowed from and depended only upon the syntactical *structure* of the theory.

[8] This is not to say that there are not problems in giving the stimulus and the response appropriate definitions; certainly S-R psychology can be defended on this score, but this is not the place to do it.

servable environment—physiological need. Hull's plan was to submit the theory for test, filling in both the semantic and syntactical relationships as the relevant data became available, modifying or even abandoning hypotheses when the data required.

A second hazard in this type of theory construction is that the theorist can well expect to have his hypotheses attacked by others, both on conceptual and on empirical grounds. When a theorist makes as many tentative proposals, or guesses, as Hull did, and reaches as far beyond the accumulated knowledge as Hull did, he can be sure that many of his hypotheses will be experimentally invalidated. It was in this connection that Hull revealed a unique, or at least rare, virtue. He constantly put himself in the position where he could be proven wrong because he believed that was how he could best serve his science. The next few chapters show something of the magnitude of this service and of our debt to Hull.

OVERVIEW

We have already devoted a considerable part of this book to just laying a conceptual and historical background for our main task which is to analyze the application of motivational concepts in contemporary behavior theory. We may profitably pause at this point to summarize some of the highlights of what we have already seen, and to anticipate some of the main features of the terrain we are about to explore.

Retrospect. All systematic explanations of behavior are set against the perennial background of rationalism. The traditional position of rationalism asserts that a man's behavior is explained by personal and private events going on in his mind. This position persists because it has the support of the clergy, our legal institutions, and, indeed, most of the institutionalized parts of our culture. This variety of explanation seems to be particularly popular among those who wish to attribute praise or blame to others. In order to hold men personally responsible for their actions the rationalist typically denies, or at least fails to recognize, that behavior itself may be lawful.

One ancient alternative to the rationalist position is the mechanistic doctrine which maintains that man is either like a machine or, in fact, is a machine. The mechanist asserts that he can account in principle for all behavior by means of the laws that have been found to apply in physics and in biology. The phenomena of psychology are then reduced to the phenomena already known (and presumably explainable) in these other sciences. The faith that the laws from other areas of science can be applied equally well to the explanation of behaving organisms no doubt accounts for the strong physiological orientation which persists in psychology. The great shortcoming of this variety of explanation is that so far it remains a faith; it fails to recognize that progress in the development of the different sciences depends upon the development of theoretical models in each science.

Another alternative to the rationalistic position is that approach which although it also attributes man's behavior to mental events differs from rationalism in that it attempts to explain how the mind works. Historically, the most important development of this sort has been that of the British associationists, starting with Hobbes and Locke. Laws of association were proposed which led toward the end of the last century to the systematic study of the contents of the mind. William James represents another variation of this same general type of approach. The most serious limitation of this approach lies in the difficulty of studying the mind systematically.

Many of our current motivational concepts have come to us out of the compromises which have been effected between the preceding varieties of explanation. Thus, the mechanist has frequently urged hedonism as an explanatory principle. The critics of the mechanistic position have long pointed to the incongruity of the mechanist explaining some behavior on the basis of a hedonistic principle which is fundamentally mentalistic. On the other hand, although the rationalist would like to be able to explain all behavior on the basis of the rationality of the individual, he has been forced to recognize the existence of instinctive behavior, i.e., behavior that appears to be automatic, and even machine-like.

The resolution of these apparent incongruities has led, gradually and painfully to be sure, to a new variety of explanation of behavior. Hedonism with Spencer, and particularly with Thorndike, was no longer a principle of mental life but merely a regularity of behavior. At about the same time (after McDougall's ill-fated attempt to make instincts more mentalistic) the instincts lost their mechanical connotation and became, again, merely a feature of behavior. More specifically, the concept of instinct became through the efforts of Tolman, Craig, and others merely a recognition of the fact that behavior frequently occurred in a manner that made it look as though it were purposive.

One characteristic of this transitional period was the emergence of what constitutes almost a new variety of explanation which was based upon the premise that behavior is explained by the operation of underlying *forces* within the organism. These forces themselves had a compromise character in that they were merely analogous to physical forces; they were said to be psychological forces. This conception of motivating forces had first been proposed by Freud who made them mentalistic, or at least psychological, but denied that they were either rational in character (as the will had been) or even that they were wholly available in awareness to the individual upon whom they operated. Later theorists, such as Lewin, took what may have been a step backward in asserting that the individual always perceived his psychological forces. However, Lewin softened this assertion somewhat with the contention that forces made themselves known to the individual by making certain objects (those to which the forces were directed) of perceived value to the individual. What he perceived was the value of the goal, not the force itself. Those who, like the ethologists, were particularly interested in the explanation of animal behavior have also urged that behavior be explained in terms of forces. Although the proponents of the psychological-force doctrine have argued that a static or purely structural account of behavior is inadequate, the situation actually seems to be that as we discover more about the structure of behavior the less adequate and certainly the less necessary a concept of force appears to be.

The 1920s was the time of transition during which many of these changes came about. At that time psychology became the study of behavior rather than the study of the mind. Our basic motivational concepts had by that time been formulated, at least roughly. Hedonism had become translated into what we call reinforcement. The instincts had been translated into what we call drives. Most important, traditional speculation about the behavior of organisms had given way to experimentation. It seems that when the old simple explanatory principles became translated into behavioral terms so that for the first time they were testable, psychologists rushed to their laboratories to begin testing them. At first motivation was "measured" in terms of the tendency of an animal to approach appropriate goal objects, in terms of certain localized sensations, in terms of the overall level of general activity, or in terms of the organism's behavioral adaptation to particular needs imposed upon it. In all of these instances the formulation was found to be too simple; none of these early formulations of the 1920s was able to cope adequately with the increasing diversity of the behavioral phenomena that were being discovered.

In retrospect, it seems that all of the traditional explanations and some of the early explanations of the modern period suffered from oversimplicity. What was being sought was a single rule, principle, or concept that would suffice to explain all behavior. But the behavior of organisms is too complicated for such an approach to succeed. It now seems likely that what is necessary is a theory, or if you like, a model, of behavior.

We can say with some certainty what the properties of an adequate theoretical model would be. It must have some minimum amount of syntactical complexity. That is, it must have at least a certain richness of hypothetical relationships to give structure to the model. It must also have a number of semantic relationships, i.e., relationships connecting the theoretical or unobservable terms of the model to terms which are observable. Thirdly, an adequate model must have among its terms some which already are, or which readily can be translated into everyday language so that we can show without too much difficulty what it is we are talking about. It is only if it meets this third criterion that we have any possibility of testing the model empirically, and testability more than anything else is what makes a theory valuable.

So far in psychology we have had only one such theoretical structure (if we consider the variations upon it as variations and not as separate theories in their own right), and this is the theory proposed by Hull (1943). Hull's theory of behavior, when appropriately stated, involves no assumptions about an underlying reality; it does not require us to make any assumptions about what is going on in the physical or biological world, or in the mind of the organism. It consists simply of a set of relationships among terms, some of which are directly observable and others of which are not. But it specifies or hypothesizes what these relationships are; and it entails sufficient syntactical complexity and semantic niceties to make it possible on the one hand to generate from the model many predictions of how behavior should occur under particular conditions, and, on the other hand, to test the model for its adequacy.

Prospect. We shall not consider in any detail all of Hull's theory, but only those aspects that relate directly to the problem of motivation. First we will consider the accumulated evidence that bears directly upon the hypothetical properties of Hull's drive construct D.

We may identify in Hull's theory seven propositions which relate to D:

1. *Antecedent Conditions of D.* Drive is supposed to be directly related to an organism's physiological needs. In Chapter 7 we will consider some of the problems that are involved in specifying these relationships systematically. We will find that it does seem possible to find relationships between many of the needs of organisms and certain invariant properties of behavior.

2. *Drive Stimuli.* Although all of the conditions that produce drive are said to produce characteristic stimuli as well, drive itself is not to be identified with these stimuli. We will see in Chapter 9 that a good deal of research has been directed to locating these alleged drive-related stimuli, or to obtaining circumstantial evidence that they exist. And we will discover that such stimuli have been extremely difficult to localize. Most of the experimental evidence seems to point not to drive stimuli but to the crucial role played by incentive motivation factors in motivated behavior.

3. *The Independence of Drive and Habit.* Although neither drive nor habit is manifest in behavior, their multiplicative product does determine behavior. In Chapter 9 we will consider the evidence that has been addressed to this proposition and we will find that, in effect, the proposition is untestable. The lack of decisive evidence either to support or to discredit this principle does not leave the issue in a state of suspension however since, as was the case with the other associative property of

drive, the connection with drive stimuli, the evidence points to the viability of alternative formulations. The ultimate effect of such evidence, then, is to lessen the utility of the drive construct.

4. *The Energizing Effect of Drive.* The most fundamental single property of drive is its hypothetical activating effect upon habits. The evidence here, and there is a great deal of it, leads to no simple conclusion. As we will see in Chapter 8, much evidence provides unquestionable support for the energizing principle; but there is also an abundance of evidence not in line with the theoretical prediction. The resolution of the discrepancy has had two important consequences, one is that it has forced experimenters to consider much more carefully the structure of behavior, and second, as behavior becomes better understood we have discovered a variety of ways for accounting for what appears to be an energizing effect of drive without invoking the energization principle.

5. *The Reinforcing Effect of Drive Reduction.* Drive reduction is said to constitute the sole basis of primary reinforcement. This principle has attracted a great deal of attention and again the evidence is somewhat contradictory. Although the principle appears to be a good first approximation, there are abundant exceptions to it.

6. *The Generalized Character of D.* Drive is hypothesized to be nonspecific and nondirectional. Therefore different sources of drive should summate or substitute for each other. The evidence bearing on this proposition is clearly against it, as we shall see in Chapter 10.

7. *Individual Differences in D.* If we could safely infer characteristic individual differences in drive this would provide considerable support for the construct. The small amount of evidence that is available, however, points not to individual differences in D but rather to differences in the associative determinants of behavior.

In Chapter 11, the last chapter addressed directly to the drive construct, we will look at the extensions that have been made to what are called learned drives, such as fear and frustration. We will find once again that the drive construct and its theoretical properties do not seem adequate for the task. The conclusion therefore is inescapable, both in the case of the primary sources of drive and in the case of the acquired drives, that Hull's drive construct cannot do the job that we had hoped it would be able to do. What we will learn from this rather lengthy analysis of the data bearing upon drive theory is that it is necessary in the explanation of behavior to pay a great deal of attention to the structure of the behavior being explained, i.e., to determine just what stimuli control it, what responses are in fact occurring, and what are the sources of reinforcement. We will find that when these structural features of behavior are known they provide an adequate enough account that little more is added by invoking the drive construct.

Finally, in the last chapters of the book we will examine in some detail some alternatives to drive theory. We will look at the various types of incentive theory that have been proposed—those which are motivational in character as well as those which are purely associationistic or structural. We will look at the evidence from secondary reinforcement, avoidance, and punishment studies and see that in all these areas current findings are leading us in the direction of reinforcement theory and away from motivation theory. We will conclude with a look at the concept of reinforcement itself and some of the implications of this concept for contemporary behavior theory.

7

ANTECEDENT

CONDITIONS OF DRIVE

❖❰❰

> . . . *It has been assumed that behavior goes off, in the last analysis,*
> *by virtue only of certain final physiological quiescences, which are*
> *being sought, or of certain final physiological disturbances which*
> *are being avoided.*
>
> E. C. TOLMAN

A number of related events occur when an animal is deprived of food. There are changes in the blood, in the nutritional state of the body's cells, and in a host of metabolic processes. There are also a number of changes in the central nervous system which lead to further alterations in the animal's body chemistry and even to changes in its behavior. Any definitive statement about hunger motivation must indicate which of these events, or what combination of them is most simply and directly tied to the behavior consequences we are interested in. When this is done for hunger and for the other sources of drive, D will be anchored on the antecedent side.

The antecedent anchoring of D is not a simple matter. It cannot be done in isolation because in testing any one part of the total definition of D at least some tentative assumptions have to be made about the other parts of the definition. Anchoring D on the antecedent side is thus ultimately as large a task as confirming the whole structure of the drive theory of motivation. In practice most psychologists have done what Hull did, formulate certain hypotheses about drive-producing conditions and about how to measure the resulting drive strength, and then see if these hypotheses could be maintained in the face of accumulating evidence. In the specific case of hunger (which has received more attention than any other type of motivation) the usual strategy has been to relate D directly to hours of deprivation, thereby bypassing the question of what physiological effects of deprivation produce drive. We will see in the present chapter, however, that enough evidence is now available to indicate that this is not a particularly useful convention; the animal's weight loss seems to have much more to recommend it than deprivation time as an index of hunger.[1]

We will consider thirst also and discover again that in spite of its frequent use hours of deprivation is probably not the best possible antecedent determinant of thirst-produced drive. Then we will see that in the case of other sources of drive it has been extremely difficult to find *any* set of antecedent conditions that can reasonably be said to produce drive. Finally we will consider the problem of quantifying or scaling drive.

Throughout this chapter, while the antecedent conditions of drive are being scrutinized, the equally important question of how to measure drive on the consequent side will be held in abeyance. A number of different response measures will be cited in the discussion, so that the question of consequent anchoring can be left open for systematic consideration in subsequent chapters.

HUNGER

Procedurally, hunger is produced by limiting an organism's food intake. Deprivation may be continuous, i.e., food may be totally withheld up until the time the animal is tested or until it dies (terminal deprivation). Under continuous deprivation the animal's deficit increases continuously so that the animal may only be tested once at a given stage. The animal's hunger-produced drive also, presumably, increases continuously, although most behavior measures show decrements if deprivation is continued past a certain point. The generality of this latter effect led Hull (1952) to postulate an inanition factor which progressively reduces the effective

---

[1] Hence, if we are to speak unambiguously about these matters we must be careful to distinguish between drive and the conditions that produce it. I will sometimes use Brown's (1961) phrase "drive-producing condition," sometimes the simpler phrase "drive condition," and sometimes merely hunger or thirst or whatever the particular conditions are, to refer to the antecedent conditions. I will refer to the physiological state correlated with a particular drive condition as the "drive state," and let "drive" stand alone only when it is clear that what is meant is Hull's behaviorally defined construct, D.

value of D. Unfortunately there has been almost no systematic research on inanition effects to permit us either to confirm or reject Hull's postulation of a general demotivating effect of hunger-produced debilitation.

Deprivation may also be intermittent, i.e., food may be alternately withheld and made available. With an appropriate schedule of feeding, animals may be maintained more or less indefinitely at a more or less constant stage of deprivation. Maintenance schedules make it possible to test animals repeatedly under, say, 23-hr. food deprivation. The practical advantages of such a procedure are apparent, and it is not surprising that maintenance schedules are widely used. But such schedules leave the animal's state of deprivation rather inadequately defined; it is now apparent that other, more direct indices of the drive state may prove more serviceable. Specifically, the evidence we are about to consider indicates that the principal determinant of the animal's hunger motivation is its weight loss.

It should be noted that in the present chapter and throughout the book when reference is made to hunger we will be speaking about general hunger, the hunger that results from a deficiency in total caloric intake. Possibly general hunger is a misnomer because what it may involve is a hunger specifically for calories. If this is the case, then what is called general hunger is really only one of a number of known specific hungers. Young (1949) and Hall (1961) give a good introduction to this difficult problem area and the scattered literature.

Some Properties of Maintenance Schedules. In some experiments reported rather briefly Hebb (1949) noted that upon being deprived and offered food for the first time, rats ate very little, not enough to make up their food deficit, and not even enough to sustain them through to the next day without further weight loss. Hebb also reported that after 9 or 10 days of successive testing rats would eat enough wet mash at one time to maintain themselves until the next day. These findings, confirmed by Ghent (1951), suggest that the animal's tendency to eat in a given situation at a given time is as much related to its past experience as to its current deprivation.

Subsequent studies (Hall et al., 1953; Lawrence & Mason, 1955; Reid & Finger, 1955) indicate that the naive animal needs a period of at least approximately two weeks to reach a stable level of activity-wheel running and/or food intake. During this two-week period the animal's food consumption rises markedly at first and then more gradually until a stable maximum is reached. At the same time the animal's weight drops off sharply and then more slowly until, by two weeks or so it too reaches a relatively stable value. Capaldi and Robinson (1960) report that rats that have been on a daily maintenance schedule for 10 days run significantly faster in an alley and make significantly fewer errors in a T maze than rats with the same current deprivation but lacking the prior deprivation experience.

There is nothing really new in these findings. In fact, it had been the practice for some time to put animals on a maintenance schedule for several days prior to putting them into an experimental situation in order to obtain "adaptation to the feeding cycle" or "habituation." This procedure guarantees that the animals will be motivated; unfortunately, it also disguises the nature of the motivation. Is the result of being on a one-hour-a-day schedule merely to eliminate prior eating habits? Or is the animal changed by virtue of the fact that it receives a number of potent reinforcements? Does r_G become conditioned to external cues? Or is the animal merely being brought down to a reduced body weight?

Ramond et al. (1955) have found that it makes some difference in the rat's running speed in a simple instrumental situation whether its maintenance has been on the basis of a limited amount of time per day in which to eat, or whether it was given a limited amount of food per day to eat (see also Moll, 1959). It was also found to make a difference whether the animals were male or female. Unfortunately, Ramond et al. made no allowance for the initial differences in weight of males and females, nor were the limited amounts and limited times adjusted to produce any sort of equivalence. Although the different groups show marked differences in performance when hours deprivation was held constant, there must have been a fairly impressive correlation between performance and weight loss across the different groups.

It looks then as though the results obtained with a variety of response measures show an erratic relationship when considered just as a function of hours deprivation. On the other hand, these discrepancies all support the hypothesis that hunger motivation is largely a function of weight loss. The results of Ghent (1951) and others on the development of eating, Hall et al. (1953) and others on the development of general activity, Capaldi and Robinson (1960), and Ramond et al. (1955) are all consistent with the proposition that it is the animal's weight (or more correctly, its relative weight loss) rather than the period of time without food which determines its motivation.

The Importance of Weight Loss. Physiologists have recognized for some time that it is caloric deficit (equivalent to weight loss) which primarily governs eating. Adolph (1947) observed that food acceptance and the urge to eat in rats have relatively little to do with any "local condition of the gastrointestinal canal," little to do with the "organs of taste," and very much to do with the "quantitative deficiencies of currently metabolized materials" (p. 122). Adolph reported that when protein food is diluted with water, the animal eats an increased amount of it, and passes the excess water; when protein is diluted with nondigestible cellulose, the animal eats a lot of that, too, and passes the residue. "Within limits, rats eat for calories" (p. 113). This conclusion has been arrived at by a number of other investigators using different testing conditions (Cowgill, 1928; Hausmann, 1932; Harte et al., 1948; Janowitz & Grossman, 1949). Thus, as far as the consummatory response is concerned, we may expect that its occurrence, and presumably, its motivation, would be governed by its consequences so that the animal would maintain normal weight.

The idea that the weight of the animal might be manipulated as an antecedent condition to control its motivation has, however, gained acceptance only rather slowly. There is some precedent in the procedure of varying the size of the rat's meal in order to make him more or less motivated by some behavioral criterion (Stone, 1929; Ruch, 1932; Skinner, 1940). There is also a prior tradition of maintaining constant drive conditions in *pigeons* by controlling their weight. [2] But the credit for first manipulating motivation in rats by maintaining them at a fixed percentage of their ad lib. body weight must go to Stolurow (1951). Stolurow found, of course, that instrumental behavior was a function of weight loss. He also discovered that although it made some difference in the animal's ultimate survival, it made little difference in its instrumental behavior whether the animal was maintained for long periods of time at a fixed percentage of normal ad lib. weight, brought down suddenly to that level, or switched from some other long-maintained level.

Eisman (1956) ran five groups of animals on a discrimination problem. Three of these groups were on a 48-hr. feeding cycle but were run 45, 22, or 4 hr. after the last feeding. A fourth group was on a 24-hr. cycle and was run after 22-hr. deprivation; and the fifth group was 4-hr. deprived (after 44 hr. ad lib.). There was no difference in the discrimination performance of the first three groups, groups which differed markedly in deprivation time but which had comparable total deprivation experience. The fourth and fifth groups, which were matched to two of the previous groups in terms of deprivation time but under conditions of less severe total deprivation, showed poorer performance. Eisman presents no weight data, but it seems extremely likely that discrimination performance was correlated with weight loss.[3] Similar findings were reported by Eisman et al. (1956).

[2] Skinner (personal communication) has indicated that he used this technique right from the beginning of his work with pigeons (in 1941), but he could not say how the practice arose.

[3] Eisman has proposed a two-factor theory of hunger motivation, one factor involving whether the stomach is full or empty, and the other depending upon the animal's long-term food deprivation experience. The short-term effect, lasting perhaps 4 hr. after ingestion of a full meal may act to inhibit the second, and principal, motivation factor, which is evidently highly correlated with, if not identical to, weight loss (see also Eisman et al., 1960). Jensen (1960) presents further evidence for such a two-factor interpretation of hunger. See also Fig. 8-13.

In contrast to the findings of Reid and Finger (1955) and others that the rat requires about 2 weeks on a maintenance schedule to reach stable performance levels, Brownstein and Hillix (1960) found that only 5 days were necessary in their study to stabilize running performance in a 9-ft. alley. Two groups were compared, a group with 15 days prior deprivation experience, and a group with 5 days prior experience. No weight data are reported except that it is noted that the 15-day and the 5-day prior deprivation conditions did not produce a difference in weight. Consequently, it is no wonder that only 5 days were necessary to accommodate to the deprivation conditions. We may presume that Brownstein and Hillix were more generous with food than Reid and Finger (1955) whose animals showed a close parallel between performance and weight loss.

Bolles and Petrinovich (1956) found that it was loss in body weight rather than the nature of the deprivation, the nature of the consummatory activity, or the particular incentive, which determined an apparent difference in instrumental alternation behavior between hungry and thirsty animals. Moskowitz (1959) and Treichler and Hall (1962) have reported that the rat's behavior in an activity wheel appears to be directly (and highly) correlated with its percentage weight loss. Ehrenfreund (1960) has recently confirmed Stolurow's finding that performance may be controlled by controlling weight, and has, in addition, developed an apparatus for the rather precise and systematic maintenance of an animal at a given desired weight.

It looks, then, as though the manipulation of motivation of an instrumental response is more meaningful when it is done in terms of the weight loss of the animal than when it is done in terms of hours deprivation. Whether this newer procedure will continue to enjoy an advantage over the older one in terms of more consistent functional behavioral relationships remains to be seen. There are already certain interpretive difficulties. For one thing, as Ehrenfreund (1959) has pointed out, when the animal is maintained at a given weight loss, its deprivation condition is not related to the amount of food consumed or the rate of consumption at the next eating opportunity (Bousfield & Elliott, 1934; Baker, 1955; Moll, 1959). Ehrenfreund has suggested that the amount of food consumed in a meal is more highly correlated with the amount of weight lost in the immediately preceding deprivation period (e.g., the immediately prior 23 hr.) than the animal's cumulative weight deficit. Ehrenfreund's data suggest that this is the case. However, this is evidently not the whole story since on the first deprivation day, when animals lose the most weight, their consumption is the least. It is the case, however, that once the animal's food consumption has stabilized, its consumption is proportional to the weight loss during the prior interval, otherwise, of course, weight loss would not be stabilized.

The fact remains that the motivating potential of a given weight loss can be balanced off against other motivational variables. In particular, the animal's prior experience with a given level of deprivation may partly determine how effective that level is in motivating the animal's behavior. Moll (1964a) maintained rats 1, 5, 10, or 20 days at either 80% or 90% of normal body weight and found increasing bar-pressing rate with increasing experience of deprivation. This effect was small, however, and did not obscure the overall difference between 80% and 90% animals. On the other hand McMahon and Games (1964) gave their animals much more handling and apparatus experience and did find a washing out of the difference between 80% and 90% animals. Such findings are not inconsistent, however, with the proposition that percentage weight loss is the best antecedent index of the hungry rat's drive strength; results such as those of McMahon and Games only show that no single antecedent index of drive strength can be expected to be perfectly correlated with behavior strength.

A second problem arising from considering weight loss as the basis of hunger is whether the base line for estimating the animal's weight loss should be the ad lib. weight prior to deprivation (which is the usual reference) or the weight of the animal had it been allowed to grow at the normal rate. According to the usual procedure, if a study is continued for an appreciable period of time and the animal maintained at, for instance, 80% of its initial ad lib. weight, then the animal might be expected to show gradually increasing motivation. Some of the available evidence suggests that the best reference is to the animal's normal growth weight. Thus, Moskowitz (1959) reports that on the basis of normal growth weight activity-wheel performance is a simple linear function of weight loss; while Ehrenfreund (1960), using the other procedure of taking weight loss relative to the initial weight criterion, found a gradual long-term increase in apparent motivation. However, when Davenport and Goulet (1964) adjusted the weights of animals to constant values of 80% or 90% of an ad lib. (and growing) control group, they found a gradual loss of motivation over an extended period of testing. The optimum procedure for constant motivation might well be an adjustment to some compromise between initial weight and the normal growth weight.

A third problem with regard to using weight loss as the antecedent motivating condition is that there are discontinuities and individual differences in weight, even in inbred strains of rats (Kaplan et al., 1959). In adult animals of the same age it is usually found that the heavier ones lose relatively more weight on either a fixed-time or fixed-amount maintenance schedule, although there are individual differences in this as well. More important is the gross difference in weight loss under a given set of deprivation conditions as a function of age (Stone, 1929). Campbell et al. (1961) weighed rats of different ages after a given number of hours deprivation and found that younger animals do lose weight at a faster rate than the older ones, and that younger animals die sooner in terminal deprivation. However, Campbell et al. found that all animals died at about the same relative weight loss, 43%; and if deprivation time was translated into time relative to expected survival time, then all of the weight loss curves for all animals became neatly superimposed (see Fig. 7-1). This solution of the problem of differential weight loss with age

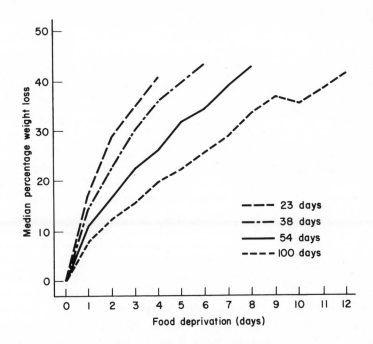

Fig. 7-1. Percentage weight loss of rats of different ages as a function of continuous food deprivation. Weight loss is taken relative to initial weight. (From Campbell et al., 1961)

was also validated by using another independent measure of motivation, viz., acceptance of quinine in the food (Williams & Campbell, 1961) (see Fig. 7-2).

These data may be refined somewhat by separating the results of males and females; the irregularity in the lowest curve in Fig. 7-1 can be attributed to the survival of males after the smaller females had perished. It also seems that plotting both weight loss and deprivation time logarithmically helps to clarify the relationship between them. Weight loss data of this sort (Bolles, 1965) are shown in Fig. 7-3. The values shown are for weight loss relative to the weights of undeprived (growing) animals

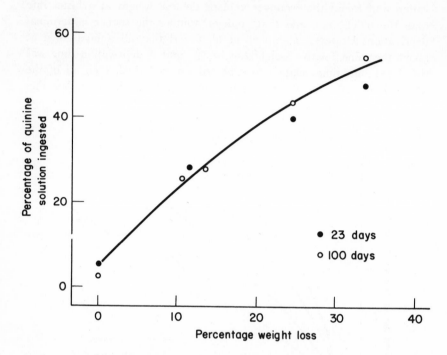

Fig. 7-2. Ingestion of quinine-flavored food relative to the amount of unflavored food consumed by control animals with the same weight loss, as a function of weight loss. (From Williams & Campbell, 1961)

rather than to the weights of the animals before deprivation. Note that females lose weight considerably more slowly than do males of the same weight (but faster than males of the same age). The curious reversal between the top two curves results from the fact that 27-day-old rats grow so much faster than 19-day-old ones.

Such data tempt one to start fitting equations; the percentage weight loss is given by $(260/W_0) h^{.71}$ for males, and $(190/W_0) h^{.71}$ for females, where W_0 is the normal weight, and h is hours deprivation (Bolles, 1965). It seems therefore that by the simple expedient of measuring the animal's need for food in terms of *percentage weight loss* we may obtain an index of need, and perhaps motivation, which is independent of the size of the animal.

Physiological Indices of Hunger. Granting that weight loss of the food-deprived animal is a reasonably serviceable index of its need, and that this may be a reasonably serviceable index of its motivation for food, there are still two intriguing questions which ultimately must be answered. One is whether it is possible to bypass the issue of need altogether and correlate the organism's hunger-motivated behavior directly with

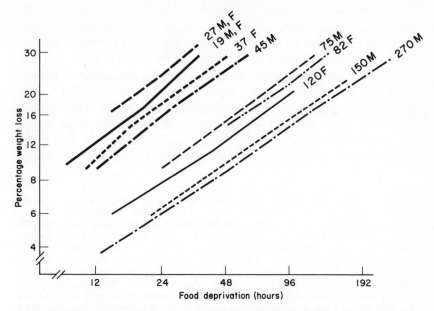

Fig. 7-3. Weight loss of male and female rats of different ages as a function of continuous food deprivation. Weight loss is taken relative to the weight of undeprived controls, and age in days is indicated. (From Bolles, 1965)

some physiological event or state. The second question is whether it is possible by proceeding to a more physiological mode of analysis to find conditions or states of the organism which will provide a better and more direct index of its need for food than the rather gross measure of bodyweight loss. In recent years attention has focused mostly on the first question, and a great deal of research has been generated by the glamorous idea that certain structures or areas in the hypothalamus are directly connected with, and hence determine, the animal's hunger-motivated behavior. The growing volume of work on this problem (reviewed by Anand, 1961; Ehrlich, 1964) offers high promise of a significant breakthrough, particularly as modern workers begin to employ more sophisticated and more diverse behavioral measures, e.g., as they include measures of instrumental behavior along with the more usual measures of consummatory behavior.

It seems likely that as the picture of the neurophysiological machinery becomes complete, it will show us primarily what the consequences of hunger are. It will still be necessary to discover what are the controlling antecedent conditions.[4] At the present stage of our knowledge, the biolog-

---

[4] The efforts to determine the role of the hypothalamus in motivation are often considered as attempts to find an *alternative* explanation of motivation, alternatives which would preclude explanations in terms of organ systems, biochemistry, cellular

ical concept of need of the organism serves as a useful intervening variable between the antecedent conditions of deprivation and the consequent tendency to eat. Let us therefore consider the second question: are there better physiological indices of need for food than weight loss?

It might seem reasonable to suppose that the concentration of blood sugar would provide a useful measure of hunger, since blood sugar, glucose, is the principal source of energy for most bodily activities.[5] This is not the case, however. Verbal reports of hunger in people are not correlated with changes in blood sugar level (Janowitz & Ivy, 1949); there is no systematic change in blood sugar level with continued depriva-

---

physiology—or behavior. We are given the impression that physiologists are either in the neural or "centralist" camp or in the "systemist" camp, and that the two camps are vying with each other to solve the problem. Actually, both types of research are necessary to provide a complete answer. No reasonable centralist would contend that finding out everything about a hunger center in the hypothalamus would solve the problem of hunger; there is still the problem of what the hunger message is and how it gets to the brain. Similarly, finding out all about how the hormonal or neural message gets to the brain doesn't solve the problem; we still have to know how the message comes to mediate appropriate behavior.

[5] *A technical note:* All of the body's demands for energy have to be supplied in the form of food taken at one time or another. (See Kleiber's excellent *The fire of life,* 1961.) The calorie therefore can be taken as a common unit of energy measurement, whether the expenditure of energy takes the form of mechanical work done by or heat generated by the muscles (which may amount to 1000 calories a day in man), chemical energy involved in the operation of bodily processes, including the maintenance of temperature (which may amount to 1500 calories a day) or various kinds of energy expended in the performance of special functions such as growing, excreting and digesting food (another 500 calories a day). The primary immediate source of energy for all kinds of cellular functioning throughout the body is glucose carried in the blood. All of these functions (except muscular work which is quite variable) are obligatory in the sense that they are carried out even when the body as a whole cannot afford the expenditure of energy, e.g., when food is withheld. The blood sugar is the "pocket money" of the system; it is immediately available, but there is not much of it—rarely more than 20 calories at any one time. Even when glucose is ingested, it is promptly converted to glycogen and stored away for later reconversion to glucose. Glycogen "banks" are found in the muscles, which place the most urgent and sudden demands upon the system, and in the liver, which does most of the converting and keeps accounts on all of the transactions. The bodily stores of glycogen rarely amount to more than about 500 calories, so that the liver frequently must draw upon the much larger "reserve banks" of body fat and convert this to glycogen. In better times, the liver converts digested food back to fat and pays off the debt, sometimes with interest. When this huge reserve of energy (from 10,000 calories in a very lean person to 500,000 calories or more in a very obese person) begins to be exhausted, the liver has one more recourse—to draw upon and convert the body's own protein. There is a regular schedule for how this is done. The gonads, spleen, and muscles are called on first; and neural tissue is called up last. This protein is replenished when and if protein is again made available in the diet. So, biologically, hunger means that the liver is recruiting energy from the body's fat reserves (Kennedy, 1953). (A different kind of hunger may result from the recruitment of body protein.) Physiologically, hunger is probably the presence in the blood of some biochemical messenger or hormone which brings about this recruitment. Presumably, when this messenger gets to the hypothalamus, it initiates neurological events which bring about psychological hunger.

tion (Scott et al., 1938) ; intravenous glucose injections do not alter stomach contractions as measured with a stomach balloon (Morrison et al., 1958). Again, intraperitoneal administration of glucose had no more effect upon subsequent food consumption than the administration of a like amount of nonnutritive substance (Janowitz & Grossman, 1948). Nor does injection of insulin, which produces a rapid and marked drop in blood sugar level and a prompt onset of stomach contractions, lead to reports of increased hunger in humans (Janowitz & Ivy, 1949), or to increased food consumption in rats (Morgan & Morgan, 1940a).[6]

There is considerable controversy over the interpretation of these findings, so that it is still possible to defend a modified "glucostatic" theory of hunger (Mayer, 1953, 1955), particularly if attention is directed not at the overall glucose concentration but at the difference between arterial and venous glucose concentrations, which provides a measure of the cellular demand for energy. On the other hand, it is not surprising that blood sugar is maintained at a relatively constant level; it is the business of the liver to keep it constant. At any one time the amount of blood sugar is so low that it must constantly be replenished. Blood sugar should probably be considered only an intermediary between cellular demand and the more substantial sources of energy.

More in keeping with present knowledge of the physiology of hunger is the idea that there is a hormone liberated from somewhere in the bloodstream which triggers the physiological adjustments to the deprived state and the behavior appropriate to it, such as eating. Carlson (1916) had provided early support for the hormonal theory of hunger with the report that blood transfusions from a hungry dog to a satiated dog produced stomach contractions in the satiated animal. Subsequent findings have been discouraging, however. For example, Siegel and Taub (1952) and Siegel and Dorman (1954) found that such transfusions failed to affect consummatory behavior.

There are a number of other possible physiological concomitants of food deprivation, some of which have been suggested as possible indices of motivation. For example, Fearing and Ross (1937) have proposed body temperature and Werthessen (1937) suggested the respiratory quotient (which is the ratio of CO_2 exhaled to O_2 absorbed, and hence indicates whether the animal is metabolizing sugar-related sources of energy or fat and protein sources of energy). Others have suggested other indicators such as heart rate and oxygen consumption. Of course, such physiological indicators may derive their validity as measures of motivation from their dependence upon the animal's overall general activity level, rather than from any inherent connection they have with the drive-

[6] Teitelbaum (1961) has reported that rats will gain weight on continued insulin injections, provided they are given enough insulin and provided they can be kept alive.

producing condition itself. That is, some of these physiological measures reflecting the animal's general metabolic condition may be the consequences of motivation rather than the antecedents of it. They could therefore serve as potentially useful indices of drive, but not as antecedent indices.

Malmo (1958, 1959) argues that perhaps that is all we can hope for; it may be virtually impossible to anchor drive on the antecedent side because there are too many other psychological factors also antecedent to motivated behavior for us to isolate the role of the drive conditions. Malmo therefore suggests that we look for invariant physiological consequences of drive, such as oxygen consumption, and measure drive in this manner. Now, while there is little question that physiological correlates of motivation are of considerable interest in themselves, it seems doubtful that they are to be preferred for the description of motivated behavior over the direct observation of the behavior itself. The one advantage that they might have would be as indicators of generalized drive, i.e., D, as opposed to the specific drive-producing conditions. The trouble with this strategy is that these physiological indices seem to vary differentially with the strength of the drive-producing conditions as a function of what these conditions are. For example, body temperature decreases with increasing hunger, but increases with increasing thirst (Brobeck, 1960). Moreover, the attempts to introduce other sources of drive, such as frustration, do not seem to have the effects upon heart rate and the other indices that a theory of generalized drive would indicate (e.g., Gerall & Berg, 1964).

In short, we seem to be left with no prospects in the immediate future for any conception better than anchoring hunger to the animal's need for calories and measuring this by weight loss.

The Scaling of Hunger. A number of findings have been published with the claim that they represent the true relationship between hours deprivation and drive strength. Warden et al. (1931) made such a claim (see Fig. 5-1), and a whole generation of textbook writers seems to have agreed with them. On the other hand, Hull thought that Yamaguchi (1951) had obtained the true scaling of hunger. The claim might also be made for Kimble's data (1951) (see Fig. 8-13) or Bolles' (1962) (see Fig. 8-5). However, any definitive statement of the quantitative relationship between drive strength and response strength must be based upon some solution of what Kimble (1961, p. 110) has called the *psychometric problem.* This is the set of problems arising from the fact that a response, and to some unknown extent the underlying habit, appears to have different strengths when it is measured in different ways. Kimble summarizes some studies in which speed and rate of responding, resistance to extinction, and the amplitude and latency of the response are negligibly and sometimes even negatively correlated (see also Hall & Kobrick, 1952;

Kobrick, 1956). Probably animals can be shaped up through differential reinforcement to show behavior with any topographical characteristics we want (Ferster & Skinner, 1957); we may make an animal respond vigorously or slowly or persistently or whatever through differential reinforcement of these characteristics. The question is whether drive affects different response measures in some "natural" way, apart from possible reinforcing effects.

In addition to the psychometric problem, there is another problem that prevents us from scaling hunger, viz., the failure to settle upon a convention to identify the appropriate antecedent condition. Sometimes it is possible to translate rather simply from experimental reports of the conditions of deprivation to the more meaningful consequences of deprivation, the animal's weight loss, for example by means of the equations given on p. 156. But the translation is not always simple or direct. What is needed is a systematic determination of how weight is lost as a function of various deprivation conditions; data such as those of Campbell et al. (1961), shown in Fig. 7-1, constitute a promising beginning. In the meantime we are required to infer what the animal's hunger might be as a result of the deprivation conditions that have been imposed. In many cases the only inference we can draw is that animals that are more deprived than others are hungrier, so that the most we can say regarding the anchoring and scaling of hunger is that we have an *ordinal* scale of drive. We may assume, for example, that if an animal is deprived of food for 40 hr., it will have a higher drive than if it had only been deprived for 6 hr. Just how much higher we are not able to say now.

Until this problem is solved we have to accept that whenever we attempt to "measure" drive we can learn only how some specific response, or a certain measure of that response, depends upon the conditions of deprivation. We will consider a number of such relationships in the next chapter but by that point we should no longer be tempted to consider any of them the "true" measure of drive.

THIRST

The use of water deprivation to motivate animals has lagged behind the use of food deprivation. This is shown not only by the small number of studies that have been conducted, and by the lack of concern expressed over the conditions produced by water deprivation, but also by the relatively shallow analysis that has been made of the consequent behavior of thirsty animals. Warner (1928), Elliott (1929), Omwake (1933), Skinner (1936a), and Bruce (1937) seem to have been the first to have run thirsty rats. By this time, of course, thousands of hungry rats had been run in hundreds of mazes. We may infer that thirst was thought to be much like any other source of drive. The title of Skinner's study, "Thirst as an arbitrary drive," is indicative of the attitude that thirst was just another drive-producing condition with little to distinguish it from hunger beyond the requirement that a different goal object had to be used.

Just as in the case of hunger, thirst has ordinarily been manipulated by imposing a water deprivation of some number of hours. But just as an animal's hunger motivation appears to be more highly correlated with its weight loss than with hours deprivation, so it may be that water balance is a more direct index not only of the animal's need for water, but also of its thirst motivation. It may be only when factors such as diet, temperature, and other determinants of water balance are equated that hours without water provides any indication of the animal's thirst. In this connection, Robinson and Adolph (1943) say it is "Not the time elapsed (which could be much reduced by heating the dog), but the shortage of water itself which appears to set off ordinary drinking. And not the absolute amount of water but the decrement in the proportion of water to other body constituents (which could be varied by feeding the dog) seems to arouse the drinking" (p. 43). Robinson and Adolph indicate that under typical laboratory conditions the dog starts to drink when it has lost .5% of its body weight in water.

A number of physiologists, such as Wolf (1958), hold that the origin of thirst is central, and that it probably arises from specialized osmoreceptors in the central nervous system. Andersson (1953) and Andersson and McCann (1955) located a drinking "center" in the hypothalamus of the goat. Within one minute of injecting less than .01 cc. of 2% salt solution in this area, animals would start to drink large quantities of water. Andersson (1951) has also reported that electrical stimulation of the lateral anterior hypothalamus produced some of the autonomic functional activities that accompany drinking in goats, such as licking and salivation. Thus, it would appear that these areas in the forward part of the hypothalamus may release drinking behavior in response to local hypertonic conditions, conditions which would result from a general water deficit. There are cases of hypotonic thirst, however, which present certain problems for such an interpretation; but in general, there seems to be little question that animals drink primarily to maintain an adequate water balance (Wolf, 1958).

If we grant that the thirst condition should be defined in terms of cellular dehydration, there still remains the practical problem of how to measure it.[7] Water balance can be assessed by actual measurement of

---

[7] *A technical note:* The body of the typical animal consists of about 70% water altogether, about 70% of which normally resides within the different cells (*intracellular* water). This is the water the cells require for normal functioning. Water and the various solutes pass in and out through the cell membrane which separates the cell from the *interstitial* spaces. Water in the interstitial spaces, which constitutes about 10% of the total body, is a pool, an internal environment, serv-

the body's water content, but the procedure is irreversible, unfortunately. Water deficit can be assessed by measuring the animal's total weight loss. This is the procedure advocated by Adolph (1939) and subsequently widely used by physiologists working with thirst. Campbell and Cicala (1962) have recently reported extensive data on weight loss as a function of the number of hours without water for rats of different ages (Fig. 7-4).

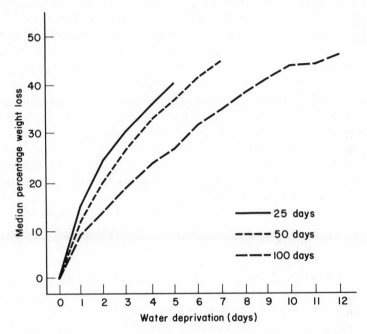

Fig. 7-4. Weight loss of rats of different ages as a function of continuous water deprivation. Weight loss is taken relative to initial weight. (From Campbell & Cicala, 1962)

Notice the similarity between these data and those obtained by Campbell et al. (1961) under similar conditions for weight loss due to food deprivation (Fig. 7-1). Also, as in the earlier hunger study, Campbell and

---

ing the cells. This water comes into the pool by diffusion through the capillaries of the blood stream, which, in turn, receives water transported through the intestinal wall. Some of these processes are reversible so that if hypertonic saline is ingested, it will be partly diluted by water passing into the intestine from the blood stream; some salt will be transported out, however, and will be carried along to the cell membrane, at which point it encounters a barrier. Water will diffuse out of the cells, however, to reduce the extracellular tonicity. The result is cellular dehydration and thirst.

When the animal is deprived of water, there is obligatory loss of water in the feces; more is pumped out in the form of sweat; some is expired; and more diffuses out through the kidneys as they pump sodium, nitrogen, and other materials

Cicala found that converting from absolute time to time relative to final survival made the different age curves coincident. They also found that the quinine suppression scores were an invariant function of weight loss over the different ages, just as they had found in the case of hunger (Fig. 7-2). These results suggest that the weight loss produced by water deprivation may be an optimum measure of thirst-produced drive.

There are a number of interesting questions that arise from the possibility that weight loss may define the strength of both hunger and thirst. One problem is how much of the thirst-produced weight loss represents a water deficit, and how much represents a food deficit incurred by the animal's reduced intake of food? It would seem from Campbell's data and also from the work of Dufort (1963) that the weight loss produced by water deprivation follows very nearly the same course as the weight loss produced by food deprivation. Weight was lost at nearly the same rate and death ensued at nearly the same point. Schmidt-Nielsen et al. (1948) have reported that rats in terminal water deprivation lost body solids almost as fast as they lost water so that they did not become appreciably dehydrated; the percentage of water comprising the total body weight only dropped from 68.5 to 65.5. A proportionate amount of thirst-produced weight loss therefore must be from the loss of protein and fat. Consequently some of this weight loss must represent a general state of malnutrition. Some of the loss represents various bodily processes that go into effect to mobilize water (by the oxidation of fat, for example). Or it may be that the all-important factor to be defended is the relative balance of water to the other body constituents, rather than the absolute amount of water available in the body; as water is lost, a proportion of fat and protein must be lost too (Collier, 1964).

Some of these questions may be answered by research in which environmental temperature is systematically introduced as a variable. It is already known that survival under terminal deprivation varies markedly with environmental temperature (Rixon & Stevenson, 1957; Brobeck, 1960; Campbell, 1964). Moreover, the percentage weight loss at death increases with temperature in hungry rats. Hence, the similarity previously noted in weight loss of hungry and thirsty animals is partly an artifact of the particular laboratory temperature that was used.

---

out of the bloodstream. These losses of water from the extracellular fluid create an osmotic pressure gradient at cell boundaries, just as a surplus of a solute would, and water is drawn out of the cells. Thus, biologically, thirst is cellular dehydration; psychologically, it is probably the dehydration of particular cells in the hypothalamus or the neurological consequences of this dehydration. Procedurally, thirst is what happens when there is not enough water, or too much of some solute, in the extracellular fluid; and this may occur by hypertonic injection, hypertonic ingestion, or obligatory secretion of water. If the extracellular fluids are hypotonic, the kidney just takes the excess out of circulation.

Weight loss can be related much more directly to hours of water deprivation than it can to hours of food deprivation. The reason is that a 24-hr. water deficit can be made up in a single drinking session, whereas, at least for animals as small as the rat, a 24-hr. food deficit cannot be made up in a single meal; successive food deprivations leave a cumulative deficit. Therefore, one of the serious limitations of hunger-maintenance schedules does not seriously affect thirst-maintenance schedules.

There are other possible physiological indices of thirst. Belanger and Feldman (1962) suggested that heart rate could be used as an index of thirst, since they found it to rise continuously with deprivation. However, O'Kelly et al. (1965) gathered together a good deal of evidence to show that heart rate decreases with thirst. Other researchers (e.g., Rust, 1962; Hahn et al., 1962, 1964) have encountered a number of difficulties in trying to find any simple relationship between heart rate and thirst motivation. One of the difficulties is that heart rate is very much a function of the animal's level of activity, quite apart from the antecedent conditions that lead to drive, so that a change in heart rate cannot be attributed with any certainty to physiological events specific to thirst, to "arousal" conditioned to the test situation, to the consequences of the behavior occurring in the test situation, or to the effects of ingesting water. Much of this work with heart rate has been stimulated by Malmo (see the discussion on p. 160), and the same conclusion holds that we found before. To use such response-dependent measures of behavior as indices of drive is to conceive of drive far over on the consequent side, and virtually to eliminate the possibility of anchoring it on the antecedent side. Such a strategy is, of course, possible and perhaps even to be recommended, but it should be clearly recognized that drive, defined in this way, then becomes a very different construct than the one Hull proposed. It becomes, in effect, synonymous with the energy output of the organism, rather than a determinant of the organism's behavior.

One of the most exciting developments in this area is the technique of Novin (1962) with implanted electrodes by which the electrical resistance of an animal's body tissues can be measured continuously without disturbing the animal's on-going activity.[8] Novin placed electrodes in the brain, but there seems to be nothing in his results that would be peculiar

---

[8] Rasmussen (1959) had previously measured skin resistance as a function of deprivation. He observed that a rise in resistance means a loss in sensitivity to electric shock, and that therefore the results of Warner (1928) on grid crossing as a function of thirst may contain an artifact. Kaplan and Kaplan (1962) have described a method for measuring skin resistance through the floor in a free situation, i.e., one in which there are no wires attached to the animal. Resistance data should be able to provide information not only about thirst, but also about autonomic reactivity, emotion, tension, arousal, stress, and drive (Kaplan, 1963; Walker & Walker, 1964).

to neural tissue. Novin reported, using this technique, that general hydration of the body starts almost immediately after water is put into the stomach, much sooner than had been thought. It is as if the extracellular fluids somehow know that water is soon to be forthcoming and therefore are willing to release water to the dehydrated cells. Some mechanism evidently must operate in this manner in order to account for the termination of drinking before any appreciable amount of water has left the stomach.

"Artificial Thirst." The need for water can be produced not only by depriving the animal of water so that water is lost by obligatory secretion in the urine, feces, and perspiration, but also by injecting hypertonic saline solutions. The first observations on drinking as a function of hypertonicity produced by salt injection seem to be those of Gilman (1937). Holmes and Gregersen (1950) and Wayner and Reimanis (1958), developing this procedure further, found that the more salt they injected the more water the animals drank.

Unfortunately for our demands for parsimony, the story doesn't stop there. O'Kelly and Heyer (1948) and Heyer (1951) report that whereas subcutaneous saline injections appeared to increase the rats' motivation as measured by consummatory behavior, instrumental performance was poor, as if the rats were unmotivated. To complicate matters further, O'Kelly and Heyer (1951) found that before the saline-injected animals would appear motivated it was necessary to impose a certain amount of additional deprivation time (several hours) before the test. They proposed a "deprivation-trace" hypothesis, according to which it is not the animal's immediate need state which determines its motivation but rather the duration of the need state. It is as if thirst motivation has to ripen before the animal is really motivated. A similar phenomenon has been demonstrated by Wayner and Emmers (1959) who tested rats in an alley at various times up to 4 hrs. after saline injections. They found that alley running increased markedly as the time of testing was advanced. They state that the animal's water need was constant throughout this period, but it seems more than likely that it increased as the animals lost water in excreting the excess NaCl. More recently, Wayner et al. (1962) have reported anomalous results both in physiological measures of salt concentration of the blood and in drinking behavior when they gave large salt injections. The only conclusion that seems safe at this point is that "artificial" thirst produced by salt injection is different in some respects from thirst resulting from water depletion. Further study should clarify both.

There have been few serious attempts to scale or quantify thirst except in terms of the amount of drinking that occurs under the test conditions. We will see some of the relevant data in the next chapter when we consider the energizing function of drive.

SEX

As soon as we leave hunger and thirst and move on to other sorts of motivation, it becomes more difficult to apply Hull's drive theory. The chief reason for this difficulty in most instances is that D becomes less securely anchored on the antecedent side. This conclusion may seem paradoxical in the case of sex because we know a good deal about the antecedent conditions that control sexual behavior in a number of animal species.[9] The trouble is partly that while these antecedent conditions control behavior which appears to be motivated, the conditions themselves do not seem to goad the animal into activity; they only seem to provide a necessary background for the occurrence of certain highly specific forms of behavior.

Consider the following: Suppose we have a male animal alone busily doing all the diffuse sorts of things that animals of his species characteristically do—he does not "look" sexually motivated. We know, though, that if we were to present him with a female we might get startling changes in behavior. The question is this: What sense does it make to attribute a "sexual drive" to the animal when it is alone? If it makes no sense, if drive is "produced" by the stimulus conditions that control the motivated behavior, e.g., the sight and smell of a female in heat, then what sense does it make to introduce the drive concept? There are just two thin strands of evidence to suggest that the conditions that are antecedent to sexual behavior contribute to D. One is that running in an activity wheel is correlated with hormone concentration. The other is that contact with animals of the opposite sex can reinforce an instrumental response. Both sorts of evidence lead to further interpretive difficulties, as we will see.

One factor that distinguishes species-specific sexual behavior from other kinds of behavior is its dependence upon the presence of hormones, estrogen in the female and testosterone in the male. We will look shortly at some of the data showing the dependence of the primary sexual response, copulation, upon these hormones. But it should be emphasized that even though copulation is itself a complex heterogeneous chain of highly specific reactions, it is only a small part of the animal's total chain of reproductive behavior. After mating, estrogen (and in some species testosterone as well) is inhibited by an increase in the production of the hormone progesterone. At this stage, mating is replaced in the animal's repertoire by nest building and other activities characteristic of gestation. After the young are born, prolactin becomes the dominant hormone and it inhibits all the others. Prolactin gives rise to maternal behavior and

---

[9] The reviews by Beach (1956) and Larssen (1956) are excellent. Young's chapter in *Sex and internal secretions* (1961) is more recent, expansive, and extensively referenced; the book gives a most exhaustive account of the physiology of sex.

parental behavior in general such as nursing in mammals, food gathering in birds, and caring for the young in most species.[10] The whole complex chain of species-specific reproductive behaviors has an entirely different temporal pattern and biological purpose from those of eating and drinking. With hunger, for example, the animal is always either digesting the last meal or looking for or ingesting the next one; the hunger-eating pattern is a continuing adaptation to a continuing problem. The antecedent conditions that motivate the appropriate behavior are, accordingly, relatively easy to find and specify. But sexual behavior is an interlude, an episode that occurs when the occasion for it and the hormonal background necessary for it happen to occur. It is perhaps not surprising then that it is difficult to force sexual behavior into the same model of need $\rightarrow$ drive $\rightarrow$ motivated behavior. Indeed, it is often difficult to conceive of sexual behavior being "motivated" in any sense.

There are two possible approaches, however, that can be followed to force the case of sexual behavior into the mold required by drive theory. We can attempt to find the necessary antecedent conditions either in sexual deprivation or in the presence of hormones. First, we have to find out more about the primary sexual response itself.

Once the male rat begins to mate (and there are marked individual differences in initial latency) he makes a series of very brief encounters involving mounting and intromission at irregular intervals until the first ejaculation. This requires approximately 6 intromissions. Following ejaculation there is a temporary refractory period during which the male appears to be sexually unmotivated.[11] In a few minutes the male again begins to mount. A second series of intromissions, shorter than the first, leads to a second ejaculation. This is followed by further refractory periods, progressively longer, and further ejaculations, which occur after progressively fewer intromissions. Thus, the refractory periods become longer, which suggests that the animal is "running out of" motivation, that he is becoming satiated, whereas the ejaculations are coming sooner with a progressively smaller number of intromissions which suggests that the animal is becoming more and more motivated. Finally the male leaves the female, not because he loses potency, but because he loses interest in her.[12] This ap-

---

[10] See Lehrman's extensive review (1961). One intriguing aspect of reproductive behavior is that while segments of it depend upon specific hormones, the production of these hormones in mammals and especially in birds depends upon the animal's behavior and upon the behavior of its mate and offspring (Lehrman, 1962), so that not only do hormones control behavior, but behavior controls the production of hormones, too.

[11] It has been reported that something like a refractory period occurs in the female rat also. If permitted to, she will leave the scene for an interval after an intromission (Peirce & Nuttall, 1961) and be reluctant to admit the male (Bermant, 1961).

[12] It has been found that substituting a fresh female can suddenly "rejuvenate" a satiated male rat (Fowler & Whalen, 1961; Fisher, 1962; Wilson et al., 1963).

parently paradoxical pattern, and the different consequences of deprivation for the different components of the consummatory act, are interpreted by Beach (1956) as evidence for there being two separate mechanisms, one for arousal, or responsiveness to the female, and the second having to do with intromission and ejaculation performance, i.e., the consummatory act itself. (A similar dichotomy has been discussed by Soulairac, 1952, and Young, 1961.) [13]

It is presumably the arousal mechanism which is correlated with both the animal's instrumental behavior and the initiation of the consummatory behavior. Accordingly, it is the possible contribution of sexual arousal to D that concerns us here, and not the consummatory mechanism itself.

Sexual Deprivation. We can draw analogies between sexual behavior and eating and drinking behavior so as to put sex within the domain of drive theory. We may think in terms of a need (the species needs sex in about the same way as the individual needs food or water). On the antecedent side, we may "deprive" the animal of sexual behavior by withholding mates. Jenkins (1928) found that male rats segregated from female rats for 12 hr. showed essentially full drive strength as measured by the Columbia obstruction-box method, and with deprivation (separation from the female) greater than 24 hr. there began a slight decrease (Warner, 1927). Stone et al. (1935) have argued that since the Columbia investigators had preselected potent males, rather than pooling performance scores of both potent and impotent animals, their results are not representative of sexual motivation in male rats in general. Furthermore, the exclusive use of potent males in the Columbia studies had led to a poor correlation between instrumental and consummatory measures of sexual motivation. Stone et al. showed that when the whole range of individual differences in consummatory behavior was included, a much higher correlation between consummatory and instrumental behavior was found. In contrast with Jenkins' results, Seward and Seward (1940) found that sexual behavior in the male guinea pig increased in strength over several days of separation.

One difficulty with these early studies was the failure to control or

----

[13] Peirce and Nuttall (1961a) found that the duration of intromission rises sharply with successive ejaculations, however, suggesting that the ejaculatory mechanism does undergo some satiation. It has been observed that the time course of the ejaculatory mechanism can be altered by imposing an enforced intercopulatory interval on the male rat (Larssen, 1956; Bermant, 1964) or guinea pig (Gerall, 1958). When the interval is shorter than about 5 min. ejaculation comes with fewer intromissions, whereas with enforced intervals longer than 5 min. the ejaculatory mechanism is depressed, even to the point where with long enough intervals ejaculation may not occur at all. One explanation, based upon the dual mechanism idea, is that following an intromission the arousal mechanism recovers from its refractory period faster than the ejaculatory mechanism, so that the animal is aroused to make a new contact before the ejaculatory mechanism has fully recovered. Then, after a few min., the ejaculatory mechanism begins to fail while the arousal mechanism remains more or less intact.

specify the amount of consummatory behavior that had preceded deprivation. Hence, it is not known how satiated the animals were at the start of the separation. Beach and Jordan (1956) have recommended placing males and females together and letting them mate until a criterion of exhaustion has been met (30 min. elapsed without mounting). Using this criterion, Beach and Jordan tested the performance of male rats after 1, 3, 6, or 15 days of separation. Fig. 7-5 shows the results.

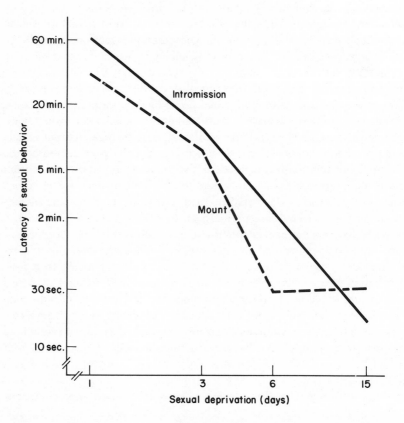

Fig. 7-5. Median latency of mounting and intromission as a function of deprivation of sexual activity. Note that both ordinate and abscissa have been given logarithmic scales. (Data reported by Beach & Jordan, 1956)

No one seems to know what would be the result of "depriving" a female rat of sexual activity. However Beach (1958) has noted briefly that females fail to learn an instrumental response in order to get to a mate.[14]

The Hormonal Background. The second approach to the antecedent

[14] Although Rapp (1963) has confirmed Beach's finding that mating is not reinforcing for the female rat, Bermant (1961) has come to the opposite conclu-

anchoring of sexual motivation is based on the evidence that sexual behavior requires a background of appropriate hormones. Let us look first at some of this evidence.

The patterns of reflective behavior (i.e., species-specific behavior) that constitute female sexual activity, as well as the stimulus conditions that control them, are also relatively well understood, at least for some animals such as the rat and the guinea pig. Sexual behavior in the female appears to consist of a number of reflex patterns of courting or anticipatory behavior, and the primary sexual behavior itself. In the case of each component there are particular postures, locomotory and investigatory movements, all of which occur in a highly predictable way in response to certain features of the male animal's behavior. Stone (1926) has emphasized the immediacy and apparent innateness of these reflex patterns in the female rat; naive females in heat may copulate within a few seconds when placed for the first time with a male. (Beach, 1956, and Larssen, 1956, have made similar observations about males.) One curious feature of this reflexive behavior is that it does not appear to depend upon any particular sense modality. Bard (1936) found that totally decorticate cats showed the complete sequence of female behavior, although they lacked initiative. Bard (1939) found that the pattern of female behavior persisted when the entire genital area was denervated and the sympathetic tracts cut. Indeed, the only simple way to abolish the behavior seems to be to remove the male animal.

Without estrogen none of the female's behavior and none of the physiological changes necessary for the development of her reproductive machinery occur. But with a normal estrogen level (whether it is produced naturally by the ovaries or whether it is given by injection) the mating behavior "runs off." After castration, the female rat's "sex drive" appears nonexistent whether it be measured in terms of receptivity to males, running in activity wheels, or by some physiological index (Beach, 1948; Young, 1961).

In male rats the situation is similar, although sexual behavior seems to be less highly dependent upon the presence of hormones. Thus, male animals that have been castrated as adults gradually, over a period of months, lose their potency and responsiveness (in that order), and it makes little difference whether they were naive or sophisticated at the time of castration (Stone, 1927). Males castrated before puberty, on the other hand, do not show normal sexual behavior as adults. Whether the reflexive patterns are destroyed by castration or prevented from develop-

---

sion. Bermant found that females would press a bar to have a male put into the test arena, although their latency to press was an increasing function of the completeness of the male's previous contact (i.e., mounting, intromission, ejaculation). It is necessary to distinguish clearly between the failure of reinforcement and the female's refractory period in these situations.

ing by castration, they can be reinstated by the administration of testosterone. With injections the male acquires normal responsiveness and potency, in that order (Stone, 1939). Although the male's behavior is, in general, somewhat more dependent upon sensory factors than is the female's, he too can engage in normal sexual activity minus any one or several of his senses (Beach, 1942a, 1947).

Perhaps, then, since sexual behavior is so dependent upon gonadal hormones, the organism's hormonal level might provide a direct measure of its sexual motivation. A nice demonstration of a relationship between testosterone and male sexual behavior has been reported by Beach (1942a). Beach tested for stimulus generalization in male rats, giving them appropriate and inappropriate sex objects such as unreceptive females, males, and animals of other species. Beach found that large amounts of testosterone injected just before a test markedly broadened the range of acceptable sex objects.

There are, however, inherent difficulties with hormonal concentration as an index of drive strength. In Beach's study very large amounts of testosterone had to be injected, whereas it is known that vast behavioral differences in sexual responsiveness occur when there are only slight differences within the normal range of hormonal levels. It has been found that both the male rat (Beach & Fowler, 1959) and the male guinea pig (Grunt & Young, 1952) show marked individual differences in sexual aggressiveness, and that these differences are only in small measure attributable to individual differences in hormonal level. When animals are castrated and then given fixed amounts of hormones the precastration differences in sexual motivation are still evident. Such individual differences are thus apparently not due to differences in hormone level but to differences somewhere in the nervous system.

Consider also that the male becomes refractory after an ejaculation. Where would one look for the sudden drop and subsequent recovery of hormone concentration to account for the loss and recovery of motivation? The refractory period is evidently due to events occurring in the nervous system rather than to hormone depletion. The appearance of sexual motivation seems to depend as much upon the context of the animal's behavior as on any other factor. Studies that have compared instrumental behavior with consummatory behavior (e.g., Denniston, 1954; Schwartz, 1956) find that in spite of the complexity of the latter it proceeds in a much more orderly and predictable manner than the former as the context of the consummatory behavior changes. In conclusion, hormonal conditions would seem to constitute a necessary background but hardly a sufficient condition for sexual motivation. We are left therefore with no substantial set of antecedent sexual conditions which can be said to produce drive.

EXPLORATION

As we move from hunger, thirst, and sex and go on to other drives (or in the Hullian framework, other sources of drive), antecedent anchoring becomes distressingly insecure. Fortunately for the study of behavior, however, our loss of contact with the drive construct in these areas does not interfere seriously with our investigation or understanding of the behaviors themselves.

Pavlov considered exploration to be a reflex; he spoke of "investigatory reflexes." During the 1930s and 1940s exploration was generally regarded as a kind of general activity which was energized by the animal's drive state (we will consider in Chapter 10 whether or not such energization actually occurs). But in 1950, exploration began to be regarded as an autonomous drive (Harlow, 1950; Harlow et al., 1950; Berlyne, 1950). Harlow et al. found that over 12 daily test sessions rhesus monkeys showed increasing virtuosity in working mechanical puzzles. During the course of the 12 days the number of errors made in correctly manipulating the puzzles dropped nearly to zero. Harlow (1953) rejected the idea that such manipulatory behavior has any historical or contemporary basis in physiological motives such as hunger and thirst.[15] He also emphasized the fact that monkeys improve their performance in the absence of food or other irrelevant reward; in fact, Davis, Settlage, and Harlow (1950) found that making the monkey hungry disrupts its puzzle-manipulating ability. This manipulatory behavior is also quite resistant to extinction. On these grounds Harlow postulated a new "manipulation drive." The thing that characterizes such a drive, in contrast with the physiological drives of hunger and thirst, is that the stimuli which arouse it are external (which makes it more akin to sexual motivation).

There are several possible interpretations of Harlow's argument. First of all, he presents no evidence in his earlier studies of any learning other than the increased facility of manipulation itself; the learned behavior which is taken as evidence of the drive is not an instrumental response, as in most instances of learning, but exploration. Admittedly, we have already recognized the phenomena of learning to eat and learning to drink. However, if these were all we had observed about eating and drinking, we surely would not have invented hunger and thirst drives. What Harlow et al. have discovered is that manipulation is one kind of self-reinforcing activity.[16] Subsequently Harlow and others have found

[15] Mason and Harlow (1959) have toyed with the idea that hunger may be an acquired drive derived from exploration! In any case, manipulatory behavior develops normally in monkeys that have had no opportunity to manipulate food objects (Mason et al., 1959). Woods and Bolles (1965) found that this is true of the rat also.

[16] Exploring is one of a number of behaviors whose strength is increased by its

that instrumental behavior can be reinforced by permitting the animal to explore (see below) and, accordingly, Harlow now refers to exploration as a kind of incentive rather than a kind of drive.

Berlyne (1950) attempted to build a conceptual model for exploratory behavior which fit Hull's theory more closely. Berlyne viewed exploratory responses as the consummatory response of a drive, which he called the curiosity drive, the antecedent condition of which was simply novel stimulation. Berlyne assumed, in accordance with Hull's system, that any behavior which led to this consummatory response of exploring would be reinforced, but that after a time something like inhibition of reinforcement would occur and the consummatory behavior, exploration, would stop. Finally, after an interval of time this inhibition would be dissipated and exploration would be renewed.[17]

Montgomery also argued for exploration as an autonomous drive. The principal point of difference between his and Berlyne's positions was that he attributed the termination of exploratory behavior to loss of novelty rather than to inhibition. At first, Montgomery was interested in spontaneous alternation. He reported a study (1951) in the Hullian tradition, explaining the phenomenon in terms of reactive inhibition. But then it was found that the animals varied their behavior independently of the amount of work involved (Montogomery, 1951a), which argued against this interpretation. Further evidence that rats alternated because of an "exploratory tendency" rather than because of reactive inhibition came with the discovery (Montgomery, 1951b, 1952) that rats alternated the places they went rather than the responses they made. Montgomery then reported a pair of transitional studies (1952a, 1953b) concerned with the spontaneous recovery and the generalization of the exploratory tendency, but the purpose was still to try to explore the spontaneous alternation phenomenon. He next found that exploration decreased rather than increased when animals were made hungry or thirsty (1953), and that it failed to change when the animals were prevented from being normally active before the test (1953a). Hence, he concluded that the tendency to explore could not be a manifestation of hunger or thirst motivation or an indication of any "general activity drive," and so it must be an autonomous drive. Subsequently, it was found that fear inhibited rather than facilitated exploration (Montgomery, 1955; Montgomery & Monk-

---

own occurrence (although satiation may decrease the strength of the response). This is, in fact, a tolerably good general definition of consummatory activity: it is self-reinforcing. In fact, this effect provides a reasonably good way to identify the different drive conditions (or different drives, if one accepts the concept of specific drives). Those activities which are self-reinforcing are just the ones we like to engage in, the ones we are motivated for, as Woodworth (1918, 1958) has always emphasized.

[17] Berlyne (1960, 1963) has recently elaborated his position, and in addition, reviewed much current research and theorizing on exploration.

man, 1955); so the tendency to explore could not be explained on the basis of a fear drive, but must, again, be attributed to an autonomous drive to explore. The logic of this conclusion left something to be desired but it was considerably strengthened by the finding (Montgomery, 1954; Montgomery & Segall, 1955) that animals would learn an instrumental response in order to get into a situation where they could explore. Animals learned either a position habit or a black-white discrimination in a T maze when the goal was a Dashiell-type maze, and they learned a reversal when the discriminanda were reversed.

The alternative to the Dashiell-maze "goal" in Montgomery's experiments was a small confining box, and Chapman and Levy (1957) have pointed out that Montgomery's animals might simply have been learning to avoid confinement rather than to approach the exploration situation. Chapman and Levy vindicated the original interpretation, however, by showing that learning also occurred where the two end boxes were the same size, and novelty was produced by changing the color and texture of one of them. Berlyne and Slater (1957) have also found that rats would learn to go to that goal which offered the more complex of two sets of stimuli. Miles (1958) has reported learning in order to explore in kittens. Thus, there seems little doubt that exploration can be considered a kind of consummatory behavior which can serve to reinforce instrumental behavior; on this account we are perhaps justified in considering exploration as a source of drive.

In his interesting review of these matters, Fowler (1965) points out that prior to the discovery of the reinforcing value of exploratory activity there was really little similarity between the new "exploratory drives" and Hull's conception of generalized drive. One difference was that Harlow, Berlyne, and Montgomery had all been speaking about a special, directive drive, a drive to explore, and not Hull's D. Much more in keeping with the generalized drive construct were the formulations of Glanzer (1953, 1958), Myers and Miller (1954), and Brown (1955). This approach emphasizes the aversive side of the coin: Boredom is a source of drive. When the animal is confined to constant stimulation it becomes "bored" or "satiated," and in this state any response which brings the animal into contact with new or different stimuli will reduce drive by diminishing boredom. Finding that novel stimuli were reinforcing therefore provided the first substantial link with drive theory. According to Fowler, and a number of other recent drive theorists, drive conditions are defined by the properties that (1) their occurrence is motivating and (2) their termination is reinforcing. In the case of exploration, or boredom, the second property was established. There still remains some question about the motivating function of boredom, since in drive theory a motivating condition must motivate any and all behavior, and not just a single class of behaviors such as exploration. Moreover, to demonstrate the motivating function of D it is necessary to show that the strength of the motivated behavior varies with the severity of the drive-producing condition. This latter requirement in turn requires us to be able to specify how much D is produced by the particular antecedent conditions.

The fascinating puzzle of exploration is that it does not have any obvious antecedent conditions. Many writers have followed Harlow (1953) in emphasizing that exploration is aroused externally by novel or interesting stimuli that suddenly confront the animal. Recent writers, such as Berlyne (1963), have emphasized that exploration has no physiological basis, and Berlyne has suggested that the lack of physiological determinants may be, in fact, the defining property of exploration.[18] How, then, can we relate exploration-produced, or boredom-produced, drive to some set of antecedent conditions?

Exploratory Deprivation. There have been attempts at depriving an animal of the opportunity to explore by confining it. Montgomery (1953a) found confinement for an 8-day period had no effect on subsequent exploratory behavior. (In all these studies exploration was defined in terms of locomotion.) Charlesworth and Thompson (1957) confined rats for various periods of time, from 3 to 6 days, in a homogeneous environment while a control group was maintained in the normal laboratory situation; they found no difference in subsequent exploratory behavior. Montgomery and Zimbardo (1957) did a similar study with three groups of animals which were confined in (1) a normal environment, (2) an environment in which motor activity but not sensory stimulation was reduced, and (3) an environment in which both sensory and activity restrictions were imposed. Again, no differences were found. Ehrlich (1959) also reported negative results.

On the other hand, Butler (1953) imposed a restricted visual environment upon monkeys for various periods of time ranging from 0 to 8 hr. The animals were then tested to determine how often they would make an instrumental response in order to open a window (which they had learned to do earlier) in order to view a rich visual world (looking at Butler) for 30 sec. Visual deprivation of this sort was found to be effective in increasing the rate of looking outside; the maximum rate of responding was reached with restrictions of 4 hr. or more (see also Fox, 1962). Butler and Harlow (1954) have reported that this behavior is also quite resistant to satiation. One trouble with the earlier rat studies, and the reason they yielded negative results with exploration deprivation, may be that they used deprivation times of the wrong magnitude. Fowler (1963) used confinements ranging just up to 15 min. in a study where rats confined

[18] Berlyne has also proposed, as Fiske and Maddi had earlier (1961), that exploration may be one means the animal has of maintaining an optimum level of stimulation. We will not go into this development, or Fowler's (1965) spirited attack of it, or Fowler's own more conventional drive-incentive theory of exploration.

to a start box of one color for a few minutes could run to a goal box of a different color. First Fowler found that the longer confinement led to *slower* running to the goal. Then, when certain procedural artifacts were eliminated, he found some evidence that the animals ran faster with longer confinements. If such findings prove to have generality they can put the exploration problem in an entirely new light, for they would present evidence of both the long-missing antecedent conditions and a genuine energizing function of boredom.

OTHER DRIVE CONDITIONS

Activity. Probably related to exploration, but in a way which is not yet clear, are those sorts of behavior that get measured in certain sorts of apparatus and are called "general activity." General activity is usually considered to be a symptom of (or index of) D rather than a source of D. But being active can also be though of as an autonomous kind of behavior for which animals have a need. Evidence that general activity (more specifically, running in an activity wheel) can be used to reinforce other sorts of behavior comes from a study by Kagan and Berkun (1954). They were able to show that rats would learn to press a bar in order to be able to run in a wheel when access to the wheel was limited to 30 sec. at a time and was contingent upon the bar press. (See also Premack, 1962.)

Although a number of factors are recognized as increasing or decreasing the rat's activity (e.g., food deprivation, castration), the underlying mechanisms are not understood. The rat runs some times and not others, and the various conditions that play a part in the overall level of activity only make running more or less probable; none of them can be said to control it.

There have been some attempts to manipulate activity by imposing something like activity deprivation upon animals. The results of these studies depend to a remarkable extent upon the apparatus used, and hence, presumably, upon the criterion response. Shirley (1928), using activity wheels, found that confinement in small cages for 1 or 2 days had no effect, but that confinement for longer periods of time reduced subsequent running. Siegel (1946a) reported that activity as measured by photo-beam interruptions in the homecage decreased with 6-hr. confinement but returned to the level of the control group with longer confinements and perhaps eventually increased beyond the level of the control group with a 24-hr. confinement. Montgomery (1953a), as we have already noted, found that locomotor activity in a maze was not affected by an 8-day confinement. Hill (1956, 1958), using stabilimeter tilt cages, found activity to be a continuously rising function of confinement for periods up to 4 days. Hill also was able to confirm Shirley's finding that long confinements produced decrements in tests with activity wheels (Hill, 1958a), but the duration and type of confinement are evidently not the only variables operating here (Hill, 1961, 1961a).

Hill has suggested that the difference between tilt-cage and activity-wheel reactions (and presumably reactions to other apparatus also) indicates the specificity of reactions that can express a general activity drive.

> . . . animals confined in small cages canalize their activity drive into those small, restless movements which are the only form of activity possible. After release from confinement, these animals show more of the canalized form of activity and less of other forms than do control animals. Hence, their tilt-cage scores are raised and their activity-wheel scores depressed. (Hill, 1958a, p. 772)[19]

Although subsequent work (Baron et al., 1961, 1962; Neiberg, 1964; Woods & Bolles, 1965) has shown effects of restricted environmental conditions on the incidence of different forms of exploratory behavior and activity which are in line with Hill's hypothesis, these effects have generally been small in magnitude. We are left with the conclusion that activity, like exploration, is only very slightly dependent upon any conditions of prior behavior deprivation.

Sleep Deprivation. The need for sleep is not ordinarily considered a drive condition (perhaps because it does not energize general activity), although it could undoubtedly be shown to be one. There is, however, a good deal known about the conditions that affect sleep (the definitive work is Kleitman, 1963), and there have been some attempts to study sleep deprivation in rats (Licklider & Bunch, 1946; Webb, 1957). Webb's data on the latency to sleep as a function of hours sleep deprivation are presented in Fig. 7-6.

Aversive Conditions. There is a wide variety of conditions whose termination is reinforcing. Animals therefore learn to terminate these conditions and man, in addition, learns to call them unpleasant or painful or aversive.[20] Psychophysical techniques with human subjects have led to a

---

[19] Canalization is a term invented by Murphy (1947) to describe the fact that an activity once undertaken in the service of some motive comes with repetition to be preferred over other possible means of satisfying the motive: habits become habitual. This is the first of many instances we will discover where a series of investigations designed to tell something about drive has led to an associative account of the behavior that drive was supposed to explain.

[20] Throughout the book the basic definition of aversiveness will be in terms of negative reinforcement, i.e., a stimulus will be said to be aversive if the organism will learn to escape it. Whether the organism will learn to avoid it, or will be punished by it, or whether it elicits any particular response from the organism— all of these are open questions. As far as drive theory is concerned, it is only necessary to add the hypotheses that the presentation of aversive stimuli increases drive and that their removal reduces drive. The question we are concerned with here is whether some property of aversive stimuli, such as their intensity, can be systematically related to the strength of the resulting drive.

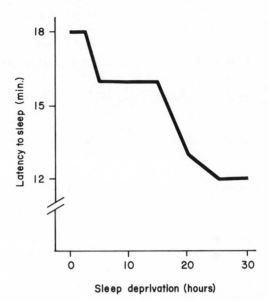

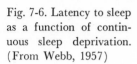

Fig. 7-6. Latency to sleep as a function of continuous sleep deprivation. (From Webb, 1957)

number of quantitative scalings of the stimulus properties (if not the motivational properties) of some of these conditions as a function of their stimulus intensity (e.g., Stevens et al., 1958). Such research has only begun with animals. Campbell (1955, 1956) has developed a procedure in which a small reduction in noise intensity (1955) or shock intensity (1956) is produced when the animal moves to one side of a tilting cage. By varying the initial intensity and the reduction in intensity in a systematic manner, it is possible to determine a threshold such that statistically significant learning is just obtained. Larger reductions in intensity for a given base intensity lead to more dramatic learning, while smaller differences lead to nonsignificant performance changes. Campbell calls the critical value a reinforcement difference limen. Presumably a number of such differential limens for different points of the stimulus dimension could be added up in classical Fechnerian style to provide a psychophysical function relating physical intensity of the stimulus to its psychological motivational properties. A similar technique has been used by Bolles (1962a) to scale hunger motivation. Such techniques should ultimately yield ratio scales for a construct which, if it had the right invariant behavioral consequences, we might want to call drive.

Such ambitious scaling programs are uncommon. Usually it is deemed sufficient to establish that the animal's motivation can be related by an ordinal scale to some dimension of physical intensity. We are satisfied to know that the animal suffering a 2-ma. electric current is more motivated than one suffering a 1-ma. current. Careful observation of animals being shocked, however, suggests that this formulation may be a little too pat. With short bursts of electricity it may make relatively little difference, but when exposed to prolonged shock the animal may learn certain characteristic modes of adjustment to gain some partial relief, even when total relief from shock is impossible. Thus, when a constant-current shock is used (such as provided by high voltage and a series resistor), and the shock is relatively mild, the animal tends to freeze and hold tight to the shock grid, thereby decreasing its skin resistance and consequently the voltage drop across its body (Bolles & Warren, 1965). On the other hand, when a constant-voltage shock source is used (such as provided by an autotransformer like the *Variac*), the animal tends to step lightly and jump around, thereby maximizing its skin resistance and decreasing the current flow. Campbell and Teghtsoonian (1958) have suggested on the basis of such observations, together with certain other behavioral data, that perhaps the motivational invariant is the electrical power (i.e., voltage times current) dissipated in the animal. Until such basic procedural questions have been answered we cannot hope to quantify drive produced by electric shock, even though we may know quite well qualitatively what the motivating antecedent conditions are and how to manipulate them.

The quantification of drive produced by electric shock is further obscured by the fact that the rat has a whole gamut of responses which are elicited, perhaps unconditionally, by shock (e.g., jumping, squealing, freezing, biting). These responses may interfere so effectively with efficient instrumental escape that it is difficult to know what behavior to use as an index of drive (Kimble, 1955; Trabasso & Thompson, 1962).

The situation is still more complicated in the case of *conditioned* physiological reactions (fear) which arise after a neutral stimulus (the one to be feared) has been paired with an already aversive stimulus. Although the concurrent physiological and behavioral manifestations are well known, we have tended to ignore the very difficult problem of quantifying fear in tying it to its antecedent conditions. Indeed, fear is almost always introduced ad hoc, its occurrence being assumed from the behavior it is introduced to explain. A few experimenters (e.g., Wynne & Solomon, 1955; Black, 1959; Runquist & Spence, 1959) have tried to validate the inferred fear drive from changes in the autonomic activity of the subject, but this sort of attempted cross-validation is rare, and, so far, the results have been discouraging (Black, 1965). As a consequence, the so-called aversive drives are, at best, anchored only qualitatively to their antecedent conditions. In a word, shock is easy to measure but pain and fear are not.

There are many different varieties of stimulation that animals will escape, noise, bright light, heat, cold, and water immersion, to name a few. These kinds of stimuli probably entail fewer methodological problems than shock because they elicit less of an emotional reaction, and less competing unconditioned behavior than shock does within the practical range of stimulation. Campbell (1955) and Woods et al. (1964) have begun to scale the motivational effects of noise and cold water. There may be still other, less obvious, sources of drive. Zajonc (1965), for example, has suggested that the presence of another animal of the same species increases drive; this hypothetical increment in drive is then used to explain the social facilitation effect upon eating and other behavior.

The Problem of Generality. An imposing problem for the Hullian drive theorist is to demonstrate that a given value of D produced by one set of conditions has the identical quantitative motivational effects as the same value of D produced by any other set of antecedent conditions. This may be a good deal to ask for, but it is what Hull's generalized drive construct requires.

Perhaps the only serious attack on this problem has been the proposal made by some theorists that the concept of *arousal* can handle the facts. A tentative identification of the hypothetical physiological state of arousal (Lindsley, 1951) with the Hullian drive construct has been suggested by Duffy (1951, 1957), Stellar (1954), Hebb (1955), Malmo (1959), Bindra (1959), and others. It is argued that the diffuse projection system in the reticular formation has the desired property of augmenting the reception of specific stimuli. Thus it would appear to magnify whatever S-R connections are operating at a given moment, just as D is supposed to do. Much of the experimental evidence cited by Duffy, Malmo, and others to support these arguments is of the increased muscle tonus and autonomic reactivity that accompanies the various drive-producing conditions. This evidence, some of which was sampled earlier in the chapter, does not yet require us to put away our old behavioral data, concepts, or theories.

SUMMARY

We have come a long way toward the understanding of motivated behavior and its antecedents since the day Canon listened to stomach rumblings. No attempt will be made to summarize what has been learned about the physiological basis of behavior, but it may be useful to survey some of the implications for the drive concept.

In general, it has been found that a variety of behavioral measures are more closely correlated with the physiological condition (the drive state) than with the antecedent conditions of deprivation or stimulation that produce them. Thus, in the case of hunger and thirst, motivated behavior appears to be better correlated with the *need* of the animal as measured by weight loss than it is with any simple set of experimental manipulations, such as deprivation time, that can produce the need condition. This finding should not be too surprising because it reflects the obvious fact that a given state of depletion can arise from a number of different experimental treatments. In support of Hullian drive theory, it can be said that both the instrumental and consummatory behavior of the hungry rat appear to increase systematically in strength with the animal's percentage body-weight loss.

On the other hand, a great deal of the research that has been done on animal motivation is either methodologically unsound or difficult to interpret because experimenters have tended to concern themselves with manipulating (and reporting) the wrong variables, e.g., hours deprivation. If we are to interpret some of the experimental literature, we are required to deduce from the specification of experimental conditions what the animals' weight loss, and hence, hunger, might have been. This problem together with our failure to solve the "psychometric problem" has resulted in our having, at best, only an ordinal scale of hunger. A parallel situation appears to exist with regard to thirst but the data are seriously incomplete.

The other sources of drive all seem to present special problems. Some of them, e.g., sex and exploration, don't represent "needs" in any real sense. Deprivation also seems to have little or no effect upon sexual or exploratory behavior (except in the case of sex to provide for the dissipation of the animal's postcopulatory refractory period). Excluding the presentation of novel or changing stimulation, there is no obvious set of antecedent conditions that lead to the motivation of exploratory behavior. On the other hand, sexual behavior depends upon so many different antecedent conditions that it is difficult to see which of them are motivational. For example, mating requires a background of hormonal stimulation, yet it does not seem sensible to say that hormones "motivate" sexual behavior.

Both fear and sleepiness could probably be quantitatively related to D, but the data are too sparse at this time to suggest what the relationships might be. In no case, except perhaps for hunger, do we have more than an ordinal scale relating the severity of a drive-producing condition to the resulting strength of drive.

8

ENERGIZING EFFECTS
OF DRIVE

❖⟨✦⟨⟨✦⟨⟨

*Psychology as a systematic science is relatively young. As a conse-
quence it is to be expected that as time goes on marked changes
will continue to be made in the fundamental assumptions underlying
the systematizations. The fearless performance of critical experiments and the continuous quantitative use of the relevant postulates
and corollaries will hasten the elimination of errors. . . .*

C. L. HULL

In all versions of the drive concept it is given the role of energizing
behavior. The unique feature of Hull's version is that drive is supposed
to energize any and all behavior. In any given situation only that behavior occurs which has the strongest associative connections, and drive
merely determines the strength of the dominant behavior. Thus, according to Hull, any source of drive is potentially able to energize any kind
of consummatory behavior, any instrumental response, and any kind of
general activity. In Chapter 10 we will consider the attempts that have
been made to test some of the broader implications of this formulation
but we will start here by looking at experimental situations in which the
motivated behavior has the greatest relevance to the drive-producing
condition.

First we will examine the basic question of whether the strength of a consummatory response varies systematically with the severity of the relevant drive-producing condition. For example, does eating increase in strength with percentage weight loss? Note that it is not enough to show that the response occurs in some strength in the presence of the drive condition; it must be shown that they vary in strength together. This may be taken as the definition of the hypothetical energizing effect.[1]

The same basic question will then be asked of instrumental responses; do they vary in strength with the strength of the relevant drive-producing condition? For example, does running to food increase in strength with percentage weight loss?

The present chapter is an attempt to do two things at once. We will consider the evidence bearing on the chief theoretical issue just defined, and we will find that much of it supports the energization hypothesis. Our second task will be to find out something about behavior itself, for example, how best to measure the strength of consummatory and instrumental behavior. We will find that different explanatory principles seem to apply to different kinds of responses, and even to different measures of a response. It should become clear that although the hypothetical energizing effect can be validated in many instances, it alone has little explanatory power. An adequate explanation of most consummatory or instrumental behaviors must include an account of their associative characteristics.

THE ENERGIZING OF CONSUMMATORY BEHAVIOR

For years psychologists have tended to consider the strength of an animal's consummatory behavior as a direct measure of drive strength. Thus we have tended to think of hunger-produced drive as leading directly and immediately to the energization of eating. But a growing mass of evidence requires us to question this conceptual shortcut. Recent investigations of consummatory activities have shown that, like any other responses, they are dependent upon controlling stimulus conditions and they are subject to reinforcement. We will see in the present section, first for the case of hunger, that it is necessary to distinguish among proba-

---

[1] To show that a drive condition will facilitate some particular behavior provides little convincing support for the drive concept. Thus, an oft-cited study by Brown et al. (1951) demonstrated that fear facilitated the startle reflex. But startle is one of the unconditioned reactions to fear, or to fear-producing stimuli. Before the claimed evidence of drive can carry much weight, it must be shown that any other drive condition, such as sexual excitement or hunger, also facilitates the startle reflex (Meryman, 1952), or that sexual behavior or eating is also facilitated by the fear condition. Much more dramatic support for the concept of drive, as a generalized energizer is Carlson's finding (1913a) that the knee jerk reflex is facilitated by hunger. Curiously, incentive motivation seems to have little or no effect upon startle (Trapold, 1962; Armus et al., 1964).

bility measures, amplitude measures, and persistence measures of eating. We will find that these different measures of the consummatory response are differentially affected by their controlling stimulus factors and are governed by different kinds of physiological mechanisms. After we have surveyed some of these regulatory mechanisms, and have gotten an over-all view of eating behavior, we will be able to ask meaningfully whether hunger-produced drive energizes eating in the technical sense that eating increases monotonically with the severity of drive-producing conditions. This section will conclude with a look at some of the less-well-studied consummatory behaviors, drinking, mating, and exploration, and we will then be in a position to arrive at some general conclusions about the energizing of consummatory behavior.

Normal Eating Behavior in the Rat. In the last chapter we noted that the rat eats primarily to maintain its energy reserves. It eats episodically to supply the energy expended more or less continuously. This is accomplished by physiological machinery not yet fully understood, which keeps track of debits and credits. It should be noted that because the rat is a small animal, eating plays a larger part in its total daily activity than it does for a larger animal. The rat must consume five times the calories per gram of body weight that a man consumes; it cannot accomplish this with one meal a day unless it has had some practice and unless it has a high-calorie diet such as laboratory food. Even with laboratory food the rat may spend nearly three hours a day eating (Bolles, 1960).

It is known that under a rather wide range of experimental conditions the rat ordinarily eats about 11 meals a day (Baker, 1953; Teitelbaum & Campbell, 1958; Bolles, 1961). Bolles (1961) has reported that the number of meals does not depend appreciably upon whether water is available with the meal; and Teitelbaum and Campbell found that it made very little difference whether the meal was given in liquid or the usual solid form—there were still about 11 meals a day. In fact, Teitelbaum and Campbell found that making rats hyperphagic with lesions in the ventromedial hypothalamus (which approximately doubles the daily food intake) had only a slight effect upon average number of daily meals. Richter (1927) reported that rats take only 5 to 10 meals a day, but the discrepancy between his results and the more recent findings may be because Richter's animals had to go to their food; it was not immediately available in their living space.

Richter (1922, 1927) also reported that rats have an approximate 4-hr. eating cycle, although his data showed that they did not adhere very strictly to a fixed cycle. If food is made more easily accessible, then the mean intermeal interval drops to something of the order of 2 hr. Figure 8-1 shows data on the distribution of intermeal times obtained by Bash (1939) under these conditions.

Richter also noted that rats do the majority of their eating at night,

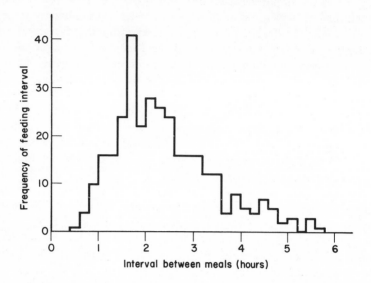

Fig. 8-1. Distribution of time intervals between periods of eating in normal rats. (From Bash, 1939)

during the dark part of the light-dark cycle. Siegel and Stuckey (1947) measured food consumption every 6 hr. and found that approximately 70% was consumed during the 12 dark hours of the diurnal cycle. This same general pattern has been reported by Gilbert and James (1956), Bare (1959), Bare and Cicala (1960), and Siegel (1961). (Siegel's data are shown in Fig. 8-2.) Bare found that the animal's tendency to confine eating to the evening can partially override a need to make up a previously incurred food deficit. Thus, animals that were deprived and then given food in the early afternoon ate some food when it was first presented, but they ate much more later at the regular evening feeding time.[2]

Elliott (1935), Bousfield and Elliott (1936), and Young and Richey (1952) have pointed out that a rat deprived in the morning may hardly be deprived at all, whereas one deprived in the evening, when it is ordinarily taking a large part of its daily food, may be suffering a relatively much greater deprivation. Siegel (1961) confirmed this speculation in the case of short deprivation times; he found that animals would eat relatively little after a 4-hr. morning deprivation, and much more, more

[2] There have been some good recent systematic studies of eating behavior in other species, e.g., dormouse (Mrosovsky, 1964), salamander (Goldstein, 1960), fish (Tugendhat, 1960; Rozin & Mayer, 1961), blowfly (Dethier, 1962), and spiders (Gardner, 1964).

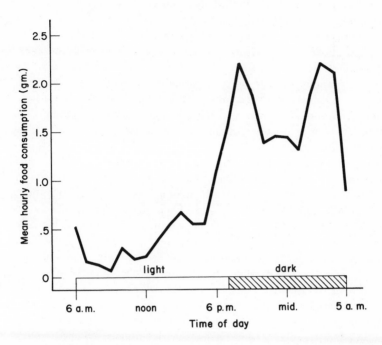

Fig. 8-2. The diurnal course of food consumption of rats maintained ad lib. and on a natural light-dark cycle. (Adapted from Siegel, 1961)

than control animals on ad lib. feeding, following a 4-hr. evening deprivation. It is possible that rats eat in the evening simply because they lose weight during the day when they are sleeping. In the morning they are slightly overweight and therefore sleep. In these terms, a short deprivation in the morning cannot bring the animal's weight down to the point where it would ordinarily eat, but an equal deprivation in the evening does bring its weight well below a weight loss threshold for eating. More data would be welcome here, particularly a correlation of weight data and consumption data.

Temporal Factors in Eating. Although the rat's diurnal cycle is rather durable, there are factors that can change it, such as being fed regularly in the middle of the day, or living in continuous illumination. Gilbert and James (1956) found little disturbance in the normal eating cycle after 3 days of continuous illumination, but others (Brody, 1945; Siegel, 1961) have reported that the cycle breaks down or disappears after about a week of constant illumination.[3] Gilbert and James have

[3] It should be noted that what breaks down is the cyclicity of the group. The

suggested that the cyclicity of eating breaks down sooner, within 3 days, if animals are in constant light and also deprived of water.

It has been suggested that the mere introduction of fresh food and water supplies at a regular time of day can trigger the 24-hr. consummatory cycle (Bolles, 1961). Naive animals were trained to press a bar for food, confined to the test situation, and given fresh supplies each day at noon. Continuous records of consummatory activity indicated that its greatest incidence occurred shortly after noon, rather than during the usual evening hours. Calvin and Behan (1954) report a similar willingness of rats to give up their usually preferred eating time when brought into a new situation.

The temporal regularity of feeding determines not only when but also how much the rat eats. Bousfield and Elliott (1934) trained rats for 3 weeks to eat for 1 hr. a day, by which time their intake during the consumption test had become stabilized. Then the feeding session was delayed 3, 12, 24, or 48 hr. The food consumption on the delayed tests, relative to the baseline established under regular feeding is shown in Fig. 8-3. Note that there is a general overall decline with increasing delay, which is partially offset when the test time coincides with the regular feeding hour. Bousfield (1935) found that delaying a regularly scheduled feeding also leads to a reduced rate of eating.

Baker (1955) compared the food intake and rate of eating of animals maintained on regular 24-hr. feedings with animals switched randomly between 12, 24, and 36 hr. deprivation. Again, he found that increased deprivation time led to decreased intake, and that the irregularly deprived group ate less on the average than the regularly fed group. In a related study, Lawrence and Mason (1955a) gave one group of animals a counterbalanced series of deprivations, ranging from 4 to 48 hr., which fell at different times of day; a control group at first received a regular series of 24-hr. deprivations, was then tested with sessions at irregular hours interspersed between feedings scheduled at the regular time. The control group therefore yielded consumption data for deprivations of 4 to 24 hr. tested at the regular feeding time, and also tested at unusual feeding times. For a given deprivation, intake was about 1 gm. greater at the regular feeding time than at the irregular feeding time, and maximal with 24-hr. deprivation. The experimental group also showed a maximum intake with 24-hr. deprivation, suggesting that a 24-hr. feeding cycle can, to

---

records of individual animals may continue to show a fairly good approximation to a 24-hr. cycle, although the period may drift and the swing in activity during the period may not be as marked as normal. At least this seems to be the story with regard to the diurnal cyclicity of general activity (Richter, 1927; Hunt & Schlosberg, 1939a). Animals usually fail to adjust to new environmental periodicities imposed on them (Hemmingsen & Krarup, 1937; Browman, 1943, 1952), although some subjects do (Browman, 1943a, 1944), at least some of the time (Browman, 1952).

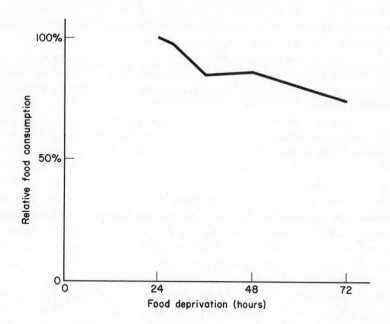

Fig. 8-3. Food consumption as a function of deprivation time, consumption taken relative to the mean amount consumed at regularly scheduled
24-hr. tests. (Data reported by Bousfield & Elliott, 1934)

some extent, be established with a single feeding (see also Bolles, 1965a).

This whole set of studies on the temporal determinants of eating behavior suggests two conclusions. The first is that eating appears to have
an inherent 24-hr. cyclicity in addition to the short-term cyclicity observed by Richter and Bash. We will see later that there are other types
of evidence to support this conclusion. Here it is sufficient to note the
implication that one of the factors which governs eating behavior quite
independently of the animal's need for food is the temporal pattern of
eating to which it is accustomed, especially when this involves feeding
on a regular 24-hr. rhythm.

The second conclusion follows from the first: The deprived animal's
energy deficit increases monotonically with deprivation time, but its consumption does not, so that we have a lack of correspondence between
the severity of the drive state and the strength of this relevant motivated
behavior. To this extent we have a failure of the principle that a drive
condition energizes its own consummatory response. Even if it is argued
that this does not invalidate the relationship between drive strength and
consummatory-response strength, but is only an additional factor that has

to be considered, this is a serious qualification. Once it has to be admitted that it is necessary to postulate two kinds of factors, drive factors and associative factors, to explain this aspect of motivated behavior, the door is open for an associative explanation of all aspects of motivated behavior. And in any case, we have another of the many illustrations we will find in these chapters of the general rule that when we go looking for motivational determinants of behavior, we end up finding associative determinants.

Associative Factors in Eating. Another important factor in eating behavior is the animal's experience in the test situation. Ghent (1951), Lawrence and Mason (1955), Reid and Finger (1955), and Moll (1959) have all noted that on repeated eating tests over a period of two weeks or so, the rat comes to eat more during the tests (but see Dufort, 1964). As we noted in the last chapter, however, the learning effect in these studies was obscured by the fact that the animals were no doubt losing weight over the course of the tests, so that what appears to be learning to eat was confounded with whatever increased energization may have resulted from cumulative weight loss. Moll (1964) made use of a much superior procedure in which animals were first brought down to reduced weight, either 80% or 90% of normal weight adjusted for growth, before being run on consumption tests. Under these conditions, Moll still obtained large learning effects measured either in terms of latency to start eating, amount consumed in the first 5 min., or the amount of time spent eating in the first 5 min. The rapidity of learning and the level of performance attained was evidently a function of the age of the animals used, but clearly there was learning in animals of all ages (from 33 to 93 days).

Whether we think of this learning effect as being due merely to the extinction of competing behavior, such as exploration (Beck, 1964), there can be no question about the overall conclusion, which is that the rat's familiarity with the eating situation is a significant associative determinant of the strength of its eating behavior.

Another kind of learning may also be involved in consummatory behavior, namely, familiarity with the particular test food. Young (1948) has surveyed some of the earlier studies showing that the rat's preference for particular foods depends in part upon its prior experience with them. More recently, Wetzel (1959) has reported that previous opportunity to drink sugar solutions made such solutions more reinforcing for rats.

Still another question is whether after the animal has become familiar with the eating situation it makes any difference if it has had previous experience with deprivation in the situation. For example, can the rat learn from prior deprivation experience to increase its intake? After being deprived for 24 hr., and then given food for 24 hr., the rat eats somewhat more than his normal ad lib. consumption (Adolph, 1947; Finger,

1951; Finger & Reid, 1952; Lawrence & Mason, 1955; Bolles, 1961). However, this extra food intake (which is part of what Finger labeled the Satiation Syndrome) ordinarily only amounts to 40% to 60%; it is never sufficient to return the animal to a normal physiological condition (Adolph, 1947). The rat does not pay off its food debt immediately, nor, according to Lawrence and Mason, does it learn to do so with repeated testing.[4] Similarly, the reduction in food intake that is found when rats are deprived of water is not overcome with the experience of eating in the absence of water, nor does the food consumption rise appreciably above normal when water is again made available (Bolles, 1961). Beck and Horne (1964) found that when water was made available only 30 min. a day, the rat's food intake during and immediately after water is available may increase with experience, but that there is no systematic increase in total daily food intake. It appears therefore that although the rat learns to eat more in a short eating session (Moll, 1964), its consumption over a 24-hr. period is relatively independent of its prior deprivation experience and even of its current cumulative deficit; it does not learn to increase its 24-hr. food intake to compensate for a previous deficit.

On the other hand, there have been some studies of long-term effects of deprivation experience. Marx (1952) found that rats put on a maintenance schedule for 10 days at the time of weaning ate faster than controls when deprived and tested as adults. Levine (1957) and Mandler (1958) have reported similar effects of early deprivation experience. Even when the early-deprived animals recovered to normal weight, they showed an exaggerated reaction to subsequent deprivation which was apparent not only in their consummatory behavior but in their instrumental and general activity as well. Evidently the rat's consummatory behavior is determined in part by associative (i.e., learned) factors over and beyond those involved in the current conditions of testing.

Some writers, notably Katz (1937), have emphasized that consummatory activity can sometimes be governed by what appear to be purely perceptual influences. Ross et al. (1962) are severely critical of this interpretation of the relevant facts, however, and have attempted to deal with them in motivational terms. There can be little question, however, of the reality of "social facilitation" of eating, even in rats (Harlow, 1932).

The Problem of Measurement. In the preceding sections we have been considering rather indiscriminately a number of different measures of the consummatory response, e.g., latency, vigor, and amount consumed. But now we must note that there are some serious difficulties with interpreting consumption as a measure of the strength of consum-

---

[4] According to Adolph (1947), the rat uses another technique in recovery: it reduces its activity level to maintain a lower overall metabolism.

matory behavior. (We should already have seen enough to be rather skeptical about taking the amount of food consumed as a direct index of D.) We have seen something of the important dependence of consummatory behavior upon associative factors. Even so, consumption criteria of motivation would be acceptable if amount consumed proved to be highly correlated with the other behavioral measures we believe should be an indication of the animal's motivation. But, in fact, such correlations are not very high, as Miller (1955, 1956) has vividly demonstrated. Miller (1956) compared four different measures of behavior as a function of hours of food deprivation. The results are shown in Fig. 8-4. The

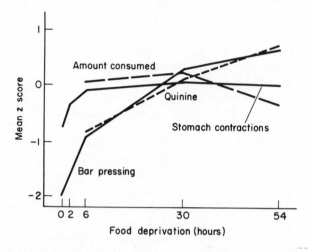

Fig. 8-4. A comparison of four measures of "hunger." Each measure is plotted as a standard score derived from the average within-test-condition variability on the last three deprivation conditions; this makes the different measures directly comparable. (From Miller, 1956)

four measures of behavior were (1) the concentration of quinine that would be tolerated in the food, (2) the rate of bar pressing on a variable-interval schedule, (3) the occurrence of stomach contractions as measured by a permanently implanted stomach balloon, and (4) the amount of food consumed during the test period. Clearly, the four behavior measures do not correlate over the range of deprivation times. Miller's conclusion that we should not place too much confidence in any one measure of drive strength certainly seems appropriate.

The lack of correlation among measures is admittedly discouraging, but perhaps the situation here is not hopeless. Notice that bar pressing and acceptance of quinine are response measures which tell us, essentially, how likely the consummatory response is to be initiated. Thus, both of these measures indicate the strength of the consummatory response before the animal has ingested enough food to materially affect its condition; they are *preingestion* measures of motivation. These measures, like latency (compare Fig. 8-5), increase continuously as the deprivation becomes more severe. On the other hand, Miller's fourth measure, amount consumed, not only depends upon the factors that initiate eating, but in addition upon all the new factors that come into play because of ingestion, i.e., all the *postingestion* factors that may operate under the particular test conditions. (It is not clear how the third measure—stomach contractions—should be interpreted, possibly only as stimuli to which eating can be conditioned.)

If the rat nearly always eats about 11 meals a day, it follows that if it is to regulate its caloric intake in accordance with its energy requirements it must do so by regulating its average meal size. Since the rat does, in fact, regulate its overall intake reasonably well, it must also, on the average, eat an appropriate amount per meal. Accordingly, there is a clear relationship between the severity of the motivating antecedent conditions (weight loss) and the subsequent consummatory response (amount of calories consumed). But this adjustment is a long-term achievement; it really only works on the average, for example, in regulating the animal's consumption from day to day or from week to week. If we look at any one meal, we may find considerable disproportionality between caloric need and caloric intake, and to that exent we have a failure of the energization principle.

In many cases we can cite specific factors which disrupt the short-term balance. Let us consider first some of the "psychological" factors that can disturb temporarily the regulation of food intake. One factor is the "dessert phenomenon": foods change palatability as they are consumed, and as the state of deprivation changes. Curiously, although there is a mountain of data on growth as a function of the nutritive content and balance of foods, there are very few data on growth as a function of the palatability of food. There is a good deal of evidence to show that rats will adjust their caloric intake rather well when offered different foods and foods of different caloric value (e.g., Cowgill, 1928; Adolph, 1947; Kleiber, 1961), but at this stage of our knowledge we can only guess at the palatabilities of the different foods that have been used. It has been found (Hamilton, 1964a; Corbit & Stellar, 1964), however, that rats get fat on high-fat diets which, we may presume, are highly palatable.

It has been noted (Siegel, 1957) that humans tend to have a "completion compulsion"; they usually eat all of whatever is set before them. It is my observation that rats also tend to finish up a pellet of food before stopping. We may note also that all of the temporal and associative determinants of eating that were considered above might induce overeating, or inhibit eating; certainly they will do so on a short-term basis. The chief factor, of course, which inhibits eating is competing behavior. Other factors regulating consummatory behavior are all insignificant compared with the effects produced by giving the animal an electric shock, or distracting it with novel stimuli, or presenting a mate, or in some other way initiating more prepotent responses.

Physiological Mechanisms That Terminate Eating. In contrast with the meager amount of work that has been done on the psychological determinants of satiation, there has been a good deal of attention focused upon the physiological factors that regulate intake, or produce satiation, or (more simply) terminate eating. One thing which puts an end to eating is eating itself. When dogs are prepared with esophageal fistulas so that food taken into the mouth does not reach the stomach, they sham eat an amount of food which is considerably larger than they would need to make up their deficit, but which nonetheless varies continuously with the extent of their food deficit (James, 1963).[5]

It should not be concluded from sham-eating studies that, because the stomach has been anatomically disassociated from the mouth, events occurring in the stomach play no part in the regulation of sham eating. We have known since the turn of the century when Pavlov (1902) did his classic work with sham eating, that food taken into the mouth produces a copious flow of digestive juices into the stomach. This "psychic secretion" may play a part in the termination of sham eating, either because the secretion fills the stomach, or leads to cellular dehydration, or in some other way affects the ordinary satiation mechanisms.

Loading the stomach with food given through a tube, or inflating a balloon in the stomach, inhibits eating (Janowitz & Grossman, 1948, 1949a; Kohn, 1951; Share et al., 1952; Berkun et al., 1952). It is commonly reported that the regulation of eating by preloading the stomach is only relatively effective, since there is only a partial reduction in the amount of food subsequently consumed. The animal eats less than it would if the preload were not given, but the total intake may be appreciably greater than the animal would have otherwise consumed. Indeed the animal must be preloaded with an amount larger than a normal full meal if the inhibition of subsequent eating is to be complete. When Share et al. gave dogs a 30% preload, there was virtually no inhibition of eating; animals subsequently ate as much as controls that had not had the prefeedings.[6]

[5] There are some serious discrepancies in the sham-eating literature. For example, Hull et al. (1951) reported that a dog would sham eat tremendous quantities of food before stopping. Hull also concluded from his findings that stomach tubing was relatively more reinforcing than sham eating, whereas James (1963) has come to just the opposite conclusion.

[6] Share et al. reported, however, that the animals under these conditions of increased total intake did not gain weight. How was the extra caloric value of the extra intake disposed of? This remains a mystery.

The inhibition of eating which follows preloading is less than that obtained by the oral ingestion of the same amount of food (Janowitz & Grossman, 1951; Kohn, 1951). This does not necessarily mean an inherent inferiority of the stomach satiation factor since we would expect orally ingested food to be accompanied in the stomach by additional gastric secretion, and greater osmotic pressure because of the more rapid enzymatic breakdown of ingested food (Smith & Duffy, 1957). Finally, it has been noted that there is an improvement with experience in the effectiveness of food regulation by the partial inhibition of eating following regular stomach preloads. After a few weeks, food regulation becomes more accurate, although in dogs it never becomes very accurate (Janowitz & Hollander, 1955).

There is now an impressive accumulation of evidence that the inhibition of eating following stomach tubing preloads of material does not depend upon the caloric value of the material but rather upon the osmotic pressure that it establishes (McCleary, 1953; Smith & Duffy, 1957; Smith et al., 1959; Schwartzbaum & Ward, 1958; Mook, 1963). Mook made use of an elegant double-fistula technique in which animals could sham drink one substance, say a concentrated glucose solution, while an equivalent amount of another substance, say, water, was tubed directly into the stomach, so that essentially complete separation could be made between the oral factors and the stomach factors in satiation. Mook found that the consumption of foods as a function of their concentration was dependent almost wholly upon the osmotic pressure of the substance tubed into the stomach. For example, rats sham drank huge quantities of 40% sucrose solutions when pure water was tubed, but inhibited their drinking of glucose when concentrated sugar or concentrated saline solutions were tubed. It is already known that the rat's preferred concentration of sugar is much lower if the preference is measured in terms of consumption over a long period of time, such as 24 hr. (Young & Greene, 1953), than if it is measured in terms of an initial choice or a short-term preference test.

Mook obtained preference data which are markedly different from those obtained when taste factors are confounded by postingestion factors, as they usually are. For example, he found rats would sham drink appreciable quantities of rather concentrated salt solutions when they were tubed with water, i.e., when their drinking had no postingestion consequences.

There is some question about the precise nature of the osmotic satiation mechanism. Smith et al. (1959) and McCleary (1953) found that inhibition of eating could be obtained by dehydration following subcutaneous injection of hypertonic salt solutions. The result of such injections is cellular dehydration, a block imposed upon water moving into the stomach, and a subsequent inability to normalize ingested food. So evidently dehydration and/or the concomitant increase in osmotic pressure inhibits food intake.[7]

Since water is necessary both for digestion and for reducing the tonicity of ingested foods, we would expect the availability of water to be an important factor in regulating food intake. Bing and Mendel (1931), Strominger (1946), Adolph (1947), Finger and Reid (1952), Verplanck and Hayes (1953), and Gilbert and James (1956) all report that rats deprived of water will "voluntarily" reduce their food intake to roughly one-half the normal amount over a 24-hr. period. Similar results have been reported for men (Adolph, 1947a), rabbits (Cizek, 1961), dogs (Pernice & Scagliosi, 1895; Cizek, 1959), and doves (McFarland, 1964). With deprivation of water continued past 24 hr. it is generally found that the consumption of food drops even farther. Moreover, the inhibition effect is apparently continuous in the sense that rats kept for 23 days on a half-normal water ration reduced their food intake to 75% of the normal value, and rats kept on one-fourth- to one-eighth-normal water ration reduced their food consumption accordingly still further (Adolph, 1947). The availability of water evidently is an important determinant of satiation and does help to regulate how much an animal consumes. In this connection, Hamilton (1963) has shown that the rat's failure to eat at high ambient temperature (above 90°F.) is due to its failure to take enough water. After a day or two of high temperature, water consumption rises sharply and an increase in food consumption follows.

There is another stomach-related satiation mechanism that we may note, and this is the sheer bulk of stomach contents. Mook (1963) found that when rats sham drank water but were tubed with a 3% saline solution they consumed (sham drank) large quantities of water. Under these conditions, it was obviously impossible for the animal to sham drink enough water to dilute its ever mounting salt load. We may ask why the animal ever stopped sham drinking. The answer is evidently the stomach distention produced by the bulk of material that had been tubed. Smith and Duffy (1957) have demonstrated rather nicely that rats given preloads of insoluble material, cellulose or kaolin, reduce their food consumption accordingly (see also Towbin, 1949; Smith et al., 1962). Whether stomach distention plays much of a role in the normal regulation of food intake is quite another matter. Chances are it is not important in the rat. Harper and Spivey (1958) made measurements of stomach contents of rats after meals of different osmolarities and found that the total con-

---

[7] There is still considerable uncertainty about how these mechanisms operate. For example, Jacobs (1964) has shown that while the osmotic theory may account for the regulation of subsequent food intake, it fails to make sense out of data on subsequent water intake. Thus, he reports that animals that have been tubed high-tonicity foods will inhibit subsequent food intake, but if the intubed material is a saline solution of the same osmolarity, they will continue to ingest water.

tent was (1) far less than the animal's capacity, and (2) only slightly dependent upon the osmotic potential of the meal. However, the results of James and Gilbert (1957) and others suggest that stomach distention may normally be an important satiation factor in the dog.[8]

Brobeck (1945, 1960) has emphasized the potential role in satiation of what is called the Specific Dynamic Action (SDA) of foods. It seems that whenever foods are digested, a certain portion of their latent caloric energy is used to provide the energy necessary for their digestion. This effect is particularly large in the case of certain protein foods where as much as 30% of the available energy may be lost in the digestion process. This lost energy is assumed to appear in the form of heat; and, whereas this obligatory heat production gives the animal no advantage against cold (Hamilton, 1963), at high ambient temperatures—above 90°F.— the animal is unable to control the increase in body temperature except by reducing its intake of high-protein foods (which it does). Hamilton and Brobeck (1962) have shown that the rat may perish if it is force-fed high-protein foods at high ambient temperatures. Most of the evidence for Brobeck's thermoregulatory theory of satiation is of this sort, i.e., rather circumstantial. Quite substantial evidence against it has recently been obtained by Rampone and Shirasu (1964) by measuring the temperature of the brain during feeding. They found a rise in temperature with eating which lasted for 2 hours or so after eating stopped. However, the temperature effect was attributed to reflexive circulatory changes (reduction in brain circulation) rather than to SDA because it (1) was mirrored by a reduced rectal temperature, (2) had a latency of seconds, and (3) failed to increase with high SDA foods.

To summarize this material on the satiation of eating, it can be said that there are a number of rather poorly explored and ill-defined psychological variables, such as food palatability. Then there are a number of more thoroughly investigated, but still somewhat controversial, physiological mechanisms, the best established of which seem to be an increase of osmotic pressure, secretion of digestive fluids, stomach distention, and cellular dehydration, all of which are caused by the ingestion of food, and are accompanied by an influx of water into the stomach. It is not yet clear how these factors are interrelated, whether, for example, they may all be different aspects of a single satiation mechanism. We have noted too that under certain circumstances, other factors such as the amount

[8] Taken altogether, the stomach mechanisms in satiation are quite effective, at least over intervals as long as 24 hr. Thus, Epstein and Teitelbaum (1962) have shown that the rat is able to regulate his total caloric intake when all food reaching the stomach is obtained by the rat pressing a bar to inject small amounts of food into the stomach. The bar-pressing rate was found to vary correspondingly, and quite accurately, when the caloric payoff of bar pressing was altered. All of this was in the total absence of consummatory behavior or oral effects of any kind.

of consummatory activity and the SDA of ingested foods may serve to terminate on-going consummatory behavior.

Most of these factors are different from those that control the onset of eating. There we found that it is primarily the stimulus properties of foods, e.g., their palatability (this is one factor which is common to both the initiation and termination of eating), plus the energy balance or need for food that initiates eating. Neither stomach contractions nor blood sugar level appear to have much to do with satiation, nor does the nutritive value of the food consumed, except on a lcng-term basis, over a period of 24 hrs. or more.[9] It would surely have been more convenient if all of the different measures of consummatory behavior showed the same functional dependence upon motivating antecedent conditions. However, the situation is not that simple. The regulation of energy over a period of time is apparently a fact which we may accept as a descriptive principle, but the principle tells us relatively little about the relation between the antecedent conditions of deprivation and the consummatory response which makes the regulation possible. In particular, in view of the complex relationships that have been discovered between drive-producing conditions of the rat and the occurrence of consummatory behavior, the choice among possible measures of the consummatory response will have to be made with some care if we are to have an appropriate test of the proposition that the intensity of hunger is monotonically related to the strength of the eating response.

Since our principal concern with hunger-produced drive is to derive a drive construct which will permit us to explain motivated behavior, i.e., instrumental behavior, it may prove more useful in the long run to use as a measure of the consummatory response one which is unalloyed by the postingestion effects of eating food. This consideration would limit us to probability measures such as the latency of the response. The latency of the consummatory response would seem, simply on this account, to be functionally more like instrumental behavior than other measures such as vigor, or persistence, or how much eating occurs. This may have been the point of Hall's cryptic footnote (1961, p. 139) where in talking about the latency to eat he says: "The time or latency measure is an instrumental response, not a consummatory one."

[9] Some of the most interesting research bearing on the distinction between the initiation and the satiation of eating comes from studies in which animals are given certain hypothalamic lesions which greatly increases their total food intake. Miller et al. (1950) have shown that such animals become enormously fat, but show decreased motivation in terms of their performance for food in an instrumental situation. Teitelbaum (1957) and Teitelbaum and Campbell (1958) have shown that the hyperphagic rat is actually quite finicky about its food, and is characterized primarily by its reluctance to stop eating once it has started, even though its initiation of eating is approximately normal. The hypothalamic hyperphasia literature has recently been summarized by Teitelbaum (1961) and Teitelbaum and Epstein (1962). Teitelbaum now believes that the hyperphagic animal also eats for calories, but that the caloric intake level for which it eats is abnormally high.

A Restatement of the Problem. All of the evidence discussed so far suggests that eating is only partly controlled by the animal's deprivation conditions. Like any other response, the probability of eating is also determined by situational factors and by the animal's history of reinforcement. If the consummatory response is viewed as being like any other response, and consequently conditionable to internal and external stimuli, then we cannot use it as an index of strength of drive unless we are prepared to say something about the strength of the consummatory habit in the test situation. Just because eating may be presumed to be of near maximum strength in some situations (e.g., the animal's homecage in the evening), we cannot assume it would be of maximum strength in an arbitrary test situation. The experimenter who would use the consummatory response as a measure of drive strength has the burden of showing that the stimuli occurring at the time of testing do, in fact, control the response and do so through a habit of near maximum strength.

In one sense, the question is only academic since certainly deprived animals eat while satiated ones do not. But our search is for a systematic quantification of the relationship between hunger and eating. Zimbardo and Montgomery (1957) and Bolles (1962, 1965) have measured the latency to eat as a function of hours deprivation, using naive animals and testing them in novel situations. The results, shown in Fig. 8-5, indicate that the strength of the eating response measured in terms of probability of occurrence is approximately a power function of deprivation time. Expressing the latency to eat as a function of weight loss rather than deprivation time does not destroy the orderly relationship; indeed, it increases the regularity, for it makes deprivation conditions comparable for animals of different sizes, as shown in Fig. 8-6. So it appears that the probability of eating in naive animals is indeed an increasing function of the severity of the deprivation conditions.

This relationship between the latency of eating and the strength of the drive-producing conditions is undoubtedly a function of associative factors, too, but the associative effects seem to be small relative to the impressive motivational effect (Bolles & Rapp, 1965). Welker (1959) and Candland and Culbertson (1963) have shown that rats show a considerable latency to eat, even when they are tested in their own homecages. Candland and Culbertson found that infant rats, deprived of either food or water showed less ability to go to the appropriate object when tested under short (1-hr. or 12-hr.) deprivations than older rats. Perhaps the weanling rat has to learn to go to food when it is hungry. Verplanck cites a study by Berry in which it was discovered that the latency to eat a piece of food is a function of the size of the piece because: "Rats eat small pieces of food at the place where it is found and transport large pieces to another place before eating it. This finding has implications for experiments . . . on habit strength as measured by running speed and resist-

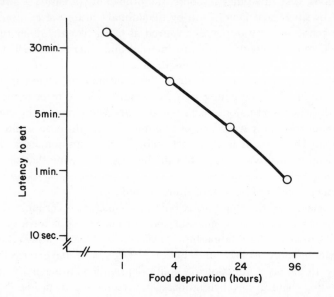

Fig. 8-5. The latency to eat as a function of deprivation time. Note that both coordinates are on logarithmic scales. (From Bolles, 1962)

ance to extinction . . . [and latency to eat]" (Verplanck, 1958, p. 102).

An alternative measure of the probability of eating was once suggested by Bousfield and Sherif (1932). They measured the speed with which eating is resumed after it is interrupted by a sudden loud noise. They found that rabbits and chickens resumed eating sooner if they had been deprived longer. A similar finding has been reported by Siegel and Correia (1963) for the rat.

Bayer (1929) and Bousfield and Spear (1935) have reported that in chickens the vigor of the eating response increases with deprivation (the chickens peck harder). Other animals may fail to show a vigor effect. Thus, Moll (1964) has found that rats maintained at 80% body weight ate significantly slower although they ate with a higher probability than animals maintained at 90% body weight.

If one must have data on the consumption of food as a function of hours of food deprivation, then Dufort and Wright's (1962) are of some value because their animals were naive, subjected to just a single test deprivation, and all tested at the same time of day. Therefore the associative factors that control food consumption were at least equated for all animals. Moreover, their subjects were tested over an extremely wide range of deprivation conditions. Their results are shown in Fig. 8-7.

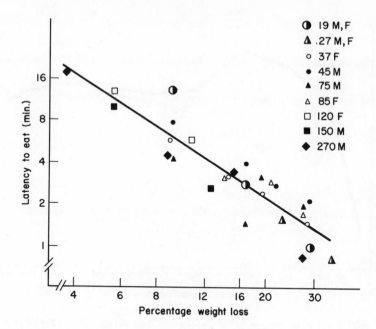

Fig. 8-6. The latency to eat as a function of weight loss for male and female rats of different ages. (From Bolles, 1965)

Finally, Allison (1964) has measured the proportion of time rats in a test arena stay near food rather than near another rat, or near play things. This index of consummatory behavior was found to increase systematically with deprivation time (Allison & Rocha, 1965). All of these measures of eating, particularly those involving the probability of eating, show that the consummatory response increases systematically in strength with the severity of the deprivation conditions. We can conclude that there is that much support for the hypothesis that hunger-produced D energizes eating.

Drinking. Just as eating has often been taken to be an a priori valid measure of hunger, so the drive strength resulting from water deprivation has often been uncritically "measured" in terms of the amount of water an animal will drink. And just as in the case of hunger, further consideration indicates that drinking should be considered first as a response, and then its relation to the antecedent conditions of deprivation and its relationships to other sorts of behavior have to be determined in their own right. Again, as in the case of hunger, some cues to the nature of the drinking response can be obtained from observing drinking under normal conditions.

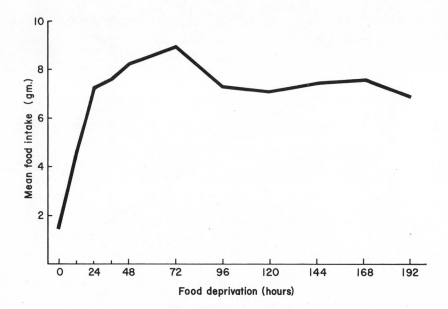

Fig. 8-7. Food consumption as a function of deprivation time. (From Dufort & Wright, 1962)

Normal Drinking Behavior. Smith and Smith (1939) found that when the cat drinks, it does so at an essentially constant rate; it cannot drink fast or slowly. Stellar and Hill (1952) showed that a constant rate of drinking is also found in the rat for a wide range of deprivation times —from 6 to 168 hr. (see Fig. 8-8).

The gradual increase in consumption found over a 2-hr. test period results from the greater persistence of drinking during the test rather than from an increased rate of drinking. Stellar and Hill report that the rat laps about 6 times a sec., taking .004 or .005 cc. per lap, which results in a fixed intake of about 1 cc. per min. as long as drinking continues. Lick rate is independent of age and experience (Schaeffer & Premack, 1961; Schaeffer & Huff, 1965). Davis and Keehn (1959), Keehn and Arnold (1960), and Keehn and Barakat (1964) have reported that this constancy of licking rate is disturbed only very slightly, perhaps to the extent of one lap per sec., by individual differences, by "local" variation, or by day-to-day variation in individual rats. Moreover, Davis and Keehn (1959) and Schaeffer and Huff (1965) have shown that the lick rate is independent of whether the liquid is sweet, salty, or plain.[10] It is also known that rats

[10] Sometimes drinking behavior is described in terms of a rate obtained by dividing the total number of licks by the duration of the test session (Premack & Hillix, 1962; Hulse et al., 1960, 1962). It is important to recognize that such

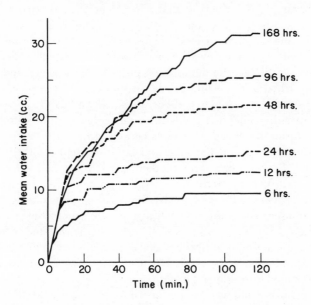

Fig. 8-8. Mean cumulative water intake in a 2-hr. test session following deprivations ranging from 6 to 168 hrs. (From Stellar & Hill, 1952)

drink approximately 20 drafts a day when they have water and food ad lib. (Young & Richey, 1952; Bolles, 1961), and that the number is not much affected by withdrawing food (Bolles, 1961).

The Relationship Between Drinking and Eating. It has been found that the diurnal course of drinking closely follows that of eating (Siegel & Stuckey, 1947). Moreover, when food is withheld, the rat's total daily water consumption drops to approximately one-half the normal value (Siegel & Stuckey, 1947a; Finger & Reid, 1952; Verplanck & Hayes, 1953; Calvin & Behan, 1954; Bolles, 1961). This phenomenon has also been reported with dogs (Kleitman, 1927; Gregersen, 1932; Robinson & Adolph, 1943). The reduction of drinking when food is withheld probably occurs in most animals but not in all. Schmidt-Nielsen et al. (1956) report that the camel is nearly immune to this problem, and Cizek (1961) found that the rabbit shows a great increase in water intake when food is withheld.

---

rate indices, in the case of the drinking response, are essentially persistence or probability measures rather than speed or vigor measures of the response, since what produces differences in such rates is only the persistence of drinking. It has been found, however, that the first few licks of a test session are appreciably faster (Collier, unpublished), take in more water per lick, and involve more tongue pressure (Imada, 1964) than later steady licking.

Gregersen (1932) observed that when dogs are fed once a day most of their water is taken in one draft immediately after eating; he suggested that the digestion of food creates a direct and immediate demand for water which is met by drinking if water is available. If drinking water is not available, the digestive system will make its demand anyhow, producing dehydration of other body tissues. A quarter of a century after Gregersen formulated this hypothesis, Lepkovsky et al. (1957) confirmed it experimentally. They fed dry food to rats either with or without water available during the meal. At various periods of time after eating the animals were sacrificed and the solid and liquid contents of their stomachs determined. It was found that whether or not water had been available with the meal, the stomach content was approximately 50% water. Evidently, immediately after dry food is ingested, or even during the meal, water is transported to the stomach at the expense of other body tissues (which Lepkovsky also assayed and found to be dehydrated in those rats that had not been allowed water). Some of this water is, of course, later returned to the rest of the body; but in the meanwhile the animal is dehydrated and will drink if possible.

This discovery has very important implications for what is referred to as "the interaction problem," which is the set of problems arising from the fact that depriving an animal of food or water results in the animal being not only hungry or thirsty as intended, but also, in some sense, thirsty or hungry as well. The Lepkovsky et al. results permit us to make a good guess at the particular sense in which thirsty animals are also hungry and hungry animals are also thirsty. We may also say on the basis of these results that although the total reduction in intake is nearly symmetrical for hunger and thirst, the underlying mechanisms are quite different in the two cases.

In the first place, the animal needs nearly all the food it consumes ad lib. to meet its various metabolic requirements; its intake, as noted above, is primarily regulated by calories. On the other hand, water intake is regulated by long-term metabolic requirements, plus the short-term demands created by the ingestion of dry food.

Hence, the nominally hungry animal drinks less because it needs less. The dependence of water intake upon food intake is diagrammed in Fig. 8-9. If no food is given, then water intake will be approximately equal to obligatory water loss. As more food is eaten, there is a proportional increase in water consumption. Any experimental manipulation that changes food intake, such as changing the temperature or altering the animal's metabolism, merely slides the animal up or down the curve (Strominger, 1946; Cizek, 1959). One such operation is restricting the animal to one meal a day. Upon being given its daily meal of dry food it will eat enough to maintain itself until the next day (if it has had some training), and it will also drink shortly thereafter a quantity of water

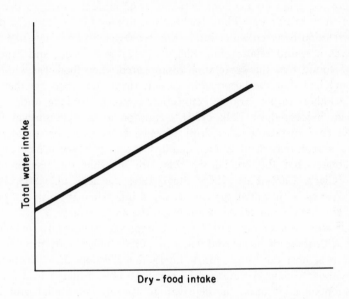

Fig. 8-9. Diagram of the relationship between average daily food and water intake. Total water includes the water content of the food, while food intake excludes this water. Both the intercept and the slope are higher for the rat than they are for the dog. (Strominger, 1946; Cizek, 1959)

necessary to meet the new demand created by the sudden ingestion of food.

On the other hand, when the animal is deprived of water its food requirements remain unchanged, so that the reduced food intake must represent some sort of "inhibition" of eating. The nature of this inhibition is not yet clear, but it could be that eating becomes aversive because it increases thirst. Or it could be that food loses palatability, because of dryness of the mouth. To support this interpretation is the finding (Reid & Campbell, 1960; Pliskoff & Tolliver, 1960) that thirsty animals avoid a stimulus that had previously been associated with food. Collier (1964) has suggested that thirsty animals reduce food intake in order to lose weight and thereby maintain water balance. Grossman (1962) has found evidence of reciprocal inhibition of eating and drinking within the hypothalamus. When water is again made available, the animal will drink what it needs, and then, the source of "inhibition" removed, will eat freely and nearly make up its self-imposed food deficit (Verplanck & Hayes, 1953).

In summary, to oversimplify slightly, the "thirsty" animal doesn't want to eat and the "hungry" animal doesn't need to drink.

There are other connections between drinking and eating in the rat, some of them artifactual. Thus, Richter and Brailey (1929) found a positive correlation between water intake and body weight, and suggested that there was a causal relationship. Siegel (1947) and Siegel and Stuckey (1947a) found that this correlation disappeared when food was withheld and concluded that the larger animals only drink more because they eat more. Another, rather strange connection between drinking and eating has been discovered by Falk (1961). Rats on a variable-interval food schedule tend to take a short drink after each food reinforcement, and during a session may drink a huge quantity of water. There is little agreement about what the crucial variables are or what the phenomenon means (Clark, 1962; Falk, 1964; Stein, 1964; Segal et al., 1963, 1964, 1965). It may be just that the rat usually drinks when it finishes a piece of food and has no immediate means of getting another piece.

Associative Factors in Drinking. Comparing the results of Siegel (1947) with those of Siegel and Talantis (1950) (Fig. 8-10) provides an indication of how the hunger-thirst interaction develops as a function of hours without water. We also see in Fig. 8-10 how drinking in a 5-min. test session depends upon hr. deprivation. Recall that Stellar and Hill (1952) found almost no difference in the amount drunk during the first 5 min. of testing (Fig. 8-8). The apparent discrepancy here may be explained on the grounds that Siegel's animals were naive since this was their first test in the situation, whereas Stellar and Hill's animals were highly familiar with their test conditions. The difference between the two sets of data therefore indicate a learning-to-drink phenomenon similar to the learning-to-eat phenomenon reported by Ghent (1951), Lawrence and Mason (1955), and Reid and Finger (1955). Subsequently, Ghent (1957) and Bolles (1962, 1965a) have shown that the latency to drink is a function of experience in the test situation and prior deprivation experience outside the test situation.

Collier et al. (1961) and Collier (1962a) have reported that in a situation where drinking has become really well established it may come so completely under the control of the test conditions that even the latency of drinking becomes relatively independent of deprivation conditions. Further evidence of the importance of the associative control of the drinking response has been reported by Fink and Patton (1953). They found that rats drank less as the stimulus conditions in the test situation were changed from those they were accustomed to. We may also note that, just as in the case of hunger, whereas the rat's drinking behavior in a short test session is clearly a function of experience in the situation, its water consumption over a 24-hr. period is relatively independent of its

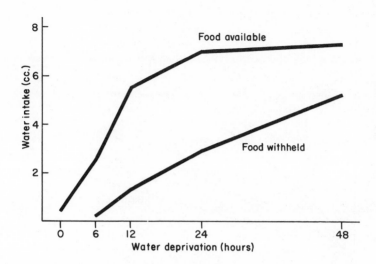

Fig. 8-10. Consumption of water during a 5-min. test as a function of hours water deprivation for animals with food (from Siegel, 1947), and for animals without food during the water deprivation. (From Siegel & Talantis, 1950)

experience with deprivation (Bolles, 1961; Beck, 1962; Dufort & Blick, 1962).

It has been found that just as the hungry rat will not eat enough to pay off its food debt, so the thirsty rat does not drink enough to regain a normal water balance. However, other species do. Adolph (1950) proposes that the ratio of consumption to deficit is fairly constant over a range of deprivation conditions for a given animal species, and that this ratio is relatively species-specific (see Fig. 8-11).

The regularity of the time of testing has also been found to be an important factor in the control of drinking. Kessen et al. (1960) maintained rats on a regular 24-hr. drinking cycle for 5 weeks. The animals were then tested under different deprivation times ranging from 0 to 47 hr. All tests were interspersed with drinking sessions scheduled at the regular accustomed time. Water consumption for a given deprivation time was greater at the regular test hour than at the irregular hours, and maximal at 24 hr. deprivation (the same pattern of results Lawrence and Mason, 1955a, found in eating). Kessen et al. interpret their results as indicating the importance of drinking habits established on the basis of regularly scheduled drinking. The best evidence for the dependence of drinking upon temporal cues is the fact that all animals showed a sharp increase

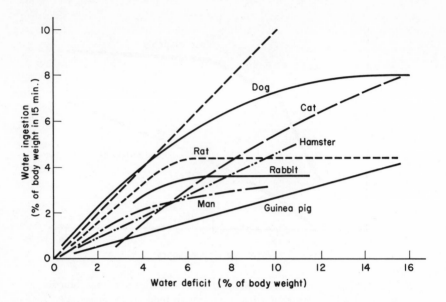

Fig. 8-11. Water consumption as a function of water deficit for different species. (Adapted from Adolph, 1950)

in drinking at or near 24 hr. deprivation, a time of testing which would correspond to the regular time of drinking.

The available evidence therefore seems to indicate that the onset of drinking is controlled by many of the same factors that control eating. Furthermore, many of the same satiation mechanisms appear to be as applicable to thirst as to hunger. Bellows (1939) and Adolph et al. (1954) have found that a dog will sham drink only a little more than its deficit, so evidently there is a "mouth factor," some sort of metering of what is drunk. There is also evidence of at least one "gut factor." Stomach loading without oral ingestion reduces subsequent drinking (Miller et al., 1957; Moyer & Bunnell, 1962) and this inhibition of drinking occurs before appreciable water assimilation can occur. This effect is probably not just a matter of stomach distention (although Towbin, 1949, has shown that distention can inhibit drinking) but rather is due to some local effect of water on the stomach which signals the central nervous system that repletion of body water is imminent (Adolph et al., 1954). A frequently proposed mechanism is the change in extracellular tonicity or osmotic pressure produced by water loading. There is, however, a growing body of evidence that this simple mechanism is inadequate. For example, intravenous saline injections make an animal thirsty, but subsequent intravenous water fails to alleviate the thirst (Holmes & Montgomery, 1960; Holmes, 1964), and in fact, the dog prefers to drink saline solutions following saline injections. Animals depleted of salt increase rather than decrease their water intake (Cizek, 1961; Falk, 1965). Of course it is well known that following heavy sweating man will drink to replace the water loss even though this throws the tonicity of the body fluids further out of balance. Because of these anomalies, and because of the great difference among species, Adolph (1964) has suggested that the hypothetical osmotic satiation mechanism must be supplemented by a host of other devices if we are to explain drinking and its satiation.

The amount consumed would seem therefore to be a rather poor measure of the strength of the drinking response; latency to drink should have an advantage in that it is free of satiation effects. There are apparently no data on the probability of drinking as a function of weight loss. However, the latency to drink has been investigated as a function of deprivation time (Bolles, 1962, 1965a) (see Fig. 8-12). These studies and the one by Siegel (1947) seem to be the only ones showing energizing effects of water deprivation upon drinking behavior which are free from, or at least not confounded with, possible postingestion and associative effects. These results, like the similar results with hungry animals, support

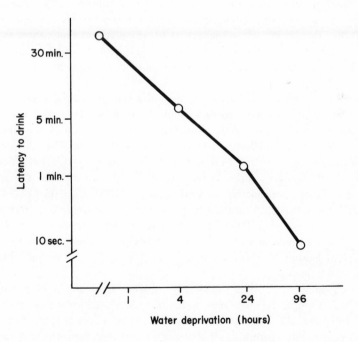

Fig. 8-12. The latency to drink as a function of deprivation time. (From Bolles, 1962)

the hypothesis that the strength of the consummatory behavior increases systematically with the severity of the relevant drive-producing condition.

Sex. We considered in Chapter 7 some of the interpretive problems that arise from the fact the consummatory response in sexual behavior is so complicated. For both the male and the female rat the chain of responses that constitute the consummatory reaction are highly dependent upon a complex of hormonal and stimulus factors, none of which really seem to "motivate" the consummatory response. In most cases, as we consider animals higher on the phylogenetic scale, sexual behavior is found to be relatively less dependent upon hormonal conditions and more dependent upon sensory and other "psychological" factors, such as previous experience.

On the consequent side, we may measure the "vigor" or "insistence" of sexual responses in a way not applicable to eating or drinking. Thus, Stone (1926), Hemmingsen (1933), and Ball (1937) have all observed that there are 10 or 12 distinguishable reactions, such as quivering and lordosis, which characterize the female rat in heat. Since these reactions appear to fall into a hierarchical order indicating the degree of arousal or receptivity, the occurrence of such patterns may be used as an index of the strength of female sexual motivation. For the most part, however, these finer possible gradations are ignored and the female is ordinarily judged on a two-point scale; she is either receptive or not receptive. Hence, we do not yet know the extent to which sexual motivation as defined by an ordinal scale such as Stone's relates to the instrumental behavioral consequences which drive is supposed to have in the Hullian system.

Young and his co-workers have devised a similar ordinal scale for the male guinea pig and have correlated instrumental performance with the resulting arousal scores. Each animal is scored in terms of the highest point achieved in a 10-min. test in terms of the hierarchy of arousal reactions ranging from mild interest in the female to ejaculation (Young & Grunt, 1951). This index is used to define the strength of the male animal's sex motivation. Grunt and Young (1953) have proceeded to use this scale to demonstrate the persistence of individual differences, and Valenstein et al. (1955) have studied the dependence of sexual behavior upon various factors of previous experience. This work holds high promise of leading to a genuinely quantitative analysis of sexual motivation in the guinea pig.

Exploration, Etc. The customary measure of exploratory behavior (and by inference, the customary index of strength of exploratory motivation) has been the amount of it that occurs in a test period. The test period is typically 10 min., and the specific response measure is typically the total distance traversed, or the total number of parts of the apparatus entered during the test period. Thus, the "drive strength" is judged in terms of the amount of the consummatory response that occurs. This convention is no more satisfactory in the case of exploration than it has proven to be for eating, drinking, and sexual behavior, but other possible measures of the consummatory response are difficult to apply in practice. Thus, the vigor of exploratory behavior has yet to be defined, and probability measures are almost meaningless in view of the fact that the rat starts almost immediately to sniff and to locomote in any strange environment, or to investigate in one way or another any novel stimulus that is suddenly introduced into the situation. However, by using a relatively uncommon response as a criterion of exploration it is possible to get meaningful latency measures of exploration (Fehrer, 1956; Bolles & de Lorge, 1962).

De Lorge and Bolles (1961) have argued that another source of confusion in research on exploratory behavior arises from the use of a single component (which is usually locomotion) as a criterion of exploration. If locomotion is conceived to be just one expression of a more general tendency of the animal to expose itself to novel stimulation, and if all the varieties of behavior which serve this purpose (such as sniffing, manipulating, rearing, etc.) are grouped together, a quite different view of exploration is obtained. For one thing, exploration involves a variety of possible consummatory behaviors rather than just one, such as eating or drinking. For another, we discover that the domesticated rat is more or less always exploring.

The fundamental difficulty with exploration (and this holds for the "activity drive" as well) is that it is difficult to keep consummatory activity from occurring. The animal can explore or be active whenever it wants to; we have very little control over it. The best we can do is to present the animal with a novel and complex situation, hoping thereby to increase the amount of exploration that will occur. And in the absence of antecedent anchoring of an exploratory source of drive we cannot say whether the antecedent conditions energize the consummatory behavior.

In the case of aversive motivation there is a failure of the conceptual distinction between consummatory and instrumental behavior since any response that is instrumental in, for example, escaping shock, is also necessarily an escape response, and therefore consummatory. We will turn shortly to the question of whether instrumental escape behavior is "energized" by aversive stimuli.

It might be that flight, activity, exploration, and sex, like eating and drinking, would be found to be energized by relevant antecedent drive conditions, if appropriate antecedent conditions could be found for all of them, and if the consummatory response was measured appropriately. At the present stage these ifs appear rather imposing; it certainly cannot be stated as a general rule that drive conditions energize their respective consummatory behaviors. Much more needs to be determined about each of these kinds of behavior before such a statement could be defended.

THE ENERGIZING OF INSTRUMENTAL BEHAVIOR

Probability Measures—Latency. The latency of a simple noncompetitive instrumental response becomes shorter when the drive-producing conditions are made more severe. This is the case for escape from shock (Trapold & Fowler, 1960), and for food deprivation (Kimble, 1951; Horenstein, 1951; Deese & Carpenter, 1951; Ramond et al., 1955).[11]

The most comprehensive data are Kimble's, shown in Fig. 8-13.

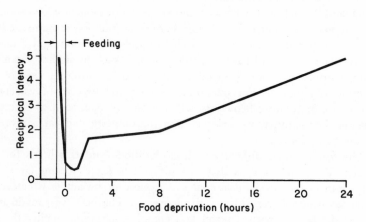

Fig. 8-13. Speed of a panel-pushing response after an interruption in feeding or after a period of deprivation. (Adapted from Kimble, 1951)

Kimble trained rats to press a panel to obtain food, and then tested them at various times after they had finished a regularly scheduled meal. Some very short deprivation periods were used; in fact, under some conditions the animals were interrupted during their meal and tested. Hence, the declining speed scores shown on the left-hand side of Fig. 8-13 indicate

[11] The expected relationship is not always found, though; Reynolds (1949a) reported an increase in latency with increasing hunger, and Woods et al. (1964) found that when amount of reinforcement was held constant there was little effect of water temperature in a water-escape situation. By a "noncompetitive" instrumental response we mean merely a learned response which has a much higher probability of occurrence than any other response in the situation. It should be noted in passing that response speed, the reciprocal of latency, has been sanctioned by Spence (1956) and Logan (1952a) as a direct measure of effective excitatory reaction potential.

what might be regarded as a decline in motivation as a function of pre-feeding the animal a certain portion of its daily meal. It is interesting to note that the speed of responding decreases for some time after the animal has stopped eating, as though an aversion to food develops after a meal is eaten. Another interesting feature of the curve is the sudden rise in speed of responding which occurs about 2 hr. after the meal. Finally, the instrumental response continues to gain in strength as the deprivation is increased from 2 to 24 hr. This portion of the function indicates the principal relationship between hrs. deprivation and hunger motivation. A similar relationship, including the sharp rise between 1 and 2 hr., has been found in other studies involving short deprivation times (Horenstein, 1951; Koch & Daniel, 1945; Saltzman & Koch, 1948) using both latency and resistance to extinction measures. The shape of the curve above 24 hr. is still open to question.

Resistance to Extinction. There also seems to be little question that resistance to extinction in a simple noncompetitive situation increases with hrs. deprivation (Perin, 1942; Saltzman & Koch, 1948; Strassburger, 1950; Yamaguchi, 1951). Sometimes negative results have been reported (Skinner, 1936; Sackett, 1939; Finan, 1940), but perhaps they can be attributed merely to the tremendous variability typically found in resistance to extinction scores. Even at best the effects are small. For example, Yamaguchi used deprivations ranging from 3 to 72 hr. and found that the median resistance to extinction scores varied only from 12 to 28, while the overall range under each condition was from 0 to 100 or more. Consequently, we can say that the conditions of deprivation have relatively little to do with the resistance to extinction of an instrumental response, although deprivation evidently does have some effect in the expected direction.

A number of writers have emphasized that what really characterizes the motivated animal is its persistence in those activities upon which reinforcement is contingent.[12] Persistence can be measured in a number of ways: as the number of unreinforced responses that occur, i.e., resistance to extinction, or as the rate of responding in the presence of reinforcement. The latter provides a difficult measure to interpret, since the overall rate of responding depends not only upon the probability of responding, but also upon the time spent in responding and the time spent taking reinforcement. Another possibility is to present reinforcement, but in very small amounts, so that little time is spent in consummatory activity. This

---

[12] Atkinson (1964) has pointed out that persistence is one property of motivated behavior for which Hull made no provision in his drive theory. Atkinson (1964), Atkinson & Cartwright (1964), and Feather (1962) review some of the theory and research on the persistence of behavior. The importance of reinforcement in making behavior persistent is often overlooked; these recent writers overlook it, and so did older writers, such as McDougall, who stressed persistence.

was the technique of Warden et al. (1931) with the Columbia obstruction box.

On the other hand, with the judicious use of minimal reinforcement, e.g., providing it on an intermittent schedule, animals can be differentially reinforced for persistence. Under these conditions the rate of responding increases with the severity of food deprivation (Skinner, 1936; Heron & Skinner, 1937; Weiss & Moore, 1956; Clark, 1958). Figure 8-14 shows

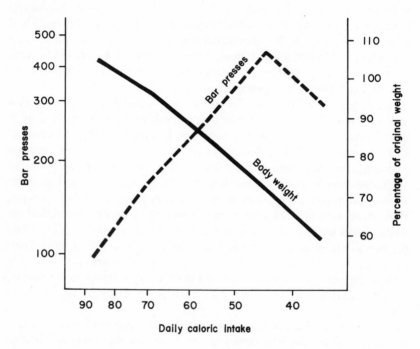

Fig. 8-14. Bar pressing for sucrose on an FR20 schedule by rats maintained on a fixed daily caloric intake. The resulting body weight is also indicated.

some unpublished data of Levitsky and Collier on the rate of bar pressing of hungry rats reinforced with sucrose on a fixed ratio of 20. The animals were adult and had been maintained for 56 days on limited caloric intake. All animals, except the most deprived, had reached asymptotic weight loss.

Response-rate measures require a considerable amount of prior training before they become stable and are usually obtained by averaging the rate over a large number of responses. Hence it is difficult to relate such measures to measures of response probability and speed. Rate measures are sometimes assumed to be elemental or primary in their own right, and the functional differences between them and other possible response measures are attributed to deficiencies in the latter (Skinner, 1950). Sometimes there are anomalous differences between rate measures and other measures. For example, we have just seen that the rate of bar pressing may increase with deprivation up to a 25% weight loss, whereas obstruction-box scores reach a peak at about 48 hr. (or about 15% weight loss), and other measures may reach a peak at 24 hr. (or about 10% weight loss). What is needed is more analysis of what animals are doing when they are pressing a bar, and how drive conditions affect the different components of the integrated response chain (e.g., Gollub, 1964).

Delayed Responding. One situation which presents an apparent exception to the general rule that response probability increases with an increase in the severity of the drive conditions is that in which the subject is differentially reinforced for responding slowly. Conrad et al. (1958) trained rats and a monkey to wait for 20 to 24 sec. after reinforcement before pressing the bar for the next reinforcement. The subjects did learn the temporal discrimination (with considerable training) and when it was once established, performance on the problem was relatively unaffected by wide variation in the deprivation conditions. The only effect of deprivation was that for very short deprivation periods the subjects did not seem able to wait adequately. With animals less able to make the necessary temporal discrimination, overall response rate increases with deprivation and, as it does, the discrimination performance may become either better or worse (Revusky, 1963; Reynolds, 1964).

How do we account for such findings? Let us think of the animal engaging in a series or chain of responses of which pressing the bar is only the last one. Observation of animals in delayed-response situations indicates that they do, in fact, acquire ritualistic patterns of behavior to fill the interval, and it seems likely that what is involved here is the acquisition of a pattern of responses the occurrence of which is indeed made more probable by increasing drive. Under low drive, responses in competition with the initial responses of the chain recur, and as a consequence the animal cannot "wait" as it has learned to do. So there is nothing necessarily inconsistent between these results and the general rule that increasing drive increases response probability, provided we define the response properly. There is still a host of problems connected with delayed responding and delayed reinforcement, however. We will consider some of them in Chapter 12.

Amplitude Measures. All of the response measures discussed above, latency, resistance to extinction, and the like, may be taken as alternate indices of a common behavioral property, namely, the probability that the response will occur in a given interval of time. In contrast with all of these probability measures there are response measures that tell us something about the amplitude or strength or vigor of the response. The question then arises whether these measures also are functionally dependent upon drive conditions. The bulk of the evidence on this question indicates that responding does become more vigorous as motivation conditions are made more severe (Notterman & Mintz, 1965).

Zener and McCurdy (1939) found that as hunger is increased the strength of a conditioned salivary reflex in the dog becomes stronger relative to the unconditioned salivary reflex. In fact, Zener and McCurdy have suggested that the ratio of conditioned to unconditioned reflex strengths (saliva secretion) could be used as an index of drive strength.

An energizing effect of drive conditions was first found with speed in a runway by Szymanski (1918). This effect was subsequently confirmed with hunger (Davis, 1957; Barry, 1958; Butter & Campbell, 1960; Lewis & Cotton, 1960), sexual motivation (Beach & Jordan, 1956a), and escape from shock (Trapold & Fowler, 1960; Karsh, 1962). Trapold and Fowler's results are shown in Fig. 8-15. There are of course many, many other studies reporting increases either in running speed or in overall speed, i.e., the reciprocal of latency plus running time.

Everything would seem to be in order with respect to the energizing of behavior, and in accordance with the Hullian drive construct, but the situation is not quite that simple. The first serious challenge for the energization hypothesis we will consider comes from the area of discrimination learning.

Discrimination Performance.   Performance on a discrimination problem is important for theories of motivation because of the arbitrary contingencies that can be established between the animal's behavior and reinforcement. The discrimination situation can be contrasted with the type of noncompetitive response situation we have been considering in that in the former we attempt to associate the response with specific stimuli, while on the latter the response may be associated with any stimulus on the situation. There is, accordingly, less obvious relevance between the hungry rat running to vertical stripes as against horizontal ones, or a white card as against a black card, than there is when the hungry rat merely runs, or salivates; in the latter case the vigor and the probability of the response seem in some intangible way appropriate to the drive condition.[13]

In Hull's system, whether or not increasing drive level will facilitate discrimination performance depends upon whether the habit strength of

[13] This may have been what Thorndike meant by "belongingness" (see p. 438). The whole point of the S-R approach in recent years has been to show that training can overcome whatever belongingness there is in the naive animal between particular sorts of behavior and particular rewards, or else to show that such relationships which appear innate are actually due to prior training. Lorge (1936) showed that animals would learn to groom as an instrumental response when reinforced by food, and Skinnerians have been emphasizing the importance of the "pure operant" ever since. What the question comes down to experimentally is whether all responses are trainable with equal ease. For example, can a rat be trained to stand still for food as easily as it can be trained to run? If it cannot (Blough, 1958), then we have some need for a concept like belongingness.

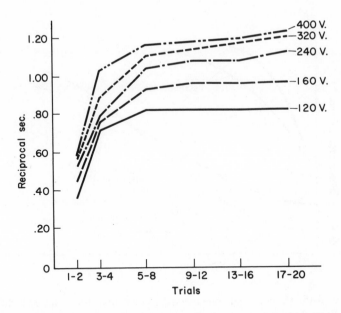

Fig. 8-15. Acquisition of running speed in escape from shock as a function of shock intensity in the runway. (Acquisition of starting speed was generally more gradual and the asymptotic speeds were not monotonically related to voltage.) (From Trapold & Fowler, 1960)

the correct response is greater than the habit strengths of competing responses. Thus, if we were to compare the performance of high-drive and low-drive animals in a difficult discrimination-learning task the percentage of correct responses under the two conditions should depend upon whether the comparison was made early or late in learning. The situation should be something like that diagrammed in Fig. 8-16. If the correct response is governed by a relatively weak habit, then early in learning discrimination should be worsened by the multiplicative effect of increasing drive, whereas later in learning, after the habit has become dominant, any increment in drive should lead to improved discrimination. Data to support such an analysis has been obtained by Ramond (1954a) with rats and by Glucksberg (1962) with humans in complex learning situations.

In the usual discrimination-learning situations the relative frequency with which the animal responds correctly and incorrectly is a consequence of the initial strengths of the two habits. Spence (1958) has suggested that if the correct response is permitted to occur more frequently

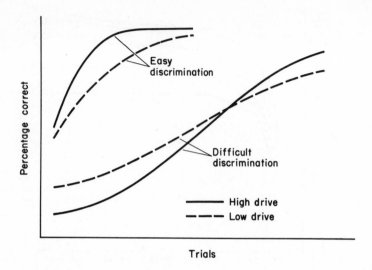

Fig. 8-16. Hypothetical interaction between drive level and task difficulty in discrimination learning.

than the incorrect response, then when the discrimination is learned a facilitory effect of drive upon performance is generally found (Dodson, 1917; Tolman & Honzik, 1930; Tolman & Gleitman, 1949; Hillman et al., 1953; Ramond, 1954; Eisman, 1956; Eisman et al., 1956). On the other hand, Spence observes, if animals are forced to make the correct and incorrect response an equal number of times, then the expected facilitory effect is not found (Teel & Webb, 1951; Teel, 1952; Spence, Goodrich & Ross, 1959).[14] But there are exceptions to this pattern. For example, Carper (1957), Armus (1958), and Jensen (1960) found drive conditions to have no effect in T-maze problems; and Lachman (1961) found no effect of drive conditions on the relative frequency of correct and incorrect responses in a visual discrimination task. Sometimes drive conditions produce effects in the unexpected direction (Birch, 1955; Bruner et al., 1955). Sometimes (e.g., Myers, 1952; Champion, 1954; Carlton, 1955) no difference in performance as a function of drive conditions can be found anywhere during the course of learning. This is notoriously true in the case of primates (Meyer, 1951; Miles, 1959).

Lachman (1961) has pointed out one reason why discrimination per-

[14] This empirical generalization is partly what led Spence (1956, 1958) to give up Hull's drive-reduction hypothesis of reinforcement. It appears that it is the number of times the animal makes the correct and incorrect responses that determines their habit strength.

formance may be so slightly dependent upon drive conditions. The animal that is highly motivated may be in a great hurry (because of the energizing effect of drive on the speed of the running response) and hence not expose himself sufficiently to the stimuli to be discriminated. Lachman attempted to test this hypothesis by delaying animals so that they would have adequate opportunity to see the stimuli, but he found no interaction between the delay conditions and the drive conditions. Because discrimination error scores showed no effect of drive conditions whereas speed of responding did, Lachman concluded that discrimination learning is, to a degree, independent of the concurrent locomotor behavior. Some sort of multiple habit hypothesis may be necessary to explain the effects of motivation upon discrimination performance.

Perhaps we have been too ready to oversimplify the discrimination situation and think of it as involving a competition between just two responses, the correct one and the incorrect one. For some purposes such an analysis may be adequate; but evidently in the case of evaluating the effect of motivation upon discrimination performance, or selective learning, such an account is too simple to do justice to the facts. Notwithstanding the great promise of Spence's (1958, 1960) analysis of selective learning, it seems quite possible that the behavioral rules which are applicable here are not the same as those which can account for behavior in a noncompetitive situation. Lachman's suggestion is that we begin to consider discrimination learning as involving responses over and beyond those that are actually involved in getting the animal through the apparatus. Locomotory behavior clearly varies with drive conditions; the orienting responses, or whatever, upon which the discrimination is based seem to be independent of drive.

All of the discrimination situations we have considered so far have involved spatial discrimination in which subjects are required to respond differentially in space, locomoting toward one stimulus and away from another. In the case of nonspatial discrimination, in which subjects are required to respond by, say, pressing a bar in the presence of one stimulus but not to press in its absence, Dinsmoor (1952) and Coate (1964) have reported that the rate of responding increases both in the presence and in the absence of the discriminative stimulus, but that the rate under the two conditions was always in a constant ratio, so that the accuracy of the discrimination was not affected by deprivation conditions.

In classical discriminative avoidance conditioning Spence and Farber (1954) and Runquist et al. (1959) report only a nonsignificant increase in discrimination performance with US intensity. Tentatively, then, it may be said that an energizing effect is found in discrimination performance, first, when (as Spence has argued) the correct response has greater habit strength than the incorrect response, and second, when the correct response involves approaching a particular stimulus. Under other conditions, discrimination performance seems to be relatively independent of drive conditions.[15]

Complex Learning Situations. The naive view of motivation and complex learning is that as the animal becomes more motivated it tries harder to solve the problem in order to get more quickly to the reward. If such a view was ever tenable, it had to be abandoned after a study by Yerkes and Dodson (1908) showed that performance in a maze-learning situation improved with increased motivation (intensity of an electric shock) up to a point beyond which it deteriorated. This point of optimum motivation was found to be high for easy tasks and lower for more difficult problems. This relationship has become generally known as the *Yerkes-Dodson Law.* The law suggests that there is an optimum motivational level for a given complexity of learning task, and that the harder the task the lower the optimum level is. This is a fairly serviceable, if crude, generalization. Its crudity is due to the fact that the decrements produced by more than optimum motivation of different sorts probably are due to different effects, for example, overvigorous responding or ina-nition in the case of hunger, and competing emotional behavior in the case of electric shock.[16]

To the degree that the Yerkes-Dodson law has empirical validity it would seem to require an amendment to the principle that drive ener-gizes habits; the amendment needs to indicate that it is true only for motivations up to a moderate intensity. Actually, what most drive theo-rists have done is to introduce an alternative oversimple amendment to the energizing principle, namely, that the energizing drive condition must not itself introduce response tendencies that compete with the criterion response.

In spite of the considerable amount of work (some of which we will consider in the next chapter) that has been done on the effect of moti-vation on complex learning, we have yet to derive any principles more fundamental than the Yerkes-Dodson law. So, while complex learning situations could potentially shed much light on the nature of motivation (because of the arbitrariness of the response-reinforcement contingencies that can be established), that potential has not been realized. Hence, the data from discriminative and complex learning situations have neither strengthened nor weakened the case for the drive construct.

[15] We will come to a similar conclusion in Chapter 12 regarding the effect of incentive motivation on discrimination performance.

[16] Those who think of drive in terms of arousal (e.g., Bindra, 1959; Malmo, 1959) have usually emphasized that there is an optimum level of arousal for optimum performance with a given task complexity. Presumably too much arousal floods the nervous system with stimulation which breaks up behavioral coordina-tion. The optimum-stimulation argument has also been advanced by those (e.g., Hebb, 1949; Leuba, 1955) who oppose the "Nirvana" and homeostatic models of motivation developed by Freud, Cannon, Hull, and others.

In conclusion, most of the support for the energizing principle comes from simple noncompetitive learning situations. In such situations most measures of response probability and response vigor increase with the severity of the drive conditions. This is the case, within limits, for hunger, thirst, sex, and escape; and it might be the case for other varieties of motivated behavior if appropriate antecedent conditions could be found for them. We thus have a fair amount of experimental support for a hypothesis which has been assumed almost from the beginning to be valid. Recent work, however, has not only questioned some of the evidence supporting the energization hypothesis, but has also offered us a powerful alternative, which we may now consider.

ASSOCIATIVE EXPLANATIONS OF ENERGIZATION EFFECTS

The correlation of drive-condition severity with *response probability* does not itself constitute sufficient grounds for inventing a construct such as D which brings this correlation about. One could suppose, to consider just one alternative, that the correlation is due to the effects of the stimuli arising from the drive conditions rather than to any energizing effect of these conditions. If we assume that the animal learns an instrumental response in the presence of certain drive stimuli, S_D, then these stimuli should acquire some associative control over the response. Then, as the severity of deprivation is increased, S_D acquire a more dominant place in the total set of stimuli controlling the response, and the response, accordingly, should have greater probability. Similarly, when the drive conditions are reduced in severity, S_D diminish in intensity and in prominence in the total stimulus situation and, insofar as they do control the instrumental response, it should occur with less strength. Such an amotivational explanation of the apparent energizing of behavior with deprivation is similar to the view expressed long ago by Guthrie (1935). This view has been revived and given currency by the recent writings of Maatsch (1954), Denny and Adelman (1955), Estes (1958), and others.

Brown (1961), who has presented the best recent case for a Hullian type of drive theory, regards this associationistic explanation of motivational phenomena as the principal alternative. According to Brown, the crucial finding, which can be handled by drive theory but which cannot be handled by the usual associationistic theory, is that when the drive conditions are suddenly shifted upward in severity, performance shifts in an appropriate manner. A dropping-off in performance with a shift downward in drive conditions presents no problem for either theoretical position; the drive theorists can argue that there is less D to energize the instrumental response, and the associationist can argue that the animal is being tested under conditions which depart from the training conditions so that a performance decrement is to be expected. But when deprivation is made more severe, or in the case of aversive learning, when stimulation is made more intense, the associationist ought to predict, again, a decrement in performance due to departure from the test conditions, whereas the drive theorist is prepared to predict an improvement in performance. The evidence for improvement under these conditions is rather substantial. First of all, there are studies in which drive conditions are suddenly shifted after learning has occurred in order to see if performance shifts appropriately. It does (Deese & Carpenter, 1951; Hillman et al., 1953; Davis, 1957).[17] There is also evidence from latent-learning experiments of the sort where the animal explores the maze, finds food some place but doesn't eat because it is not deprived, and then is later tested deprived to see if it will go to the food place. The majority of experiments of this type have produced positive results (see Kimble, 1961), and thereby provide more support for the drive-theory interpretation.

As Brown is careful to point out, even this evidence is not crucial, however, because it is possible to reformulate the associationistic position so that it too can cope with the facts. What is needed is an assumption like Estes' (1958) that as the severity of deprivation is increased there is a reduction in the prominence of stimuli, which we may call satiation cues, to which have been conditioned responses (e.g., resting, lying down, being inactive) that compete with the criterion response. According to this view, a decline in performance with reduced motivation can be attributed to the introduction of new tendencies which compete with the instrumental response. Similarly, as deprivation is made more severe these satiation cues drop out; there results less competition for the instrumental response, and so it occurs with greater probability. This is an elegant conception. But it is not readily applicable to measures of response amplitude or vigor. Why should an instrumental response be executed with more energy as drive conditions are made more extreme? This, in my opinion, is the one phenomenon that confounds associationistic explanations of behavior as they are now formulated and developed.

Estes has attempted to deal with this problem by assuming that a certain amount of elapsed running time is spent not in actual running but in competing behavior, such as grooming and exploring the environment. It is quite possible that what is recorded as faster running under high drive may not be, in fact, more vigorous responding, but only responding which is more probable than the responding under low drive;

---

[17] There have been a number of other "drive shift" studies. But these seem to be the only ones in which performance on the first postshift trial can be determined. This is the only critical trial, the only one not contaminated by possible effects of extinction, or change in incentive, or something else, resulting from the shift in the experimental conditions.

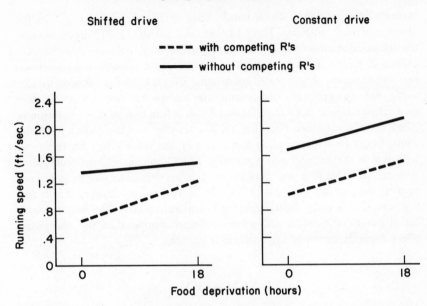

Fig. 8-17. Speed of running as a function of deprivation on trials on which competing responses were recorded and on trials free of overt competing responses. On the left are shown the results of animals trained and tested under the different drive conditions and on the right are shown the results of animals trained and tested only under a single drive condition. (Adapted from Cicala, 1961)

what is recorded as greater vigor may only be greater probability. Estes (1958) in particular has offered this explanation for what appears to be one of the energizing effects of drive. Empirical support for this position comes from a study by Cotton (1953). Cotton ran animals in a runway under 0, 6, 16, and 22 hr. food deprivation and compared running time on those trials where there was no overt competing behavior, such as grooming or exploring, with running times on trials where competing behavior did occur. The results indicate the usual relationship suggestive of an energizing effect of drive on response vigor when competing response trials were included. But considering just the noncompeting response trials, running speed was almost independent of deprivation conditions, lending support to the response-competition interpretation.

A serious criticism of Cotton's study may be raised, however. Cotton ran one large group of animals and trained them under all four of the deprivation conditions in a mixed order. His animals had a great deal of running experience in the apparatus under each of the different conditions prior to testing. It is possible that this extensive training under different deprivation conditions had the effect of eliminating differences in vigor of responding which would have occurred naturally, i.e., in the absence of such training. King (1959) and Cicala (1961) have recently conducted response-competition experiments in a runway using a procedure in which different groups of animals were trained and tested under the different deprivation conditions. Cicala's results (shown in Fig. 8-17) are unequivocal; discounting the competing response trials does give shorter times, but not differentially as a function of drive conditions. That is to say, either counting or discounting the competing response trials, hours food deprivation has precisely the same effect on the vigor with which the rat will run a runway. The Cotton-Estes interpretation is a most attractive one and perhaps further investigation will help to confirm it. But, so far, it seems that if the animal is very hungry it will run fast and if it is only slightly hungry it will run slowly. The best recourse for the associationist would seem to be to assume that the energizing effect depends somehow upon previous learning.

SUMMARY

If there is any one phenomenon which psychologists can agree provides the basic core of motivation, it is the energization of behavior. Unfortunately the evidence on energization does not seem to present as coherent a picture as is usually taken for granted. For example, the usual evidence that a rat is hungry is that it will learn an instrumental response to get to food; the usual evidence that a male rat is sexually motivated is that it will engage in the consummatory behavior; and the usual evidence that the female rat is sexually motivated is that she runs in a certain way in an activity wheel. Research on these problems has tended to become specialized so that there is relatively little evidence to show that the same male rat would be motivated according to a general activity criterion, or that the same female rat would be sexually motivated by an instrumental response criterion. What is needed, not just to save the concept of drive, but to make sense out of animal behavior is data to fill in these gaps. We really do not know if the energization of behavior has the generalized properties it is usually assumed to have.

Even more perplexing than the failure of generalization across different kinds of behavior has been the failure to show generalized energizing effects across different measures of the same kind of behavior. Thus, we may find probability measures showing the expected effects and amplitude measures not showing them.

But after much confused searching and many false alarms, we seem to be arriving at some general principles. In some cases, such as hunger, there is a very good correlation between the severity of the drive-producing conditions and the probability and vigor of responding. This energizing effect, which Hull hypothesized to be universal for all behavior, seems to be rather limited. It has only been well demonstrated for instrumental behavior, i.e., behavior which has been reinforced by a prompt change in the correlated motivating conditions. The energizing effect is also seen in consummatory behavior, where reinforcement is also operative, but as we will see in Chapter 10, it seems to disappear when the contingencies between behavior and reinforcement are removed, e.g., in general activity.

Two considerations indicate the basic importance of response vigor: (1) We will see in the chapters to follow that there are few empirical links for the drive construct, and that one of the best established of these involves the energizing of instrumental behavior. (2) If energization means no more than increasing response probability, then this can be readily handled without invoking drive either in purely associative terms, in terms of the greater drive reduction or incentive value of the reinforcer that occurs with more severe drive conditions, or in terms of stimulus sensitization effects. However, if substantial evidence could be found that drive changes lead to changes in vigor it would provide an additional and much-needed empirical link for the drive construct.

9

ASSOCIATIVE ASPECTS OF DRIVE

❖❰❁❖❰

If we are to understand the behavior of adults or even of children we need not bother ourselves much with tissue needs. We do well to give our attention to what the child or adult has learned.

E. R. Guthrie and A. L. Edwards

In Hull's theory of behavior, the construct D is not itself involved in determining the direction of behavior; it merely energizes whatever habits exist in a given situation. Nevertheless, drive is implicated in two different ways in the formation of habits. Hull hypothesized first of all that drive reduction was the mechanism whereby habits are strengthened, and second, that the conditions which produce drive, such as hunger, have characteristic stimulus consequences, S_D, such as stomach contractions, which may enter directly into the formation of habits.

In the present chapter we will consider the experimental evidence relevant to these two propositions. Before discussing these two problems we will consider the evidence that has resulted from the attempts to provide a direct test of Hull's hypothesis that D and H are independent. The tests of all of these hypothesized properties of D have usually been undertaken in good faith, i.e., in the hope of supporting Hull's theory. However, the results are not as gratifying as had been hoped. All three of these propositions about drive have turned out to have some predictive value but in each case they have a number of difficulties and limitations.

The present chapter will lead us to three very broad conclusions: (1) The explanation of behavior cannot be carried out as easily as we might have thought; both the motivational factors and the habit factors that determine behavior are much more complicated than had been anticipated. (2) Partly as a result of this complexity, behavior must be analyzed very carefully to determine just what stimuli and responses do, in fact, enter into association. (3) There is a growing tendency to explain the motivational components of behavior in terms of incentive rather than in terms of drive. What we will find, in short, is that Hull's three propositions about the associative aspects of drive are not so much empirically wrong as they are practically inadequate. To that extent the case for the drive theory of motivation is weakened.

THE INDEPENDENCE OF D AND H

Hull conceived of habit as a more or less permanent change in the nervous system, and drive as a more or less transient motivational state of the organism. Then by hypothesizing that habit structure and motivation were functionally independent, and that overt behavior was a joint function of the two, he gave a clear syntactical form to the old but imprecise distinction between learning and performance.[1] Hull's assumption of independence involves two propositions, that $_sH_R$ is independent of drive level, and that D is independent of learning. We will be concerned here with just the first proposition—that what the animal learns does not depend upon its motivation during learning.[2]

[1] In recent times, the learning-performance distinction seems to have been first made by Elliott (1930) who was working with Tolman. Tolman (1932) made capital of it, citing the early latent learning studies as evidence in support of his cognitive theory as against a law of effect reinforcement sort of theory. (Kimble, 1961, has provided a recent excellent summary of the latent-learning literature and indicated some of the contemporary implications of the findings for reinforcement theory.) Tolman (1933) himself gave credit for the distinction between learning and performance to Elliott. In olden times the distinction was well known; it was an essential part of the traditional rationalistic explanation of behavior, and always had been. Humphrey (1950, ch. 1) indicates how the separation of having habits and using them came back into systematic psychology through the Würzburgers, Lewin, and others. The fact that Tolman, Lashley, and their contemporaries could once again "rediscover" the distinction suggests only that it had become lost during Watson's heyday just as it had during the era of the structuralists.

[2] The second proposition—that D is independent of learning—would seem to be belied by the obvious fact that much of the organism's total motivation is quite apparently learned. Hull (1943, 1952) guaranteed the correctness of this proposition by introducing secondary or acquired motivation as a separate theoretical term, keeping the unlearned part identified with D. Many recent drive theorists have tended to part with Hull on this. Brown (1961) has been the most

There are two major lines of evidence. One involves the comparison of learning curves obtained under different drive conditions. The question then becomes whether subjects under different drive conditions approach their different asymptotic performance levels at the same rate. (Recall that it was this feature of the Perin-Williams data that led Hull to postulate independence.) Quite often in studies of instrumental performance, variation in drive conditions produces little effect upon performance; but in studies where effects are found, it is usually the case that drive conditions affect the asymptote but not the growth rate (e.g., Tolman & Honzik, 1930, errors in a complex maze; Hillman et al., 1953, speed of running in a maze; Ramond, 1954, discrimination errors; Barry, 1958, runway speed; Deese & Carpenter, 1951, latency in a runway).

Clark (1958) has reported that with a highly practiced bar-press response on fairly strenuous variable-interval reinforcement schedules (1 min., 2 min., and 3 min.), a range of from 1-hr. to 23-hr. food deprivation affects the rate on these three schedules proportionately (see Fig. 9-1). Hence, whatever discriminative and reinforcement processes occur under these different schedules of reinforcement, their effects are multiplied by the motivational effects of hours deprivation.

Davenport (1965) recently carried out a large systematic analysis of learning curves of rats under 3, 22, or 41 hr. food deprivation. Hullian exponential curves were fitted to the trial-by-trial speed scores of each animal, and then the individual growth constants and constants describing asymptotic performance level were estimated. It was found that mean asymptotic performance increased significantly with deprivation time, but the mean growth constant did not. The slight increase found in the growth constant could probably be attributed to the failure of a few animals to perform properly in the instrumental situation under 3-hr. deprivation. It would seem then that in simple appetitive instrumental situations the learning curves of animals under different drive conditions approach their respective asymptotes at the same rate.

Spence (1956, 1958) has suggested that D and H may not be independent in aversive learning situations.[3] He cites two studies of instrumental-escape conditioning in which divergence of the learning curves was not found (Amsel, 1950; Campbell & Kraeling, 1953). The results of these two studies are difficult to interpret because the initial (and presumably unconditioned) strength of the criterion response seems to depend upon the intensity of the drive-producing conditions (Campbell & Kraeling, 1953). Moreover there appears the further complication that

---

articulate member of this group; he refers to all determinants of motivation, learned and unlearned alike, as "sources" of D.

[3] Spence takes as a criterion of independence the divergence of the learning curves under different drive conditions. This is not quite sufficient since curves with different rates of growth may also diverge. Spence's criterion also depends upon the assumption, which he makes, that $_sE_R$ is related linearly to the speed

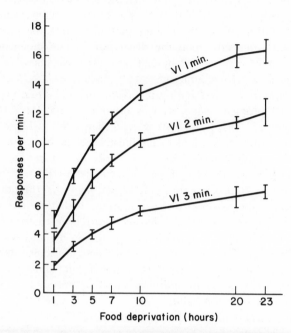

Fig. 9-1. Rate of bar pressing under three different schedules of reinforcement as a function of deprivation time. The variances under each condition are indicated. (From Clark, 1958)

the intensity of the drive-producing conditions is one of the things that determines the nature and strength of the responses that compete with the criterion response. Thus, it seems that animals that are supposedly under different intensities of drive may also inadvertently be at different stages in the course of learning the response. In general, then, the evidence of the first sort, i.e., direct comparison of acquisition performance under different drive conditions, is not conclusive; but it is at least consistent with Hull's assumption of independence.

The second line of evidence comes from those experiments in which a response is learned under one set of drive conditions and then tested under another set either during further learning or during extinction. Attention is then focused on whether performance follows the shift in drive conditions or whether there are residual carry-over effects of the old drive conditions. Performance after the shift can be attributed to (1) the moti-

---

of responding. Without some such assumption, of course, the question of convergence, or for that matter any question about the shapes of learning curves, becomes pointless.

vational effects of the drive state current after the shift, (2) residual effects of the prior drive state, and (3) the interaction between the two which represents the effect of shifting, per se (presumably, generalization decrements resulting from the change in that part of the total stimulus situation which depends upon the drive state). The independence hypothesis is supported to the extent that postshift performance is independent of the preshift drive condition.[4]

Drive-Shift Studies of Bar-Pressing Behavior. The first experimental attack on the problem came, as was often the case, from Hull's own laboratory (Finan, 1940; Heathers & Arakelian, 1941). These and some of the subsequent investigations nicely illustrate some of the methodological and interpretive complexities in this sort of research, so it will be worth our while to consider them in some detail. Finan trained four groups of rats to press a bar under 1, 12, 24, or 48 hr. food deprivation, following which the response was extinguished with the drive conditions equated for all groups at 24-hr. deprivation. The greatest resistance to extinction was found in the 12-hr. group; the 24-hr. and 48-hr. groups were a little lower; the 1-hr. group had the least resistance to extinction. The first inference from Finan's data would be that for a given number of reinforcements there is an optimum (and moderately low) drive level for producing the strongest habit.

However, certain methodological features of Finan's study cast some doubt on this conclusion. For example, we are told that the time for learning under the 30 reinforcements was about the same for the four groups, approximately 24 min. This similarity in initial acquisition performance suggests that motivation differences were not as great as the nominal hours of deprivation would suggest, and this seems likely also in view of the fact that all groups had had 6 days experience with a 10-gm. food ration prior to the introduction of the acquisition-drive conditions. Another problem is the possibility that the animals under the different drive conditions had acquired and/or had extinguished different responses during the course of training, and that differences in the subsequent extinction performance reflected these associative effects rather than residual effects of motivation. For example, it may be that the high-drive groups during early acquisition attacked the bar or otherwise engaged in "excited" behavior. The reinforcements received by this behavior would not have gone into shaping the response. Moreover, this behavior would have undergone some extinction and hence would be less likely to occur in the extinction period, so the animal's extinction score might be still further depressed. Finan did not exercise sufficient control over the animal's be-

---

[4] One advantage of this design over the comparison of learning curves is that it doesn't require any assumptions about the scaling of drive strength or of behavior strength beyond the rather weak ones of an ordinal scale and a monotonic rise of D with hours deprivation within the range of conditions used.

havior during the acquisition period to be able to offer any assurance that all animals were in fact receiving an equal number of reinforcements on the same habit.

Reynolds (1949a) attempted to improve Finan's procedure. Differential motivation was controlled by prefeeding the animals 25% or 100% of their daily ration. The instrumental response in this case was panel pushing for food pellets (presumably the topographic details of this response are less crucial than those of bar pressing). Acquisition training was with well-spaced trials. But, like Finan, Reynolds found that the low-motivation group was significantly more resistant to extinction than the high-motivation group. Something unusual had evidently occurred during training, however, since a superiority of the low-motivation group had already been established (shorter latency of responding) in acquisition. Reynolds explained this anomalous finding by postulating that more inhibition had been built up under the high-motivation condition. So, rather than discarding the independence hypothesis, he concluded that performance may be governed to a large degree by mechanisms other than or in addition to the simple multiplication of D and H. Thus, whatever effect D may have in the determination of behavior, it may be overcome by the acquisition of inhibition effects also acquired in the learning situation.

Kendler (1945a) trained two groups of rats to press a bar for food with 15 reinforcements. One group was 22-hr. hungry plus 12-hr. thirsty (no water was present in the situation so the thirst was "irrelevant"), and the other group was 22-hr. hungry plus 22-hr. thirsty (also irrelevant). The bar-press response was then extinguished with half of the animals under their acquisition conditions and half with the deprivation conditions reversed. The resistance to extinction results are shown in the table.

TABLE 9-1

Resistance to Extinction of a Bar-Press Response under 22 hr.
Hunger plus 12 or 22 hr. Irrelevant Thirst (geometric means).
(Adapted from Kendler, 1945a.)

| | | *Extinction Condition* | | |
		12 hr.	*22 hr.*	*Means*
Acquisition	12 hr.	28.1	18.3	23.2
Condition	22 hr.	22.9	16.2	19.0
	Means	25.5	17.2	

By comparing row means we may evaluate the overall residual effect of prior drive. The difference suggests a carry-over effect, but is not statistically significant. The column means reveal a significant effect of the deprivation conditions during extinction. A comparison of the two diagonals indicates that there was no appreciable interaction, i.e., there was little effect of altering deprivation conditions apart from the main effects. Thus Kendler's results would seem to indicate that extinction performance is affected by current but not by prior deprivation conditions, and that there is little evidence that the stimuli arising from specific deprivation conditions have appreciable control over the behavior. The strange feature of these results is that current deprivation had an unexpected effect; the animals with low irrelevant drive showed greater resistance to extinction than the high-irrelevant-drive animals. The question arises whether this decrement is due to differences in total effective drive or to differences in habit strengths that develop as a result of the irrelevant-drive condition. Although Kendler controlled the learning situation by spacing the acquisition trials and making the distribution of practice equal for all groups, it is still possible that animals with high irrelevant thirst had learned something different from the animals with the low irrelevant thirst. Kendler's results, however, are at least consistent with the assumption of independence.

Other experimenters (Heathers & Arakelian, 1941; Strassburger, 1950; Brown, 1956) have also worked with the resistance to extinction of a bar-press response. In these three studies the motivating conditions and acquisition performance were carefully controlled; large numbers of subjects were run; and prefeeding techniques, hours-deprivation techniques, and secondary reinforcement procedures were used as motivating conditions. In each case a pronounced effect of current deprivation was found in resistance to extinction scores, but no significant effect of prior deprivation. The Heathers and Arakelian study introduced an interesting variation of this design. All animals had acquired the response under identical deprivation conditions, then the high- and low-deprivation conditions were imposed for a first extinction under distributed trials. Finally, in the critical phase of the experiment, motivation conditions were equated for a second extinction. The results indicate that whether extinction is viewed as an acquisition of competing behavior, or a building up of inhibition, or as some other kind of alteration of the habit structure, it is not significantly affected by drive level.

Eisman et al. (1961) have pointed out that in the Strassburger study and in some of the others we have noted, the performance of the different groups was not reported to be sufficiently different during acquisition to give any assurance that they were under appreciably different motivation conditions. These authors point out that if the deprivation conditions have no effect on acquisition performance, we can hardly expect a valid test of the independence hypothesis. The point is not really applicable because the current motivation conditions did have a significant energizing effect on extinction performance in all the experiments that are cited.

Eisman imposed weight losses of approximately 7% to 8% for the low-drive condition and approximately 20% for the high-drive condition and obtained significant carry-over effects. The bar-press response was more resistant to extinction when it had been learned under high drive than when it had been learned under low drive. Eisman et al. were able to report that the initial bar-press training had been nearly twice as fast under the high- as under the low-drive conditions, thus "validating" their use of weight loss as the antecedent variable. Unfortunately, another variable in the study was confounded with weight loss, viz., the duration of the deprivation state; weight was brought down to the reduced value over a 2- or 3-week period, during which time the subjects were maintained on limited rations. Consequently, under the high-drive condition ample opportunity was provided for the acquisition of all those signs of motivation which suggest the operation of incentive motivation, and we are left with the question of whether Eisman's high-drive animals really had high D or high K or high something else. A second difficulty with this study is that the rate of acquisition was not controlled (in fact the difference in rate was used to demonstrate the energizing effect of the deprivation conditions). Therefore, we do not know for sure that the animals under the high- and low-drive conditions had acquired the same response, or had received the same number of reinforcements for the same habit.[5] In summary, the bulk of the evidence from bar-pressing situations does not seem to be inconsistent with Hull's assumption of the independence of D and H, but only because the evidence itself is so inconsistent.

Drive-Shift Studies of Running Behavior. In the case of running speed in a straight alley, the results have generally been quite different from those obtained with bar pressing. The indication is that when all animals are extinguished under equated drive conditions there is some carry-over of the speed of responding characteristic of acquisition-drive conditions at least during the first few trials of extinction (O'Kelly & Heyer, 1948; Campbell & Kraeling, 1954; Lewis & Cotton, 1957; Davis, 1957; Barry, 1958; Theios, 1963). This effect is illustrated in Fig. 9-2.

These results show a clear difference in running speed in acquisition as a function of drive conditions, and a carry-over of these differences for 6 to 10 trials in extinction. This group of studies covers a wide range of deprivation times from 0 to 60 hrs., and covers acquisition under both

---

[5] The experimenter appears to have a dilemma here: if he demonstrates that current drive conditions have an effective influence upon acquisition performance, then he cannot in general assume that the same response has been involved in the learning. But if he controls the learning session to guarantee topographic identity of the response under different drive conditions, then he loses the evidence that variation in those conditions has any effect. The dilemma might be escaped by taking note of more than one measure of the response, e.g., by using latency scores to demonstrate the effect of variation in the drive conditions and amplitude or speed scores to demonstrate the constancy of the response.

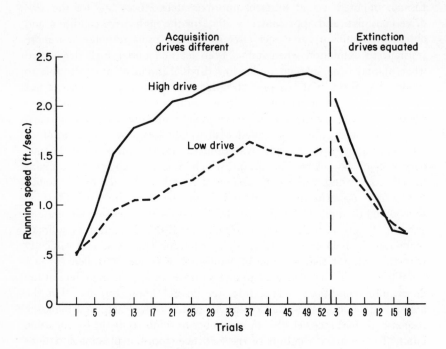

Fig. 9-2. Running speed in acquisition and extinction as a function of drive-condition differences in acquisition. (From Barry, 1958)

distributed and massed trials. Hence, we may place some confidence in the generality of the finding.

The discrepancy between these results involving the speed of running and the other results involving resistance to extinction of a bar press may hinge upon the fact that running at a particular speed is one of the things that the animal learns during acquisition. We might say that the high-drive animal learns to run whereas the low-drive animal learns to walk. Such qualitatively different responses would transfer to the extinction situation, so that the previously high-drive animals would be extinguishing running and the previously low-drive animals would be extinguishing walking. Campbell and Kraeling (1954) seem to have been the first to suggest this possibility. Hull had assumed that the same habit is learned for all levels of drive whenever animals are trained in a particular situation. But according to Campbell and Kraeling:

Observation of the present experimental animals, however, suggests a quite different formulation. The animals trained under conditions of high motivation appeared to learn responses which were qualitatively different from the responses learned by animals trained under low motivation. High-drive animals, for example, learned to crouch facing the starting-box door, ready to respond immediately by dashing down the runway when the door opened. Low-drive animals, in contrast, seldom exhibited this habit of "attending" to the starting-box door, and never appeared to acquire the skill of running rapidly down the alley. Thus, when drive is shifted during extinction, animals trained under low drive and extinguished under high drive do not show an immediate increase in running speed since they have not learned the responses constituting the skill of running rapidly in the experimental situation [and since reinforcement is no longer present, they do not acquire it]. (Campbell & Kraeling, 1954, p. 102)

King (1959) has suggested that the carry-over effect on running speed is not actually due to the strength of the running response itself, but rather to the occurrence or nonoccurrence of competing responses that become extinguished under high drive but not under low drive. King trained rats under 12- or 60-hr. food deprivation to run to food in a runway, and then extinguished them with the drive conditions reversed by half of each group. King measured not only the overall running time in the usual way, but also the amount of time the animals spent just running, i.e., the overall running time minus the time they spent engaged in competing, nonrunning behavior. The latter measure showed, as we might hope, that the prior acquisition-drive level had no residual effect on extinction performance. But for reasons which are not clear, King's total time measure also failed to show an effect of the acquisition-drive level. Thus, he was not able to replicate the results of the other runway studies he was attempting to explain and so we cannot assess his explanation of them.

The carry-over effect of prior drive conditions, which seems reasonably well established for response amplitude measures might be expected in other response measures. The response with more vigor might be expected to occur sooner and to be more resistant to extinction. Lewis and Cotton (1957) did find a carry-over effect in resistance to extinction using a more extended extinction test than Campbell and Kraeling (who failed to find it), but the effect was slight. On the question of latency of running, however, Deese and Carpenter (1951) and Davis (1957) report a very curious asymmetrical carry-over effect. Deese and Carpenter found that animals switched from low to high hunger dropped from approximately 10-sec. to 2-sec. latencies on the first trial, but that the animals switched from high to low hunger retained a short latency of about 2 sec. This pattern of performance cannot be predicted from Campbell and Kraeling's argument, nor does it follow from King's analysis.

One conclusion is clear: It does not seem advisable to anchor D × H on the consequent side directly to the speed of responding as Hull (1943) and particularly Spence (1956) have done. This convention apparently cannot be maintained simultaneously with the assumption that D and H are independent. In any case, the experimenter who wishes to show that D and H are independent carries the burden of showing first that the responses acquired under high and low drives are equivalent, and second, that their habit strengths are equal. Logan (1956, 1960) has addressed himself to this problem and has developed a "micromolar" modification of Hull's theory, in which different response amplitudes or magnitudes are viewed as generated by different habits.

Drive-Shift Studies of Maze Performance. Teel (1952), Carper (1957), Armus (1958), and Kendler (1945) have reported similar drive-switching experiments with rats in T mazes. In these four studies no differences in resistance to extinction or in errors were found which could be attributed to any residual effect of the acquisition drive. Unfortunately, we do not know what sort of differences to expect. In three of these studies there was no apparent effect of the acquisition-drive level on acquisition performance, while Kendler reported that the higher irrelevant-drive condition led to more errors in learning than the low irrelevant-drive condition. The difficulty here is that we do not have a very clear picture of how either acquisition or extinction performance in a T maze depends upon either habit strength or drive; consequently, it does not make too much sense to use the situation as a test for their functional independence.

In still more complex learning situations—mazes (MacDuff, 1946; Hillman et al., 1953) and brightness discrimination (Eisman et al., 1956) —it has been found that rats who learn under different drive conditions and are then tested under equated drive conditions show no differences in error scores. In contrast to the T maze studies noted above, acquisition-drive conditions did have the expected effect in all these studies upon acquisition performance. Hillman et al. also report no residual effects of acquisition-drive conditions in resistance to extinction of the maze habit, but Eisman et al. found that the high-drive habit is abandoned more slowly than the low-drive habit.

The Effect of Drive Conditions on Generalization. When an animal is tested under conditions which depart in some respect from those under which it was trained, a decrement in performance is usually found. Does the animal's motivation at the time of testing have any effect upon the gradient of generalization? For example, does the animal under high drive show a broader generalization gradient than the animal under low-drive conditions? Spence (1956) has argued that since generalization is really a consequence of altering the habit structure, the shape of the generalization gradient should be independent of D. He cites a study by Newman (1955) to support this interpretation, pointing out that the performance curve under high drive is merely a multiplication of the performance curve under low drive, as it should be on the assumption that D and H multiply. But there are problems here. Consider some results reported earlier by Rosenbaum (1951). Rosenbaum trained rats to press a bar for food every 60 sec. The bar was removed and presented at regular 60-sec. intervals, and the latency of the bar press was recorded. After training, the bar was presented at test intervals shorter than 60 sec. Two groups were run, both maintained on 24-hr. food deprivation but one, the low-drive group, was prefed a large part of its daily ration just before testing. Rosenbaum's results are shown in Fig. 9-3.

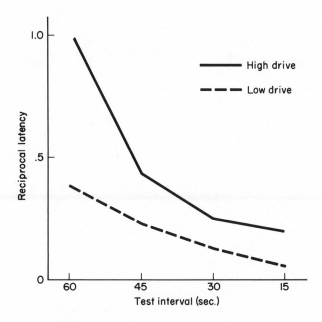

Fig. 9-3. Generalization of response strength as a function of departure from training conditions (60 sec.) under high-drive and low-drive conditions. (Adapted from Rosenbaum, 1951)

It is clear from the figure that performance is higher under high drive than under low drive, and it is also clear that the high-drive curve is sharper than the low-drive curve. There is a greater decrement in response speed for the high-drive animals as test conditions depart from the 60-sec. training condition. An analysis of variance of the data probably would show a significant interaction between drive and stimulus conditions. We might conclude from this that Spence is wrong and that D sharpens the generalization gradient. But such a conclusion would be hasty. In his original analysis of these data Rosenbaum treated them as latency scores rather than as reciprocal latencies or speeds. Under this transformation of the data the conclusion has to be reversed; Spence is still wrong, but because D broadens the generalization gradient! The interaction is still significant but in the opposite direction. There is another possibility: the interaction can be eliminated, and the curves given the same shape by considering the ratio of speeds or the ratio of latencies under high- and low-drive conditions. These are indeed interesting and docile data.

The main point is that it is possible to arrive at any of a number of conclusions by appropriate transformations of the data, and in the absence of any firm convention regarding how $_sE_R$ is to be measured and scaled, there is no way to say that one transformation is any better than another. A number of different response measures (e.g., rate of responding, heart rate, percentage occurrence) have been studied by Bersh et al. (1956a), Jenkins et al. (1958), Thomas and King (1959), Porter (1962), Golin and Bostrum (1964), and Healey(1965). The most usual claim is that D broadens the gradient. But it should be noted that there are really two questions here; one is whether D broadens the gradient, and a second distinct question is whether these generalization studies support the hypothesis that D and H combine multiplicatively. The first question, whether D broadens the gradient, is settled rather simply by considering not analyses of variance or slopes of curves, or how to scale $_sE_R$ but merely whether the subject responds to a broader range of stimuli under higher drive. The answer is clearly yes; if any arbitrary response criterion is established, such as requiring the subject to respond to the test stimulus in a given time interval, then certainly it is more likely to do so under high drive than low drive.[6] The second question, regarding the combination of D and H, can also be settled, at least tentatively. If we can accept the convention that $_sE_R$ is linearly related to speed of responding then the results of Rosenbaum (Fig. 9-3) together with the recent results of Newman and Grice (1965) make a very convincing case for a multiplicate relationship between D and H.

Drive-Shift Studies of Eyelid Conditioning. Finally, something should be said about the studies with humans which show (in general) that human learning under high motivation leads to better retention when the acquisition-motivation conditions are no longer applicable. At first sight such studies would seem to be analogous to those we have just discussed.

---

[6] This conclusion suggests a mechanism for how the hypothetical energizing effect of D comes about. Let us think of the evocation of a response in statistical terms, so that on any given occasion there is only some probability that the response will follow a given set of stimuli, but a higher probability that it will follow some other stimuli, S^1. Then any operation that broadens the given set so that it includes more stimuli, and has a greater likelihood of including the more potent stimuli, S^1, will increase the probability of the response. And that is just what increasing the severity of drive-producing conditions seems to do.

However, one difficulty with human subjects is that they tend to incorporate the instructions (or whatever) which produce the original motivational differences and to retain them as well as the behavior being tested. The subject who is ego-involved or frightened in the original learning is certainly apt to be ego-involved or frightened in the subsequent test situation even though he is not explicitly made so. Consider, for example, a study by Spence (1953) which he cites later (1956) in support of the view that D influences H in aversive learning. Spence conditioned the human eyeblink using either a 5-lb. (high drive) or a .25-lb. (low drive) air puff to the eyeball as the US. Subjects were given 30 stimulus pairings the first day; then, on the second day, drive conditions were switched for half the subjects in each group, and everybody was run another 20 trials. The results are indicated in Table 9-2.

TABLE 9-2

The Number of CR's Occurring in 20 Trials as a Function
of Prior and Current Air-Puff Intensity
(Adapted from Spence, 1953.)

		Test Condition		*Means*
		.25 lb.	5.0 lb.	
Prior	.25 lb.	5.65	8.80	7.23
Condition	5.0 lb.	7.45	13.00	10.23
	Means	6.55	10.90	

Both current and prior drive conditions have a significant effect. Note, too, a slight but not significant difference in diagonal totals, due to generalization effects. Spence has suggested (1956, 1958) that the difference between these results and those usually found with hunger is that with eyelid conditioning reinforcement involves more nearly total reduction of the drive, and that the drive is primary whereas in the case of hunger only partial drive reduction is ordinarily accomplished, and the drive probably is secondary.[7]

Further support for the idea that the habit strength of a defensive reaction may depend upon the amount of drive reduction rather than just the number of reinforcements comes from a pair of studies by Spence et al. (1958). The experimental question they asked was whether the facilitory effect of a strong US requires that it be paired with the CS, or whether it is sufficient that intense air puffs be presented in the context

[7] This curious twist—food as a secondary reinforcer and the avoidance of pain as primary—should make one wonder what the distinction between primary and secondary reinforcement is worth.

of the experimental situation to maintain drive at a high level. Two groups of subjects were conditioned, both of which got a strong air puff on half the trials and a weak air puff on the other half, but one group always had the CS paired with the strong puff, while the second group always had it paired with the weak one. Thus, the two groups were equated in terms of the presumed average drive level, whereas they were quite different in terms of the amount of reinforcement given the CS-CR habit (i.e., the US intensity on paired trials). Stronger conditioning was found in the higher reinforcement group. In a second study the rationale was the same; but instead of varying the intensity of the air puff, the time interval between the CS and the air puff was varied so that for one group it was too long for the eyelid habit to be reinforced. Again the results suggested it was the amount of reinforcement rather than the drive level that produced different strengths of conditioning (see also Spence & Tandler, 1963). However, the rationale of the delayed US procedure has been questioned by Moore and Gormezano (1963), who found that delay of the US produced a higher level of conditioning than omission of the US.

We may legitimately ask whether Spence's different procedures might have produced different amounts or kinds of motivation instead of or in addition to different amounts of reinforcement. For example, it is possible that the CS (the brightening of a light) becomes more frightening when it is followed by a strong air puff than when it is followed by a weak one. Spence and his colleagues ordinarily attribute differential performance to differential drive (they invariably do so when different groups of MAS scores yield different levels of performance) so why not here? Trapold and Spence (1960) ran a study to see if the alleged differences in habit strength would shift as expected with a shift in the drive conditions. Two groups, differing in whether the strong or the weak air puff was paired with the CS (in a manner similar to Spence et al., 1958), had these conditions reversed after 180 trials. Those switched from low to high reinforcement picked up, and those switched from high to low maintained their level of performance. A third group, for which no more strong air puffs were given after 180 trials, showed a marked drop in performance. This is just the pattern of results one would expect on the assumption that it is not drive but drive reduction with strong US that determines performance (see also Spence et al., 1958a; Ross & Hunter, 1959; Woods et al., 1964). The strong air puff facilitates performance because it leads to greater reinforcement, in addition to whatever motivational consequences it may have.

Probably no one would disagree with Spence that the strong air puff elicits an emotional reaction (r_E) from the subject, and that the emotional reaction is ultimately responsible for superior performance in the defensive conditioning. The question is whether we can properly attribute this series of events to an increase in D in the absence of substantiating evidence that r_E has the other hypothetical properties of D. One property D is supposed to have is independence with respect to habit strength. Spence would now have us surrender this property. Another property usually attributed to D is the ability to energize any and all habits in a given situation. By contrast, it seems likely that whatever "motivates" the defensive eyelid reaction is quite specific to it (Hilgard et al., 1951).

In defensive or avoidance situations, it is extremely difficult to say which aspects of the behavior are best attributed to D, which to other sources of the total motivation, and which to purely associative factors. The critical question then is what is the source and the nature of the motivation that applies in the eyelid conditioning situation. The reason motivation is not attributed directly to the CS itself (nor to r_E controlled by the CS) is that the CS-US interval used in these studies (about .5 sec.) is considered too short for any mediated motivation to occur. Spence and Runquist (1958) have shown in this connection that electric shock given .5 sec. before the US does not augment the UR. Hence, they conclude that no event occurring .5 sec. before the CR can have a motivational effect upon it. Nor does it seem reasonable to attribute a key motivation-eliciting role to the "ready" signal (which is given in the Iowa studies a few seconds before the CS) since experiments in which it has been given or withheld as an experimental treatment generally find that this makes no difference (Dufort & Kimble, 1958; Spence & Weyant, 1960; Baron & Connor, 1960; King et al., 1961; Klinger & Prokasy, 1962; Goodrich, 1964). The motivational state thus would seem to be a relatively persistent condition which is dependent upon the average air-puff intensity across a series of trials.[8] However, much remains to be done to establish the nature of the motivation in eyelid conditioning before any conclusion can be drawn about whether it is best conceptualized as D, and whether, if it is, it is one of the determinants of H.

Summary. It would appear that although there is some question in the case of avoidance behavior the assumption of independence of D and H seems justified by the evidence for appetitive behavior. However, even here we must add certain qualifications to Hull's original formulation. In

---

[8] If the air puff is presented alone, without being paired with the CS, for a series of trials interpolated in the training series so that the drive level is maintained, then the strength of the CR might be expected to continue to rise even in the absence of CS-US pairing. Kimble and his associates have reported just such findings (Kimble et al., 1955; Kimble & Dufort, 1956; Kimble & Ost, 1961). At Iowa, however, it is found that the missing CS-US pairings lead to a decrement in the strength of the response (Goodrich et al., 1957; Ross & Spence, 1960). Spence has initiated still another series of studies to show that the physiological concomitants of aversive conditions, such as a strong air puff, behave as they are supposed to (Runquist & Spence, 1959a; Runquist & Ross, 1959). In this same vein, Spence and Goldstein (1961) have found that the mere threat of pain can lead to stronger conditioning. All these matters, and others, have recently been reviewed by Ross and Hartman (1965).

a simple noncompetitive situation, measures of response probability such as resistance to extinction and latency usually support the assumption of independence, but measures of response amplitude and vigor do not. In more complex learning situations the assumption of independence is apparently justified for a wide variety of performance measures. However, the evidence in this case does not provide substantial support for independence because it is not clear in highly response-competitive situations how D is supposed to combine with the various H's to determine performance.

One further qualification seems necessary. The test of the independence assumption assumes that habits acquired under different drive conditions will be qualitatively the same. But from a strictly practical point of view it is now apparent that an impressive amount of experimental control and know-how must be exercised in order to guarantee that animals under different drive conditions will not learn different habits. From a more theoretical point of view it now seems that the question of the independence of D and H is not really an empirical matter after all, but a matter to be settled semantically. What has happened in some cases is that D has been redefined so as to make the independence postulate true. This is what Hull did in effect (see footnote 2 on p. 227) by attributing all the learned components of motivation to incentive factors and all the deprivational ones to drive. On the other hand, Spence (1956), in calling drive whatever it is that motivates eyelid conditioning, has essentially abandoned the independence postulate; and, by pooling the learned and the unlearned sources of motivation here is sure to find that H and D interact. Brown (1961) and, as we will soon see, Miller (1956, 1957) have followed the same course. This, of course, markedly changes the status of D.

THE REINFORCING FUNCTION OF
DRIVE REDUCTION

One of the fundamental propositions in Hull's drive theory is that any condition of the organism that can serve to produce drive can also serve as reinforcement when it is reduced. Certainly this sometimes occurs. In the natural order of events the animal is hungry, it makes some instrumental response, it finds food, it consumes the food. Subsequently, the animal has less drive and more habit strength for the instrumental response. But there are several questions here. Does the consumption of food, the stimulus consequences of consumption, or the subsequent reduction in drive constitute the critical event in reinforcement? Or on the other hand, is it possible the animal would have learned the instrumental response just by making it and the presence of food merely makes learning demonstrable because it motivates the animal to run?[9] We cannot settle these questions merely by observing the natural order of events; it is necessary to make some unusual manipulations of and interventions in the natural order if we are to isolate the crucial factor in reinforcement, and to determine if, in fact, there is one.

Reinforcement by Need Reduction. Hull et al. (1951) trained a dog to go to one side of a T maze to receive fistula feeding. On the other side of the maze the animal was permitted to sham eat. (This was a double-fistula preparation with one tube discharging the contents of the mouth and the other tube leading to the stomach.) In the course of 8 test days the animal overcame its original preference for the sham-eating side and learned to go to the fistula-feeding side. Hull et al. interpreted these findings as evidence for the need-reduction interpretation of reinforcement.

But this conclusion is perhaps a little too strong; the results indicate only that the dog learned to satisfy its need for food, not that learning occurred because the need was satisfied. There are some difficulties here. First of all, if the need-reduction interpretation is taken literally, then it has to be explained how the learning could occur with so few or such long-delayed reinforcements. If there is some mechanism for bridging the temporal gap, whether it be an innate or an acquired cue to reinforcement (such as stomach distention, change in the circulatory system, or change in the extracellular water pool), then the triggering of that mechanism might well be what constitutes reinforcement in the fistula-feeding situation. It is not even possible to rule out head factors in this situation. Thus, it may be that food loses palatability for sham-eating animals when it is eaten but doesn't go anywhere. In this connection, Hull noted that on the first trial the dog sham ate 80% of its body weight before quitting. Perhaps such an experience is sufficient to debilitate the mechanisms that ordinarily control the head factors in eating.[10] In Hull's own terms, per-

[9] And there are other possibilities. Maybe the animal does not learn the response in any literal sense, but only comes to make it with greater assurance as it develops a stronger expectancy of food (Tolman). In his excellent review of these matters Kimble (1961) has emphasized that there are at least three separate issues here: (1) Should behavior be explained in S-R terms or some alternative set of terms? (2) Granting the S-R orientation, is there some discrete event which reinforces the response? And (3) granting that there is a specific reinforcement event, what is its nature? Kimble concludes that continuing research has led most S-R reinforcement theorists to develop mediational theories in order to maintain their position on the first two questions, and to accept the idea that there is no one simple answer to the third question. Our first concern in the present section is merely to examine Hull's particular drive-reduction hypothesis of reinforcement. Later we will consider some of these broader questions.

[10] It is curious that the dog would sham eat so much. We know from studies of drinking that, whether it be real or sham drinking, dogs will usually take an amount that approximately matches the water deficit and then stop. Perhaps the situation is different with eating. Hull's finding and the similar results of Janowitz and Grossman (1949) and James and Gilbert (1957) suggest that the dog's principal mechanism for satiation is stomach distention.

haps so much consumption of the same foodstuff leads to a tremendous accumulation of conditioned inhibition; it was noted that the dog would still sham eat outside the experimental situation. Perhaps all Hull et al. observed was the extinction of the consummatory response and subsequent incentive motivation, rather than the reinforcement of the instrumental response. Clearly, much more work needs to be done on the sham-feeding problem.

Reinforcement without Need or Drive Reduction. One alternative to the drive-reduction hypothesis of reinforcement has been suggested by Sheffield, namely, that the mere occurrence of the consummatory response may reinforce instrumental behavior. Sheffield et al. (1951) found that sexually naive male rats would learn an instrumental response if they were rewarded by being permitted to copulate with receptive females. This in itself is not surprising, but there was a gimmick in the experimental conditions—ejaculation was not permitted. Although some sort of consummatory behavior occurred, drive was, presumably, not permitted to be reduced. In fact, it seems reasonable to suppose that the animal's sexual excitement, and hence drive, was increased by that part of the consummatory behavior that was permitted to occur. Nonetheless, there was learning.

This general finding has been replicated by Kaufman (1953), Kagan (1955), and Whalen (1961). In Kagan's study, three groups of animals were run—one was permitted only to mount, another was permitted intromission, and the third was permitted to ejaculate. It was found that mounting alone was a relatively ineffectual reinforcement; the instrumental response was not maintained. Intromission without ejaculation led to somewhat better learning, and somewhat faster running, and better maintenance of the running.[11] But learning was fastest for the group for which ejaculation was permitted. Thus, it would appear that whereas the occurrence of the consummatory response, or even some components of it, can be reinforcing, greater reinforcement occurs when drive is reduced. So Kagan argues. But, as we saw in the discussion of the sexual consummatory response, it is not clear that a reduction in drive can be equated with occurrence of ejaculation, since the copulatory mechanism seems to be sensitized rather than satiated by ejaculation. What does weaken with ejaculation is interest in the female, i.e., the arousal mechanism. Thus, we have the paradox that either the weakening of arousal (the ejaculation condition) or the increase in arousal (the intromission condition) can be reinforcing.

According to Sheffield's theory of reinforcement, it is not the reduction in hunger or thirst that makes eating or drinking reinforcing, but the occurrence of the consummatory behavior itself. Further evidence in

[11] Whalen (1961), using a nonchoice type of instrumental situation, found no extinction of the instrumental response when just intromission was the reinforcer.

support of Sheffield's argument comes from a pair of studies (Sheffield & Roby, 1950; Sheffield et al., 1954) in which it was found that hungry animals would learn an instrumental response when reinforced by the drinking of saccharin. Saccharin is not supposed to have any nutritive value, hence the possibility of reinforcement by drive reduction would seem to be ruled out.[12]

There is a considerable literature (see the review by Lockard, 1963) showing various reinforcing effects of illumination change. Even if such cases are put under the heading of exploratory behavior, they pose serious problems for the drive-reduction hypothesis.

Reinforcement as Drive Reduction. Miller (1955, 1956, 1957) has placed a somewhat different emphasis upon the results of the saccharin-drinking studies and arrived at a quite different conclusion. Miller et al. (1952) found that animals that had drunk saccharin solutions showed a reduction in the amount of it that was drunk immediately afterward. It was also found that the prior drinking of saccharin inhibited bar pressing for saccharin, although no such inhibition was found when it was placed directly into the stomach through a tube. From these findings Miller concludes that saccharin is a reinforcer (since it maintained the instrumental response), but he also concludes that *drinking saccharin reduces drive.* It is important to note that this latter conclusion implies a definition of drive that is different from Hull's. For Hull, drive was always very closely linked with the needs of the organism. In fact, Hull often used "need" and "drive" interchangeably. Miller, on the other hand, is one of those who have taken the decisive step of cutting the usual antecedent ties of the drive construct in order to obtain a more coherent picture of its behavior consequences.

Although Miller has said repeatedly that for him "drive" means any strong source of stimulation, this definition only seems to pertain to the case of aversive motivation. In the appetitive case we have little evidence of any strong noxious stimulation which drives the animal into activity, and which it seeks to terminate. What we find instead is that there are certain conditions of the organism which are correlated with consummatory behavior, the alleviation of which serve to reinforce instrumental behavior. These behavioral properties are the criteria Miller uses to define drive in all practical cases of appetitive behavior. Thus we find him accepting any reduction in motivation as evidence of drive reduction.[13]

A pair of studies by Kohn (1951) and Berkun et al. (1952) showed that milk injected directly into the stomach inhibited eating more than

[12] Jørgensen (1950) and Smith and Capretta (1956) have indicated that there is some interaction between saccharin and blood sugar. Thus, e.g., Smith and Capretta report that saccharin ingestion increases the rat's resistance to insulin shock.

[13] It should be emphasized that Miller would never accept any one index of

did an equivalent injection of saline solution, but failed to inhibit eating as much as an equivalent amount of milk drunk by mouth. Moreover, the same relative drive reduction under these three conditions was found for the criterion of bar pressing for food (see Fig. 9-4). Hence, Miller argued, there is evidence for two factors in drive reduction, a factor involving food in the stomach, and a factor involving food in the mouth. Both together produce more drive reduction than one alone.

An exactly parallel experiment with thirst (Miller et al., 1957) yielded parallel results. Water by stomach loading was drive reducing by a con-

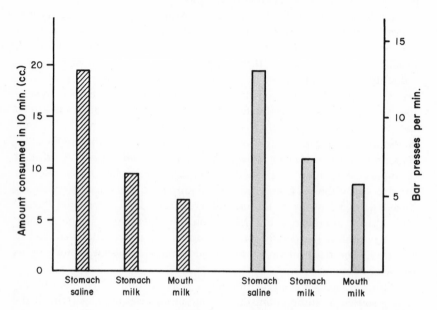

Fig. 9-4. Amount of milk consumed and performance of an instrumental response after injection of saline, injection of milk, or ingestion of milk. (Adapted from Berkun, Kessen, & Miller, 1952, and Kohn, 1951)

summatory criterion, but not as much so as normal drinking by mouth.

Better evidence of reinforcement than the mere maintenance of behavior comes from another study (Miller & Kessen, 1952) of stomach loading with milk.[14] It was found that the injection of milk directly into

---

drive as definitive if there were any possibility of multiple anchoring. For example, he reports (1957) that blowing up a stomach balloon inhibits eating in hungry animals, but he rejects the possibility that this operation involves drive reduction because it fails to reinforce instrumental learning. It should also be noted that after defending it so staunchly for so many years Miller (1963) has begun to give up the drive-reduction hypothesis. We will consider this development shortly, but first we must look at Miller's defense of the hypothesis and some of the important research it has generated.

[14] What makes new learning a better criterion of reinforcement than the main-

the stomach through a tube not only depressed subsequent consummatory behavior but also served to reinforce the acquisition of a new instrumental response. The learning curve is shown in Fig. 9-5.

While it is evident that the stomach-injection group showed learning, its performance always lagged far behind the performance of a group which was permitted to drink milk in the usual manner. As the speed-of-running scores make clear, the mouth-drinking group always showed much more impressive motivation for their particular reinforcement than the stomach-injection group did for theirs. It would seem extremely un-

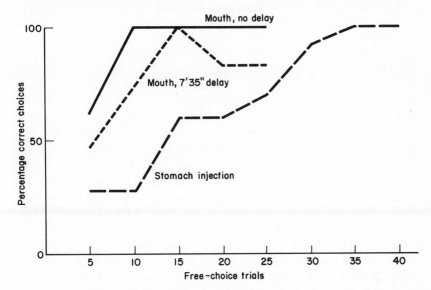

Fig. 9-5. Acquisition of T maze performance by animals previously given milk in different ways. (From Miller & Kessen, 1952)

likely that food in the stomach is the principal source of reinforcement in normal eating. Miller and Kessen ran another group of animals that were permitted to drink, but only after a delay of several minutes. This group showed performance which was approximately intermediate, both in choice behavior and running speed, between the other two groups. Consequently, Miller argued, the reason the stomach-injection group did

---

tenance of a well-learned response is purely definitional; reinforcement *means* strengthening an S-R relationship. Maintenance of response strength can be accomplished by any number of mechanisms other than giving a reinforcer, such as increasing D, increasing the incentive, changing the situation, reducing response competition, redefining the response, etc. By the same token, a drop in performance can indicate a failure of reinforcement (i.e., extinction), or lost motivation, or stimulus change, or almost anything else. The best assurance we have that Miller's stomach-injection technique doesn't, for example, make the animals nauseous is that Miller and Kessen could get new learning with it.

not perform any better than it did was because of the delayed reinforcement produced by food in the stomach; it took an appreciable time (7 mins.) to perform the loadings.

Even so, in comparing the results of Miller and Kessen with those of Kohn (1951) and Berkun et al. (1952), it appears as though the reinforcing effect of stomach loading is somewhat slower than the satiating effect. If this is the case, then it partially negates the proposition that those manipulations of the organism that reduce drive also reinforce. The temporal difference suggests that two mechanisms are involved, one for reinforcement, and another, faster one, for satiation.

This impressive series of studies by Miller and his students suggests four important conclusions. First, there does seem to be (in rats) a reinforcing effect of giving food or water directly through a fistula; such a procedure can be used to produce new learning. But this reinforcement is clearly far less effective than reinforcement involving the usual sequence of ingestion, oral activity, and sensory consequences of ingestion. Hence for all practical purposes Sheffield is right: the animal learns when it is permitted to make the consummatory response. It is probably also true that sham eating will reinforce instrumental behavior.[15] Nonetheless there is evidence for both a head factor and a gut factor in reinforcement.

Second, the speed with which the head factor (and perhaps also the gut factor) operates is such that we cannot attribute the reinforcement to any change in the animal's nutritive condition. Miller has said: "The prompt effects produced by these two factors relieve the drive-reduction hypothesis of reinforcement . . . from the burden of trying to account for learning in terms of the long-delayed effects of the restoration of tissue needs" (Miller et al., 1957, p. 4). Hull and others who have wondered whether the crucial reinforcing state of affairs is alleviation of the animal's need have their answer—it cannot be.

A third point in connection with Miller's findings is that the antecedent anchoring of the drive condition is in terms of prior consumption, or ingestion, rather than in the traditional terms of deprivation, or weight loss, or dehydration. Thus, it is entirely possible that the energizing effect of drive upon the consummatory response and the reinforcing effect of drive reduction to which Miller refers do not apply to the same "drive" that results from hours deprivation. Perhaps a parametric investigation of the relationship between the prefeeding technique and the deprivation technique for producing hunger and thirst will show that there are systematic and predictable relationships between them. But until there is

---

[15] This is true of the dog. We have unpublished data indicating that sham eating is aversive to the rat. Generalization across species is hazardous; thus, in contrast with Miller's abundant evidence that stomach tubing is reinforcing for the rat, James (1963) and Angermeier et al. (1964) have reported that stomach tubing is not reinforcing for the dog or the pigeon.

evidence to the contrary, we must remain skeptical of the view that the amount consumed is functionally equivalent to other measures of motivation (see Chapter 8). Indeed, the studies of Kohn (1951) and Berkun et al. (1952) provide one of the few cases where consummatory measures and instrumental measure of motivation have yielded comparable results.[16] And even here the comparability may not represent any general lawfulness but only reflect the fortunate use of particular parametric values (e.g., 24-hr. deprivation and 14 cc. of milk).

A fourth point is that by severing the connection between need and drive, and by taking purely behavioral criteria of drive, Miller has obliterated the distinction between primary and secondary drive. The two are lumped together because they affect behavior the same way. Thus, we are no longer in a position to distinguish between that component of the animal's total motivation which depends solely upon the conditions of deprivation and that other component that requires prior experience with the incentive in the test situation. This move (also recently advocated by Brown, 1961) is perhaps the only one that can be made at this point without losing the game. That is, a defense of the primary-secondary distinction might prove more disastrous in the long run for drive theory than relinquishing the antecedent anchoring of D which in earlier days had promised to be its safest line of development.

Verbally, the distinction has been made on the grounds that primary drives are innate whereas secondary ones are acquired. Secondary drives are supposed to be aroused by external stimulation which in the past has been associated with a primary drive, such conditioning being reinforced by the reduction of the primary drive. Thus, the sight and smell and oral contact with food are supposed to produce secondary motivation in the animal because they have been associated with ingestion and assimilation of food which is primary-drive reducing. The evidence for this conceptualization has never been very compelling. The temporal intervals between ingestion and the subsequent reduction of need are much too long to be explained by any principles of learning yet discovered. Sexual activity, as we have just noted, serves as an incentive in the absence of any demonstrable prior association with sexual drive reduction. Saccharin is a reinforcer even though the laboratory animal can not have had any opportunity to associate sweetness with nutrition since it was weaned.[17]

Procedurally, primary and secondary drives are distinguished by the different antecedent conditions that produce them, deprivation or intense

[16] It is interesting to note that there have been few attempts to correlate drive as given by its reinforcement property with drive as given by its property of energizing instrumental behavior; Miller and Kessen (1952) is one.

[17] Some animals that nurse, like cats, don't care for sweets. Some animals, like rats and men, are reinforced by sweets even though they aren't hungry (Young & Shuford, 1955). Some milk isn't sweet. Nonetheless, it would be interesting to know if rats tube-fed a nonsweet diet from birth would find saccharin reinforcing.

stimulation in one case, and prior experience with the reinforcer in the other. Abolishing the distinction does not imply that drive conditions cannot be anchored antecedently, but only that it must be done differently. And we may also expect that it will be considerably more difficult.

Reinforcement without Sensory Feedback. Another alternative to the drive-reduction hypothesis of reinforcement is that the stimulus consequences of the consummatory response, food in the mouth, erotic stimulation, or whatever, is the vital factor in reinforcement, rather than drive reduction, or the occurrence of the consummatory response. Ordinarily, of course, the consummatory response and its stimulus feedback occur together. But there have been some attempts to effect a separation. For example, Thomson and Porter (1953) ran animals in a T maze to a salt solution after the animals had been made sodium deficient and had been surgically deprived of their sense of taste. The animals gave some indication of learning even though, presumably, they could not sense the salt. However, such findings are no harder for reinforcement theory to explain than the finding that animals who can taste salt also will learn to go to it if they need it.

Coppock and Chambers (1954) found that animals would learn an instrumental head-turning response in order to get an intravenous injection of glucose. A control group given injections of xylose (a nonnutritive sugar substitute) also showed some indication of learning but not as much as the glucose group. Although these results provide evidence of reinforcement in the absence of the consummatory response, it is not so clear that the sensory consequences of the injections have been ruled out. Chambers (1956) has suggested that there may be an immediate reaction of the taste mechanism to sugar injections; this appears to be the case in human subjects. It has also been found that glucose injection leads to a slight but prompt temperature rise which surely has some stimulus consequences, and which may even be reinforcing in itself (Chambers & Fuller, 1958; see also Chambers, 1956a).

Epstein (1960) has developed a very elegant procedure with which it is possible to maintain rats without letting them drink (or eat, Epstein & Teitelbaum, 1962). A stomach tube is permanently installed in the

---

The only other possible reason for considering saccharin a secondary reinforcer is that Carper (1957) reported it gradually loses its reinforcing power for instrumental behavior. However, Carper found that animals would continue to drink as much of it for extended periods of time, and so did Carper and Polliard (1953) and Smith and Capretta (1956). Moreover, Sheffield and Roby (1950) failed to get instrumental extinction with saccharin reinforcement. Capretta (1962, 1964) has suggested that the acceptability of saccharin decreases with hunger. By contrast, Smith and Kinney (1956) and Campbell (1958) found that the acceptability and preference for sucrose increase with hunger. Moreover, palatability of non-nutritive sugars, saccharin and xylose, drops relative to sucrose as deprivation increases (Sheffield & Roby, 1950; Smith & Duffy, 1957a; Smith & Capretta, 1956), but this is probably true of Purina too.

esophagus and connected to an external feeding tube by a swivel attached to the cranium. The animal is thus able to move around freely and can be maintained more or less indefinitely. A small amount of water is delivered by the tube whenever the rat presses a bar. Although the learning of a new response has not been reported under these conditions, (evidently bar pressing has to be previously established), the animals were able to regulate their water intake over an extended period of time. Epstein and Teitelbaum were also able to show that rats would adjust their bar-pressing behavior very quickly and accurately to provide a constant daily caloric intake when the caloric payoff of a bar press was varied over a wide range. If this variation in the animal's daily amount of bar pressing can be attributed to the reinforcing effect of nutritive input, then we have very good evidence of reinforcement in the absence not only of any consummatory behavior but also many of the usual stimulus consequences of consummatory behavior. Certain stimuli are still present, however, from among those normally resulting from ingestion, e.g., those arising from stomach distention. On the other hand, it is not safe to conclude that the stimulus consequences of ingestion that are eliminated by Epstein's technique play no role in the normal control and reinforcement of consummatory behavior; it is likely that even the lowly rat uses or can learn to use a variety of different mechanisms in regulating intake.

Reinforcement by Brain Stimulation. A still more unusual and violent intervention in the usual consummatory behavior → need reduction → drive reduction order of events is effected in those situations in which reinforcement is produced by direct stimulation of the brain. Electrodes located in the lateral hypothalamus deliver brief mild electrical stimulation whenever the animal presses a bar (Olds & Milner, 1954). Under these conditions animals rapidly learn to press the bar at a very high rate and persist in doing so until overcome by sheer exhaustion. Almost simultaneously with, and independent of, Olds' work was the discovery by Delgado et al. (1954) of areas in the brain where electrical stimulation appeared to have negative reinforcing effects. Cats were trained to make an instrumental response to a cue in an ordinary avoidance learning. The cue (a buzzer) was then paired with an electric shock presented in several different areas of the brain. It was found that the animals made the learned response in avoidance of the brain stimulation. Subsequently, it has been found that in certain areas of the brain, direct stimulation can, under certain conditions, produce fear reactions (Delgado et al., 1956), or it can be used as an unconditioned stimulus for avoidance learning (Cohen et al., 1957). Sometimes escape without avoidance is found (Roberts, 1958). Some of these different effects may result from differential electrode placement (Olds, 1956). But sometimes both rewarding and punishing effects of stimulation can be found with the same electrode placement (Roberts, 1958a). Sometimes different results may be due to the different species involved. And they may be due to different durations or electrical properties of shock (Bower & Miller, 1958). For example, it appears that when current is presented to an area that has been found to be positively reinforcing, then its onset has a positive effect, whereas its continued presentation may make it aversive (Stein, 1962). (See also Keesey, 1962, 1964; Poschel, 1963; and the excellent review by Olds, 1962.)

In many of these studies it has been noted that the behavior elicited unconditionally by the stimulation seemed to be related in some way to other consummatory behaviors. Olds (1955) has noted: "All electric stimuli seem to evoke postures or automatisms that have something to do with approach to food, or attack on prey, or defense, or ingestion, or other behaviors associated with self-preservation" (p. 123). This suggests that one of the mechanisms underlying these reinforcing effects is that stimulation is being presented to the lower brain coordination centers for these different kinds of motivated activity. Olds has reported that an electrode placed in an area associated with hunger loses its direct reinforcing effect when the animal is satiated, and that the rate of pressing for stimulation goes up when the animal is hungry. If androgen is injected, a treatment which should make sexual behavior particularly reinforcing, then again self-stimulation in the "hunger" area occurs at a lower rate. Similarly, it appears to be the case that when the animal is deprived of food its rate of pressing will decrease if a high rate of pressing had been obtained under the effect of androgen. Thus, there seems to be good evidence for interactions between hunger, sex, and perhaps other drives, and the reinforcement effects of electrical self-stimulation (Olds, 1958a).

There can be very little doubt that, when conditions are right, direct brain stimulation can be used not only to reinforce bar-press behavior but also the learning of a runway and even the correct path through a maze (Olds, 1956a; Spear, 1962; Mendelson & Chorover, 1965). The vexing question here for the diehard drive-reduction theorist is what is the nature of the drive that is reduced by electrical stimulations. Perhaps an appropriate drive can be invented. Perhaps it will turn out that stimulation in appropriate areas bypasses ordinary drive conditions and produces some immediate effect which is comparable to the more commonplace effect of drive reduction. On the other hand, it may be that stimulation of the "joy center" constitutes reinforcement independently of what the drive or drive-reduction conditions may be in the organism just because it is pleasurable. Maybe pleasure constitutes reinforcement whether it be brought about directly by stimulation or whether it be produced naturally by the animal engaging in those sorts of behavior it enjoys. Gallistel (1964) has suggested that lateral hypothalamic stimulation not only stimulates reinforcement centers of the brain but also stimulates motivation centers at the same time. Such a dual action would help account for (1) the poor resistance to extinction generally found in self-stimulation studies; (2) the poor carry-over of performance from one session to the next; (3) the breakdown of behavior under stringent intermittent schedules; and (4) the failure of Stein (1958), Mogenson et al. (1965), and others to find substantial secondary reinforcement based on brain stimulation.[18] The simplest conclusion to draw (and the one most frequently drawn) is that these self-stimulation studies provide evidence of reinforcement which is independent of drive reduction and, hence, violates Hull's dictum that drive reduction constitutes reinforcement.

Drive Induction as Reinforcement. A number of writers during the 1950s invoked drives to account for learning on the grounds that learning must require drive reduction. For example, when an animal spends time in a part of the apparatus where there is no food or mate or anything else except the novelty of the apparatus itself, we may say that the animal has a tendency to explore. But when it learns a response in order to get to where it can explore, then we are tempted to talk about a drive to explore (Nissen, 1930; Montgomery, 1954; Myers & Miller, 1954). There are two difficulties here. In the first place, there is usually no evidence other than the learning at hand to indicate the existence of drive. There-fore, invoking it represents the worst kind of circularity. The situation would be more secure if there were multiple anchoring of exploration; but, as we saw in Chapter 7, there don't seem to be any nonstimulus determinants of exploration.

In the second place, even if there is such a drive there seems to be little justification for attributing the learning to its reduction. By any gen-eral activation criterion of drive it would seem to be increased by the animal's exploratory behavior.

When the animal "seeks" a novel situation in order to explore it would appear as though it is the *induction* of the exploratory drive con-dition that reinforces the instrumental response. If, in fact, the drive is aroused by novelty as Harlow insists (1953), then whatever makes the animal leave a familiar situation? On the other hand, although not beset by such logical difficulties, the attempts to explain exploration and spon-taneous alternation by introducing the concept of a "boredom drive" (e.g., Myers & Miller, 1954; Brown, 1955; Dember & Earl, 1957) have not been completely convincing (O'Connell, 1965). In considering Shef-field's work with incomplete sexual consummation we found a similar situation; it seems much more in accord with all observations of animals (including man, Hardy, 1964) that the behavior which gets the animal to the goal is reinforced by the excitement, or arousal, or increase in drive that occurs there, rather than the quiescence that may follow some time

[18] All of these effects, plus some others, can probably also be explained on the basis of Bail and Adam's (1965) hypothesis that brain stimulation is not itself necessarily reinforcing but its short-term after-effects are aversive. The rat pressing the bar for brain stimulation is, in this view, like the drunkard who doesn't partic-ularly care for alcohol but drinks to get rid of a hangover.

later. It has also been argued (e.g., Maltzman, 1952; Campbell, 1958) that in the case of hunger it is the increase in excitement or stimulation provided by food that reinforces running to food. These arguments apply equally well to the case of the alleged activity drive, to thirst, and to the aversive drives. The special problems encountered by the drive-reduction theory of reinforcement in accounting for avoidance learning are so complex and so important that we will devote most of a later chapter to them. Suffice it to say here that these problems are so imposing that they have led a number of behavior theorists (Mowrer, 1947; Solomon & Wynne, 1954; Seward, 1956; Spence, 1956; Miller, 1963) to abandon the drive-reduction hypothesis, at least in part.

Summary. Three conclusions are suggested by this diverse array of considerations. (1) Reinforcement is very highly correlated with the reduction in the needs of the organism, and inasmuch as needs are correlated with drive conditions, drive reduction often provides reinforcement. This is a serviceable empirical rule. On the other hand, there seems to be a great number of circumstances under which reinforcemnt occurs in the absence of anything that can be called need reduction, or anything that can reasonably be called drive reduction. (2) In order to retain the drive-reduction hypothesis as part of the nomological net of the drive construct it appears necessary to sever the antecedent parts of the net so as to make drive by definition that which reinforces when it is reduced. Drive thereby comes to include all of the incentive factors in motivation. (3) The drive-reduction hypothesis might fruitfully be replaced by a drive-induction hypothesis of reinforcement. While such a strategy might provide a simpler account of a number of findings it would surely entail a loss of antecedent anchoring and make drive essentially synonymous with incentive motivation.

THE STIMULUS CONCOMITANTS OF DRIVE

Virtually all theories of motivation make some provision for a special class of stimuli which do something more than provide associative control of behavior. Sometimes these stimuli are said to goad the animal into activity or to make the animal do something to end the stimulation. Sometimes these stimuli are said to motivate the animal, to motivate behavior, or to motivate learning. In Hull's system this class of stimuli has no special properties. Stimuli such as those arising from stomach contraction or from a dry mouth or from erotic stimulation or from electric shock are not considered to provide motivation, but to be mere concomitants of the drive-producing conditions. They have no special properties other than some significance for the animal's survival, i.e., these are the stimuli to which the animal must associate adaptive behavior if it is to survive.[19]

In view of the functional importance of these stimuli, Hull (1933) must have been a little surprised to find that the rat required a great deal of training in order to discriminate between hunger and thirst, and that even with extensive training discrimination was not very reliable. Hull had trained rats to turn one way in a T maze to obtain water and the other way to obtain food. The animals were run alternately hungry and thirsty. It appeared as though the rat cannot easily tell when it is hungry and when it is thirsty.

Leeper (1935) reported a similar study in which considerably faster learning was found. Part of the improvement could be attributed to the fact that Leeper used two goal boxes, one for hunger and one for thirst, which were spatially separated, whereas Hull had used one box and required the animals to learn different paths to it when hungry and thirsty. Leeper argued that of course the animal knows when it is hungry and when it is thirsty and that the only difficulty it has is in learning where the food and water are located. Leeper's interpretation has engendered some discussion (Seeman & Williams, 1952; Deutsch, 1959).[20] But in spite of Leeper's protests it was generally felt that the drive-discrimination studies demonstrated what had been suspected, namely, that there are discernible stimulus consequences of food deprivation and water deprivation to which the animal can associate differential responses.

The Selective Association Hypothesis. Kendler (1946) reported a drive-discrimination study that required a different interpretation. He trained rats simultaneously hungry and thirsty in a situation where food was on one side of a T maze and water was on the other; the animals were forced alternately to the two sides. After surprisingly few trials, the animals showed that an appropriate discrimination had been acquired. That is, when made just hungry or just thirsty on a test trial the animals went to the appropriate side significantly more frequently than would be expected by chance. While this result is intuitively plausible, it presents

[19] In 1943, but especially in 1952, Hull suggested that S_D reduction was involved in primary reinforcement. Since Hull believed the reduction in s_G (the feedback from r_G) constituted secondary reinforcement, the two were thereby made parallel. He still expressed some doubt, however, about the fundamental nature of reinforcement, and offered this arrangement on a trial basis only (Hull, 1952, p. 152).

[20] That animals would learn to make different responses depending upon their motivation in spite of the fact that the external stimulus situation remained unchanged proved to Leeper that (1) a useful distinction could be made between the acquisition of knowledge (learning) and using it (performance), and (2) animals are not bound to respond in a purely mechanical stimulus-response manner. Leeper evidently failed to understand the point of Hull's study, which was that there could be internal stimuli that could mediate behavior. Hence he was led to betray his fear (common at that time) that explanations of behavior in S-R terms had necessarily to be mechanistic, and to deny the whole approach.

some embarrassment for any simple S-R account of learning. Consider the situation when the animal is, say, both hungry and thirsty, makes a turn to the left, finds food, and eats. The turning-left response should become equally conditioned to the stimuli arising from hunger and the stimuli arising from thirst. But what happens in fact is that the hunger-produced stimulus evidently acquires greater associative loading than the thirst stimulus does. Otherwise, the animal would not have been able to make the appropriate response when tested under food deprivation. Obviously, it would not suffice to view hunger-produced and thirst-produced stimuli as being exactly like any other stimulus; they must have some special properties. Kendler suggested that drive-produced stimuli have the special property of "selective association"; they only enter into associative connection with a response when the response leads to a reduction in the stimulus (i.e., reinforcement).

A crucial test of the selective-association hypothesis should be possible. One possibility is to train animals on a discrimination in which the hypothesized stimuli arising from hunger and thirst are to be used as cues even though neither hunger or thirst is a relevant drive condition. The first such study was by Amsel (1949) who trained animals on a shock avoidance that was arranged so that when the animal was hungry one response terminated the shock, while another response terminated the shock when the animal was thirsty. Some learning was demonstrated, but only after a great amount of training. Amsel and others who have done similar studies (Winnick, 1950; Baker, 1950; Levine, 1953; Bailey, 1955) conclude that a strict selective-association hypothesis such as Kendler originally proposed cannot be correct.

The principle of selective association of drive stimuli encountered more trouble from studies such as that by Woodbury and Wilder (1954). They ran two groups of rats in a complex maze. The experimental group was made alternately hungry, and hungry plus thirsty, and was reinforced alternately with food and water. The control group was also tested alternately hungry, and hungry plus thirsty, but was reinforced consistently with food. Thus both groups had an equal number of reinforcements but according to the selective-association hypothesis, the experimental group should learn more slowly and should perform better if tested thirsty. No difference in learning was found, although the experimental group did have a superiority in the thirst test.

Kendler and Law (1950) attempted to bolster the selective-association principle with the evidence that irrelevant-drive stimuli failed to acquire any associative loading in a position-reversal situation. Kendler and Law found that the presence of an irrelevant drive during acquisition failed to impair performance on reversal learning even when the originally irrelevant drive condition was made relevant during reversal. Any possible effect here, however, was overwhelmed by the large decremental effect that the irrelevant drive condition had upon original learning. This latter finding is difficult to interpret in terms of the selective-association hypothesis, but it also raises difficulties for any account of motivation which affords drive-produced stimuli a purely associative role in the determination of behavior. Still more troublesome was the finding that irrelevant thirst produced a much more serious impairment in original learning than did irrelevant hunger.

Kendler had recognized at the outset that there was a good alternative to the selective-association explanation. He noted that discrimination in his situation might not be based upon the drive-produced stimuli at all but upon the operation of an incentive mechanism such as r_G. This could work somewhat as follows: During training the animal eats and drinks in the presence of stimuli which are similar to those occurring at the choice point. Hence, it is apt to make anticipatory goal responses of eating and drinking at the choice point. Now, if the left side of the T maze is the food side, stimuli at the choice point to the left side will produce a stronger r_G for eating than those to the right. Correspondingly, stimuli to the right side of the choice will tend to elicit stronger anticipatory drinking reactions than those to the left. Then, on the crucial test day when the animal is under just one deprivation condition it will tend to approach that side of the apparatus which elicits the stronger of the two r_G's, and this is, of course, the correct side.

Subsequently Kendler abandoned the selective-association hypothesis. Kendler and Levine (1951) found that thirsty animals appeared to be actively avoiding the place where food had been eaten; it was not just a matter of associative interference. Kendler et al. (1952, 1954) concluded that all of these phenomena—the original drive discrimination, the decrement produced by irrelevant drive, and the asymmetry in the decrement—could be best explained in terms of r_G mechanisms rather than in terms of drive stimuli. To handle the avoidance of food by thirsty animals it is only necessary to suppose that the r_G's elicited under hunger and thirst are to some extent incompatible so that one may inhibit the other.

We may note how nicely the r_G interpretation accounts for the Hull-Leeper difference. Spatially separated goal boxes permit the r_G's for hunger and thirst to come under the control of different environmental stimuli, whereas the common goal box situation leads to the same stimuli controlling both r_G's. Then, at the choice point the two responses have a chance to be discriminatively associated with different environmental cues in the first case, but not in the second. The r_G interpretation is thus able to account for the rapid acquisition of drive discrimination in situations where it is rapid (e.g., Leeper, 1935; Kendler, 1946) and also the poor performance reported in other situations. In particular, it makes sense of the fact that when hunger and thirst are irrelevant the acquisition of discrimination is always found to be very slow (Amsel, 1949; Baker, 1950; Winnick, 1950; Levine, 1953; Bailey, 1955), for if there is no eating or drinking it is not likely there would be much conditioning of the appropriate r_G's. Actually the minimal drive-discrimination learning found with irrelevant hunger and thirst may also depend upon r_G. For one thing, there may be some generalization to the test situation from those situations where consummatory behavior does occur. Moreover, minimal r_G's may occur as a direct consequence of the deprivation conditions, more or less independently of the environmental conditions. Hence, it may be that even when drive discrimination proceeds poorly the acquisition that it obtained is also attributed to r_G mechanisms; this possibility should not be ruled out. But in any case, we can say that when the experimental situation is arranged so that r_G mechanisms can be used, then the animal learns the discrimination very quickly, in 30 trials or less. But, when the situation is arranged to minimize the use of r_G mechanisms, so that discrimination is more dependent upon S_D, then animals have great difficulty learning the discrimination. It is obvious that if there are S_D's they gain relatively little associative control over instrumental behavior. In recent years a few voices could be heard asking whether there really are any drives (e.g., Postman, 1953; Bolles, 1958; Estes, 1958). Perhaps now we will begin to hear the next question: Are there really any drive stimuli?

The Locus of Drive Stimuli. It can be argued that S_D discrimination is difficult to get, not because there are no stimuli, but because S_D's have a slow onset—they arise gradually over a long period of time. Bolles and Petrinovich (1954) attempted to overcome this handicap by means of a drive-switching procedure in which rats to be made hungry were first deprived of water for 22 hr. and then offered water in the absence of food for 1 hr. The animal presumably suddenly finds itself hungry during the course of this drinking. A parallel procedure was used to produce a more rapid onset of thirst: animals were food deprived and then fed food in the absence of water. Unfortunately, Bolles and Petrinovich did not run the controls necessary to determine whether it was the relatively rapid onset of the drive conditions or some other feature of their procedure that facilitated learning. Bolles and Petrinovich originally attributed the rapid acquisition of discrimination to the fact that the onset and termination of the discriminanda occurred at the choice point and goal respectively, as in the usual discrimination, and also to the "purity" of the drive states produced by the drive-switching procedure. Subsequent work with similar procedures (Bolles, 1962a) suggests that the presence of good differential extramaze cues is at least as important. Actually, there have been few systematic studies to indicate what variables affect the ease of drive discrimination. Besch et al. (1963), using an irrelevant-drive procedure, found that the noncorrection method led to much faster learning than the correction method.

It seems unlikely that the slow onset of the stimuli to be discriminated is a relevant factor in the slow acquisition of drive discrimination. Eninger (1951) and Bailey (1955) have discovered that, with auditory stimuli as discriminanda, stimulus durations as long as 15 sec. almost preclude discrimination learning. In view of this finding it is quite remarkable that the rat can make any discrimination of hunger and thirst stimuli whose onset is spread over a period of hours or minutes as in the Bolles and Petrinovich procedure (see also Greenberg, 1954).

There is some question whether hunger produces stimuli, or thirst produces stimuli, or both do, or whether neither does but discrimination results from some experimental artifact such as the stomach-distention cues suggested by Heron (1949). Bailey (1955) has studied drive discrimination under a variety of appropriate control conditions and reports that rats could learn to press one of two panels to turn off a light according to whether they were hungry vs. satiated, thirsty vs. satiated, or hungry vs. thirsty. In another study Bailey and Porter (1955), working with cats, obtained further evidence to support the argument that animals can, in fact, discriminate unique stimuli arising from food and water deprivation. Learning in all these cases was quite slow.

Further Circumstantial Evidence of Drive Stimuli. While the search for the locus of deprivation-produced stimuli goes on there is a tendency to invoke such stimuli for theoretical reasons whenever the behavior of animals shows some sort of associative dependence upon the conditions of deprivation. Thus S_D almost acquires the status of a theoretical construct. For example, Eninger (1951a) found that a T maze shock-escape response was more resistant to extinction when the animals were both trained and extinguished under the same irrelevant drive condition (either hunger or thirst) than when they were switched from hunger to thirst or thirst to hunger. Hence it would appear that changing the irrelevant drive conditions decreased the stability of performance in extinction, suggesting that the irrelevant-drive-produced stimuli can acquire appreciable stimulus control over the escape response. This clear-cut effect with nondiscriminative stimuli is a bit surprising in view of the aforementioned difficulty others have had in demonstrating associative control in a discrimination setting. Unfortunately, Eninger's acquisition results are not presented, so that it is not possible to determine whether, for example, there may have been some asymmetry in the acquisition results perhaps based on the interaction of thirst and susceptibility to shock.

In a similar study, Wickens et al. (1949) found that reversal and relearning of a T maze position habit occurred more quickly if the animal's relevant drive condition (hunger or thirst) was changed so that a given position in the maze was associated with a given drive condition (and relevant consummatory response). This finding was interpreted in terms of the classical associative and retroactive inhibition paradigm, and taken as evidence for the reality of S_D.

Bolles (1958a) replicated the overall effect found by Wickens et al., but noted that there were marked asymmetries in the pattern and number of errors made both in the reversal learning and in the relearning phases of the experiment. The superiority of the reversed-drive groups in reversal learning appeared to be largely due to the performance under one condition, namely, where a hunger-learned habit was reversed by thirsty animals (H-T). Animals under other conditions (T-H, H-H, and T-T) all showed comparable performance. Error scores were analyzed by distinguishing between those made prior to the first correct reversal response, "preerrors," and errors made after the first correct response, "posterrors." It was observed that animals tested while hungry tended to make far fewer preerrors but more posterrors than animals tested while thirsty. On the other hand, in reversing a hunger-learned habit, there were characteristically fewer preerrors and more posterrors than in reversing a thirst-learned habit. This pattern of results could be explained on the basis of Petrinovich and Bolles' hypothesis (1954) that hungry animals tend to be more variable in such situations than thirsty animals, or on the basis of the tendency of thirsty animals to avoid a place associated with food (Kendler & Levine, 1951).

Another argument for there being discriminably different stimulus consequences of different conditions of deprivation are the demonstrations that animals can learn different responses to different intensities of deprivation conditions, i.e., so-called "drive-intensity discrimination." Drive-intensity discrimination has been reported by Bloomberg and Webb (1949), Jenkins and Hanratty (1949), and Bolles (1962a). Although Bolles got relatively rapid learning, discrimination has usually required extensive training and then only rose to a limited level of proficiency. The demonstration of drive-intensity discrimination opens up again, of course, all the same questions of the locus of the stimulus. Are such animals making the discrimination on the basis of stomach distention, or some sort of metering of the consummatory response? Are the animals discriminating different consequences of r_G? We do not know.

Another sort of circumstantial evidence for drive stimuli comes from those studies (Rethlingshafer et al., 1951; Manning, 1956) in which animals are trained to get water on one side of a T maze and food on the other, and then tested under a combination of different hunger and thirst conditions. Presumably, response competition will occur by virtue of associative interference of the stimuli arising from hunger and thirst. Both Rethlingshafer et al. and Manning agree in finding that with 23 hr. of water deprivation indifferent performance (50–50 on the T maze) occurred when the irrelevant food deprivation was something like 16 hr. When the hunger and thirst roles were reversed Rethlingshafer found again a crossover point at about 16 hr., whereas Manning reports the value to be somewhere above 23 hr. of irrelevant water deprivation. This discrepancy, and indeed all of these results, seem rather unimportant in view of the fact that the incentive variables, which play such a dominant role in hunger and thirst motivation, were not equated in value.[21]

Generalization Effects with Drive Stimuli. There have been a number of studies in which the motivation conditions of the animals are shifted during the course of acquisition either once (Elliott, 1929; Hillman et al., 1953) or many times (Daily, 1950; Teel, 1952). Moreover, there are all those latent learning experiments in which the animal responds in the old way when drive conditions are shifted to a new set of conditions (Kimble, 1961). There are in addition (as we saw in discussing the independence problem) a number of studies in which drive conditions are shifted in intensity during the course of learning. Thus, high-drive and low-drive groups are trained, and then split in half and tested either under the same or under the shifted drive conditions. Any asymmetry in the pattern of results indicates a generalization decrement insofar as the performance of animals tested under shifted conditions is inferior on the average to the performance of animals tested under the same conditions. Although a number of such drive-shift studies have been conducted, only one gives any indication that the particular level or intensity of drive conditions had entered into the associative control of the criterion behavior. In this study (Yamaguchi, 1952) animals were trained under 3, 12, 24, 48, and 72 hr. deprivation and then switched in a factorial design to 3, 24, 48, and 72 hr. for testing. Although the transfer effects were all in the direction predicted by an associative interpretation, the effects were all small, and in fact only one comparison was significant. Once again, then, it seems that if drive stimuli enter into the associative control of behavior at all they do so only very weakly.

A study by Birch et al. (1958) looked at first as though it might provide more substantial evidence of hunger-produced stimuli. Animals were maintained for 35 days in a specially constructed living cage equipped

[21] The Manning paper has many virtues, including that of being the first (or one of the first) animal motivation studies to use estimation statistics rather than traditional inference statistics. But how can any conclusion be drawn about the relative strengths of drive prior to some assessment of incentive motivation? Manning equated the amount of time for eating and drinking, but this does not guarantee an equation of the incentive values of the food and the water. (Rethlingshafer et al. did not even describe their incentive parameters.) Hence these results would seem to have no more claim to indicating the relative strengths of hunger and thirst motivation than those of Warden et al. (1931). There is the interesting reciprocal problem of how one could equate incentives in any psychological sense prior to some assessment of the relative strengths of the different drives.

with a food trough which contained food only for 2 hr. during a 24-hr. period. The principal response measure was the number of food trough contacts. Early in training the number of approaches to the food trough was more or less constant over the 24 hours. But by the 35th day the animals rarely approached the food trough except in the hours immediately before the regularly scheduled meal, indicating a rather precise temporal discrimination. A striking result of the study was found when the regular feeding was omitted on the last day. As the time for eating passed, the number of approaches to the food trough again dropped back down, suggesting that the particular stimulus magnitude resulting from a 24-hr. food deprivation had acquired discriminative control over the response of approaching the food trough.

It would appear that Birch et al. had found, at last, substantial evidence to demonstrate the existence of deprivation-produced stimuli. Unfortunately, however, it is entirely possible that the stimuli controlling food-trough contacts in the Birch study did not arise from the stomach or the head or anywhere else as a consequence of the particular deprivation state, but rather were strictly temporal in origin. Over the course of 35 days, external cues to the time of day might acquire associative control over the criterion response; and perhaps it was such external stimuli rather than anything that can be called S_D that produced the gradient. Supporting such an alternative explanation was the fact that as the 48th hour without food drew near, there was a second increase in the number of approaches to the food trough.[22]

Bolles (1961a) attempted to test this "external" or "appetitional" hypothesis by letting rats press a bar for 1 hr. for food either every 24 hr. or every 29 hr. On the 24-hr. cycle, time of day and possible internal stimuli arising from deprivation were confounded, as they were on the experiments just discussed; while under the 29-hr. condition the effects of deprivation-produced and time-of-day-produced stimuli could be isolated. Animals were maintained under the appropriate conditions for 15 deprivation cycles following which different groups received the opportunity to press the bar after the usual deprivation time, or at deprivation times 5 hr. longer or 5 hr. shorter than the training deprivation time. The 24-hr. animals showed significantly shorter latency to press and greater resistance to extinction when tested at 24 hr. than when tested at either 19 hr. or 29 hr. These results confirm those of Birch et al. However, the animals trained on a 29-hr. cycle showed no such symmetrical generalization gradient. Both response measures increased continuously with deprivation time, and fell uniformly below those of the 24-hr. animals tested

---

[22] In a study similar to that of Birch et al., Brown and Belloni (1963) failed to obtain evidence of the anticipation of feeding, perhaps because their animals were isolated from 24-hr. environmental stimulation. There were other methodological differences, however, that might account for the difference in results.

at 24 hr. Bolles and de Lorge (1962b) obtained similar results with activity wheels; rats fed every 19 hr. or every 29 hr. in wheels failed to show any anticipation (i.e., increased running) of the regularly scheduled but adiurnal feeding. Rats fed every 24 hr. of course showed a large anticipation of the regularly diurnal feeding.

These findings strongly suggest that deprivation time per se has little to do either with the anticipation of cyclic feeding or with the maintenance of the rat's normal activity cycle. All of these studies leave open the question of whether the temporal cues that do control the rat's activity and anticipation of daily feedings are internal or external in origin. That is, we do not know if the animal's cycle is bound up with some sort of intrinsic biological clock with a period more or less fixed at 24 hr., or whether the animal is responding to external cues provided by the normal 24-hr. cycle in the laboratory. A subsequent study by Bolles and Stokes (1965) attempted to answer this question. Groups of animals were born and reared in well-controlled environments in which the lighting, noise level, feeding, and maintenance of animals were all geared to 19 hr., 24 hr., or 29 hr. The animals were run when adult either in activity wheels or in Skinner boxes while being fed for 1 hr. at a given point in their light-dark cycle. None of the 19-hr. or 29-hr. subjects showed any evidence of anticipation either in the wheels or in the bar-press situation, while all of the 24-hr. subjects developed anticipatory behavior. Thus, the controlling stimuli seem to be external, but in the peculiar sense that if the environment provides stimuli with a 24-hr. periodicity, then they will control the animal's motivated behavior, perhaps through the elicitation of r_G. But, if the environmental stimuli provide no 24-hr. periodicity, then the animal ignores them and shows some evidence of responding to internal stimuli which have a period near 24 hr. Thus, some of the 29-hr. animals showed 25-hr. and 26-hr. anticipation effects. These results suggest once more that the direct stimulus consequences of deprivation or of deprivation time play a very small role in the determination of behavior.

There is no more apt summary than that written by Webb a decade ago (1955) after reviewing much of the same material we have covered here:

> The data support a notion that the conditioning of responses to drive stimuli is not easy, and, where external cues are readily available, drive stimuli are likely to play only limited roles in mediating behavior. There is a trend, with increasing supportive data, to further restrict the role of the drive stimulus. There are indications that the "fractional anticipatory responses" may provide mediating stimuli in drive situations in place of the drive stimuli themselves. The situation may be quite different for drives other than hunger and thirst and in

the human. From the data here reviewed, it is easy to suggest, however, that extensive theoretical use of the concept of drive states alone as cues is likely to be charming but unsupportable. (Webb, 1955, p. 296)

Summary. We may note that none of the available evidence, with the single exception of Eninger (1951a), is inconsistent with the proposition that rapid drive discrimination requires the operation of r_G. In those experimental situations where r_G cannot reasonably be invoked (e.g., where eating and drinking are not permitted), very slow discrimination learning has been the rule. Other types of studies in which the associative properties of the hypothetical S_D's are tested also seem more compatible with an r_G interpretation than with an S_D interpretation. This remarkable finding casts grave doubt upon all pure stimulus theories of motivation, such as Guthrie's and perhaps Estes' (1958).[23] We also now have very strong evidence that seems almost to demand some sort of incentive-motivation mechanism. This conclusion has an indirect but very real bearing on Hull's drive theory: If we have to introduce r_G to explain some of the phenomena that D and S_D were supposed to be able to explain, then we may begin to wonder if perhaps r_G can carry the entire explanatory burden.

SUMMARY

We have summarized the status of each of the other two propositions about the associative aspects of the drive construct at the conclusion of the respective sections of this chapter. The independence of D and H, we have found, has not really been verified, it has only been assumed. The hypothesis that drive reduction is the basis of reinforcement seems to be true much of the time but certainly not all of the time. In the present section we have seen that the stimulus concomitants of drive states cannot or have not been identified in any way which would support the role that Hull gave them.

Hull introduced these three propositions to deal with the apparent fact that even a motivational explanation of behavior must make some

[23] Estes has introduced the concept of "satiation cues" which may be able to carry enough of the explanatory burden that r_G won't have to be invoked. The results discussed here also make it a little difficult for those who would argue, like Miller, that drives are just strong stimuli. They have to explain the anomaly of stimuli that can energize all sorts of responses but to which no particular response can be conditioned. It appears now that animals cannot tell whether they are hungry or thirsty unless some feature of the environment makes them do something about whichever it is. On the other hand, most of the confusion would be dispelled by a methodological breakthrough demonstrating that animals can, indeed, readily discriminate irrelevant drive conditions.

allowance for the nonmotivational or associative determinants of behavior. Hull's D × H formula was a simple device to separate the two kinds of determinants. But the simplicity turns out to be deceptive. We have discovered that by the time we have analyzed any simple bit of behavior to determine what events control it and what events reinforce it, there is very little left for the D × H formula to explain. We have also begun to discover that there are some motivational phenomena for which an incentive concept seems indispensable, and this seriously undermines drive theory.

10

GENERALIZED DRIVE

❖‹C❖‹C❖‹C❖‹C❖‹C❖‹C❖‹C❖‹C❖‹C❖‹C❖‹C❖‹C❖‹C❖‹C❖‹C❖‹C❖‹C❖‹C❖‹C❖‹C❖‹C❖‹C

*One might suppose, of course, that drives are all alike save that
each is the result of its own distinctive motivational variable. But
if this is the case, then we no longer have different drives, as behavior determinants, but only* different sources of drive.

J. S. BROWN

Hull made a clear conceptual distinction between the associative and the
energizing determinants of behavior, attributing the former to H and
the latter to D. One consequence of this separation is that different
sources of D should be mutually intersubstitutable, at least as far as their
contribution to D is concerned. A response established under hunger, for
example, should also be energized by thirst. If the original hunger condition is still present, then there should be a *summation* of the hunger- and
thirst-produced contributions to D, and the response should occur with
greater strength than under the original hunger condition alone. On the
other hand, if the original hunger condition is completely satisfied, the
response should still occur with some strength because of the *substitution*
of thirst-produced D. Hull's generalized-drive concept therefore generated
two new experimental problems: is there, in fact, drive summation; and
is there, in fact, drive substitution? We will consider first the experimental
literature that was intended to answer these two questions.

Next we will consider one of the oldest and most honored types of
evidence that has been cited in support of the generalized-drive hypothesis. The argument that has been made from the earliest days of research

on the subject is that the motivated animal will increase its activity level even in the absence of any relevant goal object. It was soon found that, in animals, running in activity wheels was correlated with hunger, thirst, and the sexual state; psychologists interested in human motivation emphasized a similar increase in general tension in people when the normal outlets for motivated behavior were not available. Hull systematized this kind of thinking with the hypothesis that regardless of its source, drive would energize any on-going behavior, including behavior such as running in wheels which has no immediate relevance to the drive-producing condition. We will consider whether such behavior really is irrelevant, and whether it really is energized by the various drive-producing conditions.

A final implication of Hull's theoretical formulation of the drive construct is that individual differences in D should have some generality across different situations and even perhaps across different drive-producing conditions. The case for the D construct would be appreciably strengthened if such generalized individual differences could be demonstrated. But we will see that the evidence provides little support for any such generality. In fact the evidence appears to point toward the importance of associative determinants of behavior, even in those instances commonly accepted as demonstrating motivational factors in behavior. We will conclude from the material in this chapter that there is little empirical justification for the generalized-drive hypothesis.

THE ENERGIZING EFFECTS OF IRRELEVANT DRIVE

Recall that Perin (1942) extinguished a bar-press response in groups of animals under 3-, 16-, and 22-hr. food deprivation (see Fig. 6-2). Hull (1943), quite reasonably, extrapolated backward from the data points and concluded that even at 0 hr. deprivation the response would be maintained at something in the order of 25% of its maximum strength. Hull attributed this activation in the absence of the hunger drive condition to the energizing of the bar-press habit by irrelevant drive conditions such as thirst, fear, exploration, and sex, which are still present in the test situation. These states of the organism are called *irrelevant* because they remain unreduced in the hunger-food situation.[1]

[1] There have been a few studies comparing the effect of two relevant drive conditions with the usual procedure with just one. Porter and Miller (1957) found that animals alternated between hunger and thirst (and reinforced alternately with food and water) performed no worse in extinction than control animals trained under a single drive condition; i.e., there was little evidence of drive competition. Powloski (1953) ran animals under concurrent hunger and thirst, offering them both food and water, and found that they did no better than control animals with just one drive condition, i.e., there was little evidence for drive

The empirical basis for Hull's assumption of activation under very low levels of hunger was examined by Koch and Daniel (1945) and Saltzman and Koch (1948). They used procedures and apparatus as much like Perin's as they could, and hence the results provide something of an indication of what Perin might have obtained had he run these groups in the original study. The results, shown in Fig. 10-1, indicate that as food deprivation is reduced below 3 hr. there is a dramatic drop in the strength of the response. Koch and Daniel found that performance at 0 hr. was only 2% of the 24-hr. level instead of the 25% Hull had expected

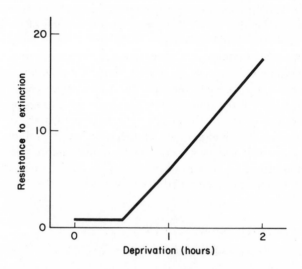

Fig. 10-1. Median resistance to extinction as a function of deprivation time for short deprivation times. (From Saltzman & Koch, 1948)

from his extrapolation. These results with a resistance-to-extinction measure were nicely corroborated by Kimble (1951) and Horenstein (1951) using other response measures (compare Fig. 8-13).

The issue would seem to have been settled, but it was not. For one thing, Hull had other evidence besides Perin's (e.g., Elliott, 1929; Finch, 1938; Zener & McCurdy, 1939). For another, the concept of generalized drive (i.e., the idea that one source of tension might activate an activity relevant to another source of tension) was not new; it had already been given considerable emphasis in the writings of Freud and Lewin. But what probably gave the generalized-drive hypothesis the greatest accept-

---

summation, but this was on a discrimination problem where differential effects of motivation would be hard to predict. (See also Wunderlich, 1961; Kleinmuntz, 1963; and Babb, 1963.)

ance was the publication of irrelevant drive experiments stemming from Hull's formulation which appeared, at least for some time, to give it empirical support.

The history of the irrelevant-drive problem divides itself with little overlap into two periods, first a hunger and thirst period, and then a more recent period in which an appetitive source of drive, usually hunger, is combined with other sources of drive, usually aversive. Let us consider the hunger and thirst studies, taking up the summation question first.

The Summation of Hunger and Thirst. Hull was never one to be vague even when being concrete meant he was likely to be proven wrong. He proposed, on the basis of no data at all, that relevant and irrelevant drive states might combine according to the equation

$$\overline{D} = \frac{D + \dot{D}}{M_D + \dot{D}}$$

where $\overline{D}$ = total effective drive,
 D = strength of the relevant drive,
 $\dot{D}$ = strength of the irrelevant drive,
and M_D = maximum attainable value of D.

Hull's law of drive summation was first tested by Kendler (1945a), who trained 5 groups of rats under 22-hr. food deprivation to press a bar for food, and then extinguished them. Throughout the experiment the different groups were under 0, 3, 6, 12, and 22 hr. irrelevant water deprivation (water was never available in the test situation). The four lower irrelevant-drive groups gave a monotonic rise in resistance to extinction, just as Hull's combination law required. But there is a marked and statistically significant reversal with the last group. As Kendler observed, Hull's combination law appeared to require modification, at least in the case of a strong irrelevant drive state.

There might be some question here, though, whether the obtained differences in resistance to extinction reflect differences in $_sH_R$ built up in acquisition, differences in total effective drive strengths in extinction, or some combination of acquisition and extinction effects. It may well be that although all animals received the same number of reinforcements, different groups may have learned topographically different responses; and although the rate of acquisition was controlled by the experimenter, different groups may have acquired different amounts of inhibition, etc. during the acquisition trials. Possible differences in habit structure would seem to be excluded, however, in a study by Danziger (1953) in which some subjects were free of irrelevant drive during acquisition. In Danziger's study all animals learned to bar press for food under 22-hr. food deprivation, but some had an irrelevant 17-hr. water deprivation. Extinction performance was tested under either hunger, or thirst, or both hunger and thirst. The response measure (reaction time during extinction) showed slightly superior performance as a result of the irrelevant drive during acquisition, but extinction performance was markedly superior under hunger alone than when it was combined with any of the irrelevant drive conditions.

Siegel (1946) also found that animals trained while hungry to press a bar for food showed somewhat less resistance to extinction if a 22-hr. irrelevant thirst was added to the 22-hr. hunger. These studies, then, are in accord in showing that strong irrelevant thirst reduces the resistance to extinction of a hunger-learned response.

Kendler and Law (1950) extended these studies by considering both food and water as both the relevant and the irrelevant drive conditions, and also by examining behavior during acquisition. It was found that whether the irrelevant condition was hunger or thirst, more errors were made in learning a maze than were made by control groups run without an irrelevant drive. The inhibition effect was highly asymmetrical however; the thirst-relevant groups made many more errors than the hunger-relevant groups, and the thirst-with-irrelevant-hunger group made a particularly large number of errors. This general pattern of findings was corroborated by Levine (1956), who also found that both irrelevant hunger and irrelevant thirst increased errors in learning a T maze, and that the learning was slower for the thirst-relevant groups than for the hunger-relevant groups.

While the decremental effect of a strong irrelevant drive in both acquisition and extinction seems well established, there remains some possibility of a genuine facilitory effect with relatively weak irrelevant drive conditions such as Kendler reported (1945). To check on this possibility, Bolles and Morlock (1960) ran animals to food under 24-hr. hunger and 0, 12, 18, 24, 36, or 48 hr. irrelevant thirst. To check on the generality of Kendler's finding of summation, another group was run with the roles of hunger and thirst reversed, and performance was measured during the acquisition of an alley-running response; latencies and running times were recorded. The animals in the Bolles and Morlock study served as their own controls, running under the different irrelevant drive conditions in a counterbalanced order. It was found that performance under the low irrelevant thirst conditions was significantly better (faster starting speeds and running speeds) than under hunger alone. And, as Kendler had found with resistance-to-extinction scores, high irrelevant thirst impaired performance. The effect was not symmetrical, however, since *all* levels of irrelevant hunger produced decrements (relative to the 0-hr. irrelevant condition) for the thirsty animals running to water. Thus, only part of the findings was compatible with Kendler's conclusion that low levels of irrelevant drive facilitate acquisition performance.

Whether the superposition of an irrelevant drive condition will facilitate or inhibit performance seems to depend upon what the particular relevant and irrelevant drive conditions are. Bolles and Morlock's results suggest another qualification based upon the fact that . . .

> neither the facilitory nor the decremental effects of irrelevant drives were present initially; both types of effect develop during successive testings, and even develop during the three daily trials. Hence, the animal's performance in the situation cannot be wholly determined by the deprivation conditions under which it runs. These conditions are too static to account for the dependence of performance upon the animal's prior experience, particularly its experience on the immediately prior trial. It is as if the animal does not know how fast to run under a given deprivation condition until it has [just] encountered the goal box under that particular condition. This aspect of these results suggests the operation of an incentive factor. . . . (Bolles & Morlock, 1960, p. 378)

Once again we find that a motivational phenomenon that seemed at first to offer the possibility of quantifying the energizing property of drive has turned out upon further analysis to be inconsistent with the hypothetical properties of the drive construct. And once again we find that the behavior in question seems to call for an incentive theory of motivation.

The Substitution of Hunger and Thirst. Hull's treatment of irrelevant drive also involved the hypothesis that a response established on the basis of one drive condition would be activated by a second drive condition even when the first drive condition no longer existed. Webb (1949) was the first to test this hypothesis using a drive substitution paradigm. He trained 5 groups of rats under 23-hr. food deprivation to press a panel for food. Four groups were then satiated for food but deprived of water for different periods of time, 0, 3, 12, and 22 hr.; the fifth group was maintained under the original 23-hr. food deprivation. Resistance to extinction of the food-learned panel-pushing response was measured. The results are shown in Fig. 10-2. Webb's finding has been replicated by Brandauer (1953) and McFarland (1964). Earlier, Miller (1948a) had found that rats that had been trained to run for water, when satiated for water ran faster under irrelevant hunger than without it. Miller interpreted this finding in terms of generalization of the drive stimuli; the animals could not, as it were, tell the difference between hunger and thirst, and so tended to run under the inappropriate conditions.

There are other explanations, though, for Miller's results, as well as

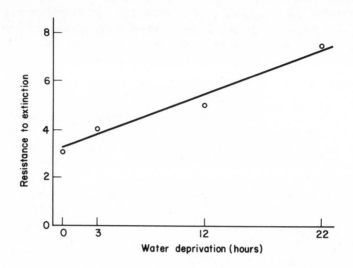

Fig. 10-2. Median resistance to extinction of a hunger-learned habit as a function of hours irrelevant thirst in rats satiated for food. (From Webb, 1949)

those of Webb and Brandauer. In Miller's case, for example, the previously relevant reward was present during the testing under the irrelevant drive, suggesting a possible secondary reinforcement factor, i.e., the sight and smell of food may not only be secondary reinforcement for hungry rats (Grindley, 1929), but for thirsty ones as well (Estes, 1949a). Zeaman and House (1950) have pointed out two other difficulties. First, how does one define absence of the relevant drive? Should one just let the animal stop eating as Kimble (1951) did, tempt it with new food as Koch and Daniel (1945) did, induce it to overeat by social facilitation (James, 1953), or punish it for not eating (Williams & Teitelbaum, 1956)? The trouble, Zeaman and House point out, is that hunger has no natural zero point, and we have not yet arrived at any convention to define satiation operationally. The second methodological problem with the early studies of drive substitution was that they failed to take into consideration the operant level of the criterion response (i.e., the strength of the response prior to the acquisition training).

There have been several reports (Elliott, 1929; Teel, 1952; Teel & Webb, 1951) of cases where animals after being trained to run to food were not markedly disrupted when their motivation was suddenly shifted from hunger to thirst. Such a finding lends some further support to the hypothesis that different sources of drive may be substituted for each other.

Doubt was cast over this whole set of drive-substitution studies using hunger and thirst, however, by Verplanck and Hayes' systematic investigation (1953) of the interaction of hunger and thirst. What Verplanck and Hayes discovered was that hunger and thirst could not be manipulated independently, at least not by the simple procedure of picking out food pellets or taking away water bottles a given number of hours before testing. We have noted before (p. 204) that there is a real possibility that when an animal is made nominally thirsty it is in some sense both hungry and thirsty. Therefore, perhaps the animal that is shifted from an "old" hunger condition to a "new" thirst condition is not under new conditions at all. Verplanck and Hayes therefore pulled the rug out from under all those who had worked on the irrelevant drive problem. (They also took the fun out of the latent learning controversy which had been waged almost exclusively with hungry and thirsty rats.)

Grice and Davis (1957) tested the Verplanck-Hayes interpretation of the Webb-Brandauer results against the generalized-drive interpretation. Four groups of rats, all under 22 hr. food deprivation, were trained to press a panel for food, and then extinguished under the acquisition condition (22-hr. food deprivation). A second group was extinguished while satiated for both food and water. These two control groups thus provide the upper and lower limits for performance that might be expected under other drive conditions. One experimental group was extinguished thirsty—with the usual 22 hr. water deprivation. Now the inference from Verplanck and Hayes is that the motivation of this "thirsty" group which determined extinction performance was not the irrelevant thirst, but rather the interacting or "voluntary" hunger (which is perhaps one-half as strong as the full 22-hr. hunger). The fourth group had also been water deprived 22 hr. prior to extinction, but had been given water *in the absence* of food just before testing. Both experimental groups, then, should have the same motivation in terms of the interacting relevant hunger, but quite different motivation in terms of the irrelevant thirst drive. Resistance to extinction, response speed, and the rate of responding were recorded. The thirsty group which had been allowed to drink and was therefore hungry was significantly *higher* than the other two groups, the satiated control group and the standard 22-hr. thirsty group, which did not differ by any of the three measures.

There are two conclusions: (1) The intensity of irrelevant thirst is not itself correlated with extinction performance, and (2) "The fact that reducing the thirst drive produced more vigorous responding implies that the presence of the [irrelevant] drive was actually depressing the response" (Grice & Davis, 1957, p. 350).

Water deprivation thus appears to actively inhibit a response which has been reinforced by food. The one peculiarity of the Grice-Davis results is that the group which was switched from hunger to thirst showed somewhat inferior performance to the completely satiated group, in direct opposition to the Webb-Brandauer results. It is not clear what feature of the apparatus or experimental procedure this particular discrepancy should be attributed to. In discussing it, Grice and Davis note that ". . . the rationale of the design was the same and there is no apparent reason why it should not provide an equally good test of the generalized drive hypothesis. The hypothesis should lead to the same prediction in both cases. This negative finding may indicate a serious restriction upon its generality, and we must at least state that a response learned with food reward will not always be activated by an irrelevant thirst drive" (p. 350). We can also say that even when an irrelevant thirst does activate a hunger-relevant response it may not be due to the energizing power of the irrelevant thirst condition, but to the interacting "voluntary" hunger.

So the hunger and thirst period in the history of the generalized-drive concept was brought to an end. Although there continues to be some interest in the area of hunger and thirst and their interaction, the area no longer seems a proper place to investigate drive summation and substitution.

The Substitution of Hunger and Other Drive Conditions. There is an important methodological lesson to be learned from a drive substitution study reported by Miles (1958a). Miles trained rats to press a bar for food, and then tested for the strength of the bar-press response in groups that were satiated for food but motivated by reduced temperature and/or cocaine injections, both of which are known to increase the rat's activity level. It was found that both kinds of stimulant led to increased bar pressing when animals were tested in a small box, but not when they were tested in a larger box. Miles argued that the bar so dominated the small box that any increase in general activity was reflected in what looked like activation of the previously hunger-learned response. In the large box, with more behavioral opportunities, there was also a general increase in activity, but it was no longer confined to the specific bar-press response. Another possible control for the general activation effect would be to run a group of animals that had never been trained on the bar. Then any surplus of responding found in the experimental group would be attributed to the specific energization of the bar press response.

Webb has reasserted his leadership in the drive-substitution problem with a well-controlled study (Webb & Goodman, 1958) in which animals were taught to press a bar for food, and tested satiated either under ordinary circumstances or under irrelevant aversive conditions. Webb and Goodman reported (and Siegel & Sparks, 1961, have confirmed) that the satiated animals increased their rate of bar pressing significantly when the apparatus was flooded with water! Webb and Goodman had a control for the general activation effect that Miles (1958a) had noted: they presented the animal with two bars, only one of which had ever produced food. Both bars received more presses when the floor was flooded, but there was a greater increase on the previously positive bar. Thus, the Webb and Goodman results indicate a general energizing effect of the new irrelevant drive condition, and beyond that, a specific energizing of the previously reinforced response. It is difficult to imagine any interaction such that animals become hungry again when their feet are wet. It is also hard to think of an alternative explanation, so perhaps the drive-substitution idea can be vindicated after all. But there is some question about the generality of the drive-substitution phenomenon. Dees and Furchtgott (1964) found little evidence of the intersubstitutability of drive-producing conditions when they switched rats from hunger to shock or vice versa in a T maze. It seems that the conditions under which, and the extent to which, different drive conditions may be substituted for each other must be determined the hard way. Hull's systematic statement of 1943 has turned out to be provocative rather than definitive. Even by 1952 Hull had retreated to the position that "At least some drive conditions tend partially to motivate into action habits which have been set up on the basis of different drive conditions" (Postulate V, part D).

The Summation of Hunger and Other Drive Conditions. More work has been done on the drive-summation problem using either hunger or thirst in combination with other, usually aversive, drive conditions. Siegel and Siegel (1949) deprived two groups of rats of food and water for 4 hr. and then measured water consumption during a 2-hr. test session. The experimental group was shocked just before the drinking session, while the control group was not. It is quite possible that the experimental group drank more than the control group but the data are not compelling, nor is the statistical treatment convincing (see Bolles, 1962b). Siegel and Siegel's original interpretation was that additional thirst was induced by the fear produced by shock (in the manner Cannon, 1934, had indicated, i.e., by inhibiting salivation), but this interpretation was soon given up for one involving the drive-summation hypothesis (Siegel & Brantley, 1951). Siegel and Brantley ran two groups again, this time under cyclic 24-hr. food deprivation, and they measured the daily food consumption in a 1-hr. eating session. After 5 days, food intake was judged to have reached a maximum, and on the sixth day the experimental animals were shocked just prior to their feeding.

The only valid comparison which is unconfounded by the quite probable continued increase in consumption is between the experimental and control groups on day six (these groups had been matched on the basis of their consumption on day 5). This comparison was significant. Siegel and Brantley took care to give the electric shock in a stimulus situation which was quite different from the test environment. The reason for this was that they wanted the irrelevant drive condition to be the residual or lingering effects of the shock rather than the immediate emotional reaction to it. The distinction, as we will now see, is an important one both theoretically and procedurally.

Amsel (1950) measured the running speed of animals in an alley which was arranged so that they had to leave the start box and run the alley in order to escape electric shock. The animals were run 15 trials a day under either 0-hr. or 22-hr. irrelevant hunger. On the first two training days there was virtually no effect of the irrelevant hunger on the speed of the shock-escape response. (Muenzinger & Fletcher, 1936, also found no such effect.) On the third day, when the shock was only applied on the first trial, the irrelevant-hunger group ran faster than the control group; this was true not only on the first trial but on the subsequent 14 trials. The effect was highly significant. Here, then, it looks as though there was a summation of hunger-produced drive and the residual effects of the electric shock. However, there was a reshuffling of subjects between groups, so it is hard to tell what part of the difference can be attributed to inadvertent selection in sampling. There is another strange feature of these data: it is apparent that on the second training day and on the first trial of the third day the animals were slowing down. Whereas they were running very fast toward the end of the first day (about 4 feet per sec.), they were only running about one foot per sec. by the start of the third day. This seems unreasonable performance on the part of rats escaping shock, and whatever was going on here was confounded with the change from training to testing conditions.

Amsel and Maltzman (1950) trained animals for 14 days to drink water in a test situation for 10 min. after having been deprived for 12 hr. After this 14-day training period the animals were shocked in a different experimental situation prior to the drinking test. Water consumption was significantly higher after the shock, but since no control data are presented it is not really clear that the increase is not due to the continued learning to drink in the situation. In fact, Amsel and Cole (1953) have subsequently indicated that water intake continues to rise well beyond 14 days under these conditions.

Amsel and Maltzman (1950) stressed that decrements in performance should be expected wherever the irrelevant drive is very strong, especially if it has had conditioned to it responses which will compete with the criterion response. Of course, it is well established that if strong shock is presented *during* eating it will almost totally inhibit food consumption or a response leading to food (Estes & Skinner, 1941).[2] Even the presenta-

---

[2] This is clearly the case with strong shock; when weak shock is used, e.g., 0.2 ma. or less, the results are more complicated. Sterritt (1965) has reported

tion of a stimulus that has been paired with shock can suppress food-related behavior (see also Amsel, 1950a). Amsel and Maltzman therefore distinguished *pain* which they defined as the reaction to noxious stimulation, *anxiety* (or fear) defined as the conditioned pain reaction, and *emotionality* defined as the continuing reaction following pain. "Pain and emotionality have the status of primary needs, since they are independent of learning; anxiety (fear) has the status of a secondary (learned) need" (p. 564). Amsel argued that both pain and anxiety were apt to introduce competing responses, those that have proven instrumental in the reduction of these needs, whereas emotionality, in the naive animal at least, would have no particular responses already conditioned to it. Amsel also argued that emotionality differed from anxiety in having an internal source rather than being generated by external stimuli. The theoretical importance of making the test situation distinct from the shock situation should be clear: any similarity between the two would be expected to reinstate responses acquired during the initial presentation of shock. Amsel and Cole (1953) supported this interpretation by finding that the extent of the inhibition of the consummatory response was proportional to the similarity between the shock and test situations. On the other hand, Miller (1948a) had reported that rats shocked before running to food, whether they were shocked in the maze apparatus itself or in a separate apparatus, ran faster and more accurately. Perhaps in Miller's situation the shock-elicited running response was not incompatible with what they had learned to do under the relevant drive, viz., run.

It seems then that introducing an irrelevant aversive drive condition can either inhibit or facilitate the performance of a response acquired on the basis of another drive condition depending upon how the situation is arranged. If the aversive stimuli, innately or through prior conditioning, control responses that compete with the criterion response, then the criterion response will be inhibited. If not, there may be facilitation; there could presumably also be no effect. The crucial theoretical question is how can the motivational effect be separated experimentally from the associative effect? Typically, the drive theorist argues that when a decrement is found in a drive-summation experiment it is due to response competi-

---

that with weak shock there may be increased eating during shock; Moyer and Baenninger (1963) and Moyer (1965) have found that even at intensities where shock depresses consummatory behavior (drinking), the depression may last only a few days after which there is facilitation. Moyer suggests that the depression phase is due to the distracting novelty of emotionality rather than to emotionality itself, and that the facilitation phase may be due to a genuine drive summation. It seems likely that it may be due to a simple interaction effect: if the shocked animal reduces its intake for a few days (Sterritt, 1965; and especially Pare, 1965), a subsequent increase in intake may be merely homeostatic readjustment to the normal. In any case both of these factors, novelty of the situation and overall daily intake, have to be controlled before any assessment of drive summation can be made.

tion, but when facilitation is found it is taken as evidence of genuine drive summation. However, the available evidence seems reasonably consistent with the following alternative hypothesis, which is offered here— only partly in jest—for experimental disproof: Irrelevant drive conditions (those that remain unreduced in the experimental situation) *inhibit* responses established under another drive condition, unless they happen to introduce response tendencies which facilitate the criterion response. Although I have little faith in the future prosperity of this hypothesis, it does raise the interesting question of how one would test it empirically against its more famous alternative.

A number of questions remain, however, regarding Amsel's third aversive state, emotionality, the residual of a prior aversive experience which is purported to be free of associative ties. Ellis (1957) was unable to replicate Siegel and Brantley's emotionality-hunger summation with either latency or running-time measures in a runway. Nor could Levine (1958) get it in consummatory behavior. Levine et al. (1959) were able to show that animals swam a water maze faster and more accurately when they were shocked immediately before swimming than when they were not, but we may note that there may have been a good deal of natural response generalization between the two escape situations.

The status of the "emotionality drive" is therefore uncertain. The studies in which positive summation effects have been reported have not always provided the sort of evidence that would be convincing. The lack of antecedent anchoring and the poverty of functional properties on the consequent side pose further interpretive problems. "Emotionality" is presumed to be some sort of internal state of the organism which persists for an hour or two after aversive stimulation. There are presumably physiological correlates of the state, but we know nothing about them. This state also presumably energizes behavior by making a contribution to D, and accordingly, it should lead to learning when it is reduced. Was it reduced by the consumption of food and water in Amsel's and Siegel's studies? If it was, then is it still to be considered an irrelevant drive? Can it persist long enough to explain what it is supposed to? We cannot say.

The effects of irrelevant hunger or thirst upon other sorts of instrumental escape behavior seem, tentatively, to be negative when the aversive condition is bright light (Strange, 1954; Dachowski, 1964) or escape from shock (Dinsmoor, 1958), positive when the condition is cold water (Braun et al., 1957) or avoidance of shock (Ley, 1965). Jarmon and Gerall (1961) failed to get any drive summation with irrelevant hunger and relevant sex in guinea pigs. Ball (1926) found that irrelevant estrus motivation in rats failed to summate with hunger in a maze.

Summary. The evidence of drive substitution and drive summation does not lend much support at this time to the generalized-drive construct. About the most that can be said is that some combinations of need states may sometimes lead to a facilitation of behavior. Spence has admitted that ". . . it would appear that there is no general quantitative law that holds for all need combinations but that, for the time being at least, more specific laws will have to be worked out for various combinations of needs" (1956, pp. 195–196). It has been found that it is much more important to determine just what responses occur in a particular situation and under a particular set of drive conditions than anyone had anticipated. In fact, the associative consequences of the drive state appear to play so prominent a role in the determination of behavior that they completely hide whatever contribution the drive state might make to D.

In all this work there is very little support for the concept of generalized drive, as distinguished from the concept of specific drives produced by specific drive conditions. Particularly in view of the demonstrably great importance of the associative consequences of deprivation, there now seems little justification for the assumption that all of the different possible sources of drive contribute to the determination of behavior by the qualitatively equivalent contribution they make to D. It seems rather more plausible (although admittedly less parsimonious) to suppose that each source of motivation provides its own sort of motivation.

THE ENERGIZING OF GENERAL ACTIVITY

Traditionally, general activity has been characterized by the fact that it occurs in the absence of reinforcement by the reduction of any drive condition. It was considered to be goalless activity. The goallessness of being active has recently been called into question, so that now we may, if we wish, regard it either as a new kind of consummatory behavior, or as a learned reaction activated by other drive conditions and reinforced by their reduction, i.e., as a kind of instrumental behavior.

The history of research on general activity can be divided into two periods, a long early one that was theoretically simple and constructive, and a short recent one that has been rather wild and woolly. This history is of some interest because it closely parallels the rise, vogue, and decline of the drive concept. The early period (which has been ably reviewed by Shirley, 1929; Reed, 1947; and Munn, 1950) was marked by the pioneer work of Slonaker, Szymanski, Richter, Hitchcock, and others. The theoretical framework for these early studies involved the simple notion that the activity wheel measures the drive level of the organism, and that activity scores indicate its general health and welfare. Since the conditions that influence general activity are also the antecedent conditions of drive as measured by instrumental or consummatory behavior, there resulted a rather simple and popular picture of the relationship between drive and activity: drive causes activity.

There were, however, even in some of these early studies some grounds for caution in assuming that activity was a direct indication of drive level. A few experimenters (e.g., Richter, 1927; Shirley, 1928) had taken activity scores every hour rather than, as was the custom, every 12 or 24 hours. Hourly records indicated that sometimes as much as one-half of the animal's total activity occurred in a few hours immediately preceding a regular feeding. Such a finding suggests that activity is controlled by the time of day or by the "anticipation" of food, rather than by any immediate consequence of deprivation itself. A second disturbing finding in some studies was that some of the effects obtained with activity wheels seemed to be specific to wheels; they did not always show up in other sorts of activity-measuring devices. For example, Hunt and Schlosberg (1939a) found that whereas castration might reduce activity scores 95% or more when measured with a wheel, in their stabilimeter-type cage (1939) castration produced only a 9% reduction in activity.

The Campbell-Sheffield Studies. In 1954 Sheffield and Campbell suggested an interpretation of general activity which was quite different from the traditional one. They remark:

Casual observation of hungry rats, however, gives a different picture of the effects of hunger on activity: (a) Left to themselves, caged hungry rats appeared to sleep much of the time and do not move about restlessly. (b) Very hungry rats have a lowered threshold for startle to a sudden stimulus, and when awake they are more active than satiated rats only if there is variation in the external stimulation. (c) Hungry rats become maximally active when exposed to external stimulation which has regularly preceded feeding in the past experience of the animal. (Sheffield & Campbell, 1954, p. 97)

Campbell and Sheffield (1953) had tested animals in stabilimeter-type cages (Campbell, 1954) which were located in a room providing a relatively homogeneous auditory and visual environment. After 4 days ad lib. to provide a base line, the animals were deprived for 72 hr. At noon on each of the 7 days activity was recorded for the preceding 24 hours, and also for a 10-min. "stimulation" period during which an environmental change was introduced (the continual masking noise was turned off, and the lights were turned on). It was found that activity (tilting of the cage) occurred at a much higher rate during the 10-min. stimulation period than during the remainder of the 24 hours. This effect, the arousal effect of stimulation, was significantly enhanced by the 3 days of deprivation. Although the total 24-hr. activity counts increased during the deprivation period, there was a much greater relative increase in activity during the 10-min. stimulation tests.

Campbell and Sheffield hypothesized from these findings that hunger seems to involve a lowering of the thresholds for responding to stimuli which normally control activity, rather than any internal stimulation to activity. The slight rise that was obtained in 24-hr. activity scores could easily be attributed to the sensitized animal's reactions to minimal stimulus changes occurring in the relatively homogeneous environment.

In a subsequent experiment Sheffield and Campbell (1954) gave animals daily feedings which were immediately preceded for the experimental group by a 5-min. period of stimulus change (visual and auditory), and which were preceded irregularly an hour or two by a similar 5-min. stimulation period for the control group. The results are shown in Fig. 10-3. Note that the control animals, for which the stimulus change did

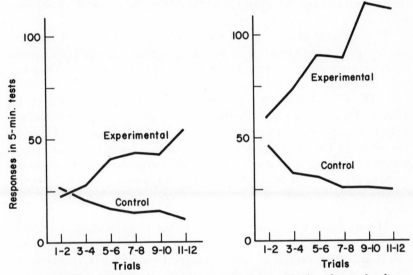

Fig. 10-3. Acquisition of activity in response to a 5-min. change in the environment that regularly preceded daily feeding (experimental groups) compared with adaption to the change when it was not correlated with feeding (control groups). For the groups on the left the change consisted of masking noise off and lights on, and for the groups on the right noise on and lights off. (From Sheffield & Campbell, 1954)

not serve as a cue to feeding, showed a gradual adaptation to stimulation but that the experimental animals, for which the stimulus change was a cue for food, showed a marked increase in activity in response to it.

These results pose a number of interesting theoretical questions. For example, what is the unconditioned stimulus for the learned activity? It cannot be hunger or stimuli arising from the hunger state because, as Campbell and Sheffield (1953) had just shown, hunger does not initiate activity. Nor can it be the food which follows because the unconditioned response to food is eating rather than being active; furthermore, such learning would require backward conditioning. Consequently, the authors conclude that the basic mechanism here must be the conditioning of the consummatory response to environmental cues. This behavior is reinforced by the subsequent eating, and its frustration during the 5-min. test period generates the motivation that produces the observed results in the experimental group. In the control group the consummatory response does not get conditioned to the same external cues. In these terms, then, the learning of activity is evidence of the progressive conditioning of the consummatory response, or of fractional components of it, to external stimuli. Amsel and Work (1961) and Amsel et al. (1962) replicated the Sheffield and Campbell study; Campbell (1960) has demonstrated a similar phenomenon for thirst; and Hall (1956, 1958) obtained the same effect with activity wheels.

Most of these studies showed that there was not only a responsiveness to cues preceding regular food or water, but also a significant overall effect of deprivation on activity scores over 24 hours. Such a finding suggests the action of a drive component in the motivation of general activity in addition to whatever learning mechanism there may be. But on the other hand, it is quite possible that such regular 24-hr. periodic activity reflects merely a large increase of activity in the few hours immediately preceding feeding. It may be that some internal biological clock type of mechanism makes it relatively easy for an animal to become active approximately every 24 hours. Or, the stimulus control for such periodic activity might be minimal cues arising from diurnal changes in the environment.

The results of the studies described in the previous chapter (p. 263) suggest that a large part of the activity characteristic of the hungry animal is under the control of some rhythmic 24-hr. stimulus events arising from either the external environment or from within the animal.

Teghtsoonian and Campbell (1960) have reported that animals in an isolated and homogeneous environment show very little increase in tilt-cage activity in the absence of reinforcement (food) during the first few days of deprivation, although activity may rise somewhat above the ad lib. base line just before death. On the other hand, animals maintained in the normal laboratory environment where, presumably, there is far more heterogeneity in the prevailing stimulus conditions, also show no immediate rise in the first few days of deprivation, but subsequently show a marked rise in activity. Two conclusions are suggested: (1) that the animal's activity is in large measure dependent upon some sort of external stimulation (as Campbell and Sheffield, 1953, had indicated); and (2) that in the absence of reinforcement by feeding, activity as measured by tilt cages declines rather than rises at least for the first 72 hours or so of deprivation.

Other Reinforcement Effects in General Activity. At the same time that this reinforcement phenomenon was being discovered, a related phenomenon was being studied by a number of investigators (Hall et al., 1953; Hall & Hanford, 1954; Eayrs, 1954; Reid & Finger, 1955; Seward & Pereboom, 1955, 1955a). If a rat is fed once a day while it is confined to an activity wheel, its activity will gradually increase over 15 days of testing from an initial level of something like 500 revolutions a day to 5,000 or 10,000 revolutions a day. The question arises whether the animal's "drive" increases during this period to produce the increase in activity, or whether it is some sort of learning phenomenon. Most investigators have interpreted the phenomenon in learning terms. Thus, Seward and Pereboom (1955) see wheel running as being self-reinforcing for the hungry animal.

Finger et al. (1957) have shown that if animals are delayed in a box for 1 hr. after coming out of an activity wheel before their meal they show significantly less increase in running than animals that are fed immediately after coming out of the wheel. Finger et al. suggest that animals tend to be active and to run just prior to the regular feeding time and that when this activity is followed by feeding the tendency becomes strengthened. By introducing a delay between the opportunity to run and the reinforcement, the effect is minimized. The effect still exists in some strength, however, since even with the imposed delay Finger et al. found a sizable increase in activity. This effect too may be due to reinforcement resulting from accidental contingencies established in the animal's early life. We know that there are cyclic patterns of activity and ingestion. And we know that activity tends to precede the ingestion. Hence, it is entirely possible that the rat creates for itself reinforcement contingencies between being active and eating.

In another study (Finger et al., 1960) animals were maintained under very lenient hunger conditions (in an attempt to duplicate the 3- or 4-hr. deprivations that occur when animals have food available constantly) to see if reinforcement could be effective under these conditions. Animals had their food removed 3 hr. before testing, and they were put into activity wheels for just 1 hr. Animals in the experimental group were taken directly out of the wheels and fed, whereas animals in the control group were taken from the wheels, delayed for 1 hr., and then fed. The results demonstrate rather convincingly the reinforcing effect of feeding upon the immediately prior running since the control group showed no increase over subsequent test days, and the experimental group increased its 1-hr. activity score about five-fold. It is important to note that these animals were under extremely low hunger conditions, conditions under which there would ordinarily be no increase in activity (Hall & Connon, 1957; Moskowitz, 1959). Certainly, one of the factors that controls the amount of running that occurs in activity wheels is the reinforcing effect of a regularly scheduled feeding.

This cannot be the whole story, however. Another factor in activity is a weight-loss effect which can probably work either independently of or in conjunction with the reinforcement effect. Reid and Finger (1955) have noted that during the two weeks or so that activity is rising to a stable high value, the animal's weight is dropping to a stable low value. Hence the increase in activity might be attributed to a change in drive (in fact, this is one of the phenomena that suggest that weight loss should be taken as an antecedent condition of drive).

Moreover, rats tested in the absence of reinforcement still show a pronounced rise in activity as a function of food deprivation (Wald & Jackson, 1944; Reid & Finger, 1957; Finger & Reid, 1952; Treichler & Hall, 1962). In fact, Duda and Bolles (1963) have shown that there is a very high correlation between an animal's weight loss and its activity-wheel performance even during the first 3 hours of the animal's experience in the wheel, and that this relationship holds regardless of the deprivation conditions under which the weight loss was incurred. That is, it made little difference whether Duda and Bolles' animals had lost weight by having been on a strict maintenance schedule or from a single severe privation. (No food was available in the wheels themselves.) It was the resulting weight loss rather than the conditions of deprivation which determined the activity level of naive animals in the wheels. This finding has been recently confirmed by Treichler and Collins (1965).

The Specificity of General Activity. Further evidence against a purely reinforcement concept of general activity comes from studies of thirst. Although the water-deprived animal is known to run significantly more than the satiated animal (Wald & Jackson, 1944; Finger & Reid, 1952; Hall, 1955; Campbell, 1960), this rise in activity does not increase progressively on subsequent days but seems to stabilize almost immediately at a value which is about twice the base-line value. Hence, the progressive rise over a two-week period obtained with hunger appears to be specific to hunger.[3] It also appears to be specific to activity wheels, although admittedly there are not yet sufficient data using other types of apparatus over long enough periods of time to permit more than a tentative conclusion. Campbell and Cicala (1962) have reported that rats under terminal water deprivation show progressive decreases in activity measured in stabilimeters. Eayrs (1954) has shown that in a stabilimeter-type cage activity scores stabilize in 1 day. He also reports a relatively low correla-

---

[3] If this is the case, and if thirsty animals lose nearly as much weight as hungry ones (see p. 164), and if weight loss determines activity in hungry animals, then we have a paradox. Treichler (1960) has offered a plausible explanation. He suggests that previous experimenters have not used tough enough water deprivation conditions to boost the activity level as high as it might go. Treichler ran animals under extremely severe thirst conditions and found that activity levels were almost identical to those of hungry animals that had lost the same weight. The data give very elegant support to the idea that activity-wheel performance is determined by weight loss regardless of how the weight is lost.

tion of .18 between scores in wheels and scores in stabilimeter cages. Strong (1957) has found that it is possible to get nearly any functional relationship one might imagine between deprivation conditions and activity merely by varying the sensitivity of a tilt cage so that it is made either sensitive to or immune to minute movements of the animal. Similarly, Weasner et al. (1960), Treichler and Hall (1962), and Finger (1961) have emphasized the marked differences in functional relationships that result as a function of the activity-measuring device.

Stranger still is that the activity-wheel effect may be specific to the rat. Nicholls (1922) has reported that hunger *depresses* the activity-wheel running of guinea pigs. In a more recent comparative study Campbell et al. (1966) failed to confirm this specific finding but did obtain striking confirmation of the main point, which is that different species of animals react to hunger and to thirst in characteristic ways. Some become more active when hungry and less active when thirsty, other animals may show just the opposite pattern.

So this is how the simple picture that had been built up in the first half of the century has been destroyed by the work done in the last decade. We can no longer accept general activity as a direct measure of drive strength. We have discovered that activity as measured by any device, but particularly by activity wheels, consists of certain specific responses which are reinforceable just like any instrumental response and that, in fact, much of the rise in activity which had traditionally been taken as evidence of drive now appears to be the result of a change in the animal's habit structure rather than an increased drive level. The fact that different species and activity-measuring devices yield different functional relationships presents a further predicament for any easy interpretation of general activity as an index of drive. The traditional conception of drive and its relation to general activity was based primarily upon the results of running hungry rats in activity wheels; now we find that these results appear to be specific to hunger, to the rat, and to activity wheels.

Two problems emerge from this conceptual reorganization. One is how to account for the apparent energizing effect of food deprivation upon activity-wheel scores. If the effect cannot be explained in terms of increased drive, how can it be explained? While psychologists have gradually become disenchanted with the idea that general activity is a measure of the animal's need or drive (e.g., Baumeister et al., 1964), they have failed to provide alternative conceptions.[4] Part of the effect can be attrib-

---

[4] Stevenson and Rixon (1957) have suggested that running in wheels in particular and activity in general may have little to do with the animal's hunger or thirst but a lot to do with its temperature regulation. Thus, it is proposed that the hungry animal runs to keep its metabolism and temperature up, even though the increased demand for energy only makes the animal's nutritional condition worse. The evidence cited in support of this hypothesis is that the activity of hungry rats is negatively correlated with ambient temperature.

uted to reinforcement, as we have seen above, but there is also a component of activity-wheel running that has to be attributed to some kind of unlearned connection with hunger. The puzzle is that there is no obvious a priori reason why running in an activity wheel should be more reinforcing for the hungry rat than it is for the satiated rat, but it is.

The second problem that confronts us is this: If neither the activity wheel nor the stabilimeter tilt cage can be accepted without qualification as an instrument for measuring an animal's activation, then how can general activation be measured; or does it even make sense to try to measure the strength of behavior which bears no relation to the current drive condition? This is the question to which we now turn.

A Molecular Descriptive Approach to General Activity. New interpretations of general activity have led to inquiries into what animals do when they are being generally active (Bindra, 1961). Bindra and Blond (1958) developed a behavior-sampling method for analyzing the rat's general activity into its various component responses. It is found that in a novel situation the animal sniffs, investigates, locomotes, grooms, and sometimes freezes. It is then natural to ask how the distribution of the animal's activities varies as a function of deprivation conditions. Using a behavior-sampling procedure, Bolles (1960) found that a single 24-hr. water deprivation had the expected effect of waking up the animals and making them more active than when they were satiated, but that a 24-hr. food deprivation slightly depressed the level of activity. A subsequent study of the rat in its own homecage (Bolles, 1963) found that hunger had only a slight effect upon the incidence of any of the different sorts of behavior that occur in the homecage, at least during the first 2 days on the maintenance schedule. (Siegel and Steinberg, 1949, had found a more impressive increase in homecage activity when it was measured with photobeams; it is not clear why the apparatus should make so much difference.) During the first 2 days of deprivation, the hungry animals slept and groomed and ran around about as much as they did under ad lib. conditions. However, as the maintenance schedule was continued for 12 days, the animals became somewhat more active; they slept and groomed less than normally, and spent a proportionately larger part of the time exploring and walking around in their cages. (Compare the first and last columns of Table 10-1.) The animals in this later study were maintained in a normal laboratory environment which provided them with numerous cues to the time of day and made it possible for them to anticipate the daily feeding. It was found that the mere approach of the observer tended to rouse the animals and make them more active.

A more recent, unpublished, study of the same type was conducted with animals maintained in isolation in order to minimize stimuli that might be cues to feeding. Temperature and noise were held constant, and the animals were viewed through a one-way window. Under these condi-

TABLE 10-1

The Incidence of Different Kinds of Activity in the Homecage
as a Function of Deprivation Conditions (in Percentages of
the Animals' Activity over a 24-hr. Period)

	Ad Lib.	Continuous (Isolated)	Cyclic (Isolated)	Cyclic (Normal)
Sleep	61	60	58	51
Lying	4	6	4	10
Grooming	18	19	15	11
Sniffing	4	6	11	
Standing	1	2	5	26
Rearing	2	3	4	
Walking	1	1	2	
Eating	6	–	–	–
Drinking	3	1	1	1

tions some activation effects were still found (compare columns 1 and 3 in Table 10-1), but they were somewhat smaller than before. The diurnal course of activity under these conditions, shown in Fig. 10-4, suggests that the animals were using temporal cues (probably of internal origin) to anticipate the regular feeding time. Another group of animals tested under the same isolation conditions but never fed in the test situation (deprived 96 hr.) showed very little evidence of being more active than ad lib. animals (see column 2). When the animals did become more active, under cyclic deprivation, the only significant shift in behavior was a decrease in eating and drinking and an increase in exploration and in lying (the least active category of things the subjects did). Results with thirsty animals have been essentially the same.

The same observational technique has been applied to female rats (Bolles, 1963b) to determine if there is any indication in the homecage activity of a 4- or 5-day estrus cycle comparable to that often seen in general activity measured in activity wheels. No evidence of a reliable cycle was found. Once again it appears that effects found in activity wheels may be specific to wheels.

Exploration. To the extent that exploration has not been previously reinforced in the life history of an animal, it may be considered as a form of general activity. The question naturally arises whether hunger, thirst, sexual motivation, fear, or any of the other drive-producing conditions leads to an increase in the incidence of exploration. It is plausible to suppose that the motivated animal would be more likely to explore since a species with such a behavioral tendency would have considerable advantage in survival over a species that lacked it. Dashiell (1925) reported

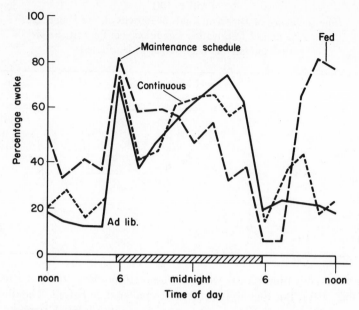

Fig. 10-4. The proportion of time rats are awake and active in their homecages at different times of day when they are maintained ad lib., continuously deprived of food, or fed regularly once a day.

positive findings—hungry animals explored more in his complex maze than did satiated animals. No one questioned Dashiell's finding, nor the kind of interpretation just cited, for a quarter of a century.

But then Montgomery (1953), who was concerned with showing that exploration was an autonomous drive condition rather than subservient to other drive conditions, reported that hungry animals explored *less* than satiated animals. Dashiell's study has been repeated with equivocal results (Hall et al., 1960; Bolles & de Lorge, 1962a). Others have used complex apparatus like Dashiell's (Adlerstein & Fehrer, 1955), and simple apparatus like Montgomery's (Carr et al., 1959; Glickman & Jensen, 1961). Again the results have been contradictory. Males and females have been compared (Thompson, 1953; Zimbardo & Montgomery, 1957; Zimbardo & Miller, 1958) and different kinds of behavioral criteria have been used (Hurwitz, 1960; Chapman & Levy, 1957; Welker, 1959; Fehrer, 1956). (See also Richards & Leslie, 1962; Hughes, 1965.) None of the variables seems to be a crucial factor in the contradictory results. Curt Stern once wrote that contradictory findings indicate not that someone is wrong and someone else is right but that the underlying principles are not generally understood. Surely exploration is a function of some antecedent conditions; for example, it is known that young animals explore more and are generally more active than old ones (Furchtgott et al., 1961; Finger, 1962), and that males ordinarily explore less than females. But as we noted in discussing its antecedent conditions, exploration in the domestic rat is overwhelmingly under the control of the novelty and complexity of the stimulus conditions under which it occurs; this may be at the bottom of the contradictory findings. The unconditioned strength of exploration is so strong in novel situations that it will almost surely dominate the animal's reaction to novelty. Moreover, the particular form of exploratory behavior that occurs in the situation is also largely dictated by the stimulus properties of the situation.

If exploration is defined broadly, so as to encompass the whole array of responses that increase stimulation from the environment, then we find that animals in novel situations typically are constantly exploring.[5] They walk around and sniff, rear up on their hind legs and sniff, pick up bits of dust and debris from the floor, manipulate and look at objects, and look at and listen to other things in the situation. If the animal is hungry, and food is available, it will ultimately stop exploring to eat; if food is not available, it will take some time out from its exploration to groom. If the situation is relatively simple, it will ultimately lie down and go to sleep (Woods, 1962). The question then of whether hunger or any other drive-producing condition facilitates exploration is operationally synonymous with the question of whether such drive-producing conditions inhibit grooming, or fear reactions, or eating, or going to sleep. Viewed in this way, the experimental question is somewhat less interesting than the traditional question of whether hunger makes the animal go out and hunt for food, but perhaps it is somewhat easier to answer.

Bolles and de Lorge (1962a) found that rats in a Dashiell maze engage in some form of exploration for approximately 95% of a 10-min. test session. The result of making the animal hungry was to increase this figure significantly, but only by one or two percentage points. Using a less complex apparatus, but one in which more manipulatory and investigatory behavior could occur, de Lorge and Bolles (1961) found that deprivation raised the incidence of exploration (again counting all forms) occurring in 10 min. from about 80% to 90%. The predominant competing behavior in both cases was grooming since food was not present and since almost no freezing or other kinds of competing behavior occurred. In another study Bolles and de Lorge (1962) took as a criterion of exploration a response which is relatively rare (leaving a familiar environment) and found that food deprivation made it about ten times as probable, i.e., made it occur with one-tenth the latency. Even so, the response

---

[5] It should be emphasized that the present discussion is limited to the domesticated white rat, with which most of the systematic research has been done. Barnett (1958, 1963) has indicated how the wild rat, like most wild animals, reacts in a much more sensible and cautious manner to novelty.

remained relatively improbable for all values of the deprivation conditions. Its overall improbability therefore seems to depend upon the fact that the environment provided relatively weak stimulus support for it. In this, and in the previous studies where exploration was the dominant behavior, the incremental effect of deprivation upon exploration is small, even when it is statistically significant. So, if our interest is in the question of whether drive-producing conditions, such as hunger, have any effect upon exploration, the answer is yes, it does. But if our concern is with exploratory behavior, we can safely ignore deprivation conditions as not having an important effect upon it; its main determinants are associative.

Fehrer (1956) has framed the old question in what appears to be a new and more meaningful way. She asks if the deprived animal is more likely to leave a familiar environment than a satiated animal. Fehrer gave subjects a 24-hr. familarity or adaption period and found that the deprived ones did indeed leave it sooner. We have just noted that Bolles and de Lorge (1962) found the hungry rat was more likely to leave its own homecage. Once more, it is necessary to ask whether this effect might be due simply to a reduction in the strength of the predominant competing behavior. In this particular case perhaps what keeps the satiated animal at home is fear, the natural timidity to which Barnett (1963) refers, which still exists to some extent in the albino rat. Although some writers have suggested that exploration is primarily motivated by fear, most investigators agree with Montgomery (1955), Montgomery and Monkman (1955), Hayes (1960), and Baron (1964), that exploration is inhibited by fear. Welker (1959) has made the important distinction between extrinsic exploration, in which the animal is "looking for" food or escape from a frightening situation, and intrinsic exploration, which is exploration for its own sake. Fear may be relevant to the former and not the latter.

Finally, it has been found that food deprivation may facilitate other forms of exploration, such as manipulation (Miles, 1962) and the acquisition of orienting responses (Forgays & Levin, 1958).[6]

In conclusion, there is evidently a wide range of situations in which the hungry rat generates more behavior than the satiated rat. It is more active in activity wheels, tilt cages, or its homecage; it appears to enter a novel situation more readily, and it certainly leaves a familiar one sooner.

---

[6] Schoenfeld, Antonitis, and Bersh (1950a) reported that increased deprivation raised the operant rate of bar pressing, which could also be considered a form of general activity. It is strange though that such an effect would be found in view of the relative rarity of bar pressing prior to reinforcement. Drive is supposed to facilitate only the dominant behavior. Prior to reinforcement, bar pressing is surely not dominant. Perhaps the sensory feedback from the response, the click of the microswitch, etc., provides some sort of sensory reinforcement. Although the effect is not always found (Segal, 1959), it usually is (Murray, 1953; Brandauer, 1953; Davis, 1958; Crocetti, 1962).

However, such general classes of behavior as running in a wheel or walking in a maze cannot be prejudged to be independent of reinforcement.

It may prove to be the case that there is no such category as "general activity"; it may be that the behaviors that have been assumed to be independent of prior reinforcement always bear some relationship to some reinforcing conditions. Our ignorance of these conditions and of the animal's history with them is no warrant for supposing that they do not exist. Consequently we cannot accept any measure of general activity as an a priori index of the animal's drive. Ultimately we must view them as specific responses and study them as such.

INDIVIDUAL DIFFERENCES IN DRIVE STRENGTH

The vast majority of the studies done in the S-R reinforcement tradition (and this includes the bulk of all studies done with primary drives) has been normative. That is, the interest of the experimenter is focused upon the mean performance obtained from a group of experimental subjects, or upon differences between the means of different groups of subjects. In the normative approach, variation of scores by subjects all treated alike is generally considered either to be an embarrassment, or at best, a nuisance. The implication of individual differences is that the experimenter has failed to control the variables that relate to his criterion measure. Even to take the most optimistic view, the experimenter has failed to control all the variables and must therefore run large enough numbers of subjects under a given condition so that at least the mean of the group can be reliably determined relative to the "error" variance.

However, there is a refreshingly different approach to the phenomenon of variation. We may focus our attention not upon the mean of the group but upon individual departures from the mean. Deviations from the group mean constitute a set of scores which is different from, and in many cases as interesting as, the original set of scores. From time to time Hull (1939, 1945, 1952) conjectured that whereas the same qualitative laws probably applied to different individuals, there might well be some variation in the coefficients and exponents of his equations which could be used to describe and characterize individual subjects. In this view individual differences change the basic laws quantitatively but not qualitatively.

In most animal research there has grown up the tradition of using only naive subjects and discarding animals as soon as publishable data have been derived from them; this precludes any systematic study of individual differences. Consequently, there have been distressingly few systematic correlational studies of rat behavior. This neglect is a little surprising in view of the possible significance that generalized individual differences would have. If individual differences in drive level could be demonstrated to have generality across different drive conditions or across different test situations, they would provide a potent source of empirical support for the drive construct.

Factor-Analytic Studies of Animal Motivation. One large-scale correlational study was undertaken by Anderson (1938). Anderson observed a large number of measures of different kinds of behavior obtained under hunger, thirst, sex, and exploratory motivation. Altogether 47 different behavioral indices were measured, any of which could be construed as a measure of motivation. Anderson found that with sex and exploration there was some consistency of individual differences across different situations, but that with hunger and thirst individual differences were almost exclusively dependent upon nonmotivational factors. Moreover, he found that there was no evidence of generality of individual differences from one drive condition to the next except insofar as the same response measure was taken in the same situation under the different drive conditions. These results led Anderson to conclude that for hunger and thirst, differences in motivated behavior were reflecting the effect of situational factors rather than differences in drive strength. In the case of exploration and even more particularly in the case of male sexual motivation, systematic generalized individual differences were found; animals that were more active sexually as measured in one situation tended also to be more active in other test situations. But, even here, the correlations were so low that prediction on the basis of general traits seemed to be unjustified.

Very similar findings have been reported in a more recent factorial study involving only hunger and thirst (Bolles, 1959). Fifty-one subjects were run in 4-day cycles of deprivation conditions including high and low hunger and high and low thirst. Behavior under each condition was tested in an open field, in a feeding-drinking box, in an elevated runway, in an alley runway, and in activity cages. The consummatory behavior in the animals' own homecages was also recorded. Counting the different deprivation conditions in the different behavioral situations, a total of 66 potential motivational measures were obtained and intercorrelated. The intercorrelations suggested several conclusions. One was that performance in any situation was poorly correlated with any response measure obtained in any other test situation; individual differences in response strength seemed to be governed largely by associative factors. The second finding was that nearly all significantly high correlations were for performance under the different deprivation conditions in the same test situation. That is, different deprivation conditions yielded intercorrelations that clustered together on the same behavioral task but were uncorrelated with tasks in other situations regardless of the deprivation conditions. Finally, it was found that these clusters of correlations within the same task had no structure in themselves; there was no consistent effect upon the correlation coefficients that were attributable to deprivation conditions as such.

In general, then, it appeared as though any individual differences with respect to motivation, if they existed, were too small and inconsistent, compared with individual differences obtained from associative factors, to be observed. A factor analysis of the correlation matrix, again, showed only situation-specific factors. Both this study, and the earlier one by Anderson (1938) argue rather convincingly against the advisability of attributing any difference in performance to individual differences in strength of drive, especially where hunger and thirst are involved.

There is one other interesting implication of these findings. If we regard the total motivation of an animal as being dependent upon primary motivation (drive) plus secondary motivation (aroused by environmental stimuli), then we may ask what portion of the total motivation of an animal in any particular situation, say when it is running for food, is attributable to primary and how much to the secondary sources of motivation. One of the few possible means of distinguishing between primary and secondary motivation is on the basis of being able to attribute individual differences in performance to characteristic differences in drive which hold up across variation in environmental conditions. The few studies that have looked for such differences have failed to find them. This leads us to wonder just how important the primary sources of motivation are.

> . . . If drives are held to constitute a relatively large component of total motivation, then the present results require that drives have the unlikely property that individual differences in strength of drive are negligible. An alternative interpretation is that drives make a relatively small contribution to total motivation. (Bolles, 1959, p. 585)

Other Correlational Studies of Animal Motivation. There is perhaps some significance in the finding that the most internalized drive conditions, hunger and thirst, fail to reveal individual differences; whereas those which are generally agreed to be highly dependent upon external stimulation, such as sexual behavior, exploration, and fear, have yielded some consistency in transsituational correlations. With sex, most investigators have found persistent individual differences, that is, differences which hold up correlationally in situations as different as runway speed, activity-wheel scores, and persistence in consummatory activity (Hitchcock, 1925; Stone et al., 1935; Stone & Ferguson, 1940; Sheffield et al., 1954; Young, 1961). With exploration, Carr and Williams (1957) and Anderson (1938) have also noted some generality of individual differences.

It has been known ever since Yerkes' pioneer work (1913) on the temperament of rats that there were strain differences in such response criteria as biting, squealing, gnashing the teeth, urinating, and defecating. Hall (1934) proposed that defecation and urination should be used as the defining measures of emotionality. He observed animals in a standard-ized open-field situation, the strangeness of which he assumed would elicit emotion. Subsequent work by Hall, his supporters, and detractors, has involved two questions: (1) whether eliminative behavior is a valid index of anything that we want to call emotionality, and (2) even if it is valid, whether it provides a basis for drawing any interesting conclusions about the animal's behavior. In regard to the first question, Hall (1934, 1934a) found that the eliminative signs disappeared with repeated testing, and that they were highly inversely correlated with the animal's willingness to eat $(r = -.82)$. It is also apparent that emotionality, as given by this criterion, can be inherited (Hall, 1941; Broadhurst, 1960). Tryon et al. (1941) found a correlation in females of .83 between defecation scores and other ratings of emotional behavior such as hiding and vocalizing (in males the correlation was only .34).

But in a subsequent study, Tryon et al. (1941a) found that their different criteria of emotionality were intercorrelated only within a given situation, and showed little generality across situations. Similarly, Billings-lea (1942), factor analyzing a number of "emotional" responses such as biting, runway latency, and activity-wheel running, found not one but three factors, which he labeled emotionality, timidity, and freezing. Again, the factors were relatively dependent upon specific situations in which behavior was observed. Willingham (1956) in a factor-analytic study of individual differences in a variety of criteria of emotionality and fear reactivity found no less than six distinctive factors in mice. Further doubt about the validity of the eliminative criterion of emotionality has been raised by O'Kelly (1940), Bindra and Thompson (1953), Hunt and Otis (1953), and Tobach and Schneirla (1962). Tobach and Schneirla, in a very extensive, very careful cross-sectional and longitudinal study of the defecation response, conclude that it too appears to be situa-tion-specific rather than a characteristic general reaction of individual animals. Thus it would appear that breeding for defecation has turned out to be breeding for defecation in a particular test situation.

It is certainly possible that there will prove to be genetically deter-mined differences in what we might want to call emotionality, and even that the tendency to defecate in a strange environment is a good index of it. There still remains the more important question of whether this has anything to do with the animal's behavior and, more specifically, whether such differences in emotionality can be identified as differences in drive strength. Broadhurst (1957, 1957a) has reported some work on this prob-lem, and his results have been rather discouraging. He has shown first of all that animals that have been bred for emotionality (by the defecation criterion) are more responsive to situational stimulation than are non-

emotional animals; they respond particularly by retreating from or reacting emotionally to the situation. Essentially this tells us what we already
knew: animals bred to react emotionally do react emotionally. It remains
to show that the "motivation" thus bred into the animals serves to
provide additional energization for an arbitrary instrumental response.
Broadhurst (1957a) ran emotional and nonemotional animals on three
brightness-discrimination problems which differed in the difficulty of the
required discrimination. Some motivation was provided by virtue of the
fact that the animal was required to respond to the discriminanda while
under water and hence "air deprived." Additional motivation was provided by holding the animal under water for varying periods of time before permitting it to make the instrumental response. The chief finding
of this study was that as discrimination was made more difficult, the
optimum air deprivation for the best discrimination learning decreased,
thus confirming the Yerkes-Dodson law. But the finding that is of interest
to us here is that the emotional and nonemotional animals failed to differ
in performance in the manner that they should (on the assumption that
genetically determined emotionality adds to the total drive in the same
way that experimentally produced air deprivation does) as a function
of the three levels of difficulty and the various air-deprivation conditions.

Individual Differences in Arousal. There have been attempts to
measure individual differences in general arousal; Duffy (1962) provides
an excellent survey of the literature. Differences can be found for almost
any autonomic index, but again we have our two questions of whether
any such index or any combination of them is valid, and whether even a
valid index can be interpreted as a measure of motivation.

Schnore (1959) has addressed himself to the first question. He obtained nine autonomic reactivity measures, and found that each subject
had his own characteristic pattern relative to the group as a whole. Thus,
some subjects might characteristically have a high heart rate, low pressure, and average skin conductance. Under instructions or a task situation designed to produce arousal it was found that some measures would
go up a little, others would come down a little, but on the whole the
pattern characteristic of the individual remained essentially intact. There
is at this time, in our present state of ignorance about the patterning of
these things, little evidence for individual differences in a general arousal
factor, less evidence for the validity of such a concept, and still less that
such a factor would indicate an individual's level of motivation.

"Manifest Anxiety" as a Measure of Drive—Eyeblink Studies. There
is another set of studies that promised to capitalize on possible individual
differences in strength of drive, and to anchor the resulting measure of
drive by means of the generally accepted behavioral criteria of drive.
These are the investigations of "manifest anxiety" begun at Iowa by
Spence and Taylor. This research starts with a set of items from the

MMPI which have been judged to be indicative of overt anxiety symptoms (Taylor, 1951, revised by Taylor, 1953). These items together with other, buffer items, are used to constitute a scale which is administered to introductory psychology students. The top and bottom 10–20% are selected and designated as high and low MAS subjects. High and low MAS subjects should act, it is hypothesized, in situations other than the paper and pencil test as though they had high and low drive. To confirm this prediction Spence and Taylor (1951) ran four groups of subjects in a factorial design involving high and low MAS, and high- and low-intensity air puff as the US in an eyelid conditioning. The MAS variable had the expected effect on the acquisition of the CR. The US intensity variable did not, which is surprising in view of the earlier study of Passey (1948) and a host of subsequent studies from Iowa demonstrating a US effect. In a similar study, Taylor (1951) ran high and low MAS subjects under anxiety-provoking and anxiety-relieving instructions and found again that MAS scores had the expected effect but that the attempt to manipulate motivation directly did not.

The basic question raised by these findings is whether the differences in performance as a function of MAS scores represent differences in habit structure or differences in D. One way to try to find out is to run an extinction series. This Taylor (1951) did, and found some but not significantly greater resistance to extinction under the high MAS condition. Subsequently Spence and Farber (1953) have reported an extinction effect, but relatively little is known about the extinction of the eyeblink. Usually, it fails after just a few elicitations but Spence et al. (1963) have begun to develop techniques for extending extinction performance.

Spence has repeatedly discussed the possibility that in aversive learning (such as the defensive eyelid conditioning situation), habit strength may grow more quickly under high drive than under low drive because of the greater amount of drive reduction that is possible with each reinforcement. As we saw in the previous discussion of the $D \times H$ independence problem, the evidence is not binding one way or the other; in fact, it is pretty much a matter of definition whether one chooses to regard D and H as independent. The Iowa group has invariably interpreted the MAS studies as demonstrating motivational differences. The implication is that the independence of D and H is not really subject to serious question, certainly not on the basis of the MAS results alone. Independence is presupposed; it has the status of a postulate in Spence's hypothetico-deductive system, to be questioned only if the whole structure of the system is found to be inadequate.

Spence has argued, and who would disagree, that whether MAS scores should be taken as indices of characteristic drive level depends upon whether MAS differences affect behavior the same way as the other manipulations of drive conditions. The trouble with putting this strategy into practice is that we know so little about how to measure or control motivation in the classical conditioning situation, or what the effects of motivation might be on eyeblink performance. As just noted, the first attempts to manipulate drive level experimentally (Spence & Taylor, 1951; Taylor, 1951) produced negative results. Subsequently, some apparently motivational effects of US intensity have been demonstrated (e.g., Spence, 1953) but it is by no means certain yet that even these effects can most profitably be attributed to differences in D.

The results reported by Spence and his coworkers have occasionally been replicated by investigators not at or from Iowa (e.g., Caldwell & Cromwell, 1959); but, more typically, other investigators have failed to corroborate the results of the Iowa group. This trend in the published findings suggests that the effect of MAS score on conditioning (and this applies to the verbal learning situation as well) is not a simple one but depends upon procedural details, only some of which have ever been recognized. One which appears to be important is whether or not a "ready" signal is given a few seconds before the CS (Dufort & Kimble, 1958; King et al., 1961; Prokasy & Whaley, 1962; Klinger & Prokasy, 1962). Another very important consideration is how or whether data from "voluntary" responders should be discarded (Spence & Ross, 1959; Gormezano & Moore, 1962).

Jenkins and Lykken (1957) have pointed out that in some cases (e.g., Franks, 1956) high MAS subjects may show better performance than low MAS subjects on the first conditioning trial, i.e., before the CS and the US have been paired. This suggests either that the response in question, the eyeblink, has a higher initial probability in high MAS subjects, or that some of the subsequent conditioning may well be pseudoconditioning. Perhaps as the discrepancies in the MAS literature become resolved we will come to a better overall understanding of eyelid conditioning.

"Manifest Anxiety"—Verbal Learning Studies. What the initial MAS studies showed was a pattern of results which was consistent with the theory, but which failed to provide substantial support either for the proposition that D and H are independent or the proposition that MAS measures D.[7] Spence's nomological net had not been damaged, but it wasn't clear that he had really caught anything with it either. The next move (Taylor & Spence, 1952) was to cast the net a bit farther. High and low MAS subjects were run on very simple (high association value)

---

[7] Experimental evidence lends *substantial* support to a theory when it is better able to handle the evidence than any alternative theory. This is to be contrasted with *circumstantial* support which occurs when some alternative theory can just as easily handle the evidence. In general, the MAS studies have provided only circumstantial support for drive theory.

verbal learning tasks and on more difficult (low association value) verbal learning tasks. It was found that the higher MAS subjects did relatively better than low MAS subjects on the simple tasks but this relationship was reversed with the difficult material. This can be deduced: If we assume that the correct responses have the highest or among the highest association values in the easy material to be learned, then increasing the drive level (or selecting subjects characterized by a heightened drive level) should raise the excitatory potentials of the correct responses further above those of the incorrect responses. On the other hand, if the correct responses are low in the hierarchy of response strengths, then increasing drive should only bury them further beneath the stronger competing responses. This general pattern of interaction between association value and MAS score has been confirmed by Lucas (1952), Montague (1953), Ramond (1953), Spence, Farber, and McFann (1956), Spence, Taylor, and Ketchel (1956), Standish and Champion (1960), and others.

It could be objected that the earlier studies in this series had accepted old and obsolete standardizations of the association values of nonsense syllables. It could be objected further that low association value may make learning difficult not because of response competition (which is the mechanism the theory uses to make its predictions) but because of the absence of *any* verbal response. Thus, the relative difficulty of difficult material for high MAS subjects might be due not to the effects of response competition but to some characteristic reaction elicited by difficulty per se. Saltz and Hoehn (1957) attempted to separate difficulty and competition as experimental variables; their results strongly suggest that difficulty is indeed the critical factor as far as producing an interaction with MAS scores is concerned. The more recent studies by Spence, Farber, and McFann (1956) and Standish and Champion (1960) have made allowance for this by using procedures that guaranteed that the appropriate conditions with respect to response competition would be present. For example, more than one list may be used and the interlist similarity of items manipulated independently of their association values. Even after such refinements the results may come out the wrong way (Bernstein, 1963). Trapp and Kausler (1960) have recently pointed out another problem here, in that high MAS subjects seem to yield systematically higher individual association values for the same items than do low MAS subjects. To add to these difficulties, a number of investigators have been unable to replicate the initial findings (e.g., Mandler & Sarason, 1952; Hughes et al., 1954; Silverman & Blitz, 1956; Buchwald, 1959; Lovaas, 1960).

The Iowa investigations of MAS have gone farther afield. Farber and Spence (1953) reported that high MAS subjects did more poorly on a stylus-maze task than low MAS subjects, and that the size of decrement as a function of MAS score was highly correlated with the difficulty of the individual choice points (as determined by the errors made by an unselected group of subjects). Since the rate of learning was reversed between high and low MAS groups in eyelid conditioning, Farber and Spence concluded that both differences could not be attributed to a general learning-ability difference between the two groups but have to be attributed to a difference in drive level.[8] Axelrod et al. (1956) were not able to replicate these results, and, in addition, suggest that the correlation reported by Farber and Spence may have been artifactual due to their failure to correct for overall performance levels. It does seem a little strange that the high MAS subjects did not make any higher proportion of their total errors on the more difficult choice points than the low MAS subjects. It also seems a little strange that for Farber and Spence's subjects the correct response was never higher in the response hierarchy than the incorrect response (inferred from the fact that at no choice point did the high MAS subjects do better). This inference is belied by the finding that at many choice points the probability of correct responding on any trial was better than .5.

Spence and Taylor (1953) sought to test the clinical validity of the MAS by comparing eyelid conditioning in neurotics, psychotics, and normals. It was found that while the neurotics and psychotics conditioned faster than normals their respective performances were not predictable from their MAS scores. On the other hand, other experimenters (e.g., Welch & Kubis, 1947; Bitterman & Holtzman, 1952) had found that clinical anxiety was positively correlated with the speed of GSR conditioning.

Since the original elaboration of MAS research at Iowa in the early 1950s, it has expanded prodigiously in all directions.[9] Most of this work is of no immediate concern to us here since it has to do with other problems, but much of its bears indirectly on the question of whether MAS measures drive. This work can be put under the following headings:

1. *Personality structure.* What are the people like who say "Yes, there seems to be a lump in my throat much of the time"? MAS scores are highly correlated with various MMPI scales, which isn't surprising in view of the scale's origin, and they can be related to the Rorschach (Levy & Kurz, 1957). At least one factor analysis of the MAS (O'Connor et al., 1956) found it to involve at least five factors. The relevance of

[8] The first part of the conclusion is much easier to agree with than the second, which doesn't seem to follow at all. However, if we begin to entertain the idea of two or several or many ability factors, then we are coming close to explaining the results in associative terms.

[9] Often lost in the welter of data and discussion is that the original sponsors of the Manifest Anxiety Scale were not concerned with anxiety, qua anxiety, nor in human individual differences, but in designing an instrument for assessing D in humans (Taylor, 1956; Spence, 1958a). I have tried to limit the present discussion to the same issue.

personality structure here is the possibility that what passes for a difference in motivation may be a difference in intelligence, or clerical ability
(Grice, 1955), or anxiety specific to mechanical things such as the conditioning apparatus (Kamin, 1955).

2. *Personality dynamics.* Do high and low MAS subjects differ in
chronic anxiety, or defensiveness, or in their reactivity to stressful situations? Do instructions designed to create threat or ego-involvement have
different effects on them? Do inhibitory and facilitory MAS effects develop or dissipate during prolonged testing? Much ingenious work has
gone into the attempts to answer these questions (e.g., Deese et al., 1953;
Eriksen, 1954; Silverman & Blitz, 1956). It has been suggested in this
connection that even if the impairment of performance on difficult tasks
suffered by the high MAS subjects is due to specific defensive reactions,
the fact that the reaction only comes in with the difficult situation
doesn't rule out a drive interpretation; it does however require us to
change our definition of drive to make it a situation-specific rather than
a generalized motivator.

3. *Clinical anxiety.* Does the MAS measure it? Although it is possible
to get predictions of MAS scores from psychiatric interviews that correlate very highly with actual MAS scores (Buss, 1955), it seems unlikely
that the judges were basing their prediction on judgments of "real" anxiety. Jenkins and Lykken (1957) after reviewing much of the work to
that time decided that MAS is useless as a predictor of clinical anxiety.
This is too bad because certainly much of the research popularity of the
MAS stems from the common desire to have a simple measuring instrument with both experimental validity and clinical utility. On the other
hand, it is not quite obvious that human anxiety, as it is seen in the
clinic, is a drive condition. It is certainly a condition, but is it a drive
condition, a source of D? As Jensen (1958) astutely points out, we have
become so acceptant of the traditional view that anxiety is a drive that
no one has bothered to demonstrate that people actually do learn those
responses or defenses which are instrumental in reducing it! In the absence of such a demonstration we might not wish to call anxiety a drive.

4. *Other indices of drive and drive conditions.* Is the MAS correlated with other measures that could be taken as indicative of individual
drive level? MAS scores fail to correlate with level, reactivity, or condi-
tionability of the GSR (Bitterman & Holtzman, 1952; McGuigan et al.,
1959). Although some investigators have found MAS to correlate with
individual differences in reaction time (e.g., Wenar, 1954), Farber and
Spence (1956) in an extensive series of investigations failed to get any
coherent reaction-time effects as a function of MAS scores. Meyer et al.
(1953) and Meyer and Noble (1958) have found rather substantial evidence to support the idea that MAS measures muscle tonus (see also
Rossi, 1959; Lovaas, 1960). If we accept with Meyer (1953) the idea

that drive is no more than muscular tension, then there is some promise. But there are also some difficulties with this interpretation.

Bindra et al. (1955) opened a window on the problem and let in some light and fresh air. They tested high and low MAS subjects on salivary conditioning. Now, it is well known that the salivary CR increases with hunger motivation, which can be accepted as a drive condition; if Manifest Anxiety is a source of drive, the same effect should be found. It was not. Bindra et al. suggest, like Hilgard et al., 1951, that the extra "drive" of high MAS subjects may just be a set of defensive reactions elicited by the noxious situation.

Then, finally, there is the other side of the coin. What would be the effect in the eyelid and verbal learning situation of varying drive in an "approved" manner rather than selecting subjects with allegedly different drive levels. Kamin and Fedorchak (1957) compared hungry and satiated subjects in verbal learning and found no effect. Franks (1957) compared satiated subjects with subjects that had been deprived of food, water, and tobacco for 24 hours in eyelid conditioning. Again no effect was found.

From the outset there were critics to point out that it was at best gratuitous to attribute MAS effects to variation in motivation, especially to variation in D, in view of the likelihood that individuals scoring differently on the MAS also differ with respect to a number of other variables—personality, prior experience, values, and so on. Hilgard et al. (1951) found that MAS scores did not predict performance in discriminative conditioning (where the US follows one stimulus, the CS, but not another, similar stimulus).[10] Their results suggested to Hilgard et al. that the high MAS subject is a worried, defensive individual who comes into the conditioning situation with strong response tendencies to wince, to startle, to blink, in short to make just the sorts of responses the experimenter is trying to condition. They do condition sooner and better than low MAS subjects, but because of their special habit structure rather than because of any greater motivation. Similar associative accounts of the superior conditioning found with high MAS subjects have been urged by Mandler and Sarason (1952), Child (1954), Kamin et al. (1955), Kimble and Dufort (1956), and others.

It is, of course, all too easy to attribute difference in performance to a difference in drive level and simply ignore any possible associative difference that might be correlated with performance. Drive theorists often use the ploy "of course we mustn't overlook the possibility of differences in habit strength," or "Hull made use of S_D, you know," and then pro-

---

[10] Spence and Farber (1954) and Spence and Beecroft (1954), using slightly different procedures, were able to get the results they expected in a discriminative conditioning situation; there was a greater difference in asymptotic performance to the positive and negative stimuli for the high MAS subjects than for the low MAS subjects. The effect wasn't statistically significant though.

ceed to overlook associative differences and the stimulus concomitants of the drive condition. Or the drive theorist may say "even if an ad hoc associative explanation for this particular phenomenon can be found, the findings still lend support to drive theory because they fit in with (or better, were predicted from) the whole theoretical structure." But the facts we have surveyed in the present chapter indicate that D dwells in a pretty shabby structure.[11]

Some drive theorists are exceptional in this respect however. Brown (1953, 1961) has cautioned against the wholesale invocation of drives for explanatory purposes, pointing out that much of what is often called an acquired drive (for money, for example) is better accounted for even within drive theory as an acquired response tendency. Similarly, Farber has questioned whether there was at that time (1955) *any* evidence demonstrating an unequivocal effect of motivation upon verbal behavior. After examining a number of research techniques—perceptual defense, instruction-induced failure, frustration, and achievement—Farber concluded that in each case associative accounts of the "motivational" effects were at least as plausible as accounts couched in motivational terms. Perhaps, he suggested, it is only with the MAS technique that enough control of the situation can be maintained to demonstrate a genuine effect.

One difficulty with MAS scores is that in order to demonstrate any relationship at all between them and other kinds of behavior it is necessary to exclude the middle scores and work with extreme subgroups. The resulting research then may yield a distorted picture of the functional relationships involved. For example, although correlations are maximized by taking extreme subgroups, the linearity of the correlation cannot in general be checked. Studies that have used whole populations in genuinely correlational analyses have typically found the correlation between MAS score and performance to be near zero (e.g., Hilgard et al., 1951). Other studies (e.g., Montague, 1953; Trapp & Kausler, 1960; Standish & Champion, 1960) have typically found that the mid-range MAS subjects score beyond the lows rather than lying between the high and low MAS subjects, as they should according to the theory. Finally, many of the studies done at Iowa have made use of large numbers of subjects, e.g., 40 high MAS and 40 low MAS from a population of 400, and have managed even so only to find marginally significant differences. Thus, even if some of the effects are there, some question can justifiably be raised regarding their utility. We seem to have the same conclusion we had regarding individual differences in animal motivation: if there are characteristic differences in motivation for different individ-

11 Moreover it seems that D is in no condition to make the necessary repairs alone. That is why K was invited in. But now it is beginning to look as though K may throw D right out, take over the premises, and do some extensive remodeling.

uals they are minute compared with the individual differences in the associative determinants of motivated behavior.

SUMMARY

The attempts to obtain drive summation and drive substitution, the investigations of general activity, and the attempts to show transituational individual differences in drive have provided little support for the hypothesis that all sources of drive contribute in the same way to the organism's motivation. The results of these studies have been sometimes affirmative and sometimes negative so that the generality of the generalized-drive concept is still controversial. But there can be little controversy over the finding that the general drive factor is only a minor determinant of behavior. Behavior is predominantly determine by the specific drive conditions, specific stimulus situations, and specific habit structures that characterize an individual at a given time. Generalized drive has turned out to be a puny fellow compared with the big D we had expected to find; he cannot carry much explanatory weight.

The impressive dependence of behavior upon associative and incentive factors, and the relatively slight impact of events independent of these factors, suggest that if we are to keep "drive" at all we ought to change its definition to make it include the learned sources of motivation. This is essentially what we will do in the following chapter, where we will examine "acquired-drive" theories of motivation.

11

ACQUIRED DRIVES

✤❮❮❖❮

People are not born with a tendency to strive for money, for the discovery of scientific truths, or for symbols of social status and security. Such motives are learned during socialization.

N. E. MILLER

The concept of acquired drive is sometimes said to be a necessary one in the explanation of behavior because adult humans have sources of motivation other than those of infant humans or animals. If we are to explain adult human behavior in motivational terms and particularly if we are to invoke drives (or D) in the explanation, we must have some variety of acquired drives. Considerable ingenuity has gone into proposals of how original or primary sources of motivation might become diverted, or modified in some way, to produce new or secondary sources of motivation. Some of the most promising and provocative hypotheses have been made by drive theorists, both those in, and those breaking away from, the Hullian tradition. But we will see in the present chapter that the attempts to expand drive theory in this direction have generally failed to strengthen it. While a few drive theorists, most notably Miller, have remained relatively true to Hull's original set of principles, most have preferred to abandon one or another of the hypothetical properties of drives, or even to reject the drive concept altogether. What we will find, then, in the present chapter is that the search for unifying motivational principles which will encompass even the most primitive of acquired drives, fear, has led us away from the drive concept and toward new and more powerful explanations of behavior.

EARLY ACCOUNTS OF ACQUIRED DRIVE

There is something prophetic in the fact that Woodworth no sooner introduced the concept of drive, or at least the word "drive," into psychology in 1918 than he cautioned against overemphasizing its importance. Thus, he made the basic distinction between drive and mechanism, indicating that drive supplied the energy that made the habit mechanisms go, and then declared that any well-exercised mechanism might itself acquire the dynamic properties that drive seems to have. Accordingly, any well-established habit could be viewed as a variety of acquired drive.

Other early proponents of the drive concept offered similar accounts of acquired motivation. For example, Tolman (1926) suggested that there were really two kinds of drives: one, the primary or unlearned drives, which have some discernible physiological basis; and two, the secondary or derived drives, the physiological bases of which are either lacking or unknown. He supposed that the derived drives depend in some yet to be determined manner upon the primary drives. For example, curiosity (a derived drive) might be assumed to vary according to some functional relationship with hunger (a primary drive). Later (1932), Tolman developed the idea that the social drives develop "in the service of" the primary drives. Thus, the young individual may become socially cooperative, gregarious, and so on, as a means toward satisfying some more basic primary drive such as hunger or comfort.

Still later (1942, 1943), Tolman suggested a mechanism for this learning, namely, that social drives arise when primary drives are frustrated. Thus, if the young organism is frustrated in its satisfaction of hunger, it might become more independent and self-assertive thereby obtaining food, as it were, by force. Alternatively, the organism might become more dependent and self-abasive thereby obtaining food by subversion. Then, when one or another of these "modes of adjustment" meets with success it tends to become stabilized and habitual, and to the extent that it generalizes to other situations, one of these modes of adjustment could become what we call a social motive.[1] This "biosocial"

---

[1] A social motive thus emerges as any well-established highly generalizable response tendency. Such social habits provide their own motivation without depending (except historically perhaps) upon other extrinsic sources of motivation. It is curious that writers such as Woodworth and Tolman who stressed that the secondary or acquired drives might be merely well-established response tendencies failed to see that the so-called primary drives might also be only well-established response tendencies either well-learned or innate.

approach to human motivation is clearly reminiscent of Freud's developmental account of behavior.

A quite different view of social motivation has been expressed by Maslow (1954). Maslow asserts that the various drives are arranged in a natural hierarchy of urgency. If the organism must spend all its time satisfying the most urgent drives, such as obtaining food and water and air, then it will not have the opportunity to engage in other sorts of activity such as seeking comfort or safety. When these matters of survival have been dealt with adequately the individual then may engage in self-aggrandizement, the seeking of prestige, etc. Finally, Maslow tells us, when everything else has been dealt with satisfactorily, the individual may seek self-actualization.

Functional Autonomy. Allport (1937) has opposed the idea that human motives have anything but the most remote connection with man's physiological needs. He has proposed instead that the adult's motives are self-sustaining contemporary systems which are functionally independent of the historical conditions that initially may have produced them; man's motives are "functionally autonomous." Notice here that Allport does not deny the historicity of primary drives in human motivation but only their relevance to understanding the adult. The label "functional autonomy" merely reminds us, in case we should need reminding, that man's social motives have no contemporaneous connection with his physiological drives.

All of these schemes, and certainly many others as well, have considerable intrinsic interest, and perhaps provide useful descriptions of behavior. But in no case do they come close to approximating an adequate explanation of social behavior. For the most part these schemes are based upon logical considerations and flourish without support from systematic empirical findings. Logic requires that if we are to have drives to explain behavior, then we must have social drives to explain social behavior. Logic tells us that since so much of man's behavior is learned the reasons of his behavior must also be learned. But in point of fact there are essentially no data on the acquisition of human social behavior and these conceptual schemes have not been conducive to the collection of data. Fundamentally, the problem of the learning of motives awaited an adequate theory of behavior, one which met the criteria of theoretical adequacy such as having explicit semantics and syntactical rules.

Brown (1953) has emphasized that ordinarily what is referred to when speaking of a social drive or an acquired drive is simply the occurrence of some particular behavior which is relevant to a social situation. Thus, we speak of a "drive for money." But, Brown observes:

> In many instances, if not all, where adult human behavior has been strongly marked by money-seeking responses there appears to be little

need for postulating the operation of a learned money-seeking drive. One does not learn to have a drive for money. Instead, one learns to become anxious in the presence of a variety of cues signifying the absence of money. The obtaining of money automatically terminates or drastically alters such cues, and in so doing, produces a decrease in anxiety. (Brown, 1953, p. 14)

The only "drive" here is the anxiety which may occur in the absence of money. This is not to say that money may not be a reinforcer; presumably it is, because it terminates anxiety which is a drive-producing condition. Moreover, money may come to be a secondary positive reinforcer through its association with anxiety reduction, and through its association with food and other good things in life. But to invent a drive specifically to explain money-seeking behavior is, at best, only to give the behavior a name. The same argument applies, of course, to all the alleged social motives.

CONDITIONED HUNGER

Dashiell (1937) had suggested that the motivational state resulting from food deprivation was only partly elicited by the internal or nutritional condition of the organism and that motivation to eat was also controlled in part by external stimuli, namely, stimuli in the presence of which eating had previously occurred. In this view the whole motivational system involved in hunger was a plastic thing which could be attached to internal stimulation, such as stomach contractions, to external stimuli, such as a familiar food dish, or to both internal and external stimuli.

Seward and Seward (1937) extended this argument with the proposition that different drives occupy different positions on a continuum of internal vs. external arousal (see also G. Seward, 1942). Thus, sexual behavior was said to be relatively more dependent upon external stimulation than hunger but less so than exploration. Moreover, the Sewards suggested that through learning there is a tendency for all motivational states to shift in the direction of external arousal. We will see in a later chapter that J. P. Seward and others have gone on from these assumptions to develop some very powerful theories of incentive motivation. The modern treatments of incentive motivation deal with the externally aroused component of motivation as being something other than, something added to, the initial component of drive arising from the animal's physiological state. But in the early 1940s the more common assumption, and the assumption of Dashiell and the Sewards, was that somehow the internal state of hunger was itself aroused by external stimuli.

This concept of an external arousal of an internal state was advanced most vigorously by Anderson (1941), who introduced the phrase "externalization of drive" for the hypothetical mechanism. Anderson reported several studies designed to demonstrate the properties of externalized drive. Perhaps the most important was one (1941a) in which a group of rats was trained on a maze with food as a reinforcement, then satiated, and then run on a second maze without food reinforcement. This group performed better on the second maze than did a control group that had not had the prior experience with hunger, or with the first maze. From the superior performance of the experimental group over the control group Anderson argued that, because of its similarity to the first maze, the second maze had aroused hunger in the experimental group. This interpretation is, however, fraught with difficulties. For one thing, Anderson ran small groups and presents no statistical analysis of the differences, which were small. But even if Anderson was correct that the experimental group had a higher drive, presumably aroused by the stimulus conditions, why should learning occur? Where was the reinforcement? And if there was a reinforcer, then why speak of a conditioned drive? More disturbing is the fact that the experimental and control animals differed not only in the opportunity to acquire a condition hunger, but also in prior experience in mazes, prior experience with handling, and prior experience with deprivation. Siegel (1943) in a careful experimental attempt to duplicate Anderson's findings was unable to do so.

Calvin et al. (1953a) reported that they had conditioned consummatory behavior to external stimuli. They fed two groups of animals 30 min. a day for 24 days in a distinctive box. One group ate while 22 hr. deprived and the other ate while only 1 hr. deprived. On a test day both animals were deprived for 12 hr. and the amount consumed was measured and found to be higher for the group that had had the eating experience in the box under high hunger. Calvin et al. argued that the prior experience in the box under high hunger had conditioned the hunger state to the distinctive test environment. Unfortunately, proper control groups were lacking. We do not know, therefore, whether the same results would have been found if the prior eating experience had been in some other environment, say, the animals' homecage. Nor do we know that weight loss was the same for the two groups at the time of testing. Siegel and MacDonnell (1954) and Scarborough and Goodson (1957) were unable to replicate the findings of Calvin et al.

There are a number of methodological difficulties in demonstrating the externalization of hunger, perhaps the most important of which is the difficulty of defining satiation (see p. 272). Another methodological problem here is that attaching a physiological state to an external stimulus may be impeded by the slowness of development of the physiological condition. In an attempt to obviate this difficulty, Greenberg (1954) produced thirst quickly by giving rats saline injections. An external cue was then paired with the rapidly produced thirst. Subsequent measures of drinking in the presence of the cue but without prior saline injection indicated no more drinking than occurred in the appropriate control group. Hence, there was no evidence of an acquired thirst drive. Other attempts to obtain conditioned hunger, as evidenced either by increased consummatory activity or strengthened instrumental behavior, have been made by Myers and Miller (1954), Solomon (1956), Dyal (1958), and Howard and Young (1962); and, for thirst, by Novin and Miller (1962). The results in every case have been negative.[2]

What evidence is now available forces us to conclude that as plausible as the hypothesis sounds, and as theoretically important as supporting evidence would be if it could be obtained, there is little indication that satiated animals can be made hungry or thirsty by the presentation of external stimuli.[3]

FRUSTRATION AS AN ACQUIRED DRIVE

It has been known for some time that an animal may respond more vigorously in extinction (when reinforcement is withheld) than in acquisition (when reinforcement is given) (e.g., Miller & Stevenson, 1936; Finch, 1942; Marzocco, 1951). Marzocco found that when the force exerted in lever pressing had stabilized at about 30 gm. it increased sharply to nearly 40 gm. as soon as reinforcement was withheld. This effect, the momentary increase in vigor of an instrumental response as a consequence of withholding reinforcement (or delaying reinforcement), is called the Frustration Effect.

Interpretations of Frustration. Although the Frustration Effect is frequently interpreted as evidence of an increase in drive as a result of thwarting, this interpretation is not always compelling. First of all it should be noted that a Frustration Effect can arise as an artifact. For example, if the rate of bar pressing is measured instead of the vigor of the response, it too is commonly seen to rise momentarily at the beginning of extinction. However, this effect can be attributed to the dropping out of the animal's eating behavior. The animal achieves a higher rate of bar pressing because its bar pressing is not interrupted by eating. Accordingly, artifactual frustration effects are more often seen with continuous

[2] Zeaman and House (1950) and Howard (1962) have shown what appear to be conditioned aversions, but, as we will see shortly, the aversive case is quite different from the appetitive case.

[3] This is not to deny that there are stimuli which will produce eating in the "satiated" animal; we know that there are. The introduction of either another hungry animal or a more palatable food will reinstate eating after it has terminated. It would be interesting to see whether the rat can learn an instrumental response while satiated, in order to get to the goal where a hungry animal is eating, i.e., to determine if socially facilitated eating is reinforcing.

reinforcement schedules than with intermittent reinforcement schedules.

It is also possible that the effect on response vigor itself is an artifact resulting from the animal's prior learning experience. For example, in the case of Marzocco's animals there were surely many instances during acquisition when they pressed with less than 30-gm. force, failed to get reinforcement, then pressed with more force, and got it. Thus, we can be sure the animals had been differentially reinforced specifically for "pressing harder," and this may have occurred in extinction because the stimuli controlling it (nonreinforcement) were present.

It is also entirely possible to view the effects of thwarting as genuine but being due to associative rather than motivational factors. (We will refer to the *procedure* as "thwarting" and to the hypothetical or observed consequence of thwarting as "frustration.") Thus, we may think of thwarting a response as producing a state or condition of the organism, the frustration condition, which elicits either innately or through prior learning particular responses or particular modes of responding, such as pressing harder or being aggressive. Experimental work in the area of frustration has in fact been dominated as much by this view as by the view that frustration is a kind of motivation. One reason for this is the notable book *Frustration and aggression* by Dollard et al. (1939), the fundamental thesis of which is that frustration is a necessary and sufficient condition for aggression. The point of view taken is that aggressive behavior is not so much motivated by frustration as it is elicited by it. It is well known that when bar pressing suddenly fails to produce food pellets, the rats' behavior becomes considerably more variable, and comes to include components such as biting the bar. These features of the behavior can most cogently be viewed as specific associative reactions to the failure of reinforcement.

In short, we find that prior to systematic experimental investigation of frustration phenomena, the Frustration Effect was variously attributed to the associative effects of thwarting (Dollard et al., 1939), to the motivational effects of thwarting (Rohrer, 1949; Brown & Jacobs, 1949), or to both (Brown & Farber, 1951). And even though different sorts of hypothetical frustration mechanisms had been postulated to account for a variety of motivational effects (e.g., Rohrer, 1949; Brown & Jacobs, 1949), and frustration had been incorporated within the broader framework of Hull's drive theory of motivation (Brown & Farber, 1951), there was little real evidence that frustration had the functional properties of a drive condition.

Indeed, some of the earliest behavioral research indicated rather clearly that the Frustration Effect was governed largely by associative factors. For example, Lambert and Solomon (1952) found greater excitement in rats if they were extinguished close to the goal box than if they were extinguished some distance from it. Holder et al. (1957) found that

rats could be trained to respond less vigorously following a failure of reinforcement and that this effect was nearly equal in size to the increase in
vigor found under normal training and thwarting conditions. Such findings led Marx (1956) and Lawson and Marx (1958) first to doubt the
validity of many claimed Frustration Effects, and second, to attribute
such effects, when they were not artifacts, to purely associative relationships. More recently, serious doubt has been raised about whether there
is any inherent connection between frustration and aggression (e.g., Feshbach, 1964). Perhaps this too is learned; certainly instrumental aggression pays off, not only in the animal colony but in the Western culture.[4]

Amsel's Studies of Frustration. Recent work on frustration has been
largely dominated by Amsel and his coworkers. Amsel and Roussel (1952)
used a frustration procedure which provided the prototype for much subsequent work. They trained rats to run a 2-unit alley for food. Subjects
would run the first unit of the alley to the first goal box, eat, and then
move on to the second unit and to the second goal box for a second piece
of food. After the running response had been acquired, food was withdrawn from the first goal box on half of the trials. The other half of the
trials were reinforced both at the first and at the second goal box, as in
acquisition. Thus, each animal served as its own control to indicate the
effect of presenting vs. withholding reinforcement in the first goal box.
Both the speed of leaving the first goal box and the speed of running the
second unit of the alley were significantly faster on those trials in which
food was withheld (see Fig. 11-1). Amsel argues that this effect provides
a clearer demonstration of frustration than the usual Frustration Effect
because it involves a response other than the one which was thwarted.

Subsequently, Amsel and Ward (1954) and Amsel and Prouty (1959)
have elaborated this procedure by replacing the second unit of the alley
with a choice situation which is arranged so that on trials when food is
withheld in the first goal (frustration trials) the animal must make one
response to obtain food in the second goal box, while on trials when food
is presented in the first box (reinforced trials) the opposite response must
be made to obtain food in the second goal box. This discrimination is
learned, and the performance of the appropriate control groups appears
to indicate that the discrimination is based upon some immediate consequences of frustration itself, rather than upon stimulus consequences of
food in the mouth vs. no food in the mouth.

But even granting for the moment that frustration has an energizing
effect upon behavior, there remains the question of whether its contribution to motivation should be considered as an increment in drive, or as a

---

[4] The best recent review of the response vigor problem and defense of the
associationistic position is Notterman and Mintz (1965); for programatic applications to human motivation problems and a historical treatment see Lawson
(1965).

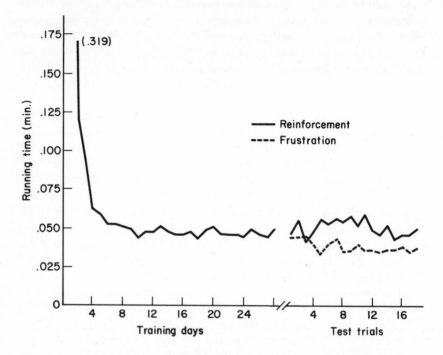

Fig. 11-1. Running time on the second part of a runway in acquisition and on subsequent test trials when reinforcement is either presented or withheld at the end of the first part of the runway. (From Amsel & Roussel, 1952)

new kind of incentive motivation factor. To some extent this is only a semantic question; it hinges upon whether drive itself is regarded as a feature of motivated behavior or as an antecedent of motivated behavior; or, put another way, it depends upon whether incentive motivation is regarded as something contributing to drive (Brown, 1961) or as something relatively independent of drive (Spence, 1956).

It turns out that the effects of frustration appear only after some acquisition training has occurred, that these effects can be elicited by presenting stimuli that have been paired with thwarting, and that under these conditions the effects can move forward in a chain of responses so that the animal appears to anticipate frustration. These and other considerations have led Amsel (1958, 1962) to view frustration as acting upon incentive factors in motivation rather than generating drive. If, on the other hand, frustration effects could be shown to lead to learning when they dissipate, or be shown to energize general activity, or to have intersubstitutability with other drive conditions, then a case could be made for frustration as a source of drive. But little of this sort of evidence has been adduced. It seems safe to conclude that Amsel and others who think of frustration as an incentive effect have taken a good course. Those who view it associatively may, however, be following a better one.

Conclusions on Acquired Appetitive Drives. In summary, then, we have found little or no evidence to show that there are any acquired appetitive drives. Claims of such demonstrations seem to be more profitably interpretable in associationistic terms or in terms of some motivational mechanism other than drive. The enormous gap between the sorts of appetitive behavior which can be found in the laboratory and those which appear to apply in human social situations seems, if anything, to be wider now than it was 40 years ago when psychologists made the first attempts to close it. This unhappy conclusion suggests that either the gap cannot be bridged because animal behavior and human behavior are somehow incommensurate, or else that something has been fundamentally wrong with the basic premises of drive theory.

ACQUIRED AVERSIVE DRIVES

Curiously perhaps, after all the work that has been done on the problem, we have really identified only one acquired drive—fear. With fear we have one point at which we can almost close the gap between human social motivation and animal laboratory motivation. Unfortunately, we have not yet gained much from this closure; avoidance learning, which is what fear is supposed to explain, is undoubtedly the least well understood of all the varieties of learning. Consequently, avoidance is a pivotal phenomenon for all theories of motivation. Hull's drive theory, and the many variants of Hullian theory (which have arisen largely in the attempt to explain avoidance) all falter over the problems it presents.

We will begin a discussion of avoidance shortly, to see if the drive concept is of any use in explaining it, and then continue the discussion in subsequent chapters as we encounter other theories of motivation. But first, we must cite some evidence that fear is an acquirable drive, and has some of the functional properties that drives are supposed to have.

Fear as an Acquired Drive. Miller (1941, 1948) shocked rats in a white compartment and then trained them to escape the white compartment by running through a doorway into a neighboring black compartment. (The animals showed no marked color preference prior to being shocked.) They were then placed in the white compartment in the absence of shock and with the door to the black compartment shut. To open the door the animals were required to make an instrumental response (rotate a small wheel). About half of the animals did learn the wheel-turning response (the other half just froze). Subsequently, the wheel-turning response was extinguished, and the animals were required to press a bar in order to open the door. They learned this response too. According to Miller, the white compartment, where the shock was presented, had come to elicit fear.

Therefore, according to Miller, fear is a response, a reaction primarily of the autonomic nervous system, which can be brought under stimulus control. Fear is also a stimulus, because any of a number of responses can be conditioned to it. But most important, fear is a drive, because any response which is instrumental in providing an exit from the fear-eliciting situation is learned by its reduction. It should be emphasized that the learned responses, wheel turning and bar pressing, never previously occurred in the presence of shock or shock termination; they were, Miller argued, new responses which depended on the reinforcing function of the fear, and not just its activating function.

Brown and Jacobs (1949) further strengthened the case for the acquired-drive position by seemingly ruling out the possibility that the source of drive in Miller's situation was frustration resulting from thwarting the animal's exit from the box. Brown and Jacobs simply did not let the escape response occur in the first phase of training as Miller had done. An unavoidable shock was presented in one compartment and it was paired with a visual and auditory cue. Subsequent learning occurred when the door between the two compartments was opened and the animal had to go from the one to the other in order to turn off the light-tone combination. As in all of these studies, no shock was presented in the second phase of the experiment. May (1948) conducted a similar study with an additional group to control for the possibility that learning might be due just to a generalized energizing effect. Control animals were tested after they had the same amount of shock and light-tone experience but without the stimuli being paired in a systematic manner. The experimental animals learned to terminate the light-tone stimulus and the controls did not, indicating once again the plausibility of assuming fear to be an acquired drive. Mowrer and Lamoreaux (1946) have also reported learning in a situation where one response escapes the "warning signal" and a quite different response escapes shock.

This series of experiments from the Yale laboratory left little doubt that fear was a conditionable drive state. There was additional evidence, if any were needed, both from the classical conditioning situation and from the conditioned suppression situation (Estes & Skinner, 1941) that fear could be conditioned to previously neutral stimuli. This conclusion from these studies still stands securely. What seems less secure today is the conclusion that conditioned fear is a drive condition with the properties drive conditions are supposed to have. Notice that an inherent feature of these early acquired-drive studies is that they reveal only one of the several hypothetical properties of drive, viz., the reinforcing property. The requirement that learning of a "new response" be demonstrated

prevented the demonstration of the energizing property. Actually, it is difficult to show that fear can energize an arbitrary "new response" because
the predominant response to fear is freezing. Miller and his colleagues
were well aware of this and exercised much experimental ingenuity in
maintaining the activity level of their animals. In effect, the case for
fear as an acquired drive in the technical sense rests entirely on the supposition that the animal does learn a "new" response. In the present
chapter we will pretend that this is the case, and proceed to see how
the acquired-drive argument was applied to the problem of avoidance
learning.[5]

Avoidance Learning. Consider the following phenomenon. A rat is
placed in a box with a metal grid floor and given an electric shock every
few minutes. Once the shock comes on it stays on until the rat presses a
bar which is available in the box. Characteristically, the rat may take 1
min. to press the bar the first time. On successive presentations of the
shock the latency of the bar-press response which is instrumental in terminating, i.e., *escaping,* the shock becomes progressively shorter until it approaches 1 sec. or so. Learning in this situation may be called escape
conditioning, or instrumental escape conditioning, or, more simply, escape
learning. This learning is generally rapid, durable, and presents no particular problem of interpretation.[6]

Suppose now we complicate the situation slightly by presenting a light
5 sec. before the shock comes on and arrange it so that pressing the bar
not only terminates the shock but also turns off the light. The light thus
serves as a cue or a signal of a forthcoming shock. As before, the rat will
learn to escape the shock and, again, the bar-press response will occur
with shorter and shorter latency. But there comes a point at which the
bar-press response occurs before the shock comes on. Now, if the situation
is arranged so that preshock responses prevent shock, the response will
come under the control of the light stimulus. With continued training
the latency of the bar press will continue to decrease until it comes to
occur regularly a second or two after the light comes on. At this point the
rat will be effectively avoiding the shock.

[5] We will drop the pretense toward the end of Chapter 13; there we will
consider the possibility that the "new" response isn't new at all but merely one
of the unconditioned escape responses elicited by aversive stimulation. At the outset Miller (1948) gave an intimation that something was amiss. In discussing possible improvements in the procedure he suggested that the acquisition of the new
response would proceed much better if the situation were arranged so that the
new response would be topographically similar to the old escape response!

[6] There is the problem of whether the termination of shock is itself reinforcing,
or whether shock elicits pain or fear reactions which produce drive and it is the
termination of drive which is reinforcing. But for all practical purposes, shock may
be classed as a negative reinforcer because, empirically, its termination reinforces.
I will take this as the fundamental property of aversive or noxious stimuli rather
than the property that they elicit withdrawal, or are unpleasant or painful.

Learning in the avoidance situation is quite different from learning in the escape situation because if the shock is the reinforcer in the avoidance situation, then successful avoidance would prevent further reinforcement, so that avoidance behavior should start extinguishing as soon as it appears. It should be a transient phenomenon. However, it is sometimes found that once the response to the light becomes established, it may be exceedingly resistant to extinction. The drive theorist, therefore, finds it difficult to maintain that the termination of shock reinforces the avoidance response.

The drive theorist can postpone his difficulties for a time by invoking an acquired drive. If it is assumed that the light comes to elicit fear, then it can be argued that the avoidance of shock is merely a byproduct of the escape from the fear conditioned to the light cue. With the conception of fear as a learnable reaction (albeit autonomic rather than overt) which motivates the rat and the reduction of which is reinforcing, the drive theorist would seem to have a workable account of avoidance learning. There are still some difficulties. One of the most embarrassing questions is why the fear doesn't extinguish as soon as avoidance behavior is established. Another vexing question is how does the fear become acquired? Is it reinforced by the termination of the shock, or by its own termination? Or is it acquired by some mechanism other than drive reduction? What grounds are there for calling fear a drive? These are some of the crucial issues for the drive theorist. But we are getting ahead of the story, and there are a number of lessons to be learned from the early part of it.

The Failure of Classical Conditioning to Explain Avoidance. Pavlov always worked just with the salivary reflex; but by 1904 Bechterev had extended the principles and methods of classical conditioning to other responses and, most notably, to withdrawal reactions to aversive stimuli. Bechterev used a CS, such as a buzzer, and a US, such as an electric shock applied to the foot. The electrodes were strapped to the foot so that when conditioning had occurred, i.e., when the buzzer had come to elicit the foot flexion, the electric shock was still applied. The shock was only omitted on certain test trials where it was desired to demonstrate that the CS had in fact gained control of the foot flexion. Now, the defining characteristic of the classical aversive conditioning procedure is that the US cannot be avoided. It is assumed in Pavlovian theory that the occurrence of the US is necessary to "reinforce" the connection between the CS and the CR. To omit it is to lead immediately to extinction.

When Hull first considered avoidance (i.e., 1929), before he had formulated his drive theory, he adhered to the view that avoidance occurred simply because the classically conditioned defense reaction generalized forward in time. He noted with some discomfort, though, that there would have to be continued cycles of acquisition and extinction of avoidance, a state of affairs which didn't seem biologically very useful.[7] Conditioning, of a sort, does occur using the classical procedure, as had been shown by Bechterev in Russia and by Liddell (1926), Schlosberg (1934), and others in this country. But the method seems to work best when the CR is not an overt defense reaction but a "physiological" reaction such as the GSR.[8]

Some writers (Hilgard & Marquis, 1940; Solomon & Brush, 1956) have noted that the possibility for true avoidance learning was introduced as a more or less accidental variation in the classical procedure. The classical procedure was modified so that the US was withheld if the CR occurred before it was scheduled to come on. Immediately, it became possible to compare learning under the classical procedure (unavoidable shock) with learning under avoidance procedures. Although some of the first comparisons (Schlosberg, 1934, 1936) yielded equivocal results, others (Hunter, 1935; Brogden et al., 1938) indicated that the avoidable shock procedure led to vastly superior learning.

Brogden et al. (1938) ran guinea pigs in an activity cage arranged so that a shock could be presented to the floor 2 sec. after a tone CS was presented. For one group the shock could be escaped or avoided and for the other it was unavoidable. A dramatic difference between the two groups was found (see Fig. 11-2). Because running is an unconditioned reaction to shock, it occurred on about 20% of the trials. It seems intuitively clear that with unavoidable shock the subject would be punished some proportion of the time for making the criterion response, whereas under the avoidable-shock condition, the animal could successfully avoid the shock by running more or less continually.

But here Brodgen et al. have come upon a dilemma: what reinforces the successful avoidance? It cannot be the shock if the animals learn better when they avoid it. A simple Pavlovian interpretation seems unable

---

[7] Hull could only suggest that in the case of a very intense US, i.e., when the issue of survival is urgent, the conditioned defensive reaction might prove to be peculiarly resistant to extinction. By 1952 Hull could only add to this the idea that secondary reinforcement might enter into the picture to delay extinction.

[8] Upton (1929) and Wever (1930) were among the first American psychologists to study classical aversive conditioning; they used it to test animals' sensory sensitivity. They paired a tone with shock in the classical fashion; and then, with tones that were very high or low, or loud or soft, tested animals' limits of hearing. It is of some interest that even in these first studies with the procedure, both Upton and Wever emphasized that the conditioned respiratory reaction was an unusual sort of "fluttering" response which bore no resemblance to the initial unconditioned reaction to shock, a sharp inspiration of air. Thus, right from the beginning of research on conditioning in this country it was apparent that it involves not just the substitution of stimuli but also a replacement of the response.

Hilgard and Marquis (1940) have noted that there was roughly a decade from about 1916, when Watson first promoted conditioning, to at least 1926, during which conditioning was accepted as a valid explanatory device and, sometimes even proposed as the basis for all learning. All this time there was virtually no empirical support for the claims made for conditioning.

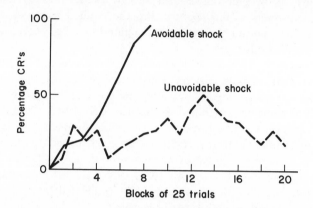

Fig. 11-2. Avoidance learning compared with classical aversive learning. Note that the performance of the avoidance animals is given in a Vincent learning curve. (From Brogden, Lipman, & Culler, 1938)

to cope either with the failure of the unavoidable animals to learn, or the fact that avoidable animals did learn. Brogden et al. suggest that it is the nonoccurrence of the shock which reinforces the animal. While this appears to be empirically true, it presents a further dilemma: how can the nonoccurrence of any stimulus constitute reinforcement? The Brogden et al. results seemed not only to exclude a classical Pavlovian conditioning explanation but to demand some sort of cognitive explanation of avoidance learning. The only way in which the nonoccurrence of a stimulus could be reinforcing would be if the organism anticipated or expected the stimulus and realized some sort of reinforcing relief when it fails to appear.

Mowrer (1938) arrived quite independently of Brogden et al. at a similar position. Mowrer was working with the GSR (because it is not under voluntary control, as had generally been the case with earlier studies of aversive conditioning). He found that when the conditioned GSR had been well established it could be instantly abolished by the simple procedure of removing the shock electrodes from the subject's finger. Mowrer also emphasized the fact that the GSR appeared to increase while the CS (a light) was on and to drop when the US (a shock) finally came on. Even though the shock was brief, it might have been expected to produce a persistent reverberatory reaction, but this was not the case. The subjects reacted as though (and their verbal report gave some confirmation) the light flash bothered or disturbed or worried them, and that it was almost with a sense of relief that they experienced the shock. Therefore, Mowrer concluded that, although the conditioned reaction may be historically traced to the experience of shock, it does not continue to be motivated by it, but rather by the expectation or anticipation or preparation for the shock. We have a commonplace name for this phenomenon, Mowrer said, we call it fear or anxiety.

These two studies published in 1938, one by Brogden et al., and one by Mowrer, provided a critical point in the history of the problem because they presented data which seem quite beyond a Pavlovian interpretation. They seemed to require either some sort of cognitive account or an explanation in terms of some new theory of learning and motivation.

Some Alternative Accounts of Avoidance Learning. A quick review of the theories of learning extant in 1940 reveals that none of them could handle avoidance learning comfortably. Hilgard and Marquis (1940) suggested that Tolman's cognitive theory (1932) had some direct applicability, particularly to data like Mowrer's. But others (e.g., Osgood, 1950) have pointed out that the application is not really very direct. The vague syntax of Tolman's theory leaves one convinced that the rat probably can learn to avoid, but not at all clear as to how it does so.

Some writers have been unwilling to give up either classical conditioning or instrumental trial and error as valid forms of learning (e.g., Schlosberg, 1937; Hilgard & Marquis, 1940). But the proposed two-process account doesn't really solve the problem of avoidance conditioning, because the nonoccurrence of shock can't be a reinforcer in either Pavlov's or Thorndike's systems.

Guthrie's contiguity theory of learning would appear at first to be no better able to explain avoidance. Sheffield repeated the Brogden et al. experiment in 1948 and got the same overall pattern of results. But Sheffield obtained additional findings which seem to rescue the contiguity position. Sheffield analyzed the behavior of his animals to determine what they were doing at the onset of shock, i.e., whether they were running or engaged in some other behavior. He found that under the unavoidable-shock condition, if the animal had been running when the shock came on, it tended to stop running; and if it was standing still when the shock came on, it would start running. The effect of shock, therefore, was to change the animal's behavior from what it had been before. Sheffield found that under the avoidable-shock condition, where repeated running did occur, the probability of a successful avoidance run was *lower* after a successful avoidance than after the occurrence of a failure to run. Hence, it cannot be said that it is the nonoccurrence of shock which reinforces avoidance, because in the absence of shock the avoiding response does extinguish. The superior learning of the avoidance animals is therefore some sort of statistical artifact. The truth of the matter is, Sheffield says, that learning to run occurs in one trial and will persist as long as it is not interfered with or punished by shock on a subsequent trial.[9] These findings lend considerable support to Guthrie's learning theory.

Although Hull said almost nothing about the problem in 1943, his collaborators at Yale had already begun to indicate how avoidance could be handled. Fear is an acquired drive. We have seen above how fear could be conceived as a conditionable response, and it had stimulus consequences which might be assumed to be intense enough to constitute a drive condition. It is presumably fear that energizes behavior in the avoidance situation and gives the avoidance response such a short latency when the CS appears. And it is presumably the reduction in fear that reinforces the avoidance response. The acquired-drive account of avoidance was concise, neat, compatible with the phenomena of appetitive motivation, and was supported by a number of systematic experimental findings. Miller could paint a quite convincing picture of fear and avoidance in 1951.

But there was trouble already. Mowrer had defected from the drive theorists' camp in 1947. Solomon and Wynne (1950, 1953) were making some startling discoveries about the extinction of avoidance; for example, the cycles in performance that were supposed to be there were not there. Schoenfeld (1950) was suggesting some new and powerful explanatory schemes to account for avoidance without invoking drive. Let us consider these developments.

Two-Factor Theory of Avoidance Learning.　In 1947 Mowrer abandoned the proposition he had done so much to promote, that drive reduction is the universal basis of reinforcement.[10] He gave a long list of reasons (which was lengthened further in 1950) why the proposition was untenable. What the reasons come to is that fear is basically a reaction of the autonomic nervous system so it might be expected to follow differ-

---

[9] It is possible, at least in principle, to explain avoidance entirely as a punishment phenomenon: The avoidance response gains in apparent strength as all other responses that occur in the situation are weakened by the punishing effects of shock. Subsequently, Schoenfeld (1950) and Sidman (1953) have entertained this possibility.

[10] There might, justifiably, be some doubt about just what Mowrer's position is. He has shifted his position so often and so far. He started in 1938 with what amounted to a cognitive or expectancy type of theory, but one which emphasized the motivational properties of tension and of the reinforcing effects of tension reduction. In 1939 and 1940 Mowrer emphasized the drive-reducing effect of fear reduction. In this he was in league with Hull, Miller, Brown, and the other pioneers of drive theory. He maintained this position until 1947 when he gave up the universal drive-reduction doctrine in favor of the two-factor position we are considering here. Subsequently (1956) Mowrer has split completely from drive theory and moved to the position which we will describe elsewhere as an incentive theory. In his latest formulation (1960), Mowrer attributes the learning of emotions to both drive reduction and induction, and denies that instrumental behavior requires reinforcement. We will discover that he has come almost full circle back to a cognitive position.

ent rules from those that apply to the skeletal motor system. Mowrer proposed that the drive-reduction theory of reinforcement only applied to the skeletal system, and that fear and other emotional reactions were acquired in accordance with the principles of classical conditioning, i.e., purely on the basis of contiguity. There are, he said, two kinds of learning for the two kinds of motor systems. In the avoidance situation both occur. First, the fear reaction becomes classically conditioned to the CS; and then, fear being a drive, whatever instrumental-avoidance response reduces the fear will be reinforced by the drive reduction it produces.

The point of departure for Mowrer's two-factor theory is that the acquisition of fear should be reinforced by the onset of the US rather than by its termination. A crucial experiment ought to be possible, one where learning when the CS is paired with the onset of shock is compared with learning when the CS is paired with the termination of shock. Barlow (1952), making use of this design, studied acquired drive under conditions where the US was always 10 sec., the CS 5 sec., and the time relationship between the two was varied between groups. For one group the CS terminated at the onset of shock; for a second group the CS terminated with the shock; and a third group, a backward conditioning group, was presented with the CS after the shock had terminated. Control groups received either the shock alone or the CS alone and so provided some control for the possibility of pseudoconditioning. After a single pairing of CS and US animals were tested in a situation where contacting a bar would turn on or off the CS. It was found that the group that had had the light paired with the onset of shock showed the strongest tendency to turn off the light.[11] Davitz (1955) ran two groups of rats with a 2-sec. CS starting either 1 sec. before shock onset or 1 sec. before shock termination. Again, the results indicated that shock onset rather than termination was effective. Mowrer and Suter (1950) and Traum and Horton (1950) have reported similar findings.

Alternatively, it ought to be possible to vary the duration of shock while maintaining a constant temporal relationship between it and the CS. Bitterman et al. (1952) varied the duration of the shocks in (classical) conditioning of the human GSR, while maintaining a constant interval between CS and US onset, and found no difference. This result led Bitterman et al. to conclude that shock onset rather than termination reinforced the GSR (and presumably the whole fear reaction).

The same relatively greater importance of shock onset has been found in yet another situation. Mowrer and Solomon (1954) trained rats to press a bar for food, and then investigated the strength of this behavior when a stimulus was presented which had been previously paired with

[11] The extra control groups in Barlow's study establish a zero reinforcement base line which reveals what may be an acquired positive reinforcement effect for stimuli associated with shock termination (see below, p. 390).

shock. The experimental groups were defined by the conditions under which the CS and the US were paired; the US was either short or long and was terminated either suddenly or gradually. It should be assumed from the Hull-Miller drive-reduction theory of reinforcement that the acquisition of fear would be poorer with a long shock (because of the delay of reinforcement), or with a gradually terminated shock (because of the relative ineffectiveness of the subsequent drive reduction). The CS always terminated with the onset of shock. After CS-US pairing, Mowrer and Solomon presented the CS alone in a different situation to observe its effect on bar pressing for food. No differences between groups were found. Mowrer and Solomon argued that, since the CS had been presented under the same conditions relative to the onset of shock, shock onset must be the critical factor in the acquisition of fear. Mowrer and Aiken (1954) introduced further variation in the fear-acquisition conditions by presenting the short CS at different points, before, during, or after a long US. Later, the different groups were presented with the CS to see the relative depressing effects upon bar pressing for food. Here differences were again found in the direction predicted by Mowrer.

Miller has admitted, speaking in behalf of the hypothesis that fear is learned by the termination of shock: "This seems to be a direct contradiction of all that is reasonable. . . . I agree that this application of the principle of drive reduction goes against common sense; I feel uncomfortable every time I am forced to make it." But he goes on to point out: "Once in a great while, however, when common sense is tested, it proves to be wrong . . ." (Miller, 1951a, p. 375).

Elsewhere, Miller (1951) has suggested two possible artifacts that would make the onset of shock appear to be the crucial event in reinforcement even if this were not really the case. One involves the well-known physiological fact that there is apt to be a rapid adaptation at the sensory surface from any strong stimulus, so that when shock is first presented it may produce extreme stimulation (and hence a high drive level) which is immediately followed by rapid diminution in stimulation (and drive) which reinforces whatever behavior occurs at shock onset. The second involves the fact that a temporary drive reduction will occur when the animal jumps into the air, or in any other way temporarily minimizes the current flow through its body.

The difficulty here, as throughout the drive theorist's account of avoidance learning, is the technical one of finding some index of the strength of drive that is independent of the instrumental behavior that the drive is invoked to explain. But even if Miller is right, we are still required to explain data such as Mowrer and Solomon's and Mowrer and Aiken's by considering the onset of shock to be the functionally effective factor.

Miller's hypotheses should not be dismissed out of hand, however.

Their value lies not just in that they rescue the drive-reduction theory of reinforcement but also in the fact that they call attention to an extremely important methodological consideration, namely, that learning may well take place during the presentation of the US. It is certainly the case that behavior changes during the session when repeated shocks are given. We have noted (in Chapter 7) that if the animal is given any opportunity to gain a relative advantage by engaging in some sort of behavior such as jumping or clinging tightly to the shock grid this behavior will quickly become acquired.[12] But even when short bursts of electricity are given and even when extreme precaution is taken to minimize the animal's opportunity to reduce the shock intensity, alterations in behavior during the course of shock are characteristically observed. We do not know whether these changes can be attributed to the gradual addition of fear to the pain component of motivation, whether they reflect learning which occurs because of some reinforcement mechanism such as Miller has suggested, or whether behavior changes just because one response after another becomes punished by occurring in the presence of shock.

But the situation here is much as it was in the case of appetitive learning: if we are to understand the changes in behavior that occur because of a learning trial, then we have to determine what goes on during the trial. Most cases of anomalous experimental findings can probably be attributed to a failure to make this analysis. For example, MacDonald (1946) has reported that avoidance learning is seriously impaired if the US is presented a number of times prior to CS-US pairing. The animals appear to suffer a motivational loss. On the other hand, there are data (Bolles, unpublished) to indicate that a weak shock, one which initially elicits no appreciable reaction, may with repeated presentations come to be highly aversive. Here we find an apparent gain in motivation through repeated presentations of a shock (see also Kurtz & Pearl, 1960). We may assume that in the absence of intentional reinforcement some unauthorized response becomes learned with repeated shock and interferes with the criterion response in the one case, and facilitates it in the other.

The Partial Irreversibility of Fear. A number of writers have noted that avoidance behavior is sometimes extremely resistant to extinction (e.g., Mowrer, 1950; Miller, 1951; Gantt, 1953). Solomon and his students have, however, promoted this fact into a major crisis for drive theory.

Solomon and Wynne (1953) and Solomon et al. (1953) found that dogs after only a few extremely intense shocks would learn an avoidance response (jumping a hurdle within 10 sec. after the CS) and that after

---

[12] Dinsmoor has aptly called such unintentionally reinforced responses "unauthorized responses."

the avoidance had been acquired it was well-nigh impossible to extinguish. Some dogs ran as many as 650 trials before the experimenters extinguished. The learning curve for a typical animal is shown in Fig. 11-3. Note that after 7 escape responses (jumps with latencies longer than 10 sec.) there is a sharp transition from escape to avoidance. This is to

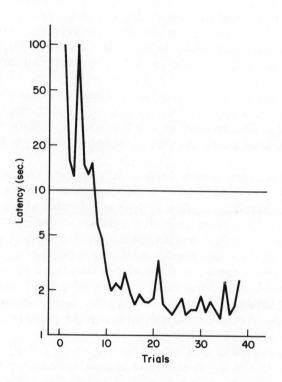

Fig. 11-3. Acquisition of avoidance for a "fairly typical" subject. (From Solomon & Wynne, 1953)

say that after the escape response has stabilized for a few trials about 5 sec. after the shock, it suddenly moves forward so that it occurs several seconds before the shock. Solomon's dogs frequently received no more shocks after the first avoidance. There is no indication here of the cyclicity of performance which we should expect from the drive-reduction hypothesis of fear acquisition. The avoidance response appears suddenly and performance continues to improve for 200 trials or more in the absence of primary reinforcement.

Solomon and Wynne report several other rather puzzling observations. Occasionally a relatively long latency response (approaching 10 sec.) would occur. These were typically followed by much shorter latency avoidances on subsequent trials rather than continued deterioration of avoidance behavior. It is as if the animal had no inclination at all to test reality, but on those occasions where it almost did so by approaching the 10-sec. limit it reenhanced its fear. Another curious observation was that when avoidance behavior became well established it had a latency in the order of 1 or 2 sec., which is so short that the autonomic nervous system can hardly do more than begin reacting to the CS (see Champion, 1964). There can be little or no feedback from the autonomic system (i.e., fear) so soon. In fact, it appears that it is on the trials on which the animal for some reason makes a long latency avoidance that the autonomic symptoms of fear (shivering, defecation, etc.) are observed. Thus, it would seem that when the avoidance response is well established, it not only prevents shock but also to a considerable degree prevents the fear which is supposed to motivate the behavior and maintain the behavior by its reduction.

These phenomena pose a vexing set of facts to be explained. Solomon's own explanation involves several assumptions. First, there are the assumptions that fear becomes conditioned during the trials on which the shock is given, and that fear exists and motivates the avoidance response early in the avoidance phase of learning. The great dilemma of avoidance performance, i.e., the relative failure of the fear to extinguish, is explained by Solomon by means of the principle of "anxiety conservation." The general notion is that the latency of the well-learned response (1 or 2 sec.) is indeed too short to permit fear to occur; it is too short for the autonomic nervous system to react to the CS. Fear does not extinguish because it is protected by the avoidance response. The reason the avoidance response does not extinguish is because as soon as it starts to do so the fear reaction is given time to be reinstated and this gives an extra boost to the avoidance habit to improve performance on subsequent trials. The scheme is that the behavior borrows drive to build habit.[13]

Solomon admits that even with the conservation principle the behavior should ultimately extinguish. Perhaps it does. But the quantitative

[13] Here we have a new dilemma. The old dilemma was that if a rat runs (thereby avoiding shock) he must be doing it to relieve fear. But then, why is he fearful? Solomon's findings suggest that the animal runs essentially to prevent fear. The new dilemma then is that if the rat isn't frightened, why does it run? Eglash (1952) has expressed the problem concisely. He observes that we have invoked an acquired drive to explain autonomous behavior, but now we have to explain an autonomous drive. We are essentially where Mowrer was in 1938, and where Freud was in 1926, i.e., still trying to account for the self-defeating and self-perpetuating behavior that arises from fear.

relationships here seem to be wrong; extinction is too slow. Moreover, if short latency responding prevents fear from occurring, then what motivates (i.e., energizes) the response? To get out of this difficulty Solomon and Wynne (1954) proposed that fears are strange reactions which just do not extinguish quickly like other classically conditioned responses such as salivation. Solomon has suggested that this whole analysis may only apply in the case of an extremely intense, i.e., traumatic, US. More moderate intensities might change the whole situation. Brush (1957) has subsequently reported, however, that partial irreversibility is also found with far weaker shocks than Solomon and his students usually use. Thus, it seems likely that if Solomon's results are a departure from those usually reported, it is not because of the shock intensity used, but the species of the animal.

It has been suggested by a number of writers (including Sheffield & Temmer, 1950; Logan, 1951; Jones, 1953) that the relatively great resistance to extinction of avoidance behavior results from partial reinforcement during acquisition. This argument may be valid in some cases but it is clearly inapplicable in a case like that illustrated in Fig. 11-3.

Subsequently, Solomon and his students have focused their attention upon the locus of the fear reaction and the relationships between fear learning and instrumental learning in the avoidance situation (Black et al., 1962). Wynne and Solomon (1955), for example, have found that sectioning the autonomic nervous system *after* avoidance training produced relatively little effect upon subsequent extinction. This helped to confirm their view that the full-blown occurrence of fear is not an essential part of the successful maintenance of avoidance. On the other hand, sectioning of the autonomic nervous system *before* training impaired learning somewhat and produced marked decrements in the resistance to extinction of the avoidance response. Bersh et al. (1956) have found that during avoidance conditioning of human subjects the cardiac response (acceleration) does extinguish, especially when avoidance is effectively brought under discriminative control (see also Kamin et al., 1963; Kimmel, 1963).

Alternatives to Drive-Theoretical Explanations of Avoidance Learning. At a time when the acquired-drive explanation of avoidance learning seemed most promising it was attacked by Schoenfeld (1950) in what is surely one of psychology's classical polemical pieces. In the best tradition of the polemicist, Schoenfeld flailed out not only at real live adversaries but at a few straw men as well. For example, he insisted that avoidance learning cannot be attributed to the nonoccurrence of shock and he indicated that Mowrer, for one, held this view. Nor, he says, can shock termination be the reinforcing agent, because, there is no way that the response which is instrumental in escaping shock can "move forward" in time so as to precede the shock without passing through a phase where it would be more or less simultaneous with shock and therefore punished. Mowrer was also singled out for attack for holding this position when, in fact, the whole point of the acquired-drive position was to provide an alternative to that which Schoenfeld was attacking.[14]

Even so, the point is well made that whatever reinforces the avoidance response cannot have more than a historical connection with the shock. The avoidance response is only incidentally, or functionally, an avoidance. It is really an escape from some other set of stimulus conditions. On this Schoenfeld is in complete agreement with the drive theorist. The remaining question is what is the nature of the stimuli the escape from which constitutes reinforcement for the avoidance response? The question for the drive theorist is whether they have all the necessary properties of a drive condition. Perhaps, Schoenfeld suggests, they have only the power of reinforcement by their reduction or termination.[15]

Here Schoenfeld offers a positive contribution by proposing a clear alternative to the acquired-drive explanation of avoidance learning. He maintains, as Skinner (1938) had earlier, that by being paired with a reinforcing stimulus (either positive or negative) a neutral stimulus would come in time to have reinforcing properties of its own (either positive or negative). By pairing a tone with a shock, the tone acquires some of the negative reinforcing power of the shock; it becomes a conditioned negative reinforcer; and the animal will learn whatever response is instrumental in terminating it, just as it would learn any response that would be instrumental in terminating the shock. And that, Schoenfeld assures us, is all there is to the explanation of avoidance learning. There is no need to invoke drives, fears, drive reductions, and all the rest.

In one sense, the distinction between Schoenfeld's analysis and the drive theorist's analysis is mainly semantic. Schoenfeld appears only to

---

[14] In 1942 Mowrer and Lamoreaux did maintain that shock-termination provided the reinforcement for the response to move forward. They attributed the appearance of the instrumental response during the tone-shock interval to "parasitic" reinforcement. But by 1947 Mowrer had adopted the position that it was the termination of fear conditioned to the tone the reduction of which reinforced intertrial responding. He argued (Coppock & Mowrer, 1947) that the occurrence of the instrumental responses, insofar as its occurrence was possible, spontaneously in the intertrial interval, evidenced that the response was motivated by fear. He assumed, moreover, that it should be reinforced by the resultant reduction in the fear it produces. To test this, two groups of animals were given avoidance training, one of which was permitted to make intertrial responses (touching a bar) and the other was not. As predicted, the group that was given the opportunity to make intertrial responses learned the avoidance response faster than the controls.

[15] Another important question concerns the locus of the controlling stimuli. We usually assume that these stimuli arise from the autonomic nervous system, but Schoenfeld points out that they might also come from the animal's own proprioceptive feedback. Thus, engaging in certain kinds of behavior might be aversive.

have thrown out the word drive and emphasized the word reinforcement in his explanation of the phenomenon. In this connection he says:

> Discussions of escape . . . have, like those of anxiety, been complicated by the introduction of extraneous concepts. . . . Thus, it has variously been held that "fear" is conditioned to [the CS], that "fear" is a drive as well as an "emotion," that the escape is from the "fear" induced by [the CS], and so on. At times, fear is spoken of as a response, a drive, a stimulus, and an emotion within one, or a few adjacent, sentences. The multiplication of assumptions and intervening variables is not at all helpful when they are not specified clearly enough for us to test their utility. For example, the properties of fear are not specified; we cannot tell whether the same fear arises from varieties of [US], and there seems to be no way of testing whether a response "escapes from, or reduces fear" as opposed to escape from [the CS] as operationally used and measured. Actually, the experimental observations are describable in terms of concrete operations, and are capable of statement in summarizing principles such as the following: if the occurrence of an operant response is followed by the removal or reduction of a stimulus associated in the past with a noxious stimulus, the strength of the response will increase. (Schoenfeld, 1950, p. 82)

Schoenfeld would by no means deny that the rat that has been shocked may be in a state of fear, or may even be suffering an emotion. His attack is directed at the a priori assumption that fear, by being a drive, motivates, and the circular argument that fear reduction reinforces the instrumental response. Drive as inferred from the behavior occurring in the avoidance situation has quite a different set of functional properties than drive defined by, say, food deprivation. The only evidence of any drive in the avoidance situation is that learning occurs there. Does fear (or electric shock for that matter) increase the general level of activity? The answer is clearly no, although the alibi would be that both shock and fear have an unconditioned reaction, viz., freezing, which competes with all other behavior. No one has seriously urged that the escape response is a variety of consummatory behavior. No one has even shown that the acquired drive "energizes" the instrumental response, in the strict sense. No one seems to have concerned themselves with the question of whether hungry animals learn avoidance faster than satiated animals, which would demonstrate something akin to a generalized-drive effect.

In short, the whole elaborate structure of theoretical relationships that has been proposed to validate the drive concept does not seem applicable to the case of avoidance learning; there is little hint of transituational or other kinds of validating evidence that fear as an acquired drive has the syntactical properties that drives are supposed to have. The only justification, in the last analysis, for calling fear an acquired drive is the drive theorist's conviction that because learning occurs in the avoidance situation, drive reduction must occur there.

We will have occasion to discuss Schoenfeld's paper again in another context, but we must stop our consideration of avoidance at this point in order to bid adieu to the drive concept.

A FINAL WORD ON THE DRIVE CONCEPT

The same troubles have plagued us in the area of acquired drives that bothered us in the area of the primary drives. The attempt to find supporting evidence has led us to an understanding of behavior which cannot be improved by talking about drives (or D). Wherever we investigate motivated behavior, its associative determinants, i.e., the stimuli and reinforcements that give it structure, loom ever more important, while the role played by drive becomes ever less clear.

The first chapters of our survey of the data on drive indicate that what Hull proposed for drive in general had only been demonstrated for hunger. There is a further limitation, however, in that not all of what Hull proposed for drive is valid even for hunger. Indeed, about all we can say with assurance is that the rat's hunger-produced weight loss is directly related to the strength of its eating behavior and of the instrumental behavior upon which eating is contingent. As soon as the contingencies between behavior and reinforcement are removed, the evidence for any kind of motivational effects begins to collapse. It is true that the hungry rat explores and runs in activity wheels more than non-hungry rats, but this seems more parsimoniously explained in terms of specific connections between hunger and these kinds of behavior. In other areas, we have failed to find that D and H are independent, that the stimulus concomitants of drive have any real existence, that drive reduction constitutes reinforcement, that different sources of drive are motivationally equivalent, or that there are consistent individual differences in drive strength. The different sources of drive seem to be marked more by their different effects than by their common properties, and even in the case of hunger, which conforms best with the theoretical requirements, its effects suggest that it is more like a source of incentive than a source of drive. However, the worst failure of the drive concept continues to be that it does not help us to explain behavior.

We can find some semblance of acquired aversive drives, but, again, having found them, we discover that we cannot explain behavior very well with them.

The drive concept is like an old man that has had a long, active, and, yes, even useful life. It has produced a notable amount of conceptual and empirical work; it has, perhaps indirectly, made a great contribution to our understanding of behavior. But the fruitful days are nearly gone. The time has come when younger, more vigorous, more capable concepts must take over. So, as sentimental as we may feel about our old friend, we should not despair at his passing.

12

INCENTIVE THEORIES

OF MOTIVATION

❖《

Increase in response strength does not necessarily mean increase in strength of S-R connections; it may mean simply that when a situation is repeated the response is more likely to occur. As we shall see, there are other ways than learning by which the probability of a response may be increased.

J. P. SEWARD

An incentive theory is one which emphasizes that organisms can in some sense anticipate reinforcement, and that such an anticipation serves in some way to facilitate instrumental behavior. According to some writers (e.g., Brown, 1961) anticipation of reinforcement is merely a learned source of drive which adds to the antecedent sources of drive, such as deprivation, to increase the total effective drive strength. Other theorists (e.g., Spence, 1956) separate the two and consider drive and incentive to be parallel and supplementary sources of total motivation. A few theorists (e.g., Mowrer, 1960) put the entire explanatory burden on incentive factors, leaving drive with virtually no part in the motivation of behavior. Thus, it is possible to conceive of incentive as a component of drive, as parallel to drive, or as replacing drive.[1]

[1] "Incentive" means various things. Sometimes it is used operationally to

The incentive concept shares with the drive concept some of its logical and philosophical background. Just as the concept of drive arises from the notion that there are conditions which impel an organism to some sort of action, so the concept of incentive arises from the notion that there are objects in the environment to which the organism is attracted. Drives push and incentives pull; the two complement each other in providing a motivational explanation of behavior. The question is how much of motivation is push and how much is pull.

There are important points of differences between drives and incentives so that the two concepts are not interchangeable. One difference arises from the distinction between primary and secondary (i.e., between unlearned and learned) sources of motivation; the organism is presumed to come into the test situation with some innate drives but it has to learn about incentives. A second difference is that drives pertain to the momentary state of the organism whereas incentives have explicit reference to its history of reinforcement. A third point of difference is that the concept of drive usually implies something other than a stimulus whereas, as we shall see, modern treatments of the incentive concept are rapidly moving in the direction of providing an associative account of behavior. The best claim that can be made for drives is that they energize behavior; if that claim cannot be maintained, then there is no reason for retaining any form of the drive concept. By contrast, incentive theory is just as viable without a hypothesized energizing function as with one. Incentive theory, therefore, permits us to explain the apparent energization of behavior without postulating a fundamental motivational *process* of energization. And having seen in the preceding chapters that the energization effect is only really evident in that behavior upon which reinforcement is contingent, i.e., in instrumental and consummatory behavior, it should perhaps not be surprising to find that the apparent energization of these kinds of behavior can be better explained in terms of the conditions of reinforcement than it can in terms of deprivation conditions.

Incentive theories of motivation have developed partly from theoretical considerations and partly from empirical studies of the effects of the conditions of reinforcement upon behavior. We will begin with a brief outline of hypothetical incentive mechanisms, then survey some of the research on the conditions of reinforcement, and conclude with a further analysis of some theoretical possibilities.

---

refer to certain procedures, namely, the conditions of reinforcement. Thus a fixed quantity and quality of food is an incentive. But sometimes incentive appears to be a property of the animal. Thus, after the first trial, when the animal can anticipate food, it has an incentive. I will tend to use "reinforcement" for the procedure and consider incentive as a theoretical construct, the defining functional properties of which are not yet quite established.

SOME EARLY STUDIES AND INTERPRETATIONS

Systematic investigation of incentive began nearly as early as work on the drive concept. Richter reported his "behavioristic study of drive" in 1922 and just two years later Simmons reported a study of the "Relative effectiveness of certain incentives." (Simmons found, among other things, that rats would not perform as well in a maze when they were rewarded with sunflower seeds as when they were rewarded with their usual fare, which was bread and milk!) Thus, almost at the outset of research on motivation it was evident that the nature of the reinforcer is an important consideration.

Tolman (1932) has summarized a number of studies done in the late 1920s, many of them under his direction, which vividly demonstrated the importance of incentive factors in animal performance. For example, Elliott (1928) demonstrated that when animals were shifted from a less-preferred to a more-preferred reinforcer, their maze performance improved; and when they were shifted to a less-preferred reinforcer, their performance worsened. The change in performance in both cases was immediate. When the improvement in performance arises from a shift from no reinforcement to some reinforcement, we have the basis of the latent learning phenomenon (Blodgett, 1929). Tinklepaugh (1928) showed that when monkeys were shifted from a highly preferred to a less-preferred reinforcer they became quite disrupted and disturbed. Elliott (1929) also demonstrated that a complete shift in reinforcement—from water to food—failed to disrupt behavior seriously if the animal's drive condition was shifted appropriately—from thirst to hunger. Tolman concluded from these and related studies that performance is determined in large part by the expectation of reward. Tolman treated drive and incentive variables more or less equivalently and afforded them more or less equal importance. He assumed that they operate jointly so that the animal's physiological state plus its expectation of a particular goal object combine to determine the "demand for" a particular goal object.

In succeeding years Tolman reaffirmed this position, but he was unable to extend it, and in particular he was unable or unwilling to specify how such expectancies and demands were acquired; they just were. Two things were needed to advance incentive theory: (1) some explicit rules regarding how an organism's expectancies become established, and (2) some explicit rules regarding how the expectancy of a particular incentive affects behavior.

As early as 1930, Hull had offered a program to deal with both of these sets of problems; but little was done for the next 15 or 20 years to follow up his suggestions. Hull's early formulation, we we saw in Chapter 6, involved the hypothesis that when the consummatory response (R_G) occurs in the goal box it tends to become conditioned to all of the stimuli present there. Then, when stimuli are present which are similar to those in the goal box, e.g., those in the start box, some compatible fraction of the goal response (r_G) will be elicited which anticipates the final goal response. In 1930 Hull proposed that the way this affects behavior is that r_G has proprioceptive consequences (s_G) which enter associatively into the determination of behavior. And, Hull supposed, it is this persistent core of stimulations (s_G) which explains in S-R terms that the animal knows there is food in the goal box. How does this mechanism operate? According to the laws of classical conditioning, Hull assured us.

In 1943 when Hull became a reinforcement theorist, he incorporated the r_G-s_G mechanism into the new theory. When reinforcement occurs, the quality, quantity, and delay of the reinforcing agent are assumed to determine the amount of reinforcement that occurs, and hence the growth of habit strength. Accordingly, Hull inserted terms into his equations for habit strength involving the amount and delay of reinforcement. It is interesting to note that Hull spoke of incentive factors as motivational, but to the extent that he treated the incentive concept at all in 1943 he handled it as a factor affecting habit.

Crespi's Study. Crespi (1942, 1944) was quick to point out that this was a mistake; incentive variables should be motivational in character rather than registering permanently upon the organism's habit structure. Crespi ran different groups of rats in a straight alley to large or small quantities of food and found that the large-amount animals performed better than those receiving a small amount of food. So far there is nothing here to force a choice between Hull's habit interpretation and Crespi's motivational interpretation. But Crespi switched half of each group after 20 trials, from high to low or from low to high; performance changed rapidly to levels appropriate for the new incentive values. The shift in running time occurred more rapidly than could reasonably be attributed to changes in habit structure (see Fig. 12-1).

The main features of Crespi's study have been replicated by Zeaman (1949) and Metzger et al. (1957), so that this pattern of results seems well established both for latency and running speed. Notice that the different amounts of reinforcement affect the asymptote of performance but not the rate at which the asymptote is approached. Notice too the speed with which the animals' performance changes with the change in incentive, within one or two trials. And finally, note that after the shift the animals' performance settles down to a value which corresponds to the performance that might have been expected from animals that had not

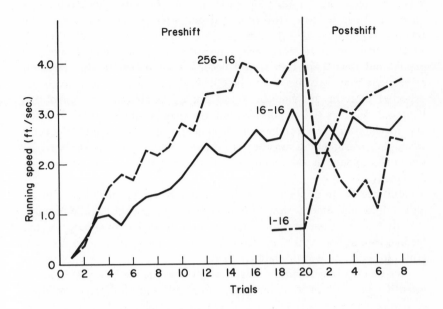

Fig. 12-1. Speed of running in a long runway as a function of amount of rein-forcement. For the first 19 trials different groups were given 1, 16, or 256 pellets of food (acquisition data for the 1-pellet group are not presented); from trial 20 on subjects all were given 16 pellets. (Adapted from Crespi, 1942)

been shifted. That is, there are no carry-over effects.[2] All of these consid-erations suggest the operation of a motivational factor which multiplies the habit strength of the running response.

Hull's Incentive Theory. Hull's reaction to these findings (1952) was to introduce a new motivational construct, K, which altered the old D × H equation to read K × D × H. In this formulation, K was postu-lated to be a function of the size or vigor of the consummatory response, R_G, which may be assumed to depend upon the amount and quality of reinforcement. Hull also incorporated into this formulation other incen-tive mechanisms, one to account for the effects of delayed-reinforcement situations in which the animal makes other responses during the delay period, as, for example, when it is running through a chain of responses, and a second mechanism for situations in which no other behavior inter-

[2] Fig. 12-1 shows that animals shifted upward to 16 pellets perform better than animals kept at 16 pellets. Crespi (1942) called this the *elation* effect, and attributed it to a sort of emotional contrast. There is a corresponding *depression* effect for animals shifted downward. The former incentive-contrast effect has only rarely been replicated while the latter has been found occasionally. Both have proven extremely difficult to study systematically.

venes between the response in question and the subsequent reinforcement. In the latter case Hull proposed that whatever stimuli exist at the time the organism makes the instrumental response, traces of those stimuli could persist until reinforcement (provided that the delay is not too great) and that there they would become conditioned to R_G. Then on subsequent trials r_G will tend to be elicited by those stimuli. It might be expected that this mechanism would not be as effective in bridging a temporal delay as the secondary reinforcement possibility implied in the first mechanism. The common environmental stimulus elements present when the instrumental response is initiated and when it is replaced by the next response in the chain permits the operation of secondary reinforcement.

Hull merely multiplied these three different factors together with D, although he had at that time little evidence to support either the assumption that all of these incentive factors were indeed motivational or the further assumption that they combined multiplicatively. As we will see, Hull's formulation was probably premature.

Let us turn our attention now from the speculative interpretations of incentive and look at some of the research indicating how the conditions of reinforcement affect behavior. There are several questions that should be kept in mind as we survey this literature. One is whether the effects of variation in incentive conditions appear to be motivational or whether they involve habit formation. We can judge this on the basis of the speed of shift, the lack of interaction between acquisition and extinction performance, and, in general, all of the criteria we used in assessing the independence of D and H. We may look also for similarities and differences between the effects of delay of reinforcement and the effects of the amount of reinforcement. And finally we may note the crucial importance in all of this research of the learning task: large, easily verifiable incentive effects in one situation may be difficult or impossible to get in a different situation.

The anticipatory goal response is the only serious proposal that has been made for a mechanism to account for incentive motivation, so hopefully we will discover in the research on incentive motivation what the behavioral properties of this mechanism have to be.

DELAY OF REINFORCEMENT

Decremental Effects. It has been found almost universally that instrumental behavior suffers a decrement when there is a delay of reinforcement. Effects have been observed in a Columbia obstruction box (Hamilton, 1929), where there are fewer grid crossings. Delays also lead to decrements in problem boxes (Roberts, 1930), in various kinds of bar-pressing apparatus (Perin, 1943; Logan, 1952; Ramond, 1954a; Harker, 1956), in different sorts of mazes (Warden & Haas, 1927; Hamilton, 1929; Muenzinger & Fletcher, 1937; Gilhousen, 1938; Cooper, 1938; Brown et al., 1948; Fehrer, 1956a; Pubols, 1962), and in straight runways (Peterson, 1956; Holder et al., 1957; Wike & McNamara, 1957; Logan, 1960; Wist, 1962). The effect has been found mostly with hunger, but also with thirst (Fehrer, 1956a) and escape from shock (Fowler & Trapold, 1962).

It would be convenient if all these studies demonstrated the same quantitative relationship, or if one study could be selected from the rest as showing the delay effect in its simplest or most universal form. Unfortunately this is not possible, partly because the psychometric problem remains unsolved, and partly because of the fact that in any study of delayed reinforcement there must almost of necessity be some opportunity for the operation of secondary reinforcement. To the extent that the stimuli eliciting the instrumental response bear any resemblance to those present in the goal box at the time of reinforcement, we may expect secondary reinforcing effects. Thus it is not surprising that in some of the older studies (e.g., Wolfe, 1934), appreciable performance was found with delays as long as 20 min. Perin (1943) and Perkins (1947) attempted to eliminate secondary reinforcement effects but were not able to do so, apparently—judging from the relatively substantial performance that was obtained with intervals as long as 1 min. Grice (1948) solved this problem, not by eliminating secondary reinforcers at the choice point but by making them uncorrelated with the response measure. Grice used a discrimination problem and studied acquisition of the discrimination as a function of the delay between presentation of the discriminanda and reinforcement. Under these conditions he got an extremely short gradient of delay (see Fig. 12-2).

Grice's evidence of the rat's limited ability to bridge a delay in the absence of secondary reinforcement and its much more substantial ability to do so in the presence of secondary reinforcers led Spence (1947) to argue that reinforcement must be immediate if it is to have any efficacy. All instances of learning with delayed primary reinforcement were thus to be construed as cases where the behavior was strengthened by the immediate occurrence of secondary reinforcement.

The secondary reinforcement hypothesis itself, briefly, is this: When the consummatory response occurs in the goal box it should become conditioned to all stimuli present there, most notably, it should become conditioned to environmental stimuli present in the goal box. Then the occurrence of such stimuli, or similar stimuli, anywhere in the apparatus should tend to elicit at least some fractional component of the consummatory response, r_G. As the animal encounters stimuli which more closely resemble goal box stimuli, r_G should occur with greater vigor which pro-

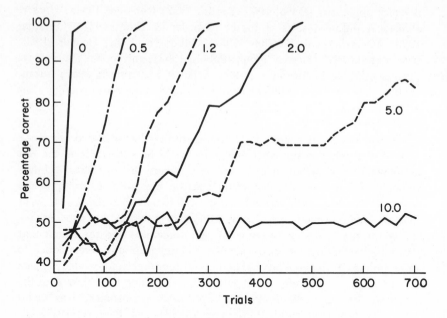

Fig. 12-2. Acquisition of a black-white discrimination as a function of the delay, in seconds, of primary reinforcement. (From Grice, 1948)

vides, first of all, a source of secondary reinforcement for the responses which lead to such stimuli, and in addition, a source of incentive motivation for whatever responses have been associated with these stimuli.[3]

Incremental Effects. Although decrements in performance are usually found with delayed reinforcement, the effect is not produced by a massive or generalized inhibition. In fact, it turns out that if the animal is delayed part way through a chain of behavior, e.g., in the middle of a runway, then only the portion of the run which precedes the delay is adversely affected (Brown et al., 1948; Gilhousen, 1938; Cooper, 1938; Holder et al., 1957; Wist, 1962). When one looks at the behavior which occurs after the delay, facilitory effects may be found (Amsel & Roussel, 1952; Holder et al., 1957), although sometimes no effect is reported (Wist, 1962, 1963). It may be important that Wist's experiments were run in an extremely well-insulated runway so that external cues were minimal and, consequently, so was the opportunity for the elicitation of r_G. We noted in Chapter 11 that the facilitory effect upon postdelay be-

[3] We will see shortly that all sorts of trouble result from the assumption that r_G plays a role both in incentive motivation and in secondary reinforcement because of the dual, and contradictory, functions thereby assigned to it. Renner (1963) gives a good review of the history of incentive theory, linking it up with Tolman's early work on the length of path to a goal and Hull's "goal gradient" hypothesis.

havior is cited by Amsel and others as evidence for a frustration-produced drive. But now we must note that Amsel cites the predelay slowing down as evidence of the introduction of competing responses in anticipation of frustration. These competing responses are assumed to be the consequence of a fractional anticipatory frustration reaction, r_F. Thus, Amsel invokes the drive-producing properties of frustration to account for facilitory effects and a negative incentive effect of frustration to account for decrements in performance.[4]

Another apparently verifiable finding with delayed reinforcement is that an instrumental response acquired under conditions of delay shows increased resistance to extinction (Crum et al., 1951; Fehrer, 1956a; Peterson, 1956; Sgro & Weinstock, 1963). This finding has also been used to argue for a competing-response interpretation. The basis of the argument is that the animal learns to run (because ultimately it is reinforced for doing so) in the presence of cues to nonreinforcement, so that in extinction the withdrawal of reinforcement merely reinstates learned cues for running (Weinstock, 1958).

Effects of Varying Delay. An important question relative to whether the delay effect is associative or motivational is how performance of animals changes when there is a sudden shift in the delay of reinforcement. Hamilton (1929) reported an immediate improvement in maze performance following elimination of a delay; but Harker (1956), using a barpress situation, found a very gradual shift requiring at least 15 trials when a delay was shifted from 10 sec. to 1 sec. Harker also reported that when the shift was in the other direction, from 1 sec. to 10 sec., there was no apparent worsening in bar-pressing behavior. More peculiar, too, for a motivational interpretation, is the fact that Harker's short-delay animals had approached very close to the apparent asymptote of performance by the 88th trial, whereas the long-delay group was still showing improvement; it seems likely from Harker's learning curves that all groups ultimately would reach the same asymptote.

Spence (1956) has offered what is essentially an associative explanation of Harker's findings based upon the incidental observation that animals under the 10-sec. delay condition seemed unable to wait at the food cup during the delay interval, whereas animals under shorter delays

---

[4] Amsel (1958) and Spence (1960) have suggested the following convenient notation: r_G for anticipatory consummatory response which is conditioned by eating or drinking (we might call it appetite), r_E for the anticipatory response conditioned by pain, or escape from pain (we could call it fear), and r_F for the anticipatory form of frustration presumably conditioned by removal from the frustrating situation (we might tentatively call it anger). We may note that the drive-reduction hypothesis looks no better in accounting for the reinforcement of anger than it does for fear. We may also wonder how many other anticipatory reactions there are. Is there one for each emotion we can name, or only for some set of "basic" emotions? Or are there just two, one positive and one negative?

could. Thus, the problem was evidently a more difficult one for the long-delay animals. We may think of the difficulty either in terms of uncontrolled variation in the response to be acquired, or we may think of it as a disruption in the chain of behavior bridging the gap between pressing the bar and obtaining reinforcement. Carlton (1954) attempted to test the hypothesis that the activity occurring in the goal box during the delay interval is a crucial variable in the effects of delayed reinforcement. He ran animals in a situation similar to Harker's but in which one group was tested in a very narrow apparatus to restrict the animal's behavior, while another group was tested in an open box where competing behavior could occur. The results (see Spence, 1956, p. 162) of restricting the animal's repertoire by confinement tended to confirm the competing-response prediction and indicated that when competing responses are controlled, the effect of delay is upon performance rather than learning (see also Brown et al., 1949).

One of the strange findings in this area has been reported by Cogan and Capaldi (1961). They ran two groups of subjects, one that was reinforced only on alternate trials and one that was delayed for 20 sec. on alternate trials. Performance both in acquisition and extinction showed that the animals learned to discriminate the alternation pattern when it involved being fed and not being fed (as Crum et al., 1951, had found) but they failed to discriminate the pattern when it involved being fed immediately and being fed with delay. Burt and Wike (1963) have replicated this finding for acquisition performance but not for extinction performance, and Capaldi and Cogan (1963) have found subsequently that rats can learn to discriminate an alternating pattern of amount of reinforcement. Such divergent patterns suggest that the different dimensions of reinforcement, amount, delay, withdrawal, and quality contribute to incentive motivation in different ways and through different mechanisms. Perhaps one dimension has its effect directly through the r_G mechanism and another indirectly through frustration or competing-behavior effect.

To return to the delay phenomenon, Pubols (1961) has reported that rats would learn a one-choice maze problem in which one side of the maze offered variable delayed feeding and the other side a constant mean value of delay. Pubols found that the animals would learn to go to the variable side. Logan et al. (1955) had previously found that rats ran faster in an alley when the delay of reinforcement was varied randomly between high and low amounts than did a group consistently fed at a delay equal to the mean delay. In fact, Logan et al. reported that performance was approximately equal under the variable condition and under the shortest delay condition. Such a finding could be explained in many ways; it could be interpreted as further evidence for a frustration-produced drive. In this connection it may be noted that the differential effects only show up after a number of trials (approximately 30, according to Logan et al., 1955). It has also been discovered that when more than one trial a day is run, the decremental effect of delay develops over the course of daily trials (Gilhousen, 1938; Holder et al., 1957). Evidence that this effect may not be due to frustration or an incentive factor is that it does not appear to be important where in a long runway the delay is imposed (Wist, 1962); nor, when delays are imposed in the goal box, do there seem to be any systematic differential effects upon the speed of running in different portions of a long runway (Logan, 1960).

We are left with a variety of explanatory devices to account for the fact that animals are able to bridge a temporal gap between the stimulus for a response and its subsequent reinforcement. Hull had proposed that stimulus traces decay more or less gradually with time and that learning is possible as long as these traces still have some strength at the time reinforcement occurs. There seems to be no direct evidence either for or against such a mechanism. Hull also suggested that learning would occur if the animal could fill the temporal gap with a chain of responses, either a heterogeneous chain (different responses) or a homogeneous chain (repetition of the same response, as in running a long alley). Ferster (1953) has argued that the occurrence of some intervening chain of behavior is a necessary condition for the maintenance of behavior with delayed reinforcement. It seems likely, however, that the critical factor here is that engaging in a series of responses presents the animal with a series of stimulus changes which serve to break up the interval into a set of shorter intervals. It is usually contended that each stimulus change is a source of secondary reinforcement which helps maintain the chain of behavior. Elegant support for such a mechanism was found by Grice (1948), as we noted on p. 337. In Grice's situation the response required after both the positive and the negative stimuli was the same, i.e., running; under these conditions, any delay greater than about 5 sec. made discrimination learning impossible. It looks, then, as though the learning of a delayed discrimination requires the presence of differential stimuli during the delay interval.

There are some confusing properties of these alleged secondary reinforcing stimuli, however. For example, Myers (1958a) and Lawrence and Hommel (1961) have found that once a delayed discrimination has been established in the presence of differential stimuli, the interval can be lengthened, or .the differential stimuli removed, without destroying the discrimination. Moreover, Renner (1963) has reported that while the presence of differential stimuli facilitates a delayed discrimination it gives no advantage to animals learning a discrimination without delay, which it should if it really contributes to incentive motivation. We will discover some further embarrassing findings for the secondary reinforcement hypothesis as we proceed.

Finally, there is the possibility of accounting for some of these effects of delayed reinforcement in terms of competing responses. The basic notion here is that during the delay interval the animal will engage in behavior such as exploring or grooming which either fails to fit into the instrumental behavior chain or actively competes with parts of it.

AMOUNT OF REINFORCEMENT

A great deal of research has been done on the effect of the amount of reinforcement upon performance. Some of this work has involved subjects receiving no reinforcement during some trials or some group of trials. We will not consider this case in any detail in the present chapter. It is mentioned here only to draw attention to the fact that a really adequate theory of incentive motivation would be able to deal with partial reinforcement and extinction as limiting cases. Although we will have occasion here to mention some of these partial reinforcement and extinction effects we will be primarily concerned with cases in which some definite amount of reinforcement is given.

Learning vs. Performance. We have already mentioned the studies of Crespi (1942), Zeaman (1949), and Metzger et al. (1957) which show that animals in an alley run sooner and faster for larger quantities of food. We noted that the acquisition curves under different quantities of reinforcement reach different asymptotes but approach the respective asymptotes at approximately the same rate of growth. And we noted that when incentive conditions were switched after a given number of trials, the animal's behavior shifted rapidly in an appropriate manner to suggest that the effect of the amount-of-reinforcement variable is on performance rather than on learning.

It has been reported (Pereboom & Crawford, 1958; Kintsch, 1962; Marx & Brownstein, 1963) that the effect of incentive magnitude on the speed of running an alley is obtained even when trials on which there is competing behavior are discounted. The case of incentive in the runway situation would seem to be much the same as the case of drive; incentive motivation affects not only the probability of running but also the vigor of running. However, in bar-press situations this conclusion may not hold; e.g., DiLollo et al. (1965) found that the force of a bar-press response varied inversely with the amount of reinforcement it produces. Such findings suggest the operation of a frustration effect. So do the data of Hill and Spear (1963) on the relative speeds of running to high and low amounts of reinforcement in a choice situation. Less amenable to any simple interpretation is the result of Beer and Trumble (1965) that DRL behavior is better with lower amounts of reinforcement.

Another approach to the problem of whether incentive affects learning or performance is by way of performance in extinction. Lawrence and

Miller (1947), Reynolds (1950a), Fehrer (1956a), Metzger et al. (1957), and Ison and Cook (1964) have reported that although the rat tends to take into extinction the level of performance it had acquired prior to extinction, the amount of reinforcement obtained in acquisition has little effect upon the ultimate resistance to extinction. Thus, Metzger et al. (1957) found substantial performance differences in extinction but found that when acquisition differences were removed by analysis of covariance the extinction differences disappeared also.[5] The picture we begin to get then is of a multiplicative motivational factor; performance curves diverge uniformly as instrumental behavior is acquired under different quantities of reinforcement, and then in extinction the curves converge again.[6] Notice that this is *not* the picture we obtained with the delay-of-reinforcement parameter. Evidently incentive motivation as generated by amount of reinforcement involves different mechanisms from those involved in immediacy of reinforcement.

One implicit aspect of incentive motivation in most interpretations is that it is supposed to depend upon the animal's relatively recent history of reinforcement conditions. Thus, we might expect to find incentive-transition effects for a few trials whenever incentives are shifted, e.g., Crespi's elation and depression effects. We might also expect trial-by-trial changes in performance as a function of the particular reinforcing conditions that applied on the immediately preceding trial, more or less independently of the animal's prior history of reinforcement (Beach & Jordan, 1956a). And we might expect an animal to show trial-by-trial changes in incentive motivation over the course of a series of daily trials (Bolles & Morlock, 1960). In short, we might be able to apply incentive motivation concepts to any case where variation in performance is not attributable to the animal's drive conditions or to permanent modifications of its habit structure. Collier and Marx (1959) have shown rather convincingly that performance can be a function of a rat's specific history of reinforcement independently of the number of reinforcements or the current drive conditions. These intermediate speed effects, slower than the effects of cur-

[5] These results are difficult to interpret. The principal issue here is whether differences in extinction can be found that must be attributed to learning, or whether all differences reflect merely differential motivation. The trouble is that the incentive motivation factor is itself admitted to be a learned determinant of behavior. Hence the differences removed by the covariance analysis must include the differences we are looking for. What is needed is some technique for equating incentive motivation in extinction.

[6] To the extent that incentive motivation tends to depend primarily upon only the recent history of reinforcement, incentive differences should dissipate in a few extinction trials. Then later extinction performance should reflect differences in habit strength, if there are any. Sometimes there don't seem to be any, but sometimes there are (Armus, 1959). Pubols (1960), who has reviewed a number of lines of evidence, concludes that the incentive motivation effects are upon performance rather than learning. This is perhaps true for amount of food but probably not true for concentration of sucrose (Marx et al., 1963).

rent drive conditions, but too fast to be explained by habit acquisition, would seem to prevent us from formulating any simple account of incentive motivation based exclusively either upon multiplicative motivation or upon habit acquisition.

Incentive Effects in Different Situations. All of the studies that we have mentioned so far, plus some other early studies (Grindley, 1929; Wolf & Kaplon, 1941; Gagné, 1941), that have made use of runways have invariably reported some effect of reinforcement magnitude on performance. By contrast, studies using maze situations usually find little or no effect of reinforcement magnitude (Heyer, 1951; Furchtgott & Rubin, 1953; Maher & Wickens, 1954; McKelvey, 1956), although there are exceptions (Cross & Boyer, 1964; Cross et al., 1964).

Negative results have been found repeatedly with rats in brightness-discrimination problems; they do not learn the discrimination any faster with large amounts of reinforcement than they do with small amounts of reinforcement (e.g., Reynolds, 1949, 1950; Hopkins, 1955; Schrier, 1956). Most of these writers have reported that rats run faster for a large incentive, but that they do not learn the discrimination any sooner. On the other hand, incentive effects have usually been demonstrated with primates in discrimination problems (Fletcher, 1940; and a number of studies cited by Schrier, 1958). Superficially, this looks like a species difference but a better solution of the dilemma was suggested by Meyer (1951) and apparently confirmed by both Lawson (1957) and Schrier (1958). It seems that in primate studies, experimenters are economical of animals and tend to use the same ones over again under different conditions, thereby permitting each subject eventually to find out about large and small amounts of reinforcement. In rat studies, however, different subjects are used under the different conditions, each under a fixed amount of reinforcement. This difference in methodology, the difference between absolute vs. differential training, or between shift and nonshift training, has been shown to be an important variable by both Lawson (1957) for rats and Schrier (1958) for monkeys. To be sure, there are some exceptions to the general rule (e.g., Reynolds, 1950a; Lawson et al., 1959) but it seems safe to conclude that the training method is an important variable here; animals that are trained under differing amounts of reinforcement show much clearer incentive-magnitude effects in selective learning situations than do groups of animals that are trained under constant amounts of reinforcement.[7]

Another attempt to explain the apparent absence of an incentive

[7] Several investigators have found differences attributable to incentive magnitude using the absolute method when very small magnitudes were used (Schrier, 1956; Furchtgott & Salzberg, 1959; Pubols, 1961). It has been suggested that the absolute method works when the absolute amounts are near the threshold of reinforcement.

effect in discrimination performance has been suggested by Reynolds (1949) in terms of his "R hypothesis." According to the R (for replication) hypothesis, the amount of reinforcement (and presumably the magnitude of incentive motivation) can only affect an instrumental response if that response is a replicate of the goal reaction, R_G. Running in an alley to food presumably is a replicate of the goal reaction, whereas responding to black vs. white cues in a discrimination problem is not. Lawson (1957) has attempted to spell out the details of this hypothesis more explicitly. He compared rats trained by the absolute method with rats trained by the differential method on a discrimination problem and then tested subsequently for secondary reinforcing effects of the stimuli that had accompanied the different amounts of reinforcement. Secondary reinforcing effects were shown only for groups that had had differential training. Hence, Lawson concluded: (1) that the facilitory effect of large amounts of incentive could be attributed to the increased secondary reinforcement effects they produce, and (2) that whether the instrumental response preceding the secondary reinforcer is affected is determined by whether the response elicited by the secondary reinforcer can generalize back to compete with or to facilitate the instrumental response. Thus, if the reaction to the secondary reinforcer is to run forward then this would be expected to facilitate runway performance; but it would not be expected to provide differential facilitation of responding to black and white alleys. Of course, if the goal box associated with a large amount of food were black and the box associated with a small amount were white, then we might expect a black-white discrimination to be learned rather easily; and this is just what Greene (1953) has found.

Discrimination learning under different amounts of reinforcement should not be confused with the learning to discriminate different amounts of reinforcement. Festinger (1943), Denny and King (1955), Pereboom (1957), Reynolds and Anderson (1961), and Davenport (1963) have all demonstrated that rats in a simple two-choice situation can learn to go to that side which offers a greater amount of reinforcement as against a small amount of reinforcement on the alternate side. Denny and King, Pereboom, and Davenport ran reversal training with the large- and small-incentive sides reversed. Their rats were able to learn both the original discrimination and the reversal; but it is of some interest to note that the reversal required 10 trials or so in contrast with the 1 or 2 trials necessary to obtain shifted performance in a noncompetitive situation such as Crespi (1942) used, and that reversal learning gets worse with practice (Davenport). We do not know enough about behavior in competitive situations, or in selective-learning situations, to indicate why the shift should be so slow. We also do not know enough about the behavior occurring in bar-pressing situations to be able to explain the fact that the rate of bar pressing is correlated with the amount of reinforcement it provides on an FI schedule with small amounts (Hutt, 1954) but not with FR schedules and larger amounts (Keesey & Kling, 1961).

The conclusion, then, would seem to be that the amount of reinforcement usually facilitates responses such as running in an alley but usually does not facilitate more complex selective-learning performance, although sometimes it may. Perhaps greater amounts of reinforcement lead to greater incentive motivation which makes the rat run faster in complex problems so that it does not have an opportunity to make the appropriate discriminations. Experiments in this area have largely focused upon the acquisition of discrimination; perhaps once a discrimination has become well established incentive magnitude would be found to affect the asymptotic level of performance on it, in the manner suggested in Fig. 8-16. Attempts have been made to balance off different factors of the reinforcement condition, e.g., by giving animals a choice between some amount of reinforcements and some probability or delay of reinforcement (Davenport, 1962; Spear, 1964; McDiarmid & Rilling, 1965). Some balancing evidently can be effected.

The Dimensions of Consummatory Behavior. A number of writers have pointed out that in the typical study of the amount of reinforcement there are several factors which must necessarily be confounded to some extent, such as the amount of time in the goal box, the amount consumed, the rate of consumption, the amount of consummatory behavior, and the amount of stimulation resulting from this consummatory behavior. Wike and Barrientos (1957) reported that drinking from a small-bore water tube has more incentive value than drinking from a large-bore tube (rats learned to go to the one rather than the other in a T maze). This argues for the importance of the amount of consummatory activity as against the amount consumed or the amount of drive reduction involved, since Wike and Barrientos equated the consumption under the two conditions. (They chose to confound the duration of consummatory behavior with its vigor and rate.) This conclusion has been supported by Hall and Kling (1960) and by Goodrich (1960) using sucrose; but Hellyer (1953) and Kling (1956) have reported incentive effects positively correlated with rate of consumption. Perhaps all these dimensions are relevant.

One of the most interesting findings in this area has been reported by Black and Elstad (1964). They gave rats either 10 sec. or 30 sec. to eat in the goal box, and found that the 10-sec. animals, although receiving less reinforcement, ran faster and ate faster than the 30-sec. animals. This paradoxical result could perhaps be explained in terms of frustration; the 10-sec. animals would be more likely to be interrupted during consummatory behavior and hence would be more likely to have frustration conditioned to the situation. But a more elegant explanation can be framed in competing response terms: If the 10-sec. animals engage in competing behavior prior to starting to eat, they are not likely to have time to eat and hence such behavior is not likely to be reinforced. Exploratory behavior is more likely to be reinforced in the 30-sec. animals and hence is more likely also to generalize throughout the apparatus.

There are a number of studies demonstrating what may be perceptual factors in the acquisition of incentive motivation. Apparently there is greater incentive value in incentives that "look" larger independently of how much is actually consumed (Yoshioka, 1930; Wolf & Kaplon, 1941; Fay et al., 1953; Davis, 1956; McKelvey, 1956; Rehula, 1957; Dyal, 1960; Schrier, 1961a).

QUALITY OF REINFORCEMENT

Early studies by Simmons (1924), Young (1928), and others had shown that the kind of food was as important as the amount of food in determining performance. But until recently little was done to develop such findings systematically. Recent work on the behavioral effect of quality of reinforcement stems largely from the attempt to isolate the several dimensions of the consummatory response that are confounded in most studies of the amount of reinforcement. Guttman (1953), who was the first to attempt such an isolation, trained rats to press a bar for a sucrose solution, and then tested them with different concentrations of sucrose, so that amount of consummatory behavior could be operationally distinguished from the amount of reinforcement. He found that when the amount of drinking was held constant, the rate of bar pressing generally increased with concentration, although there was a reversal with the highest concentration condition (32%). Similar findings have been reported by Young and Shuford (1955); Dufort and Kimble (1956); and, with monkeys, Conrad and Sidman (1956).

It has also been found that when sucrose concentration is shifted suddenly, performance shifts appropriately (Guttman, 1953; Dufort & Kimble, 1956; Homzie & Ross, 1962; Rosen & Ison, 1965). Collier and Marx (1959), Pieper and Marx (1963), and Marx et al. (1963) have reported effects that appear similar to elation and depression effects when sucrose concentrations are shifted upward or downward. These contrast effects are quite large in magnitude, highly reliable, and quite durable. They seem, therefore, to be something different from the elation and depression effects reported by Crespi. In all of these studies, as well as in those which obtain incentive-shift effects without the contrast effects, the effects develop slowly, over the course of 10 trials or so. This slowness also suggests that they are governed by different mechanisms than those that come into play when the amount of solid food is varied experimentally. Under some circumstances, sucrose-concentration shift effects fail to appear (Spear, 1965). Ison (1964) did an incentive reversal study in a T maze analogous to the drive-reversal studies that were discussed in Chapter 9; he found significant effects on postshift performance of preshift incentive, postshift incentive, and the interaction. Evidently variation in sucrose concentration has behavioral effects quite different than those produced by variation in food deprivation conditions.

A drop-off in consumption with high concentrations of sucrose has frequently been reported. This drop-off effect occurs even when the animal has not ingested enough sucrose to supply an appreciable fraction of its daily caloric need, nor enough to create an appreciable osmotic pressure. It is known that in preference tests (Young & Greene, 1953), and in consumption tests where consumption is measured just in the first few minutes (Collier & Siskel, 1959), and under partial reinforcement (Guttman, 1953) performance is monotonically related to concentration. Collier and Siskel (1959) and Collier et al. (1961) have argued from their data, and others', that this drop-off is some sort of postingestion effect (see above, p. 195) even though it may not be due to satiation.[8]

Findings very similar to those obtained with bar pressing have been demonstrated in runways; sometimes sucrose concentration has relatively little effect upon instrumental behavior (Snyder and Hulse, 1961), but usually speed does increase monotonically (Collier and Marx, 1959; Goodrich, 1960; Brush et al., 1961; Kraeling, 1961). The usual finding is that the amount of consummatory activity and the concentration of sucrose both, and independently, contribute to the incentive effect. But it has been commonly reported that the variables that affect the consummatory response, drinking, do not operate in the same manner upon an instrumental response (e.g., Young & Madsen, 1963).

Different concentrations define a new dimension of *quality,* although they are often described as "amounts" of reinforcement. The mistake probably stems from the idea that since the animals are hungry and need calories they receive a bigger reward with a higher concentration. But many of the same incentive effects have been demonstrated in satiated

---

[8] Collier and his collaborators have done considerable work on the problem; they conclude that there are three principal factors affecting performance, sweetness, hunger, and this postingestion factor. But there are also a number of interactions and other complications (Collier & Willis, 1961; Collier & Myers, 1961). All of these effects with sucrose pose problems for the r_G interpretation of incentive motivation. Are different consummatory responses involved with different concentrations, or different vigors of responding, or what? What evidence is available indicates that the consummatory response itself, drinking, changes very little with changes in concentration.

animals. And probably all of the effects that have been obtained with sucrose can be demonstrated with saccharin (Hughes, 1957; Collier, 1962; Hulse & Firestone, 1964). The variable that does seem to be crucial with sucrose is sweetness. Guttman (1954) has determined equal reinforcing values for sucrose and glucose and found that it is not concentration (and hence calories) that produces equivalent reinforcement values but judged sweetness. Guttman determined the reinforcement threshold for concentration and found that it lies very close to the sensory detection threshold. Further evidence, both behavioral and physiological, has been summarized by Pfaffmann(1960). The conclusion seems inescapable that the reinforcing effect of sugars is the sensory stimulation they provide, or if you like, their sweetness.

P. T. Young (1955, 1959, 1961) has developed a potentially broad theory of incentive motivation presupposing, and based mainly upon, this general finding. According to Young, the incentive factor works because of "affective arousal"; the animal likes sweet-tasting substances, is affectively aroused by them, and the sweeter they are the more the animal is aroused. This affectivity determines consummatory behavior, provides the basis of the animal's motivation, and is the fundamental mechanism underlying learning. Motivation for Young is exclusively incentive; it is directly proportional to the strength of effective arousal. Motives may be either plus, as in the case of sweet substances, or negative, as in the case of aversive stimuli like bitter substances. Young's treatment of learning is also relatively simple and straightforward; any stimulus which is consistently paired with affective arousal tends to produce a similar affective arousal. Thus, animals learn instrumental responses to the extent that there are stimuli to elicit incentive motivation and to support the instrumental response. Young attributes a negligible role to any kind of drive concept. He makes the assumption that has to be made by any theorist relying exclusively upon incentive at the expense of drive, namely, *deprivation increases the incentive value of the goal object*. The goal substance and the stimuli that have been associated with it produce a more intense affective arousal if the animal is deprived (1961, p. 180).[9]

The data from the study of the quality of reinforcement indicate the need for a little interpretive caution: in almost every respect in which quality has been compared with quantity or delay we have found different functional properties of these dimensions of reinforcement. More specifically, it seems almost certain that the laws of incentive motivation, which have been worked out primarily from studies of amount of reinforcement for hungry rats, will turn out not to be applicable to the other dimensions or to nonhungry animals.

[9] There have been a number of studies of the change in preferences among foodstuffs with hunger but no one seems to have shown, or considered how it could be shown, that deprivation increases incentive motivation.

SOME SPECIAL PROBLEMS IN INCENTIVE MOTIVATION

The Combination Law for D and K.   Hull (1952) proposed that drive, D, and incentive motivation, K, multiply to determine the organism's total motivation. On the basis primarily of a study by Ramond (1954), Spence (1956) has proposed that the proper combination law is additive; D and K should add together and jointly multiply habit strength to determine behavior. A number of ingenious experimental designs have been used in an attempt to perform the crucial experiment (Reynolds, Marx & Henderson, 1952; Besch & Reynolds, 1958; Reynolds & Pavlik, 1960; Weiss, 1960; Hulicka, 1960; Stabler, 1962; Brush et al., 1961; Ehrenfreund & Badia, 1962; Pavlik & Reynolds, 1963). Results of these studies have indicated either additive laws, multiplicative laws, or some combination of the two. The conclusion in all of these studies, however, rests upon some a priori assumption about how $_sE_r$ should be measured. The usual assumption is that $_sE_r$ is linearly related to response speed and to response probability, and the usual conclusion is that D and K add. But as we noted in Chapter 9, quite different conclusions can be obtained if one is willing to make other assumptions. The point is that any quantitative analysis of performance curves presupposes a quantitative scaling of performance.

Reynolds and Anderson (1961) have cleverly avoided this problem. They ran animals in an amount-of-reinforcement discrimination with a large amount of food on one side of the T maze and a small amount of food on the other. Two groups were run, one under high drive and one under low drive. It can be shown algebraically that if D and K multiply, then the high-drive group should learn the discrimination faster than the low-drive group. According to Spence's additive hypothesis, there should be no difference between groups provided the competing habits can be assumed to be equal. Since an equal number of reinforcements was given on both sides (by using forced trials), discrimination would have to be based solely upon the differential K factors involved and hence be independent of drive. The results indicated virtually identical acquisition for the two groups, thereby nicely supporting Spence's additive hypothesis.

There is a complication, however, in that incentive motivation seems to require some minimum amount of drive; Seward and Procter (1960) and Seward et al. (1958, 1960) found that if the animal has little or no hunger, then no amount of food will be adequate for reinforcement. Thus, the additive formula appears to fail in the area near zero drive.

Black (1965) has proposed a solution to this problem. He suggests that K be reconceptualized so that it becomes a function of deprivation time (or weight loss). Then, as the deprivation condition disappears, both D and K would approach zero; and the additive relationship can be retained. We may wonder, however, why D should be kept at this point.

The Locus of r_G. Implicit in most theoretical interpretations of incentive motivation is that it is mediated by an anticipatory goal reaction, r_G. But the precise nature of r_G is rarely ever specified; it is ordinarily treated as a hypothetical construct and given just enough functional properties to tie it down in a theoretical network. Few psychologists today have seriously entertained the possibility of directly observing r_G. The few studies (e.g., Lewis et al., 1958; Lewis, 1959; Lewis & Kent, 1961; Kintsch & Witte, 1962; Shapiro, 1962; Miller & DeBold, 1965) that have attempted to manipulate or observe r_G or responses correlated with it, such as salivation, have not obtained encouraging results. These attempts to locate r_G have shown some of the correlations with subsequent instrumental behavior that are expected, but these correlations so far have been too low to permit anyone to say that r_G has been located or even that it has all of the properties it is supposed to have. In short, the efforts to substantiate r_G have not paid off. This is not to say that r_G cannot be anchored operationally, but only that it is a very serviceable explanatory device in the absence of direct operational anchoring (and maybe because of this absence).

Spence's contention that incentive motivation results from the elicitation of r_G by environmental stimuli similar to those to which R_G becomes conditioned in the goal box is easily tested indirectly by experimentally manipulating the similarity of alley and goal box cues in a runway and determining what effect this similarity has on the animal's motivation. One of the first such tests was performed by Moltz (1957) in a "latent extinction" experiment. Animals were trained to run in the apparatus to food and when their performance had stabilized they were placed in an empty box, so that r_G would begin to extinguish. The decrement in subsequent running behavior was found to increase with the similarity between the extinction box and the goal box. Similar studies (Stein, 1957; Gonzalez & Diamond, 1960; Hughes et al., 1960; Koppman & Grice, 1963; DiLollo, 1964) have generally yielded opposite results; the effects of extinction, or of a change in incentive magnitude, are in the wrong direction, and in at least one case (Gonzalez & Diamond, 1960) support Tolman's S-R-S theory as against the r_G theory.

We may conceive of r_G not just as a fraction of a consummatory response, but also as a fraction of any response occurring in the goal box. This suggestion had been made as early as 1935 by Miller, who also adduced some evidence for it. Miller required animals to assume unusual postures while eating in the goal box and found that the instrumental response of getting to the goal box was either facilitated or interfered with in accordance with the compatibility of the behaviors required at the choice point and in the goal box. These results do not demand a motivational interpretation; we may consider them simply as a case of generalization and transfer. Performance improves to the degree that the stimuli and responses are similar in a test situation (the choice point) to what they are in the situation where reinforcement occurs (in the goal box). But the point remains that responses occurring in the goal box, whether they be inherently relevant to reinforcement, like eating, or only relevant by circumstances, as in Miller's experiment, can antedate or anticipate reinforcement and hence affect instrumental behavior. The question is whether any response is potentially able to occur in fractional anticipatory form; and, if it can, whether such an anticipation necessarily constitutes incentive motivation, or whether it must be restricted to an associative role. Perhaps only fractional antedating consummatory responses can make a contribution to incentive motivation.

On the other hand, perhaps there is no incentive motivation apart from the purely associative effect of the antedating response. Regardless of whether it is a fraction of the consummatory response or of some incidental behavior, perhaps the antedating response serves only to provide stimulus feedback which adds to the total stimulus configuration controlling instrumental behavior. Still another possibility is that incentive motivation involves a genuine energization factor in addition to the associative factor, but that it is not very specific to the antedating reaction. Thus, incentive motivation may involve only a basic polarity of approach and aversion. In this view the r_G conditioned by eating produces an approach to any stimulus that elicits it, and the r_E conditioned by shock produces withdrawal from any stimulus that elicits it. In this connection we may note Hall and Kling's (1960) suggestion that it is the searching for and going to the food cup which provide incentive motivation rather than the amount of consummatory behavior that occurs (see also Denny & Martindale, 1956). Surely one of the most compatible fractions of the goal reaction, at least in the alley-running situation, is the tendency to approach, to move forward; perhaps this is what constitutes incentive motivation.

Nissen (1950) has pointed out that in the traditional discrimination learning situation the organism's behavior is often defined in terms of the stimuli to be discriminated, for example "turning right vs. turning left," or "going to the white vs. going to the black." Nissen suggests as an alternative that in these situations the organism really has at its disposal only two responses, approach and avoidance, and that what is involved in a typical discrimination problem is the competition between approach and avoidance responses as they are associated with the correct stimulus on the one hand and the incorrect stimulus on the other. It is noteworthy that the great majority of the discrimination studies done with the rat have been in locomotion situations. We almost invariably study drive discrimination, black-white discrimination, the effect of secondary reinforcers and of incentive variables in situations in which the rat is required to run to one stimulus and not to run to another. It may be not just a coincidence that it is precisely in these situations that incentive motivation interpretations have gained the greatest currency and apparent applicability. It is entirely possible that the basic incentive motivation mechanisms involve incipient approach and avoidance tendencies rather than salivation and the like. Schneirla (1959) has suggested the dominant role such tendencies must have in biological adaptation.

If such an interpretation is valid, it might also permit us to apply incentive theory to aversive learning. There has been a serious neglect of the possibility of negative incentives. Some writers, notably Amsel (1962), have given r_E and r_F (fear and anger) the property of being aversive, but much more frequently they are assumed merely to have an energizing role; they are usually assumed to contribute to drive or to be acquired drives. In either case fear serves as a generalized energizer rather than as an anticipatory escape tendency or as a specific tendency to withdraw. Skinnerian psychologists often refer to acquired aversiveness and are quite willing to attribute such a property to the stimulus feedback from covert and anticipatory responses, but as we will see in subsequent chapters, they consider aversiveness to be a condition for reinforcement rather than a variety of motivation. The animal is not motivated to turn away from aversive stimuli, it is merely reinforced for doing so.

In Chapter 9 we noted some of the problems involved in distinguishing between learning and performance factors in aversive learning. Recall that Campbell and Kraeling (1953) found performance in shock-escape was a function of the amount of drive reduction (voltage drop), and that Spence (1956) attributed the different level of performance to differential increments in habit strength. Spence may possibly be making the same mistake here for aversive behavior that Hull made in 1943 for appetitive behavior. The little evidence now available is not conclusive. Bower et al. (1959) reported a Crespi-type of experiment using reduction of electric shock as the reinforcer, with different groups getting different amounts of shock reduction. After 15 trials conditions were switched. The results indicate a fairly rapid adjustment to the postshift conditions, within about 5 to 10 trials. However, the original preshift acquisition had also been just about this rapid. This is faster than instrumental behavior is usually learned but slower than the usual acquisition of positive incentive-motivation effects. Thus, we do not yet have very substantial evidence for negative incentive learning as distinguished from instrumental escape learning. The possibility that anticipatory withdrawal is a basic element in avoidance or escape behavior remains relatively unexplored.

THEORETICAL INTERPRETATIONS OF INCENTIVE MOTIVATION

When we consider the effects of reinforcement conditions from a purely empirical viewpoint we may find some extremely well-established principles, e.g., rats run faster for larger amounts of food. While this is a useful generalization there is always the hope that it can be incorporated by a still more general statement at a theoretical level.

In the present section we will consider briefly some of the more promising approaches toward a theory of incentive motivation, and we will see that what distinguishes the different positions is the treatment of three fundamental problems: (1) the motivation problem—how does the incentive motivating mechanism work, does it reinforce instrumental behavior, motivate it, or simply provide stimulus control for it? (2) The learning problem—how is the incentive mechanism acquired? (3) The asymmetry problem—how are we to account for the evident asymmetry between the appetitive and aversive cases?

The Hull-Spence Position.   Between 1943 and 1952 Hull gave increasing emphasis to the hypothetical K factor and to the still more hypothetical r_G mechanism to account for it. Many of the phenomena which had earlier been explained in terms of drive, drive summation, and generalized drive, were later explained in terms of r_G. However, Hull always held to the drive-reduction hypothesis for both instrumental response learning and incentive learning. The occurrence of drive reduction (or S_D reduction) at the termination of a chain of instrumental responses was assumed to provide both delayed reinforcement for all the members of the chain and reinforcement for the conditioning of R_G or components of it, r_G, to stimuli present in the goal box. Other theorists have parted company with Hull on this point; Mowrer (1947, 1950) maintained that instrumental responses were reinforced by drive reduction but that the responses involved in incentive motivation were not. Mowrer and a number of subsequent writers hold the position that the emotional reactions aroused by the organism's encounter with shock and food are established by contiguous association, i.e., classical conditioning. Spence (1956), on the other hand, has tentatively proposed just the opposite two-factor hypothesis: instrumental responses are established by contiguity and r_G is established by drive reduction.

Strange to say, although these divergent views illustrate profound differences of opinion, and suggest that great theoretical issues are at stake, they are often not really contradictory. It turns out that these discrepant hypotheses arose mainly from considering different sorts of evidence. Hull concerned himself almost exclusively with the appetitive case, and he theorized almost exclusively about hungry rats in simple situations. Spence's 1956 position was based partly on the same evidence Hull cited, but also on discrimination-learning data. Mowrer, on the other hand, arrived at his position from a consideration of avoidance learning. In Chapter 11 we noted that Mowrer supported his position with the finding that it was onset of electric shock rather than shock termination that seemed to be important in the establishment of fear.

A crucial test of the reinforcement theories of Hull (1952), Spence (1956), and Mowrer (1950) is extremely difficult to envisage. For one thing, it is difficult to see how primary and secondary motivation can be distinguished either in the aversive or the appetitive case; and secondly, it is hard to see how primary and secondary reinforcement can be distinguished operationally. Thus, are we to attribute avoidance learning to fear as an acquired drive or to fear as a negative incentive? Are we to consider the sight of food and the ingestion of food primary reinforcers or secondary reinforcers?

There is a related difficulty which besets Hull's formulation (and Spence's), a very profound and difficult problem, which has led as much as anything else to the proliferation of theoretical positions. The difficulty may be called *Hull's Paradox*. Hull said that a stimulus associated with drive reduction comes to acquire secondary reinforcing power; it acts the same way as drive reduction. So, if the assumed mechanism is r_G, then the occurrence of r_G is like a reduction in drive. On the other hand, secondary motivation, or incentive motivation, is explicitly attributed to the occurrence of r_G so that r_G acts like an increase in drive. The paradox is this: how can the occurrence of r_G be like both drive reduction and drive induction? Put another way, how can it be both reinforcing and motivating? The paradox can only be resolved by some major conceptual readjustment, such as denying one of the functions attributed to r_G, or denying one of those attributed to D, or redefining motivation or reinforcement.

One resolution of the paradox has been suggested by Sheffield (Sheffield & Campbell, 1954; Sheffield et al., 1954). Sheffield denies the drive-reduction hypothesis of reinforcement and emphasizes the role of r_G both in motivation and reinforcement. The occurrence of r_G is reinforcing if the momentary conditions permit it to proceed to its complete form (R_G), and is motivating if the momentary conditions preclude its completion. Thus, as the rat runs toward the goal it is motivated by the frustration of the consummatory response, but when it gets to the goal where R_G can occur the frustrating running is reinforced. This is tantamount to a drive-induction hypothesis of reinforcement; it is also similar to the response-completion hypothesis proposed many years ago by White (1936).

Hull, of course, never resolved the paradox himself. In fact he is sometimes accused of having fallen into it unknowingly (Hilgard, 1956). Perhaps so, but other features of Hull's treatment of secondary reinforcement make it likely that he believed the occurrence of r_G could be both reinforcing and motivating.[10] We may note in closing this section that the paradox disappears for Hull (and Spence) in the aversive case. Fear, for example, reinforces responses when it terminates and motivates those that are concurrent with it. Thus, fear is a source of drive rather than a negative incentive, and everything is in order. The appetitive and aversive cases turn out quite differently.

Logan's Position. Logan's position (1960) is very much like Hull's, the outstanding difference being that he has rejected speed of responding as a measure of $_sE_r$, preferring to attribute responses of different speeds to different habits. Logan has also changed Hull's treatment of the factors involved in inhibition. But he has kept the same variables in motivation. The occurrence of r_G is still held to be the mechanism underlying both secondary reinforcement and incentive motivation. Logan almost slips out of Hull's Paradox by attributing the incentive effect of r_G to the occurrence of the instrumental response on the following occasion or trial: "The occurrence of R_G or r_G immediately following a response produces incentive motivation . . . for *repetition* of that response to the coincident stimulus traces" (Logan, 1960, pp. 105–106, italics mine). This doesn't really resolve the paradox however because, presumably, secondary reinforcement also would be manifest on subsequent trials, so we still do not know if r_G is fundamentally a reinforcer or a motivator. Logan's formulation, like Hull's, is apparently based entirely upon a consideration of appetitive behavior.

Logan has described an integrated series of three dozen carefully executed studies of the effects of the parameters of reinforcement all within a single experimental context. It is possible, for example, from his work to compare the effects of delay of reinforcement with the effects of amount of reinforcement. Recall the earlier discussion of the study by Logan et al. (1955) of varied delay, in which it was found that rats ran faster to variable short and long delays than to a constant mean delay. By contrast, varied amounts of reinforcement lead to performance which is about the same as obtained with a constant mean amount and far

---

[10] The argument is based on the assumption that r_G can be concurrent with a *chain* of instrumental responses. Whenever it occurs in the chain its feedback can reinforce antecedent responses of the chain and also motivate subsequent responses or those in progress. We will find though that even this simple attempt to resolve the paradox requires a reconsideration of the nature of secondary reinforcement.

below performance of animals run to the larger amount (Grimsley & Mc-Donald, 1964, however, failed to obtain this). This is explained on the basis of the assumption that different amounts of reinforcement produce r_G's that are not only quantitatively but qualitatively different. Under the varied-magnitude condition, the different r_G's compete; and the resultant incentive motivation is determined by a compromise r_G. On the other hand, under conditions of varied delayed reinforcement there is no competition since the same r_G can be conditioned to different stimuli or different stimulus traces. The resulting incentive motivation therefore should be at least equal to that produced by conditions of no delay, and this advantage should be especially marked in extinction. Sometimes the results come out this way, but sometimes they do not (Logan et al., 1956; Leventhal et al., 1959; Yamaguchi, 1961). It has been suggested that perhaps the quantitative relations involved depend not only upon the relative amounts of reinforcement that are used but upon the absolute amounts as well.

Another feature of Logan's theory is that incentive motivation ought to have a greater effect as the animal approaches the goal where, presumably, stimuli eliciting r_G are more similar to those to which it has been conditioned. Logan's results seem to indicate that this is true for the amount variable but that the delay of reinforcement has effects which are more or less uniform throughout the course of an alley. Other experimenters (e.g., Goodrich, 1959; Wagner, 1961) have not always agreed with these findings. The focus of contention seems to concern mainly the results obtained under partial reinforcement. Should a nonreinforced trial be considered the limiting case of the delay variable (infinite delay) or the limiting case of the amount variable (zero amount)? Or are other factors such as frustration involved? Further research may tell us.

When rats run in an alley to food they usually accelerate from one trial to the next—we ordinarily call this learning. But notice that if we have an incentive factor in our theory, improved performance does not necessarily mean an increase in habit strength. When the rats run more quickly, reinforcement occurs with less delay. Thus, reinforcement can not only produce an increment in the strength of the running habit, it can also increase the incentive motivation which alone would make the rat run faster on the next trial. Logan would say that this experimental situation is one in which there is an arbitrary, if more or less natural, positive correlation between speed of running and immediacy of reinforcement. Logan and his students (e.g., Bower, 1961) have been able to instrument runway situations in which this positive correlation is abolished, or even converted into a negative correlation. This is done by giving the animal increasing amounts of food for correspondingly slower running times. It is found that by 100 trials or so the rat will reach a stable speed of running which presumably balances the various incentive, habit, and inhibition factors determining the behavior. The model describing this balance is admittedly complex, but it is the best thing we have in incentive theory aimed at providing a genuinely quantitative account of both response probability and the vexing problem of response vigor.

Amsel's Position.   Amsel (1958, 1962) has also followed Hull (1952) and Spence (1956) on the basic premises of incentive motivation, but he has added an important new element, frustration. According to Amsel, when the hungry rat runs to the goal box any one of three things may happen: it may be rewarded, in which case the consummatory response will occur and tend to become conditioned to the prevailing stimuli. A second possibility is that the rat may be punished. Amsel assumes that these first two cases are relatively well understood and focuses his attention on a third case, which arises when reinforcement is withheld after it has been regularly given. This state of affairs is said to produce frustration, which is assumed to have all the properties of a drive condition such as contributing to D and giving rise to a characteristic S_D. Some of the evidence Amsel and others have cited for the drive-like and response-eliciting properties of frustration was mentioned in Chapter 11. Now something must be said about the negative incentive character of frustration.

Amsel assumes that something akin to incentive motivation can occur in the form of a classically conditioned anticipatory frustration reaction, r_F. This reaction, he argues, can account for some of the effects of partial reinforcement, discrimination learning, and ordinary extinction. Wilson, Weiss, and Amsel (1955) have described how r_F is supposed to work. Early in learning the animal makes an instrumental response in the presence of some stimulus, which takes it to the goal where the goal response, R_G, occurs. In the case of discrimination learning, the instrumental response tends to occur about equally in the presence of the positive and the negative stimuli (S^+ and S^-), the only difference being that R_G does not follow a response to S^-. But when the animal responds to S^+, R_G occurs so that the generalizable part, r_G, can be elicited by S^+ and also, because of generalization, by S^-. So far this is a traditional account of discrimination training, but Amsel assumes that once the instrumental response has become fairly well established then the nonreinforced trials will lead to frustration. A fraction of this too will generalize back to S^- and, by further generalization, to $S+$. At this stage of learning, the choice-point situation will tend to elicit both r_G and r_F, the one tending to make the animal approach and the other tending to make the animal avoid. The animal will finally learn the discrimination when differential reinforcement overcomes the tendency of the stimuli to elicit the inappropriate anticipatory reaction. The discrimination will become well established at the time S^- regularly elicits r_F and withdrawal, and S^+ regularly elicits r_G and approach.

Several implications of this analysis have been confirmed. One is that the animal must make errors in order to learn the discrimination because it is only by making errors that r_F can become conditioned to S^- (Amsel, 1962). Various sorts of warm-up effects have been reported in a number of discrimination-learning situations, as though r_G and r_F had to be reinstated at the beginning of a test session in order to be effective. Some of the most compelling evidence comes from those studies in which the similarity of the stimulus situation at the correct and incorrect end boxes is varied relative to the stimulus situation at the choice point. For example, Eninger (1953) ran animals in a black-white discrimination problem and found that acquisition was much faster when the discriminanda were the same color as the goal boxes than when they were the opposite color. Grice and Goldman (1955) have reported similar findings; moreover, they found that when, for example, a white goal box is correct and a black one is wrong, the rat in some sense both approaches the white alley and avoids the black alley. Control groups that had a grey positive box or a grey negative box or grey for both showed the discrimination decrements consistent with the idea that both positive and negative incentives are involved.[11]

There are some difficulties with Amsel's interpretation. Recall that he indicates three things may happen when a rat runs to the goal box, reward, punishment, or frustration. In the case of reward we know what the goal response is. The animal eats, or drinks, and accordingly we may suppose that r_G consists of fractional responses such as salivation, tongue movements, and the like. In the case of punishment we may suppose that the goal response is withdrawal and that the anticipatory form of withdrawal is also withdrawal. But what is the reaction in the goal box in the presence of frustration; what is R_F? There is a logical puzzle here because if we assume that frustration is fundamentally a stimulus to which the animal learns responses and that it is these responses that constitute R_F, then we have the problem of what produces the stimulus. On the other hand, we might assume that frustration is fundamentally a learned (or innate) reaction and that it is the feedback from the frustration reaction that constitutes the characteristic stimulus associated with frustration. But in this case we have the problem of what elicits R_F. Amsel's own partial solution to the puzzle is that the failure of r_G to become R_G is the state of affairs producing frustration; before any frustration effects can be demonstrated it is necessary that r_G be well established. But, however

---

[11] We may think in terms of positive and negative incentives or alternatively, in terms of positive and negative secondary reinforcers; it makes little difference in this case.

R_F comes about, Amsel's analysis of partial reinforcement and nonreinforcement and discrimination learning hinges on the assumption that the occurrence of r_F is aversive in a way parallel to the manner in which r_G is appetitive.

Seward's Position. One of the fundamental problems in motivation theory is how much of the animal's motivation in any given instance should be attributed to D and how much should be attributed to incentive factors. This question was first put in explicit form by Seward (1942) in a "Note on the externalization of drive." Seward, in commenting on Anderson's (1941) externalization hypothesis, observed that there are two possible interpretations of externalization, one, the one favored by Anderson himself, is to conceive of drive as an intervening construct which itself becomes conditioned to environmental cues, and the other is to equate the hypothetical mechanisms underlying motivated behavior with Hull's associative construct, r_G (it was associative in 1942). Seward noted that even an associative r_G had all the properties that we want drive to have. Seward was suggesting, in effect, two hypotheses: (1) incentive motivation can, at least in principle, be extended to include all motivation, and (2) motivation is the behavior-eliciting effect of stimuli that have been associated with reinforcement. Seward has continued to defend both of these hypotheses although he has altered them from time to time.[12]

After questioning the indubitable concept of drive, Seward (1943) attacked the unassailable concept of reinforcement. He suggested that r_G might provide enough stimulus control over an instrumental response that it would occur without having to have habit strength of its own. What appears to be reinforcement of an instrumental response may be simply the progressive increase in incentive motivation that occurs through the continued conditioning of r_G in the goal box and the continued elicitation of r_G in the alley. Extinction is explained by the similar development of negative incentive motivation, avoidance. Seward suggested further that learning could occur in the same way in complex situations since when the animal looks one way and then another at the choice point the environment will provide differential elicitation of r_G, which will lead to differential motivation of the correct response and the incorrect response. Thus, Seward was able to do away with reinforcement, at least for instrumental behavior (it was still very much a part of the estab-

[12] These alterations make it difficult to summarize Seward's position precisely. Perhaps it would be fair to say that over the years Seward has struggled with a number of very basic issues without committing himself to any final stand on them. I have taken the liberty here of simplifying Seward's notation. He symbolizes drive and incentive as sr_d and sr_g, partly to emphasize the part they play in the associative determination of behavior, partly to indicate their mediational and intervening position between stimuli and responses, and partly, I suspect, to indicate that we really do not know where these constructs are to be localized.

lishment of r_G). To do this, however, he had to reintroduce some sort of motivational hypothesis. Seward proposed that when the animal makes incipient running responses, when it starts to run, r_G is aroused; and this provides incentive motivation for running. Running thus becomes further energized until overt running occurs. Seward offered no hypotheses at this time to explain how this mechanism might work except: "A portion of a response exerts a tendency to arouse the total response."[13] Seward extended this explanation to the case of latent learning (1947) and to all sorts of other learning phenomena (1948); r_G (and its stimulus consequences) act as a symbol, as an expectancy, as an incentive, and as a goad to action.

In 1950 and 1951 Seward began to reintroduce drive, D, while still excluding the concept of reinforcement (for instrumental behavior).

> . . . an animal in a state of need is motivated not only by a primary drive (D) and drive stimulus (s_D) but by a secondary drive consisting of a set r_G to make a characteristic consummatory or goal response (R_G). When a response (R) is followed by a reward, R_G is conditioned to concurrent stimuli. By generalization of this conditioning, stimuli accompanying R now serve to intensify r_G . . . this intensification called tertiary motivation [is] endowed with the property of facilitating R, the activity in progress. (Seward, 1951, p. 130)

Here Seward jumped from 1 to 3 motivators. There is D which is necessary to produce (and reinforce) a set, r_G, for the consummatory response. Set is a sort of nonspecific, nonassociative incentive motivator. Then there is the special Sewardian incentive factor, tertiary motivation, which facilitates any response with which it is correlated.

Up to this point Seward had avoided the difficulties of the asymmetry between aversive and appetitive behavior and also the troublesome question of how r_G became established. He addressed himself to these questions in 1952 and 1953 and arrived at what is essentially an associationistic account.[14] A r_G which occurs when drive decreases becomes conditioned to it and its s_G becomes a secondary goal or incentive. (This is just a restatement of the 1951 hypothesis and, like it, is designed to take care of the appetitive case.) On the other hand, when a r_G accompanies an

[13] This is the beginning of what Seward later called tertiary motivation. The hypothesis is by no means new; we first saw it in Chapter 2 in the form of Hobbes' concept of endeavor and again in Spencer's concept of nascent excitation.

[14] However he also felt it necessary to introduce drive, primarily to deal with the aversive case. At this time Seward had a motivational system which was very much like Spence's 1956 position, even to the assumption that primary and secondary motivating factors add together to produce total motivation. r_G itself was assumed to be conditioned in the same way. Both Seward and Spence gave r_G an associative as well as an incentive motivating role. Seward, however, attributed all of the strength of instrumental behavior to incentive (and tertiary) motivation, Spence only some of it.

increase in drive it becomes conditioned to it and its s_G becomes a secondary drive (which takes care of the aversive case). Thus, Seward postulates that incentive or tertiary motivation arises whenever there is a change in a second-order drive or goal.

In Seward's latest statement (1956), both r_G and drive (or at least drive stimuli) are present and both are assumed to have energizing and reinforcing powers, evidently not only in the appetitive case but in the aversive case as well. This assembly of factors is deemed necessary in view of the fact that learning appears to occur on the basis of consummatory behavior in the absence of drive reduction (e.g., Sheffield et al., 1954) as well as drive reduction in the absence of consummatory behavior (e.g., Miller & Kessen, 1952).

The asymmetry between the appetitive and the aversive case, as well as Hull's paradox, are resolved in Seward's final statement by means of a new special hypothesis, namely, that there are two kinds of goal responses, R_G: one which includes the ordinary class of consummatory responses such as eating, and the other which consists of responses coincident with the removal of an aversive drive condition. The rat running along an electrified grid is assumed to be able to make some sort of little anticipatory "whee, I'm getting away" responses. The attempt to make such a response in the absence of stimulus support for it produces tertiary motivation, so that the rat is motivated to run on the electrified grid in much the same way that it would run to food. This unusual hypothesis ought to permit Seward to do away once again with drive; but he retains it, partly because of its assumed associative possibilities. Drive reduction and induction are discarded for a Guthrian account of r_G learning: r_G is acquired as the stimuli controlling it change in the goal box.

Seward's system is evidently still in flux. His contribution has consisted largely in the proposal of a number of profound and startling hypotheses. There are no drives; there are no reinforcers; incipient behavior becomes motivated into overt behavior; frustrated r_G produces tertiary motivation; and so on. Probably most of these hypotheses will not endure; the important thing is that some of them may. Somewhere here is the key to the understanding of incentive motivation.

Mowrer's Position. In his most recent writings Mowrer (1956, 1960) has extended the incentive concept about as far as it can logically go; it carries almost the whole burden of directing and motivating behavior. According to Mowrer, the associative control of behavior, its motivation, and what appears to be its reinforcement are all consequences of the operation of hypothetical mechanisms which appear to be on the one hand like r_G, and on the other hand, like emotions. The concept of reinforcement is not applied to instrumental behavior but only to these incentive factors; it is they that are learned or extinguished by presenting or withholding reinforcement rather than the instrumental responses they govern. Mowrer's latest system affords drive a single limited but crucial function, viz., the reinforcement of emotions. Such emotion learning can occur either by drive reduction or drive induction.

Mowrer (1960) argues for the existence of four principal emotions. Let us consider these four, taking them up in the order of the amount of substantiating evidence now available for them.

First there is fear, which is established by (reinforced by) an increase in drive such as is produced by the onset of shock. Any stimulus present at the time of an increase in drive or present immediately preceding an increase in drive we may call a cue to the increase; it will acquire the ability to elicit fear. This cue presents a threat; it means that an increase in drive is impending. The effect on the animal's overt behavior is a withdrawal from the cue. The evidence for such a mechanism comes from avoidance learning situations, and the supporting evidence is excellent in this case. It is important to note that Mowrer does not assume that the cue gains direct associative control over the avoidance response; it merely elicits the motivation for such behavior.

One of the most elegant conceptions in this system is that the cue which comes to elicit the mediating emotion may be external or internal. If it is external the animal will make an overt avoidance or escape response or whatever response withdraws from or eliminates the cue. But the cue may also be internal; it may be the proprioceptive consequences of some response that the animal itself has made. Just as we may frighten the animal by presenting stimuli that have been associated with the onset of shock, so the animal can frighten itself by making responses which were contiguous with the onset of shock. The animal will tend to avoid or escape these internal cues, which it does by withdrawing from the stimuli, which means in effect that it will inhibit the responses that produce them. Thus, according to Mowrer, the difference between avoidance learning and learning through punishment is the locus of the cue which elicits fear in the two cases.[15]

Whenever a drive is reduced, either by the consumption of food or by the termination of shock, a second emotional mediator will be established, "hope." Hope will be subsequently elicited by any cues to the reduction in drive, and such cues will present a promise. The effect upon behavior is to facilitate any response that produces an approach to or retention of such cues. Evidence for such an effect is found in some of the studies of secondary reinforcement which we will consider in the next chapter and in some of the studies of incentive motivation which we

[15] Here, curiously, Mowrer has come around almost to the position advocated by Schoenfeld (1950), Dinsmoor (1954), and other Skinnerians. The only real point of difference is that for Mowrer the aversive stimulus, of whatever origin, *motivates* withdrawal, while for the Skinnerian it (actually, its removal) can only *reinforce* withdrawal.

have considered in this chapter. This evidence is rather substantial. In opposition to fear, hope has the effect of motivating any behavior which produces a cue that has been associated with drive reduction. Again, such cues may be external, as in the typical secondary reinforcement study, or they may be internal as an incentive motivation.

Hope and fear are Mowrer's two primary mediating mechanisms but he does not stop with them. He introduces two other mechanisms of a secondary nature which are reinforced by the onset and termination of drive respectively but which are elicited by cues to the onset and termination of cues rather than the onset and termination of drive. "Relief" is elicited by the presentation of a cue to the removal of drive. This occurs, for example, when a light signals the impending termination of shock. Such a higher order cue signals the withdrawal of threat and it too should motivate approach behavior. The empirical evidence for a relief mechanism (which we will consider in the next chapter) is not altogether compelling. Finally, Mowrer suggests that "disappointment" is reinforced by increase in drive and that this is elicited by the presentation of a cue which signals the withdrawal of a cue eliciting hope. Such a second-order cue signals the withdrawal of promise, or disappointment. Its effect upon behavior should be to produce withdrawal from the stimuli that elicit it. Such a mechanism could be used to explain a phenomenon reported by Konorski (1948), and Ferster (1958), viz., the aversiveness of nonreward. Table 12-1 summarizes the assumed properties and effects of these four emotions.

Evaluation of Mowrer's Position.　On the one hand Mowrer has presented a coherent, broad, consistent case for positive and negative incentive effects. Hull's Paradox has been avoided by attributing learning to both drive induction and reduction. The asymmetry between the appetitive and the aversive case has been reduced to the fundamental (i.e., unanalyzed) axiom that the organism retreats from bad things and approaches good ones. Drive is only implicated in the reinforcement of positive and negative incentives; it no longer affects behavior associatively, or energizes it, or has anything to do with the reinforcement of instrumental behavior.

The explicitness and frankness with which Mowrer has spelled out his theory invite us to find fault with it. I will note three difficulties. First, it is not clear that the hypothesized relief and disappointment effects have been sufficiently documented, nor is it clear that such mechanisms are necessary. With fear and hope we have a basic set of negative and positive incentive factors that ought to be able to explain all motivated behavior. Relief and disappointment appear to be redundant; they have entered the system by way of not too compelling logical arguments rather than empirical demonstrations.

Second, we may view Mowrer's system either as explaining emotions

TABLE 12-1
Summary of the Properties and Effects of Mowrer's
Motivation Constructs

Emotion	Reinforced by	Elicited by	Meaning of Cue	Behavioral Effect	Learning Situation	Evidence
Fear	Increase of D	Cue to increase of D	Presents threat	Remove or withdraw from cue	Avoidance escape	Excellent
Hope	Decrease of D	Cue to decrease of D	Presents promise	Approach or retain cue	Incentive	Good
Disap-point-ment	Increase of D	Cue to increase of D	Withdrawal of promise	Withdrawal	——	Slight
Relief	Decrease of D	Cue to decrease of D	Withdrawal of threat	Approach	——	Poor

and their consequences in terms of behavior theory, or as the attempt to explain behavior by invoking emotions. Since the early days of behavior theory we have been trying to do the former; and now it would appear that Mowrer is calling for us to do the latter. We can all agree that animals withdraw from fear-eliciting stimuli. The question is whether this fact should be taken as a definition of fear or an explanation of withdrawal. Mowrer (1960) says: ". . . there can be no adequate theory of behavior and behavior change which does not accept the reality and functional relevance of such subjective states as fear and . . . other emotions" (p. 48). Mowrer's theory has reduced all behavioral adaptations to the approach to and withdrawal from internal and external stimuli, but he insists that this is not as fundamental as the fact that such stimuli evoke fear and hope.

Third, although the emotions are held to be reactions to stimulation, instrumental responses are not. The animal presses the bar at a high rate because it is motivated to do so rather than because it is reinforced for doing so. According to Mowrer, when we reward bar pressing we do not teach the rat how to press the bar; it already knows how. We teach it to *want* to press the bar. What this means is that when the rat starts to press the bar, proprioceptive feedback is produced which elicits hope, which facilitates the response, and the overt bar press occurs. But what makes the animal start to press the bar? And what makes the animal press the bar the first time?

During the first quarter of the present century the phenomenon of learning was said to involve two problems, explaining the selection of the correct response, and explaining the fixation of the correct response. The two problems were seen as separate. Thorndike, Hull, and most subsequent behavior theorists have accepted a concept of habit which, whether we regard it in neurological and realistic terms, or in purely empirical and associationistic terms, reduces this two-fold problem to one, namely, how does the association between stimulus and response become strengthened? What Mowrer has done, in effect, is to reintroduce the old two-fold concept of habit and give us an incentive theory of motivation to account for the fixation of behavior. But he leaves us quite unprepared to explain the selection of behavior. This may indeed be the logical limit to which the incentive concept, or any motivation concept, can be extended.

SUMMARY

There is a rapidly growing mass of data showing how performance depends upon the conditions of reinforcement. When reinforcement is delayed, or withheld, or presented only in small amounts, the animal does not respond as surely or as vigorously as when a lot of reinforcement is promptly given. These effects appear to be flexible in the sense that they can change rapidly when the conditions of reinforcement are changed; they seem to depend primarily upon the animal's recent history of reinforcement rather than the whole history, or just current conditions. These and other findings lead us to the conclusion that the conditions of reinforcement have a motivational effect upon behavior rather than determining what is learned or how well it is learned.

The flexible nature of these incentive effects, the fact that they obviously involve learning, and the fact that they depend upon external stimulus conditions suggest that they are due to the operation of some response system. The leading candidate is r_G, a hypothetical covert fractional part of R_G, the response the animal makes to the reinforcer. Usually r_G is assumed to be much like any other response, but there is now enough evidence to suggest that it may be a very unusual sort of response: (1) While other responses become associated with drive stimuli only with great difficulty (see Chapter 9), it is necessary to assume that r_G is readily associated in order to account for the rapid changes in behavior that follow a change in the conditions of reinforcement or deprivation (e.g., the latent learning situation; Kendler, 1946; Seward, 1947). (2) r_G comes associated with external stimuli by different principles than those that apply to instrumental responses (see evidence cited by Mowrer, 1956; Seward, 1956; Spence, 1956). (3) r_G and its stimulus consequences or the stimuli arising from its frustration, are sometimes held to have an energizing function, in addition to whatever part they may play in the associative control of instrumental behavior. Sometimes this energization is assumed to be general or nonspecific, but more often it is assumed to have either an appetitive or aversive nature, so as to provide an additional element of control over behavior. Thus, Spence affords K, the incentive motivator, which he assumes is based upon r_G, the role of a generalized energizer, like D. But others, like Seward, have proposed that r_G has special motivating properties, e.g., that the organism approaches stimuli that elicit it. Mowrer (1960) has argued that incentive motivation is essentially emotional, and that what we call r_G is very much like what we call hope and that it can have quite diversified effects upon behavior.

If the r_G mechanism must operate too differently from other response systems it will not be easy to keep it within the domain of S-R psychology and a potentially powerful explanatory device may be lost. Mowrer's latest formulation shows that there is considerable strain already. Another reason for caution in accepting the r_G mechanism is the failure so far to localize it in the organism. Should we look for it only in the mouth? Or can the feedback from any response acquire incentive value? Does it necessarily involve the autonomic nervous system? Or is it really covert, a neural response occurring somewhere in the brain?

Whatever the status of r_G, incentive theories of motivation offer a clear alternative to drive theories. The antecedent conditions are different: drives are anchored in the prior conditions of deprivation whereas incentives are anchored in the conditions prevailing at the time of reinforcement, and in the organism's history of reinforcement. The behavioral consequences are similar: both drives and incentives are assumed to provide some combination of energization and associative control of behavior. Thus, incentives can explain anything drives can explain, and they can explain a vast number of transient and short-term effects that drives cannot explain. In fact the chief danger with incentives is that they tend to be too facile—they can go anywhere and do anything. This danger can, of course, be overcome by the collection of data and the development of systematic hypothetical models. The amount of current activity in the area offers some hope that this danger will be overcome, and that a durable account of incentive motivation will soon be forthcoming.

We may expect from such a theory a major reorganization of some of our traditional conceptions such as, for example, Seward and Mowrer have already proposed. We must have some solution of the problem of how incentives are learned; some resolution of the apparent differences between appetite and aversion; and more than anything else, some answer to the question of whether incentives elicit behavior, motivate it, or provide for its reinforcement. This is the question to which we now turn.

13

SECONDARY

REINFORCEMENT

In order to act as a secondary reinforcer for any response, a stimulus must have status as a discriminative stimulus for some response.
F. S. KELLER AND W. S. SCHOENFELD

There is probably no concept in all of psychology that is in such a state of theoretical disarray as the concept of secondary reinforcement. We know that there are secondary reinforcers because we know that the bulk of human behavior is learned by means of socially instilled rewards and punishments. But we know essentially nothing about how this instilling is done. The attempts to conduct systematic laboratory investigations to disclose how secondary reinforcers are established have as often as not failed to obtain any effects at all, much less show how they depend upon experimental parameters. A number of recent writers have suggested that there may not even be such a phenomenon as secondary reinforcement; or that if there is such a thing, then it has properties that make it quite different from what we had expected.

On the other hand, some theorists seem to have been so eager to find laboratory evidence of secondary reinforcement that they have been willing to accept purported claims that simply were not substantiated by the data. We will have occasion in the present chapter to look at some of these amazing discrepancies between data and interpretation; we will find that they have arisen mainly because there has been relatively little agreement about either (1) what conditions are supposed to be necessary to establish secondary reinforcers or (2) what role they are supposed to have in the determination of behavior once they are established. In the present chapter we will consider a number of specific proposals pertaining both to their establishment and to their functional properties.[1] Although many of these matters are still unsettled we will be able to come to some tentative conclusions about secondary reinforcement. Let us consider first the appetitive case and then the aversive case.

EARLY EXPERIMENTS ON SECONDARY REINFORCEMENT

The first experimental validation of the secondary reinforcement concept appears to have been Frolov's study of "higher order conditioning" which has been described by Pavlov (1927). Frolov first obtained classical conditioning of salivation in dogs, using an auditory stimulus as the CS. Then, in the crucial second phase of the experiment, a new visual CS was paired with the auditory stimulus which now supposedly had reinforcing powers. Pavlov reports that salivation did become conditioned to the visual stimulus, although he admitted that the effect was quite fragile. But Frolov's results do fit the paradigm of secondary reinforcement: a once-neutral stimulus (the auditory one) is paired with a reinforcer (food) and then when subsequently tested it appears itself to have the power of reinforcing.

Williams (1929) reported an experiment in which animals were taught a black-white discrimination in one apparatus, using food reinforcement; and then this apparatus, without food, was placed at the end of a maze in lieu of a goal box. The animals performed better, although not significantly so, under these conditions than when a plain empty box was placed at the end of the maze. In the somewhat mixed terminology of that era, Williams claimed that the conditioned stimulus in the discrimination problem had acquired the power of reinforcing learning in a new task.

A third early experiment was reported by Grindley (1929). Grindley ran chicks down an alley to food which was behind a glass partition so that it could be seen but not eaten. Grindley's chicks showed an increase in running speed for a few trials and then they slowed down again, presumably indicating the extinction of the secondary reinforcing power of the sight of food.

[1] Some good recent reviews of the secondary reinforcement literature are Myers (1958), Beck (1961), Kimble (1961), and Kelleher & Gollub (1962). More partisan but highly provocative is Mowrer (1960).

None of these experiments furnished convincing evidence of secondary reinforcement. In each case the alleged learning was transient and disappeared in a few trials. Frolov included no control groups to assess the possibility that the alleged higher order conditioning might be just pseudoconditioning. Pavlov cautioned that the effect could only be obtained under very specialized conditions. Moreover it has not been possible, in general, to replicate Frolov's results. Razran (1955), after surveying a mass of Russian and American literature, concludes that higher order conditioning is at best a laboratory curiosity. It is surely not the sort of effect that can explain social learning and motivation.

In the Williams and Grindley experiments there were no appropriate control groups to indicate that the "secondary reinforcer" was actually producing any new learning. We have no assurance that there may not have been weak primary reinforcers operating in the situation, e.g., the handling Williams gave her animals at the goal. Although we cannot give much weight to the claims of these early studies, a great number of theorists have. Hull (1943), for example, accepted all of these findings not only as evidence for the reality of secondary reinforcement, but also as indicating some of the functional properties of secondary reinforcement.

Token-Reward Studies. There is a remarkable early series of experiments by Wolfe (1936) and Cowles (1937), which provides much more convincing evidence of secondary reinforcement. Both Wolfe and Cowles trained chimpanzees to insert tokens (poker chips) into vending machines in order to receive raisins or peanuts. After this behavior had become established the situation was made more difficult by requiring the animals to accumulate 20 poker chips before they could be spent for food. Then to determine whether the poker chips had acquired secondary reinforcing value, the animals were required to learn a discrimination problem in order to get poker chips (Cowles, 1937). The chimps were able to learn relatively complicated new habits on the basis of poker chip reinforcement, even when the chips were not immediately exchangeable for food but had to be accumulated throughout the day's session. Learning with poker chips appeared to have many of the properties of learning with primary reinforcement; extinction, generalization, discrimination, and reversal learning effects could all be produced. Appropriate control conditions were run to demonstrate that the learning was not based on any inherent reinforcing properties of the chips themselves.

These studies with token rewards demonstrate that laboratory-controlled secondary reinforcement can have the sort of durability and persistence that are necessary to explain social learning and motivation. But this finding raises the question of why token rewards with chimps are so effective whereas secondary reinforcement procedures in other situations are so ineffective. One possible source of the difference is the organism itself; perhaps chimpanzees, like humans, are able to make use of tokens, or symbolic reinforcements, whereas lower animals are not. This is undoubtedly true to some extent, but Smith (1939) was able to get learning in cats based upon token rewards by modifying the procedure to allow for the different response repertories of cats and chimps. Smith taught cats to pull strings to get balls which could be used in a vending machine to obtain food. Ellson (1937) obtained similar results with dogs.

Another unique feature of the token-reward studies which may account for their success is that the animals had the tokens in hand between the time they were acquired and the time they were exchanged for primary reinforcement. Cowles found that the chimps would no longer work for their poker chips if they had to part with them. Thus, it may be that the possession of the token rewards rather than merely obtaining them constitutes the reinforcing state of affairs, and that this is what bridges the gap and explains the long delays that are possible between obtaining the token rewards and cashing them in for food. In this connection, Kelleher (1958) has reported that when chimps are put on a very difficult fixed ratio schedule so that they must press a bar 50 or 100 times for each chip, they start responding very slowly and only gradually accelerate bar pressing as the required number of tokens is approached. Kelleher also found that the rate of responding could be sharply increased by starting the animals with 50 tokens. Thus it would appear that it is the number of poker chips which matters, and that it is the possession of a large number of chips rather than obtaining a chip which produces a high rate of responding. One implication of these results is that responding for chips is *elicited* by the number of chips possessed rather than being reinforced by obtaining chips.[2]

One further consideration, the importance of which will become apparent later, is that the token reward serves as a subgoal, or as an invariant link between the instrumental behavior and the ultimate primary reinforcement. In the studies by Frolov, Williams, and Grindley primary reinforcement was withheld during the test of the effectiveness of the secondary reinforcer. In Cowles' study primary reinforcement was still present to support learning, and the secondary reinforcer or token reward became just a link in the chain of events leading to primary reinforcement.

THE BEHAVIORAL EFFECTS OF SECONDARY REINFORCERS

The current uncertain status of the concept of secondary reinforcement is partly a result of the fact that the term has never been anchored firmly

[2] This is just the first of a number of instances we will discover where what looks like a reinforcement effect turns out to be partly, or perhaps totally, a matter of the behavior being elicited.

on the behavioral side. We have already noted four different and largely independent properties of behavior that have been attributed to different explanatory aspects of secondary reinforcers. We have seen them invoked to explain higher order conditioning, the maintenance or motivation of instrumental behavior, the reinforcement of instrumental behavior, and the various effects of token or subgoal rewards. In the present section we will extend this list to include still other aspects of learned behavior. But we will also try to see if some common underlying principle is involved in all the manifestations of secondary reinforcers. This survey will be easier if we can anticipate the answer, which is: secondary reinforcers are merely stimuli that hold together chains of behavior.

The Reinforcement of New Responses. The term "secondary reinforcer" implies an agency of some sort that has acquired the power to reinforce, i.e., to produce new learning. Unfortunately most of the time the term is used it is applied in situations where there is little or no evidence of acquisition. Thus, in the four studies discussed in the last section, only Cowles had an unequivocal demonstration of learning; the others show at best only momentary increments in performance in the absence of primary reinforcement. To make the situation worse, learning is often claimed in cases where the data clearly do not support the claim. For example, D'Amato (1955) fed rats in a distinctive box, and then put this box and a neutral box, both empty, on opposite sides of a T maze and tested to see if the animals would learn to go to the distinctive "secondary reinforcing" box where they had previously eaten. The trial-by-trial performance is indicated in Fig. 13-1.

Notice that there is no rise of any consequence in the learning curve. D'Amato acknowledged this but pointed to the fact that the curve averages significantly above 50%; he took this as evidence of secondary reinforcement (see Bolles, 1962b).

One of the few convincing demonstrations of acquisition of new behavior in rats has been reported by Saltzman (1949). Saltzman's animals were trained to run a straight alley to a distinctive box for food, and then this box was placed in one side of a T maze on the nonpreferred side for each subject. On the opposite side was a box which for one group (the continuous-reinforcement group) was novel, and which for another group (the differential-reinforcement group) had been used in the straight alley on trials when food had been withheld. A control group was run with primary reinforcement in the T maze. The learning of the T-maze habit for these three groups is shown in Fig. 13-2. (Saltzman also ran other groups the results for which are not indicated in the figure.)

Several features of Saltzman's experiment should be noted. One is that the rats could not see the goal boxes at the choice point; hence it cannot be said that they were merely making approach responses to

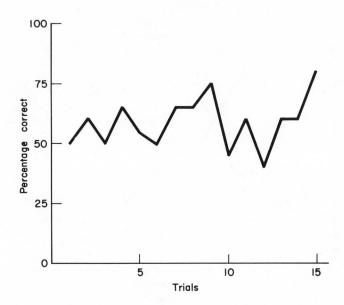

Fig. 13-1. Alleged learning on the basis of secondary reinforcement. (Data from D'Amato, 1955; figure reproduced from Bolles, 1962b)

stimuli they had learned to approach in the alley. Note that the apparent effect of secondary reinforcement was considerably more durable for the animals in the differential-reinforcement group than for the continuous group, and that for the latter the secondary reinforcing effect was quite short-lived. It has been suggested that the poor showing of the continuous group is due to frustration effects that occur when the empty box is encountered for the first time, or to exploratory effects produced by the novelty of the situation. In this connection, Reynolds et al. (1963) have attempted, with some success, to control these competing tendencies, and they report somewhat more stable performance with continuous prior training than Saltzman found in the same type of situation.

Klein (1959) has also confirmed the main findings reported by Saltzman. There seems little question that the acquisition of a new habit can be reinforced by running to a distinctive box in which eating has occurred, and that this learning leads to more permanent performance if the animal has had prior discrimination training. However, no one has yet run the control groups necessary to show whether this learning indicates an approach to a positive box or an avoidance of an aversive one.[3]

[3] Grice & Goldman (1955) have reported a study suggesting that both effects exist (see p. 359). While their results do not require a secondary reinforcement

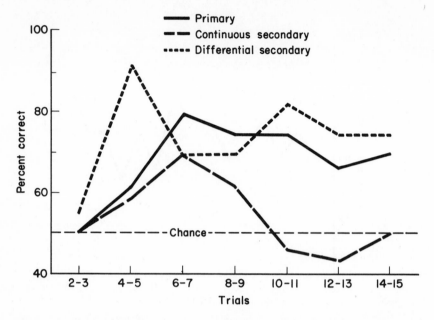

Fig. 13-2. A comparison of T maze performance reinforced by food or by going to a box previously associated with food. Previously all subjects had run an alley and eaten in the box. For the continuous group, alley running had always been reinforced, but for the differential group running had been reinforced in this box but not reinforced in a box of a different color which was later put on the incorrect side of the T maze. (Adapted from Saltzman, 1949)

Skinner (1938) has described a case where a rat was trained to press a bar using just the click as a reinforcer.[4] When the animal had been magazine trained, the bar was presented but the food magazine was emptied so that it continued to click but no longer delivered food. Skinner reported that the rat did indeed learn to press the bar under these conditions. However, it is clear from Skinner's brief report and from similar reports of others (e.g., Estes, 1949) that the performance under these conditions falls far short of that obtained with the usual bar-press

interpretation, they are consistent with such an interpretation. They are also consistent with a frustration interpretation. Actually, the procedures used to study frustration effects are sometimes identical to those used to study secondary reinforcement effects.

[4] When rats are trained to press a bar they are first usually "magazine trained," i.e., trained to approach a food cup and eat when the food delivery mechanism makes a characteristic "click" in presenting a pellet of food. Ordinarily, when the animal has been magazine trained, the bar is presented for the first time and it is arranged so that the magazine presents food when the bar is pressed. Then when the bar is pressed the click occurs, the animal goes to eat the food, and the bar press is reinforced. The rat accordingly learns to press the bar.

training with food. This deficiency has supposedly been repaired by Zimmerman (1957) who demonstrated that under the proper conditions animals would generate thousands of bar-press responses in the absence of any primary reinforcement. The procedures that are necessary to produce this result, according to Zimmerman, consist first in pairing the secondary reinforcer (a buzzer in his experiments) with primary reinforcement on an intermittent schedule so that the animal obtains food during the magazine-training phase of the experiment only a fraction of the times the buzzer is sounded. Under these conditions the buzzer acquires very strong associative control over the response of turning to the food cup. Then, in the test for the secondary reinforcing powers of the buzzer, only a fraction of the bar presses result in producing the buzzer. Unfortunately, Zimmerman did not run the appropriate control groups to permit a firm conclusion to the effect that the buzzer has secondary reinforcing effect. Thus, he has no group which got the buzzer in the absence of prior pairing with food, nor does he have groups that had secondary reinforcement training but had it on a continuous rather than intermittent schedule. The evidence for secondary reinforcement is presumptive; Zimmerman got many more bar-press responses out of his subjects than prior experimenters had been able to.[5]

The Maintenance of Previously Learned Responses. Bugelski (1938) trained two groups of rats to press a bar for food and when the behavior was well established extinguished them, one group with the click and the other group without the click (food was withheld from both groups). Bugelski reported that subjects undergoing extinction without the click extinguished more quickly than those with the click. Presumably the click helped to maintain the learned bar-pressing response, and for this reason is called a secondary reinforcer.

These results suggest alternative explanations, however. Bitterman et al. (1953) have pointed out that Bugelski's findings and much of the other evidence then cited to support the concept of secondary reinforcement could be interpreted simply on the basis of what is called the discrimination hypothesis. Bitterman et al. argue that, of course, Bugelski's animals extinguished more slowly with the click than without it, because the click had been present in acquisition; the subjects without

---

[5] Zimmerman (1959) has attempted to extend these procedures to a situation where pressing a bar opened a door to where food had been. Extremely durable learning was found; but, again, the appropriate controls were not run. McNamara & Paige (1962) and Wike et al. (1962), who have run additional control animals, have indicated that Zimmerman's 1959 results are not attributable to secondary reinforcement. It seems, for example, that getting out of the bar-pressing box is inherently reinforcing. (See also Zimmerman, 1961, 1963, 1963a; Keehn, 1962; Wike & Platt, 1962; McNamara, 1963; Wike et al., 1963). A further peculiarity of Zimmerman's data is that the secondary reinforcer does not seem to extinguish with continued use.

the click were extinguished under conditions which differed more from the acquisition conditions than they did for subjects extinguished with the click. The difference can be discriminated and accordingly behavior decrements occur.

A similar but somewhat more pointed alternative has been suggested by Bugelski himself (1956). Bugelski contends that the click has no special properties; it is simply one of the stimuli that elicit one of the responses in the chain of behavior leading to food. He says:

> . . . it would appear that rather than talking about secondary rein- forcement we might more logically conceive the click to be a stimulus which happens to become associated with one segment of a chain of responses, namely, that part of the pattern which we can label "going to the food cup." . . . When it is dropped out of the picture, the pattern is to that extent weakened or altered so that the behavior is less likely to occur and will be eliminated more rapidly as the rest of the pattern gets extinguished. (Bugelski, 1956, p. 93)

Bugelski's argument differs from that of Bitterman et al. in that he attributes the difference in extinction performance to the fact that a chain of behavior is broken for one group but not for the other. White (1953), a student of Bugelski's, trained several groups of rats to press a bar, and observed them in the situation to determine the nature of the behavior during the course of acquisition and extinction. As Bugelski describes it:

> When all the rats were trained they were given different *pre-extinc- tion* training. Some rats were placed in a box without a bar present and were presented with the click at an average of 30 seconds. The click was followed ordinarily by an approach to the food cup, now empty. As the clicks continued the fruitless trips began to decline until they stopped altogether (usually within a period of 30 clicks). It would appear that the food-cup approach was extinguished as far as the click was concerned. The next day the rats were replaced in the box with the bar present and underwent ordinary extinction (that is, no food was dropped to them after the bar-presses). Allowing for "spontaneous recovery" and for the probable short-circuiting of the behavior so that the click might not be particularly important if food was present, we could expect the rats to make some food-cup ap- proaches, which they did. However, an interesting chain of events began to unfold. The rats began to cut down on the number of trips to the food cup after bar-pressing, compared with the normal (non- pre-extinguish) group. Their behavior toward the food cup became less regular, frequently they failed to reach it at all, and frequently

they failed to "search" it for food. As the food-cup behavior began to break down, the entire pattern of return to the bar also weakened and broke down. Now the rat did not get to the bar and consequently could not press it. When it did get around to the bar and pressed, it failed to go to the cup, and consequently spent more time in the bar area. Spending more time in the bar area permitted a few more bar-presses than might be ordinary, but even that behavior began to weaken. The pre-extinguished rats met an extinction criterion sooner than did the control animals. (Bugelski, 1956, pp. 91–93)

The results from White's study are shown in Fig. 13-3. One of the great virtues of these data, and Bugelski's description of the animals' behavior, is that they suggest how the strength of the criterion response,

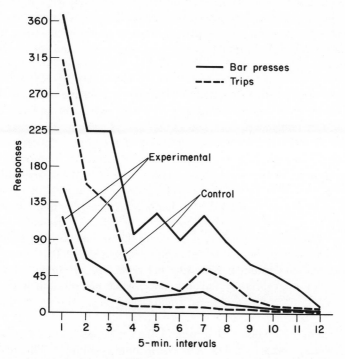

Fig. 13-3. Extinction performance of bar pressing and trips to the food cup in successive 5-min. intervals in a 1-hr. extinction session. The experimental group had a 30-min. preextinction session with the click presented irregularly but without the bar being present. The control group also had 30-min. preextinction experience but without the click. Note how the prior extinction of going to the food cup depressed bar pressing for the experimental group. (Data from White, 1953; figure reproduced from Bugelski, 1956)

the one being maintained by secondary reinforcement, depends upon the strength of the subsequent response in the chain.

These findings point to two quite different questions. The one we are concerned with at this point is whether a stimulus paired with primary reinforcement helps to maintain a previously learned response. The answer is clearly yes; this is evidently one of the functional properties of secondary reinforcers. But Bugelski is raising a much more profound and exciting question: Does a secondary reinforcer have any other functional properties beyond its ability to maintain behavior? More particularly, if we can assume that such stimuli maintain behavior by eliciting the next response in a response chain, is there any reason to make the additional assumptions that they have the ability to reinforce? Bugelski leaves little doubt about where he stands:

> The click is part of the stimulation that is associated with approaching the food cup which automatically puts the animal in position for pressing the bar. To select out the click and glamorize it into a "secondary reinforcer" is totally unnecessary, gratuitous, and theoretically harmful. (Bugelski, 1956, p. 271)

We will return to this assertion with more supporting evidence shortly but first we must continue the survey of the proposed behavioral effects of secondary reinforcers.

The Motivating Function of Secondary Reinforcers. An effect which is rarely adequately allowed for in studies of secondary reinforcement is the component of the animal's response to the click that I will call "excitement." Whether or not the effect is due to the arousal of r_G mechanisms, it is apparent that the click does increase the animal's energy output and activity level. Perhaps, then, one effect of the click early in the acquisition of bar pressing is to excite the animal so that it clings to or attacks the bar, thereby boosting the response score. It is well known that the animal's initial bar-pressing behavior tends to include bursts of activity. An appropriately "micro" analysis of bar-press acquisition in secondary reinforcing situations could show how important such an effect is.

It is also well known that stimuli that have been closely associated with feeding produce excited behavior in hungry animals. This has been systematically demonstrated by Cowles (1937) and others in token-reward situations. Miller (1951) has described this phenomenon: "The sight of a learned reward can be used as an incentive to induce striving" (p. 457). Granting that this is so, we are brought back once again to the question of elicitation vs. reinforcement vs. motivation. This incentive effect could be due simply to the fact that excited behavior is the behavior which typically precedes feeding. That is, excited behavior, the striving for food, is an early member of the eating chain, one which is frequently reinforced. The question with regard to the secondary reinforcement properties of such exciting stimuli is whether there is any necessary relationship between the excitement produced by a secondary reinforcer, i.e., the sudden increase in incentive motivation, and the reinforcement of a preceding response.[6]

The Facilitation Hypothesis. Even if the click does not markedly "excite" the animal, it should, as a consequence of magazine training, increase the probability of pressing the bar, if only because it elicits approach to the food cup which keeps the animal near the front of the box and consequently near the bar (Wyckoff et al., 1958; Myers, 1958). Crowder et al. (1959, 1959a, 1959b, 1959c) have controlled for this facilitation effect and shown with a variety of tests that there are secondary reinforcement effects over and beyond it. Their control for facilitation was accomplished by using a "yoked" control procedure in which two animals are given secondary reinforcement training and then tested together in two boxes arranged so that one of the pair can produce the secondary reinforcer for both animals, but the responses of the other animal do not have any stimulus consequences. Thus, both animals have the advantage of whatever facilitation the click produces; but this facilitation is only correlated with the behavior of one of the pair. It is unfortunate that Crowder and his colleagues did not run other controls to determine, for example, whether the yoked controls did in fact have a higher rate of responding than animals that had no secondary reinforcement, as the facilitation hypothesis requires.

The Mediation of Discrimination Learning. Denny (1948) found that rats would learn a simple position habit in a T maze more quickly if the two goal boxes (the correct one and the incorrect one) were different colors than if they were the same color. Denny argued that the color of the positive goal box acquired secondary reinforcement by virtue of being present at the time of primary reinforcement, and that if this stimulus was also present in the incorrect end box it would tend to produce an increment in the strength of the incorrect response by virtue of its secondary reinforcing power. This would hinder discrimination learning.

---

[6] We may note that Kimble (1961) has confused the issue here somewhat. He cites studies such as those of Crespi (1942) and Zeaman (1949) to show that the amount of primary reinforcement has a motivational effect on instrumental behavior, and then proceeds to argue that secondary reinforcers also provide for the instigation or motivation of instrumental behavior. Kimble cites Dinsmoor's finding (1950) that a discriminative stimulus would help maintain behavior in extinction. But it is clear that neither Dinsmoor nor anyone else has shown that such stimuli motivate behavior; the most that has been shown is that such stimuli control behavior.

This general set of findings has been confirmed by Saltzman (1950), Ehrenfreund (1949, 1954), Webb and Nolan (1953), Bauer and Lawrence (1953), and Grice and Goldman (1955).

The Mediation of Temporal Delays. Perkins (1947) showed that running an alley for food was seriously impaired by delaying the animal in a box which was dissimilar from the goal box, and that there was less decrement when the delay box presented stimuli that were similar to those in the goal box. Hence, it has been argued, behavior may be maintained by the secondary reinforcing value of stimuli like those that have been associated with primary reinforcement.

Grice (1948), as we noted in Chapter 12, reported that a black-white discrimination was extremely difficult if not impossible to learn if the delay of reinforcement was longer than just a few seconds (see Fig. 12-2). Of course, previous experimenters had reported successful learning with considerably longer delays of primary reinforcement. But, Grice argued, in those studies sufficient care was not exercised to prevent the possibility of learning by secondary reinforcement. That is, typically, the delay of primary reinforcement is imposed in the goal box, and because eventually the stimuli in the goal box become associated with food and the eating of food they acquire secondary reinforcing power which strengthened the response sufficiently to make learning evident. In Grice's apparatus, however, delay was imposed in a stimulus situation which was distinct from the goal box, and, as Grice's data show, animals were then virtually unable to bridge any temporal gap.

Spence (1947) used this and similar findings to propose that the gradient of delay of primary reinforcement was quite short, and that whenever learning occurs with relatively long delays it is on the basis of the immediate action of secondary reinforcement.

Secondary Reinforcement and the Chaining of Behavior. In some of the previous discussions we have noted that some importance must be given to the fact that secondary reinforcement effects seem to work best when a chain of behavior is involved. This raises the possibility that the maintenance of a chain of behavior may be the principal effect of stimuli called secondary reinforcers. Cowles (1937) has found that token rewards lose their efficacy if the animal is not hungry or if the token no longer is allowed to produce food; that is, the token loses its power to reinforce if the terminal element of the behavior chain does not occur. Zimmerman (1957), who has gotten perhaps the most vivid evidence of response acquisition based on secondary reinforcement, has emphasized that there must be a very strong association between the buzzer and the next response (turning to the food cup) if the buzzer is to reinforce a new response.

It is possible to apply the same type of argument to the case of what appears to be the acquisition of bar pressing with only a click reinforcement (Skinner, 1938). Here we can raise Bugelski's question (p. 378) of whether the click is really functioning in any way which distinguishes it from any other stimulus to which a response has been conditioned.

Wyckoff et al. (1958) trained rats to approach and lick a water dipper in response to the sound of a buzzer. The rats were then tested in a situation in which lever pressing produced the buzzer but no water. The data showed that the buzzer did become a discriminative stimulus for approaching the water dipper and that the animal did learn to press the bar for a buzzer reinforcement. However (and this is the important finding), the acquisition of bar pressing was not significantly better for these subjects than for subjects for whom pressing the bar turned the buzzer off! Wyckoff et al. suggest that a large part of the literature that appears to support the concept of secondary reinforcement may be more readily interpreted in terms of the response-eliciting effects of the alleged secondary reinforcer.

Weiss and Lawson (1962) have observed that Wyckoff's animals were run on a variable-interval schedule where considerable "pausing" after the buzzer might be expected. An analysis of their own data, also obtained under VI conditions, showed that this was the case. This does not alter the force of the argument; the data still suggest that the function of the buzzer was not primarily that of reinforcing the response that preceded it, but rather to produce the behavior that had previously been conditioned to it. Whether the eliciting effect produces an increase or a decrease in the strength of the response which is supposedly being reinforced would seem to depend entirely upon whether the elicited response carries the animal back into or further away from the situation in which the "reinforced" response is likely to occur. Thus, the buzzer in Wyckoff's situation took the animals away from the bar and therefore depressed bar pressing; but if the animal has learned to get excited, or attack the apparatus when the buzzer sounds, then it may get excited or attack the bar and show a large increase in bar pressing. Other experimenters (e.g., Hulicka & Capeheart, 1960; Bolles, 1961b; Kelleher & Fry, 1962) have also observed these kinds of associative effects. Such results suggest that when the response-eliciting properties of the secondary reinforcer have been fully accounted for there may be nothing left over for the hypothetical secondary reinforcing property to explain.

In one study (Ratner, 1956), approaching the food cup (or water dipper) was extinguished prior to testing for the reinforcing effects of the click. In other studies (Ratner, 1956a; Morrow et al., 1965), although no explicit extinction was given, the goal-approach response was found to extinguish during testing. In either case it would be expected that as the click lost the ability to elicit the next response, approaching the goal, it would lose the ability to reinforce the new bar-press response. These studies are consistent only in showing extremely small and transient effects; they do not constitute a test of the chaining hypothesis because in none of them is it clear that approaching the goal, or any other response, had come under strong discriminative control of the click.

A curious feature of acquisition studies of this type, which does not seem to appear in published reports, is that the cumulative records of the new response are negatively rather than positively accelerated, as if extinction rather than acquisition were being recorded. The new response never seems to have any more strength than it does when it first starts to appear. We may suppose that the first occurrence of the buzzer produces a sudden increment in incentive motivation or conditioned excitement, which then rapidly extinguishes. Such a finding is rather damaging to any interpretation requiring the secondary reinforcer really to reinforce new responses, but it is entirely consistent with a hypothesis that emphasizes the role of the elicited response. The importance of the elicited response is implicit, of course, in the excitement and facilitation effects of secondary reinforcement. And in each case the stimulus which excites the animal or holds it near the vicinity of the bar does have associative control over responses which have previously received primary reinforcement. In the studies of delayed reinforcement (e.g., Grice, 1948) and discrimination learning (e.g., Denny, 1948), the secondary reinforcer is the goal box so that the next member of the response chain is approaching food, and this is followed by eating.

The situation in which delays are imposed in the goal box itself also poses little difficulty in view of Skinner's discovery (1948) of superstitious behavior in such situations. Skinner noted that if pigeons are fed at fixed intervals they soon develop stereotyped sequences of responses which he called "superstitious behavior." Animals will "invent" chains of responses to fill the delay interval. What is involved is a complex chain in which the animal may preen its feathers, walk around the experimental chamber, stand on one foot for a while and then the other, and so occupy itself until food is presented. Skinner and his followers have argued that the whole chain of behavior, capable of lasting a minute or more, is held together by secondary reinforcement. Each response of the chain leads to certain internal and external stimulus events which come in turn to elicit the next response and reinforce the last, so that the whole sequence is not only linked together by the sequence of stimuli and responses but is glued together by the operation of secondary reinforcing elements all along the line. Ferster (1953) has suggested that such chains are always involved when temporal gaps are successfully bridged. To the extent that such chains are formed, they can be expected to maintain the eliciting effects of the stimuli that initiate them, so that more antecedent responses can always be added to the chain.

There can be no doubt that chaining occurs. If we are to have a concept of reinforcement, then it is applicable to the new responses that accrue to the beginning of a chain. It follows from any empirical law of reinforcement that the stimuli which initiate chains reinforce these new responses. Thus, the phenomenon of chaining reveals an empirical law of secondary reinforcement.

Our interest then turns from the question of whether such stimuli do reinforce, to the question of whether secondary reinforcement (according to any of the behavioral criteria) ever occurs *except* in situations where the secondary reinforcer controls a subsequent response, or chain of responses. There are three slim lines of evidence suggesting a possible negative answer. One is the finding of Saltzman (1949) and Klein (1959) that rats will learn a new response to get to a goal box where they have previously eaten. At the time the test for secondary reinforcement occurs the terminal response of the chain (eating) cannot occur because food is not present. Nonetheless, learning occurs. It is fragile, however, and Saltzman and a host of others have recognized this, and postulated that secondary reinforcement extinguishes rapidly. To apply the elicitation hypothesis, it is only necessary to add that secondary reinforcement extinguishes rapidly to the extent that the chain which gives the goal box its secondary reinforcing effect is disrupted.

The second line of contrary evidence comes from a study by Stein (1958) in which he was able to give a buzzer secondary reinforcing properties by pairing it with direct brain stimulation. The experimental design was not the best for isolating secondary reinforcement effects from possible confounding factors, and the reported effect was rather small, but that it was there at all raises a problem because there is no a priori reason to suppose that any response had been conditioned to the buzzer, or that direct stimulation of the brain had elicited any particular response. However, Pliskoff et al. (1964) have found that .5 sec. is a sufficiently long interval for animals to make a peculiar "postural" response after the secondary reinforcer is presented and before brain stimulation is turned on. They suggest that this postural adjustment could easily have become conditioned to the secondary reinforcer during training and henceforth act in a manner analogous to the theoretically required goal-approach response in other situations. The fact that the presentation of the primary reinforcer is not made contingent upon the animal making such a postural adjustment does not mean that such responses will not be acquired, nor even that their acquisition may be necessary for the mediation of a secondary reinforcement effect. It is primarily the failure to determine by observation whether the secondary reinforcer actually had any response conditioned to it during training that permitted us to discount so easily Ratner's study (p. 381).

The third line of evidence comes from a study reported by Landauer (1964) in which short delays were introduced between the new response to be learned (bar pressing) and the click. Landauer found a sharp temporal gradient and maximal secondary reinforcing effects (i.e., maximum number of bar presses in the session) at a delay of .8 sec. A further interesting finding was that the maximal effect of the first click was found at 0 sec. delay instead of .8 sec. Landauer suggests that the principal beneficial effect of the first reinforcement might result from the reinforcement of responses just prior to bar pressing, such as approaching the bar. Approaching the bar has to be reinforced before the effect of reinforcement upon the bar press itself can be manifest. Landauer's results pose a problem for the response-elicitation hypothesis because it is not clear how that hypothesis can account for the approach to the bar being acquired before the bar press itself, if that is what does happen. In any case, this is the kind of detailed analysis that is much needed to clarify how response chains are built up.

THE ESTABLISHMENT OF SECONDARY REINFORCERS

Although they frame the principle in different ways, nearly all motivation theorists have subscribed to the principle that stimuli become secondary reinforcers by virtue of being paired with primary reinforcement. A cognitive theorist might argue that under such conditions the stimuli are seen as "related" to valued objects and therefore acquire value themselves. Everyday experience supports this view and no doubt a large part of the appeal of S-S theories of learning is due to the belief that some events become good (or bad) "by association." However, S-S theorists have been lax in spelling out the syntactical rules of this sort of association, so we must look to S-R theorists for explicit hypotheses and conjectures regarding the establishment of secondary reinforcement.

Contiguity with Primary Reinforcement. One of the simplest hypotheses is that neutral stimulus acquires reinforcing properties merely by being contiguous with the events constituting primary reinforcement. This was Pavlov's position and provided the basis of his explanation of higher order conditioning. Hull (1943) accepted the contiguity hypothesis of secondary reinforcement as a general working hypothesis, although he supplemented it with certain specific hypotheses, which we will examine shortly.[7] If contiguity were sufficient for the establishment of a secondary

---

[7] Hull probably accepted the contiguity hypothesis because he accepted the case Pavlov had made for higher order conditioning. Hull also had previously (1930) committed r_G to an associative role in the explanation of behavior, and except for the hypothesis that drive reduction was involved in conditioning r_G he kept it that way. By 1952, when he had attributed reinforcing, motivating, and eliciting powers to r_G, he still adhered to the position that a stimulus "which occurs repeatedly and consistently in close conjunction with a reinforcing state of affairs, . . . will itself acquire the power of acting as a reinforcing agent" (p. 6).

reinforcer, this would imply that whenever primary reinforcement occurs, e.g., whenever the animal eats, all of the stimuli impinging on the organism would gain some tendency to act as reinforcers. Some writers have handled the concept of secondary reinforcement as though contiguity were sufficient (e.g., Spence, 1947).

The Discriminative-Stimulus Hypothesis. Skinner had suggested as early as 1938 that a necessary condition for establishing a stimulus as a secondary reinforcer is that it be a discriminative stimulus.[8] This implies that it is not sufficient that the stimulus be contiguous with reinforcement in order for it to acquire reinforcing properties. Experimental evidence to support this hypothesis comes from a study by Schoenfeld et al. (1950). These workers trained two groups of rats to press a bar for food. For the experimental group, a light of 1-sec. duration was turned on at the onset of eating. Considerable care was taken to make this stimulus accompany rather than precede the consummatory response as it does in most secondary reinforcement situations. The control group received no light stimulus. After acquisition, both groups were extinguished under conditions such that a bar press no longer produced food but did present the 1-sec. light. No difference in performance between the groups was found. Schoenfeld et al. did not run a group where the light preceded the consummatory response by a short interval—such as is the case when the click of the feeding mechanism is used as a secondary reinforcer— to show that a group trained with the light would have greater resistance to extinction than the control group. But they could cite studies in which such an effect had been found. The crucial point is that being present at the time of primary reinforcement did not make the stimulus a secondary reinforcer.

Dinsmoor (1950) gave two groups of animals discrimination training on bar pressing. In extinction, one group produced the S^D for 3 sec. by pressing the bar (i.e., this group was extinguished while using the S^D as though it were a reinforcer—following the response). The second group was extinguished under conditions similar to those in acquisition in that the light was on except for 3 sec. immediately after a response (i.e., it was still being presented as though it were an S^D). No difference between the two groups was found in extinction. Dinsmoor concluded that there is no functional difference between the discriminative and the reinforcing functions of a stimulus as far as the organism is concerned; any differ-

---

[8] What this means in Skinnerian terminology is that the response may be reinforced when the discriminative stimulus (S^D) is present, but is never reinforced in its absence. What happens under these conditions, of course, is that the animal learns to respond more or less exclusively in the presence of S^D. After this learning has occurred the stimulus is said to "set the occasion" for responding, or to be a "discriminative stimulus" or, according to this hypothesis, to be a secondary reinforcer.

ence is merely a matter of temporal relationship as seen by the experimenter.

The hypothesis that a secondary reinforcer must necessarily be a discriminative stimulus has become pretty much accepted doctrine in Skinnerian psychology. Kelleher and Gollub (1962) have reviewed a mass of evidence that has accumulated to support the hypothesis. And it seems undeniable that in lever-pressing and key-pecking situations, and using rate of responding as the response measure, this hypothesis explains what is known. But unfortunately the restrictions of apparatus and data analysis make it very difficult to give the hypothesis a fair test. Thus, when the animal generates 1000 responses an hour under a given set of stimulus conditions, we cannot tell whether the behavior is occurring because it is being elicited by these conditions (i.e., that they are serving as discriminative stimuli) or whether these conditions are reinforcing the behavior to keep it at that level. Unfortunately too, the Skinnerian psychologist often does not care to distinguish between the discriminative and the reinforcing properties of stimuli; as long as the maintenance of behavior can be correlated with the presence of the stimulus, it may not matter to him whether he regards it as possessing discriminative or reinforcing properties.

On the other hand, Ferster and Skinner (1957) have developed some very elaborate and sophisticated techniques in the attempt to tease apart the reinforcing and discriminative roles of stimuli. One of the most ingenious designs (first used by Skinner, 1936b) and the one to which Kelleher and Gollub devote most of their attention, is the "chain" schedule of reinforcement in which the animal must press the bar on one schedule to turn on the S^D, in the presence of which it must respond on another schedule to receive reinforcement. For example the animal might work on a fixed ratio of 50 (be required to make 50 responses) to turn a light on and then have to work for 1 min. in the presence of the light to produce food. The presentation of food then puts the animal back into phase one where it has to press the bar to turn the light back on. The experimental question here is whether the presentation of the light (i.e., the S^D for pressing for food) has the same reinforcing properties that food might have upon the behavior occurring under the first part of the chain. The answer seems to be yes. Chain schedules have been developed in which the animal responds quite differently on the two parts of the chain, e.g., at a very slow rate to obtain food in the presence of the reinforcer, and a very high rate in order to produce the S^D. In fact Autor (1960) was able to develop behavior which consisted of a very high rate of responding for S^D and then a zero response rate in the presence of S^D. The subject had to keep from pressing for an interval of time in the presence of a light in order to receive food. Thus the emphasis has to be upon the pattern of responding that gets reinforced, and not just the raw response rate. In contrast with the studies described above where the initial acquisition of the bar-press response was in question, and where typically only 20 or 30 responses occur, the situation here involves extremely well-learned bar pressing involving often hundreds of hours of training. After so much training, it is extremely difficult to separate the many subtle and complex stimulus factors that control not only the response itself but its temporal pattern.

Saltzman (1949) and Klein (1959) have lent some support to the discriminative-stimulus hypothesis by showing that discrimination training facilitates the secondary reinforcement effect. On the other hand, these studies as well as a number of others demonstrate some secondary reinforcement effects in the absence of prior discriminative training. The reported secondary reinforcement effects in most discrimination-training studies are usually small, fragile, and short-lived, both in animals that receive discrimination training and in control animals that do not. Evidently discriminative training per se is not a particularly important variable in the secondary reinforcement effect.

The trouble lies partly in the concept of discriminative stimulus. The Skinnerian distinguishes a discriminative stimulus from other kinds of stimuli on the basis of the experimental procedures that define it rather than in terms of its hypothetical or observed behavioral properties; it is merely a stimulus in the presence of which reinforcement is given. Following the procedures, however, certainly does not guarantee that the stimulus in question will gain associative control over any piece of behavior. It seems extremely likely that what is crucial is not that the stimulus be presented differentially with reinforcement but that it actually does gain control over some response, either eating, or approaching food, or running over to the food cup, or running forward. The majority of studies in which animals are given differential training, e.g., fed in a black box and not fed in a white box, probably have established different responses to the differential stimuli; but these differences may well have disappeared during the time when the secondary reinforcing effects of the stimuli were being tested. We may suppose that the poor performance so often noted in these studies is due either to the failure of the positive stimulus to gain control over a suitable response, or to the failure to maintain this response-eliciting power in the test situation when primary reinforcement is withheld. No other fact is more striking in the whole secondary reinforcement area than the difference in ease with which responses can be chained when primary reinforcement is at the end of the chain and when primary reinforcement is withheld.

The Informational Hypothesis. Miller (1961) has suggested a hypothesis of secondary reinforcement which is in many ways like the discriminative-stimulus hypothesis, although he calls it by a different name which endows it with somewhat different conceptual properties. According to Miller a primary reinforcer ordinarily follows a series of other stimulus events. The question he raises is whether all of the stimuli preceding primary reinforcement have secondary reinforcing powers, or whether this is reserved just for those that have some special function. Miller suggests that there is a special function involved and that what it is is the informational value of the stimulus. There is ordinarily considerable redundancy in the sequence of stimuli arising from seeing food, approaching it, having food in the mouth, swallowing it, and so on. There is no new information, no gain in predictive power, in the case of the normal hungry animal, in these subsequent stimuli. Once the animal sees the food, primary reinforcement (whatever its ultimate basis) will follow. The sight of food in this case is the last information-conveying stimulus in the chain, and as such, it supplies the reinforcement for the chain. We might change the information value of seeing food by means of a fistula procedure, in which case we ought to find, as Hull et al. (1951) found, that seeing food and even the stimuli arising from food in the mouth lose their reinforcing effect. In other words, Miller is saying that the last informative or nonredundant stimulus preceding primary reinforcement acquires secondary reinforcing powers; subsequent stimuli have no reinforcing power because they convey no new information. Notice that this hypothesis makes sense out of the finding of Schoenfeld et al. that stimuli concurrent with eating fail to acquire secondary reinforcing powers; they are redundant. If Miller's interpretation is right, then the traditional contiguity-with-primary-reinforcement hypothesis is not only incomplete, it is quite wrong.

Egger and Miller (1962, 1963) have reported an extensive experimental test of the informational hypothesis. Basically what they did was to train two groups of rats to press a bar for food; extinguish this response (in order to get rid of some of the variability found in the resistance to extinction measure) ; and then test the resistance to extinction in a second session where pressing the bar produced a stimulus, S_2, that had been associated in various ways with reinforcement during training. For both groups S_2 had been regularly presented immediately prior to reinforcement; it was technically a discriminative stimulus. But for one group it had been redundant because it had been regularly preceded by another stimulus, S_1, while for the second group it had been irregularly preceded by S_1, so that it was a more reliable predictor of food than S_1 and, hence, not redundant. The results indicated that S_2 was a significantly more effective secondary reinforcer under the second, informative, condition than under the first, redundant, condition. (Unfortunately we cannot assess from the report of the results whether the redundant stimulus had any secondary reinforcing value, nor do we know if the same analysis would be applicable to other response measures of secondary reinforcement besides the maintenance of a learned response.) Various control procedures make it quite likely that the secondary reinforcement effects were not due to facilitation effects or to pseudoconditioning.

The Elicitation Hypothesis. Hull (1943) conjectured that a stimulus acquires secondary reinforcing properties to the extent that it comes to elicit another response. Although none of the evidence then available really required this hypothesis, all of the early work was at least consistent with it, and some of it (Frolov, 1927; Cowles, 1937) strongly suggested it. And, as we have seen, subsequent investigation of secondary reinforcement has continued to lend support to this position; much of the work with extended chains of operant behavior had made explicit use of some variety of elicitation hypothesis. The next question is whether the response elicited by the secondary reinforcer has to have any special properties.

Hull advanced the specific hypothesis that a stimulus acquires secondary reinforcing properties to the extent that it becomes capable of eliciting a fractional anticipatory goal response, r_G. The principal use that Hull and his followers made of this hypothesis, as we observed in the last chapter, was to explain the phenomena of incentive motivation. It is often called secondary reinforcement but the explanatory emphasis is usually upon the motivating aspects of r_G rather than its possible reinforcing powers.

It should be noted that the elicitation hypothesis is not incompatible with the other hypotheses we have just considered. Even Hull's special r_G hypothesis is consistent with them, or at least could be made consistent with them. It is quite possible that a discriminative stimulus works as a secondary reinforcer just to the degree that it comes to elicit r_G; the "discrimination" in discriminative training might well involve the differential association of r_G and r_F to the presence and absence of S^D, respectively. Much the same argument could be applied to the informational hypothesis. In any case we may ask what is a discriminative stimulus, or an informotional stimulus either, if it is not just a stimulus which has acquired associative control over some criterion response. If we do not give discriminative training but merely present the stimulus in question, it may or may not gain such control; we cannot tell. But after discrimination training we know whether it does. Similarly, the only way we know that the informational stimulus conveys information is that the animal does what the stimulus tells it to do, i.e., responds to it in the way we have designated. It should be noted also that the elicitation hypothesis, at this point in our understanding of it, is nonspecific. We do not know any more than Hull did 20 years ago about whether the elicitation of any response is sufficient for secondary reinforcement, whether r_G must be elicited, whether the elicited response must ultimately lead to primary reinforcement, as much of the data suggest, or whether anticipatory approach must be involved, as Maatsch (1954) has suggested.

Nakamura et al. (1963) have shown the importance of attaching a vigorous approach response to a stimulus that is to become a secondary reinforcer. They ran rats in a competitive situation where, upon presentation of the stimulus, only the animal that ran faster to the food received any food. After this differential reinforcement of vigorous running the cue for such running was found to be a relatively durable secondary reinforcer.

An important question about the elicitation hypothesis is whether the response elicited during the test of a secondary reinforcer must be the same response the stimulus elicited when it was being established as a secondary reinforcer. Keehn (1962) seems to have shown that it must be the same. Subjects required to make a new response to a secondary reinforcer failed to show acquisition of a new response that produced it, whereas subjects that could make the old response to the secondary reinforcer did show acquisition of a new response that produced it. This not only provides an ingenious confirmation of the elicitation hypothesis but shows also that secondary reinforcers are not autonomous; we cannot consider the secondary reinforcer as the end-point of a segment of behavior, we also have to consider the following response. (Kent et al., 1960, have made the same point for the aversive case.) It is clear that this is a logical implication of the informational hypothesis, the elicitation hypothesis, and the discriminative-stimulus hypothesis. These three hypotheses have a great deal in common, but they also have somewhat different conceptual properties and theoretical implications. What we need now is more research like Keehn's to sharpen up our statements of these hypotheses so that we may see which of these various properties and implications are the crucial ones.

Shock Termination and Secondary Reinforcement. A fundamental assumption in Mowrer's theory of learning (1960) is that stimuli which signal the termination of aversive stimulation should acquire positive reinforcing value; they should come to elicit "relief." Barlow (1952, 1956) first put the question in empirical terms: will an animal learn a new response which produces a stimulus that has previously been associated in time with the termination of shock? Barlow gave rats 10-sec. shocks near the end of which a light was presented. The next day they were put in a situation where for half of them a certain response (touching a bar) turned the light on, and for the other half touching the bar turned the light off. Barlow did not report data to show whether learning occurred in the test session, but he did report that the animals tended to have the light on more than off. Beck (1961) has suggested an uncontrolled artifact that might result from this measure of behavior: perhaps the light elicited fear rather than relief, and the rats froze on the bar whenever they produced the light.

Beck (1961) describes several variations on this theme, most of which have failed to support Barlow and Mowrer's position. Smith and Buchanan (1954) and Buchanan (1958) have found some supporting evidence in a somewhat different situation. In these studies, hungry rats were trained to approach one box to get food and terminate shock, and to approach another box to get food (no shock). Later they were given a preference test between the two boxes (no shock). Comparison with control animals indicated a significant preference (stronger approach behavior) for the box that had been associated with shock termination. It should be noted, however, that this situation provided no real test of learning. Therefore, the results cannot be taken to indicate a reinforcement effect of secondary reinforcement. Beck (1961) has reviewed the problems here with considerable care and insight, and concluded that at that time there was little evidence to show that stimuli contiguous with shock termination become secondary reinforcers. However, Beck points out that perhaps the hypothesis has not been given a fair test. No one has tested it using the optimum procedures known from other situations to facilitate the establishment and use of secondary reinforcers, namely, intermittent or discriminative training, the use of optimum drive conditions, and control for elicitation effects.[9]

Since Beck's review, more support for Barlow's hypothesis has been found (Evans, 1962; Wagman & Allen, 1964; Lawler, 1965); but the demonstrated effects remain small and rather fragile, and still no learning curves have appeared. Mowrer (1960) suggested that the positive value of safety cues (cues paired with shock termination) might only appear when the original drive state (fear) was reinstated. Lawler (1965) has tested this proposition and failed to confirm it.

Other Kinds of Conditioned Reinforcers. It has been widely accepted that stimuli associated with the interruption of feeding are aversive. In order to complete his hypothetical set of motivators Mowrer (1960) assumed that withdrawal of positive reinforcement, or a cue to its withdrawal, would be aversive. Mowrer cited a series of studies by Ferster (1958) in which animals in operant situations learn to terminate or avoid a "time out," i.e., a period during which, typically, the animal's lights are turned out and the schedule of reinforcement is suspended. Leitenberg (1965a) has reviewed a number of experiments in which time outs have been introduced into various kinds of reinforcement schedules and subjects appear to find the time out aversive. However, Leitenberg points out that in virtually all of these experiments there is serious confounding between the avoidance of time out and the increase of rate of

[9] Beck conceives the elicitation property of secondary reinforcers to be a factor which should be eliminated or controlled in some way in order that their reinforcing effects can be demonstrated. He does not consider the possibility suggested implicitly by Hull (1943) and Keller and Schoenfeld (1950), and stated explicitly by Maatsch (1954) and Wyckoff (1959), that the reinforcing effect *is* the eliciting effect.

positive reinforcement, so that we cannot tell if the animal is avoiding the time out or merely maximizing the amount of food it receives per unit time. The one exception is a study by Wagner (1963) done in the context of frustration theory. Wagner found that animals would learn a new response to terminate stimuli in one situation that had been paired with nonreinforcement in another situation. Actually, Wagner could not report learning of the new response but only that it was maintained at its initial strength better by the experimental animals than it was by controls who did not have the "reinforcing" stimulus previously paired with nonreinforcement. We are left, therefore, with little substantial evidence that cues to the withdrawal of food can be conditioned reinforcers.

There is even less evidence for the existence of what are supposed to be generalized conditioned reinforcers. Commenting upon the fact that the efficacy of social reinforcement in people appears to be independent of current deprivation conditions, Skinner (1953) suggested that their generality was due to their having been associated with a number of different primary reinforcers. Somehow Skinner came to the deduction that if a stimulus was associated with enough different kinds of motivation-reinforcement procedures it would remain effective in the absence of any motivation condition. Experimental support for this conception has been sought by running animals alternately hungry and thirsty, or both hungry and thirsty, and showing that the instrumental behavior is more durable than it is when animals are run under just a single drive condition (Reid & Slivinske, 1954; Wike & McNamara, 1955; Wike & Barrientos, 1958; Wunderlich, 1961). It is not clear what implications such findings have for the generalized conditioned reinforcement hypothesis in view of the known interactions of hunger and thirst (see Chapter 8) and the fact that any variability in acquisition conditions can be expected to lead to more durable behavior.

SOME CONDITIONS AFFECTING THE ESTABLISHMENT AND USE OF SECONDARY REINFORCERS

A good deal of research has gone into the quest for factors that affect the strength of secondary reinforcement effects. The studies comprise a heterogeneous group because, as we have seen, there has been little agreement about either what a secondary reinforcement is (what its effects upon behavior are supposed to be) or how it is established. The temptation is to invoke a secondary reinforcer whenever we observe more behavior than can readily be attributed to primary reinforcement.

Intermittency of Presentation. Ordinarily secondary reinforcers are used continuously, i.e., they are presented with every occurrence of the response. Dinsmoor et al. (1953) and Clayton (1956) have found that it makes relatively little difference whether the secondary reinforcer is presented on every trial or only intermittently. However, Zimmerman (1957) has argued that a pronounced benefit is obtained by the intermittent use of a secondary reinforcer presumably because that way it is saved from extinction. The subsequent findings of Fox and King (1961) indicate that Zimmerman is right, but they also show that before the intermittent use of a secondary reinforcer can have any benefit there must have been intermittent pairing of the secondary reinforcer with primary reinforcement during its establishment.

Saltzman (1949), Notterman (1951), McClelland and McGown (1953), D'Amato et al. (1958), Klein (1959), Armus and Garlich (1961), and others have found that intermittency and variability during the acquisition phase of secondary-reinforcement training facilitates the effect of secondary reinforcement in subsequent tests. We may think of the animal being required to discriminate between situations in which there is a secondary reinforcer and situations in which there is none. Such discriminative training of course helps to bring the animal's behavior under the associative control of the stimulus in question, and it may be this effect which is then subsequently manifest in the test for secondary reinforcement.

Amount of Primary Reinforcement. The importance of the amount of primary reinforcement in establishing a secondary reinforcer has been studied by several investigators (Lawson, 1953; D'Amato, 1955; Hopkins, 1955; Butter & Thomas, 1958). The discrepant findings probably result from the different sorts of incentive, the different test situations, and the different experimental designs that have been used. In the case of sucrose concentration Butter and Thomas (1958) and Stebbins (1959) showed that increasing concentrations lead to stronger apparent secondary reinforcement effects. It may also be important to note here that with the sucrose-concentration variable the amount of time spent in consummatory activity can be equated for different incentive values, and consummatory time is a variable which evidently is important (Powell & Perkins, 1957) in the strength of a secondary reinforcer.

The Temporal Interval Between Secondary and Primary Reinforcement. Recall that Schoenfeld et al. (1950) found that a stimulus which came on during primary reinforcement failed to acquire secondary reinforcing powers. Schoenfeld et al. argued that in order to become a secondary reinforcer a stimulus had to be a S^D, but what this may mean in effect is only that it must precede reinforcement. The temporal parameter here has been studied systematically by Bersh (1951), who presented food to different groups of rats during magazine training at various intervals of time after the onset of a light. After 160 reinforcements in magazine training, the bar was made available and the situation arranged so that pressing the bar produced a 1-sec. light, but no food. The results showed that the optimum interval is about .5 to 1 sec. That is, to be a secondary reinforcer the stimulus should be presented approximately 1 sec. prior to primary reinforcement. Similar results have been reported by Jenkins (1950) (see Fig. 13-4).

Kimble (1961) has noted the similarity between these time functions and those commonly found in classical conditioning studies, and has

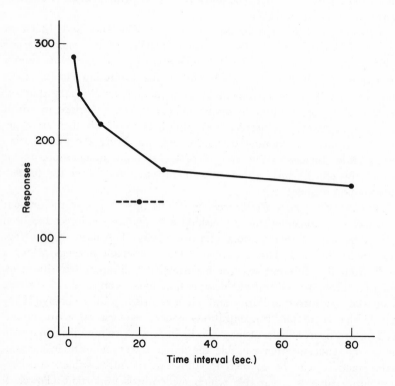

Fig. 13-4. Mean number of bar presses for a buzzer in 6 hrs. as a function of the interval between buzzer and food during acquisition. The isolated point indicates the performance of animals with no buzzer. (From Jenkins, 1950)

argued that this similarity suggests that secondary reinforcement develops as a result of classical conditioning. Kimble notes, however, that ". . . substantial amounts of secondary reinforcement were obtained at intervals considerably longer than one would think possible from comparable studies of the interstimulus interval in regular classical conditioning" (p. 184). In Jenkins' study the stimulus to become the secondary reinforcer was presented for 3 sec., and the interval that was varied was the time between termination of the stimulus and the presentation of food. It is indeed remarkable that trace conditioning would occur with intervals in the order of 1 min.

The effect of the number of pairings of the stimulus to be a secondary reinforcer with primary reinforcement has been studied by Bersh (1951), Hall (1951), and Miles (1956). Their results generally agree. Miles' data are shown in Fig. 13-5.

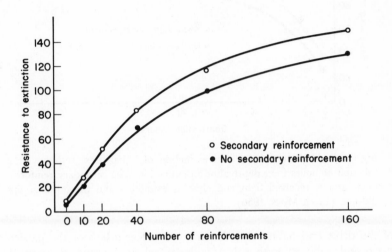

Fig. 13-5. Median resistance to extinction of a bar-press response as a function of the number of reinforcements in acquisition. The secondary reinforcement groups received light and click in extinction and the other groups did not. (From Miles, 1956)

The Effects of Drive Conditions. Miles (1956) has shown that the resistance to extinction of a bar-press response maintained by a secondary reinforcer is an increasing function of the severity of the animal's food deprivation at the time of testing (Fig. 13-6).

One feature of Miles' results requires comment. The data shown in Figs. 13-5 and 13-6 can be presented in other ways. The *differences* can be plotted to give curves showing how many additional extinction responses can be attributed to the secondary reinforcer; the resulting curves are monotonic and have been frequently cited by writers desiring to show that there really is such a thing as secondary reinforcement. The curves shown here suggest, by contrast, that secondary reinforcement is a minor factor in extinction performance. The data can also be plotted as *ratios*, showing what proportion of the extinction performance can be attributed to secondary reinforcement. Miles himself emphasized that the ratio is very nearly constant and that this constancy holds throughout the range

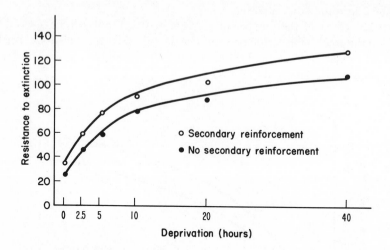

Fig. 13-6. Median resistance to extinction of a bar-press response as a function of hours food deprivation in extinction. The secondary reinforcement groups received light and click in extinction and the other groups did not. (From Miles, 1956)

of the drive and habit strength parameters. Regardless of the particular drive and habit strength values under which it is tested, the secondary reinforcer accounts for about 15% of the animal's performance. From these elegant data Miles drew the elegant conclusion that the associative and motivating processes involved in secondary reinforcement are no different from those involved in primary reinforcement—the secondary reinforcer is just one of the many stimuli controlling the behavior in the situation.

It has been found that drive conditions in acquisition have little or no effect upon the secondary reinforcing power of a stimulus subsequently tested with drive conditions equated (Hall, 1951a; Brown, 1956; Wike & Farrow, 1962). In fact, it has been found that rats can be shifted from hunger to thirst (or vice versa) between acquisition and extinction tests of secondary reinforcement without seriously impairing the effectiveness of a secondary reinforcer (Estes, 1949, 1949a; Wike & Casey, 1954a; D'Amato, 1955). It should be noted however that, at best, only marginal evidence of secondary reinforcement was reported in these studies. And, as we noted on p. 392, the generality of secondary reinforcement across different drive conditions should be regarded somewhat lightly in view of the possibility of hunger-thirst interaction in all these studies.

Then there is the special question of whether there are secondary reinforcement effects when the acquisition-drive condition no longer exists and there are no other interacting drive conditions operative at the time. Estes (1949a) and Schlosberg and Pratt (1956) failed to find secondary reinforcement effects in satiated animals. However, Wike and Casey (1954), Seward and Levy (1953) and Seward et al. (1953) have reported what is, if not acquisition of new behavior, at least reinstatement or instigation or motivation of previously learned behavior. Platt and Wike (1962) have attempted to explain the discrepancy on the grounds that satiated animals might go to a food-baited loaded goal box in order to explore or manipulate food objects.[10]

It seems reasonably safe to say that a secondary reinforcer cannot be used to produce a new learning in satiated animals (Simon et al., 1951; Calvin et al., 1953; Miles & Wickens, 1953). These same studies seem to indicate, however, that a secondary reinforcer can have the effect of energizing or motivating or activating instrumental behavior in motivated animals. It is as if a secondary reinforcer makes the hungry animal hungrier but has no effect upon the satiated animal. The only exceptions to this pattern seem to be the results reported by Anderson (1941).

NEGATIVE SECONDARY REINFORCERS

We tend to think of secondary reinforcement when we see an organism maintaining its performance in the absence of primary reinforcement. This is precisely the situation in avoidance learning when the organism is successfully avoiding the shock. We may note that at first the warning stimulus (the CS) is closely and consistently contiguous with shock (the US). According to the contiguity hypothesis it should become a secondary reinforcer, i.e., its termination should be reinforcing. And to the extent that the organism does learn to avoid, to respond before the shock comes on, the avoidance is evidently reinforced by CS termination.

But there is an element of circularity in this argument if the only evidence of secondary reinforcement is the occurrence of avoidance. What is needed is independent confirmation by a demonstration of the variety

---

10 There is some question whether the various sources of drive that could operate in a secondary reinforcement situation could ever be eliminated to test whether a secondary reinforcer could have a motivating effect. This is really a semantic question in that if incentive motivation is viewed as a source of drive and if it is attributed to secondary reinforcement, then we have the logical impossibility of testing for an effect in the absence of the effect we are looking for. But on the other hand, if we accept ordinary satiation procedure as producing zero drive, then the question is meaningful, and the answer to it is evidently no; a secondary reinforcer does not reinstate hunger (Danziger, 1951; Schlosberg & Pratt, 1956; Seward & Handlon, 1952; Seward & Levy, 1953), although the animal may make the response it had previously learned to make. (Sometimes it doesn't even do that, Koch & Daniel, 1945.)

of behavioral effects secondary reinforcers are supposed to have. Can evidence of new learning be demonstrated? Yes, it can; Miller (1948) showed learning of a new avoidance response in the absence of reinforcement by shock termination. Although Miller used these results to argue for an acquired-drive interpretation of avoidance (see Chapter 11), they can just as easily be taken to support an acquired reinforcement interpretation.[11]

We have here all of the problems we had in the appetitive case, plus a few more. The chief questions are: what are the behavioral consequences of secondary negative reinforcers, and how are they established? These questions have attracted relatively little direct attention; most of our understanding has to come indirectly from an analysis of avoidance learning because that is where the research has been concentrated.

The Role of the CS in Avoidance Behavior. The main point of Schoenfeld's 1950 paper had been to emphasize the role of the CS in the acquisition of avoidance. He proposed that the CS serves as a conditioned negative reinforcer, whose termination maintains the instrumental response in the absence of primary negative reinforcement (on trials when the response prevents shock). The drive theorist also stresses a unique role for the CS, but a quite different one. It elicits fear, and it is the reduction in fear which makes the termination of the CS reinforce the instrumental response. These alternative positions might be tested by searching for a temporal lag between the onset and termination of the CS and the behavioral effects of the hypothesized arousal and reduction of fear. The fear reaction should show some latency both coming and going. Mowrer and Lamoreaux (1942) found that avoidance learning is much more effective when the CS is terminated simultaneously with the avoidance response than when it is terminated several seconds before, or continued 5 sec. after the response. These intervals were apparently too gross to permit us to identify a lag between CS and fear. The main effect was clear, however—the optimum interval between response and CS termination is near zero.

Kamin (1956) attempted to assess the relative importance of CS termination and US prevention in avoidance learning. He ran four groups in a shuttle box, with a 5-sec. CS-US interval. For one group,

---

[11] In the next several pages we will be considering the problem of avoidance behavior from the point of view of secondary reinforcement theory, and our mission will be to evaluate the fruitfulness of this approach. However, it should be kept in mind that the acquired drive theory, which we considered in some detail in Chapter 11, and the secondary reinforcement theory, which we are considering here, are not fundamentally very different. Both are in effect "two-factor" theories requiring first the conditioning of fear (or the establishment of a secondary negative reinforcer) and then the acquisition of the avoidance response itself through the reduction of fear (or the termination of the conditioned negative reinforcer). What we find regarding the one theory can be applied to the other.

under usual avoidance conditions, the criterion response of running from one side to the other both terminated the CS and prevented the onset of the US. This group showed rapid and stable learning. A second group could neither terminate the CS nor prevent the US but, like all the other groups, could terminate the US by responding after the inevitable CS-US sequence had run off. This "classical conditioning" group showed slow and unstable learning. The two interesting groups were these for whom running *either* terminated the CS without preventing the US, or prevented the US without terminating the CS. The two groups showed approximately equal acquisition intermediate between the other two groups. This pattern of results is often superficially interpreted as indicating that both CS termination and US prevention can effectively and independently reinforce in the avoidance situation, and the US prevention effect is sometimes seen as a point for a cognitive explanation of avoidance behavior (e.g., Solomon & Brush, 1956).

Kamin's own interpretation seems much sounder. He argues that the animals who only terminated the CS would have demonstrated much better learning had not their running been subject to punishment by the continuation of the US. Similarly, the animals who only prevented the US also had the possible advantage of delayed CS termination. (The immediacy of punishment and the delay of CS termination depend upon the latency of the running response.) Hence, Kamin suggests that CS termination may be the principal, or even the exclusive, source of reinforcement in this situation (see also Wickens & Platt, 1954).

A crucial test between Kamin's and Solomon and Brush's interpretations would be provided by a replication with a longer (or shorter) CS-US interval to change the intervals between the response and the hypothetical reinforcement effects. Kamin (1957a) repeated the study with a 10-sec. CS-US interval and found a complex pattern of results which could be handled (after some ad hoc assumptions) by his model, but which provided little support for the cognitive position of Solomon and Brush. What Kamin's interpretation requires is that the temporal gradient of punishment by the continuation of shock be much flatter than the temporal gradient of delayed reinforcement by CS termination. Kamin (1957) has confirmed part of this pattern: a very sharp gradient for the synchronization of CS termination with the avoidance response. He found that if the termination of the CS (a buzzer) was delayed as much as 2.5 sec. after the running response had occurred, the proportion of successful avoidances was sharply reduced (see Fig. 13-7).

In another study Kamin (1959) found that terminating the CS just before the avoidance response occurred also weakened avoidance performance considerably. The importance of synchronizing CS termination with the avoidance response appears not only when immediate termination is applied to avoidance (1957b) but also when it is applied just to escape

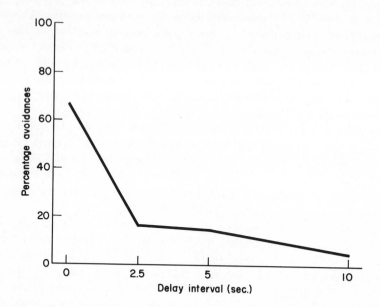

Fig. 13-7. Median percentage of avoidances in 100 trials as a function of the delay of CS termination after a response. (Data from Kamin, 1957)

responses, i.e., mostly early in training (Kamin et al., 1959). This argues rather strongly for the position that termination of the CS reinforces the response, not only on the trials when shock is avoided, but also on the trials when it is not avoided, i.e., on escape trials where shock termination is usually afforded the principal reinforcement role.[12]

The other part of the picture, the gradual gradient of the effect of continuing the shock after an avoidance has occurred has been shown by other investigators. Church and Solomon (1956) delayed shock termination 0, .5, 2.5, and 10 sec. for different groups of subjects. Escape performance was markedly impaired by delay; the latencies were long and variable, and more so with the longer delays. But there was little or no effect on avoidance behavior once it became established. The different delays had no systematic effect upon the animal's manifest emotionality.

[12] It also suggests that the situation during the escape phase of avoidance training really involves shock plus fear, rather than only shock. Note that although Kamin has separated CS termination and US avoidance as potential reinforcers of the avoidance response, both of these factors are still seriously confounded with US escape, since the same response is required of the animal to escape shock and to avoid it. Stojkiewicz (1964) has shown that the escape-from-shock contingency is such an important determinant of response strength that it can totally obscure the relative contribution of the other two factors.

Fowler and Trapold (1962) have studied the analogous phenomenon in a runway. They trained rats to run an alley to escape shock, but different delays of shock termination were imposed for different groups. The results (shown in Fig. 13-8) show the expected decrements with continued shock. However, there is still considerable learning even with quite long delays, indicating that whereas shock termination is certainly reinforcing, continuation of shock does not have a disastrous effect upon performance.

Kamin's work provides the best systematic demonstration of the importance of CS termination in the acquisition of avoidance behavior, but there are a number of other types of evidence that can be cited to provide further support for this principle. One is the demonstration by McAdam (1964) and Biederman et al. (1964) that rats have more difficulty learn-

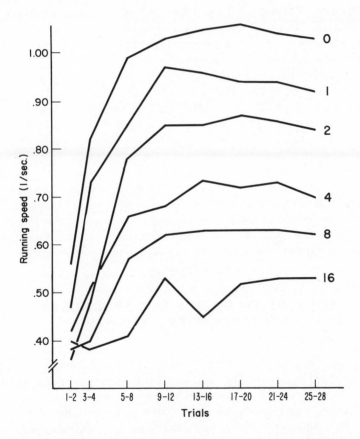

Fig. 13-8. The acquisition of running reinforced by shock termination for delays of reinforcement ranging from 0 to 16 sec. (From Fowler & Trapold, 1962)

ing avoidance when they have to approach the CS (a light) than when they can run away from it. Another substantiating piece of evidence comes from a study showing that facility in avoidance increases with the amount of stimulus change in the CS that the avoidance response produces (Bower et al., 1963). Mowrer and Lamoreaux (1946) trained rats to make one response, e.g., jumping up in the air, to escape shock and a different response, e.g., running, to terminate the CS and avoid the shock. They report that the animals could learn this "double response" problem nearly as easily as controls could learn the normal "single response" problem, either jumping or running (see also Keehn, 1959). It has been suggested that animals can learn avoidance about as fast and perform it about as proficiently as they can learn escape (Santos, 1960), and that they can learn avoidance without having to acquire an escape response first (Marx & Hellwig, 1964). All of these results support the view that the CS rapidly becomes aversive, i.e., it either comes to elicit fear or else it becomes itself a secondary negative reinforcer, and that any response which terminates it is rather effectively reinforced.

The picture we begin to get of avoidance learning is that any and all stimuli become aversive that are paired with shock, or that are similar to those that are paired with shock. The organism will be reinforced for making any response that introduces new stimuli or abolishes the old aversive ones. As avoidance learning progresses, the aversiveness of many stimuli dissipates; but some, because of the arrangement of the experimental situation, remain aversive. The animal will learn whatever response takes it from the latter to the former. A secondary reinforcement theorist (e.g., a Skinnerian) will accept this as a sufficient account of the learning; an incentive theorist or a drive theorist would insist in addition that these events produce arousal and reduction of fear, and that it is the changes in fear that produce the motivation and the learning of the response.

SOME DIFFICULTIES FOR SECONDARY REINFORCEMENT THEORY

In the last few years the secondary reinforcement interpretation has become increasingly secure. The proposition that all instances of avoidance really depend upon the escape from some secondary negative reinforcer has gained so much empirical support that it has become nearly axiomatic. However, much of the applicability of this proposition has been purchased at the cost of untestability. We will see now, first, that avoidance behavior occurs in situations where it is extremely difficult to point to any observable stimulus which can serve as the theoretically required secondary reinforcer. Then we will look briefly at an assortment of phenomena which indicates that there is something fundamentally wrong with the secondary reinforcement position.

The Locus of Secondary Reinforcement. Even if we grant that secondary reinforcement plays a crucial role in escape performance and avoidance learning, there is still the problem of isolating and identifying those stimuli in the situation which constitute the secondary reinforcer. McAllister and McAllister (1962) have suggested that any stimulus that precedes shock, whether it be a light or just the presence of environmental stimuli, will elicit the fear that governs the avoidance response. This, they say, accounts for the fact that avoidance can sometimes be learned when the nominal CS follows the shock, i.e., under conditions which appear to indicate backward conditioning. It also accounts for intertrial responding.

Sidman (1953a) has demonstrated a variety of avoidance learning which takes place in the absence of any discernible CS. In Sidman's situation very brief, fairly intense shocks are delivered at regular intervals, e.g., every 10 sec. The animal can do nothing to escape a shock, but by pressing a bar during an intershock interval it can *postpone* the delivery of the next shock by, e.g., 20 sec. Continued pressing leads to continued postponement. Under these conditions, if the animal presses the bar at all it rapidly settles down to a rate of bar pressing which spares it all but a few shocks per hour. The question is what stimuli control bar pressing and what stimuli reinforce it?

Sidman's original answer (1953, 1953a, 1954) followed Schoenfeld's suggestion (1950) that the crucial stimuli are the proprioceptive stimulus consequences of the response itself (or its anticipation). In this view, all the responses in the animal's repertory except bar pressing are liable to punishment because their proprioceptive consequences can be present when the shock comes on; only bar pressing is safe. Sidman (1953) has found that if postponement time is short, so that punishment can come only a few seconds after the bar press, then evidently even bar pressing is not safe, because the behavior deteriorates; avoidance behavior encounters a sharp "punishment gradient." With longer response-shock intervals, the criterion response also suffers the effects of delayed punishment but inevitably it enjoys longer delayed punishment than any other response the animal can make. With reasonably long response-shock times, 10 sec. or longer, all other behavior is selectively punished so that bar pressing emerges as the dominant response. Notice that once the behavior is established it will be maintained, according to this position, by just an occasional shock to maintain the suppression of competing behavior.

Sidman's argument was supported by the results of a study (1954) in which animals could press two bars providing either the same or different response-shock intervals. It was found that the subject would learn to make a preponderance of its responses to whichever bar provided the longer interval, although there was some tendency toward proportionality.

It is hard not to believe that the regular pacing of shocks is not relevant to the acquisition of Sidman's type of avoidance behavior. He has found (Sidman, 1954a) that in well-practiced behavior the temporal distribution of response (the distribution of times between responses) comes very close to what it would be if the animal were responding randomly in time. However, he observes that there are systematic departures from this pattern by some subjects. Some tend to pace their behavior regularly at a safe rate, and others tend to respond in bursts. But in another study (Sidman, 1955) it was found that if a CS was introduced after the behavior was well established (the CS was a light 5 sec. before a scheduled shock), the subject would quickly learn to respond to the light and that this pacing would persist long after the CS procedure was discontinued. This finding suggests on the one hand that the behavior prior to introducing the CS condition was independent of temporal discrimination. On the other hand, behavior in the post-CS sessions indicates how subtle, accurate, and persistent temporal discrimination can be. It is certainly possible that temporal factors are involved in the earliest stages of learning.

Another empirical difficulty with Sidman's original explanation is that at the beginning of bar pressing the response should come in slowly and when shock is discontinued it should extinguish quickly. This would be expected because the bar press is initially quite weak, and it should remain weak if it only appears to gain in strength as all other behavior is inhibited. In fact, though, acquisition is frequently precipitous after the first response occurs, and is sometimes exceedingly resistant to extinction (Boren & Sidman, 1957). It would seem that the avoidance response is reinforced by some direct process rather than merely emerging indirectly from the punishment of nonavoidance.

Recently Sidman (1962) has suggested that the reinforcing agent in this type of avoidance is the reduction in shock frequency (number of shocks per unit time) that follows bar pressing. Empirically it is true, of course, that bar pressing is correlated with reduction in shock frequency, but it seems likely that Sidman has only rediscovered the effect rather than its cause. Anger (1963) has pointed out that Sidman's new hypothesis cannot reasonably be applied to the occasional cases of rats avoiding shocks successfully for many hours at a time. How can the rat discriminate such a low rate from either no shocks at all or a slightly higher rate? How can such low rates be effective in shaping up the animal's behavior?

Anger proposes that there are stimulus consequences of responding which persist for some time after a response so that the animal can, in some sense, tell how long it has been since it last responded. Shock never occurs in Sidman avoidance just after a response, so when the "traces" of responding are short the animal is safe, and short traces are relatively nonaversive. But as time elapses since the last response the probability of a shock increases, and the conditioned aversiveness of the trace increases accordingly. Early in acquisition, learning occurs because by pressing the bar the animal produces for itself new (short) traces which are much less aversive than long traces. Learning starts as soon as the animal has responded a few times, so that long traces begin to become aversive. Later in acquisition the discrimination of different length of traces progresses rapidly as the aversiveness of all the irrelevant stimuli dissipates.

According to Anger's formulation, then, the effective CS in Sidman avoidance, the stimulus whose termination reinforces avoidance, is some interoceptive consequence of having not responded recently. Anger (1963) and Bolles and Popp (1964) have adduced some support for this formulation. A similar hypothesis was advanced by Mowrer and Keehn (1958) although, of course, they introduced the additional element of fear: Not responding produces fear, the aversiveness of which the animal escapes by responding. This mechanism was primarily designed to explain intertrial responding in the shuttle box. Black and Carlson (1959) have reported in this connection that during the course of learning intertrial responding decreases early in the intertrial interval and increases late in the interval (see also Brown, 1939).

Anger's hypothesis can be said to make sense out of the Sidman avoidance data, and to reconcile this seemingly paradoxical behavior with secondary reinforcement theory. But one may well demand to know what is the tangible reference of the hypothetical stimuli that are said to be "the consequence of having not responded recently." Just what kind of a stimulus is this? Do such hypothetical stimuli rescue the secondary reinforcement hypothesis, or make it untestable?

Other Difficulties. There are a number of avoidance phenomena which seem to run counter to what would be expected from the point of view of either the acquired drive or the secondary reinforcement positions. We will merely list some of these difficulties by putting them in a series of questions.

1. Why does reasonably well-established avoidance behavior sometimes collapse with continued training (Coons et al., 1960)? And why does this "avoidance decrement" effect appear only in avoidance situations that involve nonlocomotory responses (Anderson & Nakamura, 1964; Nakamura & Anderson, 1964; Reynierse et al., 1964)?

2. Why is it so difficult to obtain avoidance when the secondary reinforcer is on an intermittent schedule (Badia & Levine, 1964; Badia, 1965)? Is this characteristic of the aversive case (Kaplan, 1956, and Henry & Hendry, 1963, found poor performance on fixed-ratio escape), or does it depend upon the apparatus (shuttle box)?

3. Why is it so difficult to get higher order negative reinforcers or higher order conditioned fears (McAllister & McAllister, 1964)? If the CS really becomes more or less permanently aversive, then why doesn't pairing it with another stimulus make the latter aversive?

4. Why does the animal fail to avoid the CS itself? It is found that when animals are given the opportunity to avoid or postpone the CS they gradually come to respond more regularly in its presence and less frequently in its absence, as though they found its cue value to be more important than its aversiveness (Sidman, 1955; Sidman & Boren, 1957; Keehn, 1959a; Behrend & Bitterman, 1963; Graf & Bitterman, 1963).

5. Why, when rats are given unavoidable shocks, do they prefer to have them preceded by a CS than to have them come unannounced (J. S. Lockard, 1963) or immediate rather than delayed (Knapp et al., 1959)? Again it looks like the cue properties of the CS may be more important than its aversiveness.

6. How is it possible that animals can learn an avoidance response under trace conditioning procedures (Kamin, 1954; Black, 1963; Pearl & Edwards, 1963)? When the CS comes on only momentarily 5 sec. before a scheduled shock, rats can learn to avoid the shock almost as well as they can when the CS remains on and is response-terminated.

7. Why is it relatively easy to obtain avoidance learning in a shuttle box, and extremely difficult to get it in a bar-press situation (Meyer et al., 1960; D'Amato & Schiff, 1964; Chapman & Bolles, 1964)? In other situations, such as a running-wheel shock apparatus, acquisition can be superior to acquisition in the shuttle box (Stojkiewicz, 1964).

8. Why does delayed termination of the CS, which Kamin has found to have so important a decremental effect in the shuttle box situation, have little or no effect upon the acquisition of avoidance in other situations (Mogenson et al., 1965)?

Many of these difficulties for the secondary reinforcement position, the acquired drive position, and two-factor theories in general, arise from studies of the acquisition of avoidance in different situations. It is becoming apparent that the acquisition of avoidance depends in a very important way upon what response the experimenter selects to be the criterion avoidance response. Gibson (1952) emphasized this point several years ago, but the point has been largely ignored. She asked why the animal in a classical aversive conditioning situation (in which shock is presented whether or not the animal responds to the CS) continues to make a leg flexion trial after trial when this response is repeatedly punished every time it occurs. The answer seems to be in part that this is quite characteristic of punishment (see Chapter 14), but the point Gibson emphasized was that leg flexion is one of the animal's natural defensive responses. It is one of the animal's small repertory of responses regularly elicited by painful stimuli applied to the leg. It is easy to condition in the first place because it is of such high initial strength in fearful situations, and it persists presumably because it does not compete with whatever else the animal may be doing when the CS appears. Other, more gross activities such as rearing and locomoting do gradually extinguish during an experimental session, but the leg flexion persists.[13]

The situation may be essentially the same in avoidance learning. When the animal merely has to run from an environment in which it has been shocked, it learns to do so quite rapidly; all of the acquired-drive studies agree on this point. Moreover, as the number or intensity of shocks increases the learning appears to get better and better (Miller & Lawrence, 1950; Kalish, 1954). This kind of learning, withdrawal from a place where pain has been experienced, is the fastest and most durable that we have yet found in the rat. Indeed, such learning is so good that we ordinarily do not think of it as avoidance learning but as punishment or escape learning.

In the shuttle box we have some elements of the same situation, e.g., the animal does leave the place where it has been shocked, and where cues to shock, including the CS, are present. But, while the animal can make a "natural" defense response, the defensive nature of the response is compromised by the fact that the animal is required to return to a place where it has been shocked before. Hence, learning in the shuttle box proceeds considerably more slowly than it does in the acquired-drive situation. In view of this conflict it is rather remarkable that shuttle box learning occurs at all; when it does (and it is certainly not infallible) the response probably occurs for the same reason that Gibson's animals continued to make a punished response, viz., the response is a natural defensive reaction when the animal is frightened.[14]

If this idea of the animal's natural fear-elicited defense reactions is pushed to its logical extreme, it implies that the rat cannot really acquire an avoidance response which is not part of its innate defensive repertory. This extreme position would seem to be refuted by the rat's ability to learn bar-press avoidance. But in fact, as we have noted, the rat just barely is able to learn this response, and even when it is established after many trials it is not stable. Moreover, what little evidence is available strongly suggests that the common experimental parameters have different effects upon the acquisition of bar pressing and the acquisition of shuttle

[13] Gibson's subjects were goats. Other animals may not have such prepotent defensive leg-flexion reactions. Thus Schlosberg (1934) had great difficulty conditioning this response in the rat; the rat kept trying to get free of the apparatus. James (1937) could not condition leg flexion in the opossum; the animal kept playing possum!

[14] Since the acquired-drive phenomenon does not occur with weak shocks (Miller & Lawrence, 1950) we may assume that fear is an essential part of it. Here and in what follows we will make this assumption; we will not, however, attribute any drive-like properties to fear. We will assume only that it is conditionable and that it predisposes animals to make defensive reactions characteristic of their species. In the rat, fear is defined as the conditionable tendency to withdraw, freeze, or cower.

box running. What the bar-press animal does primarily is freeze (recall that freezing is another of the rat's defense reactions). If it happens to freeze while holding on to the bar then it may show extremely short latency shock-escape responses, in the order of .1 sec. (e.g., Dinsmoor, 1958; Migler, 1963; Bolles & Warren, 1965a). These short latencies suggest that the animal has not learned an operant type of bar press, but is frozen on the bar and is inadvertently making responses which are more like startle reactions than anything else. Then, if the animal is fortunate, CS onset will also produce the startle reaction so that shock will be avoided. Whatever reinforcement contingencies are operating here are shaping up the animal's posture while it is freezing and are not actually shaping up the bar press itself.

It has been argued that the avoidance response may be different from the escape response, and that under such conditions the animal is quite able to learn to avoid (Mowrer & Lamoreaux, 1946). The implication is that the avoidance response can be chosen from any response on the animal's repertory; it is a pure operant. However, other experimenters (e.g., Bixenstine & Barker, 1964; Bolles & Tuttle, unpublished) have been unable to replicate Mowrer and Lamoreaux' results. For example, Bixenstine and Barker were only able to get avoidance with a response which was different from the escape response when they made the latter ineffective by delaying shock termination. Hearst & Whalen (1963) found that prevention of the shock-escape contingency destroyed avoidance performance. In short, there seems to be room for considerable doubt whether the rat can learn any arbitrary response in an avoidance situation.

The same doubt arises in connection with escape learning, and as we will see in the next chapter, it is almost certain that in the case of punishment the learned response must be one of the defense reactions produced by the punisher. In escape learning we often find extremely fast learning and persistent performance. As before, it is generally assumed that the animal will learn any arbitrarily selected response if we make shock termination contingent upon its occurrence. In the situations where escape has been studied, alley running and bar pressing, we do find extremely fast learning. The trouble is that the performance is too good; what the rat does in the bar-press situation is freeze on the bar, as we discussed above. In the runway, of course, it runs. But running away and freezing are the two most prominent responses in the rat's innate defensive repertory, and there are virtually no data to show that the rat can learn any other response in the escape situation.[15] In the acquired-drive situation it would seem that escape from the fear-eliciting situation is an essential component of the behavior, and that the "new" instrumental response is, again, not an arbitrary response but already part of

[15] Nor is there any evidence that the pigeon can peck a key (an eating response) to avoid or even to escape shock.

the animal's escape repertory. The observation of animals in situations like Miller's (1948) reveals that they turn the paddle wheel in trying to climb out through it, and step on the bar in trying to climb out of the box.

The learning that seems to be involved in all these cases is, first, the conditioning of fear to the situation, and then, the chaining of escape responses which lead ultimately to termination of the fear-eliciting cues. Viewed in this perspective so-called negative secondary reinforcers are quite analogous in their behavioral effects to positive secondary reinforcers. The termination of stimuli that have been paired with shock is probably no more reinforcing, in the strict sense, than is the presentation of stimuli that have been paired with food, such stimuli may merely elicit species specific defense reactions.

THE PARAMETERS OF AVOIDANCE LEARNING

With a phenomenon as complex as avoidance, hypothesis may be piled on hypothesis to provide an account compatible with almost any theory of behavior. What keeps this process within bounds is the accumulation of empirical findings, particularly those that uncover the dependence of the behavior upon its basic variables. In the case of avoidance behavior, the basic variables are the characteristics of the CS, US, and response, and the interrelationships among them. Let us see what has been discovered about these variables that can clarify our theoretical accounts.

The CS-US Interval. In classical conditioning, and this includes classical aversive conditioning, the optimum time between CS and US presentation is about .5 sec. (see the review by Kimble, 1961). Moreover, the gradient is usually found to be quite sharp; if the interval is less than zero (the condition for backward conditioning) or more than about 2 sec., conditioning is found to be virtually impossible. By contrast, the optimum CS-US interval for avoidance learning is much longer and the gradient is much flatter. Brush et al. (1955), Church et al. (1956), Schwartz (1958), Schrier (1961), Low and Low (1962), and Brush et al. (1964) all report better avoidance learning with intervals in the order of 5 to 10 sec. than when the intervals are shorter or longer. This pattern, a relatively flat gradient with a maximum near 5 or 10 sec., appears with a variety of species—rats, cats, and dogs—and with a variety of CS conditions and US intensities.

But there are limitations on the generality of this finding. There are two particular conditions in all these studies which seem crucial. First, they were all of the delayed-conditioning type, which means that the CS remains on during the CS-US interval. And second, all of these studies used a shuttle box. Kamin (1954) and Black (1963) obtained a markedly different gradient, much sharper and with a maximum at shorter intervals, using a trace-conditioning procedure, which is one in which the CS is on only briefly and is off during most of the CS-US interval. The difference between the findings with the delay and trace procedures suggests that the CS-US interval is an important determinant of avoidance learning only insofar as it affects other parameters, specifically, the interval between the response and CS termination (see Fig. 13-9). The CS-US interval is sometimes reported as affecting the latency of the response during the avoidance phase of training, but not the trial on which the first avoidance response occurs (Jones, 1961).

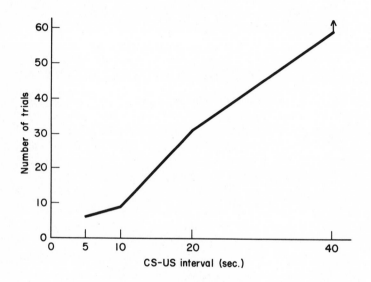

Fig. 13-9. The number of trials required to learn avoidance, i.e., to reach the last shock trial, as a function of the CS-US interval using a trace-conditioning procedure. (Data from Kamin, 1954)

Low and Low (1962) have discussed the possibility that animals trained with long intervals may show greater resistance to extinction, not because they have a stronger habit, but because they are permitted to make more avoidance responses. Then, too, animals trained under a short interval may get quicker punishment of competing nonavoidance behavior, while animals trained under long intervals suffer less punishment of competing behavior. But at the same time, long-delay animals are allowed to develop a more complete fear reaction. We cannot conclude, therefore, that animals trained under long and short CS-US intervals have different strengths of habit, because they may have acquired different habits and they may have been subjected to differential inhibition of competing habits.

Weisman et al. (1965) have found that the CS-US interval makes little difference in well-established shuttle-box avoidance, so most of the effects we have noted reflect acquisition processes and not performance processes. Kamin (1960), Levine and England (1960), and Low and Low (1962a) report discrepant results in comparing fixed with variable CS-US intervals.

Relatively little work has been done on the effects of intertrial interval on avoidance acquisition, but Levine and England (1960) and Brush (1962) have found that optimum avoidance learning in the shuttle box requires a fairly long intertrial interval, 1 min. or longer.

Another factor influencing the effect of the CS-US interval is the nature of the avoidance response itself. In classical conditioning, and this includes classical aversive conditioning, the response ordinarily occurs within .5 sec. after the CS is presented. Although such short latency responses can occur in bar pressing, they cannot occur in the shuttle box. We have already noted that the avoidance response need not wait for the CS to produce fear, but the topography of the response alone dictates that it cannot occur faster than 1 or 2 sec. In the shuttle box the avoidance response is undoubtedly further retarded because animals acquire pre-CS behavior, such as crouching at the far end of the apparatus, which competes with the post-CS behavior. These reactions are presumably acquired on the basis of fear associated with situational cues.

It appears that in the Skinner box the optimum CS-US interval is very long, in the order of 60 sec. (Pearl & Edwards, 1962), and that the optimum intertrial interval is short (Pearl, 1963), less than 40 sec. Pearl got very low levels of performance, however. It may be that the intertrial interval should be as short as possible and the CS-US interval as long as possible.

In summary, studies of the CS-US interval suggest that this interval is not itself a particularly important parameter in the acquisition or extinction of avoidance behavior, but it becomes important in relation to the avoidance response. The animal must have a fair chance to make the response, so the interval should not be too short.

The Conditioned Stimulus. A great variety of conditioned stimuli—lights, buzzers, noises, and pure tones—have been used effectively to gain control over avoidance behavior. Kish (1955) and Schwartz (1958) have found that the onset of a stimulus serves as a more effective CS than stimulus termination (but see Schwartz & Goodson, 1958). There is little indication that the intensity of the CS has an appreciable effect in avoidance learning (see, e.g., Kessen, 1953), but there is good evidence (Myers, 1959, 1960, 1962, 1964; Smith et al., 1961) that some modes of stimulation are more effective than others. These investigators indicate that a buzzer is better than a pure tone and that an auditory stimulus is better than a visual one. Myers (1959) has suggested that when the choice of the CS makes a difference it may be because of the unconditioned reaction it elicits. If the animal initially startles or freezes when the light comes on, then it may be difficult to get the light to control running. Hefferline (1950) and Baron (1959) have shown that commonly used CS's may be themselves slightly aversive. What appears as avoidance learning may therefore be partly artifactual. In the case of the primary reinforcers the experimenters were using, i.e., various weak sensory-change reinforcers, the initially weak effects of the CS may have been a relatively important factor. But it is a different story with electric shock. When the shock comes on everything in sight rapidly moves in the direction of aversiveness; and whatever initial departures there may have been from strict neutrality are almost immediately lost. As Myers (1958) has pointed out, the so-called neutral stimulus need not be strictly neutral; what matters is whether it can be moved far enough and fast enough in the direction of aversiveness (or appetitiveness, as the case may be).

E. S. Brush (1957) has assessed the effect of duration of the CS independently of CS-US interval. The CS-US interval was always 25 sec. and the CS duration was independent of the animal's response. For different groups the CS was on .25, 10, or 20 sec. With the brief CS, which imposes a 25-sec. trace conditioning procedure, subjects learned the avoidance about as fast as might be expected but extinguished relatively quickly. With the 20-sec. CS, which imposes a 5-sec. trace between CS termination and US onset, avoidance responses were acquired, again, relatively quickly. The latency of the avoidance response was only slightly longer than with the brief CS, which means that the avoidance response was "punished" by the nontermination of the CS for several seconds after it occurred. But the response was slow to extinguish. What these results tell us is that CS duration itself has little effect on the acquisition of the avoidance response, so that avoidance may be mediated by effects that occur some seconds after CS onset, e.g., a fear reaction. Moreover, the latencies for all three groups were such that the intervals between the response and CS termination were all far from optimum (Kamin, 1957). Perhaps this sort of experimental procedure can help clarify the mechanism whereby the escape response moves forward to become avoidant.

The Unconditioned Stimulus. Virtually all work in avoidance learning has been done with electric shock as the US. One reason for this is the notorious difficulty in producing much behavior with noise as an aversive stimulus (Hefferline, 1950; Harrison & Tracy, 1955; Campbell, 1955). It is not clear why other varieties of stimulation do not work better; perhaps it is because they elicit freezing rather than the freezing-running conflict state that shock does, or perhaps it is that they do not arouse fear, as shock seems to do. However, while shock as an aversive stimulus is easy to produce and measure in electrical terms, it is very difficult to quantify in behavorial or in physiological terms (see Chapter 7).

It is generally found that unlearned or well-learned escape behavior is facilitated by increasing shock intensity at least up to about 5 ma., at which point tetanization may begin (e.g., Miller & Lawrence, 1950; Kimble, 1955; Boren et al., 1959). Quite likely the effects of shock intensity on avoidance behavior will turn out to depend upon how well the behavior is established. As far as acquisition is concerned, Brush (1957) found that the proportion of dogs that learned avoidance increased with shock intensity but that resistance to extinction and asymptotic latency did not. Moyer and Korn (1964) found a clear but gradual decline in acquisition with increasing shock intensity. Moyer and Korn used rats instead of dogs and used somewhat different procedures than Brush used, so the reason for the discrepancy can only be guessed at. Bolles and Warren (1965) and D'Amato and Fazzaro (1966) found Skinner box avoidance performance clearly negatively correlated with shock intensity.

D'Amato et al. (1964) and Biederman et al. (1964) have discovered that the rat's normally poor acquisition of bar-press avoidance can be sharply improved by using discontinuous shock. Apparently the best US is one with minimal on time (.3 sec. or less) and maximal off time (2 sec. or more). This finding together with the previous findings regarding shock intensity suggest that the rat shows the best acquisition of bar-press avoidance when it receives the least possible amount of total shock. We may assume that the minimum is set by the amount of shock that will maintain fear during the acquisition.

Miscellaneous Considerations. Denny and Thomas (1960) have reported that considerable variation in the apparatus dimensions has no pronounced effect upon avoidance performance; although Kent et al. (1960) found that if the shock compartment in an acquired drive situation was really small, prohibiting responses like that later to be learned, then that learning was seriously impaired. Subsequently, Denny and his collaborators (Denny et al., 1959; Reynierse et al., 1963; Denny & Weisman, 1964) have emphasized the importance of the similarity of pre-response and postresponse stimulus situations. The argument is that the animal does something like relax after making the avoidance response, and if this behavior should generalize back to the preresponse situation it could compete with the avoidance response. The data appear to support Denny's analysis. There are effects of species and strain differences, sex, and time of day of testing (Singh, 1959; Myers, 1959, 1964; Nakamura & Anderson, 1962; Pearl, 1963). There are also a number of warm-up, incubation, and other intersession effects (Bindra & Cameron, 1953; Kamin, 1957c, 1963; Denny & Ditchman, 1962; McAllister & Mc-

Allister, 1963; Brush et al., 1963, 1964; Brush, 1964). Gerbrandt (1964) has made a valiant effort to integrate the enormous volume of recent work on the neurological correlates of avoidance behavior.

SUMMARY

Secondary reinforcement is a ubiquitous explanatory device; we have seen it invoked to explain higher order conditioning, token-reward phenomena, the reinforcement of new behavior, the maintenance of old behavior, the facilitation of discrimination learning, the bridging of temporal delays, and the acquisition of chains of instrumental behavior. Sometimes it is introduced after the fact to account for inexplicable findings. But, increasingly, these effects are being predicted on the basis of our gradually clearing understanding of what the properties of secondary reinforcers are supposed to be. As the facts become clearer some of these effects have become much more firmly established, and some of them now seem to be more fundamental than others. By the same token there now seems to be a gradually emerging picture of how secondary reinforcers are established, and of the conditions that must be fulfilled before their effects upon behavior can be demonstrated.

A secondary reinforcer appears to be merely a stimulus to which has been associated a response; usually this is an approach or a withdrawal response, and usually it has become associated with the stimulus in question by the prior action of a primary reinforcer. This means that stimuli present at the time of primary reinforcement will acquire secondary reinforcing powers to the extent that they have acquired associative control over the response. Thus, the organism will acquire a response by secondary reinforcement if that response produces stimuli which elicit another previously learned response. If the terminal primary reinforcer is still forthcoming, the organism will have acquired a chain of two responses leading to it, but if the primary reinforcer is no longer forthcoming, the chain will be established only to the degree that the secondary reinforcer maintains its control over the second member of the chain (and to the degree that new competing responses are not introduced, e.g., by frustration). The strength and durability of secondary reinforcement therefore depend upon the reliability of the eliciting power of the secondary reinforcer and this can be enhanced by discriminative training, and by the prior conditioning of the elicited response to possibly interfering concurrent stimuli, such as those arising from frustration. In short, a stimulus will provide secondary reinforcement for one response to the extent that it has associative control over another response.

All this is for the positive case; the situation for the negative case may be quite different. A secondary negative reinforcer, such as the buzzer in an avoidance experiment, is usually thought of as eliciting the same response it reinforces, such as jumping over the hurdle. The experimental situation, moreover, is usually arranged so that this is also the same response that is elicited by the primary negative reinforcer. Hence it is extremely difficult to isolate the various eliciting, reinforcing, and possible motivating effects involved in avoidance learning. It is conceivable that the same response must necessarily be involved (this may be true in the appetitive case also) or at least that some fraction of the same response, such as r_G, or anticipatory approach or avoidance, must be carried through. Recent research on avoidance suggests that this restriction may be necessary and that a negative secondary reinforcer can be effective only when the animal is required to make a response which is already part of its innate defensive repertory.

One final conclusion should be emphasized: Explanations of behavior couched in terms of secondary reinforcement are fundamentally associative rather than motivational in character. Such explanations put upon the theorist and the researcher the very healthy responsibility of having to indicate precisely what stimuli, responses, and reinforcers are involved in the behavior being explained.

14

PUNISHMENT

❖❰❰❖❰

> . . . *the strengthening of a connection by satisfying consequences seems, in view of our experiments and of certain general considerations, to be more universal, inevitable, and direct than the weakening of a connection by annoying consequences. The latter seems more specialized, contingent upon what the annoyer in question makes the animal do, and indirect.*
>
> E. L. THORNDIKE

The prescientific and traditional view has always been that our actions are guided by our anticipation of rewards and punishments. When Thorndike proposed that rewards stamp behavior in and punishers stamp behavior out he was merely giving behavioral significance and empirical testability to the almost universal belief in the practical effectiveness of rewards and punishments as determinants of behavior. In his early statements of the law of effect (which we will consider in more detail in the following chapter), Thorndike made it symmetrical: reward stamps in and punishment stamps out the S-R connections which they follow. Other early behavior theories also typically postulated reciprocal processes; Tolman spoke of demands for or against certain goal objects, Pavlov spoke of excitation and inhibition. This assumption of the symmetrical or complementary action of reward and punishment reflected man's immemorial customs of rewarding and punishing.

It is understandable, then, that learning theorists and educators alike were startled when Thorndike (1932) rejected the punishment half of the law of effect. Rewards still stamped in but punishment no longer stamped out. We will consider here the sort of evidence that led Thorndike to truncate the law. We will also look at a number of studies of the effects of punishment on animal behavior. We will find that Thorndike was right, and that the effect of punishment is indeed specialized and indirect, and does indeed depend upon what it makes the animal do.

EFFECTS OF PUNISHMENT

Punishment in Verbal Learning. Thorndike (1932) presented evidence from an impressive series of studies which, he said, left him no alternative but to reject the idea that punishment can weaken an S-R connection. In a typical experiment, a subject would be presented with a long list of words and required to guess numbers from one to ten to associate with each word of the list. Responses might be either ignored, rewarded by the verbal statement "right," or punished by the verbal statement "wrong." The subject was instructed to learn which numbers went with which words, so that on a test trial he could repeat those that were said to be right and to vary those that were said to be wrong. Thorndike found, of course, that subjects tended to repeat their "correct" responses. They also showed an above-chance tendency to repeat those responses which elicited no response from the experimenter (demonstrating, he assumed, the law of exercise—learning through mere repetition without an aftereffect). But the important finding was that subjects also tended to repeat at an above-chance level responses that they had been told were wrong.

Thorndike's asymmetrical law of effect was not universally accepted. Critics were quick to point out certain basic methodological flaws. For one thing, it is gratuitous to assume that the numbers from 1 to 10 have equal probabilities of occurring in isolation, much less in the context of the verbal associations produced by the stimulus words. Moreover, subjects tend to use numbers in systematic ways; they come into the experimental situation with well-established verbal habits for using numbers. Subsequent investigation has demonstrated that the expected repetition rate for numbers given in guessing sequences may be closer to 20% than 10%. Another difficulty here is in the possible generalization effects, such as the spread-of-effect phenomenon, which is the tendency for associations near a reinforced association to be repeated.[1]

A good deal of research effort has gone into teasing out the different variables and effects that influence performance in this sort of verbal learning situation. Sometimes Thorndike is confirmed and sometimes he is repudiated. But Stone (1953), with the wisdom from some 20 years of

[1] The details of all these matters are ably discussed by Postman (1947, 1962).

such research to draw on, conducted an experiment which seems to control the relevant factors and provide a real test of the asymmetrical law of effect. Stone made lavish use of subjects (160 in a group), precision presentation apparatus, a very carefully counterbalanced design, and a control group to establish the zero reinforcement baseline. He found under these conditions that telling the subject "wrong" strengthens the response more than telling him nothing. It appears, then, that verbal punishment is a slightly positive reinforcer.

Dinsmoor (1954) has dismissed this whole line of research on the grounds that according to the empirical law of effect a punisher is an event which stamps out, and if "wrong" fails to do so, then it is not a punisher. All we have discovered, Dinsmoor implies, from this research is that "wrong" is not a punisher in this situation; we have discovered nothing about the experimental treatments that are punishers. Stone was evidently aware of this possible interpretation, however, and accordingly he culminated his work on this problem with a study of the same sort as before in which an electric shock was used (Stone & Walter, 1951). The findings were the same as before; an electric shock is a weak positive reinforcer in this situation.

Certainly we know that electric shock can be used as a punisher in other situations, and the probability is that "wrong" can be used effectively also. Clearly, then, Dinsmoor's charge cannot stand as it is. On the other hand, it is not clear how it should be altered. We may wonder whether there are any punishers in the situation if shock is not among them. Should we conclude that there are no punishers for human subjects, or for human subjects in Thorndike's learning situation? Or are we to conclude with Thorndike that "wrong" is a punisher, but that punishers do not weaken the strength of a response? Or is it possible to arrive at some alternative explanation of why stimuli such as "wrong" and electric shock which are punishers in some situations do not punish in this situation? If we are to solve the puzzle we will have to consider punishment in other situations.[2]

Spatially Localized Punishment. Consider the following hypothetical situation. A hungry rat is put into a novel environment and allowed to explore for a few moments until it finds food. The animal is allowed to eat for a few seconds and then the shock is turned on. If the shock is brief, intense, and localized in the vicinity of the food, then the animal will quickly withdraw as far as possible from the food, crouch and show

---

[2] There are a number of studies (e.g., Brackbill & O'Hara, 1958; Meyer & Offenbach, 1962) showing that verbal punishment, saying "wrong," can be effective in more complex situations than those Thorndike used, e.g., in concept formation problems. Perhaps this is because the subject attacks such problems with relatively long-term verbal hypotheses which are more subject to the effects of the experimenter's verbal behavior than the short-term S-R associations Thorndike studied.

a number of signs of emotional disturbance. After a few moments it may approach the food again; but when it encounters shock once more, the tendency to approach will soon be reduced to near zero strength. The animal will learn not to approach the food. This learning will be very rapid and effective.[3]

How is such learning to be explained? Perhaps the most straightforward explanation is that derived from the escape paradigm: the animal learns on the basis of the reinforcement that occurs when the punishing shock is terminated. What the animal learns, according to this position, is to withdraw from food when near it. Withdrawal occurs, by generalization, to stimuli similar to those to which withdrawal is conditioned. Miller and Dollard (1941) who first offered this explanation of punishment put it this way:

> A child touches a hot radiator. The pain elicits a [withdrawal] response, and the escape from pain rewards this response. Since the sight and muscular feel of the hand approaching the radiator are similar in certain respects to the sight and muscular feel of the hand touching the radiator, the strongly rewarded response of withdrawal will be expected to generalize from the latter situation to the former. After one or more trials, the child will reach out its hand toward the radiator and withdraw it before touching the radiator. The withdrawal response will become anticipatory; it will occur before that of actually touching the radiator. This is obviously adaptive, since it enables the child to avoid getting burned. (Miller & Dollard, 1941, pp. 49–50)

What is proposed here is that the stimuli which initially control approach responses come to elicit withdrawal because of the very rapid learning (escape learning) of withdrawal in the presence of stimuli like those that initially controlled the approach.[4]

There are two points about this explanation that should be emphasized. One is that its only motivational feature is the assumption that drive reduction (removal of the painful stimulus) reinforces the response (withdrawal) that produces it. A contiguity theorist, such as Guthrie,

[3] Some instances of one-trial learning through punishment have been reported (e.g., Hudson, 1950; Maatsch, 1959; Heriot & Coleman, 1962; Essman & Alpern, 1964). Lloyd Morgan (1894) reported perhaps the first such case—chicks learn, sometimes in one trial, to avoid bitter-tasting caterpillars. Morgan had a hypothesis very close to the one stated here to explain it. Boycott and Young (1950) report very rapid learning through punishment in an animal as low as the octopus.

[4] Later Miller and Dollard speak also of fear, through punishment, inhibiting the response. The "anticipation" that Miller and Dollard refer to above means only the coming forward in time, a short-circuiting. They did not mean to emphasize the kind of anticipatory reaction involved in "the muscular feel of the hand approaching" which we are about to consider.

could use this explanation of punishment just as easily as Miller and Dollard by simply omitting the reference to drive reduction. In other words, this is basically an associative account of punishment. Specifically, it ignores fear; it attributes no behavioral significance to the common observation that the punished animal may be fearful. We may suspect, therefore, that the escape paradigm will fail to account for persistent punishment effects in much the same way, and for many of the same reasons, that accounts of avoidance learning which attribute all learning to the escape from shock are inadequate.

The second point is that punishment is assumed to lead to the acquisition of behavior which *interferes* with the punished response, rather than weakening the punished response directly. One consequence of this is that as long as there are persistent stimuli which continue to produce the punished response, e.g., hunger which continues to elicit approach to food, punishment can do no more than hold this response in abeyance. If the prepunishment stimulus situation is markedly different from the situation at the site of punishment, then we would expect punishment to have no inhibitory effect upon the strength of the punished response, because there would be no way in which the withdrawal, or whatever response is learned by punishment, could be elicited. Ordinarily, the withdrawal response should be strong in the presence of the food and weaker elsewhere (Bindra, 1963). Since the strength of the tendency to approach the food shows the same general type of gradient, the animal is effectively in an approach-avoid conflict situation.[5] Miller found early support for the hypothesis that the withdrawal gradient is sharper than the approach gradient. Thus, as long as withdrawal is stronger than approach at the food cup, the animal should withdraw to the point at which the two gradients intersect, i.e., the point where approach and withdrawal just balance. As withdrawal dissipates in time, this point should move forward, until eventually, when withdrawal has become sufficiently weak, the animal will approach close enough to start eating again.

The one assumption implicit in this analysis which we need to emphasize is that the strengths of the old approach response and the newly acquired withdrawal response must vary continuously as a function of the relevant experimental variables. On this assumption, whether punishment will prevent a previously reinforced response from occurring in this type of situation should depend upon (among other variables) the number of times approach has been reinforced and the number of times it has been punished. These functional relationships can be quantified as Kaufman

---

[5] This conception is, in fact, the source of the brilliant work done by Miller and his co-workers on conflict. We will not consider this work in any detail primarily because it lends itself, just as punishment does, directly to an associationistic interpretation without involving any new facts or concepts about motivation. The best recent review is Miller (1959).

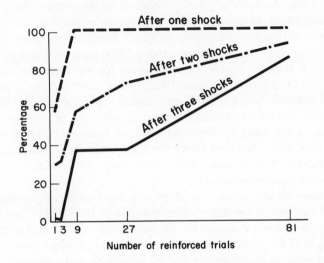

Fig. 14-1. Percentage of animals that reach the goal after they have been shocked there as a function of the number of previous training trials reinforced by food. (From Kaufman & Miller, 1949)

and Miller (1949) showed in one of the early conflict studies (see Fig. 14-1).

Subsequently it has been shown that the effectiveness of punishment in preventing a previously reinforced locomotory response varies in a continuous fashion with shock intensity (Karsh, 1962, 1963, 1964; Appel, 1963), proximity to the point of shock (Brown, 1948; Karsh, 1962), and previous strength of the response (Karsh, 1962), although sometimes the latter effect is difficult to assess (Miller, 1960). Delay of administering shock also seems to produce continuous variation in its effectiveness (Warden & Diamond, 1931; Bevan & Dukes, 1955; Coons & Miller, 1960).

Although some writers (Church, 1963; Solomon, 1964) suggest that the results of some of the studies just cited indicate general functional properties of punishment in instrumental behavior, some caution is called for. It is probably as hard, or harder, to specify the general properties of shock punishment as it is to specify the general properties of food. Food can make the rat run to it, but we have to arrange conditions with some care so that this will happen. We usually do, but we can as easily arrange the conditions, e.g., by making the rat thirsty, so that it will avoid food. However, Azrin and his collaborators have found many of the rat runway effects of punishment in the pecking response of pigeons. They have shown continuous effects in intensity (Azrin, 1959, 1960; Azrin

& Holz, 1961; Azrin et al., 1963), delay (Azrin, 1956), and schedule (Azrin, 1956; Azrin et al., 1963). With these procedures Azrin is evidently able to get an extremely delicate balance of pecking and whatever response it is that competes with pecking.[6] Thus, he has found compensation effects, both in extinction (Azrin, 1959) and in time out (Azrin, 1960), such that the bird tends to make up for lost food (see also Stein et al., 1958; Carlton & Didamo, 1960; Geller, 1960). Azrin is also able to show gradual recovery from punishment within a session. The conclusion that should be emphasized from all this work is not that punishment can have graded inhibitory effects upon behavior (Church and Solomon's conclusion) but that under the conditions where punishment does have inhibitory effects, these effects vary continuously with variation in the relevant associative variables.

We have spoken so far only about the explanation of punishment in terms of the escape paradigm. Two features of both Miller and Azrin's studies provide some difficulty for the escape theory. One is that the punishments used are typically of very short duration, frequently only .1 sec. It would seem to be impossible for the subject to make (or even begin) an escape response in so short an interval.[7] The second problem is that the subjects in these studies were quite evidently frightened, and the escape paradigm, at least in the simple form we have stated it, makes no provision for the possible effects of fear.

Both of these difficulties can be overcome by introducing an avoidance paradigm, which accounts for the effects of punishment by hypothesizing the conditioning of fear (considered either as an acquired drive or as a conditioned negative reinforcer) to stimuli in the vicinity of the food. Fear is aversive, so that the animal withdraws and is reinforced for doing so. Such a view is supported by the evidence of emotionality that occurs even after the animal has withdrawn from the food. A spatial gradient of avoidance is again derived from the fact that the stimuli anywhere in the test situation are likely to be similar to the stimuli near the food, so that some fear will occur everywhere in the situation, but in an amount that depends upon stimulus generalization. The animal can minimize its fear by minimizing the similarity between where he is and the place where the shock is. A crucial difference be-

[6] For reasons that will be made clear shortly, it would be most interesting to know what response Azrin's shocks elicit. Azrin and Holz (1961) say that when birds are on an FI schedule, shock produces some locomotory disturbance which they suggest might account for some of the response decrement. However, they find no decrement in local response rate on an FR schedule but only lengthened postreinforcement pauses. Here we might expect an overt withdrawal from the target.

[7] Moreover, Leitenberg (1965) and Bolles and Warren (1966) have found that delaying the termination of a punishing stimulus does not reduce its punishing efficacy. It appears to be the onset of the punisher rather than its termination which counts.

tween the avoidance and the escape paradigms is that according to the former the subject should show increased sensitization because repeated fear reduction should reinforce progressively further withdrawal; whereas according to the latter, withdrawal should rapidly extinguish because of the fact that it prevents further reinforcement. The animal thus not only avoids shock, and food, but to the extent that Solomon's anxiety-conservation principle can be applied, fear itself, by keeping sufficiently far away from danger.

Notice that both the escape and the avoidance accounts of punishment explain alterations in behavior by invoking the acquisition of behavior that competes with the original behavior in the punishment situation.

Punishment Correlated with a Specific Response. Even if we accept the proposition that punishment produces behavior that competes with the punished response there still remains a question whether punishment has any additional effect upon the strength of the initial tendency itself. Estes (1944) investigated this question in a now-classic series of experiments. He trained rats to press a bar for food, and when the behavior had become well established he extinguished them. If a rat is under moderate deprivation conditions we might normally expect something like 200 responses in extinction. The question Estes asked was how does this compare with the resistance to extinction of animals trained in the same way but, in addition, punished several times for pressing the bar? The answer, Estes found, is that there is no difference. To be sure, the punished animal takes longer to extinguish in the sense that the suppression of bar pressing persists for some time after punishment is discontinued. But as soon as the animal begins to press the bar again it rapidly comes to respond at a normal rate (or even at a higher compensatory rate) and from that point takes as long to extinguish as the control animal. The punishment of bar pressing does not seem to weaken the bar-press response but only to produce temporary decrements in responding, as if the animal had been prevented from pressing for a time.

Punishment Uncorrelated with Behavior—the CER. Estes (1944) also noted that it made little difference whether shocks in his situation were correlated with bar pressing (as punishment) or presented independently of the animal's behavior. Hence he argued (as Estes & Skinner, 1941, had earlier) that the effect of shock was to produce a diffuse, generalized emotional state, "anxiety," and that it was primarily this state together with its immobilizing effect upon behavior (i.e., the powerful elicitation of freezing and crouching) which competed with bar pressing. Estes and Skinner (1941) had previously developed a procedure in which a CS was paired with shock in a situation where rats were pressing a bar for food. It was found that after just a few such pairings presentation of the CS alone would inhibit or suppress bar pressing, in some cases as effectively as the shock would in control animals. Since this suppression effect occurred when bar pressing itself was never immediately punished, the conclusion was reached that shock has a generalized disrupting or inhibiting effect rather than a specific weakening or repelling effect upon behavior.

This experimental procedure, which has become known as the conditioned-emotional-response (CER) procedure, offers considerable promise of allowing us to separate, or at least to compare, the generalized emotional effect of shock with the effect produced by the acquisition of specific reactions such as withdrawal acquired by punishment. Hunt and Brady (1955) were among the first to undertake such a comparison; they compared the behavior of animals punished a few times for pressing a bar in the presence of a CS with the behavior of animals given identical shocks, also in the presence of the CS, but not contingent upon their behavior. Figure 14-2 (top) shows that under both conditions the CS rapidly came to inhibit bar pressing. This inhibition came under much weaker control of general situational cues for the punished subjects, however, as shown by the fact that they made appreciably more bar presses during test sessions when the CS was not present (Fig. 14-2, bottom). We may assume that the attachment of a specific response (withdrawal) to specific stimuli (the CS plus the proprioceptive feedback of bar pressing) produced much less inhibition of bar pressing than the attachment of a general reaction (let us call it fear) to general stimuli (from the situation). This interpretation is supported by the additional evidence that under the punishment condition there was less overt emotional behavior and more varied bar-press topography than under the condition where shock was not contingent on the animal's behavior. The conclusion, then, is that relatively little fear was conditioned to the CS under the punishment conditions, but that considerable fear was conditioned under the noncontingent (CER) condition.

Note here that there was relatively rapid recovery after shocks were discontinued. While these results do not rule out the possibility of fear being a factor in the punishment condition, they suggest that in those cases where punishment does lead to the persistent inhibition of behavior, the fear component is an important factor in producing it.

Estes and Skinner and others who have worked with the CER procedure have found that it provides a sensitive index of the effects (presumably upon the fear reaction) of a number of experimental variables. The beauty of the CER situation lies in its simplicity; the effects are governed by far fewer processes than occur, for example, in the typical avoidance situation. Perhaps for this reason there has been a tremendous increase in recent years of research using this procedure. Singh (1959) and Annau and Kamin (1961) have found that both the magnitude of the CER effect and its persistence are quite sensitive functions of the

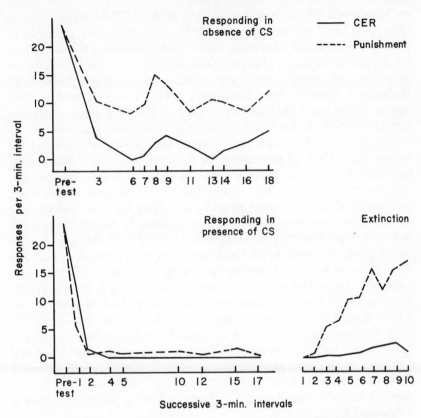

Fig. 14-2. Rate of bar pressing prior to introduction of shock, during 3-min. intervals of aversive stimulation, during interspersed 3-min. intervals, and in extinction for animals either shocked for bar pressing (punishment) or shocked independently of bar pressing (CER) in the aversive stimulation intervals. (From Hunt & Brady, 1955)

shock intensity used in establishing it. One interesting finding in the Annau and Kamin study was that punishment effects were found at lower shock intensities (.28 ma) than would yield CER effects, which illustrates again the possibility of experimentally separating the two.

Kamin has suggested that if the CER is really classically conditioned to the stimulus that produces it then its occurrence and strength should vary with the manipulation of experimental variable in the same manner as other classically conditioned responses have been shown to vary. He has found roughly similar dependence upon the CS-US interval (Kamin, 1961, 1963a; Kamin & Schaub, 1963), and CS and US intensities (Kamin & Schaub, 1963; Kamin & Brimer, 1963). Compensatory effects are sometimes reported, just as they are with the punishment procedure (see p. 422) (Brimer & Kamin, 1963; Kelleher et al., 1963). Other experimenters have noted effects upon the strength of the CER of shock duration (Storms et al., 1963; Boroczi et al., 1964; Strouthes, 1965); number of pairings (Strouthes & Hamilton, 1964); and, sometimes, the strength of the suppressed behavior (Hearst, 1963; Boroczi et al., 1964). A number of studies have shown stimulus generalization effects (Ray & Stein, 1959; Hoffman & Fleshler, 1961; Desiderato, 1964; Winograd, 1965), which further demonstrate that the dependence of the CER upon associative factors is similar to that of other classically conditioned responses.[8]

All of this kind of work holds considerable promise of clarifying the nature of the CER, of elucidating the variables that control fear, and of indicating some of the effects fear may be expected to have on behavior. Unfortunately much of this research has been done from an extremely peripheralistic point of view; much of the effort has been addressed to questions no more fundamental than, e.g., what is the effect upon the rate of bar pressing of presenting stimuli paired with different intensities of shock? We need to ask much more penetrating questions than this if we are to untangle the contributions of the punishment and CER procedures to the establishment of withdrawal and freezing in the experimental situation. We need to know more about what kind of behavior the subject is engaged in when it is not making the criterion response in the CER situation. Is it freezing; is it fearful? We particularly need more research in which punishment and CER procedures are introduced and compared in the same experimental context. Available reports (Hunt & Brady, 1955; Azrin, 1956; Hoffman & Fleshler, 1965) indicate that the animal's behavior may be quite different following punishment than it is following CER.

There is an important lesson to be learned from an experiment reported by Page (1955), who trained rats to leave an electrified box and run to a safe goal box. This response was then extinguished by withholding shock. Two groups were run, one which was free to continue making the response in extinction, and one which had the response blocked. The blocked group extinguished more quickly than the unblocked group, suggesting that fear extinguishes faster when the response is blocked. This obvious conclusion was rejected however because Page subsequently trained the animals to go back to the old shock box to get food, and on this problem the blocked animals showed poorer acquisition than the unblocked animals. It can be concluded, exactly in opposition to the first conclusion, that fear extinguishes slower when the response is blocked. The moral is that we cannot safely base any conclusion about

---

[8] There are some complications however, as we might expect. For example, Storms et al. (1963) and Boroczi et al. (1964) have emphasized that different response measures may not vary the same way with the manipulation of experimental variables.

the strength of fear on the manifest strength of any single instrumental response.

We are left with a number of important unresolved problems. Does fear have only general or diffuse suppressing effects, or can it produce specific withdrawal behavior; for example, do organisms have unconditioned withdrawal responses to stimuli that elicit fear? If fear has both effects, then how can we separate them experimentally? Can any response be conditioned to fear, or does fear-produced response suppression necessarily imply that the organism is withdrawing or freezing?

AN INTERPRETATION OF PUNISHMENT

The three situations we have considered, verbal learning, spatial conflict, and the CER situation, all yield a fairly consistent picture of punishment. We are led to the view that punishment does not itself change the strength of the response it follows, but that it provides the opportunity for other learning to occur, either directly or through the mediation of learned fear. The direct effects we have seen have been due to acquisition of competing behavior, most evident in the case of withdrawal from spatially localized shock. Fear too may cause withdrawal from fear-eliciting stimuli. However fear has a more widespread and diffuse effect; it elicits freezing and crouching, and these kinds of behavior compete most effectively with any other kind of behavior we care to punish.

The only apparent discrepancy among the results from the three situations is that in the verbal learning situation punishment seems to have no effect, even when electric shock is used as the punisher. Why doesn't the human subject develop fear in this context, or if he does, why doesn't it affect his verbal learning? The answer may be that he does feel some fear, or anxiety, or at least he may become tense and excited, but that this does not affect the specific S-R association between a given word and a given number because fear-elicited behavior does not compete with it. The subject can say "seven" while worried about the shock just as easily as he can if he is not worried about the shock. There is nothing about the reaction to shock in this situation which in any way inhibits or interferes with the response "seven."[9] The situation for the animal being shocked for approaching a particular stimulus is quite different. Here both

---

[9] One could argue that the tenseness or other motor concomitants of the subject's fear do interfere with his speech so that there might be a difference in the latency of the punished verbal response. On the other hand, the drive theorist would argue that the extra fear might produce extra drive which would simply multiply the subject's strongest response tendency, namely, the one which was most likely to have been punished on the previous trial (see also Miller, 1959).

the shock itself and the fear conditioned to the sight of the food cup evoke withdrawal which quite effectively inhibits approach.

If this interpretation of the discrepancy is valid, it brings us to the following hypothesis: *When punishment leads to learning, what is learned are the responses which the punisher elicits, including fear.* Stated another way, punishment cannot produce the learning of any behavior other than that which it elicits—e.g., withdrawal, fear, and cowering. If the punishment conditions are arranged so that punishment produces withdrawal, then the organism will withdraw. If it only produces freezing or cowering, then the organism will freeze or cower. On the other hand, if a rat is punished for running in a situation where the reaction to punishment is also running, then punishment may facilitate the behavior, as we will see shortly.[10]

The elicitation interpretation of punishment has been further supported by a beautiful study by Fowler and Miller (1963). They trained rats to run an alley for food. At the goal some animals were shocked in the hindpaws and some were shocked in the forepaws. During the course of training the hindpaw subjects ran progressively faster and the forepaw subjects ran progressively slower than a group receiving no shock. This is just what would be expected if hindpaw shocks elicited running and forepaw shocks elicited startle or withdrawal.

Adelman and Maatsch (1955) trained rats to run into a box for food and then extinguished them. One group was permitted to jump out through the top of the box to escape the frustrating situation, while another group was required to back up out of the box. The back-up group extinguished running to the box almost immediately whereas the jump-out group continued to run to the box, and jump out of it, for many trials. Again, all animals did what the punisher (frustration in this case) made them do, jump out in one case, which was not incompatible with the running response, and retreat in the other, which effectively interfered with running. Bolles and Seelbach (1964) studied the punishing effect of loud noise on different responses in the rat's repertory and found that poking the head through a window could be rapidly eliminated by making sudden noise-onset contingent upon its occurrence. However, noise punishment had no effect upon the incidence of other responses, namely, standing up on the hind legs, or grooming. Once more

---

[10] It may be noted that the great majority of punishment studies have required the animal to make locomotory responses, so that the elicitation hypothesis seems to be immediately of service in explaining, e.g., that shock in one arm of a maze facilitates the rat learning to go to food in the other arm. Church (1963) has cited about a dozen such studies. He also discusses the literature showing the paradoxical facilitory effect of giving mild shocks for going to the food side. This latter effect appears to be due to mild conflict at the choice point which has the effect of slowing up the animal so that the relevant stimuli will be more likely to register.

a hedonistic account of punishment fails utterly, but the elicitation hypothesis puts the data in order if we assume that the onset of a loud noise elicits a reflexive head jerk which interferes with head poking but not with standing or grooming.

It is important to notice that this response-elicitation or response-competition account of punishment does not commit one to any particular theory of motivation. Its essential features were spelled out by Thorndike (1932), Guthrie (1935), and stated again by Miller and Dollard (1941) and Estes and Skinner (1941). It arises just as easily from the systems of Hull (1943), Dinsmoor (1954, 1955), Mowrer (1947) or Mowrer (1960). Different theoretical systems differ not on the question of what effect punishment has, but rather on the question of whether fear is involved, and if it is, how it is acquired. Not since Thorndike abandoned the idea that punishment weakens S-R associations has a major systematist defended it.

Curiously, even though there is this uncommon agreement about punishment there have been very few systematic statements about it, and relatively little research has been done on the phenomena of punishment. Even the textbook writers tend to slight it. This neglect of punishment is especially remarkable in view of Skinner's well-known assertions that it is probably the most common means of controlling human behavior (1953), and at the same time, ineffective and morally indefensible (1948a).

The backward state of research on punishment should not lead us to believe that there are no problems here, nor any possibilities of deriving a better understanding of behavior by pursuing them. Let us consider briefly one of the most fundamental of these problems: what is the locus of the stimuli that control the avoidance response (i.e., the response that avoids punishment)?

The Locus of the Controlling Stimuli. In order for punishment to be effective the crucial stimuli must be the same as those which before punishment controlled the punished response. When punishment is effective it produces in an organism a response which is an alternative to the punished response on those occasions when the punished response might occur. The question is whether the avoidance response is under the control just of the initial stimuli or is dependent as well upon new additions to the original stimulus complex.

There are three distinct sources or varieties of stimulation that might be effective in controlling the alternative response. One is the environment, providing stimuli which, prior to punishment, controlled the punished response. The second is the feedback from the fear reaction produced by the punishment which generalizes more or less to the whole situation. And the third is the feedback (proprioceptive stimulus consequences) of the punished act itself. The first of these alternatives has been emphasized by Miller and Dollard (1941) in what I have called the escape hypothesis. However, the drive theorist can include as well the second variety of stimulation, that arising from fear acquired in the situation. (There is the restriction that fear is reinforced by the termination of the punisher, but either the termination of the punisher or the termination of fear could serve as the reinforcer for the avoidance response.) A contiguity theorist, or a classical conditioning theorist is free to invoke all three sources of controlling stimuli, but would contend, ordinarily, that it is the onset of the punisher which reinforces the fear and that it is the onset of either the punisher or the fear which reinforces the avoidance response.

The new approaches in contemporary motivation theory tend to emphasize the third source of stimulation, the proprioceptive feedback from the punished response. According to Schoenfeld (1950) and Dinsmoor (1954) the proprioceptive stimulation which arises when the punished act is initiated becomes aversive and the termination of this secondary negative reinforcer strengthens any alternative response. A contiguity theorist can join in here with the assumption (Sheffield, 1948) that any reaction to aversive stimulation which terminates it is strengthened because it alters the stimulus situation. All the drive theorist would have to do to get on the band wagon is to postulate that these proprioceptive components of the total stimulus situation become a source of drive. Although this fateful step was taken many years ago by Hull in the case of appetitive behavior, drive theorists have been reluctant to make the same move for the case of aversive behavior. The most that has been done in this direction is the assumption (made by Mowrer, 1960) that these proprioceptive cues may come to elicit fear, so that the animal becomes frightened by the initiation of the punished response. Any alternative response will reduce fear or the cues to fear, and hence be motivated to occur, according to Mowrer.

Thus, we find that the punishment situation presents the theorist with many of the problems and complexities of the avoidance situation. Consider the question of the extent to which the effectiveness of avoidance of punishment consists merely in learning an alternative response, as against the possibility that it depends upon the arousal of an emotional state which produces behavior that competes with the punished response.

A number of investigators (Libby, 1951; Bevan & Dukes, 1955; Davitz et al., 1957; Kamin, 1959a; Baron, 1965) have reported that the temporal interval between the response and the punishment is not very important. Quite broad or even flat temporal gradients have been found in these studies, most of them obtained in situations where a previously food-reinforced response was punished by shock several seconds or even minutes after the response. Kamin (1959a) punished a shock-avoidance response in a shuttle box and also obtained pronounced punishment effects with relatively long delays. Such findings suggest the operation of generalized fear reactions rather than specific withdrawal responses.

There has been considerable interest recently in such questions as whether it is possible to get adaptation to the effects of shock either by prior exposure to it or by introducing it gradually (Feirstein & Miller, 1963; Brown & Wagner, 1964; Martin & Ross, 1964; Melvin & Brown, 1964), and whether an acquired fear can be reduced by the introduction of particular stimuli, such as another animal (J. C. Hall, 1955; Davitz & Mason, 1955a; Korman & Loeb, 1961), or by the introduction of a cue to safety (Rescorla & LoLordo, 1965). The answer to all these questions seems, tentatively, to be yes.

Discrimination Learning Based on Punishment. In the earliest days of animal psychology aversive stimuli such as electric shocks were regarded as "negative incentives." The general concept was that the animal would learn to avoid negative incentives—like shock—in a way analogous to its learning to approach positive ones like food. Within this framework it was natural to ask how discrimination learning based on negative incentives varies as a function of the strength of the negative incentive. Yerkes and Dodson (1908) found that the dancing mouse would learn an easy discrimination best with a large shock but would learn increasingly more difficult discriminations best with increasingly milder shocks. (This is the famous Yerkes-Dodson Law which was discussed in Chapter 8.) This pattern of results was confirmed by Cole (1911) with chicks, Dodson (1915) with kittens, and Vaughn and Diserens (1930) with human subjects. Similar discrimination learning with a single-shock intensity was obtained by Hoge and Stocking (1912), Dodson (1917), and Warden and Aylesworth (1927).

One feature of these early studies is particularly pertinent to the question of how important fear is in punishment. The way they were ordinarily conducted was that the animal under the shock condition would be put in a choice situation where if it went in one direction it would be shocked, and if it went in the other direction nothing would happen to it. The remarkable phenomenon in this situation is that animals would perform at all! This was not an escape situation; there was no shock at the choice point, so why would the animal move one way or another? Why did the animal venture forth with the risk of being shocked rather than avoid shock by staying where it was? Admittedly, some subjects did refuse to run, sometimes as many as a third of the group, but the modal response was running. One thing that might make them go would be the tendency to explore, but it seems unlikely that any exploratory behavior would survive many shocks, and certainly not the many trials that were commonly needed to obtain discrimination learning in the Yerkes box.

A better hypothesis is that fear became conditioned, during the incorrect trials, to cues in the apparatus, and that this reaction generalized back to the choice-point situation to motivate the animal. Alternatively, when the animal ran into the shock compartment it was permitted either to run out again or to run on through the shock area to a region of safety. In either case, the last response the animal made in the presence of shock was running. Running was an escape response. Therefore we may suppose that the learning which occurred involved not only the acquisition of fear but also the acquisition of the running response and that it too would generalize back to the preshock area.

Such behavior seems perfectly inexplicable in terms of the traditional idea of motivation, which says that shock is unpleasant and the animal ought to avoid that which experience has shown to be unpleasant. But it becomes quite understandable when framed in the context of the acquired-fear drive. And we also have another case in which an animal makes a response which is likely to earn it punishment; the reason is, as before, that the punishment only facilitates this behavior because it is the behavior the punishment elicits. Gwinn (1949) punished a running escape response and found that this treatment only made the animals run faster. In fact he found that this "vicious circle" behavior continued until the animal became so frightened in the test situation that the reaction to fear was no longer running but freezing. Subsequently it has been found that once an animal has learned to run from an electrified start box and through an alley to escape, it will continue to do so even when shock is no longer present in the start box but only in the alley (Brown, Martin & Morrow, 1964). Just as in the Yerkes and Dodson study, the animal needlessly exposes itself to shock and this behavior shows great resistance to extinction; in fact all the parameters that make the situation worse for the animal seem only to make the behavior more persistent (Martin & Melvin, 1964; Melvin, 1964). Sometimes the vicious circle effect is not found (Moyer, 1957; Seward & Raskin, 1960) perhaps because the shock produces behavior other than running into the goal (see also Whiteis, 1956).

SUMMARY

Punishment, the presentation of an aversive stimulus after a response has occurred, sometimes weakens the strength of the punished response. When it does have a weakening effect the effect can be attributed to the acquisition of a response which is an alternative to the punished response on those occasions when the latter might occur. This is the whole point of punishment, from either a moral or a behavioristic point of view. But both the moral concern with, and the behavioral limitations of, punishment arise from the fact that the response acquired through punishment, the response which competes with the punished response, evidently must necessarily be that which is immediately elicited by the punishment. This may be some sort of specific withdrawal reaction, or it may be a diffuse generalized immobilization involving crouching, freezing, in short, all the overt evidence of fear. There is some evidence to support the idea that whenever punishment is shown to have long-lasting effects it is because of the elicitation of fear rather than specific withdrawal reactions. It does not seem possible to weaken the punished response itself, nor to produce by punishment competing behavior other than the particular response it elicits. Therefore punishment is not effective in altering behavior unless the reaction to punishment itself competes with the response we wish to punish.

15

REINFORCEMENT
THEORIES
OF MOTIVATION

❖❰❮❖❰

*. . . the initiation of learned, or habitual, patterns of movement or
behavior is called* motivation.

C. L. HULL

In the early chapters of this book we considered the possibility that what
we call motivation is a fact, either a fact of human experience or a fact
of behavior. We were able to come rather quickly to the conclusion that
this view had done little to advance our understanding of behavior. In
succeeding chapters we considered the possibility that what we call motivation is a theoretical construct, not directly observable but theoretically
implicated in the explanation of behavior. We have examined the evidence in some detail and concluded that while some theoretical structures
have failed to stand the test of time there are other theoretical positions
that still offer considerable explanatory promise.

Here in the final chapter it is perhaps appropriate to consider the
possibility that the explanation of behavior can proceed better without
any motivational concepts, without involving needs or drives or wants or

anything of the sort, either in our data language or among our theoretical concepts. Specifically, we will consider the possibility that what we have called motivated behavior is neither more nor less than learned behavior, and that all of the phenomena that have been called motivational can be translated, without loss, into phenomena of reinforcement. We will look at some of the implications and possibilities of such an approach. First, however, we should say something about E. L. Thorndike who started this movement even though he could not adhere strictly to it himself.

THORNDIKE'S LAW OF EFFECT

At the time when the first animal psychologists were collecting anecdotes and casual observations to prove that animals' minds were like men's minds, Thorndike began systematic experimentation on "animal intelligence." Hungry animals were put in puzzle boxes and timed to see how long it took them to get out of the box and to food. Thorndike found that consistent but gradual improvement over a series of trials was the rule. Thorndike (1898) denied the popular views of the day that the animal's actions were governed by intelligence, or by its idea or memory of the pleasure its actions brought; he contended that what the animal learns in the puzzle box is a direct association between sense impression and impulse to action. Thorndike argued further, in opposition to James' ideo-motor theory, that an idea in and of itself had no power to initiate action.[1]

Thorndike did not deny that getting out of the box and to the food dish aroused pleasure; indeed, he maintained that such pleasure played an essential part in the learning. But he denied that the animal learns in any literal sense what leads to pleasure. His position was like Herbert Spencer's (see Chapter 2) in that pleasure, or the alleviation of pain, was hypothesized to produce automatic strengthening of the S-R association.

The Law of Effect. An early statement of the law of effect was:

> Of several responses made to the same situation, those which are accompanied or closely followed by satisfaction to the animal will, other things being equal, be more firmly connected with the situation, so that when it recurs, they will be more likely to recur; those which are accompanied or closely followed by discomfort to the animal will, other things being equal, have their connections with that situation

[1] Thorndike (1913a) was able to say that at that time at least 9 out of 10 psychologists probably believed in James' ideo-motor theory of voluntary action. The law of effect was first proposed in 1908 in a paper significantly titled "A pragmatic substitute for free will."

weakened, so that, when it recurs, they will be less likely to occur. (Thorndike, 1911, p. 244)

When Thorndike was formulating the law of effect, America was preparing for the Behavioristic Revolution. The old hedonism had to be abandoned. Even the terms pleasure and pain had to be handled carefully; as we would say today, they had to be given operational definitions. Accordingly, Thorndike substituted for these terms the behaviorally defined words "satisfiers" and "annoyers." A satisfier was a state of affairs ". . . which the animal does nothing to avoid, often doing such things as attain and preserve it." Similarly, an annoyer was defined as "a state of affairs . . . which the animal commonly avoids and abandons" (Thorndike, 1911, p. 245).

Early Criticisms of the Law of Effect. In its long and colorful career, the law of effect has been subjected to constant criticism on grounds other than its empirical validity and practical utility. For example, Carr (1914) and Watson (1917) objected to what they took to be its subjective flavor. For them, "effect" implied the old and objectionable pleasure-pain doctrine with its implied mental determinants of behavior. These critics failed to distinguish between effect (consequence) and affect (pleasure-pain). The law was, perhaps, unfortunately named. But regardless of what Thorndike may have thought privately about his theoretical constructs his statement of the law was in strictly behavioral terms. Here Thorndike's critics were combating a straw man.

Another frequent objection to the law of effect was the implied retroactive action of satisfiers and annoyers. How can the consequence of an act influence the connection which it follows? Thorndike (and later Hull) suggested that the stimulus might perseverate for some time in the nervous system, and that it is this trace which acts as the effective stimulus. Carr (1914) and later Hollingworth (1928, 1931) and Tolman (1932) attempted to solve the problem by denying that what is learned is an S-R association. Postman (1947) has pointed out that retroaction is only a logical problem arising from our common presuppositions about what kinds of physiological processes have to underlie learning. If we recognize the law of effect as an empirical law describing learning, setting aside how learning is mediated, then there is no problem of retroaction.

More cogent criticism of the law of effect was made by those theorists, like Watson and Guthrie, who felt that it was unnecessary. They held that learning can be accounted for entirely in terms of frequency and recency (Watson), or contiguity (Guthrie). They point out the fallacy of assuming that the successful act is necessarily pleasant and is always the one which gets learned, and that the unsuccessful act is necessarily unpleasant and disappears with practice. But neither Guthrie nor Watson was opposed to the general terms of Thorndike's S-R-reinforcement approach; their criticism was limited to his proposed mechanism of reinforcement.

Within behavior theory the chief threat of reinforcement theory has always been to our concepts of motivation. In its early days motivation theory was less ardently defended than it was subsequently, so there was little opposition when Thorndike first proposed that the animal is reinforced by pleasure rather than being motivated by pleasure. And then, probably, the reason no serious opposition ever developed is that Thorndike, as well as those he most influenced, like Hull, supplemented their reinforcement principles with motivation principles. Even the strongest advocates of reinforcement theory seem to have overlooked, or else not trusted, its full theoretical potential. This is most strikingly the case with Thorndike himself.

Thorndike's Treatment of Motivation.   The contrast between Thorndike's reinforcement concepts and his motivation concepts was quite marked: the learning system was empirically sound, remained relatively unchanged for 25 years, and was experimentally productive; the motivation system was generally untestable, underwent continual alteration, and was experimentally sterile. At times, it appeared that the motivation system would overthrow or invalidate the learning system, so that Brown and Feder (1934) could remark that Thorndike's theory might be successfully rewritten in terms of Gestalt psychology.

In most of the formulations of the law of effect, there appears the clause "other things being equal." What "other things" are important, Thorndike could never fix in his own mind, apparently, since different "other things" were described in his different writings. Even before the law of effect was stated explicitly, Thorndike had indicated in 1898 that the strength of an S-R association was a function of (1) attention or set, and (2) the "susceptibility" or readiness of the S-R bond. Thorndike concerned himself with motivation in two other ways. In the first place, his animals were food deprived, and secondly, they were offered food incentives. Thorndike presumed that in order to have trial-and-error learning, trials have to occur and that the animal has to want to escape from the box.

In 1911 Thorndike said that the "other things" besides effect of which learning was a function were (1) frequency, energy, and duration of the connection; (2) temporal proximity of response and effect; and (3) "susceptibility" of the connection. In Thorndike's 1913 book the important motivation concept was "readiness" which was defined pseudoneurologically: when a nerve is ready to conduct, i.e., when its threshold is low, there will be a state of readiness, and if it is actually called upon to conduct when in this state, then its conduction is satisfying. At one point Thorndike asserted that readiness is the sole determinant of what can serve as a satisfier. Some nerves are highly modifiable in their condition of readiness whereas others are not. For example, the nerves that conduct noxious stimuli are never in a state of readiness. In these terms, motivation could be viewed as a particular pattern of readiness obtaining in the nervous system at a particular moment.

Some activities and conditions of the organism were supposed to put other behaviors into readiness. For example, reaching for a piece of candy puts eating mechanisms into readiness, so that the successful reaching will be immediately followed by eating. Since eating the candy is satisfying, the reaching-eating sequence will be reinforced. Thorndike believed that a large part of what people learn has to do with the development of such readiness sequences. Thorndike viewed the readiness concept as being particularly important because of its implication that behavior was not totally under simple stimulus determination. Thus, the readiness concept went a long way toward accounting for the apparent spontaneity of human responses.

In his 1932 book we find readiness replaced by "belongingness," which meant something like the appropriateness of the response, as a determinant of what constituted a satisfying state of affairs. Finally, in 1935 we find that the "OK reaction," and "want" have appeared in lieu of the previous concepts, but that they have many of the same properties.

It should be abundantly clear from Thorndike's many writings that his frequent reference to mental events and states was intended merely to simplify exposition. If he attributed reality status to any of his concepts it was to the physiological ones. But there remained some possibility of doubt, apparently, since Hull (1935a), in a review of Thorndike's *Fundamentals of learning,* accused him of not quite facing up to the issue. In particular, Hull said, Thorndike had not completed the transition from psychological hedonism to a reinforcement theory of behavior. For one thing, why use the old language of hedonism? Why speak of pleasure, satisfaction, and striving for a goal? And why introduce all the loose motivational concepts like readiness and belongingness and want?

Hull maintained that Thorndike had not squarely met the fundamental question of learning, namely: which is primary, the striving for a goal or the goal's reinforcing effect? Does the motivation (striving) produce the learning (strengthening the S-R connection) or does the learning lead to the manifestation of striving? Confronted with just these alternatives, Thorndike's choice, I believe, would have been the same as Hull's: *"The organism through the mere process of conditioning will come to strive for states of affairs which are positively reinforcing"* (p. 822).

Perhaps Thorndike never saw Hull's fundamental question so clearly as Hull did, or perhaps he did not believe it to be so fundamental. But we will now show that it is, for if we give the right answer to it, then we may leave hedonism, motivation, and most of the other subjects that we have treated here to the historian of psychology and turn our attention to a new and potentially powerful way to explain behavior. It is based on the fact that whatever can be said in the language of motivation can be said as well in the language of reinforcement.

The Equivalence of Motivation and Reinforcement. One clue to the equivalence of motivation and reinforcement involves the empirical difficulties in the ancient idea that motivated behavior is directed toward a goal. The original idea was that somehow our personal experience of striving to attain or avoid some object involves that object as an invariant end or purpose. A number of recent writers (e.g., Bindra, 1959) have embodied this idea in the assertion that goal-directedness defines motivated behavior. The hazard in this approach is the tradition of seeking the "causes" of goal-directedness. To avoid this hazard we need simply translate goal-directedness, the seeking a goal, from something the individual does to or for the goal into something that the goal does to the individual. This translation means regarding behavior from the viewpoint of what reinforces it rather than from the more familiar viewpoint of what motivates it.

A second clue to the plausibility of a reinforcement theory of motivation comes from our earlier review of the functional properties of the Hullian drive construct. Recall that of the several behavioral properties that Hull postulated for D only one, viz., the energizing property, seemed to match even approximately what we have found in the laboratory, and even it had to be amended in some respects. We found that the energizing effects of drive conditions really apply only to instrumental and consummatory behavior and not to all behavior indiscriminately. Thus, the energization of behavior seems to apply precisely to those responses which have had a history of reinforcement relevant to the specific drive conditions.

The third, and perhaps the most insistent, indication that motivational phenomena are isomorphic with reinforcement phenomena is the apparent equivalence of the properties of incentive motivation and secondary reinforcement. We find not only that, of course, both incentive motivation and secondary reinforcement are due to the same conditions of learning, but that the assumed properties of these concepts appear in many cases to be conceptually equivalent and empirically indistinguishable. We have Hull's Paradox (see Chapter 12) to suggest that the two sets of concepts are either redundant or contradictory. We may also note that the behavioral phenomena described in the last two chapters under the heading of secondary reinforcement and punishment are clearly motivational in character—administration of an electric shock is motivating if anything is—yet most of these phenomena turn out to be explicable in terms of the stimuli that control and reinforce the behavior in question rather than in terms of what motivates it. The case of the responses contingent upon fear might appear to constitute an exception to this conclusion; but notice that even in this case the only unequivocal effects of fear we have encountered were those that were produced by the responses elicited by fear, such as freezing.

One final clue to the equivalence of motivation and reinforcement is revealed in Hull's writing. The quotation which heads this chapter might appear to have been written early, perhaps around 1935, when Hull was attempting to derive motivational phenomena from the premises of classical conditioning. But these words actually appear in the introduction to the problem of motivation in *The Principles*. Thus, even at a time when he was developing the drive concept, and incentive concepts, and attempting to formulate a motivational model of behavior, he could still entertain the possibility of an alternative in which there would be no primary motivational terms. Perhaps he saw nothing inconsistent about the two possible approaches.

Translating from Motivational to Reinforcement Terms. Consider the following hypothetical situation. We have a sexually mature male rat in a novel situation with a female rat in heat. He will explore for a while, but sooner or later he will show a fairly complex, species-specific, and highly predictable response (or series of consummatory responses). The fact that we can abolish the behavior (or at least change it) either by castrating the animal, by presenting a female not in heat, or by varying a number of other antecedent conditions means that the behavior is lawful and, accordingly, we can explain it in terms of its lawfulness. But the explanation is not motivational in character because none of the explanatory antecedent conditions are motivational; they are simply the conditions in the presence of which the behavior occurs. Hence we are not inclined to consider the behavior motivated.

If we repeatedly test our male animal the latency of the response will decrease, the behavior will gradually become more stereotyped and generally predictable. At this point we may be tempted to say that the animal is motivated; it seems to be more excited, sexual activity occurs with greater persistence, and there is less competing behavior. But this evidence of motivation is precisely what leads us to say that sexual behavior is reinforcing (in this case it is seen to reinforce its own repetition).[2]

---

[2] Notice that in such a system we are not required to assert that all behavior is learned; there perfectly well may be (there undoubtedly are) varieties of behavior that occur full blown without prior reinforcement. We do not have to deny that such examples of behavior are unlearned, only that they are unmotivated. And as in the case of the sexually excited rat, there is nothing to prevent behavior which prior to reinforcement has considerable strength from being further strengthened through reinforcement. This undoubtedly happens in the case of all of the varieties of consummatory behavior. Indeed, this is essentially what we mean by consummatory behavior.

If we have any doubt either about whether the animal is sexually motivated or about whether sexual behavior is reinforcing we can make its occurrence contingent upon an instrumental response, such as running an alley to get to the female. The animal will indeed learn to run and, in addition, will learn other sorts of behavior that we had not intended it to learn such as climbing out of its home cage to our hand, jumping out of our hand into the start box, and scratching at the start box door. The evidence we use for supporting the claim of motivation is again precisely the same evidence we cite to indicate that the consummatory behavior is reinforcing. No one would deny that the animal has learned something nor would anyone deny that the animal is excited; the basic question is whether the two effects (learning and motivation) represent two highly correlated but different effects or merely two ways of regarding a single set of phenomena? What we are proposing here is that there is just a single set of phenomena to be explained, and that it can be best explained as an effect of reinforcement. This is what is meant by the designation "reinforcement theory of motivation."

In many respects, the semantics of reinforcement theory is equivalent to the semantics of the traditional motivational viewpoint. We may compile a list of reinforcers just as readily as we might compile a list of drives, and we would expect that the two lists would correspond in a one-to-one fashion.[3] We might break down our list, as used to be the custom a generation ago, into primary and derived drives, but we are also free to break down our list of reinforcers, distinguishing between those which are innately reinforcing and those which have acquired reinforcing value. And once again we ought to expect the breakdown of the two lists to correspond in a one-to-one fashion. In an analogous manner we may break down drives into those which are appetitive, due to deprivation, and those which are aversive, due to excess stimulation. This breakdown can also be carried through into the distinction between two kinds of reinforcers, those that reinforce when they are presented and those that reinforce when they are removed.

There are several respects in which a thoroughgoing reinforcement theory has a more parsimonious syntax than a motivational theory. Motivational concepts such as drive were introduced to simplify the explanation of behavior, but if we learned anything from the evidence cited in Chapters 8 through 11 it is that the attempts to validate the drive construct have led us more and more deeply into the intricacies of behavior, so that before the hypothetical drive construct can be applied at all it is necessary to find what responses are learned and what stimuli control them. A motivational theory invites us to pass over such details in the explanation of behavior; a reinforcement theory calls our attention im-

---

[3] We do not really need such lists; no one ever uses them. What we do need is analysis of the conditions under which reinforcers are effective as reinforcers.

mediately to them. As Skinner might say, the assumption of motives to explain behavior is apt to keep us from finding out about behavior, to prevent us from seeing what the problems are (see p. 18). The problems usually turn out to be associative; i.e., they typically involved determining what responses are occurring, and what stimuli and reinforcers are operative in a given situation. Thus, a motivational theory must necessarily involve all of the terms incorporated in a reinforcement theory and must include a few others in addition. If these other terms are kept strictly to the status of theoretical constructs, then the only difficulty is a loss in parsimony. But our experience so far has been that the temptation is irresistible to attach surplus meaning to motivation constructs, e.g., to equate drive with need or with r_G or with salivation or something of the sort. We do not seem to be able to overcome our heritage of regarding motives as the causes of behavior.

On the other hand, it should not be assumed that a reinforcement theory necessarily precludes the consideration of how behavioral changes are mediated. There is already a very active interest in the question of what constitutes reinforcement.

A critic of reinforcement theory might contend that in such a theory there is no place for the phenomenon of the energization of general activity, there is no place, for example, for the fact that sexually mature rats run more in activity wheels than castrated rats. The answer to such a charge is that rather than look for a source of drive in such a situation we should look for the source of reinforcement. What is it that reinforces activity-wheel running in sexually normal animals but fails to reinforce castrated ones? We discovered in Chapter 10 that whatever the reinforcer is it is quite likely specific to rats, specific to hunger and sex, and specific to activity wheels. It is certainly not as general as was once supposed.

A critic might also ask how we are to account for the increase in performance attendant on an increase in the severity of deprivation conditions. This is a difficult question and a crucial one because the energization effect is the one functional property of drives that appears to be well established. There are several possible solutions to the problem. One, the oldest and perhaps the simplest solution, the one we discussed in Chapter 8, was originally suggested by Guthrie (1935), then defended by Sheffield (1948, 1951), and recently revitalized by Estes (1958, 1961). The idea is simply that there are important stimulus changes correlated with the conditions of deprivation. The hungry animal is stimulated from sources which are not present in the satiated animal; there are stimuli such as those arising from stomach contractions and from other still unidentified locations which tell the animal it is hungry. The way that this telling comes about, presumably, is that these stimuli become conditioned to instrumental responses. The larger such stimuli loom in the total stimulus situation, the more probable these responses become. This principle fits very nicely with the finding that the energizing effect of deprivation seems applicable only to responses that have been reinforced by eating. There may very well also be stimuli signaling satiation, stimuli that tell the animal to stop eating, or running, stimuli that have acquired associative control over competing behavior.

The chief difficulty with this solution of the energizing problem is the extreme difficulty that has been encountered in attempting to attach responses to such hypothetical stimuli in well-controlled laboratory experiments. But we may introduce an incentive mechanism (one of the associative variety) to account for the effect. We may assume that one important source of stimuli controlling the instrumental response arises from some compatible fraction of the reaction to the reinforcer, such as running forward. The energization of instrumental behavior can then be reduced to an effect of the energization of the mediating or incentive response. This latter effect, the energization of the incentive response, might be partly or wholly innate.[4] The same mechanism can be applied to the case of aversive learning: the animal runs faster to escape a more intense shock partly because there is more stimulus support for it, and also because there is more stimulus support for whatever negative incentive factors may operate in escape performance.

The energization problem is just a little more complicated by virtue of the fact that response amplitude as well as response probability appears to vary as a function of the severity of deprivation conditions. Amplitude or vigor measures do not lend themselves quite as readily as probability measures to a strictly associative interpretation. Logan (1960) has called attention to the fact that a rapid or vigorous response usually leads to more immediate reinforcement than a leisurely response. Thus, if the animal runs rapidly, it not only receives greater reinforcement for running but also differential reinforcement for running rapidly. Such an associative interpretation of the energizing of behavior with amplitude measures is consistent with the finding that this response measure often changes slowly when drive conditions are shifted suddenly (Chapter 9). A lot of the details remain to be worked out, of course, but it would appear at first sight as though the results of the drive-shift studies, even those involving amplitude measures (and recall that they are the drive theorist's last stand) are quite amenable to a nonmotivational analysis.

Prior Statements of Reinforcement Theories of Motivation. We have already noted some of Guthrie's and Estes' contributions to these ideas. We may also observe that there is nothing really new in the idea that reinforcement and motivation are complementary conceptions. The idea

---

[4] We will see below (p. 447) one way to explain the apparent energizing of the incentive response without having to assume that it is energized in the technical sense.

is clearly implicit in any statement to the effect that all motivation is learned (e.g., Asch, 1952; McClelland et al., 1953). Ausubel (1956) has noted that the generality of generalized drive appears to involve a large number (but not an indefinite number) of different reaction potentials, and that this effect is produced by a reduction in the elicitation threshold of the responses involved. The effect is not completely general, however, nor is the effect of the drive state upon reaction thresholds random. As he puts it: ". . . in a state of drive the thresholds of those responses are lowered most which are most relevant to the termination of the particular drive that is operative" (Ausubel, 1956, p. 222). We need only add that the responses which are most relevant to the termination of a particular drive are those which have been reinforced by the termination of that particular drive condition.

It should be apparent that for years Skinner has been advocating a position like that we are considering here, not so much in his theoretical statements about learning and behavior (e.g., 1950, 1958) as in the attitudes he has shown toward our social problems (1948a) and toward experimental research. If behavior can be shown to be highly correlated with the conditions of reinforcement, then let us proceed with our attempt to explain behavior by studying the conditions of reinforcement.

THEORIES OF REINFORCEMENT

We may wonder whether the assertion that there is reinforcement, or even the weaker assertion that reinforcement is a useful concept, is as vulnerable to overthrow as the assertions that there is motivation, or that motivation is a useful concept. We have been assured not only by Thorndike himself (1932) but by a number of other writers (e.g., Carr, 1930, 1938; Miller & Dollard, 1941; Postman, 1947; Meehl, 1950) that there can be no question about the empirical validity and practical usefulness of the law of effect. Meehl (1950) has shown that, logically, there is no more circularity in the law of effect than in any other law because we are perfectly able to determine empirically whether the stimulus which is a reinforcer under one set of circumstances is a reinforcer under another set of circumstances. And, empirically, there are stimuli that strengthen the S-R associations they follow.

On the other hand, the law of effect is not a law if we choose not to recognize it. There has certainly been opposition to the S-R-reinforcement view of behavior right from the outset. But it turns out that much of this criticism, even that part of it which is addressed specifically to the law of effect or to the principle of reinforcement, reveals only an abhorrence of S-R analysis in general (Allport, 1946; Birch & Bitterman, 1949), or a rejection of, apparently, any sort of analysis of behavior

(Allport, 1947). If we are to analyze behavior in search of its lawfulness, then we should surely welcome the empirical law of reinforcement; it is one of the best we have found so far.[5]

But as valuable as the law of effect is as an empirical regularity and as crucial as it may be in engineering the control of behavior, there is always the hope that it may be derived as a consequence of some still more basic and powerful theoretical proposition. The search for the basis of reinforcement becomes all the more pressing as we clear away the motivational debris and find just how central a position the empirical law of reinforcement is in the explanation of behavior.

For a generation now textbook writers have told us that the basic issue in reinforcement theory is whether drive reduction constitutes the basis of reinforcement or whether learning is due merely to the contiguity of stimuli and responses. These two positions, roughly the positions of Hull and Guthrie, have been afforded so much attention that we have lost sight of the fact that there are a great number of additional possibilities, many of which seem to be at least as interesting and some of which would seem to have at least as much chance of ultimate fruition. Let us just note with little comment some of the possibilities that have been described.

Incentive Theories of Reinforcement. Hobhouse (1901) attributed learning to the confirmation and the lack of inhibition of whatever behavior the individual undertook. Any response which carried through all the existing motor tendencies without leading to their disruption was learned, according to Hobhouse. A similar position was advanced by Holmes (1911) who suggested that learned responses were simply parts of some large activity in progress, and that the part would be learned to the extent that it is congruous or compatible with the total activity. Peterson (1916) proposed that any response which was undertaken would be learned if it could be carried out to completion. For example, a rat running in a maze is running forward; if it encounters a blind alley, then that response is not completed and hence will not be as likely to be repeated on the next trial as the correct response, namely, the one which does lead to a completion of running forward (see also Peterson, 1935).

Thorndike attacked all of these hypotheses on the grounds that they

---

[5] A useful law in science is one that has some optimum balance of generality and precision. Too much of one at the expense of the other leads inevitably to a loss in utility. The empirical law of reinforcement has great generality; the danger with it is that its generality has been obtained by sacrificing its precision or specificity. This is why the continued concern with theories of reinforcement is so important. Without an effort to make our law (or laws) of reinforcement more precise there is the danger that they will endure for the same reason that common sense explanations are so tenacious, viz., explanatory assertions are stated with so little precision that they cannot be disconfirmed (Nagel, 1961).

only postponed facing the fact that it was the ultimate satisfyingness or annoyance produced by a response that determined whether or not it would be reinforced. But we may note that what all of these hypotheses, including Thorndike's, really needed was rules indicating when a state of affairs would be "confirming," "congruous," "complete," or "satisfying."

There have also been a number of eclectic statements about learning and the conditions that produce it. For example, Tolman (1949) suggested that there may be six or more kinds of learning and that these different varieties of learning may involve different reinforcement principles; the law of effect he held to be only valid as a law of instrumental performance.[6] Kimble (1961) has concluded on the basis of more recent evidence that there may quite well be more than one mechanism of reinforcement. Such eclecticism may ultimately prove justified but for the present the search for unifying principles seems worthwhile.

All of the theories of reinforcement that we have mentioned here so far have involved some assumption that reinforcement occurs when the subject makes a response, usually a consummatory response, which it has been preparing to make.[7] As we have discovered, the assumed incentive mechanism need not necessarily be motivational in nature; there are purely associative theories of incentive. But set, anticipatory tension, and the occurrence of the anticipatory goal reaction have usually been conceived as motivational variables; usually they are assumed to energize concurrent instrumental behavior in addition to providing stimulus support for it.

In contrast with all incentive conceptions of reinforcement and motivation, there has been, especially in the last few years, a growing interest in the possibility of a strictly associative theory of reinforcement and motivation. Let us consider very briefly some of these possibilities.

Associative Theories of Reinforcement. Harlow (1959) and a number of other recent writers (e.g., Sidman, 1953; Pubols, 1958) have observed that in the last analysis reinforcement may not be the occurrence of any particular event; it may not depend upon a specialized reinforcing process that occurs in certain special states of affairs, but may be simply the result of the dropping out of competing behavior. The "correct" response increases in probability as the various conflicting or competing response tendencies extinguish. Perkins (1955), also, has pointed out that what we call reinforcement is, in empirical terms, only relative. One response is always strengthened at the expense of another. If we find that an animal learns to run an alley for food all that we can conclude is that

---

[6] Waters (1956) has suggested that reinforcement affects not learning, or performance, but retention.

[7] This is the basis of the designation "incentive theories" for these otherwise diverse hypotheses about reinforcement. We should include under this heading also the hypotheses of White (1936), Sheffield and Campbell (1954), and Seward (1956).

the goal box plus hunger plus food is more reinforcing than the goal box plus hunger without food. But the latter, in turn, may be more reinforcing than some other set of conditions.

In recent years there have been some variations on Guthrie's theme that there is no special process of reinforcement and that organisms associate that response with a stimulus which is the last one to occur in its presence. A reinforcing state of affairs only reinforces to the extent that it changes the stimulus situation thereby "protecting" the S-R association which last occurred. From this it follows that any stimulus change may be reinforcing and that what appear to be differences in reliability of reinforcement involve only stimulus-sampling factors such as the proportion of the total stimulus context that changes as a result of the response. In many cases the vivid effect of the more reliable reinforcers, such as food, can be attributed to the change they produce in the stimulus situation without supposing that they have any direct effect upon the S-R associations involved. Estes describes this possibility:

> . . . there are at least two functions for rewards within a contiguity theory: (a) If the reward evokes a response which is topographically similar to the one being rewarded, as in a runway situation where the sight and smell of food evoke movements of approach, then the response evoked by reward on a given trial may become conditioned to any new cues in the stimulus pattern; and (b), more generally, if reward serves to condition approach movements to some stimuli, the result will be to make patterns including these stimuli more likely to be sampled. The latter mechanism, like Spence's r_G or Mowrer's hope, could lead to increased probability of the rewarded responses without involving a change in the associative connections of that response to any of the causes available for sampling in the situation. (Estes, 1962, p. 121)

Estes' very simple and yet powerful conception of the effect of reinforcers helps to clarify a number of points. The mechanism he suggests would, for one thing, account for the apparent energization of instrumental behavior by means of an incentive factor which also appears to involve energization but which in fact does not. This was the sort of mechanism that eluded Seward when he proposed that a portion of a response exerts a tendency to arouse the total response. We can now see that this may occur, and why it should occur, but that the effect should be limited to the case where the response involves approaching or orienting toward the stimuli that control it. This gives us a device to explain not only incentive but drive-energization effects. There is some question, though, how applicable it is to instrumental behavior other than approach. Thus how are we to explain the aversive case? If the organism withdraws from the stimuli controlling the withdrawal response, then why does it withdraw? Perhaps there is no problem here; perhaps animals in aversive situations do make only partial withdrawals. But there is still the case of behavior in nonspatial situations; can the same mechanism be applied to responses like bar pressing? Or does the relatively slow acquisition of such responses demonstrate that they do not involve incentive mechanisms? We do not have the quantitative sort of evidence we need to answer such questions.

Another important feature of Estes' analysis is that it focuses attention on the issue of whether reinforcement should be regarded in operational terms, i.e., as something the experimenter does which increases the probability of a particular response, or as a hypothetical process in the organism, i.e., as something which strengthens S-R connections. An empirical law of reinforcement, taking reinforcement in the first sense, is a useful tool in behavioral engineering; but the problems we have found in the scientific explanation of behavior are now so complex that a single, simple law of learning cannot make sense of them. We have to distinguish between reinforcement and reinforcement-like effects, which may or may not involve reinforcement, i.e., the strengthening of associations.

Kish and Barnes (1961) have suggested on the basis of their work with sensory change (the onset and termination of lights and sounds) that there are special states of affairs that are reinforcing, but all that may ultimately be involved in any reinforcement is a change in the environment. Or put the other way around: perhaps any stimulus change is reinforcing, at least to some degree (see also Caldwell, 1951).

The Elicitation Hypothesis. We found in Chapter 13 that much of the evidence on secondary reinforcement suggests the hypothesis that a stimulus acquires reinforcing powers to the extent that it comes to elicit a previously reinforced response. Although a number of writers have advanced this hypothesis for the case of secondary reinforcement, only a few, most notably a group at Michigan State University, have applied it explicitly to the case of primary reinforcement. According to the elicitation hypothesis the presentation of food reinforces a preceding response because the sight of food is a stimulus which either innately or through prior learning strongly elicits the approaching and eating of food (Maatsch, 1954; Denny & Adelman, 1955). This view has led to some ingenious research which seems to confirm the hypothesis (e.g., Maatsch et al., 1954; Adelman & Maatsch, 1955, 1956; Denny & Martindale, 1956; Maatsch, 1959).

The elicitation hypothesis appears to be as applicable to classical conditioning as to instrumental-response learning and as able to explain extinction phenomena as acquisition phenomena. According to the elicitation hypothesis, the distinction between primary and secondary reinforcement disappears; the old distinction reduces to the question of whether the reinforcing stimulus has its eliciting effect innately or has acquired it through prior learning. It seems likely, as Denny and Martindale (1956) suggest, that virtually all instrumental behavior can be attributed to the acquisition of eliciting effects, i.e., secondary reinforcement, and that what this usually involves is the conditioning of tendencies to approach or withdraw.

Premack (1959, 1965) has advanced a hypothesis of reinforcement which appears to be functionally equivalent to the elicitation hypothesis, although it is stated in somewhat different language. According to Premack, any response is reinforced when it is followed by a second response which, because of the arrangement of circumstances, has a greater probability of occurrence than the first response. For example, in the runway situation the running response has some definite prereinforcement probability of occurrence, and if the animal has been food deprived then the probability of eating will be much higher than the probability of running. Then, if we arrange the experimental situation so that the opportunity to eat is made contingent upon the occurrence of running, the probability of running on the subsequent trial will be increased. (Presumably, the probability of running will increase on succeeding trials up to the point where it is as high as the probability of eating, at which point we say that eating is no longer reinforcing, or that the animal is satiated.)

Premack (1962) deprived animals either of the opportunity to drink except for one hour a day or deprived them of the opportunity to run in a wheel except for one hour a day. The relative probabilities of the two responses, drinking and running, under these two different sets of deprivation conditions are shown in Table 15-1. Probabilities are given as the proportion of a 1-hr. ad lib. test period spent drinking and running.

TABLE 15-1

The Prereinforcement Probability of Running and Drinking During an Ad Lib. Test Hour for Rats Deprived Either of the Opportunity to Run or to Drink
(Adapted from Premack, 1962)

	Running	*Drinking*
Running-Deprived	.091	.008
Drinking-Deprived	.015	.067

It is clear that running was more probable than drinking if the animal had had water but no opportunity to run, and conversely, that drinking during the ad lib. test hour was more probable than running if the animal had been able to run but had no opportunity to drink. Hence, if the experimental situation is arranged so that running in the wheel is only permitted after the animal has drunk in the situation or drinking is only permitted after running in the wheel has occurred, then the two sorts of learning should occur during successive test periods. One group of animals should learn to run in order to drink and the other should learn to drink in order to run if Premack is correct. The results indicate that this is precisely what occurs. The question, then, of what are the conditions that govern reinforcement turns out to be the question of what conditions determine the probabilities of different responses in the experimental situation. Premack has noted (Premack, 1961; Premack & Collier, 1962) that response probability is affected by a variety of nonreinforcement variables, i.e., variables which are independent of the experimental contingencies between responses, such as the novelty of the test situation, stimulus support for the response, the natural periodicity of the response, etc.

Premack's response-probability hypothesis appears superficially to be quite distinct from the elicitation hypothesis, but the difference is primarily a matter of emphasis. If the reinforcing response, the highly probable one, is made contingent upon the occurrence of the to-be-learned response, then there must be some stimulus change transitional between the two responses. That intervening stimulus or stimulus change may be viewed either as eliciting the reinforcing response or as reinforcing the reinforced response. On the other hand, Premack's analysis has an advantage of parsimony. He explains changes in the relative probabilities of responses in a given situation on the basis solely of other response-probability figures. This may be the optimum way to view reinforcement.

In any case, we may conclude that there is nothing inconsistent or incompatible between Premack's hypothesis and the elicitation hypothesis. Both are, moreover, quite compatible with Skinner's discriminative-stimulus hypothesis. Actually, much of what we have discovered about secondary reinforcement, plus the particular associative incentive concepts of Seward and Estes, and Miller's recent hypothesis (Miller, 1961; Egger & Miller, 1962) about the importance of the information value of a stimulus in reinforcement all point to the emergence of a new consensus regarding the nature of reinforcement and the important role it plays in motivated behavior.

THE LIMITS OF REINFORCEMENT THEORY

If theories of reinforcement can be made isomorphic with theories of motivation, then we ought to be able to extend reinforcement theory at least as far as motivation theories have been extended. We should conclude, to paraphrase Murray (see Chapter 3), that no one who has to deal in a practical way with human beings can get along without some notion of what reinforces their behavior. It might be objected that the richness of human behavior cannot be contained by any finite list of possible reinforcers. But this objection is premature; no one has tried it. Surely no one would have thought, prior to his doing it, that Murray would be able to encompass the richness of human behavior or describe his explorations in personality with a list of a few dozen basic motives. Skinner (1957) has already applied what amounts to a reinforcement theory to the intricacies of verbal behavior.[8]

There are, in fact, no a priori limits to how far reinforcement theory can be extended. There was actually no a priori limit to how far the various concepts of motivation could be extended; whatever limits we now recognize for them are not imposed upon their outward extension, but are internal, based upon their inability to order the evidence obtained in well-controlled laboratory situations. Reinforcement theory, as an alternative to motivation theory, has only just begun to be tested, and many of the semantic and syntactical details of reinforcement theory have yet to be specified. Much of the specification, as we have noted, can be accomplished merely by the translation of what we know of motivational phenomena into reinforcement terms. And, as noted, we ought to be able to make the translation with no loss, or at least with no loss to our ability to explain behavior.

It should not be thought that reinforcement theory, as envisaged here, is no more than a translation of motivation theory. There are some very different implications, not only in the laboratory, but also in the wider world outside. In the practical world of everyday affairs we judge men on the basis of their motives; motives have always been used as a basis for evaluation. In the courts, for example, we judge a man guilty not so much by the acts he has committed as by his motives in committing them; we have social sanctions for doing this. But would we be as free to pronounce judgment on a man for the conditions under which he has previously been reinforced?

For ages man has attributed the social condition in which he finds himself to various sources of social motivation within himself. Society is the way it is because man's nature is the way it is, and we may despair at trying to change it. Reinforcement theory suggests at the outset that man is the way he is because of the conditions prevailing in his social situation. The sources of social reinforcement are to be found in the structure of society, and we may have some hope of being able to find them and, perhaps some day, of changing them.

[8] For example, Skinner has distinguished between the different sorts of verbal responses, tacts, mands, autoclitic responses, intraverbal responses, and so on, on the basis of the different stimulus conditions that control them, but we could just as easily make these distinctions, and continue with the analysis, on the basis of the conditions that reinforce the different kinds of behavior.

REFERENCES

Where two dates for a work are given, the first one is the date of original publication, and this is the date cited in the text. The second date, given at the end, is the date of the English translation or of the particular edition that has been quoted.

Ach N. (1905) *Ueber die Willenstaetigheit und das Denken.* Goettingen: Vandenhoeck und Ruprecht.

Adelman, H. M., & Maatsch, J. L. (1955) Resistance to extinction as a function of the type of response elicited by frustration. *J. exp. Psychol.,* **50,** 61–65.

Adlerstein, A., & Fehrer, E. (1955) The effect of food deprivation on exploratory behavior in a complex maze. *J. comp. physiol. Psychol.,* **48,** 250–254.

Adolph, E. F. (1939) Measurements of water drinking in dogs. *Amer. J. Physiol.,* **125,** 75–86.

Adolph, E. F. (1943) *Physiological regulations.* Lancaster, Pa.: J. Cattell Press.

Adolph, E. F. (1947) Urges to eat and drink in rats. *Amer. J. Physiol.,* **151,** 110–125.

Adolph, E. F. (1947a) *Physiology of man in the desert.* New York: Interscience.

Adolph, E. F. (1950) Thirst and its inhibition in the stomach. *Amer. J. Physiol.,* **161,** 374–386.

Adolph, E. F. (1964) Regulation of body water content through water ingestion. In M. J. Wayner (Ed.), *Thirst.* Oxford: Pergamon Press.

Adolph, E. F., Barker, J. F., & Hoy, P. A. (1954) Multiple factors in thirst. *Amer. J. Physiol.,* **178,** 538–562.

Allison, J. (1964) Strength of preference for food, magnitude of food reward, and performance in instrumental conditioning. *J. comp. physiol. Psychol.,* **57,** 217–223.

Allison, J., & Rocha, S. M. (1965) Time spent with food and nonfood incentives as a function of food deprivation. *Psychon. Sci.,* **2,** 63–64.

Allport, G. W. (1937) *Personality: a psychological interpretation.* New York: Holt.

Allport, G. W. (1937a) Functional autonomy of motives. *Amer. J. Psychol.,* **50,** 141–156.

Allport, G. W. (1943) The ego in contemporary psychology. *Psychol. Rev.,* **50,** 451–476.

Allport, G. W. (1946) Effect: a secondary principle of learning. *Psychol. Rev.,* **53,** 335–347.

Allport, G. W. (1947) Scientific models and human morals. *Psychol. Rev.,* **54,** 182–192.

Amsel, A. (1949) Selective association and the anticipatory goal reponse mechanism as explanatory concepts in learning theory. *J. exp. Psychol.,* **39,** 785–799.

Amsel, A. (1950) The combination of a primary appetitional need with primary and secondary emotionally derived needs. *J. exp. Psychol.,* **40,** 1–14.

Amsel, A. (1950a) The effect upon level of consummatory response of the addition of anxiety to a motivational complex. *J. exp. Psychol.*, **40**, 709–715.

Amsel, A. (1958) The role of frustrative nonreward in noncontinuous situations. *Psychol. Bull.*, **55**, 102–119.

Amsel, A. (1962) Frustrative nonreward in partial reinforcement and discrimination learning: some recent history and a theoretical extension. *Psychol. Rev.*, **69**, 306–328.

Amsel, A., & Cole, K. F. (1953) Generalization of fear motivated interference with water intake. *J. exp. Psychol.*, **46**, 243–247.

Amsel, A., & Maltzman, I. (1950) The effect upon generalized drive strength of emotionality as inferred from the level of consummatory response. *J. exp. Psychol.*, **40**, 563–569.

Amsel, A., & Prouty, D. L. (1959) Frustrated factors in selective learning with reward and nonreward as discriminanda. *J. exp. Psychol.*, **57**, 224–230.

Amsel, A., & Roussel, J. (1952) Motivational properties of frustration: I. Effect on a running response of the addition of frustration to the motivational complex. *J. exp. Psychol.*, **43**, 363–368.

Amsel, A., & Ward, J. S. (1954) Motivational properties of frustration: II. Frustration drive stimulus and frustration reduction in selective learning. *J. exp. Psychol.*, **48**, 37–47.

Amsel, A., & Work, M. S. (1961) The role of learned factors in "spontaneous" activity. *J. comp. physiol. Psychol.*, **54**, 527–532.

Amsel, A., Work, M. S., & Penick, E. C. (1962) Activity during and between periods of stimulus change related to feeding. *J. comp. physiol. Psychol.*, **55**, 1114–1117.

Anand, B. K. (1961) Nervous regulation of food intake. *Physiol. Rev.*, **41**, 677–708.

Anderson, E. E. (1938) The interrelationship of drives in the male albino rat: II. Intercorrelations between 47 measures of drives and of learning. *Comp. psychol. Monogr.*, **14** (Serial No. 72).

Anderson, E. E. (1941) Externalization of drive: I. Theoretical considerations. *Psychol. Rev.*, **48**, 204–224.

Anderson, E. E. (1941a) The externalization of drive: II. Maze learning by non-rewarded and by satiated rats. *J. genet. Psychol.*, **59**, 397–426.

Anderson, N. H., & Nakamura, C. Y. (1964) Avoidance decrement in avoidance conditioning. *J. comp. physiol. Psychol.*, **57**, 196–204.

Andersson, B. (1951) The effect and localisation of stimulation of certain parts of the brain stem in sheep and goats. *Acta Physiol. Scand.*, **23**, 1–16.

Andersson, B. (1953) The effects of injections of hypertonic NaCl solutions into different parts of the hypothalamus of goats. *Acta Physiol. Scand.*, **28**, 188–201.

Andersson, B., & McCann, S. M. (1955) Drinking, anti-diuresis and milk ejection from electrical stimulation within the hypothalamus of the goat. *Acta Physiol. Scand.*, **35**, 191–201.

Andrew, R. J. (1956) Normal and irrelevant toilet behavior in *Emberiza* spp. *Brit. J. anim. Behav.*, **4**, 85–91.

Anger, D. (1963) The role of temporal discrimination in the reinforcement of Sidman avoidance behavior. *J. exp. anal. Behav.*, **6**, 477–506.

Angermeier, W. F., Locke, D., & Harris, A. (1964) Direct stomach feeding in the pigeon. *Psychol. Rep.*, **15**, 771–774.

Annau, Z., & Kamin, L. J. (1961) The conditioned emotional response as a function of intensity of the US. *J. comp. physiol. Psychol.*, **54**, 428–432.

Appel, J. B. (1963) Punishment and shock intensity. *Science,* **141,** 528–529.

Armstrong, E. A. (1947) *Bird display and behavior.* London: Cambridge University Press.

Armstrong, E. A. (1950) The nature and function of displacement activities. *Symp. Soc. exp. Biol.,* **4,** 361–386.

Armus, H. L. (1958) Drive level and habit reversal. *Psychol. Rep.,* **4,** 31–34.

Armus, H. L. (1959) Effect of magnitude of reinforcement on acquisition and extinction of a running response. *J. exp. Psychol.,* **58,** 61–63.

Armus, H. L., Carlson, K. R., Guinan, J. F., & Crowell, R. A. (1964) Effect of a secondary reinforcement stimulus on the auditory startle response. *Psychol. Rep.,* **14,** 535–540.

Armus, H. L., & Garlich, M. M. (1961) Secondary reinforcement strength as a function of schedule of primary reinforcement. *J. comp. physiol. Psychol.,* **54,** 56–58.

Asch, S. (1952) *Social psychology.* New York: Prentice-Hall.

Atkinson, J. W. (1958) *Motives in fantasy, action, and society.* Princeton: Van Nostrand.

Atkinson, J. W. (1964) *An introduction to motivation.* Princeton: Van Nostrand.

Atkinson, J. W., & Cartwright, D. (1964) Some neglected variables in contemporary conceptions of decision and performance. *Psychol. Rep.,* **14,** 575–590.

Ausubel, D. P. (1956) Introduction to a threshold concept of primary drives. *Amer. J. Psychol.,* **54,** 209–229.

Autor, S. M. (1960) The strength of conditioned reinforcers as a function of frequency and probability of reinforcement. Unpublished Ph.D. dissertation, Harvard University. Cited by Kelleher and Gollub (1962).

Axelrod, H. S., Cowen, E. L., & Heilizer, F. (1956) The correlates of manifest anxiety in stylus maze learning. *J. exp. Psychol.,* **51,** 131–138.

Ayres, C. E. (1921) Instinct and capacity: I. The instinct of belief-in-instincts. *J. Philos.,* **18,** 561–566.

Azrin, N. H. (1956) Some effects of two intermittent schedules of immediate and non-immediate punishment. *J. Psychol.,* **42,** 3–21.

Azrin, N. H. (1959) Punishment and recovery during fixed-ratio performance. *J. exp. anal. Behav.,* **2,** 301–305.

Azrin, N. H. (1960) Effects of punishment intensity during variable-interval reinforcement. *J. exp. anal. Behav.,* **3,** 123–142.

Azrin, N. H., & Holz, W. C. (1961) Punishment during fixed-interval reinforcement. *J. exp. anal. Behav.,* **4,** 343–347.

Azrin, N. H., Holz, W. C., & Hake, D. F. (1963) Fixed-ratio punishment. *J. exp. anal. Behav.,* **6,** 141–148.

Babb, H. (1963) Transfer between habits based upon shock and thirst. *J. comp. physiol. Psychol.,* **56,** 318–323.

Badia, P. (1965) Fixed ratio discriminative avoidance responding. *Psychol. Rec.,* **15,** 445–448.

Badia, P., & Levine, S. (1964) Stable long term avoidance responding and fixed ratio avoidance training. *Psychon. Sci.,* **1,** 91–92.

Bailey, C. (1928) *The Greek atomists and Epicurus.* Oxford: Clarendon Press.

Bailey, C. J. (1955) The effectiveness of drives as cues. *J. comp. physiol. Psychol.,* **48,** 183–187.

Bailey, C. J., & Porter, L. W. (1955) Relevant cues in drive discrimination in cats. *J. comp. physiol. Psychol.,* **48,** 180–182.

Bain, A. (1864) *The senses and the intellect,* 2nd ed.

Baker, R. A. (1950) Establishment of a nonpositional drive discrimination. *J. comp. physiol. Psychol.,* **43,** 409–415.

Baker, R. A. (1953) Aperiodic feeding behavior in the albino rat. *J. comp. physiol. Psychol.,* **46,** 422–426.

Baker, R. A. (1955) The effects of repeated deprivation experience on feeding behavior. *J. comp. physiol. Psychol.,* **48,** 37–42.

Baldwin, J. M. (1913) *History of psychology.* New York: Putnam.

Ball, G. G., & Adams, D. W. (1965) Intracranial stimulation as an avoidance or escape response. *Psychon. Sci.,* **3,** 39–42.

Ball, J. (1926) The female sex cycle as a factor in learning in the rat. *Amer. J. Physiol.,* **78,** 533–536.

Ball, J. (1937) A test for measuring sexual excitability in the female rat. *Comp. Psychol. Monogr.,* **14** (Serial no. 67).

Barclay, J. R. (1959) Franz Brentano and Sigmund Freud. Unpublished Ph.D. dissertation, University of Michigan.

Bard, P. (1935) The effects of denervation of the genitalia on the oestrual behavior of cats. *Amer. J. Physiol.,* **113,** 5.

Bard, P. (1936) Oestrual behavior in surviving decorticate cats. *Amer. J. Physiol.,* **116,** 4–5.

Bard, P. (1939) Central nervous mechanisms for emotional behavior patterns in animals. *Res. Publ. Ass. nerv. ment. Dis.,* **19,** 190–218.

Bard, P. (1940) The hypothalamus and sexual behavior. *Res. Publ. Ass. nerv. ment. Dis.,* **20,** 551–579.

Bare, J. K. (1959) Hunger, deprivation, and the day-night cycle. *J. comp. physiol. Psychol.,* **52,** 129–131.

Bare, J. K., & Cicala, G. (1960) Deprivation and time of testing as determinants of food intake. *J. comp. physiol. Psychol.,* **53,** 151–154.

Barlow, J. A. (1952) Secondary motivation through classical conditioning: one trial nonmotor learning in the white rat. *Amer. Pychologist,* **7,** 273.

Barlow, J. A. (1956) Secondary motivation through classical conditioning: a reconsideration of the nature of backward conditioning. *Psychol. Rev.,* **63,** 406–408.

Barnett, S. A. (1958) Experiments on "neophobia" in wild and laboratory rats. *Brit. J. Psychol.,* **49,** 195–201.

Barnett, S. A. (1963) *The rat: a study in behaviour.* Chicago: Aldine.

Baron, A. (1959) Functions of CS and US in fear conditioning. *J. comp. physiol. Psychol.,* **52,** 591–593.

Baron, A. (1964) Suppression of exploratory behavior by aversive stimulation. *J. comp. physiol. Psychol.,* **57,** 299–301.

Baron, A. (1965) Delayed punishment of a runway response. *J. comp. physiol. Psychol.,* **60,** 131–134.

Baron, A., Antonitis, J. J., & Beale, R. H. (1961) Effects of activity deprivation upon bar pressing. *J. comp. physiol. Psychol.,* **54,** 291–293.

Baron, A., Antonitis, J. J., & Schell, S. F. (1962) Effects of early restriction and facilitation of climbing on later climbing behavior of mice. *J. comp. physiol. Psychol.,* **55,** 808–812.

Baron, M. R., & Connor, J. P. (1960) Eyelid conditioned responses with various levels of anxiety. *J. exp. Psychol.,* **60,** 310–313.

Barry, H., III (1958) Effects of strength of drive on learning and on extinction. *J. exp. Psychol.,* **55,** 473–481.

Bash, K. W. (1939) An investigation into a possible organic basis for the hunger drive. *J. comp. Psychol.,* **28,** 109–134.

Bauer, F. J., & Lawrence, D. H. (1953) Influence of similarity of choice-point and goal cues on discrimination learning. *J. comp. physiol. Psychol.,* **46,** 241–248.

Baumeister, A., Hawkins, W. F., & Cromwell, R. L. (1964) Need state and activity level. *Psychol. Bull.,* **61,** 438–453.

Bayer, E. (1929) Beitraege zur Zweikomponententheorie des Hungres. *Z. Psychol.,* **112,** 1–54.

Beach, F. A. (1942) Analysis of factors involved in the arousal, maintenance and manifestation of sexual excitement in male animals. *Psychosom. Med.,* **4,** 173–198.

Beach, F. A. (1942a) Analysis of the stimuli adequate to elicit mating behavior in the sexually-inexperienced male rat. *J. comp. Psychol.,* **33,** 163–207.

Beach, F. A. (1947) A review of physiological and psychological studies of sexual behavior in mammals. *Physiol. Rev.,* **27,** 240–307.

Beach, F. A. (1948) *Hormones and behavior.* New York: Hoeber.

Beach, F. A. (1956) Characteristics of masculine "sex drive." In M. R. Jones (Ed.), *Nebraska symposium on motivation.* Lincoln: University of Nebraska Press.

Beach, F. A. (1958) Neural and chemical regulation of behavior. In H. F. Harlow and C. N. Woolsey (Eds.), *Biological and biochemical bases of behavior.* Madison: University of Wisconsin Press.

Beach, F. A., & Fowler, H. (1959) Individual differences in the response of male rats to androgen. *J. comp. physiol. Psychol.,* **52,** 50–52.

Beach, F. A., & Jordan, L. (1956) Sexual exhaustion and recovery in the male rat. *Quart. J. exp. Psychol.,* **8,** 121–133.

Beach, F. A., & Jordan, L. (1956a) Effects of sexual reinforcement upon the performance of male rats in a straight runway. *J. comp. physiol. Psychol.,* **49,** 105–110.

Bechterev, V. M. (1904) *La psychologie objective.* Paris: Alcan, 1913.

Beck, R. C. (1961) On secondary reinforcement and shock termination. *Psychol. Bull.,* **58,** 28–45.

Beck, R. C. (1962) The rat's adaptation to a 23.5–hour water-deprivation schedule. *J. comp. physiol. Psychol.,* **55,** 646–648.

Beck, R. C. (1964) Some effects of restricted water intake on consummatory behavior in the rat. In M. J. Wayner (Ed.), *Thirst.* Oxford: Pergamon Press.

Beck, R. C., & Horne, M. (1964) Some effects of two thirst-control procedures on eating, drinking, and body weight of the rat. *J. gen. Psychol.,* **71,** 93–101.

Beebe-Center, J. G. (1951) Feeling and emotion. In H. Helson (Ed.), *Theoretical foundations of psychology.* New York: Van Nostrand.

Beer, B., & Trumble, G. (1965) Timing behavior as a function of amount of reinforcement. *Psychon. Sci.,* **2,** 71–72.

Beer, C. G. (1963–1964) Ethology—the zoologist's approach to behaviour. *Tuatara,* **11,** 170–177; **12,** 16–39.

Behrend, E. R., & Bitterman, M. E. (1963) Sidman avoidance in the fish. *J. exp. anal. Behav.,* **6,** 47–52.

Bélanger, D., & Feldman, S. M. (1962) Effects of water deprivation upon heart rate and instrumental activity in the rat. *J. comp. physiol. Psychol.,* **55,** 220–225.

Bellows, R. T. (1939) Time factors in water drinking in dogs. *Amer. J. Physiol.,* **125,** 87–97.

Berkun, M. M., Kessen, M. L., & Miller, N. E. (1952) Hunger-reducing effects of food by stomach fistula versus food by mouth measured by a consummatory response. *J. comp. physiol. Psychol.,* **45,** 550–554.

Berlyne, D. E. (1950) Novelty and curiosity as determinants of exploratory behavior. *Brit. J. Psychol.,* **41,** 68–80.

Berlyne, D. E. (1960) *Conflict, arousal, and curiosity.* New York: McGraw-Hill.

Berlyne, D. E. (1963) Motivational problems raised by exploratory and epistemic behavior. In S. Koch (Ed.), *Psychology: a study of a science,* Vol. V. New York: McGraw-Hill.

Berlyne, D. E., & Slater, J. (1957) Perceptual curiosity, exploratory behavior, and maze learning. *J. comp. physiol. Psychol.,* **50,** 228–232.

Bermant, G. (1961) Response latencies of female rats during sexual intercourse. *Science,* **133,** 1771–1773.

Bermant, G. (1964) Effects of single and multiple enforced intercopulatory intervals on the sexual behavior of male rats. *J. comp. physiol. Psychol.,* **57,** 398–403.

Bernard, C. (1878) *Leçons sur les phénomènes de la vie en communs aux animaux et aux végétaux.*

Bernfeld, S. (1944) Freud's earliest theories and the school of Helmholtz. *Psychoanal. Quart.,* **13,** 341–362.

Bernstein, A. S. (1963) Anxiety as a nondirectional drive: a test of Hull-Spence theory. *Psychol. Rep.,* **12,** 87–98.

Bersh, P. J. (1951) The influence of two variables upon the establishment of a secondary reinforcer for operant responses. *J. exp. Psychol.,* **41,** 62–73.

Bersh, P. J., Notterman, J. M., & Schoenfeld, W. N. (1956) Extinction of a human cardiac-response during avoidance-conditioning. *Amer. J. Psychol.,* **69,** 244–251.

Bersh, P. J., Notterman, J. M., & Schoenfeld, W. N. (1956a) Generalization to varying tone frequencies as a function of intensity of unconditioned stimulus. Unpublished U.S.A.F. Report. Cited by Kimble (1961).

Besch, N. F., Morris, H., & Levine, S. (1963) A comparison between correction and noncorrection methods in drive discrimination. *J. exp. Psychol.,* **65,** 414–419.

Besch, N. F., & Reynolds, W. F. (1958) Alley length and time of food deprivation in instrumental reward learning. *J. exp. Psychol.,* **56,** 448–452.

Bevan, W., & Dukes, W. F. (1955) Effectiveness of delayed punishment on learning performance when preceded by premonitory cues. *Psychol. Rep.,* **1,** 441–448.

Biederman, G. B., D'Amato, M. R., & Keller, D. M. (1964) Facilitation of discriminated avoidance learning by dissociation of CS and manipulandum. *Psychon. Sci.,* **1,** 229–230.

Billingslea, F. Y. (1942) Intercorrelational analysis of certain behavior salients in the rat. *J. comp. Psychol.,* **34,** 203–211.

Bindra, D. (1959) *Motivation: a systematic reinterpretation.* New York: Ronald.

Bindra, D. (1961) Components of general activity and the analysis of behavior. *Psychol. Rev.,* **68,** 205–215.

Bindra, D. (1963) Effects of nonreinforcement, drive diminution, and punishment on relevant and irrelevant behavior in the runway. *Psychol. Rec.,* **13,** 273–282.

Bindra, D., & Blond, J. (1958) A time-sample method for measuring general activity and its components. *Canad. J. Psychol.,* **12,** 74–76.

Bindra, D., & Cameron, L. (1953) Changes in experimentally produced anxiety with the passage of time: incubation effect. *J. exp. Psychol., 45,* 197–203.

Bindra, D., Paterson, A. L., & Strzelecki, J. (1955) On the relation between anxiety and conditioning. *Canad. J. Psychol., 9,* 1–6.

Bindra, D., & Thompson, W. R. (1953) An evaluation of defecation and urination as measures of fearfulness. *J. comp. physiol. Psychol., 46,* 43–45.

Bing, F. C., & Mendel, L. B. (1931) The relationship betwen food and water intakes in mice. *Amer. J. Physiol., 98,* 169–179.

Birch, D. (1955) Discrimination learning as a function of the ratio of nonreinforced to reinforced trials. *J. comp. physiol. Psychol., 48,* 371–374.

Birch, D., Burnstein, E., & Clark, R. A. (1958) Response strength as a function of hours of food deprivation under a controlled maintenance schedule. *J. comp. physiol. Psychol., 51,* 350–354.

Birch, H. G., & Bitterman, M. E. (1949) Reinforcement and learning: the process of sensory integration. *Psychol. Rev., 56,* 292–308.

Bitterman, M. E., Fedderson, W. F., & Tyler, D. W. (1953) Secondary reinforcement and the discrimination hypothesis. *Amer. J. Psychol., 66,* 456–464.

Bitterman, M. E., & Holtzman, W. H. (1952) Conditioning and extinction of the galvanic skin response as a function of anxiety. *J. abnorm. soc. Psychol., 47,* 615–623.

Bitterman, M. E., Reed, P. C., & Krauskopf, J. (1952) The effect of the duration of the unconditioned stimulus upon conditioning and extinction. *Amer. J. Psychol., 65,* 256–262.

Bixenstine, V. E., & Barker, E. (1964) Further analysis of the determinants of avoidance behavior. *J. comp. physiol. Psychol., 58,* 339–343.

Black, A. H. (1959) Heart rate changes during avoidance learning in dogs. *Canad. J. Psychol., 13,* 229–242.

Black, A. H. (1963) The effect of CS-US interval on avoidance conditioning in the rat. *Canad. J. Psychol., 17,* 174–182.

Black, A. H. (1965) Cardiac conditioning in curarized dogs: The relationship between heart rate and skeletal behaviour. In W. F. Prokasy (Ed.), *Classical conditioning.* New York: Appleton-Century-Crofts.

Black, A. H., & Carlson, N. J. (1959) Traumatic avoidance learning: a note on intertrial-interval responding. *J. comp. physiol. Psychol., 52,* 759–760.

Black, A. H., Carlson, N. J., & Solomon, R. L. (1962) Exploratory studies of the conditioning of autonomic responses on curarized dogs. *Psychol. Monogr., 76* (Whole No. 548).

Black, R. W. (1965) On the combination of drive and incentive motivation. *Psychol. Rev., 72,* 310–317.

Black, R. W., & Elstad, P. (1964) Instrumental and consummatory behavior as a function of length of reward-period. *Psychon. Sci., 1,* 301–302.

Blodgett, H. C. (1929) The effect of the introduction of reward upon the maze performance of rats. *Univ. Calif. Publ. Psychol., 4,* 113–134.

Bloomberg, R., & Webb, W. B. (1949) Various degrees within a single drive as cues for spatial response learning in the white rat. *J. exp. Psychol., 39,* 628–636.

Blough, D. S. (1958) A new test for tranquilizers. *Science, 127,* 586–587.

Bolles, R. C. (1958) The usefulness of the drive concept. In M. R. Jones (Ed.), *Nebraska symposium on motivation.* Lincoln: University of Nebraska Press.

Bolles, R. C. (1958a) A replication and further analysis of a study on position reversal learning in hungry and thirsty rats. *J. comp. physiol. Psychol., 51,* 349.

Bolles, R. C. (1959) Individual and group performance as a function of the intensity and kind of deprivation. *J. comp. physiol. Psychol.,* 52, 579–585.

Bolles, R. C. (1960) Grooming behavior in the rat. *J. comp. physiol. Psychol.,* 53, 306–310.

Bolles, R. C. (1961) The interaction of hunger and thirst in the rat. *J. comp. physiol. Psychol.,* 54, 580–584.

Bolles, R. C. (1961a) The generalization of deprivation-produced stimuli. *Psychol. Rep.,* 9, 623–626.

Bolles, R. C. (1961b) Is the "click" a token reward? *Psychol. Rec.,* 11, 163–168.

Bolles, R. C. (1962) The readiness to eat and drink: the effect of deprivation conditions. *J. comp. physiol. Psychol.,* 55, 230–234.

Bolles, R. C. (1962a) A psychophysical study of hunger in the rat. *J. exp. Psychol.,* 63, 387–390.

Bolles, R. C. (1962b) The difference between statistical hypotheses and scientific hypotheses. *Psychol. Rep.,* 11, 639–645.

Bolles, R. C. (1963) Effect of food deprivation upon the rat's behavior in its homecage. *J. comp. physiol. Psychol.,* 56, 456–460.

Bolles, R. C. (1963a) Psychological determinism and the problem of morality. *J. sci. study Relig.,* 2, 182–189.

Bolles, R. C. (1963b) A failure to find evidence of the estrus cycle in the rat's activity level. *Psychol. Rep.,* 12, 530.

Bolles, R. C. (1965) Readiness to eat: effects of age, sex, and weight loss. *J. comp. physiol. Psychol.,* 60, 88–92.

Bolles, R. C. (1965a) Consummatory behavior in rats maintained a-periodically. *J. comp. physiol. Psychol.,* 60, 239–243.

Bolles, R. C., & de Lorge, J. (1962) Effect of hunger on exploration in a familiar locale. *Psychol. Rep.,* 10, 54.

Bolles, R. C., & de Lorge, J. (1962a) Exploration in a Dashiell maze as a function of prior deprivation, current deprivation, and sex. *Canad. J. Psychol.,* 16, 221–227.

Bolles, R. C., & de Lorge, J. (1962b) The rat's adjustment to a-diurnal feeding cycles. *J. comp. physiol. Psychol.,* 55, 760–762.

Bolles, R. C., & Morlock, H. (1960) Some asymmetrical drive summation phenomena. *Psychol. Rep.,* 6, 373–378.

Bolles, R., & Petrinovich, L. (1954) A technique for obtaining rapid drive discrimination in the rat. *J. comp. physiol. Psychol.,* 47, 378–380.

Bolles, R., & Petrinovich, L. (1956) Body weight changes and behavioral attributes. *J. comp. physiol. Psychol.,* 49, 177–180.

Bolles, R. C., & Popp, R. J., Jr. (1964) Parameters affecting the acquisition of Sidman avoidance. *J. exp. anal. Behav.,* 7, 315–321.

Bolles, R. C., & Rapp, H. M. (1965) Readiness to eat and drink: effect of stimulus conditions. *J. comp. physiol. Psychol.,* 60, 93–97.

Bolles, R. C., & Seelbach, S. E. (1964) Punishing and reinforcing effects of noise onset and termination for different responses. *J. comp. physiol. Psychol.,* 58, 127–131.

Bolles, R. C., & Stokes, L. W. (1965) Rat's anticipation of diurnal and a-diurnal feeding. *J. comp. physiol. Psychol.,* 60, 290–294.

Bolles, R. C., Sulzbacher, S. I., & Arant, H. (1964) Innateness of the adrenalectomized rat's acceptance of salt. *Psychon. Sci.,* 1, 21–22.

Bolles, R. C., & Warren, J. A., Jr. (1965) The acquisition of bar press avoidance as a function of shock intensity. *Psychon. Sci.,* 3, 297–298.

Bolles, R. C., & Warren, J. A., Jr. (1965a) Effects of delayed UCS termination on classical avoidance learning of the bar-press response. *Psychol. Rep.,* **17,** 687–690.

Bolles, R. C., & Warren, J. A., Jr. (1966) Effects of delay on the punishing and reinforcing effects of noise onset and termination. *J. comp. physiol. Psychol.,* **61,** 475–477.

Boren, J. J., & Sidman, M. (1957) A discrimination based upon repeated conditioning and extinction of avoidance behavior. *J. comp. physiol. Psychol.,* **50,** 18–22.

Boren, J. J., Sidman, M., & Herrnstein, R. J. (1959) Avoidance, escape, and extinction as functions of shock intensity. *J. comp. physiol. Psychol.,* **52,** 420–425.

Boring, E. G. (1950) *A history of experimental psychology,* 2nd ed. New York: Appleton-Century-Crofts.

Boring, E. G., & Luce, A. (1917) The psychological basis of appetite. *Amer. J. Psychol.,* **28,** 443–453.

Boroczi, G., Storms, L. H., & Broen, W. E., Jr. (1964) Response suppression and recovery of responding at different deprivation levels as functions of intensity and duration of punishment. *J. comp. physiol. Psychol.,* **58,** 456–459.

Bousfield, W. A. (1935) Quantitative indices of the effects of fasting on eating behavior. *J. genet. Psychol.,* **46,** 476–479.

Bousfield, W. A., & Elliott, M. H. (1934) The effect of fasting on the eating behavior of rats. *J. genet. Psychol.,* **45,** 227–237.

Bousfield, W. A., & Elliott, M. H. (1936) The experimental control of the hunger drive. *J. gen. Psychol.,* **15,** 327–334.

Bousfield, W. A., & Sherif, M. (1932) Hunger as a factor in learning. *Amer. J. Psychol.,* **44,** 552–554.

Bousfield, W. A., & Spear, E. (1935) Influence of hunger on the pecking responses of chickens. *Amer. J. Psychol.,* **47,** 482–484.

Bower, G. H. (1961) Correlated delay of reinforcement. *J. comp. physiol. Psychol.,* **54,** 196–203.

Bower, G. H., Fowler, H., & Trapold, M. A. (1959) Escape learning as a function of amount of shock reduction. *J. exp. Psychol.,* **58,** 482–484.

Bower, G. H., & Miller, N. E. (1958) Rewarding and punishing effects from stimulating the same place in the rat's brain. *J. comp. physiol. Psychol.,* **51,** 669–674.

Bower, G., Starr, R., & Lazarovitz, L. (1965) Amount of response-produced change in the CS and avoidance learning. *J. comp. physiol. Psychol.,* **59,** 13–17.

Boycott, B. B., & Young, J. Z. (1950) The comparative study of learning. *Symp. Soc. exp. Biol.,* **4,** 432–453.

Brackbill, Y., & O'Hara, J. (1958) The relative effectiveness of reward and punishment for discrimination learning in children. *J. comp. physiol. Psychol.,* **51,** 747–751.

Brandauer, C. M. (1953) A confirmation of Webb's data concerning the action of irrelevant drives. *J. exp. Psychol.,* **45,** 150–152.

Braun, H. W., Wedekind, C. E., & Smudski, J. F. (1957) The effect of an irrelevant drive on maze learning in the rat. *J. exp. Psychol.,* **54,** 148–152.

Bridgman, P. (1932) *The logic of modern physics,* 2nd ed. New York: Macmillan.

Brimer, C. J., & Kamin, L. J. (1963) Disinhibition, habituation, sensitization, and the conditioned emotional response. *J. comp. physiol. Psychol.,* **56,** 508–516.

Broadhurst, P. L. (1957) Determinants of emotionality in the rat: I. Situational factors. *Brit. J. Psychol.,* **48,** 1–12.

Broadhurst, P. L. (1957a) Emotionality and the Yerkes-Dodson Law. *J. exp. Psychol.,* **54,** 345–352.

Broadhurst, P. L. (1960) Studies in psychogenetics: applications of biometrical genetics to the inheritance of behavior. In H. J. Eysenck (Ed.), *Experiments in personality,* Vol. I. London: Routledge & Kegan Paul.

Brobeck, J. R. (1945) Effects of variations in activity, food intake, and environmental temperature on weight gain in the albino rat. *Amer. J. Physiol.,* **143,** 1–5.

Brobeck, J. R. (1960) Food and temperature. In *Recent progress in hormone research.* New York: Academic Press.

Brody, S. (1945) *Bioenergetics and growth.* New York: Reinhold.

Brogden, W. J., Lipman, E. A., & Culler, E. (1938) The role of incentive in conditioning and learning. *Amer. J. Psychol.,* **51,** 109–117.

Browman, L. G. (1943) The effect of bilateral optic enucleation upon the activity rhythms of the albino rat. *J. comp. Psychol.,* **36,** 33–46.

Browman, L. G. (1943a) The effect of controlled temperature upon the spontaneous activity rhythms of the albino rat. *J. exp. Zool.,* **94,** 477–489.

Browman, L. G. (1944) Modified spontaneous activity rhythms in rats. *Amer. J. Physiol.,* **142,** 633–637.

Browman, L. G. (1952) Artificial 16 hr. day activity rhythms in the white rat. *Amer. J. Physiol.,* **168,** 694–697.

Brown, J. F. (1932) Ueber die dynamismchen Eigenschaften der Realitaet und Irrealitaet. *Psychol. Forsch.,* **14,** 46–61.

Brown, J. F., & Feder, D. D. (1934) Thorndike's theory of learning as Gestalt psychology. *Psychol. Bull.,* **31,** 426–437.

Brown, J. L. (1956) The effect of drive on learning with secondary reinforcement. *J. comp. physiol. Psychol.,* **49,** 254–260.

Brown, J. S. (1939) A note on a temporal gradient of reinforcement. *J. exp. Psychol.,* **25,** 211–227.

Brown, J. S. (1948) Gradients of approach and avoidance responses and their relation to level of motivation. *J. comp. physiol. Psychol.,* **41,** 450–465.

Brown, J. S. (1953) Problems presented by the concept of acquired drives. In *Current theory and research in motivation: a symposium.* Lincoln: University of Nebraska Press.

Brown, J. S. (1955) Pleasure-seeking behavior and the drive reduction hypothesis. *Psychol. Rev.,* **62,** 169–179.

Brown, J. S. (1961) *The motivation of behavior.* New York: McGraw-Hill.

Brown, J. S., & Belloni, M. (1963) Performance as a function of deprivation time following periodic feeding in an isolated environment. *J. comp. Physiol. Psychol.,* **56,** 105–110.

Brown, J. S., & Farber, I. E. (1951) Emotions conceptualized as intervening variables—with suggestions toward a theory of frustration. *Psychol. Bull.,* **48,** 465–495.

Brown, J. S., & Jacobs, A. (1949) Role of fear in motivation and acquisition of responses. *J. exp. Psychol.,* **39,** 747–759.

Brown, J. S., Kalish, H. I., & Farber, I. E. (1951) Conditioned fear as revealed by magnitude of startle response to an auditory stimulus. *J. exp. Psychol.,* **41,** 317–328.

Brown, J. S., Martin, R. C., & Morrow, M. W. (1964) Self-punitive behavior in the rat: facilitative effects of punishment on resistance to extinction. *J. comp. physiol. Psychol.,* **57,** 127–133.

Brown, R. T., & Wagner, A. R. (1964) Resistance to punishment and extinction following training with shock or nonreinforcement. *J. exp. Psychol.,* **68,** 503–507.

Brown, T. (1820) *Lectures on the philosophy of the human mind.*

Brown, W. L., Gentry, G., & Bosworth, L. L. (1949) The effects of intra-maze delay: IV. A gap in the maze. *J. comp. physiol. Psychol.,* **42,** 182–191.

Brown, W. L., Gentry, G., & Kaplan, S. J. (1948) The effect of intra-maze delay: I. Delay enforced by a revolving wheel. *J. comp. physiol. Psychol.,* **41,** 258–268.

Brownstein, A. J., & Hillix, W. A. (1960) Drive accommodation and learning. *Psychol. Rec.,* **10,** 21–24.

Bruce, R. H. (1937) An experimental investigation of the thirst drive in rats with especial reference to the goal-gradient hypothesis. *J. gen. Psychol.,* **17,** 49–60.

Bruce, R. H. (1938) The effect of lessening the drive upon performance by white rats in a maze. *J. comp. Psychol.,* **25,** 225–248.

Bruner, J. S., Matter, J., & Papanek, M. L. (1955) Breadth of learning as a function of drive level and mechanization. *Psychol. Rev.,* **62,** 1–10.

Brunswick, E. (1952) The conceptual framework of psychology. In R. Carnap and C. Morris (Eds.), *Int. Encycl. Unif. Sci.,* Vol. I., No. 10. Chicago: University of Chicago Press, 1955.

Brush, E. S. (1957) Traumatic avoidance learning: the effects of conditioned stimulus length in a free-responding situation. *J. comp. physiol. Psychol.,* **50,** 541–546.

Brush, F. R. (1957) The effects of shock intensity on the acquisition and extinction of an avoidance response in dogs. *J. comp. physiol. Psychol.,* **50,** 547–552.

Brush, F. R. (1962) The effects of intertrial interval on avoidance learning in the rat. *J. comp. physiol. Psychol.,* **55,** 888–892.

Brush, F. R. (1964) Avoidance learning as a function of time after fear conditioning and unsignalled shock. *Psychon. Sci.,* **1,** 405–406.

Brush, F. R., Brush, E. S., & Solomon, R. L. (1955) Traumatic avoidance learning: the effects of CS-US interval with a delayed-conditioning procedure. *J. comp. physiol. Psychol.,* **48,** 285–293.

Brush, F. R., Goodrich, K. P., Teghtsoonian, R., & Eisman, E. H. (1961) Running speed as a function of deprivation condition and concentration of sucrose incentive. *Psychol. Rep.,* **9,** 627–634.

Brush, F. R., Myer, J. S., & Palmer, M. E. (1963) Effects of kind of prior training and intersession interval upon subsequent avoidance learning. *J. comp. physiol. Psychol.,* **56,** 539–545.

Brush, F. R., Myer, J. S., & Palmer, M. E. (1964) Joint effects of intertrial and intersession interval upon avoidance learning. *Psychol. Rep.,* **14,** 31–37.

Buchanan, G. N. (1958) The effects of various punishment-escape events upon subsequent choice behavior of rats. *J. comp. physiol. Psychol.,* **51,** 355–362.

Buchwald, A. M. (1959) Manifest anxiety-level, verbal response-strength, and paired-associate learning. *Amer. J. Psychol.,* **72,** 89–93.

Bugelski, B. R. (1938) Extinction with and without sub-goal reinforcement. *J. comp. Psychol.,* **26,** 121–133.

Bugelski, B. R. (1956) *The psychology of learning.* New York: Holt, Rinehart and Winston.

Bunge, M. (1959) *Causality*. Cambridge: Harvard University Press.

Burt, D. H., & Wike, E. L. (1963) Effects of alternating partial reinforcement and alternating delay of reinforcement on a runway response. *Psychol. Rep.,* **13,** 439–442.

Bury, J. B. (1913) *A history of freedom of thought*. New York: Holt.

Buss, A. H. (1955) A follow-up item analysis of the Taylor anxiety scale. *J. clin. Psychol.,* **11,** 409–410.

Butler, R. A. (1953) Discrimination learning by rhesus monkeys to visual-exploration motivation. *J. comp. physiol. Psychol.,* **46,** 95–98.

Butler, R. A., & Harlow, H. F. (1954) Persistence of visual exploration in monkeys. *J. comp. physiol. Psychol.,* **47,** 258–263.

Butter, C. M., & Campbell, B. A. (1960) Running speed as a function of successive reversals in hunger drive level. *J. comp. physiol. Psychol.,* **53,** 52–54.

Butter, C. M., & Thomas, D. R. (1958) Secondary reinforcement as a function of the amount of primary reinforcement. *J. comp. physiol. Psychol.,* **51,** 346–348.

Caldwell, D. F., & Cromwell, R. L. (1959) Replication report: the relationship of manifest anxiety to eyelid conditioning. *J. exp. Psychol.,* **57,** 348–349.

Caldwell, W. E. (1951) Adaptive conditioning: a unified theory proposed for conditioning. *J. genet. Psychol.,* **78,** 3–37.

Calvin, A. D., & Behan, R. A. (1954) The effect of hunger upon drinking patterns in the rat. *Brit. J. Psychol.,* **45,** 294–298.

Calvin, J. S., Bicknell, E. & Sperling, D. S. (1953) Effect of a secondary reinforcer on consummatory behavior. *J. comp. physiol. Psychol.,* **46,** 176–179.

Calvin, J. S., Bicknell, E., & Sperling, D. S. (1953a) Establishment of a conditioned drive based upon the hunger drive. *J. comp. physiol. Psychol.,* **46,** 173–175.

Campbell, B. A. (1954) Design and reliability of a new activity-recording device. *J. comp. physiol. Psychol.,* **47,** 90–92.

Campbell, B. A. (1955) The fractional reduction in noxious stimulation required to produce "just noticeable" learning. *J. comp. physiol. Psychol.,* **48,** 141–148.

Campbell, B. A. (1956) The reinforcement difference limen (RDL) function for shock reduction. *J. exp. Psychol.,* **52,** 258–262.

Campbell, B. A. (1958) Absolute and relative sucrose preference thresholds for hungry and satiated rats. *J. comp. physiol. Psychol.,* **51,** 795–800.

Campbell, B. A. (1960) Effects of water deprivation on random activity. *J. comp. physiol. Psychol.,* **53,** 240–241.

Campbell, B. A. (1964) Theory and research on the effects of water deprivation on random activity in the rat. In M. J. Wayner (Ed.), *Thirst*. Oxford: Pergamon Press.

Campbell, B. A., & Cicala, G. A. (1962) Studies of water deprivation in rats as a function of age. *J. comp. physiol. Psychol.,* **55,** 763–768.

Campbell, B. A., & Kraeling, D. (1953) Response strength as a function of drive level and amount of drive reduction. *J. exp. Psychol.,* **45,** 97–101.

Campbell, B. A., & Kraeling, D. (1954) Response strength as a function of drive level during training and extinction. *J. comp. physiol. Psychol.,* **47,** 101–103.

Campbell, B. A., & Sheffield, F. D. (1953) Relation of random activity to food deprivation. *J. comp. physiol. Psychol.,* **46,** 320–322.

Campbell, B. A., Smith, N. F., Misanin, J. R., & Jaynes, J. (1966) Species differences in activity during hunger and thirst. *J. comp. physiol. Psychol.,* **61,** 123–127.

Campbell, B. A., & Teghtsoonian, R. (1958) Electrical and behavioral effects of different types of shock stimuli on the rat. *J. comp. physiol. Psychol.*, **51**, 185–192.

Campbell, B. A., Teghtsoonian, R., & Williams, R. A. (1961) Activity, weight loss, and survival time of food-deprived rats as a function of age. *J. comp. physiol. Psychol.*, **54**, 216–219.

Candland, D.K., & Culbertson, J. L. (1963) Age, type and duration of deprivation, and consummatory preference in the rat. *J. comp. physiol. Psychol.*, **56**, 565–568.

Cannon, W. B. (1918) The physiological basis of thirst. *Proc. Roy. Soc. Lond.*, **90B**, 283–301.

Cannon, W. B. (1929) *Bodily changes in pain, hunger, fear and rage*, 2nd ed. New York: Appleton-Century.

Cannon, W. B. (1934) Hunger and thirst. In G. Murchison (Ed.), *Handbook of general experimental psychology*. Worcester: Clark University Press.

Cannon, W. B., & Washburn, A. L. (1912) An explanation of hunger. *Amer. J. Physiol.*, **29**, 441–454.

Capaldi, E. J., & Cogan, D. (1963) Magnitude of reward and differential stimulus consequences. *Psychol. Rep.*, **13**, 85–86.

Capaldi, E. J., & Robinson, D. E. (1960) Performance and consummatory behavior in the runway and maze as a function of cyclic deprivation. *J. comp. physiol. Psychol.*, **53**, 159–164.

Capretta, P. J. (1962) Saccharin consumption under varied conditions of hunger drive. *J. comp. physiol. Psychol.*, **55**, 656–660.

Capretta, P. J. (1964) Saccharin consumption and the reinforcement issue. *J. comp. physiol. Psychol.*, **57**, 448–450.

Carlson, A. J. (1912) The relation between the contractions of the empty stomach and the sensation of hunger. *Amer. J. Physiol.*, **31**, 175–192.

Carlson, A. J. (1913) A study of the mechanisms of the hunger contractions of the empty stomach by experiments on dogs. *Amer. J. Physiol.*, **32**, 369–388.

Carlson, A. J. (1915a) The influence of the contractions of the empty stomach in man on the vaso-motor center, on the rate of heart beat, and on the reflex excitability of the spinal cord. *Amer. J. Physiol.*, **31**, 318–327.

Carlson, A. J. (1916) *The control of hunger in health and disease*. Chicago: University of Chicago Press.

Carlton, P. L. (1954) Response strength as a function of delay of reward and physical confinement. Unpublished M.A. thesis, State University of Iowa. Cited by Spence (1956).

Carlton, P. L. (1955) The effect of time of food deprivation on selective learning. Unpublished Ph.D. dissertation, State University of Iowa. Cited by Spence et al. (1959).

Carlton, P. L., & Didamo, P. (1960) Some notes on the control of conditioned suppression. *J. exp. anal. Behav.*, **3**, 255–258.

Carmichael, L. (1926) The development of behavior in vertebrates experimentally removed from the influence of external stimulation. *Psychol. Rep.*, **33**, 51–58.

Carnap, R. (1936) Testability and meaning. *Philos. Sci.*, **3**, 419–471.

Carper, J. W. (1957) A comparison of the reinforcing value of a nutritive and a non-nutritive substance under conditions of specific and general hunger. *Amer. J. Psychol.*, **70**, 270–277.

Carper, J. W., & Polliard, F. (1953) A comparison of the intake of glucose and saccharin solutions under conditions of caloric need. *Amer. J. Psychol.,* **66,** 479–482.

Carr, H. A. (1914) Principles of selection in animal learning. *Psychol. Rev.,* **21,** 157–165.

Carr, H. A. (1930) Teaching and learning. *J. genet. Psychol.,* **37,** 189–219.

Carr, H. A. (1938) The law of effect: a round table discussion. *Psychol. Rev.,* **45,** 191–199.

Carr, R. M., Overall, J. E., White, R. K., & Brown, W. L. (1959) The effects of food deprivation and restricted activity upon exploratory behavior of the rat. *J. genet. Psychol.,* **95,** 321–325.

Carr, R. M., & Williams, C. D. (1957) Exploratory behavior of three strains of rats. *J. comp. physiol. Psychol.,* **50,** 621–623.

Cartwright, D. (1959) Lewinian theory as a contemporary systematic framework. In S. Koch (Ed.), *Psychology: a study of a science,* Vol. II. New York: McGraw-Hill.

Carus, C. G. (1866) *Psychologie oder Seele in der Reihenfolge der Tierwelt.*

Chambers, R. M. (1956) Some physiological bases for reinforcing properties of reward injections. *J. comp. physiol. Psychol.,* **49,** 565–568.

Chambers, R. M. (1956a) Effects of intravenous glucose injections on learning, general activity, and hunger drive. *J. comp. physiol. Psychol.,* **49,** 558–564.

Chambers, R. M., & Fuller, J. L. (1958) Conditioning of skin temperature changes in dogs. *J. comp. physiol. Psychol.,* **51,** 223–226.

Champion, R. A. (1954) Drive-strength and competing response tendencies. Unpublished M.A. thesis, State University of Iowa. Cited by Spence et al. (1959).

Champion, R. A. (1964) The latency of the conditioned fear-response. *Amer. J. Psychol.,* **77,** 75–83.

Chapman, J. A., & Bolles, R. C. (1964) Effect of UCS duration on classical avoidance learning of the bar-press response. *Psychol. Rep.,* **14,** 559–563.

Chapman, R. M., & Levy, N. (1957) Hunger drive and reinforcing effect of novel stimuli. *J. comp. physiol. Psychol.,* **50,** 233–238.

Charlesworth, W. R., & Thompson, W. R. (1957) Effect of lack of visual stimulus variation on exploratory behavior in the adult white rat. *Psychol. Rep.,* **3,** 509–512.

Child, I. L. (1954) Personality. *Ann. Rev. Psychol.,* **5,** 149–170.

Church, R. M. (1963) The varied effects of punishment on behavior. *Psychol. Rev.,* **70,** 369–402.

Church, R. M., Brush, F. R., & Solomon, R. L. (1956) Traumatic avoidance learning: the effects of CS-US interval with a delayed-conditioning procedure in a free-responding situation. *J. comp. physiol. Psychol.,* **49,** 301–308.

Church, R. M., & Solomon, R. L. (1956) Traumatic avoidance learning: the effects of delay of shock termination. *Psychol. Rep.,* **2,** 357–368.

Cicala, G. A. (1961) Running speed in rats as a function of drive level and presence or absence of competing response trials. *J. exp. Psychol.,* **62,** 329–334.

Cizek, L. J. (1959) Long-term observations on relationship between food and water ingestion in the dog. *Amer. J. Physiol.,* **197,** 342–346.

Cizek, L. J. (1961) Relationship between food and water ingestion in the rabbit. *Amer. J. Physiol.,* **201,** 557–566.

Clark, F. C. (1958) The effect of deprivation and frequency of reinforcement on variable interval responding. *J. exp. anal. Behav.,* **1,** 221–228.

Clark, F. C. (1962) Some observations on the adventitious reinforcement of drinking under food reinforcement. *J. exp. anal. Behav.,* **5,** 61–66.

Clayton, F. L. (1956) Secondary reinforcement as a function of reinforcement scheduling. *Psychol. Rep.,* **2,** 377–380.

Coate, W. B. (1964) Effect of deprivation on postdiscrimination stimulus generalization in the rat. *J. comp. physiol. Psychol.,* **57,** 134–138.

Cofer, C. N., & Appley, M. H. (1964) *Motivation: theory and research.* New York: Wiley.

Cogan, D., & Capaldi, E. J. (1961) Relative effects of delayed reinforcement and partial reinforcement on acquisition and extinction. *Psychol. Rep.,* **9,** 7–13.

Cohen, B. D., Brown, G. W., & Brown, M. L. (1957) Avoidance learning motivated by hypothalamic stimulation. *J. exp. Psychol.,* **53,** 228–233.

Cole, L. W. (1911) The relation of strength of stimulus to rate of learning in the chick. *J. anim. Behav.,* **1,** 111–124.

Collier, G. (1962) Some properties of saccharin as a reinforcer. *J. exp. Psychol.,* **64,** 184–191.

Collier, G. (1962a) Consummatory and instrumental responding as functions of deprivation. *J. exp. Psychol.,* **64,** 410–414.

Collier, G. (1964) Thirst as a determinant of reinforcement. In M. J. Wayner (Ed.), *Thirst.* Oxford: Pergamon Press.

Collier, G., Knarr, F. A., & Marx, M. H. (1961) Some relations between the intensive properties of the consummatory response and reinforcement. *J. exp. Psychol.,* **62,** 484–492.

Collier, G., & Marx, M. H. (1959) Changes in performance as a function of shifts in the magnitude of reinforcement. *J. exp. Psychol.,* **57,** 305–309.

Collier, G., & Myers, L. (1961) The loci of reinforcement. *J. exp. Psychol.,* **61,** 57–66.

Collier, G., & Siskel, M., Jr. (1959) Performance as a joint function of amount of reinforcement and interreinforcement interval. *J. exp. Psychol.,* **57,** 115–120.

Collier, G., & Willis, F. N. (1961) Deprivation and reinforcement. *J. exp. Psychol.,* **62,** 377–384.

Conrad, D. G., & Sidman, M. (1956) Sucrose concentration as reinforcement for lever pressing by monkeys. *Psychol. Rep.,* **2,** 381–384.

Conrad, D. G., Sidman, M., & Herrnstein, R. J. (1958) The effects of deprivation upon temporally spaced responding. *J. exp. anal. Behav.,* **1,** 59–65.

Coons, E. E., Anderson, N. H., & Myers, A. K. (1960) Disappearance of avoidance responding during continued training. *J. comp. physiol. Psychol.,* **53,** 290–292.

Coons, E. E., & Miller, N. E. (1960) Conflict versus consolidation of memory traces to explain "retrograde amnesia" produced by ECS. *J. comp. physiol. Psychol.,* **53,** 524–531.

Cooper, J. B. (1938) The effect upon performance of introduction and removal of a delay within the maze. *J. comp. Psychol.,* **25,** 457–462.

Copeland, M. A. (1926) Desire, choice, and purpose from a natural-evolutionary standpoint. *Psychol. Rev.,* **33,** 245–267.

Coppock, H. W., & Chambers, R. M. (1954) Reinforcement of position preference by automatic intravenous injections of glucose. *J. comp. physiol. Psychol.,* **47,** 355–358.

Coppock, H. W., & Mowrer, O. H. (1947) Inter-trial responses as "rehearsal": a study of "overt thinking" in animals. *Amer. J. Psychol.,* **60,** 608–616.

Corbit, J. D., & Stellar, E. (1964) Palatability, food intake, and obesity in normal and hyperphagic rats. *J. comp. physiol. Psychol.,* **58,** 63–67.

Cotton, J. W. (1953) Running time as a function of amount of food deprivation. *J. exp. Psychol.,* **46,** 188–198.

Cowgill, G. R. (1928) The energy factor in relation to food intake: experiments on the dog. *Amer. J. Physiol.,* **85,** 45–64.

Cowles, J. T. (1937) Food tokens as incentives for learning by chimpanzees. *Comp. Psychol. Monogr.,* **14** (Serial No. 71).

Craig, W. (1918) Appetites and aversions as constituents of instincts. *Biol. Bull.,* **34,** 91–107.

Crespi, L. P. (1942) Quantitative variation of incentive and performance in the white rat. *Amer. J. Psychol.,* **55,** 467–517.

Crespi, L. P. (1944) Amount of reinforcement and level of performance. *Psychol. Rev.,* **51,** 341–357.

Crocetti, C. P. (1962) Drive level and response strength in the bar-pressing apparatus. *Psychol. Rep.,* **10,** 563–575.

Crombie, A. C. (1959) *Medieval and early modern science.* Garden City: Doubleday Anchor.

Cross, H. A., & Boyer, W. N. (1964) Influence of amount of reward in a complex learning situation. *Psychol. Rep.,* **14,** 427–432.

Cross, H. A., Rankin, R. J., & Wilson, J. (1964) Influence of amount of reward on maze learning in hooded and albino rats. *Psychon. Sci.,* **1,** 275–276.

Crowder, W. F., Gay, B. R., Bright, M. G., & Lee, M. F. (1959) Secondary reinforcement or response facilitation?: III. Reconditioning. *J. Psychol.,* **48,** 307–310.

Crowder, W. F., Gay, B. R., Fleming, W. C., & Hurst, R. W. (1959) Secondary reinforcement or response facilitation?: IV. The retention method. *J. Psychol.,* **48,** 311–314.

Crowder, W. F., Gill, K., Jr., Hodge, C. C., & Nash, F. A., Jr. (1959) Secondary reinforcement or response facilitation?: II. Response acquisition. *J. Psychol.,* **48,** 303–306.

Crowder, W. F., Morris, J. B., & McDaniel, M. H. (1959) Secondary reinforcement or response facilitation?: I. Resistance to extinction. *J. Psychol.,* **48,** 299–302.

Crum, J., Brown, W. L., & Bitterman, M. E. (1951) The effect of partial and delayed reinforcement on resistance to extinction. *Amer. J. Psychol.,* **64,** 228–237.

Dachowski, L. (1964) Irrelevant thirst drive and light aversion. *Psychol. Rep.,* **14,** 899–904.

Daily, A. D. (1950) The effect of within task drive variation on the learning behavior of the albino rat. Unpublished Ph.D. dissertation, Washington University. Cited by Webb (1955).

D'Amato, M. R. (1955) Transfer of secondary reinforcement across the hunger and thirst drives. *J. exp. Psychol.,* **49,** 352–356.

D'Amato, M. R. (1955a) Secondary reinforcement and magnitude of primary reinforcement. *J. comp. physiol. Psychol.,* **48,** 378–380.

D'Amato, M. R., & Fazzaro, J. (1966) Discriminated lever-press avoidance learning as a function of type and intensity of shock. *J. comp. physiol. Psychol.,* **61,** 313–315.

D'Amato, M. R., Keller, D., & DiCara, L. (1964) Facilitation of discriminated avoidance learning by discontinuous shock. *J. comp. physiol. Psychol.,* **58,** 344–349.

D'Amato, M. R., Lachman, R., & Kivy, P. (1958) Secondary reinforcement as affected by reward schedule and the testing situation. *J. comp. physiol. Psychol.*, **51**, 734–741.

D'Amato, M. R., & Schiff, D. (1964) Long-term discriminated avoidance performance in the rat. *J. comp. physiol. Psychol.*, **57**, 123–126.

Danziger, K. (1951) The operation of an acquired drive in satiated rats. *Quart. J. exp. Psychol.*, **3**, 119–132.

Danziger, K. (1953) The interaction of hunger and thirst in the rat. *Quart. J. exp. Psychol.*, **5**, 10–21.

Darwin, C. A. (1859) *The origin of species by means of natural selection.*

Darwin, C. A. (1872) *The expression of the emotions in man and animals.*

Dashiell, J. F. (1925) A quantitative demonstration of animal drive. *J. comp. Psychol.*, **5**, 205–208.

Dashiell, J. F. (1937) *Fundamentals of general psychology*, 2nd ed. Boston: Houghton Mifflin.

Davenport, D. G., & Goulet, L. R. (1964) Motivational artifacts in standard food-deprivation schedules. *J. comp. physiol. Psychol.*, **57**, 237–240.

Davenport, J. W. (1962) The interaction of magnitude and delay of reinforcement in spatial discrimination. *J. comp. physiol. Psychol.*, **55**, 267–273.

Davenport, J. W. (1963) Spatial discrimination and reversal learning involving magnitude of reinforcement. *Psychol. Rep.*, **12**, 655–665.

Davenport, J. W. (1965) Distribution of M and i parameters for rats trained under varying hunger drive levels. *J. genet. Psychol.*, **106**, 113–121.

Davis, C. M. (1928) Self-selection of diet by newly weaned infants. *Amer. J. Dis. Children*, **36**, 651–679.

Davis, J. D. (1958) The reinforcing effect of weak-light onset as a function of amount of food deprivation. *J. comp. physiol. Psychol.*, **51**, 496–498.

Davis, J. D., & Keehn, J. D. (1959) Magnitude of reinforcement and consummatory behavior. *Science*, **130**, 269–270.

Davis, R. C., Garafolo, L., & Kveim, K. (1959) Conditions associated with gastrointestinal activity. *J. comp. physiol. Psychol.*, **52**, 466–475.

Davis, R. H. (1957) The effect of drive reversal on latency, amplitude, and activity level. *J. exp. Psychol.*, **53**, 310–315.

Davis, R. T. (1956) Problem-solving behavior of monkeys as a function of work variables. *J. comp. physiol. Psychol.*, **49**, 499–506.

Davis, R. T., Settlage, P. H., & Harlow, H. F. (1950) Performance of normal and brain-operated monkeys on mechanical puzzles with and without food incentive. *J. genet. Psychol.*, **77**, 305–311.

Davitz, J. R. (1955) Reinforcement of fear at the beginning and at the end of shock. *J. comp. physiol. Psychol.*, **48**, 152–155.

Davitz, J. R., & Mason, D. J. (1955) Socially facilitated reduction of a fear response in rats. *J. comp. physiol. Psychol.*, **48**, 149–151.

Davitz, J. R., Mason, D. J., Mowrer, O. H., & Viek, P. (1957) Conditioning of fear: a function of the delay of reinforcement. *Amer. J. Psychol.*, **70**, 69–74.

Dees, J. W., & Furchtgott, E. (1964) Drive generalization. *Psychol. Rep.*, **15**, 807–810.

Deese, J., & Carpenter, J. A. (1951) Drive level and reinforcement. *J. exp. Psychol.*, **42**, 236–238.

Deese, J., Lazarus, R. S., & Keenan, J. (1953) Anxiety, anxiety reduction, and stress in learning. *J. exp. Psychol.*, **46**, 55–60.

Delgado, J. M. R., Roberts, W. W., & Miller, N. E. (1954) Learning motivated by electrical stimulation of the brain. *Amer. J. Physiol.*, **179**, 587–593.

Delgado, J. M. R., Rosvold, H. E., & Looney, E. (1956) Evoking conditioned fear by electrical stimulation of subcortical structures in the monkey brain. *J. comp. physiol. Psychol.,* **49,** 373–380.

de Lorge, J., & Bolles, R. C. (1961) The effect of food deprivation upon exploration in a novel environment. *Psychol. Rep.,* **9,** 599–606.

Dember, W. N., & Earl, R. W. (1957) Analysis of exploratory, manipulatory, and curiosity behaviors. *Psychol. Rev.,* **64,** 91–96.

Denniston, R. H. (1954) Quantification and comparison of sex drives under various conditions in terms of a learned response. *J. comp. physiol. Psychol.,* **47,** 437–440.

Denny, M. R. (1948) The effect of using differential end boxes in a simple T-maze learning situation. *J. exp. Psychol.,* **38,** 245–249.

Denny, M. R., & Adelman, H. M. (1955) Elicitation theory: I. An analysis of two typical learning situations. *Psychol. Rev.,* **62,** 290–296.

Denny, M. R., & Ditchman, R. E. (1962) The locus of maximal "Kamin effect" in rats. *J. comp. physiol. Psychol.,* **55,** 1069–1070.

Denny, M. R., & King, G. F. (1955) Differential response learning on the basis of differential size of reward. *J. genet. Psychol.,* **87,** 317–321.

Denny, M. R., Koons, P. B., & Mason, J. E. (1959) Extinction of avoidance as a function of the escape situation. *J. comp. physiol. Psychol.,* **52,** 212–214.

Denny, M. R., & Martindale, R. L. (1956) The effect of the initial reinforcement on response tendency. *J. exp. Psychol.,* **52,** 95–100.

Denny, M. R., & Thomas, J. O. (1960) Avoidance learning and relearning as a function of shuttlebox dimensions. *Science,* **132,** 620–621.

Denny, M. R., & Weisman, R. G. (1964) Avoidance behavior as a function of length of nonshock confinement. *J. comp. physiol. Psychol.,* **58,** 252–257.

Descartes, R. (1649) *Passions of the soul.* In E. S. Haldane and G. R. T. Ross, *The philosophical works of Descartes.* Cambridge: University Press, 1911. (Reprinted by Dover, 1955).

Descartes, R. (1677) *Tractatus de homine.*

Desiderato, O. (1964) Generalization of conditioned suppression. *J. comp. physiol. Psychol.,* **57,** 434–437.

Dethier, V. G. (1962) *To know a fly.* San Francisco: Holden-Day.

Deutsch, J. A. (1959) The Hull-Leeper drive discrimination situation—a control experiment. *Quart. J. exp. Psychol.,* **11,** 155–163.

Deutsch, J. A. (1960) *The structural basis of behavior.* Chicago: University of Chicago Press.

DiLollo, V. (1964) Runway performance in relation to runway-goal-box similarity and changes in incentive amount. *J. comp. physiol. Psychol.,* **58,** 327–329.

DiLollo, V., Ensminger, W. D., & Notterman, J. M. (1965) Response force as a function of amount of reinforcement. *J. exp. Psychol.,* **70,** 27–31.

Dinsmoor, J. A. (1950) A quantitative comparison of the discriminative and reinforcing functions of a stimulus. *J. exp. Psychol.,* **40,** 458–472.

Dinsmoor, J. A. (1952) The effect of hunger on discriminated responding. *J. abnorm. soc. Psychol.,* **47,** 67–72.

Dinsmoor, J. A. (1954) Punishment: I. The avoidance hypothesis. *Psychol. Rev.,* **61,** 34–46.

Dinsmoor, J. A. (1955) Punishment: II. An interpretation of empirical findings. *Psychol. Rev.,* **62,** 96–105.

Dinsmoor, J. A. (1958) Pulse duration and food deprivation in escape-from-shock training. *Psychol. Rep.,* **4,** 531–534.

Dinsmoor, J. A., Kish, G. B., & Keller, F. S. (1953) A comparison of the effectiveness of regular and periodic secondary reinforcement. *J. gen. Psychol.*, **48**, 57–66.

Dodson, J. D. (1915) The relation of strength of stimulus to rapidity of habit-formation. *J. anim. Behav.*, **5**, 330–336.

Dodson, J. D. (1917) Relative values of reward and punishment in habit formation. *Psychobiology*, **1**, 231–276.

Dollard, J., Doob, L. W., Miller, N. E., Mowrer, O. H., & Sears, R. R. (1939) *Frustration and aggression.* New Haven: Yale University Press.

Drever, J. (1917) *Instinct in man.* Cambridge: Cambridge University Press.

Duda, J. J., & Bolles, R. C. (1963) Effects of prior deprivation, current deprivation, and weight loss on the activity of the hungry rat. *J. comp. physiol. Psychol.*, **56**, 569–571.

Duffy, E. (1951) The concept of energy mobilization. *Psychol. Rev.*, **58**, 30–40.

Duffy, E. (1957) The psychological significance of the concept of "arousal" or "activation." *Psychol. Rev.*, **64**, 265–275.

Duffy, E. (1962) *Activation and behavior.* New York: Wiley.

Dufort, R. H. (1963) Weight loss in rats continuously deprived of food, water, and both food and water. *Psychol. Rep.*, **12**, 307–312.

Dufort, R. H. (1964) The rat's adjustment to 23-, 47-, and 71-hour food-deprivation schedules. *Psychol. Rep.*, **14**, 663–669.

Dufort, R. H., & Blick, K. A. (1962) Adjustment of the rat to a 23-hour water-deprivation schedule. *J. comp. physiol. Psychol.*, **55**, 649–651.

Dufort, R. H., & Kimble, G. A. (1956) Changes in response strength with changes in the amount of reinforcement. *J. exp. Psychol.*, **51**, 185–191.

Dufort, R. H., & Kimble, G. A. (1958) Ready signals and the effect of interpolated UCS presentations in eyelid conditioning. *J. exp. Psychol.*, **56**, 1–7.

Dufort, R. H., & Wright, J. H. (1962) Food intake as a function of duration of food deprivation. *J. Psychol.*, **53**, 465–468.

Dunlap, K. (1919) Are there any instincts? *J. abnorm. soc. Psychol.*, **14**, 307–311.

Dunlap, K. (1922) *Elements of scientific psychology.* St. Louis: Mosby.

Dunlap, K. (1923) The foundations of social psychology. *Psychol. Rev.*, **30**, 81–102.

Dyal, J. A. (1958) Secondary motivation based on appetites and aversions. *Psychol. Rep.*, **4**, 698.

Dyal, J. A. (1960) Response strength as a function of magnitude of perceived incentive. *Percept. mot. Skills*, **10**, 35–38.

Eayrs, J. T. (1954) Spontaneous activity in the rat. *Brit. J. anim. Behav.*, **11**, 25–30.

Egger, M. D., & Miller, N. E. (1962) Secondary reinforcement in rats as a function of information value and reliability of the stimulus. *J. exp. Psychol.*, **64**, 97–104.

Egger, M. D., & Miller, N. E. (1963) When is a reward reinforcing?: an experimental study of the information hypothesis. *J. comp. physiol. Psychol.*, **56**, 132–137.

Eglash, A. (1952) The dilemma of fear as a motivating force. *Psychol. Rev.*, **59**, 376–379.

Ehrenfreund, D. (1949) The effect of a secondary reinforcing agent in black-white discrimination. *J. comp. physiol. Psychol.*, **42**, 1–5.

Ehrenfreund, D. (1954) Generalization of secondary reinforcement in discrimination learning. *J. comp. physiol. Psychol.*, **47**, 311–314.

Ehrenfreund, D. (1959) The relationship between weight loss during deprivation and food consumption. *J. comp. physiol. Psychol.,* **52,** 123–125.

Ehrenfreund, D. (1960) The motivational effect of a continuous weight loss schedule. *Psychol. Rep.,* **6,** 339–345.

Ehrenfreund, D., & Badia, P. (1962) Response strength as a function of drive level and pre- and postshift incentive magnitude. *J. exp. Psychol.,* **63,** 468–471.

Ehrlich, A. (1959) Effects of past experience on exploratory behaviour in rats. *Canad. J. Psychol.,* **13,** 248–254.

Ehrlich, A. (1964) Neural control of feeding behavior. *Psychol. Bull.,* **61,** 100–114.

Eiseley, L. (1958) *Darwin's century.* Garden City: Doubleday Anchor.

Eisman, E. (1956) An investigation of the parameters defining drive (D). *J. exp. Psychol.,* **52,** 85–89.

Eisman, E., Asimow, A., & Maltzman, I. (1956) Habit strength as a function of drive in a brightness discrimination problem. *J. exp. Psychol.,* **52,** 58–64.

Eisman, E., Linton, M., & Theios, J. (1960) The relationship between response strength and one parameter of the hunger drive. *J. comp. physiol. Psychol.,* **53,** 356–363.

Eisman, E., Theios, J., & Linton, M. (1961) Habit strength as a function of drive in a bar-pressing situation. *Psychol. Rep.,* **9,** 583–590.

Elliott, M. H. (1928) The effect of change of reward on the maze performance of rats. *Univ. Calif. Publ. Psychol.,* **4,** 19–30.

Elliott, M. H. (1929) The effect of change of "drive" on maze performance. *Univ. Calif. Publ. Psychol.,* **4,** 185–188.

Elliott, M. H. (1930) Some determining factors in maze performance. *Amer. J. Psychol.,* **42,** 315–317.

Elliott, M. H. (1935) Drive and the characteristics of driven behavior. *Psychol. Rev.,* **42,** 205–213.

Ellis, N. R. (1957) The immediate effect of emotionality upon behavior strength. *J. exp. Psychol.,* **54,** 339–344.

Ellson, D. G. (1937) The acquisition of a token-reward habit in dogs. *J. comp. Psychol.,* **24,** 505–522.

English, H. B. (1921) Dynamic psychology and the problem of motivation. *Psychol. Rev.,* **28,** 230–248.

Eninger, M. V. (1951) The rate of learning a tone-no-tone discrimination as a function of the tone duration at the time of the choicepoint response. *J. exp. Psychol.,* **41,** 440–445.

Eninger, M. V. (1951a) The role of irrelevant drive stimuli in learning theory. *J. exp. Psychol.,* **41,** 446–449.

Eninger, M. V. (1953) The role of generalized approach and avoidance tendencies in brightness discrimination. *J. comp. physiol. Psychol.,* **46,** 398–402.

Epstein, A. N. (1960) Water intake without the act of drinking. *Science,* **131,** 497–498.

Epstein, A. N., & Teitelbaum, P. (1962) Regulation of food intake in the absence of taste, smell, and other oropharyngeal sensations. *J. comp. physiol. Psychol.,* **55,** 753–759.

Eriksen, C. W. (1954) Psychological defenses and "ego strength" in the recall of completed and incompleted tasks. *J. abnorm. soc. Psychol.,* **49,** 45–50.

Essman, W. B., & Alpern, H. (1964) Single trial conditioning: Methodology and results with mice. *Psychol. Rep.,* **14,** 731–740.

Estes, W. K. (1944) An experimental study of punishment. *Psychol. Monogr.*, **57** (Whole No. 263).

Estes, W. K. (1949) A study of motivating conditions necessary for secondary reinforcement. *J. exp. Psychol.*, **39**, 306–310.

Estes, W. K. (1949a) Generalization of secondary reinforcement from the primary drive. *J. comp. physiol. Psychol.*, **42**, 286–295.

Estes, W. K. (1954) Kurt Lewin. In W. K. Estes et al., *Modern learning theory*. New York: Appleton-Century-Crofts.

Estes, W. K. (1958) Stimulus-response theory of drive. In M. R. Jones (Ed.), *Nebraska symposium on motivation*. Lincoln: University of Nebraska Press.

Estes, W. K. (1961) Growth and function of mathematical models for learning. In *Current trends in psychological theory*. Pittsburgh: University of Pittsburgh Press.

Estes, W. K. (1962) Learning theory. *Ann. Rev. Psychol.*, **13**, 107–144.

Estes, W. K., & Skinner, B. F. (1941) Some quantitative properties of anxiety. *J. exp. Psychol.*, **29**, 390–400.

Evans, W. O. (1962) Producing either positive or negative tendencies to a stimulus associated with shock. *J. exp. anal. Behav.*, **5**, 335–337.

Evvard, J. M. (1916) Is the appetite of swine a reliable indication of physiological needs? *Proc. Iowa Acad. Sci.*, **4**, 91–98.

Falk, J. L. (1961) Production of polydipsia in normal rats by an intermittent food schedule. *Science,* **133**, 195–196.

Falk, J. L. (1964) Studies on schedule-induced polydipsia. In M. J. Wayner (Ed.), *Thirst*. Oxford: Pergamon Press.

Falk, J. L. (1965) Water intake and NaCl appetite in sodium depletion. *Psychol. Rep.*, **16**, 315–325.

Farber, I. E. (1955) The role of motivation in verbal learning and performance. *Psychol. Bull.*, **52**, 311–327.

Farber, I. E., & Spence, K. W. (1953) Complex learning and conditioning as a function of anxiety. *J. exp. Psychol.*, **45**, 120–125.

Farber, I. E., & Spence, K. W. (1956) Effects of anxiety, stress, and task variables on reaction time. *J. Pers.*, **25**, 1–18.

Farrer, A. M. (1959) *The freedom of the will*. London: A. & C. Black.

Fay, J. C., Miller, J. D., & Harlow, H. F. (1953) Incentive size, food deprivation, and food preference. *J. comp. physiol. Psychol.*, **46**, 13–15.

Fearing, F. (1930) *Reflex action: a study in the history of physiological psychology*. Baltimore: Williams & Wilkins.

Fearing, F., & Ross, G. (1937) Behavior factors affecting body temperature in pigeons: II. General level of activity as modified by deprivation and ingestion of food with particular reference to the hunger drive. *J. comp. Psychol.*, **22**, 231–239.

Feather, N. T. (1962) The study of persistence. *Psychol. Bull.*, **59**, 94–115.

Fehrer, E. (1956) The effects of hunger and familiarity of locale on exploration. *J. comp. physiol. Psychol.*, **49**, 549–552.

Fehrer, E. (1956a) Effect of amount of reinforcement and of pre- and post-reinforcement delays on learning and extinction. *J. exp. Psychol.*, **52**, 167–176.

Feirstein, A. R., & Miller, N. E. (1963) Learning to resist pain and fear: effects of electric shock before versus after reaching goal. *J. comp. physiol. Psychol.*, **56**, 797–800.

Fenichel, O. (1934) On the psychology of boredom. In D. Rapaport, *Organization and pathology of thought*. New York: Columbia University Press, 1951.

Ferster, C. B. (1953) Sustained behavior under delayed reinforcement. *J. exp. Psychol.*, **45**, 218–224.

Ferster, C. B. (1958) Control of behavior in chimpanzees and pigeons by time-out from positive reinforcement. *Psychol. Monogr.*, **72** (Whole No. 461).

Ferster, C. B., & Skinner, B. F. (1957) *Schedules of reinforcement.* New York: Appleton-Century-Crofts.

Feshbach, S. (1964) The function of aggression and the regulation of aggressive drive. *Psychol. Rep.*, **71**, 257–272.

Festinger, L. (1943) Development of differential appetite in the rat. *J. exp. Psychol.*, **32**, 226–234.

Fey, J. W. (1939) *American psychology before William James.* New Brunswick, N.J.: Rutgers University Press.

Finan, J. L. (1940) Quantitative studies in motivation: I. Strength of conditioning under varying degrees of hunger. *J. comp. Psychol.*, **29**, 119–134.

Finch, G. (1938) Hunger as a determinant of conditional and unconditional salivary response magnitude. *Amer. J. Physiol.*, **123**, 379–382.

Finch, G. (1942) Chimpanzee frustration responses. *Psychosom. Med.*, **4**, 233–251.

Finger, F. W. (1951) The effect of food deprivation and subsequent satiation upon general activity in the rat. *J. comp. physiol. Psychol.*, **44**, 557–564.

Finger, F. W. (1961) Estrous activity as a function of measuring device. *J. comp. physiol. Psychol.*, **54**, 524–526.

Finger, F. W. (1962) Activity change under deprivation as a function of age. *J. comp. physiol. Psychol.*, **55**, 100–102.

Finger, F. W., & Reid, L. S. (1952) The effect of water deprivation and subsequent satiation upon general activity in the rat. *J. comp. physiol. Psychol.*, **45**, 368–372.

Finger, F. W., Reid, L. S., & Weasner, M. H. (1957) The effect of reinforcement upon activity during cyclic food deprivation. *J. comp. physiol. Psychol.*, **50**, 495–498.

Finger, F. W., Reid, L. S., & Weasner, M. H. (1960) Activity changes as a function of reinforcement under low drive. *J. comp. physiol. Psychol.*, **53**, 385–387.

Fink, J. B., & Patton, R. M. (1953) Decrement of a learned drinking response accompanying changes in several stimulus characteristics. *J. comp. physiol. Psychol.*, **46**, 23–27.

Fisher, A. E. (1962) Effects of stimulus variation on sexual satiation in the male rat. *J. comp. physiol. Psychol.*, **55**, 614–620.

Fiske, D. W., & Maddi, S. R. (1961) A conceptual framework. In D. W. Fiske and S. R. Maddi (Eds.), *Functions of varied experience.* Homewood, Illinois: Dorsey.

Fletcher, F. M. (1940) Effects of quantitative variation of food-incentive on the performance of physical work by chimpanzees. *Comp. Psychol. Monogr.* **16** (Serial No. 82).

Forgays, D. G., & Levin, H. (1958) Learning as a function of change of sensory stimulation in food-deprived and food-satiated animals. *J. comp. physiol. Psychol.*, **51**, 50–54.

Fowler, H. (1963) Exploratory motivation and animal handling: the effect on runway performance of start-box exposure time. *J. comp. physiol. Psychol.*, **56**, 866–871.

Fowler, H. (1965) *Curiosity and exploratory behavior.* New York: Macmillan.

Fowler, H., & Miller, N. E. (1963) Facilitation and inhibition of runway performance by hind- and forepaw shock of various intensities. *J. comp. physiol. Psychol.*, **56**, 801–805.

Fowler, H., & Trapold, M. A. (1962) Escape performance as a function of delay of reinforcement. *J. exp. Psychol.*, **63**, 464–467.

Fowler, H., & Whalen, R. E. (1961) Variation in incentive stimulus and sexual behavior in the male rat. *J. comp. physiol. Psychol.*, **54**, 68–71.

Fox, R. E., & King, R. A. (1961) The effects of reinforcement scheduling on the strength of a secondary reinforcer. *J. comp. physiol. Psychol.*, **54**, 266–269.

Fox, S. S. (1962) Self-maintained sensory input and sensory deprivation in monkeys: a behavioral and neuropharmacological study. *J. comp. physiol. Psychol.*, **55**, 438–444.

Franks, C. M. (1956) Conditioning and personality: a study of normal and neurotic subjects. *J. abnorm. soc. Psychol.*, **52**, 143–150.

Franks, C. M. (1957) Effects of food, drink, and tobacco deprivation on the conditioning of the eyeblink response. *J. exp. Psychol.*, **53**, 117–120.

Freud, A. (1936) *The ego and the mechanisms of defence.* London: Hogarth, 1937.

Freud, S. (1895) Project for a scientific psychology. Published posthumously in *The origins of psycho-analysis.* New York: Basic Books, 1954.

Freud, S. (1900) *The interpretation of dreams.* In A. A. Brill (Ed.), *The basic writings of Sigmund Freud.* New York: Modern Library, 1938.

Freud, S. (1915) Instincts and their vicissitudes. In *Collected papers,* Vol. IV. New York: Basic Books, 1959.

Freud, S. (1917) One of the difficulties of psycho-analysis. In *Collected papers,* Vol. IV. New York: Basic Books, 1959.

Freud, S. (1920) *Beyond the pleasure principle.* London: Hogarth, 1948.

Freud, S. (1922) Psycho-analysis. In *Collected papers,* Vol. V. New York: Basic Books, 1959.

Freud, S. (1925) The resistances to psycho-analysis. In *Collected papers,* Vol. V. New York: Basic Books, 1959.

Freud, S. (1926) Inhibitions, symptoms and anxiety. In *Collected works,* Vol. XX. London: Hogarth, 1959.

Freud, S. (1940) *An outline of psychoanalysis.* New York: Norton, 1949.

Freud, S., & Breuer, J. (1892) On the theory of hysterical attacks. In *Collected papers,* Vol. V. New York: Basic Books, 1959.

Fryer, D. (1931) *The measurement of interests in relation to human adjustment.* New York: Holt.

Fuller, J. L., & Thompson, W. R. (1960) *Behavior genetics.* New York: Wiley.

Furchtgott, E., & Rubin, R. D. (1953) The effect of magnitude of reward on maze learning in the white rat. *J. comp. physiol. Psychol.*, **46**, 9–12.

Furchtgott, E., & Salzberg, H. C. (1959) Magnitude of reward and maze learning. *Psychol. Rep.*, **5**, 87–93.

Furchtgott, E., Wechkin, S., & Dees, J. W. (1961) Open-field exploration as a function of age. *J. comp. physiol. Psychol.*, **54**, 386–388.

Gagné, R. M. (1941) The effect of spacing of trials on the acquisition and extinction of a conditioned operant response. *J. exp. Psychol.*, **29**, 201–216.

Gallistel, C. R. (1964) Electrical self-stimulation and its theoretical implications. *Psychol. Bull.*, **61**, 23–34.

Gantt, W. H. (1953) Principles of nervous breakdown—schizokinesis and autokinesis. *Ann. N. Y. Acad. Sci.*, **56**, 143–163.

Gardner, B. T. (1964) Hunger and sequential responses in the hunting behavior of salticid spiders. *J. comp. physiol. Psychol.*, **58**, 167–173.

Geller, I. (1960) The acquisition and extinction of conditioned suppression as a function of the baseline reinforcer. *J. exp. anal. Behav.*, **3**, 235–240.

Gerall, A. A. (1958) Effect of interruption of copulation on male guinea pig sexual behavior. *Psychol. Rep.*, **4**, 215–221.

Gerall, A. A., & Berg, W. S. (1964) Effect of novel situation and modification in sexual drive in rate of oxygen consumption in guinea pigs. *Psychol. Rep.*, **15**, 311–317.

Gerbrandt, L. K. (1964) Generalizations from the distinction of passive and active avoidance. *Pychol. Rep.*, **15**, 11–22.

Ghent, L. (1951) The relation of experience to the development of hunger. *Canad. J. Psychol.*, **5**, 77–81.

Ghent, L. (1957) Some effects of deprivation on eating and drinking behavior. *J. comp. physiol. Psychol.*, **50**, 172–176.

Gibson, E. J. (1952) The role of shock in reinforcement. *J. comp. physiol. Psychol.*, **45**, 18–30.

Gibson, J. J. (1941) A critical review of the concept of set in contemporary experimental psychology. *Psychol. Bull.*, **38**, 781–871.

Gilbert, T. F., & James, W. T. (1956) The dependency of cyclic feeding behavior on internal and external cues. *J. comp. physiol. Psychol.*, **49**, 342–344.

Gilhousen, H. C. (1938) Temporal relations in anticipatory reactions of the white rat. *J. comp. Psychol.*, **26**, 163–175.

Gilman, A. (1937) The relation between blood osmotic pressure, fluid intake, and voluntary water intake of thirsty rats. *Amer. J. Physiol.*, **120**, 323–328.

Gilson, E. (1956) *The Christian philosophy of Thomas Aquinas.* New York: Random House.

Glanzer, M. (1953) Stimulus satiation: a construct to explain spontaneous alternation, variability, and exploratory behavior. *Psychol. Rev.*, **60**, 257–268.

Glanzer, M. (1958) Curiosity, exploratory drive, and stimulus satiation. *Psychol. Bull.*, **55**, 302–315.

Glickman, S. E., & Jensen, G. D. (1961) The effects of hunger and thirst on Y-maze exploration. *J. comp. physiol. Psychol.*, **54**, 83–85.

Glucksberg, S. (1962) The influence of strength of drive on functional fixedness and perceptual recognition. *J. exp. Psychol.*, **63**, 36–41.

Goldstein, A. C. (1960) Starvation and food-related behavior in a poikilotherm, the salamander, *Triturus viridescens. J. comp. physiol. Psychol.*, **53**, 144–150.

Goldstein, H., & Spence, K. W. (1963) Performance in differential conditioning as a function of variation in magnitude of reward. *J. exp. Psychol.*, **65**, 86–93.

Golin, S., & Bostrum, B. (1964) Stimulus generalization as a function of drive and strength of competing responses to generalized stimuli. *Psychol. Rep.*, **14**, 611–619.

Gollub, L. R. (1964) The relations among measures of performance on fixed interval schedules. *J. exp. anal. Behav.*, **7**, 337–343.

Gonzalez, R. C., & Diamond, L. (1960) A test of Spence's theory of incentive-motivation. *Amer. J. Psychol.*, **73**, 396–403.

Goodrich, K. P. (1959) Performance in different segments of an instrumental response chain as a function of reinforcement schedule. *J. exp. Psychol.*, **57**, 57–63.

Goodrich, K. P. (1960) Running speed and drinking rate as functions of sucrose concentration and amount of consummatory activity. *J. comp. physiol. Psychol.*, **53**, 245–250.

Goodrich, K. P. (1964) Effect of a ready signal on the latency of voluntary responses in eyelid conditioning. *J. exp. Psychol.,* **67,** 496–498.

Goodrich, K. P., Ross, L. E., & Wagner, A. R. (1957) Performance in eyelid conditioning following interpolated presentation of the UCS. *J. exp. Psychol.,* **53,** 214–217.

Gormezano, I., & Moore, J. W. (1962) Effects of instructional set and UCS intensity on the latency, percentage, and form of the eyelid response. *J. exp. Psychol.,* **63,** 487–494.

Goy, R. W., & Young, W. C. (1957) Somatic basis of sexual behavior patterns in guinea pigs: factors involved in the determination of the character of the soma in the female. *Psychosom. Med.,* **19,** 144–151.

Graf, V., & Bitterman, M. E. (1963) General activity as instrumental: application to avoidance training. *J. exp. anal. Behav.,* **6,** 301–305.

Graham, C. H. (1950) Behavior, perception and the psychophysical methods. *Psychol. Rev.,* **57,** 108–120.

Graham, C. H. (1952) Behavior and the psychophysical methods: an analysis of some recent experiments. *Psychol. Rev.,* **59,** 62–70.

Green, H. H. (1925) Perverted appetites. *Physiol. Rev.,* **5,** 336–348.

Greenberg, I. (1954) The acquisition of a thirst drive. Unpublished Ph.D. dissertation, University of Pennsylvania. Cited by Hall (1961).

Greene, J. E. (1953) Magnitude of reward and acquisition of a black-white discrimination habit. *J. exp. Psychol.,* **46,** 113–119.

Gregersen, M. I. (1932) Studies on the regulation of water intake: II. Conditions affecting the daily water intake of dogs as registered continuously by a potometer. *Amer. J. Physiol.,* **102,** 344–349.

Grice, G. R. (1948) The relation of secondary reinforcement to delayed reward in visual discrimination learning. *J. exp. Psychol.,* **38,** 1–16.

Grice, G. R. (1955) Discrimination reaction time as a function of anxiety and intelligence. *J. abnorm. soc. Psychol.,* **50,** 71–74.

Grice, G. R., & Davis, J. D. (1957) Effect of irrelevant thirst motivation on a reponse learned with food reward. *J. exp. Psychol.,* **53,** 347–352.

Grice, G. R., & Goldman, H. M. (1955) Generalized extinction and secondary reinforcement in visual discrimination learning with delayed reward. *J. exp. Psychol.,* **50,** 197–200.

Grimsley, D. L., & McDonald, R. D. (1964) Effect of varied magnitude of reward in runway performance. *Psychol. Rep.,* **14,** 199–202.

Grindley, G. C. (1929) Experiments on the influence of the amount of reward on learning in young chickens. *Brit. J. Psychol.,* **30,** 173–180.

Grossman, M. I. (1955) Integration of current views on the regulation of hunger and appetite. *Ann. N. Y. Acad. Sci.,* **63,** 76–89.

Grossman, S. P. (1962) Direct adrenergic and cholinergic stimulation of hypothalamic mechanisms. *Amer. J. Physiol.,* **202,** 872–882.

Grunt, J. A., & Young, W. C. (1952) Differential reactivity of individuals and the response of the male guinea pig to testosterone propionate. *Endocrinology,* **51,** 237–248.

Grunt, J. A., & Young, W. C. (1953) Consistency of sexual behavior patterns in individual male guinea pigs following castration and androgen therapy. *J. comp. physiol. Psychol.,* **46,** 138–144.

Guthrie, E. R. (1935) *The psychology of learning.* New York: Harper. (2nd ed., 1952.)

Guttman, N. (1953) Operant conditioning, extinction, and periodic reinforcement in relation to concentration of sucrose used as reinforcing agent. *J. exp. Psychol.,* **46,** 213–224.

Guttman, N. (1954) Equal-reinforcement values for sucrose and glucose solutions compared with equal-sweetness values. *J. comp. physiol. Psychol.,* **47,** 358–361.

Gwinn, G. T. (1949) Effect of punishment on acts motivated by fear. *J. exp. Psychol.,* **39,** 260–269.

Hahn, W. W., Stern, J. A., & Fehr, F. S. (1964) Generalizability of heart rate as a measure of drive state. *J. comp. physiol. Psychol.,* **58,** 305–309.

Hahn, W. W., Stern, J. A., & McDonald, D. G. (1962) Effects of water deprivation and bar pressing activity on heart rate of the male albino rat. *J. comp. physiol. Psychol.,* **55,** 786–790.

Hall, C. S. (1934) Emotional behavior in the rat: I. Defecation and urination as measures of individual differences in emotionality. *J. comp. Psychol.,* **18,** 385–403.

Hall, C. S. (1934a) Drive and emotionality: factors associated with adjustment in the rat. *J. comp. Psychol.,* **17,** 89–108.

Hall, C. S. (1941) Temperament: a survey of animal studies. *Psychol. Bull.,* **38,** 909–943.

Hall, C. S., & Lindzey, G. (1957) *Theories of personality.* New York: Wiley.

Hall, J. C. (1955) Some conditions of anxiety extinction. *J. abnorm. soc. Psychol.,* **51,** 126–132.

Hall, J. F. (1951) Studies in secondary reinforcement: I. Secondary reinforcement as a function of the frequency of primary reinforcement. *J. comp. physiol. Psychol.,* **44,** 246–251.

Hall, J. F. (1951a) Studies in secondary reinforcement: II. Secondary reinforcement as a function of the strength of drive during primary reinforcement. *J. comp. physiol. Psychol.,* **44,** 462–466.

Hall, J. F. (1955) Activity as a function of a restricted drinking schedule. *J. comp. physiol. Psychol.,* **48,** 265–266.

Hall, J. F. (1956) The relationship between external stimulation, food deprivation, and activity. *J. comp. physiol. Psychol.,* **49,** 339–341.

Hall, J. F. (1958) The influence of learning in activity wheel behavior. *J. genet. Psychol.,* **92,** 121–125.

Hall, J, F. (1961) *Psychology of motivation.* Chicago: Lippincott.

Hall, J. F., & Connon, H. E. (1957) Activity under low motivational levels as a function of the method of manipulating the deprivation. *J. genet. Psychol.,* **91,** 137–142.

Hall, J. F., & Hanford, P. V. (1954) Activity as a function of a restricted feeding schedule. *J. comp. physiol. Psychol.,* **47,** 362–363.

Hall, J. F., & Kobrick, J. L. (1952) The relationship between three measures of response strength. *J. comp. physiol. Psychol.,* **45,** 280–282.

Hall, J. F., Low, L., & Hanford, P. V. (1960) A comparison of the activity of hungry, thirsty, and satiated rats in the Dashiell checkerboard maze. *J. comp. physiol. Psychol.,* **53,** 155–158.

Hall, J. F., Smith, K., Schnitzer, S. B., & Hanford, P. V.(1953) Elevation of activity level in the rat following transition from ad libitum to restricted feeding. *J. comp. physiol. Psychol.,* **46,** 429–433.

Hall, R. D., & Kling, J. W. (1960) Amount of consummatory activity and performance in a modified T maze. *J. comp. physiol. Psychol.,* **53,** 165–168.

Hamilton, C. L. (1963) Interaction of food intake and temperature regulation in the rat. *J. comp. physiol. Psychol.*, **56**, 476–488.

Hamilton, C. L. (1964) Interaction of water, food and temperature regulation in the monkey. In M. J. Wayner (Ed.), *Thirst.* Oxford: Pergamon Press.

Hamilton, C. L. (1964a) Rat's preference for high fat diets. *J. comp. physiol. Psychol.*, **58**, 459–460.

Hamilton, C. L., & Brobeck, J. R. (1962) Temperature response of tube-fed rats. *Amer. J. Physiol.*, **203**, 383–384.

Hamilton, E. L. (1929) The effect of delayed incentive on the hunger drive in the white rat. *Genet. Psychol. Monogr.*, **5**, 133–207.

Hamilton, W. (1858) *Metaphysics.*

Hardy, K. R. (1964) An appetitional theory of sexual motivation. *Psychol. Rev.*, **71**, 1–18.

Harker, G. S. (1956) Delay of reward and performance of an instrumental response. *J. exp. Psychol.*, **51**, 303–310.

Harlow, H. F. (1932) Social facilitation of feeding in the albino rat. *J. genet. Psychol.*, **41**, 211–221.

Harlow, H. F. (1950) Learning and satiation of response in intrinsically motivated complex puzzle performance by monkeys. *J. comp. physiol. Psychol.*, **43**, 289–294.

Harlow, H. F. (1953) Motivation as a factor in the acquisition of new responses. In *Current theory and research in motivation: a symposium.* Lincoln: University of Nebraska Press.

Harlow, H. F. (1959) Learning set and error factor theory. In S. Koch (Ed.), *Psychology: a study of a science,* Vol. II. New York: McGraw-Hill.

Harlow, H. F., Harlow, M. K., & Meyer, D. R. (1950) Learning motivated by a manipulation drive. *J. exp. Psychol.*, **40**, 228–234.

Harmon, F. L. (1951) *Principles of psychology,* rev. ed. Milwaukee: Bruce.

Harper, A. E., & Spivey, H. E. (1958) Relationship between food intake and osmotic effect of dietary carbohydrate. *Amer. J. Physiol.*, **193**, 483–487.

Harriman, A. E., & MacLeod, R. B. (1953) Discriminative thresholds of salt for normal and adrenalectomized rats. *Amer. J. Psychol.*, **66**, 465–471.

Harrison, J. M., & Tracy, W. H. (1955) The use of auditory stimuli to maintain lever pressing behavior. *Science,* **121**, 273–274.

Harte, R. A., Travers, J. A., & Sarich, P. (1948) Voluntary caloric intake of the growing rat. *J. Nutrition,* **36**, 667–679.

Hartmann, H. (1958) *Ego psychology and the problem of adaptation.* New York: International Universities Press.

Hausmann, M. F. (1932) The behavior of albino rats in choosing food and stimulants. *J. comp. Psychol.*, **13**, 279–309.

Hayes, K. J. (1960) Exploration and fear. *Psychol. Rep.,* **6**, 91–93.

Healey, A. F. (1965) Compound stimuli, drive strength, and primary stimulus generalization. *J. exp. Psychol.,* **69**, 536–538.

Hearst, E. (1963) Escape from a stimulus asociated with both reward and punishment. *J. comp. physiol. Psychol.,* **56**, 1027–1031.

Hearst, E., & Whalen, R. E. (1963) Facilitating effects of D-amphetamine on discriminated-avoidance performance. *J. comp. physiol. Psychol.,* **56**, 124–128.

Heathers, G. L., & Arakelian, P. (1941) The relationship between strength of drive and rate of extinction of a bar-pressing reaction in the rat. *J. gen. Psychol.,* **24**, 243–258.

Hebb, D. O. (1949) *The organization of behavior.* New York: Wiley.

Hebb, D. O. (1955) Drives and the C.N.S. (Conceptual nervous system). *Psychol. Rev.*, **62**, 243–254.

Hefferline, R. F. (1950) An experimental study of avoidance. *Genet. Psychol. Monogr.*, **42**, 231–334.

Heider, F. (1960) The Gestalt theory of motivation. In M. R. Jones (Ed.), *Nebraska symposium on motivation.* Lincoln: University of Nebraska Press.

Heinroth, O. (1911) Beitrage zur Biologie, namentlich Ethologie und Psychologie der Anatiden. *Verh. V. Int. Ornithol. Kongr. Berlin.*

Hellyer, S. (1953) Duration of the consummatory response as a variable in amount of reinforcement studies. Unpublished Ph.D. dissertation, Indiana University. Cited by Collier and Myers (1961).

Hemmingsen, A. M. (1933) Studies on the oestrus-producing hormone (oestrin). *Skand. arch. Physiol.*, **65**, 97–250.

Hemmingsen, A. M., & Krarup, N. B. (1937) Cited by Hunt and Schlosberg (1939a).

Hempel, C. G., & Oppenheim, P. (1948) Studies in the logic of explanation. *Philos. Sci.*, **15**, 135–175.

Hendry, D. P., & Hendry, L. S. (1963) Partial negative reinforcement: fixed-ratio escape. *J. exp. anal. Behav.*, **6**, 519–523.

Heriot, J. T., & Coleman, P. D. (1962) The effect of electroconvulsive shock on retention of a modified "one-trial" conditioned avoidance. *J. comp. physiol. Psychol.*, **55**, 1082–1084.

Heron, W. T. (1949) Internal stimuli and learning. *J. comp. physiol. Psychol.*, **42**, 486–492.

Heron, W. T., & Skinner, B. F. (1937) Changes in hunger during starvation. *Psychol. Rec.*, **1**, 51–60.

Hetherington, A. W., & Ranson, S. W. (1940) Hypothalamic lesions and adiposity in the rat. *Anat. Rec.*, **78**, 149–172.

Heyer, A. W., Jr. (1951) Studies in motivation and retention: IV. The influence of dehydration on acquisition and retention of the maze habit. *Comp. Psychol. Monogr.*, **20** (Serial No. 106).

Hilgard, E. R. (1956) *Theories of learning,* 2nd ed. New York: Appleton-Century-Crofts.

Hilgard, E. R., Jones, L. V., & Kaplan, S. J. (1951) Conditioned discrimination as related to anxiety. *J. exp. Psychol.*, **42**, 94–99.

Hilgard, E. R., & Marquis, D. G. (1940) *Conditioning and learning.* New York: Appleton-Century-Crofts.

Hill, W. F. (1956) Activity as an autonomous drive. *J. comp. physiol. Psychol.*, **49**, 15–19.

Hill, W. F. (1958) The effect of varying periods of confinement on activity in tilt cages. *J. comp. physiol. Psychol.*, **51**, 570–574.

Hill, W. F. (1958a) The effect of long confinement on voluntary wheel-running by rats. *J. comp. physiol. Psychol.*, **51**, 770–773.

Hill, W. F. (1961) Effects of activity deprivation on choice of an activity incentive. *J. comp. physiol. Psychol.*, **54**, 78–82.

Hill, W. F. (1961a) An attempt to canalize activity drive. *Psychol. Rep.*, **8**, 86.

Hill, W. F., & Spear, N. E. (1963) Choice between magnitudes of reward in a T maze. *J. comp. physiol. Psychol.*, **56**, 723–726.

Hillman, B., Hunter, W. S., & Kimble, G. A. (1953) The effect of drive level on the maze performance of the white rat. *J. comp. physiol. Psychol.*, **46**, 87–89.

Hinde, R. A. (1954) Changes in responsiveness to a constant stimulus. *Brit. J. anim. Behav.*, **2**, 41–55.

Hinde, R. A. (1956) Ethological models and the concept of "drive." *Brit. J. Philos. Sci.*, **6**, 321–331.

Hinde, R. A. (1959) Unitary drives. *Anim. Behav.*, **7**, 130–141.

Hinde, R. A. (1960) Energy models of motivation. *Symp. Soc. exp. Biol.*, **14**, 199–213.

Hitchcock, F. A. (1925) Studies in vigor: V. The comparative activity of male and female albino rats. *Amer. J. Physiol.*, **75**, 205–210.

Hitchcock, F. A. (1928) The effect of low protein and protein-free diets and starvation on the voluntary activity of the albino rat. *Amer. J. Physiol.*, **84**, 410–416.

Hobbes, T. (1651) *Leviathan*.

Hobhouse, L. T. (1901) *Mind in evolution*. New York: Macmillan.

Hoelzel, F. (1927) Central factors in hunger. *Amer. J. Physiol.*, **82**, 665–671.

Hoelzel, F. (1957) Dr. A. J. Carlson and the concept of hunger. *Amer. J. clin. Nutr.*, **5**, 659–662.

Hoelzel, F., & Carlson, A. J. (1952) The alleged disappearance of hunger during starvation. *Science*, **115**, 526–527.

Hoffman, H. S., & Fleshler, M. (1961) Stimulus factors in aversive control: the generalization of conditioned suppression. *J. exp. anal. Behav.*, **4**, 371–378.

Hoffman, H. S., & Fleshler, M. (1965) Stimulus aspects of aversive controls: the effects of response contingent shock. *J. exp. anal. Behav.*, **8**, 89–96.

Hoge, M. A., & Stocking, R. L. (1912) A note on the relative value of punishment and reward as motives. *J. anim. Behav.*, **2**, 43–50.

Holder, W. B., Marx, M. H., Holder, E. E., & Collier, G. (1957) Response strength as a function of delay in a runway. *J. exp. Psychol.*, **53**, 316–323.

Hollingworth, H. L. (1928) *Psychology: its facts and principles*. New York: Appleton-Century-Crofts.

Hollingworth, H. L. (1931) Effect and affect in learning. *Psychol. Rev.*, **38**, 153–159.

Holmes, J. H. (1964) Thirst and fluid intake problems in clinical medicine. In M. J. Wayner (Ed.), *Thirst*. Oxford: Pergamon Press.

Holmes, J. H., & Gregersen, M. I. (1950) Observations on drinking induced by hypertonic solutions. *Amer. J. Physiol.*, **162**, 326–337.

Holmes, J. H., & Montgomery, A. V. (1960) Relation of route of administration and types of fluid to satisfaction of thirst in the dog. *Amer. J. Physiol.*, **199**, 907–911.

Holmes, S. J. (1911) *The evolution of animal intelligence*. New York: Holt.

Holt, E. B. (1915) *The Freudian wish and its place in ethics*. New York: Holt.

Homzie, M. J., & Ross, L. E. (1962) Runway performance following a reduction in the concentration of a liquid reward. *J. comp. physiol. Psychol.*, **55**, 1029–1033.

Hopkins, C. O. (1955) Effectivenes of secondary reinforcing stimuli as a function of the quantity and quality of food reinforcement. *J. exp. Psychol.*, **50**, 339–342.

Horenstein, B. R. (1951) Performance of conditioned responses as a function of strength of hunger drive. *J. comp. physiol. Psychol.*, **44**, 210–224.

Hoskins, R. G. (1925) Studies on vigor: II. The effects of castration on voluntary activity. *Amer. J. Physiol.*, **72**, 324–330.

Howard, T. C. (1962) Conditioned temperature drive in rats. *Psychol. Rep.*, **10**, 371–373.

Howard, T. C., & Young, F. A. (1962) Conditioned hunger and secondary rewards in monkeys. *J. comp. physiol. Psychol.,* **55,** 392–397.

Hudson, B. B. (1950) One-trial learning in the domestic rat. *Genet. Psychol. Monogr.,* **41,** 99–145.

Hughes, D., Davis, J. D., & Grice, G. R. (1960) Goal box and alley similarity as a factor in latent extinction. *J. comp. physiol. Psychol.,* **53,** 612–614.

Hughes, J. B., Sprague, J. L., & Bendig, A. W. (1954) Anxiety level, response alternation, and performance in serial learning. *J. Psychol.,* **38,** 421–426.

Hughes, L. H. (1957) Saccharine reinforcement in a T maze. *J. comp. physiol. Psychol.,* **50,** 431–435.

Hughes, R. N. (1965) Food deprivation and locomotor exploration in the white rat. *Anim. Behav.,* **13,** 30–32.

Hulicka, I. M. (1960) Additive versus multiplicative combination of drive and incentive. *Psychol. Rep.,* **6,** 403–409.

Hulicka, I. M., & Capeheart, J. (1960) Is the "click" a secondary reinforcer? *Psychol. Rec.,* **10,** 29–37.

Hull, C. L. (1929) A functional interpretation of the conditioned reflex. *Psychol. Rev.,* **36,** 498–511.

Hull, C. L. (1930) Knowledge and purpose as habit mechanisms. *Psychol. Rev.,* **37,** 511–525.

Hull, C. L. (1930a) Simple trial-and-error learning. *Psychol. Rev.,* **37,** 241–256.

Hull, C. L. (1931) Goal attraction and directing ideas conceived as habit phenomena. *Psychol. Rev.,* **38,** 487–506.

Hull, C. L. (1933) Differential habituation to internal stimuli in the albino rat. *J. comp. Psychol.,* **16,** 255–273.

Hull, C. L. (1934) The concept of the habit-family hierarchy, and maze learning. *Psychol. Rev.,* **41,** 33–54, 134–152.

Hull, C. L. (1935) The mechanism of the assembly of behavior segments in novel combinations suitable for problem solution. *Psychol. Rev.,* **42,** 219–245.

Hull, C. L. (1935a) Special review: Thorndike's Fundamentals of learning. *Psychol. Bull.,* **32,** 807–823.

Hull, C. L. (1937) Mind, mechanism, and adaptive behavior. *Psychol. Rev.,* **44,** 1–32.

Hull, C. L. (1939) The problem of stimulus equivalence in behavior theory. *Psychol. Rev.,* **46,** 9–30.

Hull, C. L. (1943) *Principles of behavior.* New York: Appleton-Century-Crofts.

Hull, C. L. (1945) The place of innate individual and species differences in a natural-science theory of behavior. *Psychol. Rev.,* **52,** 55–60.

Hull, C. L. (1951) *Essentials of behavior.* New Haven: Yale University Press.

Hull, C. L. (1952) *A behavior system.* New Haven: Yale University Press.

Hull, C. L., Hovland, C. I., Ross, R. T., Hall, M., Perkins, D. T., & Fitch, F. B. (1940) *Mathematico-deductive theory of rote learning.* New Haven: Yale University Press.

Hull, C. L., Livingston, J. R., Rouse, R. O., & Barker, A. N. (1951) True, sham, and esophageal feeding as reinforcements. *J. comp. physiol. Psychol.,* **44,** 236–245.

Hulse, S. H., & Bacon, W. E. (1962) Supplementary report: partial reinforcement and amount of reinforcement as determinants of instrumental licking rates. *J. exp. Psychol.,* **63,** 214–215.

Hulse, S. H., & Firestone, R. J. (1964) Mean amount of reinforcement and instrumental response strength. *J. exp. Psychol.,* **67,** 417–422.

Hulse, S. H., Snyder, H. L., & Bacon, W. E. (1960) Instrumental licking behavior as a function of schedule, volume, and concentration of a saccharine reinforcer. *J. exp. Psychol.*, **60**, 359–364.

Hume, D. (1739) *Treatise of human nature.*

Hume, D. (1779) *Dialogues on natural religion.*

Humphrey, G. (1951) *Thinking.* London: Methuen.

Hunt, H. F., & Brady, J. V. (1955) Some effects of punishment and intercurrent "anxiety" on a simple operant. *J. comp. physiol. Psychol.*, **48**, 305–310.

Hunt, H. F., & Otis, L. S. (1953) Conditioned and unconditioned emotional defecation in the rat. *J. comp. physiol. Psychol.*, **46**, 378–382.

Hunt, J. McV., & Schlosberg, H. (1939) General activity in the male white rat. *J. comp. Psychol.*, **28**, 23–38.

Hunt, J. McV., & Schlosberg, H. (1939a) The influence of illumination upon general activity in normal, blinded and castrated male white rats. *J. comp. Psychol.*, **28**, 285–298.

Hunter, W. S. (1935) Conditioning and extinction in the rat. *Brit. J. Psychol.*, **26**, 135–148.

Hurwitz, H. M. B. (1960) Effect of amount of food deprivation on performance of non-reinforced responses. *Psychol. Rep.*, **6**, 347–350.

Hutcheson, F. (1728) *Essay on the nature and conduct of the passions and affections.*

Hutt, P. J. (1954) Rate of bar pressing as a function of quality and quantity of food reward. *J. comp. physiol. Psychol.*, **47**, 235–239.

Imada, H. (1964) "Vigor" of water drinking behavior of rats as a function of thirst drive. *Jap. psychol. Res.*, **6**, 108–114.

Ison, J. R. (1964) Acquisition and reversal of a spatial response as a function of sucrose concentration. *J. exp. Psychol.*, **67**, 495–496.

Ison, J. R., & Cook, P. E. (1964) Extinction performance as a function of incentive magnitude and number of acquisition trials. *Psychon. Sci.*, **1**, 245–246.

Jacobs, H. L. (1964) Evaluation of the osmotic effects of glucose loads in food satiation. *J. comp. physiol. Psychol.*, **57**, 309–310.

James, W. (1890) *Principles of psychology.*

James, W. (1914) *The varieties of religious experience.* New York: Longmans, Green.

James, W. T. (1937) An experimental study of the defense mechanism in the opossum, with emphasis on natural behavior and its relation to mode of life. *J. genet. Psychol.*, **51**, 95–100.

James, W. T. (1953) Social facilitation of eating behavior in puppies after satiation. *J. comp. physiol. Psychol.*, **48**, 427–428.

James, W. T. (1963) An analysis of esophageal feeding as a form of operant reinforcement in the dog. *Psychol. Rep.*, **12**, 31–39.

James, W. T., & Gilbert, T. F. (1957) Elimination of eating behavior by food injection in weaned puppies. *Psychol. Rep.*, **3**, 167–168.

Jammer, M. (1957) *Concepts of force.* Cambridge: Harvard University Press.

Janis, I. L. (1958) The psychoanalytic interview as an observational method. In G. Lindzey (Ed.), *Assessment of human motives.* New York: Rinehart.

Janowitz, H. D., & Grossman, M. I. (1948) Effect of parenteral administration of glucose and protein hydrolysate on food intake in the rat. *Amer. J. Physiol.*, **155**, 28–32.

Janowitz, H. D., & Grossman, M. I. (1949) Effect of variations in nutritive density on intake of food of dogs and rats. *Amer. J. Physiol.*, **158**, 184–193.

Janowitz, H. D., & Grossman, M. I. (1949a) Some factors affecting the food intake of normal dogs and dogs with esophagostomy and gastric fistula. *Amer. J. Physiol.,* **159,** 143–148.

Janowitz, H. D., & Grossman, M. I. (1951) Effect of prefeeding, alcohol and bitters on food intake of dogs. *Amer. J. Physiol.,* **64,** 182–186.

Janowitz, H. D., & Hollander, F. (1955) The time factor in the adjustment of food intake to varied caloric requirement in the dog: a study of the precision of appetite. *Ann. N. Y. Acad. Sci.,* **63,** 56–67.

Janowitz, H. D., & Ivy, A. C. (1949) Role of blood sugar levels in spontaneous and insulin-induced hunger in man. *J. appl. Physiol.,* **1,** 643–645.

Jarmon, H., & Gerall, A. A. (1961) The effect of food deprivation upon the sexual performance of male guinea pigs. *J. comp. physiol. Psychol.,* **54,** 306–309.

Jenkins, J. J., & Hanratty, J. A. (1949) Drive intensity discrimination in the white rat. *J. comp. physiol. Psychol.,* **42,** 228–232.

Jenkins, J. J., & Lykken, D. T. (1957) Individual differences. *Ann. Rev. Psychol.,* **8,** 79–112.

Jenkins, M. (1928) The effect of segregation on the sex behavior of the white rat as measured by the obstruction method. *Genet. Psychol. Monogr.,* **3,** 455–571.

Jenkins, T. N., Warner, L. H., & Warden, C. J. (1926) Standard apparatus for the study of animal motivation. *J. comp. Psychol.,* **6,** 361–382.

Jenkins, W. O. (1950) A temporal gradient of derived reinforcement. *Amer. J. Psychol.,* **63,** 237–243.

Jenkins, W. O., Pascal, G. R., & Walker, R. W., Jr. (1958) Deprivation and generalization. *J. exp. Psychol.,* **56,** 274–277.

Jennings, H. S. (1906) *The behavior of lower organisms.* New York: Columbia University Press.

Jensen, A. R. (1958) Personality. *Ann. Rev. Psychol.,* **9,** 295–322.

Jensen, G. D. (1960) Learning and performance as functions of ration size, hours of privation, and effort requirement. *J. exp. Psychol.,* **59,** 261–268.

Jones, E. (1953) *The life and work of Sigmund Freud.* New York: Basic Books.

Jones, J. E. (1961) The CS-UCS interval in conditioning short- and long-latency responses. *J. exp. Psychol.,* **62,** 612–617.

Jones, M. B. (1953) An experimental study of extinction. *Psychol. Monogr.,* **67** (Whole No. 369).

Jørgensen, H. (1950) The influence of saccharine on the blood sugar. *Acta Physiol. Scand.,* **20,** 37.

Kagan, J. (1955) Differential reward value of incomplete and complete sexual behavior. *J. comp. physiol. Psychol.,* **48,** 59–64.

Kagan, J., & Berkun, M. (1954) The reward value of running activity. *J. comp. physiol. Psychol.,* **47,** 108.

Kalish, H. I. (1954) Strength of fear as a function of the number of acquisition and extinction trials. *J. exp. Psychol.,* **47,** 1–9.

Kamin, L. J. (1954) Traumatic avoidance learning: the effects of CS-US interval with a trace conditioning procedure. *J. comp. physiol. Psychol.,* **47,** 65–72.

Kamin, L. J. (1955) Relations between discrimination, apparatus stress, and the Taylor scale. *J. abnorm. soc. Psychol.,* **51,** 595–599.

Kamin, L. J. (1956) The effects of termination of the CS and avoidance of the US on avoidance learning. *J. comp. physiol. Psychol.,* **49,** 420–424.

Kamin, L. J. (1957) The gradient of delay of secondary reward in avoidance learning. *J. comp. physiol. Psychol.,* 50, 445–449.

Kamin, L. J. (1957a) The effects of termination of the CS and avoidance of the US on avoidance learning: an extension. *Canad. J. Psychol.,* 11, 48–56.

Kamin, L. J. (1957b) The gradient of delay of secondary reward in avoidance learning tested on avoidance trials only. *J. comp. physiol. Psychol.,* 50, 450–456.

Kamin, L. J. (1957c) The retention of an incompletely learned avoidance response. *J. comp. physiol. Psychol.,* 50, 457–460.

Kamin, L. J. (1959) CS-termination as a factor in the emergence of anticipatory avoidance. *Psychol. Rep.,* 5, 455–456.

Kamin, L. J. (1959a) The delay-of-punishment gradient. *J. comp. physiol. Psychol.,* 52, 434–437.

Kamin, L. J. (1960) Acquisition of avoidance with a variable CS-US interval. *Canad. J. Psychol.,* 14, 1–6.

Kamin, L. J. (1961) Trace conditioning of the conditioned emotional response. *J. comp. physiol. Psychol.,* 54, 149–153.

Kamin, L. J. (1963) Retention of an incompletely learned avoidance response: some further analyses. *J. comp. physiol. Psychol.,* 56, 713–718.

Kamin, L. J. (1963a) Backward conditioning and the conditioned emotional response. *J. comp. physiol. Psychol.,* 56, 517–519.

Kamin, L. J., Bindra, D., Clark, J. W., & Waksberg, H. (1955) The interrelations among some behavioral measures of anxiety. *Canad. J. Psychol.,* 9, 79–83.

Kamin, L. J., & Brimer, C. J. (1963) The effects of intensity of conditioned and unconditioned stimuli on a conditioned emotional response. *Canad. J. Psychol.,* 17, 194–200.

Kamin, L. J., Brimer, C. J., & Black, A. H. (1963) Conditioned suppression as a monitor of fear of the CS in the course of avoidance training. *J. comp. physiol. Psychol.,* 56, 497–501.

Kamin, L., Campbell, D., Judd, R., Ryan, T., & Walker, J. (1959) Two determinants of the emergence of anticipatory avoidance. *J. comp. physiol. Psychol.,* 52, 202–205.

Kamin, L. J., & Fedorchak, O. (1957) The Taylor scale, hunger, and verbal learning. *Canad. J. Psychol.,* 11, 212–218.

Kamin, L. J., & Schaub, R. E. (1963) Effects of conditioned stimulus intensity on the conditioned emotional response. *J. comp. physiol. Psychol.,* 56, 502–507.

Kantor, J. R. (1947) *Problems of physiological psychology.* Bloomington, Ind.: Principia Press.

Kaplan, M. (1956) The maintenance of escape behavior under fixed-ratio reinforcement. *J. comp. physiol. Psychol.,* 49, 153–157.

Kaplan, M., Campbell, S. L., Johnson, L., PapaMichael, A., Sparer, R., & Weinbaum, M. (1959) Growth of body weight and manipulation of food motivation. *Science,* 129, 1673–1674.

Kaplan, R. (1963) Rat basal resistance level under stress and nonstress conditions. *J. comp. physiol. Psychol.,* 56, 775–777.

Kaplan, S., & Kaplan, R. (1962) Skin resistance recording in the unrestrained rat. *Science,* 138, 1403–1404.

Karsh, E. B. (1962) Effects of number of rewarded trials and intensity of punishment on running speed. *J. comp. physiol. Psychol.,* 55, 44–51.

Karsh, E. B. (1963) Changes in intensity of punishment: effect on runway behavior of rats. *Science,* **140,** 1084–1085.

Karsh, E. B. (1964) Punishment: trial spacing and shock intensity as determinants of behavior in a discrete operant situation. *J. comp. physiol. Psychol.,* **58,** 299–302.

Katz, D. (1937) *Animals and men.* New York: Longmans, Green.

Kaufman, E. L., & Miller, N. E. (1949) Effect of number of reinforcements on strength of approach in an approach-avoidance conflict. *J. comp. physiol. Psychol.,* **42,** 65–74.

Kaufman, R. S. (1953) Effects of preventing intromission upon sexual behavior in rats. *J. comp. physiol. Psychol.,* **46,** 209–211.

Keehn, J. D. (1959) On the non-classical nature of avoidance-behavior. *Amer. J. Pychol.,* **72,** 243–247.

Keehn, J. D. (1959a) The effect of a warning signal on unrestricted avoidance behavior. *Brit. J. Psychol.,* **50,** 125–135.

Keehn, J. D. (1962) The effect of post-stimulus conditions on the secondary reinforcing power of a stimulus. *J. comp. physiol. Psychol.,* **55,** 22–26.

Keehn, J. D., & Arnold, E. M. M. (1960) Licking rates of albino rats. *Science,* **132,** 739–741.

Keehn, J. D., & Barakat, H. (1964) Local response rates as affected by reinforcement quality. *Psychol. Rep.,* **15,** 519–524.

Keesey, R. E. (1962) The relationship between pulse frequency, intensity, and duration and the rate of responding for intracranial stimulation. *J. comp. physiol. Psychol.,* **55,** 671–678.

Keesey, R. E. (1964) Duration of stimulation and the reward properties of hypothalamic stimulation. *J. comp. physiol. Psychol.,* **58,** 201–207.

Kelleher, R. T. (1958) Fixed-ratio schedules of conditioned reinforcement with chimpanzees. *J. exp. anal. Behav.,* **1,** 281–289.

Kelleher, R. T., & Fry, W. T. (1962) Stimulus functions in chained fixed-interval schedules. *J. exp. anal. Behav.,* **5,** 167–173.

Kelleher, R. T., & Gollub, L. R. (1962) A review of positive conditioned reinforcement. *J. exp. anal. Behav.,* **5,** 543–597.

Kelleher, R. T., Riddle, W. C., & Cook, L. (1963) Persistent behavior maintained by unavoidable shocks. *J. exp. anal. Behav.,* **6,** 507–517.

Keller, F. S. (1937) *The definition of psychology.* New York: Appleton-Century-Crofts.

Keller, F. S., & Schoenfeld, W. N. (1950) *Principles of psychology.* New York: Appleton-Century-Crofts.

Kelly, G. A. (1958) Man's construction of his alternatives. In G. Lindzey (Ed.), *Assessment of human motives.* New York: Rinehart.

Kendler, H. H. (1945) Drive interaction: I. Learning as a function of the simultaneous presence of the hunger and thirst drives. *J. exp. Psychol.,* **35,** 96–109.

Kendler, H. H. (1945a) Drive interaction: II. Experimental analysis of the role of drive in learning theory. *J. exp. Psychol.,* **35,** 188–198.

Kendler, H. H. (1946) The influence of simultaneous hunger and thirst drives upon the learning of two opposed spatial responses of the white rat. *J. exp. Psychol.,* **36,** 212–220.

Kendler, H. H., Karasik, A. D., & Schrier, A. M. (1954) Studies of the effect of change of drive: III. Amounts of switching produced by shifting drive from thirst to hunger and from hunger to thirst. *J. exp. Psychol.,* **47,** 179–182.

Kendler, H. H., & Law, F. E. (1950) An experimental test of the selective principle of association of drive stimuli. *J. exp. Psychol.*, **40**, 299–304.

Kendler, H. H., & Levine, S. (1951) Studies of the effect of change of drive: I. From hunger to thirst in a T-maze. *J. exp. Psychol.*, **41**, 429–436.

Kendler, H. H., Levine, S., Altchek, E., & Peters, H. (1952) Studies of the effect of change of drive: II. From hunger to different intensities of a thirst drive in a T-maze. *J. exp. Psychol.*, **44**, 1–4.

Kennedy, G. C. (1953) The role of depot fat in the hypothalamic control of food intake in the rat. *Proc. Roy. Soc.*, **140B**, 578–592.

Kennedy, J. S. (1954) Is modern ethology objective? *Brit. J. anim. Behav.*, **2**, 12–19.

Kent, N. D., Wagner, M. K., & Gannon, D. R. (1960) Effect of unconditioned response restriction on subsequent acquisition of a habit motivated by "fear." *Psychol. Rep.*, **6**, 335–338.

Kessen, W. (1953) Response strength and conditioned stimulus intensity. *J. exp. Psychol.*, **45**, 82–86.

Kessen, W., Kimble, G. A., & Hillman, B. M. (1960) Effects of deprivation and scheduling on water intake in the white rat. *Science*, **131**, 1735–1736.

Kimble, G. A. (1951) Behavior strength as a function of the intensity of the hunger drive. *J. exp. Psychol.*, **41**, 341–348.

Kimble, G. A. (1955) Shock intensity and avoidance learning. *J. comp. physiol. Psychol.*, **48**, 281–284.

Kimble, G. A. (1961) *Hilgard and Marquis' Conditioning and learning*. New York: Appleton-Century-Crofts.

Kimble, G. A., & Dufort, R. H. (1956) The associative factor in eyelid conditioning. *J. exp. Psychol.*, **52**, 386–391.

Kimble, G. A., Mann, L. I., & Dufort, R. H. (1955) Classical and instrumental eyelid conditioning. *J. exp. Psychol.*, **49**, 407–417.

Kimble, G. A., & Ost, J. W. P. (1961) The influence of unpaired UCS presentation on eyelid conditioning. *Psychol. Rep.*, **9**, 239–245.

Kimmel, H. D. (1963) Management of conditioned fear. *Psychol. Rep.*, **12**, 313–314.

King, M. S., Kimble, G. A., Gorman, J., & King, R. A. (1961) Replication report: two failures to reproduce effects of anxiety on eyelid conditioning. *J. exp. Psychol.*, **62**, 532–533.

King, R. A. (1959) The effects of training and motivation on the components of a learned instrumental response. Unpublished Ph.D. dissertation, Duke University. Cited by Kimble (1961).

Kintsch, W. (1962) Runway performance as a function of drive strength and magnitude of reinforcement. *J. comp. physiol. Psychol.*, **55**, 882–887.

Kintsch, W., & Witte, R. S. (1962) Concurrent conditioning of bar press and salivation responses. *J. comp. physiol. Psychol.*, **55**, 963–968.

Kish, G. B. (1955) Avoidance learning to the onset and cessation of conditioned stimulus energy. *J. exp. Psychol.*, **50**, 31–38.

Kish, G. B., & Barnes, G. W. (1961) Reinforcing effects of manipulation in mice. *J. comp. physiol. Psychol.*, **54**, 713–715.

Kleiber, M. (1961) *The fire of life*. New York: Wiley.

Klein, R. M. (1959) Intermittent primary reinforcement as a parameter of secondary reinforcement. *J. exp. Psychol.*, **58**, 423–427.

Kleinmuntz, B. (1963) One response learned to two drives. *J. gen. Psychol.*, **68**, 181–186.

Kleitman, N. (1927) The effect of starvation on the daily consumption of water by the dog. *Amer. J. Physiol.,* **81,** 336–340.

Kleitman, N. (1963) *Sleep and wakefulness,* 2nd ed. Chicago: University of Chicago Press.

Kling, J. W. (1956) Speed of running as a function of goal-box behavior. *J. comp. physiol. Psychol.,* **49,** 474–476.

Klinger, B. I., & Prokasy, W. F. (1962) A note on MAS score and the ready signal in classical eyelid conditioning. *Pychol. Rep.,* **10,** 829–830.

Knapp, R. K., Kause, R. H., & Perkins, C. C., Jr. (1959) Immediate versus delayed shock in T-maze performance. *J. exp. Psychol.,* **58,** 357–362.

Kobrick, J. L. (1956) The relationship among three measures of response strength as a function of the numbers of reinforcements. *J. comp. physiol. Psychol.,* **49,** 582–586.

Koch, S. (1941) The logical character of the motivation concept. *Psychol. Rev.,* **48,** 15–38, 127–154.

Koch, S. (1954) Clark L. Hull. In W. K. Estes et al., *Modern learning theory.* New York: Appleton-Century-Crofts.

Koch, S., & Daniel, W. J. (1945) The effect of satiation on the behavior mediated by a habit of maximum strength. *J. exp. Psychol.,* **35,** 167–187.

Kohn, M. (1951) Satiation of hunger from food injected directly into the stomach versus food ingested by mouth. *J. comp. physiol. Psychol.,* **44,** 412–422.

Konorski, J. (1948) *Conditioned reflexes and neural organization.* Cambridge: Cambridge University Press.

Koppman, J., & Grice, G. R. (1963) Goal-box and alley similarity in latent extinction. *J. exp. Psychol.,* **66,** 611–612.

Korman, M., & Loeb, J. (1961) Effects of the presence of another animal during acquisition and extinction upon the strength of a fear response. *J. comp. physiol. Psychol.,* **54,** 158–161.

Kortlandt, A. (1959) An attempt at clarifying some controversial notions in animal psychology and ethology. *Arch. Neer. Zool.,* **13,** 196–229.

Kraeling, D. (1961) Analysis of amount of reward as a variable in learning. *J. comp. physiol. Psychol.,* **54,** 560–565.

Krutch, J. W. (1956) *The great chain of life.* Boston: Houghton Mifflin.

Kuo, Z. Y. (1924) A psychology without heredity. *Psychol. Rev.,* **31,** 427–448.

Kuo, Z. Y. (1928) The fundamental error of the concept of purpose and the trial and error fallacy. *Psychol. Rev.,* **35,** 414–433.

Kuo, Z. Y. (1929) The net result of the anti-heredity movement in psychology. *Psychol. Rev.,* **36,** 191–199.

Kurtz, K., & Pearl, J. (1960) The effects of prior fear experiences on acquired drive learning. *J. comp. physiol. Psychol.,* **53,** 201–206.

Lachman, R. (1961) The influence of thirst and schedules of reinforcement-nonreinforcement ratios upon brightness discrimination. *J. exp. Psychol.,* **62,** 80–87.

Lamarck, J. B. (1809) *Philosophie zoölogique.*

Lambert, W. W., & Solomon, R. L. (1952) Extinction of a running response as a function of distance of block point from the goal. *J. comp. physiol. Psychol.,* **45,** 269–279.

Landauer, T. K. (1964) Delay of an acquired reinforcer. *J. comp. physiol. Psychol.,* **58,** 374–379.

Lange, A. (1873) *The history of materialism,* 3rd ed. trans. by E. C. Thomas. New York: Harcourt, Brace, 1925.

Larssen, K. (1956) *Conditioning and sexual behavior in the male albino rat.* Stockholm: Almquist & Wiksell.

Lashley, K. S. (1938) Experimental analysis of instinctual behavior. *Psychol. Rev.,* **45,** 445–471.

Lawler, E. E., III. (1965) Secondary reinforcement value of stimuli associated with shock reduction. *Quart. J. exp. Psychol.,* **17,** 57–62.

Lawrence, D., & Hommel, L. (1961) The influence of differential goal boxes on discrimination learning involving delay of reinforcement. *J. comp. physiol. Psychol.,* **54,** 552–555.

Lawrence, D. H., & Mason, W. A. (1955) Intake and weight adjustment in rats to changes in feeding schedule. *J. comp. physiol. Psychol.,* **48,** 43–46.

Lawrence, D. H., & Mason, W. A. (1955a) Food intake in the rat as a function of deprivation intervals and feeding rhythms. *J. comp. physiol. Psychol.,* **48,** 267–271.

Lawrence, D. H., & Miller, N. E. (1947) A positive relationship between reinforcement and resistance to extinction produced by removing a source of confusion from a technique that had produced opposite results. *J. exp. Psychol.,* **37,** 494–509.

Lawson, R. (1953) Amount of primary reward and strength of secondary reward. *J. exp. Psychol.,* **46,** 183–187.

Lawson, R. (1957) Brightness discrimination performance and secondary reward strength as a function of primary reward amount. *J. comp. physiol. Psychol.,* **50,** 35–39.

Lawson, R. (1965) *Frustration: the development of a scientific concept.* New York: Macmillan.

Lawson, R., Cross, H. A., & Tambe, J. T. (1959) Effects of large and small rewards on maze performance after different prior experiences with reward amounts. *J. comp. physiol. Psychol.,* **52,** 717–720.

Lawson, R., & Marx, M. H. (1958) Frustration: theory and experiment. *Genet. Psychol. Monogr.,* **57,** 393–464.

Leeper, R. (1935) The role of motivation in learning: a study of the phenomenon of differential motivational control of the utilization of habits. *J. genet. Psychol.,* **46,** 3–40.

Leeper, R. W. (1943) *Lewin's topological and vector psychology.* Eugene: University of Oregon Press.

Lehrman, D. S. (1953) A critique of Konrad Lorenz's theory of instinctive behavior. *Quart. Rev. Biol.,* **28,** 337–363.

Lehrman, D. S. (1961) Hormonal regulation of parental behavior in birds and infrahuman mammals. In W. C. Young (Ed.), *Sex and internal secretions.* Baltimore: Williams & Wilkins.

Lehrman, D. S. (1962) Interaction of hormonal and experiential influences on development of behavior. In E. L. Bliss (Ed.), *Roots of behavior.* New York: Hoeber.

Leitenberg, H. (1965) Response initiation and response termination: analysis of effects of punishment and escape contingencies. *Psychol. Rep.,* **16,** 569–575.

Leitenberg, H. (1965a) Is time-out from positive reinforcement an aversive event? A review of the experimental literature. *Psychol. Rev.,* **64,** 428–441.

Lepkovsky, S., Lyman, R., Fleming, D., Nagumo, M., & Dimick, M. M. (1957) Gastrointestinal regulation of water and its effect on food intake and rate of digestion. *Amer. J. Physiol.,* **188,** 327–331.

Leuba, C. J. (1955) Toward some integration of learning theories: the concept of optimal stimulation. *Psychol. Rep.,* **1,** 27–33.

Leventhal, A. M., Morrell, R. F., Morgan, E. F., Jr., & Perkins, C. C., Jr. (1959) The relation between mean reward and mean reinforcement. *J. exp. Psychol.*, **57**, 284–287.

Levine, S. (1953) The role of irrelevant drive stimuli in learning. *J. exp. Psychol.*, **45**, 410–416.

Levine, S. (1956) The effects of a strong irrelevant drive on learning. *Psychol. Rep.*, **2**, 29–33.

Levine, S. (1957) Infantile experience and consummatory behavior in adulthood. *J. comp. physiol. Psychol.*, **50**, 609–612.

Levine, S. (1958) Noxious stimulation in adult rats and consummatory behavior. *J. comp. physiol. Psychol.*, **51**, 230–233.

Levine, S., & England, S. J. (1960) Temporal factors in avoidance learning. *J. comp. physiol. Psychol.*, **53**, 282–283.

Levine, S., Staats, S. R., & Frommer, G. (1959) Drive summation in a water maze. *Psychol. Rep.*, **5**, 301–304.

Levy, L. H., & Kurz, R. B. (1957) The connotative impact of color on the Rorschach and its relation to manifest anxiety. *J. Pers.*, **25**, 617–625.

Lewin, K. (1917) Kriegslandschaft. *Z. Psychol.*, **12**, 212–247.

Lewin, K. (1922) Das Problem der Willenmessung der Assoziation. *Psychol. Forsch.*, **1**, 191–302; **2**, 65–140.

Lewin, K. (1926) Vorsatz, Wille und Beduerfnis. In D. Rapaport (Ed.), *Organization and pathology of thought.* New York: Columbia University Press, 1951.

Lewin, K. (1926a) Vorbemerkungen ueber die psychischen Kraefte und Energien und ueber die Struktur der Seele. *Psychol. Forsch.*, **7**, 294–329.

Lewin, K. (1927) Gesetz und Experiment in der Psychologie. *Symposiun,* **1**, 375–421.

Lewin, K. (1936) *Principles of topological psychology.* New York: McGraw-Hill.

Lewin, K. (1938) *The conceptual representation and the measurement of psychological forces.* Durham, N.C.: Duke University Press.

Lewis, D. J. (1959) A control for the direct manipulation of the fractional anticipatory goal response. *Psychol. Rep.*, **5**, 753–756.

Lewis, D. J., Butler, D., & Diamond, A. L. (1958) Direct manipulation of the fractional anticipatory goal response. *Psychol. Rep.*, **4**, 575–578.

Lewis, D. J., & Cotton, J. W. (1957) Learning and performance as a function of drive strength during acquisition and extinction. *J. comp. physiol. Psychol.*, **50**, 189–194.

Lewis, D. J., & Cotton, J. W. (1960) Effect of runway size and drive strength on acquisition and extinction. *J. exp. Psychol.*, **59**, 402–408.

Lewis, D. J., & Kent, N. D. (1961) Attempted direct activation and deactivation of the fractional anticipatory goal response. *Psychol. Rep.*, **8**, 107–110.

Ley, R. (1965) Effects of food and water deprivation on the performance of a response motivated by acquired fear. *J. exp. Psychol.*, **69**, 583–589.

Libby, A. (1951) Two variables in the acquisition of depressant properties by a stimulus. *J. exp. Psychol.*, **42**, 100–107.

Licklider, J. C. R., & Bunch, M. E. (1946) Effects of enforced wakefulness upon growth and the maze-learning performance of white rats. *J. comp. Psychol.*, **39**, 339–350.

Liddell, H. S. (1926) A laboratory for the study of conditioned motor reflexes. *Amer. J. Psychol.*, **37**, 418–419.

Lindsley, D. B. (1951) Emotion. In S. S. Stevens (Ed.), *Handbook of experimental psychology.* New York: Wiley.

Littman, R. A. (1958) Motives, history and causes. In M. R. Jones (Ed.), *Nebraska symposium on motivation.* Lincoln: University of Nebraska Press.

Lockard, J. S. (1963) Choice of a warning signal or no warning signal in an unavoidable shock situation. *J. comp. physiol. Psychol., 56,* 526–530.

Lockard, R. B. (1963) Some effects of light upon the behavior of rodents. *Psychol. Bull., 60,* 509–529.

Locke, J. (1690) *An essay concerning human understanding.*

Logan, F. A. (1951) A comparison of avoidance and nonavoidance eyelid conditioning. *J. exp. Psychol., 42,* 390–393.

Logan, F. A. (1952) The role of delay of reinforcement in determining reaction potential. *J. exp. Psychol., 43,* 393–399.

Logan, F. A. (1952a) Three estimates of differential excitatory tendency. *Psychol. Rev., 59,* 300–307.

Logan, F. A. (1956) A micromolar approach to behavior theory. *Psychol. Rev., 63,* 63–73.

Logan, F. A. (1960) *Incentive.* New Haven: Yale University Press.

Logan, F. A., Beier, E. M., & Ellis, R. A. (1955) Effect of varied reinforcement on speed of locomotion. *J. exp. Psychol., 49,* 260–266.

Logan, F. A., Beier, E. M., & Kincaid, W. D. (1956) Extinction following partial and varied reinforcement. *J. exp. Psychol., 52,* 65–70.

Lorber, S. H., Komarov, S. A., & Shay, H. (1950) Effect of sham feeding on gastric motor activity of the dog. *Amer. J. Physiol., 162,* 447–451.

Lorenz, K. (1935) Der Kumpans in der Umwelt des Vogels. In C. Schiller (Ed.), *Instinctive behavior.* New York: International Universities Press, 1957.

Lorenz, K. (1937) Uber die bildung Instinktbegriffes. In C. Schiller (Ed.), *Instinctive behavior.* New York: International Universities Press, 1957.

Lorenz, K. (1950) The comparative method in studying innate behavior pattern. *Symp. Soc. exp. Biol., 4,* 221–268.

Lorge, I. (1936) Irrelevant rewards in animal learning. *J. comp. Psychol., 21,* 105–128.

Lovaas, O. I. (1960) The relationship of induced muscular tension, tension level, and manifest anxiety in learning. *J. exp. Psychol., 59,* 145–152.

Low, L. A., & Low, H. I. (1962) Effects of CS-US interval length upon avoidance responding. *J. comp. physiol. Psychol., 55,* 1059–1061.

Low, L. A., & Low, H. I. (1962a) Effects of variable versus fixed CS-US interval schedules upon avoidance responding. *J. comp. physiol. Psychol., 55,* 1054–1058.

Lubbock, J. (1882) *Ants, bees, and wasps.*

Lucas, J. D. (1952) The interactive effects of anxiety, failure, and interserial duplication. *Amer. J. Psychol., 65,* 59–66.

Maatsch, J. L. (1954) Reinforcement and extinction phenomena. *Psychol. Rev., 61,* 111–118.

Maatsch, J. L. (1959) Learning and fixation after a single shock trial. *J. comp. physiol. Psychol., 52,* 408–410.

Maatsch, J. L., Adelman, H. M., & Denny, M. R. (1954) Effort and resistance to extinction of the bar-pressing response. *J. comp. physiol. Psychol., 47,* 47–50.

MacDonald, A. (1946) The effect of adaptation to the unconditioned stimulus upon the formation of conditioned avoidance response. *J. exp. Psychol.*, **36**, 1–12.

MacDuff, M. (1946) The effect on retention of varying degrees of motivation during learning in rats. *J. comp. Psychol.*, **39**, 207–240.

Mach, E. (1900) *Analyse der Empfindungen*, 2nd ed.

Madsen, K. B. (1961) *Theories of motivation*, 2nd ed. Cleveland: Howard Allen.

Magendie, F. (1831) *Précis élémentaire de physiologie*, 4th ed.

Maher, W. B., & Wickens, D. D. (1954) Effect of differential quantity of reward on acquisition and performance of a maze habit. *J. comp. physiol. Psychol.*, **47**, 44–46.

Malmo, R. B. (1958) Measurement of drive: an unsolved problem. In M. R. Jones (Ed.), *Nebraska symposium on motivation*. Lincoln: University of Nebraska Press.

Malmo, R. B. (1959) Activation: a neurophysiological dimension. *Psychol. Rev.*, **66**, 367–386.

Maltzman, I. (1952) The process need. *Psychol. Rev.*, **59**, 40–48.

Mandler, G., & Sarason, S. B. (1952) A study of anxiety and learning. *J. abnorm. soc. Psychol.*, **47**, 166–173.

Mandler, J. M. (1958) Effect of early food deprivation on adult behavior in the rat. *J. comp. physiol. Psychol.*, **51**, 513–517.

Manning, H. M. (1956) The effect of varying conditions of hunger and thirst on two responses learned to hunger or thirst alone. *J. comp. physiol. Psychol.*, **49**, 249–253.

Margenau, H. (1950) *The nature of physical reality*. New York: McGraw-Hill.

Martin, B., & Ross, L. E. (1964) Effects of consummatory response punishment on consummatory and runway behavior. *J. comp. physiol. Psychol.*, **58**, 243–247.

Martin, R. C., & Melvin, K. B. (1964) Vicious circle behavior as a function of delay of punishment. *Psychon. Sci.*, **1**, 415–416.

Marx, M. H. (1952) Infantile deprivation and adult behavior in the rat: retention of increased rate of eating. *J. comp. physiol. Psychol.*, **45**, 43–49.

Marx, M. H. (1956) Some relations between frustration and drive. In M. R. Jones (Ed.), *Nebraska symposium on motivation*. Lincoln: University of Nebraska Press.

Marx, M. H., & Brownstein, A. J. (1963) Effects of incentive magnitude on running speeds without competing responses in acquisition and extinction. *J. exp. Psychol.*, **65**, 182–189.

Marx, M. H., & Hellwig, L. R. (1964) Acquisition and extinction of avoidance conditioning without escape responses. *J. comp. physiol. Psychol.*, **58**, 451–452.

Marx, M. H., Tombaugh, J. W., Cole, C., & Dougherty, D. (1963) Persistence of nonreinforced responding as a function of the direction of a prior-ordered incentive shift. *J. exp. Psychol.*, **66**, 542–546.

Marzocco, F. N. (1951) Frustration effect as a function of drive level, habit strength, and distribution of trials during extinction. Unpublished Ph.D. dissertation, State University of Iowa. Cited by Brown (1961).

Maslow, A. H. (1954) *Motivation and personality*. New York: Harper.

Mason, W. A., & Harlow, H. F. (1959) Initial responses of infant rhesus monkeys to solid food. *Psychol. Rep.*, **5**, 193–199.

Mason, W. A., Harlow, H. F., & Reuping, R. R. (1959) Development of manipulatory responsiveness in the infant rhesus monkey. *J. comp. physiol. Psychol.*, **52**, 555–558.

May, M. A. (1948) Experimentally acquired drives. *J. exp. Psychol.*, **38**, 66–77.

Mayer, J. (1953) Genetic, traumatic and environmental factors in the etiology of obesity. *Physiol. Rev.*, **33**, 472–508.

Mayer, J. (1955) Regulation of energy intake and the body weight: the glucostatic theory and the lipostatic hypothesis. *Ann. N. Y. Acad. Sci.*, **63**, 15–43.

McAdam, D. (1964) Effects of positional relations between subject, CS, and US on shuttle-box avoidance learning in cats. *J. comp. physiol. Psychol.*, **58**, 302–304.

McAllister, D. E., & McAllister, W. R. (1964) Second-order conditioning of fear. *Psychon. Sci.*, **1**, 383–384.

McAllister, W. R., & McAllister, D. E. (1962) Role of the CS and of apparatus cues in the measurement of acquired fear. *Psychol. Rep.*, **11**, 749–756.

McAllister, W. R., & McAllister, D. E. (1963) Increase over time in the stimulus generalization of acquired fear. *J. exp. Psychol.*, **65**, 576–582.

McCleary, R. A. (1953) Taste and post-ingestion factors in specific-hunger behavior. *J. comp. physiol. Psychol.*, **46**, 411–421.

McClelland, D. C., Atkinson, J. W., Clark, R. A., & Lowell, E. L. (1953) *The achievement motive.* New York: Appleton-Century-Crofts.

McClelland, D. C., & McGown, D. R. (1953) The effect of variable food reinforcement on the strength of a secondary reward. *J. comp. physiol. Psychol.*, **46**, 80–86.

McCosh, J. (1874) *The Scottish philosophy.*

McDiarmid, C. G., & Rilling, M. E. (1965) Reinforcement delay and reinforcement rate as determinants of schedule preference. *Psychon. Sci.*, **2**, 195–196.

McDougall, W. (1908) *An introduction to social psychology,* 8th ed. Boston: Luce, 1914.

McDougall, W. (1932) *The energies of men.* London: Methuen.

McFarland, D. J. (1964) Interaction of hunger and thirst in the barbary dove. *J. comp. physiol. Psychol.*, **58**, 174–179.

McGuigan, F. J., Calvin, A. D., & Richardson, E. C. (1959) Manifest anxiety, palmar perspiration-index, and stylus maze-learning. *Amer. J. Psychol.*, **72**, 434–438.

McKelvey, R. K. (1956) The relationship between training methods and reward variables in brightness discrimination learning. *J. comp. physiol. Psychol.*, **49**, 485–491.

McMahon, R. R., & Games, P. A. (1964) Adaptation to cyclic food deprivation in the acquisition of an instrumental running response. *Psychol. Rep.*, **14**, 755–758.

McNamara, H. J. (1963) Effects of drive, discrimination training and response disruption on response strength in the absence of primary reinforcement. *Psychol. Rep.*, **12**, 683–690.

McNamara, H. J., & Paige, A. B. (1962) An elaboration of Zimmerman's procedure for demonstrating durable secondary reinforcement. *Psychol. Rep.*, **11**, 801–803.

Meehl, P. E. (1950) On the circularity of the law of effect. *Psychol. Bull.*, **47**, 52–75.

Melvin, K. B. (1964) Escape learning and "vicious-circle" behavior as a function of percentage of reinforcement. *J. comp. physiol. Psychol.*, **58**, 248–251.

Melvin, K. B., & Brown, J. S. (1964) Neutralization of an aversive light stimulus as a function of number of paired presentations with food. *J. comp. physiol Psychol.*, **58**, 350–353.

Mendelson, J., & Chorover, S. L. (1965) Lateral hypothalamic stimulation in satiated rats: T-maze learning for food. *Science,* 149, 559–561.

Merlan, P. (1945) Brentano and Freud. *J. Hist. Ideas,* 6, 375–377.

Meryman, J. J. (1952) Magnitude of startle response as a function of hunger and fear. Unpublished M.A. thesis, State University of Iowa. Cited by Brown (1961).

Messer, K. (1906) Experimentell-psychologische Untersuchungen ueber das Denken. *Arch. Psychol.,* 8, 1–224.

Metzger, R., Cotton, J. W., & Lewis, D. J. (1957) Effect of reinforcement magnitude and of order of presentation of different magnitudes on runway behavior. *J. comp. physiol. Psychol.,* 50, 184–188.

Meyer, D. R. (1951) Food deprivation and discrimination learning by monkeys. *J. exp. Psychol.,* 41, 10–16.

Meyer, D. R. (1951a) The effects of differential reward on discrimination reversal learning by monkeys. *J. exp. Psychol.,* 41, 268–274.

Meyer, D. R. (1953) On the interaction of simultaneous responses. *Psychol. Bull.,* 50, 204–220.

Meyer, D. R., Bahrick, H. P., & Fitts, P. M. (1953) Incentive, anxiety, and the human blink rate. *J. exp. Psychol.,* 45, 183–187.

Meyer, D. R., Cho, C., & Wesemann, A. F. (1960) On problems of conditioned discriminated lever-press avoidance responses. *Psychol. Rev.,* 67, 224–228.

Meyer, D. R., & Noble, M. E. (1958) Summation of manifest anxiety and muscular tension. *J. exp. Psychol.,* 55, 599–602.

Meyer, W. J., & Offenbach, S. I. (1962) Effectiveness of reward and punishment as a function of task complexity. *J. comp. physiol. Psychol.,* 55, 532–534.

Migler, B. (1963) Bar holding during escape conditioning. *J. exp. anal. Behav.,* 6, 65–72.

Miles, R. C. (1956) The relative effectiveness of secondary reinforcers throughout deprivation and habit-strength parameters. *J. comp. physiol. Psychol.,* 49, 126–130.

Miles, R. C. (1958) Learning in kittens with manipulatory, exploratory, and food incentives. *J. comp. physiol. Psychol.,* 51, 39–42.

Miles, R. C. (1958a) The effect of an irrelevant motive on learning. *J. comp. physiol. Psychol.,* 51, 258–261.

Miles, R. C. (1959) Discrimination in the squirrel monkey as a function of deprivation and problem difficulty. *J. exp. Psychol.,* 52, 15–19.

Miles, R. C. (1962) Effect of food deprivation on manipulatory reactions in cat. *J. comp. physiol. Psychol.,* 55, 358–362.

Miles, R. C., & Wickens, D. D. (1953) Effect of a secondary reinforcer on the primary hunger drive. *J. comp. physiol. Psychol.,* 46, 77–79.

Miller, N. E. (1935) A reply to "sign-gestalt or conditioned reflex." *Psychol. Rev.,* 42, 280–292.

Miller, N. E. (1941) An experimental investigation of acquired drives. *Psychol. Bull.,* 38, 534–535.

Miller, N. E. (1948) Studies in fear as an acquirable drive: I. Fear as motivation and fear-reduction as reinforcement in the learning of new responses. *J. exp. Psychol.,* 38, 89–101.

Miller, N. E. (1948a) Theory and experiment relating psychoanalytic displacement to stimulus-response generalization. *J. abnorm. soc. Psychol.,* 43, 155–178.

Miller, N. E. (1951) Learnable drives and rewards. In S. S. Stevens (Ed.), *Handbook of experimental psychology*. New York: Wiley.

Miller, N. E. (1951a) Comments on multiple-process conceptions of learning. *Psychol. Rev.*, **58**, 375–381.

Miller, N. E. (1955) Shortcomings of food consumption as a measure of hunger: results from other behavioral techniques. *Ann. N. Y. Acad. Sci.*, **63**, 141–143.

Miller, N. E. (1956) Effects of drugs on motivation: the value of using a variety of measures. *Ann. N. Y. Acad. Sci.*, **65**, 318–333.

Miller, N. E. (1957) Experiments on motivation. *Science*, **126**, 1271–1278.

Miller, N. E. (1959) Liberalization of basic S-R concepts: extensions to conflict behavior, motivation, and social learning. In S. Koch (Ed.), *Psychology, a study of a science*, Vol. II. New York: McGraw-Hill.

Miller, N. E. (1960) Learning resistance to pain and fear: effects of overlearning, exposure, and rewarded exposure in context. *J. exp. Psychol.*, **60**, 137–145.

Miller, N. E. (1961) Analytical studies of drive and reward. *Amer. Psychologist*, **16**, 739–754.

Miller, N. E. (1963) Some reflections on the law of effect produce a new alternative to drive reduction. In M. R. Jones (Ed.), *Nebraska symposium on motivation*. Lincoln: University of Nebraska Press.

Miller, N. E., Bailey, C., & Stevenson, J. A. F. (1950) Decreased "hunger" but increased food intake resulting from hypothalamic lesions. *Science*, **112**, 256–259.

Miller, N. E., & DeBold, R. C. (1965) Classically conditioned tongue-licking and operant bar pressing recorded simultaneously in the rat. *J. comp. physiol. Psychol.*, **59**, 109–111.

Miller, N. E., & Dollard, J. (1941) *Social learning and imitation*. New Haven: Yale University Press.

Miller, N. E., & Kessen, M. L. (1952) Reward effects of food via stomach fistula compared with those of food via mouth. *J. comp. physiol. Psychol.*, **45**, 555–564.

Miller, N. E., & Lawrence, D. H. (1950) Studies of fear as an acquirable drive: III. Effect of strength of electric shock as a primary drive and number of trials with the primary drive on the strength of fear. Cited by Miller (1951).

Miller, N. E., Roberts, W. W., & Murray, E. J. (1952). Cited by Miller (1957).

Miller, N. E., Sampliner, R. I., & Woodrow, P. (1957) Thirst-reducing effects of water by stomach fistula vs. water by mouth measured by both a consummatory and an instrumental response. *J. comp. physiol. Psychol.*, **50**, 1–5.

Miller, N. E., & Stevenson, S. S. (1936) Agitated behavior of rats during experimental extinction and a curve of spontaneous recovery. *J. comp. Psychol.*, **21**, 205–231.

Misiak, H., & Staudt, V. M. (1954) *Catholics in psychology*. New York: McGraw-Hill.

Mogenson, G. J. (1965) An attempt to establish secondary reinforcement with rewarding brain stimulation. *Psychol. Rep.*, **16**, 163–167.

Mogenson, G. J., Mullin, A. D., & Clark, E. A. (1965) Effects of delayed secondary reinforcement and response requirements on avoidance learning. *Canad. J. Psychol.*, **19**, 61–73.

Moll, R. P. (1959) The effect of drive level on acquisition of the consummatory response. *J. comp. physiol. Psychol.*, **52**, 116–119.

Moll, R. P. (1964) Drive and maturation effects in the development of consummatory behavior. *Psychol. Rep.*, **15**, 295–302.

Moll, R. P. (1964a) Effect of drive and drive stabilization on performance and extinction of bar pressing. *J. comp. physiol. Psychol.*, **57**, 459–461.

Moltz, H. (1957) Latent extinction and the fractional anticipatory response mechanism. *Psychol. Rev.*, **64**, 229–241.

Montague, E. K. (1953) The role of anxiety in serial rote learning. *J. exp. Psychol.*, **45**, 91–96.

Montgomery, K. C. (1951) An experimental study of reactive inhibition and conditioned inhibition. *J. exp. Psychol.*, **41**, 39–51.

Montgomery, K. C. (1951a) "Spontaneous alternation" as a function of time between trials and amount of work. *J. exp. Psychol.*, **42**, 82–93.

Montgomery, K. C. (1951b) The relation between exploratory behavior and spontaneous alternation in the white rat. *J. comp. physiol. Psychol.*, **44**, 582–589.

Montgomery, K. C. (1952) A test of two explanations of spontaneous alternation. *J. comp. physiol. Psychol.*, **45**, 287–293.

Montgomery, K. C. (1952a) Exploratory behavior and its relation to spontaneous alternation in a series of maze exposures. *J. comp. physiol. Psychol.*, **45**, 50–57.

Montgomery, K. C. (1953) The effect of the hunger and thirst drives upon exploratory behavior. *J. comp. physiol. Psychol.*, **46**, 315–319.

Montgomery, K. C. (1953a) The effect of activity deprivation on exploratory behavior. *J. comp. physiol. Psychol.*, **46**, 438–441.

Montgomery, K. C. (1953b) Exploratory behavior as a function of "similarity" of stimulation situations. *J. comp. physiol. Psychol.*, **46**, 129–133.

Montgomery, K. C. (1954) The role of the exploratory drive in learning. *J. comp. physiol. Psychol.*, **47**, 60–64.

Montgomery, K. C. (1955) The relation between fear induced by novel stimulation and exploratory behavior. *J. comp. physiol. Psychol.*, **48**, 254–260.

Montgomery, K. C., & Monkman, J. A. (1955) The relation between fear and exploratory behavior. *J. comp. physiol. Psychol.*, **48**, 132–136.

Montgomery, K. C., & Segall, M. (1955) Discrimination learning based upon the exploratory drive. *J. comp. physiol. Psychol.*, **48**, 225–228.

Montgomery, K. C., & Zimbardo, P. G. (1957) Effect of sensory and behavioral deprivation upon exploratory behavior in the rat. *Percept. mot. Skills, ***7**, 223–229.

Montgomery, M. F. (1931) The role of the salivary glands in the thirst mechanism. *Amer. J. Physiol.*, **96**, 221–227.

Mook, D. G. (1963) Oral and postingestional determinants of the intake of various solutions in rats with esophageal fistulas. *J. comp. physiol. Psychol.*, **56**, 645–659.

Moore, J. W., & Gormezano, I. (1963) Effects of omitted versus delayed UCS on classical eyelid conditioning under partial reinforcement. *J. exp. Psychol.*, **65**, 248–257.

Morgan, C. L. (1894) *Introduction to comparative psychology.*

Morgan, C. T. (1943) *Physiological psychology.* New York: McGraw-Hill.

Morgan, C. T., & Fields, P. E. (1938) The effect of variable preliminary feeding upon the rat's speed of locomotion. *J. comp. Psychol.*, **26**, 331–348.

Morgan, C. T., & Morgan, J. D. (1940) Studies in hunger: I. the effects of insulin upon the rat's rate of eating. *J. genet. Psychol.*, **56**, 137–147.

Morgan, C. T., & Morgan, J. D. (1940a) Studies in hunger: II. the relation of gastric denervation and dietary sugar to the effects of insulin upon food intake in the rat. *J. genet. Psychol.*, **57**, 153–163.

Morgan, J. J. B. (1916) The overcoming of distractions and other resistances. *Arch. Psychol., 35,* 1–84.

Morgan, J. J. B. (1923) The measurement of instincts. *Psychol. Bull., 20,* 94.

Morrison, S. D., Lin, H. J., Eckel, H. E., van Itallie, T. B., & Mayer, J. (1958) Gastric contractions in the rat. *Amer. J. Physiol., 193,* 4–8.

Morrow, J. E., Sachs, L. B., & Belair, R. R. (1965) Further evidence on the dependence between reinforcing and discriminative functions of a stimulus. *Psychon. Sci., 2,* 61–62.

Moskowitz, M. J. (1959) Running-wheel activity in the white rat as a function of combined food and water deprivation. *J. comp. physiol. Psychol., 52,* 621–625.

Moss, F. A. (1924) Study of animal drives. *J. exp. Psychol., 7,* 165–185.

Mowrer, O. H. (1938) Preparatory set (expectancy)—a determinant in motivation and learning. *Psychol. Rev., 45,* 62–91.

Mowrer, O. H. (1939) A stimulus-response analysis of anxiety and its role as a reinforcing agent. *Psychol. Rev., 46,* 553–565.

Mowrer, O. H. (1940) Anxiety reduction and learning. *J. exp. Psychol., 27,* 497–516.

Mowrer, O. H. (1947) On the dual nature of learning: a re-interpretation of "conditioning" and "problem-solving." *Harv. educ. Rev., 17,* 102–148.

Mowrer, O. H. (1950) *Learning theory and personality dynamics.* New York: Ronald.

Mowrer, O. H. (1956) Two-factor learning theory reconsidered, with special reference to secondary reinforcement and the concept of habit. *Psychol. Rev., 63,* 114–128.

Mowrer, O. H. (1960) *Learning theory and behavior.* New York: Wiley.

Mowrer, O. H., & Aiken, E. G. (1954) Contiguity vs. drive-reduction in conditioned fear: temporal variations in conditioned and unconditioned stimulus. *Amer. J. Psychol., 67,* 26–38.

Mowrer, O. H., & Keehn, J. D. (1958) How are inter-trial "avoidance" responses reinforced? *Psychol. Rev., 65,* 209–221.

Mowrer, O. H., & Lamoreaux, R. R. (1942) Avoidance conditioning and signal duration—a study of secondary motivation and reward. *Psychol. Monogr., 54,* (Whole no. 247).

Mowrer, O. H., & Lamoreaux, R. R. (1946) Fear as an intervening variable in avoidance conditioning. *J. comp. Psychol., 39,* 29–50.

Mowrer, O. H., & Solomon, L. N. (1954) Contiguity versus drive-reduction in conditioned fear: the proximity and abruptness of drive-reduction. *Amer. J. Psychol., 67,* 15–25.

Mowrer, O. H., & Suter, J. W. (1950) Further evidence for a two-factor theory of learning. Cited by Mowrer (1950).

Moyer, K. E. (1957) The effects of shock on anxiety-motivated behavior in the rat. *J. genet. Psychol., 91,* 197–203.

Moyer, K. E. (1965) Effect of experience with emotion provoking stimuli on water consumption in the rat. *Psychon. Sci., 2,* 251–252.

Moyer, K. E., & Baenninger, R. (1963) Effect of environmental change and electric shock on water consumption in the rat. *Psychol. Rep., 13,* 179–185.

Moyer, K. E., & Bunnell, B. N. (1962) Effect of stomach distention caused by water on food and water consumption in the rat. *J. comp. physiol. Psychol., 55,* 652–655.

Moyer, K. E., & Korn, J. H. (1964) Effect of UCS intensity on the acquisition and extinction of an avoidance response. *J. exp. Psychol., 67,* 352–359.

Mrosovsky, N. (1964) The performance of dormice and other hibernators on tests of hunger motivation. *Anim. Behav.,* **12,** 454–469.

Muenzinger, K. F., & Fletcher, M. (1936) Motivation in learning: VI. Escape from electric shock compared with hunger-food tension in the visual discrimination habit. *J. comp. Psychol.,* **22,** 79–91.

Muenzinger, K. F., & Fletcher, F. M. (1937) Motivation in learning: VII. The effect of an enforced delay at the point of choice in the visual discrimination habit. *J. comp. Psychol.,* **23,** 383–392.

Munn, N. L. (1950) *Handbook of psychological research on the rat.* Boston: Houghton Mifflin.

Murphy, G. (1947) *Personality: a biosocial approach to origins and structure.* New York: Harper.

Murray, E. J. (1953) The effects of hunger and type of manipulandum on spontaneous instrumental responding. *J. comp. physiol. Psychol.,* **46,** 182–183.

Murray, H. A. (1938) *Explorations in personality.* New York: Oxford University Press.

Myers, A. K. (1959) Avoidance learning as a function of several training conditions and strain differences in rats. *J. comp. physiol. Psychol.,* **52,** 381–386.

Myers, A. K. (1960) Onset vs. termination of stimulus energy as the CS in avoidance conditioning and pseudoconditioning. *J. comp. physiol. Psychol.,* **53,** 72–78.

Myers, A. K. (1962) Effects of CS intensity and quality in avoidance conditioning. *J. comp. physiol. Psychol.,* **55,** 57–61.

Myers, A. K. (1964) Discriminated operant avoidance learning in Wistar and G-4 rats as a function of type of warning stimulus. *J. comp. physiol. Psychol.,* **58,** 453–455.

Myers, A. K., & Miller, N. E. (1954) Failure to find a learned drive based on hunger; evidence for learning motivated by "exploration." *J. comp. physiol. Psychol.,* **47,** 428–436.

Myers, J. L. (1958) Secondary reinforcement: a review of recent experimentation. *Psychol. Bull.,* **55,** 284–303.

Myers, J. L. (1958a) The effects of delay of reinforcement upon an operant discrimination in the pigeon. *J. exp. Psychol.,* **55,** 363–368.

Myers, T. I. (1952) An experimental investigation of the effect of hunger drive upon the brightness discrimination learning of the rat. Unpublished Ph.D. dissertation, State University of Iowa. Cited by Spence et al. (1959).

Nagel, E. (1961) *The structure of science.* New York: Harcourt, Brace & World.

Nakamura, C. Y., & Anderson, N. H. (1962) Avoidance behavior differences within and between strains of rats. *J. comp. physiol. Psychol.,* **55,** 740–747.

Nakamura, C. Y., & Anderson, N. H. (1964) Avoidance conditioning in wheel box and shuttle box. *Psychol. Rep.,* **14,** 327–334.

Nakamura, C. Y., Smith, J. C., & Schwartz, F. W. (1963) Establishment of a lasting discriminative stimulus in rats by competition training. *J. comp. physiol. Psychol.,* **56,** 852–856.

Neiberg, A. (1964) Effect of rearing conditions on exploratory behavior. *Psychol. Rep.,* **15,** 207–210.

Newman, J. R. (1955) Stimulus generalization of an instrumental response under high and low levels of drive. *Amer. Psychologist,* **10,** 459–461.

Newman, J. R., & Grice, G. R. (1965) Stimulus generalization as a function of drive level, and the relation between two measures of response strength. *J. exp. Psychol., 69*, 357–362.

Newton, I. (1687) *Principia. . . .* See Cajori, F. (1934) *Sir Isaac Newton's Mathematical principles of natural philosophy and his system of the world.* Berkeley: University of California Press.

Nicholls, E. E. (1922) A study of the spontaneous activity of the guinea pig. *J. comp. Psychol., 2*, 303–330.

Nissen, H. W. (1930) A study of exploratory behavior in the white rat by means of the obstruction method. *J. genet. Psychol., 37*, 361–376.

Nissen, H. W. (1950) Description of learned responses in discrimination behavior. *Psychol. Rev., 57*, 121–131.

Notterman, J. M. (1951) A study of some relations among aperiodic reinforcement, discrimination training, and secondary reinforcement. *J. exp. Psychol., 41*, 161–169.

Notterman, J. M., & Mintz, D. E. (1965) *Dynamics of response.* New York: Wiley.

Novin, D. (1962) The relation between electrical conductivity of brain tissue and thirst in the rat. *J. comp. physiol. Psychol., 55*, 145–154.

Novin, D., & Miller, N. E. (1962) Failure to condition thirst induced by feeding dry food to hungry rats. *J. comp. physiol. Psychol., 55*, 373–374.

O'Connell, R. H. (1965) Trials with tedium and titillation. *Psychol. Bull., 63*, 170–179.

O'Connor, J. P., Lorr, M., & Stafford, J. W. (1956) Some patterns of manifest anxiety. *J. clin. Psychol., 12*, 160–163.

O'Kelly, L. I. (1940) The validity of defecation as a measure of emotionality in the rat. *J. gen. Psychol., 23*, 75–87.

O'Kelly, L. I., & Beck, R. C. (1960) Water regulation in the rat: III. the artificial control of thirst with stomach loads of water and sodium chloride. *Psychol. Monogr., 74* (Whole No. 500).

O'Kelly, L. I., Hatton, G. I., Tucker, L., & Westall, D. (1965) Water regulation in the rat: heart rate as a function of hydration, anesthesia, and association with reinforcement. *J. comp. physiol. Psychol., 59*, 159–165.

O'Kelly, L. I., & Heyer, A. W., Jr. (1948) Studies in motivation and retention: I. Retention of a simple habit. *J. comp. physiol. Psychol., 41*, 466–478.

O'Kelly, L. I., & Heyer, A. W., Jr. (1951) Studies in motivation and retention: V. The influence of need duration on retention of a maze habit. *Comp. Psychol. Monogr., 20* (Serial No. 106).

Olds, J. (1955) Physiological mechanisms of reward. In M. R. Jones (Ed.), *Nebraska symposium on motivation.* Lincoln: University of Nebraska Press.

Olds, J. (1956) A preliminary mapping of the electrical reinforcing effects in the rat brain. *J. comp. physiol. Psychol., 49*, 281–285.

Olds, J. (1956a) Runway and maze behavior controlled by basomedial forebrain stimulation in the rat. *J. comp. physiol. Psychol., 49*, 507–512.

Olds, J. (1958) Satiation effects in self-stimulation of the brain. *J. comp. physiol. Psychol., 51*, 675–679.

Olds, J. (1958a) Effects of hunger and male sex hormone on self-stimulation of the brain. *J. comp. physiol. Psychol., 51*, 320–324.

Olds, J. (1962) Hypothalamic substrates of reward. *Physiol. Rev., 42*, 554–604.

Olds, J., & Milner, P. (1954) Positive reinforcement produced by electrical stimulation of septal area and other regions of the rat brain. *J. comp. physiol. Psychol., 47*, 419–427.

Omwake, L. (1933) The activity and learning of white rats. *J. comp. Psychol.*, **16**, 275–285.

Osgood, C. E. (1950) Can Tolman's theory of learning handle avoidance training? *Psychol. Rev.*, **57**, 133–137.

Ovsiankina, M. (1928) Die Wiederaufnahme unterbrochener Handlungen. *Psychol. Forsch.*, **11**, 302–379.

Page, H. A. (1955) The facilitation of experimental extinction by response prevention as a function of the acquisition of a new response. *J. comp. physiol. Psychol.*, **48**, 14–16.

Pare, W. P. (1965) Stress and consummatory behavior in the albino rat. *Psychol. Rep.*, **16**, 399–405.

Passey, G. E. (1948) The influence of intensity of unconditioned stimulus upon acquisition of a conditioned response. *J. exp. Psychol.*, **38**, 420–428.

Pavlik, W. B., & Reynolds, W. F. (1963) Effects of deprivation schedule and reward magnitude on acquisition and extinction performance. *J. comp. physiol. Psychol.*, **56**, 452–455.

Pavlov, I. P. (1902) *The work of the digestive glands.* London: Griffin.

Pavlov, I. P. (1927) *Conditioned reflexes.* Trans. by G. V. Anrep. London: Oxford University Press.

Pearl, J. (1963) Intertrial interval and acquisition of a lever press avoidance response. *J. comp. physiol. Psychol.*, **56**, 710–712.

Pearl, J. (1963a) Avoidance learning in rodents: a comparative study. *Psychol. Rep.*, **12**, 139–145.

Pearl, J., & Edwards, R. E. (1962) Delayed avoidance conditioning: warning stimulus (CS) duration. *Psychol. Rep.*, **11**, 375–380.

Pearl, J., & Edwards, R. E. (1963) CS-US interval in the trace conditioning of an avoidance response. *Psychol. Rep.*, **13**, 43–45.

Pearl, R., & Fairchild, T. E. (1921) Studies in the physiology of reproduction in the domestic fowl: XIX. On the influence of free choice of food materials in winter egg production and body weight. *Amer. J. Hygiene*, **1**, 253–277.

Pearson, K. (1911) *The grammar of science,* 3rd ed. London: A. & C. Black.

Peirce, J. T., & Nuttall, R. L. (1961) Self-paced sexual behavior in the female rat. *J. comp. physiol. Psychol.*, **54**, 310–313.

Peirce, J. T., & Nuttall, R. L. (1961a) Duration of sexual contacts in the rat. *J. comp. physiol. Psychol.*, **54**, 585–587.

Penick, S. B., Smith, G. P., Wieneke, K., Jr., & Hinkle, L. E., Jr. (1963) An experimental evaluation of the relationship between hunger and gastric motility. *Amer. J. Physiol.*, **205**, 421–426.

Pereboom, A. C. (1957) An analysis and revision of Hull's Theorem 30. *J. exp. Psychol.*, **53**, 234–238.

Pereboom, A. C., & Crawford, B. M. (1958) Instrumental and competing behavior as a function of trials and reward magnitude. *J. exp. Psychol.*, **56**, 82–85.

Perin, C. T. (1942) Behavioral potentiality as a joint function of the amount of training and the degree of hunger at the time of extinction. *J. exp. Psychol.*, **30**, 93–113.

Perin, C. T. (1943) The effect of delayed reinforcement upon the differentiation of bar responses in white rats. *J. exp. Psychol.*, **32**, 95–109.

Perkins, C. C., Jr. (1947) The relation of secondary reward to gradients of reinforcement. *J. exp. Psychol.*, **37**, 377–392.

Perkins, C. C., Jr. (1955) The stimulus conditions which follow learned responses. *Psychol. Rev., 62,* 341–348.

Pernice, B., & Scagliosi, G. (1895) Ueber die Wirkung der Wasserentziehung auf Thiere. *Arch. path. Anat., 139,* 155–184.

Perrin, F. A. C. (1923) The psychology of motivation. *Psychol. Rev., 30,* 176–191.

Perry, R. B. (1918) Docility and purposiveness. *Psychol. Rev., 25,* 1–21.

Perry, R. B. (1921) A behavioristic view of purpose. *J. Philos., 18,* 85–105.

Peters, R. S. (1956) *Thomas Hobbes.* Harmondsworth, Middlesex: Penguin.

Peters, R. S. (1958) *The concept of motivation.* New York: Humanities Press.

Peterson, J. (1916) Completeness of response as an explanation principle in learning. *Psychol. Rev., 23,* 153–162.

Peterson, J. (1935) Aspects of learning. *Psychol. Rev., 42,* 1–27.

Peterson, L. R. (1956) Variable delayed reinforcement. *J. comp. physiol. Psychol., 49,* 232–234.

Petrinovich, L., & Bolles, R. (1954) Deprivation states and behavioral attributes. *J. comp. physiol. Psychol., 47,* 450–453.

Pfaffmann, C. (1960) The pleasures of sensation. *Psychol. Rev., 67,* 253–268.

Pieper, W. A., & Marx, M. H. (1963) Effects of within-session incentive contrast on instrumental acquisition and performance. *J. exp. Psychol., 65,* 568–571.

Platt, J. R., & Wike, E. L. (1962) Inaccessible food as a secondary reinforcer for deprived and satiated rats. *Psychol. Rep., 11,* 837–840.

Pliskoff, S. S., Hawkins, T. D., & Wright, J. E. (1964) Some observations on the discriminative stimulus hypothesis and rewarding electrical stimulation of the brain. *Psychol. Rec., 14,* 179–184.

Pliskoff, S., & Tolliver, G. (1960) Water-deprivation-produced sign reversal of a conditioned reinforcer based upon dry food. *J. exp. anal. Behav., 3,* 323–329.

Porter, J. J. (1962) Stimulus generalization as a function of UCS intensity in eyelid conditioning. *J. exp. Psychol., 64,* 311–313.

Porter, L. W., & Miller, N. E. (1957) Training under two drives, alternately present, versus training under a single drive. *J. exp. Psychol., 54,* 1–8.

Poschel, B. P. H. (1963) Is centrally-elicited positive reinforcement associated with onset or termination of stimulation? *J. comp. physiol. Psychol., 56,* 604–607.

Postman, L. (1947) The history and present status of the law of effect. *Psychol. Bull., 44,* 489–563.

Postman, L. (1953) Comments on papers by Professors Brown and Harlow. In *Current theory and research in motivation: a symposium.* Lincoln: University of Nebraska Press.

Postman, L. (1962) Rewards and punishments in human learning. In L. Postman (Ed.), *Psychology in the making.* New York: Knopf.

Powell, D. R., Jr., & Perkins, C. C., Jr. (1957) Strength of secondary reinforcement as a determiner of the effects of duration of goal response on learning. *J. exp. Psychol., 53,* 106–112.

Powelson, M. H. (1925) Gastric transplantation. *Science, 62,* 247–248.

Powloski, R. F. (1953) The effects of combining hunger and thirst motives in a discrimination habit. *J. comp. physiol. Psychol., 46,* 434–437.

Pratt, C. C. (1939) *The logic of modern psychology.* New York: Macmillan.

Premack, D. (1959) Toward empirical behavior laws: I. Positive reinforcement. *Psychol. Rev., 66,* 219–234.

Premack, D. (1961) Predicting instrumental performance from the independent rate of the contingent response. *J. exp. Psychol.*, **61**, 163–171.

Premack, D. (1962) Reversibility of the reinforcement relation. *Science,* **136**, 255–257.

Premack, D. (1965) Reinforcement theory. In D. Levine (Ed.), *Nebraska symposium on motivation.* Lincoln: University of Nebraska Press.

Premack, D., & Collier, G. (1962) Joint effects of stimulus deprivation and intersession interval: analysis of nonreinforcement variables affecting response probability. *Psychol. Monogr.*, **76** (Whole No. 524).

Premack, D., & Hillix, W. A. (1962) Evidence for shift effects in the consummatory response. *J. exp. Psychol.*, **63**, 284–288.

Pribam, K. H. (1962) Interrelations of psychology and the neurological disciplines. In S. Koch (Ed.), *Psychology: a study of a science,* Vol. IV. New York: McGraw-Hill.

Prokasy, W. F., Jr., & Whaley, F. L. (1962) Manifest anxiety scale score and the ready signal in classical conditioning. *J. exp. Psychol.*, **63**, 119–123.

Pubols, B. H., Jr. (1958) Delay of reinforcement, response perseveration, and discrimination reversal. *J. exp. Psychol.*, **56**, 32–40.

Pubols, B. H., Jr. (1960) Incentive magnitude, learning, and performance in animals. *Psychol. Bull.*, **57**, 89–115.

Pubols, B. H., Jr. (1961) The acquisition and reversal of a position habit as a function of incentive magnitude. *J. comp. physiol. Psychol.*, **54**, 94–97.

Pubols, B. H., Jr. (1962) Constant versus variable delay of reinforcement. *J. comp. physiol. Psychol.*, **55**, 52–56.

Ramond, C. K. (1953) Anxiety and task as determiners of verbal performance. *J. exp. Psychol.*, **46**, 120–124.

Ramond, C. K. (1954) Performance in selective learning as a function of hunger. *J. exp. Psychol.*, **48**, 265–270.

Ramond, C. K. (1954a) Performance in instrumental learning as a joint function of delay of reinforcement and time of deprivation. *J. exp. Psychol.*, **47**, 248–250.

Ramond, C. K., Carlton, P. L., & McAllister, W. R. (1955) Feeding method, body weight, and performance in instrumental learning. *J. comp. physiol. Psychol.*, **48**, 294–298.

Rampone, A. J., & Shirasu, M. E. (1964) Temperature changes in the rat in response to feeding. *Science,* **144**, 317–319.

Ranson, S. W. (1939) Somnolence caused by hypothalamic lesions in the monkey. *Arch. neurol. Psychiat.*, **41**, 1–23.

Rapaport, D. (1960) On the psychoanalytic theory of motivation. In M. R. Jones (Ed.), *Nebraska symposium on motivation.* Lincoln: University of Nebraska Press.

Rapp, H. M. (1963) Is sexual activity reinforcing for the female rat? Unpublished M.A. thesis, Hollins College.

Rasmussen, E. W. (1959) The effect of water deprivation on the skin resistance of the rat. *J. comp. physiol. Psychol.*, **52**, 626–628.

Ratner, S. C. (1956) Effect of extinction of dipper-approaching on subsequent extinction of bar-pressing and dipper-approaching. *J. comp. physiol. Psychol.*, **49**, 576–581.

Ratner, S. C. (1956a) Reinforcing and discriminative properties of the click in a Skinner box. *Psychol. Rep.*, **2**, 332.

Raup, R. B. (1925) *Complacency, the foundation of human behavior.* New York: Macmillan.

Ray, O. S., & Stein, L. (1959) Generalization of conditioned suppression. *J. exp. anal. Behav., 2,* 357–361.

Razran, G. (1955) A note on second-order conditioning—and secondary reinforcement. *Psychol. Rev., 62,* 327–332.

Reed, J. D. (1947) Spontaneous activity of animals. *Psychol. Bull., 44,* 393–412.

Rehula, R. (1957) Cited by Powell and Perkins (1957).

Reid, L. S., & Campbell, J. F. (1960) The aversive effect of food-associated secondary reinforcement upon extinction during thirst. *Amer. Psychologist, 15,* 474.

Reid, L. S., & Finger, F. W. (1955) The rat's adjustment to 23-hour food deprivation cycles. *J. comp. physiol. Psychol., 48,* 110–113.

Reid, L. S., & Finger, F. W. (1957) The effect of activity restriction upon adjustment to cyclic food deprivation. *J. comp. physiol. Psychol., 50,* 491–494.

Reid, L. S., & Slivinske, A. J. (1954) A test for generalized secondary reinforcement during extinction under a different drive. *J. comp. physiol. Psychol., 47,* 306–310.

Reid, T. (1785) *Essays on the intellectual powers of man.*

Reid, T. (1788) *Essays on the active powers of the human mind.*

Renner, K. E. (1963) Influence of deprivation and availability of goal box cues on the temporal gradient of reinforcement. *J. comp. physiol. Psychol., 56,* 101–104.

Renner, K. E. (1964) Delay of reinforcement: a historical review. *Psychol. Bull., 61,* 341–361.

Rescorla, R. A., & LoLordo, V. M. (1965) Inhibition of avoidance behavior. *J. comp. physiol. Psychol., 59,* 406–412.

Rethlingshafer, D., Eschenbach, A., & Stone, J. T. (1951) Combined drives in learning. *J. exp. Psychol., 41,* 226–231.

Revusky, S. H. (1963) Effects of hunger and VI value on VI pacing. *J. exp. anal. Behav., 6,* 163–169.

Rexroad, C. N. (1933) Goal-objects, purposes, and behavior. *Psychol. Rev., 40,* 271–281.

Reynierse, J. H., Weisman, R. G., & Denny, M. R. (1963) Shock compartment confinement during the intertrial interval in avoidance learning. *Psychol. Rec., 13,* 403–406.

Reynierse, J. H., Zerbolio, D. J., & Denny, M. R. (1964) Avoidance decrement: replication and further analysis. *Psychon. Sci., 1,* 401–402.

Reynolds, B. (1949) The acquisition of a black-white discrimination habit under two levels of reinforcement. *J. exp. Psychol., 39,* 760–769.

Reynolds, B. (1949a) The relationship between the strength of a habit and the degree of drive present during acquisition. *J. exp. Psychol., 39,* 296–306.

Reynolds, B. (1950) Resistance to extinction as a function of the amount of reinforcement present during acquisition. *J. exp. Psychol., 40,* 46–52.

Reynolds, B. (1950a) Acquisition of a simple spatial discrimination as a function of the amount of reinforcement. *J. exp. Psychol., 40,* 152–160.

Reynolds, B., Marx, M. H., & Henderson, R. L. (1952) Resistance to extinction as a function of drive-reward interaction. *J. comp. physiol. Psychol., 45,* 36–42.

Reynolds, G. S. (1964) Temporally spaced responding by pigeons: development and effects of deprivation and extinction. *J. exp. anal. Behav., 7,* 415–421.

Reynolds, W. F., & Anderson, J. E. (1961) Choice behavior in a T-maze as a function of deprivation period and magnitude of reward. *Psychol. Rep.,* **8**, 131–134.

Reynolds, W. F., & Pavlik, W. B. (1960) Running speed as a function of deprivation period and reward magnitude. *J. comp. physiol. Psychol.,* **53**, 615–618.

Reynolds, W. F., Pavlik, W. B., Schwartz, M. M., & Besch, N. F. (1963) Maze learning by secondary reinforcement without discrimination training. *Psychol. Rep.,* **12**, 775–781.

Richards, T. W. (1936) The importance of hunger in the bodily activity of the neonate. *Psychol. Bull.,* **33**, 817–835.

Richards, W. J., & Leslie, G. R. (1962) Food and water deprivation as influences on exploration. *J. comp. physiol. Psychol.,* **55**, 834–837.

Richter, C. P. (1922) A behavioristic study of the activity of the rat. *Comp. Psychol. Monogr.,* **1** (Serial No. 2).

Richter, C. P. (1927) Animal behavior and internal drives. *Quart. Rev. Biol.,* **2**, 307–343.

Richter, C. P. (1936) Increased salt appetite in adrenalectomized rats. *Amer. J. Physiol.,* **115**, 155–161.

Richter, C. P. (1939) Salt taste thresholds of normal and adrenalectomized rats. *Endocrinology,* **24**, 367–371.

Richter, C. P. (1942–1943) Total self-regulatory functions in animals and human beings. *Harvey Lectures,* **38**, 63–103.

Richter, C. P., & Brailey, M. E. (1929) Water intake and its relation to the surface area of the body. *Proc. Nat. Acad. Sci.,* **15**, 570–578.

Richter, C. P., Holt, L. E., & Barelare, B. (1938) Nutritional requirements for normal growth and reproduction in rats studied by the self-selection method. *Amer. J. Physiol.,* **122**, 734–744.

Rignano, E. (1923) *The psychology of reasoning.* New York: Harcourt.

Rixon, R. H., & Stevenson, J. A. F. (1957) Factors influencing survival of rats in fasting: metabolic rate and body weight loss. *Amer. J. Physiol.,* **188**, 332–336.

Roberts, W. H. (1930) The effect of delayed feeding of white rats in a problem cage. *J. genet. Psychol.,* **37**, 35–58.

Roberts, W. W. (1958) Rapid escape learning without avoidance learning motivated by hypothalamic stimulation in cats. *J. comp. physiol. Psychol.,* **51**, 391–399.

Roberts, W. W. (1958a) Both rewarding and punishing effects from stimulation of posterior hypothalamus of cats with same electrode at same intensity. *J. comp. physiol. Psychol.,* **51**, 400–407.

Robertson, J. M. (1930) *A history of free thought in the 19th century.* New York: Putnam.

Robinson, E. A., & Adolph, E. F. (1943) Patterns of normal water drinking in dogs. *Amer. J. Physiol.,* **139**, 39–44.

Rogers, F. T., & Martin, C. L. (1926) X-ray observations of hunger contractions in man. *Amer. J. Physiol.,* **76**, 349–353.

Rohrer, J. H. (1949) A motivational state resulting from non-reward. *J. comp. physiol. Psychol.,* **42**, 476–485.

Romanes, G. J. (1882) *Animal intelligence.*

Root, W. S., & Bard, P. (1937) Erection in the cat following removal of lumbosacral segments. *Amer. J. Physiol.,* **119**, 392–393.

Rosen, A. J., & Ison, J. R. (1965) Runway performance following changes in sucrose rewards. *Psychon. Sci.,* **2**, 335–336.

Rosenbaum, G. (1951) Temporal gradients of response strength with two levels of motivation. *J. exp. Psychol., 41,* 261–267.

Rosenzweig, M. R. (1962) The mechanisms of hunger and thirst. In L. Postman (Ed.), *Psychology in the making.* New York: Knopf.

Ross, L. E. (1959) The decremental effects of partial reinforcement during acquisition of the conditioned eyelid response. *J. exp. Psychol., 57,* 74–82.

Ross, L. E., & Hartman, T. (1965) Human eyelid conditioning: the recent experimental literature. *Genet. Psychol. Monogr., 71,* 93–136.

Ross, L. E., & Hunter, J. J. (1959) Habit strength parameters in eyelid conditioning as a function of UCS intensity. *Psychol. Rec., 9,* 103–107.

Ross, L. E., & Spence, K. W. (1960) Eyelid conditioning performance under partial reinforcement as a function of UCS intensity. *J. exp. Psychol., 59,* 379–382.

Ross, S., Goldstein, I., & Kappel, S. (1962) Perceptual factors in eating behavior in chicks. *J. comp. physiol. Psychol., 55,* 240–241.

Rossi, A. M. (1959) An evaluation of the manifest anxiety scale by the use of electromyography. *J. exp. Psychol., 58,* 64–69.

Rowell, C. H. F. (1961) Displacement grooming in the chaffinch. *Anim. Behav., 9,* 38–63.

Rozin, P. (1965) Specific hunger for thiamine: recovery from deficiency and thiamine preference. *J. comp. physiol. Psychol., 59,* 98–101.

Rozin, P., & Mayer, J. (1961) Regulation of food intake in the goldfish. *Amer. J. Physiol., 201,* 968–974.

Ruch, F. L. (1932) The effect of inanition upon maze learning in the white rat. *J. comp. Psychol., 14,* 321–329.

Runquist, W. N., & Ross, L. E. (1959) The relation between physiological measures of emotionality and performance in eyelid conditioning. *J. exp. Psychol., 57,* 329–332.

Runquist, W. N., & Spence, K. W. (1959) Performance in eyelid conditioning as a function of UCS duration. *J. exp. Psychol., 57,* 249–252.

Runquist, W. N., & Spence, K. W. (1959a) Performance in eyelid conditioning related to changes in muscular tension and physiological measures of emotionality. *J. exp. Psychol., 58,* 417–422.

Runquist, W. N., Spence, K. W., & Stubbs, D. W. (1958) Differential conditioning and intensity of the UCS. *J. exp. Psychol., 55,* 51–55.

Russell, E. S. (1916) *Form and function.* London: John Murray.

Rust, L. D. (1962) Changes in bar pressing performance and heart rate in sleep-deprived rats. *J. comp. physiol. Psychol., 55,* 621–625.

Sackett, R. S. (1939) The effect of strength of drive at the time of extinction upon resistance to extinction in rats. *J. comp. Psychol., 27,* 411–431.

Saltz, E., & Hoehn, A. J. (1957) A test of the Taylor-Spence theory of anxiety. *J. abnorm. soc. Psychol., 54,* 114–117.

Saltzman, I. J. (1949) Maze learning in the absence of primary reinforcement: a study of secondary reinforcement. *J. comp. physiol. Psychol., 42,* 161–173.

Saltzman, I. J. (1950) Generalization of secondary reinforcement. *J. exp. Psychol., 40,* 189–193.

Saltzman, I., & Koch, S. (1948) The effect of low intensities of hunger on the behavior mediated by a habit of maximum strength. *J. exp. Psychol., 38,* 347–370.

Santos, J. R. (1960) The influence of amount and kind of training on the acquisition and extinction of escape and avoidance responses. *J. comp. physiol. Psychol.*, **53**, 284–289.

Scarborough, B. B., & Goodson, F. E. (1957) Properties of stimuli associated with strong and weak hunger drive in the rat. *J. genet. Psychol.*, **91**, 257–261.

Schachter, S., & Singer, J. E. (1962) Cognitive, social, and physiological determinants of emotional state. *Psychol. Rev.*, **69**, 379–399.

Schaeffer, R. W., & Huff, R. (1965) Lick rates in cats. *Psychon. Sci.*, **3**, 377–378.

Schaeffer, R. W., & Premack, D. (1961) Licking rates in infant albino rats. *Science*, **134**, 1980–1981.

Schlosberg, H. (1934) Conditioned responses in the white rat. *J. genet. Psychol.*, **45**, 303–335.

Schlosberg, H. (1936) Conditioned responses in the white rat: II. Conditioned responses based upon shock to the foreleg. *J. genet. Psychol.*, **49**, 107–138.

Schlosberg, H. (1937) The relationship between success and the laws of conditioning. *Psychol. Rev.*, **44**, 379–394.

Schlosberg, H., & Pratt, C. H. (1956) The secondary reward value of inaccessible food for hungry and satiated rats. *J. comp. physiol. Psychol.*, **49**, 149–152.

Schmidt-Nielsen, B., Schmidt-Nielsen, K., Brokaw, A., & Schneiderman, H. 1948) Water conservation in desert rodents. *J. cell. comp. Physiol.*, **32**, 331–360.

Schmidt-Nielsen, B., Schmidt-Nielsen, K., Houpt, T. R., & Jarnum, S. A. (1956) Water balance of the camel. *Amer. J. Physiol.*, **185**, 185–194.

Schneirla, T. C. (1959) An evolutionary and developmental theory of biphasic processes underlying approach and withdrawal. In M. R. Jones (Ed.), *Nebraska symposium on motivation*. Lincoln: University of Nebraska Press.

Schnore, M. M. (1959) Individual patterns of physiological activity as a function of task differences and arousal. *J. exp. Psychol.*, **58**, 117–128.

Schoenfeld, W. N. (1950) An experimental approach to anxiety, escape, and avoidance behavior. In P. H. Hoch and J. Zubin (Eds.), *Anxiety*. New York: Grune & Stratton.

Schoenfeld, W. N., Antonitis, J. J., & Bersh, P. J. (1950) A preliminary study of training conditions necessary for secondary reinforcement. *J. exp. Psychol.*, **40**, 40–45.

Schoenfeld, W. N., Antonitis, J. H., & Bersh, P. J. (1950a) Unconditioned response rate of the white rat in a bar pressing apparatus. *J. comp. physiol. Psychol.*, **43**, 41–48.

Schrier, A. M. (1956) Amount of incentive and performance on a black-white discrimination problem. *J. comp. physiol. Psychol.*, **49**, 123–125.

Schrier, A. M. (1958) Comparison of two methods of investigating the effect of amount of reward on performance. *J. comp. physiol. Psychol.*, **51**, 725–731.

Schrier, A. M. (1961) Effects of CS-US interval on avoidance conditioning of cats. *J. genet. Psychol.*, **98**, 203–210.

Schrier, A. M. (1961a) Response latency of monkeys as a function of amount of reward. *Psychol. Rep.*, **8**, 283–289.

Schrier, A. M. (1962) Response latency of monkeys as a function of reward amount and trials within test days. *Psychol. Rep.*, **10**, 439–444.

Schwartz, M. (1956) Instrumental and consummatory measures of sexual capacity in the male rat. *J. comp. physiol. Psychol.*, **49**, 328–333.

Schwartz, M. (1958) Conditioned-stimulus variables in avoidance learning. *J. exp. Psychol.*, **55**, 347–351.

Schwartz, M., & Goodson, J. E. (1958) Direction and rate of conditioned stimulus change in avoidance performance. *Psychol. Rep.,* **4,** 499–502.

Schwartzbaum, J. S., & Ward, H. P. (1958) An osmotic factor in the regulation of food intake in the rat. *J. comp. physiol. Psychol.,* **51,** 555–560.

Scott, E. M., & Verney, E. L. (1949) Self-selection of diet: VI. The nature of appetites for B vitamins. *J. Nutrition,* **34,** 471–480.

Scott, W. W., Scott, C. C., & Luckhardt, A. B. (1938) Observations on the blood-sugar level before, during and after hunger periods in humans. *Amer. J. Physiol.,* **123,** 243–247.

Seeman, W., & Williams, H. (1952) An experimental note on a Hull-Leeper difference. *J. exp. Psychol.,* **44,** 40–43.

Segal, E. F. (1959) Confirmation of a positive relation between deprivation and number of responses emitted for light reinforcement. *J. exp. anal. Behav.,* **2,** 165–169.

Segal, E. F. (1965) The development of water drinking on a dry-food free-reinforcement schedule. *Psychon. Sci.,* **2,** 29–30.

Segal, E. F., & Deadwyler, S. A. (1964) Water drinking patterns under several dry food reinforcement schedules. *Psychon. Sci.,* **1,** 271–272.

Segal, E. F., & Deadwyler, S. A. (1965) Determinants of polydipsia in rats: II. DRL extinction. *Psychon. Sci.,* **2,** 203–204.

Segal, E. F., & Holloway, S. M. (1963) Timing behavior in rats with water drinking as a mediator. *Science,* **140,** 888–889.

Segal, E. F., & Oden, D. L. (1965) Determinants of polydipsia in rats: A reply to Stein. I. Emptying the water bottle. *Psychon. Sci.,* **2,** 201–202.

Segal, E. F., Oden, D. L., & Deadwyler, S. A. (1965) Determinants of polydipsia: III. Withholding food on a free-reinforcement schedule. *Psychon. Sci.,* **2,** 205–206.

Seward, G. (1942) The "validation" of drives. *Psychol. Rev.,* **49,** 88–95.

Seward, J. P. (1942) Note on the externalization of drive. *Psychol. Rev.,* **49,** 197–199.

Seward, J. P. (1943) Reinforcement in terms of association. *Psychol. Rev.,* **50,** 187–202.

Seward, J. P. (1947) A theoretical derivation of latent learning. *Psychol. Rev.,* **54,** 83–98.

Seward, J. P. (1948) The sign of a symbol: a reply to Professor Allport. *Psychol. Rev.,* **55,** 277–296.

Seward, J. P. (1950) Secondary reinforcement as tertiary motivation: a revision of Hull's revision. *Psychol. Rev.,* **57,** 362–374.

Seward, J. P. (1951) Experimental evidence for the motivating function of reward. *Psychol. Bull.,* **48,** 130–149.

Seward, J. P. (1952) Introduction to a theory of motivation in learning. *Psychol. Rev.,* **59,** 405–413.

Seward, J. P. (1953) How are motives learned? *Psychol. Rev.,* **60,** 99–110.

Seward, J. P. (1956) Drive, incentive, and reinforcement. *Psychol. Rev.,* **63,** 195–203.

Seward, J. P., & Handlon, J. H. (1952) The effect of satiation on the use of habit. *J. genet. Psychol.,* **81,** 259–272.

Seward, J. P., & Levy, N. (1953) Choice-point behavior as a function of secondary reinforcement with relevant drives satiated. *J. comp. physiol. Psychol.,* **46,** 334–338.

Seward, J. P., Levy, N., & Handlon, J. H. (1953) Choice behavior in satiated rats as a function of drive during training. *J. genet. Psychol.,* **83,** 3–18.

Seward, J. P. & Pereboom, A. C. (1955) A note on the learning of "spontaneous" activity. *Amer. J. Psychol.,* **68,** 139–142.

Seward, J. P., & Pereboom, A. C. (1955a) Does the activity wheel measure goal striving? *J. comp. physiol. Psychol.,* **48,** 272–277.

Seward, J. P., & Procter, D. M. (1960) Performance as a function of drive, reward, and habit strength. *Amer. J. Psychol.,* **73,** 448–453.

Seward, J. P., & Raskin, D. C. (1960) The role of fear in aversive behavior. *J. comp. physiol. Psychol.,* **53,** 328–335.

Seward, J. P., & Seward, G. (1937) Internal and external determinants of drives. *Psychol. Rev.,* **44,** 349–363.

Seward, J. P., & Seward, G. H. (1940) Studies on the reproductive activities of the guinea pig: I. Factors in maternal behavior. *J. comp. Psychol.,* **29,** 1–24.

Seward, J. P., Shea, R. A., & Davenport, R. H. (1960) Further evidence for the interaction of drive and reward. *Amer. J. Psychol.,* **73,** 370–379.

Seward, J. P., Shea, R. A., & Elkind, D. (1958) Evidence for the interaction of drive and reward. *Amer. J. Psychol.,* **71,** 404–407.

Sgro, J. A., & Weinstock, S. (1963) Effects of delay on subsequent running under immediate reinforcement. *J. exp. Psychol.,* **66,** 260–263.

Shapiro, M. M. (1962) Temporal relationship between salivation and lever pressing with differential reinforcement of low rates. *J. comp. physiol. Psychol.,* **55,** 567–571.

Share, I., Martyniuk, E., Grossman, M. I. (1952) Effect of prolonged intragastric feeding on oral food intake in dogs. *Amer. J. Physiol.,* **169,** 229–235.

Sheffield, F. D. (1948) Avoidance training and the contiguity principle. *J. comp. physiol. Psychol.,* **41,** 165–177.

Sheffield, F. D. (1951) The contiguity principle in learning theory. *Psychol. Rev.,* **58,** 362–367.

Sheffield, F. D., & Campbell, B. A. (1954) The role of experience in the "spontaneous" activity of hungry rats. *J. comp. physiol. Psychol.,* **47,** 97–100.

Sheffield, F. D., & Roby, T. B. (1950) Reward value of a non-nutritive sweet taste. *J. comp. physiol. Psychol.,* **43,** 471–481.

Sheffield, F. D., Roby, T. B., & Campbell, B. A. (1954) Drive reduction versus consummatory behavior as determinants of reinforcement. *J. comp. physiol. Psychol.,* **47,** 349–355.

Sheffield, F. D., & Temmer, H. W. (1950) Relative resistance to extinction of escape training and avoidance training. *J. exp. Psychol.,* **40,** 287–298.

Sheffield, F. D., Wulff, J. J., & Backer, R. (1951) Reward value of copulation without sex drive reduction. *J. comp. physiol. Psychol.,* **44,** 3–8.

Sherrington, C. S. (1906) *The integrative action of the nervous system.* New Haven: Yale University Press.

Shirley, M. (1928) Studies in activity: II. Activity rhythms; age and activity; activity after rest. *J. comp. Psychol.,* **8,** 159–186.

Shirley, M. (1929) Spontaneous activity. *Psychol. Bull.,* **26,** 341–365.

Sidman, M. (1953) Two temporal parameters of the maintenance of avoidance behavior by the white rat. *J. comp. physiol. Psychol.,* **46,** 253–261.

Sidman, M. (1953a) Avoidance conditioning with brief shock and no exteroceptive warning signal. *Science,* **118,** 157–158.

Sidman, M. (1954) Delayed-punishment effects mediated by competing behavior. *J. comp. physiol. Psychol.,* **47,** 145–147.

Sidman, M. (1954a) The temporal distribution of avoidance responses. *J. comp. physiol. Psychol.,* **47,** 399–402.

Sidman, M. (1955) Some properties of the warning stimulus in avoidance behavior. *J. comp. physiol. Psychol.*, **48**, 444–450.

Sidman, M. (1962) Reduction of shock frequency as reinforcement for avoidance behavior. *J. exp. anal. Behav.*, **5**, 247–257.

Sidman, M., & Boren, J. J. (1957) A comparison of two types of warning stimulus in an avoidance situation. *J. comp. physiol. Psychol.*, **50**, 282–287.

Siegel, P. S. (1943) Drive shift, a conceptual and experimental analysis. *J. comp. Psychol.*, **35**, 139–148.

Siegel, P. S. (1946) Alien drive, habit strength, and resistance to extinction. *J. comp. Psychol.*, **39**, 307–317.

Siegel, P. S. (1946a) Activity level as a function of physically enforced inaction. *J. Psychol.*, **21**, 285–291.

Siegel, P. S. (1947) The relationship between voluntary water intake, body weight loss, and number of hours of water privation in the rat. *J. comp. physiol. Psychol.*, **40**, 231–238.

Siegel, P. S. (1957) The completion compulsion in human eating. *Psychol. Rep.*, **3**, 15–16.

Siegel, P. S. (1961) Food intake in the rat in relation to the dark-light cycle. *J. comp. physiol. Psychol.*, **54**, 294–301.

Siegel, P. S., & Brantley, J. J. (1951) The relationship of emotionality to the consummatory response of eating. *J. exp. Psychol.*, **42**, 304–306.

Siegel, P. S., & Correia, M. J. (1963) Speed of resumption of eating following distraction in relation to number of hours food-deprivation. *Psychol. Rec.*, **13**, 39–44.

Siegel, P. S., & Dorman, L. B. (1954) Food intake of the rat following the intragastric administration of "hungry" and "satiated" blood. *J. comp. physiol. Psychol.*, **47**, 227–229.

Siegel, P. S., & MacDonnell, M. F. (1954) A repetition of the Calvin-Bicknell-Sperling study of conditioned drive. *J. comp. physiol. Psychol.*, **47**, 250–252.

Siegel, P. S., & Siegel, H. S. (1949) The effect of emotionality on the water intake of the rat. *J. comp. physiol. Psychol.*, **42**, 12–16.

Siegel, P. S., & Sparks, D. L. (1961) Irrelevant aversive stimulation as an activator of an appetitional response: a replication. *Psychol. Rep.*, **9**, 700.

Siegel, P. S., & Steinberg, M. (1949) Activity level as a function of hunger. *J. comp. physiol. Psychol.*, **42**, 413–416.

Siegel, P. S., & Stuckey, H. L. (1947) The diurnal course of water and food intake in the normal mature rat. *J. comp. physiol. Psychol.*, **40**, 365–370.

Siegel, P. S., & Stuckey, H. L. (1947a) An examination of some factors relating to voluntary water intake of the rat. *J. comp. physiol. Psychol.*, **40**, 271–274.

Siegel, P. S., & Talantis, B. S. (1950) Water intake as a function of privation interval when food is withheld. *J. comp. physiol. Psychol.*, **43**, 62–65.

Siegel, P. S., & Taub, D. V. (1952) A "hunger hormone?" *J. comp. physiol. Psychol.*, **45**, 250–253.

Silverman, R. E., & Blitz, B. (1956) Learning and two kinds of anxiety. *J. abnorm. soc. Psychol.*, **52**, 301–303.

Simmons, R. (1924) The relative effectiveness of certain incentives in animal learning. *Comp. Psychol. Monogr.*, **2** (Serial No. 7).

Simon, G. W., Wickens, D. D., Brown, U., & Pennock, L. (1951) Effect of the secondary reinforcing agent on the primary thirst drive. *J. comp. physiol. Psychol.*, **44**, 67–70.

Singer, C. (1959) *A short history of scientific ideas to 1900.* Oxford: Oxford University Press.

Singh, S. D. (1959) Conditioned emotional response in the rat: I. Constitutional and situational determinants. *J. comp. physiol. Psychol.*, **52**, 574–578.

Skinner, B. F. (1936) Conditioning and extinction and their relation to drive. *J. gen. Psychol.*, **14**, 296–317.

Skinner, B. F. (1936a) Thirst as an arbitrary drive. *J. gen. Psychol.*, **15**, 205–210.

Skinner, B. F. (1936b) The reinforcing effect of a differentiating stimulus. *J. gen. Psychol.*, **14**, 263–277.

Skinner, B. F. (1938) *The behavior of organisms.* New York: Appleton-Century-Crofts.

Skinner, B. F. (1940) A method of maintaining an arbitrary degree of hunger. *J. comp. physiol. Psychol.*, **30**, 139–145.

Skinner, B. F. (1948) "Superstition" in the pigeon. *J. exp. Psychol.*, **38**, 168–172.

Skinner, B. F. (1948a) *Walden Two.* New York: Macmillan.

Skinner, B. F. (1950) Are theories of learning necessary? *Psychol. Rev.*, **57**, 193–216.

Skinner, B. F. (1953) *Science and human behavior.* New York: Macmillan.

Skinner, B. F. (1957) *Verbal behavior.* New York: Appleton-Century-Crofts.

Skinner, B. F. (1958) Reinforcement today. *Amer. Psychologist,* **13**, 94–99.

Skinner, B. F. (1959) *Cumulative record.* New York: Appleton-Century-Crofts.

Slonaker, J. R. (1924) The effects of pubescence, oestration, and menopause on the voluntary activity of the albino rat. *Amer. J. Physiol.*, **68**, 294–315.

Smith, F. V. (1960) *The explanation of human behavior,* 2nd ed. London: Constable.

Smith, M., & Duffy, M. (1957) Some physiological factors that regulate eating behavior. *J. comp. physiol. Psychol.*, **50**, 601–609.

Smith, M., & Duffy, M. (1957a) Consumption of sucrose and saccharine by hungry and satiated rats. *J. comp. physiol. Psychol.*, **50**, 65–69.

Smith, M., & Kinney, G. C. (1956) Sugar as a reward for hungry and non-hungry rats. *J. exp. Psychol.*, **51**, 348–352.

Smith, M., Pool, R., & Weinberg, H. (1958) Evidence for a learning theory of specific hunger. *J. comp. physiol. Psychol.*, **51**, 758–763.

Smith, M., Pool, R., & Weinberg, H. (1959) The effect of peripherally induced shifts in water balance on eating. *J. comp. physiol. Psychol.*, **52**, 289–293.

Smith, M., Pool, R., & Weinberg, H. (1962) The role of bulk in the control of eating. *J. comp. physiol. Psychol.*, **55**, 115–120.

Smith, M. F. (1939) The establishment and extinction of the token-reward habit in the cat. *J. gen. Psychol.*, **20**, 475–486.

Smith, M. F., & Smith, K. U. (1939) Thirst-motivated activity and its extinction in the cat. *J. gen. Psychol.*, **21**, 89–98.

Smith, M. P., & Buchanan, G. (1954) Acquisition of secondary reward by cues associated with shock reduction. *J. exp. Psychol.*, **48**, 123–127.

Smith, M. P., & Capretta, P. J. (1956) Effects of drive level and experience on the reward value of saccharine solutions. *J. comp. physiol. Psychol.*, **49**, 553–557.

Smith, O. A., Jr., McFarland, W. L., & Taylor, E. (1961) Performance in a shock-avoidance conditioning situation interpreted as pseudoconditioning. *J. comp. physiol. Psychol.*, **54**, 154–157.

Smith, S., & Guthrie, E. R. (1921) *General psychology in terms of behavior.* New York: Appleton.

Snyder, H. L., & Hulse, S. H. (1961) Effect of volume of reinforcement and number of consummatory responses on licking and running behavior. *J. exp. Psychol.*, **61,** 474–479.

Solomon, R. L. (1956) The externalization of hunger and frustration drive. *J. comp. physiol. Psychol.*, **49,** 145–148.

Solomon, R. L. (1964) Punishment. *Amer. Psychologist,* **19,** 239–253.

Solomon, R. L., & Brush, E. S. (1956) Experimentally derived conceptions of anxiety and aversion. In M. R. Jones (Ed.), *Nebraska symposium on motivation.* Lincoln: University of Nebraska Press.

Solomon, R. L., Kamin, L. J., & Wynne, L. C. (1953) Traumatic avoidance learning: the outcomes of several extinction procedures with dogs. *J. abnorm. soc. Psychol.*, **48,** 291–302.

Solomon, R. L., & Wynne, L. C. (1950) Avoidance conditioning in normal dogs and in dogs deprived of normal autonomic functioning. *Amer. Psychologist,* **5,** 264.

Solomon, R. L., & Wynne, L. C. (1953) Traumatic avoidance learning: acquisition in normal dogs. *Psychol. Monogr.*, **67** (Whole No. 354).

Solomon, R. L., & Wynne, L. C. (1954) Traumatic avoidance learning: the principles of anxiety conservation and partial irreversibility. *Psychol. Rev.*, **61,** 353–385.

Soulairac, A. (1952) La signification physiologique de la période réfractaire dans le comportement sexual du rat male. *J. Physiol.*, **44,** 99–113.

Spear, N. E. (1962) Comparison of the reinforcing effect of brain stimulation on Skinner box, runway, and maze performance. *J. comp. physiol. Psychol.*, **55,** 679–684.

Spear, N. E. (1964) Choice between magnitude and percentage of reinforcement. *J. exp. Psychol.*, **68,** 44–52.

Spear, N. E. (1965) Replication report: Absence of a successive contrast effect on instrumental running behavior after a shift in sucrose concentration. *Psychol. Rep.*, **16,** 393–394.

Spearman, C. E. (1937) *Psychology down the ages.* London: Macmillan.

Spence, K. W. (1944) The nature of theory construction in contemporary psychology. *Psychol. Rev.*, **51,** 47–68.

Spence, K. W. (1947) The role of secondary reinforcement in delayed reward learning. *Psychol. Rev.*, **54,** 1–8.

Spence, K. W. (1953) Learning and performance in eyelid conditioning as a function of intensity of the UCS. *J. exp. Psychol.*, **45,** 57–63.

Spence, K. W. (1956) *Behavior theory and conditioning.* New Haven: Yale University Press.

Spence, K. W. (1958) Behavior theory and selective learning. In M. R. Jones (Ed.), *Nebraska symposium on motivation.* Lincoln: University of Nebraska Press.

Spence, K. W. (1958a) An emotionally based theory of drive (D) and its relation to performance in simple learning situations. *Amer. Psychologist,* **13,** 131–141.

Spence, K. W. (1960) *Behavior theory and learning.* Englewood Cliffs, N.J.: Prentice-Hall.

Spence, K. W., & Beecroft, R. S. (1954) Differential conditioning and level of anxiety. *J. exp. Psychol.*, **48,** 399–403.

Spence, K. W., & Farber, I. E. (1953) Conditioning and extinction as a function of anxiety. *J. exp. Psychol.*, **45,** 116–119.

Spence, K. W., & Farber, I. E. (1954) The relation of anxiety to differential eyelid conditioning. *J. exp. Psychol.*, **47,** 127–134.

Spence, K. W., Farber, I. E., & McFann, H. H. (1956) The relation of anxiety (drive) level to performance in competitional and noncompetitional paired-associates. *J. exp. Psychol.*, **52**, 296–305.

Spence, K. W., & Goldstein, H. (1961) Eyelid conditioning performance as a function of emotion-producing instructions. *J. exp. Psychol.*, **62**, 291–294.

Spence, K. W., Goodrich, K. P., & Ross, L. E. (1959) Performance in differential conditioning and discrimination learning as a function of hunger and relative response frequency. *J. exp. Psychol.*, **58**, 8–16.

Spence, K. W., Haggard, D. F., & Ross, L. E. (1958) UCS intensity and the associative (habit) strength of the eyelid CR. *J. exp. Psychol.*, **55**, 404–411.

Spence, K. W., Haggard, D. F., & Ross, L. E. (1958a) Intrasubject conditioning as a function of the intensity of the unconditioned stimulus. *Science*, **138**, 774–775.

Spence, K. W., & Ross, L. E. (1959) A methodological study of the form and latency of eyelid responses in conditioning. *J. exp. Psychol.*, **58**, 376–381.

Spence, K. W., & Runquist, W. N. (1958) Temporal effects of conditioned fear on the eyelid reflex. *J. exp. Psychol.*, **55**, 613–616.

Spence, K. W., Rutledge, E. F., & Talbott, J. H. (1963) Effect of number of acquisition trials and the presence or absence of the UCS on extinction of the eyelid CR. *J. exp. Psychol.*, **66**, 286–291.

Spence, K. W., & Tandler, B. F. (1963) Differential eyelid conditioning under equated drive as a function of the reinforcing UCS. *J. exp. Psychol.*, **65**, 35–38.

Spence, K. W., & Taylor, J. A. (1951) Anxiety and strength of the UCS as determiners of the amount of eyelid conditioning. *J. exp. Psychol.*, **42**, 183–188.

Spence, K. W., & Taylor, J. A. (1953) The relation of conditioned response strength to anxiety in normal, neurotic and psychotic subjects. *J. exp. Psychol.*, **45**, 265–272.

Spence, K. W., Taylor, J. A., & Ketchel, R. (1956) Anxiety (drive) level and degree of competition in paired-associates learning. *J. exp. Psychol.*, **52**, 306–310.

Spence, K. W., & Weyant, R. G. (1960) Conditioning performance of high and low anxious subjects in the absence of a warning signal. *J. exp. Psychol.*, **60**, 146–149.

Spencer, H. (1880) *Principles of psychology,* 3rd ed.

Stabler, J. R. (1962) Performance in instrumental conditioning as a joint function of time of deprivation and sucrose concentration. *J. exp. Psychol.*, **63**, 248–253.

Stagner, R., & Karwoski, T. F. (1952) *Psychology.* New York: McGraw-Hill.

Standish, R. R., & Champion, R. A. (1960) Task difficulty and drive in verbal learning. *J. exp. Psychol.*, **59**, 361–365.

Stebbins, W. C. (1959) Relation of amount of primary reinforcement to discrimination and to secondary reinforcement strength. *J. comp. physiol. Psychol.*, **52**, 721–726.

Stein, L. (1957) The classical conditioning of the consummatory response as a determinant of instrumental performance. *J. comp. physiol. Psychol.*, **50**, 269–278.

Stein, L. (1958) Secondary reinforcement established with subcortical stimulation. *Science*, **127**, 466–467.

Stein, L. (1962) An analysis of stimulus-duration preference in self-stimulation of the brain. *J. comp. physiol. Psychol.*, **55**, 405–414.

Stein, L. (1964) Excessive drinking in the rat: superstition or thirst? *J. comp. physiol. Psychol.*, **58**, 237–242.

Stein, L., Sidman, M., & Brady, J. V. (1958) Some effects of two temporal variables on conditioned suppression. *J. exp. anal. Behav.*, **1**, 153–162.

Stellar, E. (1954) The physiology of motivation. *Psychol. Rev.*, **61**, 5–22.

Stellar, E., & Hill, J. H. (1952) The rat's rate of drinking as a function of water deprivation. *J. comp. physiol. Psychol.*, **45**, 96–102.

Sterritt, G. M. (1965) Inhibition and facilitation of eating by electric shock: III. A further study of the role of strain and of shock level. *Psychon. Sci.*, **2**, 319–320.

Stevens, S. S. (1935) Operational definitions of psychological concepts. *Psychol. Rev.*, **42**, 517–527.

Stevens, S. S., Carton, A. S., & Shickman, G. M. (1958) A scale of apparent intensity of electric shock. *J. exp. Psychol.*, **56**, 328–334.

Stevenson, J. A. F., & Rixon, R. H. (1957) Environmental temperature and deprivation of food and water on the spontaneous activity of rats. *Yale J. Biol. Med.*, **29**, 575–584.

Stewart, C. C. (1898) Variations in daily activity produced by alcohol and by changes in barometric pressure and diet, with a description of recording method. *Amer. J. Physiol.*, **1**, 40–56.

Stewart, D. (1792–1827) *Elements of the philosophy of the human mind.*

Stojkiewicz, L. W., Jr. (1964) Do rats really avoid? The role of US-avoidance in avoidance behavior. Unpublished M.A. thesis, Hollins College.

Stolurow, L. M. (1951) Rodent behavior in the presence of barriers: II. The metabolic maintenance method; a technique for caloric drive control and manipulation. *J. genet. Psychol.*, **79**, 289–335.

Stone, C. P. (1926) The initial copulatory response of female rats reared in isolation from the age of 20 days to puberty. *J. comp. Psychol.*, **6**, 73–83.

Stone, C. P. (1927) Retention of copulatory ability in male rats following castration. *J. comp. Psychol.*, **7**, 369–387.

Stone, C. P. (1929) The age factor in animal learning: I. Rats in the problem box and the maze. *Genet. Psychol. Monogr.*, **5**, 8–130.

Stone, C. P. (1939) Copulatory activity in adult male rats following castration and injections of testosterone propionate. *Endocrinology*, **24**, 165–174.

Stone, C. P., Barker, R. G., & Tomilin, M. I. (1935) Sexual drive in potent and impotent male rats as measured by the Columbia obstruction apparatus. *J. genet. Psychol.*, **47**, 33–48.

Stone, C. P., & Ferguson, L. (1938) Preferential responses of male albino rats to food and to receptive females. *J. comp. Psychol.*, **26**, 237–253.

Stone, C. P., & Ferguson, L. W. (1940) Temporal relationships in the copulatory acts of adult male rats. *J. comp. Psychol.*, **30**, 419–433.

Stone, C. P., & Sturman-Huble, M. (1927) Food vs. sex as incentives for male rats on the maze learning problem. *Amer. J. Psychol.*, **38**, 403–408.

Stone, C. P., Tomilin, M. I., & Barker, R. G. (1935) A comparative study of sexual drive in adult male rats as measured by direct copulatory tests and by the Columbia obstruction apparatus. *J. comp. Psychol.*, **19**, 215–241.

Stone, G. R. (1953) The effect of negative incentives in serial learning: VII. Theory of punishment. *J. gen. Psychol.*, **48**, 133–161.

Stone, G. R., & Walter, N. (1951) The effect of negative incentives in serial learning: VI. Response repetition as a function of an isolated electric shock punishment. *J. exp. Psychol.*, **41**, 411–418.

Storms, L. H., Boroczi, G., & Broen, W. E., Jr. (1963) Effects of punishment as a function of strain of rat and duration of shock. *J. comp. physiol. Psychol.*, **56**, 1022–1026.

Stout, G. F. (1903) *The groundwork of psychology.* New York: Hinds, Noble, and Eldredge.

Strange, J. R. (1954) The effect of an irrelevant drive on the reaction tendency specific to another drive. *J. gen. Psychol.*, **51**, 31–40.

Strassburger, R. C. (1950) Resistance to extinction of a conditioned operant as related to drive level at reinforcement. *J. exp. Psychol.*, **40**, 473–487.

Strominger, J. L. (1946–47) The relation between water intake and food intake in normal rats and in rats with hypothalamic hyperphagia. *Yale J. Biol. Med.*, **19**, 279–287.

Strong, T. N., Jr. (1957) Activity in the white rat as a function of apparatus and hunger. *J. comp. physiol. Psychol.*, **50**, 596–600.

Strouthes, A. (1965) Effect of CS-onset UCS-termination delay, UCS duration, CS-onset UCS-onset interval, and number of CS-UCS pairings on conditioned fear response. *J. exp. Psychol.*, **69**, 287–291.

Strouthes, A., & Hamilton, G. C. (1964) UCS intensity and number of CS-UCS pairings as determiners of conditioned fear R. *Psychol. Rep.*, **15**, 707–714.

Szymanski, J. S. (1914) Eine Methode zur Untersuchung der Ruhe und Aktivitaetsperioden bei Tieren. *Arch. ges. Physiol.*, **158**, 343–385.

Szymanski, J. S. (1918) Abhandlungen zum Aufbau der Lehre von den Handlungen der Tiere. *Arch. ges. Physiol.*, **170**, 220–237.

Taylor, J. A. (1951) The relationship of anxiety to the conditioned eyelid response. *J. exp. Psychol.*, **41**, 81–92.

Taylor, J. A. (1953) A personality scale of manifest anxiety. *J. abnorm. soc. Psychol.*, **48**, 285–290.

Taylor, J. A. (1956) Drive theory and manifest anxiety. *Psychol. Bull.*, **53**, 303–320.

Taylor, J. A., & Spence, K. W. (1952) The relationship of anxiety level to performance in serial learning. *J. exp. Psychol.*, **44**, 61–64.

Teel, K. S. (1952) Habit strength as a function of motivation during learning. *J. comp. physiol. Psychol.*, **45**, 188–191.

Teel, K. S., & Webb, W. B. (1951) Response evocation on satiated trials in the T-maze. *J. exp. Psychol.*, **41**, 148–152.

Teghtsoonian, R., & Campbell, B. A. (1960) Random activity of the rat during food deprivation as a function of environment. *J. comp. physiol. Psychol.*, **53**, 242–244.

Teitelbaum, P. (1957) Random and food-directed activity in hyperphagic and normal rats. *J. comp. physiol. Psychol.*, **50**, 486–490.

Teitelbaum, P. (1961) Disturbances in feeding and drinking behavior after hypothalamic lesions. In M. R. Jones (Ed.), *Nebraska symposium on motivation.* Lincoln: University of Nebraska Press.

Teitelbaum, P., & Campbell, B. A. (1958) Ingestion patterns in hyperphagic and normal rats. *J. comp. physiol. Psychol.*, **51**, 135–141.

Teitelbaum, P., & Epstein, A. N. (1962) The lateral hypothalamic syndrome: recovery of feeding and drinking after lateral hypothalamic lesions. *Psychol. Rev.*, **69**, 74–90.

Theios, J. (1963) Drive stimulus generalization increments. *J. comp. physiol. Psychol.*, **56**, 691–695.

Thilly, F. (1957) *History of philosophy,* 3rd ed., revised by L. Wood. New York: Holt.

Thomas, D. R., & King, R. A. (1959) Stimulus generalization as a function of level of motivation. *J. exp. Psychol.*, **57**, 323–328.

Thompson, W. R. (1953) Exploratory behavior as a function of hunger in "bright" and "dull" rats. *J. comp. physiol. Psychol.*, **46**, 323–326.

Thomson, C. W., & Porter, P. B. (1953) Need reduction and primary reinforcement: maze learning by sodium-deprived rats for a subthreshold saline reward. *J. comp. physiol. Psychol.*, **46**, 281–287.

Thorndike, E. L. (1898) Animal intelligence: an experimental study of the associative processes in animals. *Psychol. Rev. Monogr. Suppl.*, **2**, No. 8.

Thorndike, E. L. (1908) A pragmatic substitute for free will. In *Essays philosophical and psychological in honor of William James.* New York: Longmans, Green.

Thorndike, E. L. (1911) *Animal intelligence.* New York: Macmillan.

Thorndike, E. L. (1913) *Educational psychology.* New York: Teachers College, Columbia University.

Thorndike, E. L. (1913a) Ideo-motor action. *Psychol. Rev.*, **20**, 91–105.

Thorndike, E. L. (1932) *The fundamentals of learning.* New York: Columbia University Press.

Thorndike, E. L. (1933) A theory of the action of the after-effects of a connection upon it. *Psychol. Rev.*, **40**, 434–439.

Thorndike, E. L. (1935) *The psychology of wants, interests, and attitudes.* New York: Appleton-Century-Crofts.

Thurstone, L. L. (1923) The stimulus-response fallacy in psychology. *Psychol. Rev.*, **30**, 354–369.

Tinbergen, N. (1940) Die Ubersprungbewegung. *Z. Tierpsychol.*, **4**, 1–40.

Tinbergen, N. (1951) *The study of instinct.* London: Oxford University Press.

Tinklepaugh, O. L. (1928) An experimental study of representative factors in monkeys. *J. comp. Psychol.*, **8**, 197–236.

Tobach, E., & Schneirla, T. C. (1962) Eliminative responses in mice and rats and the problem of "emotionality." In E. L. Bliss (Ed.), *Roots of behavior.* New York: Harper.

Tolman, E. C. (1920) Instinct and purpose. *Psychol. Rev.*, **27**, 218–233.

Tolman, E. C. (1923) The nature of instinct. *Psychol. Bull.*, **20**, 200–218.

Tolman, E. C. (1923a) A behavioristic account of the emotions. *Psychol. Rev.*, **30**, 217–227.

Tolman, E. C. (1926) The nature of fundamental drives. *J. abnorm. soc. Psychol.*, **5**, 349–358.

Tolman, E. C. (1932) *Purposive behavior in animals and men.* New York: Appleton-Century.

Tolman, E. C. (1933) The law of effect: a reply to Dr. Goodenough. *J. exp. Psychol.*, **16**, 463–470.

Tolman, E. C. (1936) Operational behaviorism and current trends in psychology. In E. C. Tolman, *Collected papers in psychology.* Berkeley: University of California Press, 1951.

Tolman, E. C. (1942) *Drives toward war.* New York: Appleton-Century-Crofts.

Tolman, E. C. (1943) A drive-conversion diagram. *Psychol. Rev.*, **50**, 503–513.

Tolman, E. C. (1949) There is more than one kind of learning. *Psychol. Rev.*, **56**, 144–155.

Tolman, E. C., & Gleitman, H. (1949) Studies in spatial learning: VII. Place and response learning under different degrees of motivation. *J. exp. Psychol.*, **39**, 653–659.

Tolman, E. C., & Honzik, C. H. (1930) Degrees of hunger, reward and non-reward, and maze learning in rats. *Univ. Calif. Publ. Psychol.,* **4,** 241–256.

Towbin, E. J. (1949) Gastric distention as a factor in the satiation of thirst in esophagostomized dogs. *Amer. J. Physiol.,* **159,** 533–541.

Trabasso, T. R., & Thompson, R. W. (1962) Supplementary report: Shock intensity and unconditioned responding in a shuttle box. *J. exp. Psychol.,* **63,** 215.

Trapold, M. A. (1962) The effect of incentive motivation on an unrelated reflex response. *J. comp. physiol. Psychol.,* **55,** 1034–1039.

Trapold, M. A., & Fowler, H. (1960) Instrumental escape performance as a function of the intensity of noxious stimulation. *J. exp. Psychol.,* **60,** 323–326.

Trapold, M. A., & Spence, K. W. (1960) Performance changes in eyelid conditioning as related to the motivational and reinforcing properties of the UCS. *J. exp. Psychol.,* **59,** 209–213.

Trapp, E. P., & Kausler, D. H. (1960) Relationship between MAS scores and association values of nonsense syllables. *J. exp. Psychol.,* **59,** 233–238.

Traum, A., & Horton, S. H. (1950) Cited by Mowrer (1950).

Treichler, F. R. (1960) The relationship between deprivation weight loss and two activity measures. Ph.D. dissertation, Pennsylvania State University. Published in part in Treichler & Hall (1962).

Treichler, F. R., & Collins, R. W. (1965) Comparison of cyclic and continuous deprivation on wheel running. *J. comp. physiol. Psychol.,* **60,** 447–448.

Treichler, F. R., & Hall, J. F. (1962) The relationship between deprivation weight loss and several measures of activity. *J. comp. physiol. Psychol.,* **55,** 346–349.

Troland, L. T. (1928) *The fundamentals of human motivation.* New York: Van Nostrand.

Tryon, R. C., Tryon, C. M., & Kuznets, G. (1941) Studies in individual differences in maze ability: IX. Ratings of hiding, avoidance, escape and vocalization responses. *J. comp. Psychol.,* **32,** 407–435.

Tryon, R. C., Tryon, C. M., & Kuznets, G. (1941a) Studies in individual differences in maze ability: X. Ratings and other measures of initial emotional responses of rats to novel inanimate objects. *J. comp. Psychol.,* **32,** 447–473.

Tsai, C. (1925) The relative strength of sex and hunger motives in the albino rat. *J. comp. Psychol.,* **5,** 407–415.

Tsang, Y. C. (1938) Hunger motivation in gastrectomized rats. *J. comp. Psychol.,* **26,** 1–17.

Tugendhat, B. (1960) The normal feeding behavior of the three-spined stickleback (*Gasterosteus aculeatus*). *Behaviour,* **15,** 284–318.

Uexkull, J. von (1909) *Umwelt und Innerwelt der Tiere.* Berlin: Springer.

Upton, M. (1929) The auditory sensitivity of guinea pigs. *Amer. J. Psychol.,* **41,** 412–421.

Valenstein, E. S., Riss, W., & Young, W. C. (1955) Experiential and genetic factors in the organization of sexual behavior in the male guinea pig. *J. comp. physiol. Psychol.,* **48,** 397–403.

Vaughn, J., & Diserens, C. M. (1930) The relative effects of various intensities of punishment on learning and efficiency. *J. comp. Psychol.,* **10,** 55–66.

Verplanck, W. S. (1955) Since learned behavior is innate, and vice versa, what now? *Psychol. Rev.,* **62,** 139–144.

Verplanck, W. S. (1958) Comparative psychology. *Ann. Rev. Psychol.,* **9,** 99–118.

Verplanck, W. S., & Hayes, J. R. (1953) Eating and drinking as a function of maintenance schedule. *J. comp. physiol. Psychol.,* **46,** 327–333.

Verworn, M. (1889) *Psycho-physiologische Protistenstudien.*

Wada, T. (1922) An experimental study of hunger in its relation to activity. *Arch. Psychol.,* **8** (Serial No. 57).

Wagman, W., & Allen, J. D. (1964) The development of a conditioned positive reinforcer based upon the termination of shock. *Psychon. Sci.,* **1,** 363–364.

Wagner, A. R. (1961) Effects of amount and percentage of reinforcement and number of acquisition trials on conditioning and extinction. *J. exp. Psychol.,* **62,** 234–242.

Wagner, A. R. (1963) Conditioned frustration as a learned drive. *J. exp. Psychol.,* **66,** 142–148.

Wald, G., & Jackson, B. (1944) Activity and nutritional deprivation. *Proc. Nat. Acad. Sci.,* **30,** 255–263.

Walker, B. E., & Walker, E. L. (1964) Learning, extinction, and relearning of running and basal skin resistance (BRL) in a segmented straight alley. *Psychol. Rec.,* **14,** 507–513.

Wang, G. H. (1923) Relation between "spontaneous" activity and oestrus cycle in the white rat. *Comp. Psychol. Monogr.,* **2** (Serial No. 6).

Wang, G. H., Richter, C. P., & Guttmacher, A. F. (1925) Activity studies of male castrated rats with ovarian transplants, and correlation of the activity with the histology of the grafts. *Amer. J. Physiol.,* **73,** 581–598.

Wangensteen, O. H., & Carlson, A. J. (1931) Hunger sensations in a patient after total gastrectomy. *Proc. Soc. exp. Biol.,* **28,** 545–547.

Warden, C. J. et al. (1931) *Animal motivation: experimental studies on the albino rat.* New York: Columbia University Press.

Warden, C. J., & Aylesworth, M. (1927) The relative value of reward and punishment in the formation of a visual discrimination habit in the white rat. *J. comp. Psychol.,* **7,** 117–127.

Warden, C. J., & Diamond, S. A. (1931) A preliminary study of the effect of delayed punishment on learning in the white rat. *J. genet. Psychol.,* **39,** 455–462.

Warden, C. J., & Haas, E. L. (1927) The effect of short intervals of delay in feeding upon speed of maze learning. *J. comp. Psychol.,* **7,** 107–116.

Warden, C. J., Jenkins, T. N., & Warner, L. H. (1936) *Comparative psychology.* New York: Ronald.

Warner, L. H. (1927) A study of sex drive in the white rat by means of the obstruction method. *Comp. Psychol. Monogr.,* **4** (Serial No. 22).

Warner, L. H. (1928) A study of thirst behavior in the white rat by means of the obstruction method. *J. genet. Psychol.,* **35,** 178–192.

Warren, H. C. (1921) *A history of the association psychology.* New York: Scribner.

Washburn, M. F. (1908) *The animal mind.* New York: Macmillan.

Waters, R. H. (1956) Reinforcement in learning theory: a proposed realignment. *J. gen. Psychol.,* **54,** 149–154.

Watson, J. (1895) *Hedonistic theories from Aristippus to Spencer.*

Watson, J. B. (1917) The effect of delayed feeding upon learning. *Psychobiology,* **1,** 51–59.

Watson, J. B. (1919) *Psychology from the standpoint of a behaviorist.* Philadelphia: Lippincott.

Watt, H. (1905) Experimentelle Beitgaege zu einer Theorie des Denkens. *Arch. Psychol.,* **4,** 289–436.

Wayner, M. J., Jr., & Emmers, R. (1959) A test of the thirst-deprivation trace hypothesis in the hooded rat. *J. comp. physiol. Psychol.,* **52,** 112–115.

Wayner, M. J., Jr., & Reimanis, G. (1958) Drinking in the rat induced by hypertonic saline. *J. comp. physiol. Psychol.,* **51,** 11–15.

Wayner, M. J., Jr., Wetrus, B., & Blank, D. Artificial thirst, serum Na, and behavioral implications in the hooded rat. *Psychol. Rep.,* **11,** 667–674.

Weasner, M. H., Finger, F. W., & Reid, L. S. (1960) Activity changes under food deprivation as a function of recording device. *J. comp. physiol. Psychol.,* **53,** 470–474.

Webb, W. B. (1949) The motivational aspect of an irrelevant drive in the behavior of the white rat. *J. exp. Psychol.,* **39,** 1–14.

Webb, W. B. (1955) Drive stimuli as cues. *Psychol. Rep.,* **1,** 287–298.

Webb, W. B. (1957) Antecedents of sleep. *J. exp. Psychol.,* **53,** 162–166.

Webb, W. B., & Goodman, I. J. (1958) Activating role of an irrelevant drive in absence of the relevant drive. *Psychol. Rep.,* **4,** 235–238.

Webb, W. B., & Nolan, C. Y. (1953) Cues for discrimination as secondary reinforcing agents: a confirmation. *J. comp. physiol. Psychol.,* **46,** 180–181.

Weinstock, S. (1958) Acquisition and extinction of a partially reinforced running response at a 24-hour intertrial interval. *J. exp. Psychol.,* **56,** 151–158.

Weir, L. G., Larson, E. E., & Roundtree, L. G. (1922) Studies in diabetes insipidus, water balance, and water intoxication. *Arch. int. Med.,* **29,** 306–330.

Weisman, R. G., Zerbolio, D. J., & Denny, M. R. (1965) Intertrial interval in the maintenance of discrete-trial avoidance. *Psychon. Sci.,* **2,** 33–34.

Weiss, B., & Moore, E. W. (1956) Drive level as a factor in distribution of responses in fixed-interval reinforcement. *J. exp. Psychol.,* **52,** 82–84.

Weiss, R. F. (1960) Deprivation and reward magnitude effects on speed throughout the goal gradient. *J. exp. Psychol.,* **60,** 384–390.

Weiss, S. J., & Lawson, R. (1962) Secondary reinforcement as a suppressor of rate of responding in the free operant situation. *J. comp. physiol. Psychol.,* **55,** 1016–1019.

Welch, L., & Kubis, J. (1947) The effect of anxiety on the conditioning and stability of the PGR. *J. Psychol.,* **23,** 83–91.

Welker, W. I. (1959) Escape, exploratory, and food-seeking responses of rats in a novel situation. *J. comp. physiol. Psychol.,* **52,** 106–111.

Wells, W. R. (1923) The anti-instinct fallacy. *Psychol. Rev.,* **30,** 228–234.

Wenar, C. (1954) Reaction time as a function of manifest anxiety and stimulus intensity. *J. abnorm. soc. Psychol.,* **49,** 335–340.

Werthessen, N. (1937) The significance of subnormal respiratory quotient values induced by controlled feeding of the rat. *Amer. J. Physiol.,* **120,** 458–465.

Wetzel, R. J. (1959) The effect of experience with a taste reward. *J. comp. physiol. Psychol.,* **52,** 267–271.

Wever, E. G. (1930) The upper limit of hearing in the cat. *J. comp. Psychol.,* **10,** 221–233.

Whalen, R. E. (1961) Effects of mounting without intromission and intromission without ejaculation on sexual behavior and maze learning. *J. comp. physiol. Psychol.,* **54,** 409–415.

White, R. K. (1936) The completion hypothesis and reinforcement. *Psychol. Rev.,* **43,** 396–404.

White, R. T. (1953) Analysis of the function of a secondary reinforcing stimulus in a serial learning situation. Unpublished Ph.D. dissertation, University of Buffalo. Cited by Bugelski (1956).

Whiteis, U. E. (1956) Punishment's influence on fear and avoidance. *Harv. educ. Rev.,* **26,** 360–373.

Wickens, D. D., Hall, J., & Reid, L. S. (1949) Associative and retroactive inhibition as a function of the drive stimulus. *J. comp. physiol. Psychol.,* **42,** 398–403.

Wickens, D. D., & Platt, C. E. (1954) Response termination of the cue stimulus in classical and instrumental conditioning. *J. exp. Psychol.,* **47,** 183–186.

Wike, E. L., & Barrientos, G. (1957) Selective learning as a function of differential consummatory activity. *Psychol. Rep.,* **3,** 255–258.

Wike, E. L., & Barrientos, G. (1958) Secondary reinforcement and multiple drive reduction. *J. comp. physiol. Psychol.,* **51,** 640–643.

Wike, E. L., & Casey, A. (1954) The secondary reward value of food for satiated animals. *J. comp. physiol. Psychol.,* **47,** 441–443.

Wike, E. L., & Casey, A. (1954a) The secondary reinforcing value of food for thirsty animals. *J. comp. physiol. Psychol.,* **47,** 240–243.

Wike, E. L., & Farrow, B. J. (1962) The effects of drive intensity on secondary reinforcement. *J. comp. physiol. Psychol.,* **55,** 1020–1023.

Wike, E. L., & McNamara, H. J. (1955) A quest for the generalized conditioned reinforcer. *Psychol. Rep.,* **1,** 83–91.

Wike, E. L., & McNamara, H. J. (1957) Some training conditions affecting secondary reinforcement. *J. comp. physiol. Psychol.,* **50,** 345–347.

Wike, E. L., & Platt, J. R. (1962) Reinforcement schedules and bar pressing: some extensions of Zimmerman's work. *Psychol. Rec.,* **12,** 273–278.

Wike, E. L., Platt, J. R., & Knowles, J. M. (1962) The reward value of getting out of a starting box: further extensions of Zimmerman's work. *Psychol. Rec.,* **12,** 397–400.

Wike, E. L., Platt, J. R., & Scott, D. (1963) Drive and secondary reinforcement: Further extensions of Zimmerman's work. *Psychol. Rec.,* **13,** 45–50.

Williams, D. R., & Teitelbaum, P. (1956) Control of drinking behavior by means of an operant-conditioning technique. *Science,* **124,** 1294–1296.

Williams, K. A. (1929) The reward value of a conditioned stimulus. *Univ. Calif. Publ. Psychol.,* **4,** 31–55.

Williams, R. A., & Campbell, B. A. (1961) Weight loss and quinine-milk ingestion as measures of "hunger" in infant and adult rats. *J. comp. physiol. Psychol.,* **54,** 220–222.

Williams, S. B. (1938) Resistance to extinction as a function of the number of reinforcements. *J. exp. Psychol.,* **23,** 506–521.

Willingham, W. W. (1956) The organization of emotional behavior in mice. *J. comp. physiol. Psychol.,* **49,** 345–348.

Wilm, E. C. (1925) *The theories of instinct.* New Haven: Yale University Press.

Wilson, J. R., Kuehn, R. E., & Beach, F. A. (1963) Modification in the sexual behavior of male rats produced by changing the stimulus female. *J. comp. physiol. Psychol.,* **56,** 636–644.

Wilson, W., Weiss, E. J., & Amsel, A. (1955) Two tests of the Sheffield hypothesis concerning resistance to extinction, partial reinforcement, and distribution of practice. *J. exp. Psychol.,* **50,** 51–60.

Winnick, W. A. (1950) The discriminative function of drive-stimuli independent of the action of the drive as motivation. *Amer. J. Psychol.,* **63,** 196–205.

Winograd, E. (1965) Maintained generalization testing of conditioned suppression. *J. exp. anal. Behav.,* **8,** 47–51.

Wist, E. R. (1962) Amount, delay, and position of delay of reinforcement as parameters of runway performance. *J. exp. Psychol.,* **63,** 160–166.

Wist, E. R. (1963) Effect of training level at the time of introduction of delay on runway performance. *Psychol. Rep.,* **12,** 899–911.

Wolf, A. V. (1958) *Thirst.* Springfield: C. C. Thomas.

Wolf, S., & Wolff, H. G. (1943) *Human gastric function.* New York: Oxford University Press.

Wolfe, J. B. (1934) The effect of delayed reward upon learning in the white rat. *J. comp. Psychol.,* **17,** 1–21.

Wolfe, J. B. (1936) Effectiveness of token rewards for chimpanzees. *Comp. Psychol. Monogr.,* **12** (Serial No. 60).

Wolfe, J. B., & Kaplon, M. D. (1941) Effect of amount of reward and consummatory activity on learning in chickens. *J. comp. Psychol.,* **31,** 353–361.

Wolpe, J. (1950) Need-reduction, drive-reduction, and reinforcement: a neurophysiological view. *Psychol. Rev.,* **57,** 19–26.

Woodbury, C. B., & Wilder, D. H. (1954) The principle of selective association of drive stimuli. *J. exp. Psychol.,* **47,** 301–302.

Woods, P. J. (1962) Behavior in a novel situation as influenced by the immediately preceding environment. *J. exp. anal. Behav.,* **5,** 185–191.

Woods, P. J., & Bolles, R. C. (1965) Effects of current hunger and prior eating habits on exploratory behavior. *J. comp. physiol. Psychol.,* **60,** 141–143.

Woods, P. J., Davidson, E. H., & Peters, R. J., Jr. (1964) Instrumental escape conditioning in a water tank: effects of variations in drive stimulus intensity and reinforcement magnitude. *J. comp. physiol. Psychol.,* **57,** 466–470.

Woodworth, R. S. (1918) *Dynamic psychology.* New York: Columbia University Press.

Woodworth, R. S. (1924) Four varieties of behaviorism. *Psychol. Rev.,* **31,** 257–264.

Woodworth, R. S. (1958) *Dynamics of behavior.* New York: Holt.

Wunderlich, R. A. (1961) Strength of a generalized conditioned reinforcer as a function of variability of reward. *J. exp. Psychol.,* **62,** 409–415.

Wyckoff, L. B. (1959) Toward a quantitative theory of secondary reinforcement. *Psychol. Rev.,* **66,** 68–79.

Wyckoff, L. B., Sidowski, J., & Chambliss, D. J. (1958) An experimental study of the relationship between secondary reinforcing and cue effect of a stimulus. *J. comp. physiol. Psychol.,* **51,** 103–109.

Wynne, L. C., & Solomon, R. L. (1955) Traumatic avoidance learning: acquisition and extinction in dogs deprived of normal peripheral autonomic functioning. *Genet. Psychol. Monogr.,* **52,** 241–284.

Yamaguchi, H. G. (1951) Drive (D) as a function of hours of hunger (h). *J. exp. Psychol.,* **42,** 108–117.

Yamaguchi, H. G. (1952) Gradients of drive stimulus (S_D) intensity generalization. *J. exp. Psychol.,* **43,** 298–304.

Yamaguchi, H. G. (1961) The effect of continuous, partial, and varied magnitude reinforcement on acquisition and extinction. *J. exp. Psychol.,* **61,** 319–321.

Yerkes, R. M. (1913) The heredity of savageness and wildness in rats. *J. anim. Behav.,* **3,** 286–296.

Yerkes, R. M., & Dodson, J. D. (1908) The relation of strength of stimulus to rapidity of habit-formation. *J. comp. Neurol. Psychol.,* **18,** 459–482.

Yoshioka, J. G. (1930) Size preference of albino rats. *J. genet. Psychol.,* **37,** 427–430.

Young, P. T. (1928) Preferential discrimination of the white rat for different kinds of grain. *Amer. J. Psychol.,* **40,** 372–394.

Young, P. T. (1936) *Motivation of behavior.* New York: Wiley.

Young, P. T. (1941) The experimental analysis of appetite. *Psychol. Bull.,* **38,** 129–164.

Young, P. T. (1948) Appetite, palatability and feeding habit: a critical review. *Psychol. Bull.,* **45,** 289–320.

Young, P. T. (1949) Food-seeking drive, affective process, and learning. *Psychol. Rev.,* **56,** 98–121.

Young, P. T. (1955) The role of hedonic processes in motivation. In M. R. Jones (Ed.) *Nebraska symposium on motivation.* Lincoln: University of Nebraska Press.

Young, P. T. (1959) The role of affective processes in learning and motivation. *Psychol. Rev.,* **66,** 104–125.

Young, P. T. (1961) *Motivation and emotion.* New York: Wiley.

Young, P. T., & Greene, J. T. (1953) Quantity of food ingested as a measure of relative acceptability. *J. comp. physiol. Psychol.,* **46,** 288–294.

Young, P. T., & Madsen, C. H., Jr. (1963) Individual isohedons in sucrose-sodium chloride and sucrose-saccharin gustatory area. *J. comp. physiol. Psychol.,* **56,** 903–909.

Young, P. T., & Richey, H. W. (1952) Diurnal drinking patterns in the rat. *J. comp. physiol. Psychol.,* **45,** 80–89.

Young, P. T., & Shuford, E. H., Jr. (1955) Quantitative control of motivation through sucrose solutions of different concentrations. *J. comp. physiol. Psychol.,* **48,** 114–118.

Young, W. C. (1961) The hormones and mating behavior. In W. C. Young (Ed.), *Sex and internal secretions,* 3rd ed. Baltimore: Williams & Wilkins.

Young, W. C., & Grunt, J. A. (1951) The pattern and measurement of sexual behavior in the male guinea pig. *J. comp. physiol. Psychol.,* **44,** 492–500.

Zajonc, R. B. (1965) Social facilitation. *Science,* **149,** 269–274.

Zeaman, D. (1949) Response latency as a function of the amount of reinforcement. *J. exp. Psychol.,* **39,** 466–483.

Zeaman, D., & House, B. (1950) Response latency at zero drive after varying numbers of reinforcements. *J. exp. Psychol.,* **40,** 570-583.

Zeigarnik, B. (1927) Ueber das Behalten von erledigten und unerledigten Handlungen. *Psychol. Forsch.,* **9,** 1–85.

Zeigler, H. P. (1964) Displacement activity and motivational theory: a case study in the history of ethology. *Psychol. Bull.,* **61,** 362–376.

Zeller, E. (1883) *Outlines of the history of Greek philosophy,* 13th ed., trans. by L. R. Palmer. New York: Meridian, 1957.

Zener, K. E., & McCurdy, H. G. (1939) Analysis of motivational factors in conditioned behavior: I. The differential effect of changes in hunger upon conditioned, unconditioned and spontaneous salivary secretion. *J. Psychol.,* **8,** 321–350.

Zigler, M. J. (1923) Instinct and the psychological viewpoint. *Psychol. Rev.,* **29,** 447–460.

Zilboorg, G. (1951) *Sigmund Freud.* New York: Scribner's.

Zilboorg, G., & Henry, G. W. (1941) *A history of medical psychology.* New York: Norton.

Zimbardo, P. G., & Miller, N. E. (1958) Facilitation of exploration by hunger in rats. *J. comp. physiol. Psychol.,* **51,** 43–46.

Zimbardo, P. G., & Montgomery, K. C. (1957) The relative strengths of consummaory responses in hunger, thirst, and exploratory drive. *J. comp. physiol. Psychol.,* **50,** 504–508.

Zimmerman, D. W. (1957) Durable secondary reinforcement: method and theory. *Psychol. Rev.,* **64,** 373–383.

Zimmerman, D. W. (1959) Sustained performance in rats based on secondary reinforcement. *J. comp. physiol. Psychol.,* **52,** 353–358.

Zimmerman, D. W. (1961) The effect of deprivation and satiation on secondary reinforcement developed by two methods. *J. genet. Psychol.,* **99,** 139–144.

Zimmerman, D. W. (1963) Influence of three stimulus conditions upon the strength of a secondary reinforcement effect. *Psychol. Rep.,* **13,** 135–138.

Zimmerman, D. W. (1963a) Influence of conditions at the time of reinforcement upon the strength of a secondary reinforcement effect. *Psychol. Rep.,* **13,** 747–752.

Zweig, S. (1932) *Mental healers.* New York: Garden City.

INDEXES

Index of Authors

Index of Subjects

DATE DUE